THE BOOK OF IRISH AMERICAN POETRY

THE BOOK OF
IRISH AMERICAN
Poetry

*from the Eighteenth Century
to the Present*

edited by DANIEL TOBIN

University of Notre Dame Press

Notre Dame, Indiana

Library of Congress Cataloging in-Publication Data

The book of Irish American poetry : from the eighteenth century to the present /
edited by Daniel Tobin.
p.   cm.
Includes bibliographical references and indexes.
ISBN-13: 978-0-268-04230-1 (alk. paper)
ISBN-10: 0-268-04230-6 (alk. paper)
1. American poetry—Irish American authors.   2. Irish Americans—Poetry.
3. Ireland—Poetry.   I. Tobin, Daniel.
PS591.I69B66   2006
811.008'089162—dc22

2006032384

For Gerard Tobin, in memoriam

For Helen Tobin, in memoriam

and for

Catherine Tobin ni Donavan, and James Tobin

and

Martin Ruane, and Nora Ruane ni Hughes,

sojourners

CONTENTS

INTRODUCTION

Irish American Poetry and the Question of Tradition

What does it mean to be an Irish American poet? The question is not just rhetorical, for it raises to consciousness the issue of a certain kind of imaginative identity that rarely, if ever, has been adequately explored. In fact, the question is so fundamental that we might want to rephrase it in such a way that something of what is at stake behind the question enters into its form. So: Does the experience of being Irish American predispose the Irish American poet to embrace any characteristic themes, subjects, or styles? Is there in such poetry something that might be identified as a uniquely Irish American sensibility, in the same way one might identify Jewish American poetry or African American poetry? And, if not, is it worth even using the appellation "Irish American Poetry," as though such a thing existed in any artistically commendable form? Such questions construe Irish American poetry as a problem to be wrestled with, and possibly constructed, rather than as an established tradition to celebrate alongside Irish American forays into politics or the entertainment industry. Charles Fanning, for one, remarks in his ground-breaking *The Irish Voice in America* that while Irish American fiction and drama constitute a distinctive and complex literary heritage, Irish American poetry has been afflicted by a "simplicity" that verges on the stage Irish:

> Over the years many Irish Americans have published poems, and by the 1880s critic E. C. Steadman was referring to an "Irish-American School" of poets. This poetry has often been popular, and the legions of green-covered volumes of verse stretching back to the 1810s and the 1820s have had their effect on the Irish-American literary self-consciousness. And yet, there have been few memorable Irish-American poems, especially before recent times. The problem has been an endemic blight of programmatic melancholy or bravado that emerged from the experience and perception of forced exile. The stock-in-trade of Irish-American poetry has been the immigrant's lament for a lost, idealized homeland and the patriot's plea for Irish freedom from British oppression. Such materials make good songs

but bad verse that exhibits simplistic strains of nostalgia and righteous indignation.[1]

Unless one is willing to elide any distinction between "popular" poetry, say, of the kind one might have found in *Gill's Irish Reciter* or *The Household Anthology of Irish Poets* (1886), and the poetry of considered literary achievement, it is fruitless to contradict Charles Fanning's judgment. Moreover, if we assume as Charles Fanning does that an Irish American literature must by definition involve distinctively Irish American "subjects, themes, styles, plot-lines and character types,"[2] then what perhaps ought to be a dominant theme in Irish American poetry—the immigrant experience—is virtually absent from the work of those Irish American poets who have assumed, in some notable cases, highly prominent positions within the pantheon of American poetry.

One prime exception to this state of affairs is the poetry of John Boyle O'Reilly, a poet and journalist of commanding presence in late-nineteenth-century America, whose work represents a more serious and complex engagement with Irish America. However, as Conor Johnston observed, for all its seriousness most of O'Reilly's poetry is finally characterized more by a "documentary style" than by any self-justifying aesthetic impulse.[3] Nevertheless, in poems like "Crispus Attucks" and "At Fredericksburg," O'Reilly's self-consciousness at being an Irish American immigrant powerfully fuels his aesthetic engagement with American history. Indeed, his identification with Crispus Attucks reveals his sympathy with the fate of African Americans, as well as the heroic struggle of a people to maintain their dignity in the face of oppression. In O'Reilly's imagination, African Americans and the emigrant Irish are joined together in a uniquely American quest for freedom. Similarly, though in "At Fredericksburg" O'Reilly commemorates Irish American dead who fought for both the North and South in one of the bloodiest battles of the Civil War, the poem ultimately celebrates the equality of all races: "Who loveth the Flag is a man and a brother, / No matter what birth or what race or what creed."[4] Such poems place the Irish American experience at the heart of the American experience and join Irish American poetry to other ethnic poetries that seek to examine the question of what it means to be an American.

John Boyle O'Reilly's is not the sole example of an Irish American poet whose work confronts such definitively American issues. Born in 1774, Thomas Branagan addresses the question of slavery head-on in his "Avenia" (1805). Branagan conceived of the poem as a tragic epic of the slave trade and, as such, something of an abolitionist's zeal infuses the poem's heroic romance. More importantly, Branagan's work, like O'Reilly's, anticipates an ongoing encounter between two ethnic groups whose relations with each other have shaped American history. Born in 1760, Mathew Carey's "The Plaigiscuriliad" and "The Porqupiniad" (1798) are by his own account "Hudbrastic poems." With their terse satirical wit, these mock epics illuminate the rich political ferment of New York City during the post–Revolutionary War period. All of these works, along with the poetry of John Boyle O'Reilly, establish the concern with American history and politics as significant themes in Irish American poetry. As such, among the multitude of Irish American poems that invoke the immigrant's lament for a lost history, there are those that intend to explore and often celebrate the history of the exile's new nation. Though not included in this volume, Charles James Cannon's "The Crowning Hour" and James Riley's "Patos, Hispaniola 1492" are nineteenth-century poems that, while not great poetry, nonetheless exemplify the desire to commemorate one of history's most significant turning points—Columbus's discovery of America. Both poems anticipate Hart Crane's "Ave Maria," the first section of his epic *The Bridge*. Indeed, their foreshadowing of Crane's great work is remarkable. "Te Deum laudamus / O Thou Hand of Fire," so Cannon's poem ends, as does Hart Crane's. In turn, the self-conscious exploration of American social relations as well as the plight of laborers in the poems of James Jeffrey Roche and Daniel O'Connell presages the work of such leftist poets as Lola Ridge and Thomas McGrath. Likewise, the place of Louise Imogene Guiney among these poets, as well as Kate McPhelim Cleary, augurs for the full flowering of American women's poetry in the twentieth century. At the very least, the work of these poets offers a more nuanced picture of the place of Irish American poetry within the tradition of American poetry as it developed over the course of the nineteenth century.

Beyond the interesting cases of John Boyle O'Reilly, Thomas Branagan, and others, the issue of Irish American poets embracing Irish American themes—if not constructing an Irish American identity—becomes even more murky when one considers those American poets for whom Ireland has no ancestral allure, and who yet have taken Ireland as inspiration for their own imaginative work. Though a minor poem, Walt Whitman's "Old Ireland" brings the Shan Van Vocht, or Old Mother Ireland, into the purview of his own democratic vision. "What you wept for was translated," Whitman writes, "passed from the grave, / The winds favored and the sea sailed it, / And now with rosy and new blood, / Moves today in a new country."[5] Here, the iconography of the Irish emigrant experience becomes assimilated into the cosmos of Whitman's America. In Wallace Stevens's "Our Stars Come from Ireland," and most notably in "The Irish Cliffs of Moher," Ireland again becomes the prism through which an American poet at once envisions and defines his work. In "Our Stars Come from Ireland," it is through contemplation of his native place that the poet's fictional Tom Mc-Greevy (as opposed to the Irish poet, Thomas McGreevy, who corresponded with Stevens) defines his sense of identity. Not surprisingly, McGreevy's immigrant consciousness is, for Stevens, illustrative of the imagination. It embodies "the westwardness of everything," as do the Irish cliffs of Moher in Stevens's poem of that title, where the imagination's return to its primal elements—"earth and sea and air"—is spurred inescapably by what Seamus Heaney might have called "the backward look" to origins: "Who is my father in this world, in this house, / at the spirit's base?"[6] In a similar vein, though without the canonical security of Whitman and Stevens, recent American poets like Chris Agee, Julie O'Callaghan, Richard Tillinghast, and Knute Skinner have found in Ireland an alternative to the contemporary consumerist landscape of America. Such poets assume more than merely a tourist's glancing encounter with Ireland, while American poets like Robert Frost, Louis Simpson, Hayden Carruth, Elizabeth Spires, and J. D. McClatchy have written notable poems that demonstrate at least a passing influence of Ireland and Irish culture, though the poets themselves claim no Irish ancestry. Does the work of these poets warrant being called Irish American? On the other hand, to muddy the waters further, there are those writers of Irish American ancestry who would find being labeled "an Irish American writer" limiting for their work. A good poet is a good poet, and defining the poetry through the lens of ethnicity detracts from and perhaps even diminishes the individual artistic achievement. Why align oneself with what Yeats called derisively "the poetry of the point of view"? Writers would prefer to steer clear of such aesthetic and critical harbors, the way Elizabeth Bishop sought to exclude her work from anthologies of women's poetry. Yet can we imagine an anthology devoted to the poetry of American women *without* Elizabeth Bishop? While some lament the loss of the ideal of a pure aesthetic judgment, and others exult in the victory of multiculturalism in politicizing our understanding of literature and culture, the reader who wishes to pursue the question of whether there is such a thing as Irish American poetry will have to negotiate these extremes by weighing the claims of ethnicity and identity against those of aesthetic integrity. Such is the intention of this volume.

From yet another perspective, however, the sheer prominence of certain Irish American poets within the history of American poetry argues for the affirmation of an Irish American tradition, especially if we refrain from narrowly defining a poet's thematic and aesthetic inclinations. Surely, one can remain open to such preoccupations, especially when one considers the work of Edwin Arlington Robinson and John Gould Fletcher, two poets on the cusp of Modernism whose Irish American heritage enters passingly, albeit obliquely, into their work.

Still, given the poet's Scotch-Irish ancestry, Fletcher's work in particular offers passage into an important estuary of Irish American poetry that anticipates the work of poets like Kathryn Stripling Byer, Carolyne Wright, Michael McFee, and Michael Chitwood—poets whose Scotch-Irish inheritance informs their sense of identity and hence their poetry. Between Fletcher and these contemporary poets, the work of A. R. Ammons stands as one of the high water marks of American poetry.

The presence of Irish American poets at the advent of Modernism offers similar vantages. In his poem "To Robinson Jeffers," Nobel laureate Czeslaw Milosz chides the preeminent American poet of nature's austerity and majesty for proclaiming "an inhuman thing."[7] Yet, as Milosz's poem suggests, the source of what he sees as Jeffers' embrace of human diminishment before brute nature lies, initially at least, in a deep-seated cultural identification. "If you have not read the Slavic poets so much the better," Milosz's poem begins, "there's nothing there for a Scotch-Irish wanderer to seek." For Milosz, Jeffers is not so much an American as someone whose Scotch-Irish ancestry and Ulster heritage—and in particular his father's Calvinist theology—shapes his imaginative identity. Unquestionably there is a stark transcendence and virility to Robinson Jeffers's vision, and while we might want to hesitate before endorsing Milosz's cultural rebuke, his insight nevertheless raises the question of whether there is something in Jeffers' poetry that is distinctly Irish American, or a variation of being Irish American: a restlessness born, perhaps, of historical circumstance, as well as a preoccupation with nature, place, and the metaphysical. So we may ask whether there is more than merely a generic thematic connection between Yeats' "rook-delighting heaven," or Heaney's victims of tribal violence, and Jeffers' own disturbing version of the sublime among California's brooding headlands.

In contrast, Marianne Moore is a poet whose imaginative proclivities and evocations of people and places and particularly animals incline toward the fabulous. Her whole sensibility stands in stark contrast to that of Jeffers. Not surprisingly, the difference is perhaps most evident in both poets' use of line. Moore's formal interest in the precision of syllabic verse appears utterly alien to Jeffers' vigorous free-verse. And if, to risk being fanciful, Robinson Jeffers braces himself like a hermit on Skellig Michael before the violent majesty of nature, then we can likewise picture Marianne Moore similar to a monk bent over an illuminated manuscript obsessively working over one of her fantastic creatures. Nevertheless, in the last line of her poem "Spenser's Ireland" she writes "I am troubled, I'm dissatisfied, I'm Irish,"[8] a declaration that resonates with the more turbulent stirrings of Jeffers' efforts to "befriend the furies." Indeed, "Spenser's

Ireland" is a noteworthy poem by an American modernist whose influence and achievement ranks her, with Jeffers, among the most significant twentieth-century American poets. Moreover, it is a highly anthologized poem that both admits and explores the poet's Irish ancestry. From yet another standpoint, however, one might object to the poem's declaration that Spenser's Ireland "has not altered;— / a place as kind as it is green," the "greenest place" the poet has "never seen,"[9] for in so doing the poem effectively disavows history even as it obscures the fact that, considering the great English poet's own administrative role in a mechanism of conquest, Spenser's Ireland was anything but kind. As such, while Marianne Moore's "Spenser's Ireland" stands as an artistically achieved moment of consciousness on the part of Irish American poetry, it also defines the limits of that consciousness within the poet's sense of identity.

Both Jeffers and Moore were born in the latter years of the nineteenth century, and taken together their work comprises a significant Irish American contribution to American modernism. Lesser figures like Lola Ridge, Ernest Walsh, and Horace Gregory became significant practitioners and exponents of modernist poetic practice. Lola Ridge's "The Ghetto" is an example of modernist poetry that stands as a corrective to the Rightist program of figures like Pound, Eliot, and Yeats. Ridge's poem rejects anti-Semitism through her imaginative identification with the Jews of New York's Lower East Side. Her's is a neglected achievement. Largely forgotten, the later poems of Ernest Walsh anticipate the experimental poetics of "postmodernity." In turn, Louise Bogan, who was born near the turn of the century and whose paternal grandfather emigrated from Derry, stands as one of this century's most important early exemplars of what Adrienne Rich called "the female sensibility" in poetry. Though known more for her novels, Kay Boyle's poetry is also significant in this regard. While the question of being Irish American does not fully enter into Louise Bogan's poetry, her terse visionary and at times incantatory poems are laudable for their willingness to engage often unconscious, irrational processes as fit subject matter for poetry. Her work crosses the Romantic tradition with depth psychology even as she breaks new imaginative ground for poetry written by women. In the poem "Hypocrite Swift," her abiding concerns find expression by exposing the great Anglo-Irish satirist for a misanthropy that belies his seeming liberality: "Stir / The bed-clothes; hearten up the perishing fire. / Hypocrite Swift sent Stella a green apron / And dead desire."[10] Bogan's critique of Swift is part of a wellspring of American feminist poetry that eventually flows into the work of Adrienne Rich and many others, and then onward and then back to Ireland through the work of Eavan Boland.

A similar spirit of directness and radical politics inheres in the poems of Thomas McGrath. Born in 1916, McGrath was a lifelong communist and campaigner for social justice who refused to testify before the McCarthy House Sub-committee on Un-American Activities, and whose poems range formally from a Whitmanesque expansiveness to the concision of haiku. While certainly his political beliefs have curtailed a general appreciation of his achievement (though his work has been lauded with numerous fellowships and prizes), there is no diminishing his poems' passionate intensity even as they avoid merely "documentary" or political cant. His concern with political exile, with social and metaphysical justice, places him prominently within a tradition of poets of dissent, of which the Irish are not excluded. In his epic, *Letter to an Imaginary Friend*, those passions find expression by reference to the Irish American working class of which his own family was a part.[11] Another "epic poet" of Irish American ancestry is Charles Olson, whose Maximus poems join Ezra Pound's influence to a uniquely American sense of place. At the same time, his "Enniscorthy Suite" and "The Grandfather-Father Poem," among others, give his postmodernist sensibility an explicitly Irish American context. To these auspicious names from these first two decades of twentieth-century American poetry we may add that of Robert Fitzgerald, a poet in his own right whose magisterial translations of Homer's *Iliad* and *The Odyssey*, and Virgil's *Aeneid*, are among the finest produced in this century.

Few American poets, of any ethnicity, have been as troubled or disaffected as John Berryman and fewer still, with the exception of Lowell, Plath, and Sexton, have dramatized their own psychomachia with as much vigilance and artistic strength. Born in 1914, of the same stellar generation of poets that produced Elizabeth Bishop, Robert Lowell, Randall Jarrell, and Delmore Schwartz, Berryman's Irish connection may be traced through his grandmother Mary Kanar whose family emigrated from County Cork. Of particular significance to seeing Berryman's work through the prism of "Irish American Poetry" is the final section of his masterwork, *The Dream Songs*. There, Berryman makes a pilgrimage to Ireland which comprises nothing less than an imaginative confrontation, if not with his ancestral roots, than with one of the most significant "hiding places" of his own artistic powers. "I have moved to Dublin to have it out with you / majestic Shade, You whom I read so well / so many years ago," so he writes in Dream Song 312.[12] The Shade is obviously William Butler Yeats, and the urgency with which Berryman seeks to "have it out" with him is testimony to the Irish poet's influence on his American disciple. Moreover, given the fact that Berryman's eastern passage is a journey through which he leaves "behind the country of the dead," we can understand the poet's self-imposed exile from America as a kind of return from Tir na nOg, an imagined reversal of the nineteenth-century immigrant's journey; or Stevens's Tom McGreevy—troubled, dissatisfied, Irish—pursuing his ghosts under the aegis of his fixed stars.

Lesser instances of an American poet's engagement with compelling Irish shades are John Logan's "At Drumcliffe Churchyard, County Sligo" and "Dublin Suite: Homage to James Joyce." Logan's work, though not of the same monumental power as Berryman's, likewise reveals a considerable autobiographical impulse as well as a fascination with the theme of the poet's peripatetic physical and metaphysical wandering. The like is true of the poetry of Alan Dugan who has won two Pulitzer Prizes and two National Book Awards, and whose work is fueled by an acerbic wit which, in the poem "Mockery Against the Irish Censorship," he turns against a country that "was better in its dream" because it has sought to curtail the imaginations of its poets.[13] In marked distinction to Dugan's poetry, the richly celebrated and highly influential work of Frank O'Hara engages the world with little if any dissatisfaction. His own wanderings through the streets of his beloved New York are occasions for discerning wonder within the quotidian and recording those spots of urban time with painterly precision. To his name we may add James Schuyler's, whose Pulitzer Prize winning *The Morning of the Poem* in both sensibility and imaginative execution emerges from O'Hara's fascination with the off-hand and occasional as a source for poetry. Still more explicitly visionary is the work of Galway Kinnell whose ecstatic religious sensibility makes him equally at home evoking the vivid street-life of a modern immigrant ghetto in "The Avenue Bearing the Initial of Christ into the New World" and embarking on a kind of metaphysical dreamquest in *The Book of Nightmares*. Less prominent, the poetry of Ned O'Gorman likewise evinces a strong religious and particularly Catholic sensitivity. In this it resembles the work of the Jesuit poet, Daniel Berrigan, though O'Gorman's is more traditionally formalist in temperament. Leo Connellan's poetry, in turn, exhibits an affinity for both the New England landscape of the poet's childhood and the urban landscape of his years as a businessman in New York. His *The Clear Blue Lobster Water Country* is yet another personal epic by an Irish American. Connellan's grandfather "The O'Dock," the central figure of the poem, may be compared to Wallace Stevens's "The McCullough," the major-man of "Notes Toward a Supreme Fiction." Both are Irish American figures, though where Stevens's giant is an imaginative invention Connellan's enjoins the real historical circumstance of a particular poet's imaginative growth.

Born to the same generation of poets as O'Hara and Kinnell as well as Connellan, X. J. Kennedy's work exhibits a wryly satirical intelligence, as well as a formalism that ties the emergence of his work in the 1950s to the New Formalists of today. In contrast, the poetry of Robert Creeley embraces a minimalist aesthetic—in his own words an aesthetic of "the hearth."[14] Creeley's poems are almost always short and focus on the moment, though with none of O'Hara's penchant for lush, seemingly off-hand description. Instead, Creeley's work operates through a pared-down clarity of perception, and so the poems assume an almost etched quality. His connection with Charles Olson through the Black Mountain School of American poetry establishes his work, as well as Olson's, in the center of the American *avant-garde*. In turn, though not as influential as Creeley's work, Robert Kelly's poems and the poems of Ted Berrigan record an Irish American presence likewise influenced by the work of the Black Mountain Projectivists. Finally, yet another Irish American who has had a profound influence on the history of American poetry is James Laughlin. A devotee of Ezra Pound, Laughlin not only wrote his own poems, but at the master's suggestion began New Directions, one of the most important *avant-garde* houses in American publishing history.

Nevertheless, despite all of these achievements, with the exception of certain individual poems and poets, few from among this diverse group places their work consistently within an explicitly Irish or Irish American context. If there are common themes—social or psychic dissatisfaction, the relationship to family, to the natural world, to history, varying brands of religious sensibility—they only occasionally refer to anything that might be identified as an specifically Irish American ethnic milieu. The same could not be said for most, if not all, important African American poets, and the recent publication of Stephen Rubin's *Telling and Remembering,* as well as Jonathan Barron's *Jewish American Poetry,* suggests the prominence of a specifically Jewish American poetry. One obvious reason for this circumstance might be that, for specific social reasons, the Irish like other peoples of European lineage were able to assimilate more fully into American society than either of these groups, despite their having been largely vilified early on as a minority whose religion and cultural practices were deemed anti-American. Alongside of African Americans, Irish Americans competed for a foothold in American society, and like "Jim Crow" and "Jim Dandy," the drunken "Paddy" of Thomas Nast's cartoons exemplifies the tendency to belittle if not dehumanize the emigrant Irish during this period in American history. Nevertheless, horrific displays of racism such as the New York Draft Riots of 1863 illuminate the extent to which the common experience of oppression and marginalization can lead to greater discord and alienation rather than a sense of common experience and purpose.

Placed against the backdrop of such social forces, the achievement of Irish American poets—great as it is through such figures as Jeffers, Moore, Bogan, Berryman, and O'Hara—reveals something of a collective cultural amnesia. As we have seen, one key exception to this set of circumstances is the work of John Boyle O'Reilly whose importance in this regard is underscored by Paul

Laurence Dunbar's poem in homage to the Irish American poet. Nevertheless, while the Irish American poetry of the nineteenth century remains largely "programmatic"[15] in its treatment of Irish America, the more notable work of those who follow largely neglects to treat substantially the historical and social circumstances from which Irish America arose.

This has not been the case among those Irish poets who have spent substantial periods of time in the United States and whose presence here has greatly influenced their work. Padraic Colum's extended sojourn in America warranted that his work be included in at least one American anthology of poetry. The like is true of Oliver St. John Gogarty.[16] Brian Coffey's "Missouri Sequence" was born of his time as visiting professor at the University of St. Louis during the late forties and early fifties, and reveals the profound influence of Wallace Stevens. Similarly, Thomas Kinsella's poem "The Good Fight," inscribed to John F. Kennedy on the tenth anniversary of his death, and Eavan Boland's poem "The Emigrant Irish" demonstrate these Irish poets' success at giving voice to what should be considered Irish American subjects. The same might be said of Derek Mahon's *The Hudson Letter* and Peter Fallon's *The Deerfield Series*. And what of Paul Muldoon's hybrid excursions—his *immrama*—into Ireland and America? Are such poets merely Irish tourists in America, or do particular poems by such poets offer a vantage from which to inquire what it is to be Irish American? Muldoon has become an American citizen, and so his work warrants inclusion on that basis alone, but what of Boland, Mahon, Fallon, and the earlier figures, Colum, St. John Gogarty, and Coffey? Why not include Heaney's "Westering," or "Remembering Malibu"? Unlike these poets, the direction of Heaney's "American" poems is retrospective. America occasions thoughts of Ireland in the Nobel laureate's work, rather than exhibiting a sustained presence in its own right, such as may be found in the American poems of these other Irish poets. For that reason I include their work in this volume.

To a much larger degree, James Liddy—who has spent over thirty years teaching and writing in the United States—has composed a hybrid body of work that may be understood as a marriage between the Whitman tradition as embodied in American Beat poetics, and Kavanagh's parish, with undertones of Beckett and Ashbery. Younger poets like Eamon Grennan, Eamonn Wall, and Greg Delanty continue a tradition of writers who to varying degrees engage Irish American themes more strongly and readily than most Irish American poets whose work has been incorporated into anthologies of American verse. Greg Delanty's poems might be said to explore the boundary between Irish-ness and American-ness, while Eamonn Wall's reveals something of a pioneer's passion for exploring the continent and its history, including Native America. Both of these poets place the new Irish emigrant experience at the forefront of Irish as well as Irish American poetry. One Irish American poet whose work is rarely seen as Irish American is John Montague. Montague's *oeuvre,* of not only Irish but international renown, is in large part the product of what he has called his "double birth"[17]—his having been born in America to Irish immigrant parents at the beginning of the Great Depression and then re-patriated back to County Tyrone in his early childhood—as well as his almost mythopoeic connection to his ancestral home. If any poet has succeeded in portraying the complex world of Irish America in light of his own "double consciousness" it is John Montague. His is a path similarly traveled by Padraic Fiacc, who emigrated from Belfast to Hell's Kitchen in New York City and returned.

In many ways John Montague is a pivotal figure, for in his work the idea of being an Irish American poet enters into and becomes to a great extent the subject of the poetry. In this regard his work at once overtly manifests an imaginative identity that has remained unexamined in most Irish American poetry until recent years, and establishes a bridge to the old world without recourse to nostalgia at the same time as it anticipates those newer Irish American poets who seem determined to include at least some of their own historically charged ethnic identity into their poems. Brendan Galvin is one such poet who understands his work as emerging from a specifically Irish American milieu. In addition to being obsessed with landscape and seascape in and around his native Massachusetts, in his *Saints in Their Ox-Hide Boat* Galvin establishes a metaphorical connection between his own identity as a poet and that of the Irish saint who, in legend at least, "discovered America" centuries before Columbus or the first Norse settlers in Newfoundland. Galvin's embrace of the natural world is as vital as Jeffers', though more palliative in its recognition of the human presence in nature and the value of human work. Likewise, Tess Gallagher's poems move with ease between both Irish and American subjects, enjoining each with a lyricism that borders on the visionary. Still other poets like Maura Stanton, Alice Fulton, Dennis Finnell, Ethna McKiernan, Nuala Archer, Thomas Lynch, Mary Swander, Maureen Seaton, Larry Levis, R.T. Smith, Gibbons Ruark, Billy Collins, Michael Heffernan, Ben Howard, Phillip Dacey, Katherine Stripling Byer, Michael Waters, and Terence Winch often write poems that emerge from a sensibility that is uniquely Irish American. Others, like Michael Ryan, James Galvin, Peter Cooley, Richard Kenney, Heather McHugh, Mekeel McBride, Diana O'Hehir, Killarney Clary, Marie Howe, Campbell McGrath, and Brigit Pegeen Kelly, while not always writing explicitly out of an Irish American context, collectively have produced a range of work that speaks to the vitality of the Irish American presence in the wide and varied world of American poetry. That variety ranges stylistically from the experimental poetries of Susan Howe, Fanny Howe, and Maureen Owen to formalist narratives. Add to that Alice Fulton's poems that cross physics with the Irish American poet's concern with metaphysics and what one discovers is a remarkable diversity of styles and subject matter within the poetry being written by Irish Americans. There are many others whose poems exhibit not only the widest possible range of sensibilities but also geographical affiliations that extend through every region of the country from Appalachia to Las Vegas, from North Carolina to Alaska. Moreover, the awards bestowed on Irish American poets range from Yale Younger Poet Awards and state poet laureateships to Pulitzer Prizes, National Book Awards, American Book Awards, the Lenore Marshall Prize, the Kingsley Tufts Award, and MacArthur Foundation grants. To observe, then, that the poetry of Irish Americans remains a vigorous presence within the heritage of American poetry, a presence that is by now well nigh indispensable, is to point out what ought to be obvious.

Yet is it the same thing to claim that the poetry of Irish Americans has an indispensable place in American poetry as it is to claim there is a tradition of Irish American poetry? Reformulated in the light of such a diverse company of poets, the question of whether there is at least a lineage of Irish American poetry is already answered—in the affirmative. More specifically, one might argue that a tradition of Irish American poets exists within the multiple traditions or schools that compose American poetry—modernists, projectivists, confessionals, Beats, New York School, deep imagists, formalists, and postmodernists of various stripes. At the same time, at least in part such an affirmation rings hollow. As T. S. Eliot observed, "tradition is a matter of much wider significance" than "the blind or timid adherence" to the literary culture's successes.[18] Crucial to Eliot's understanding of tradition is his perception that tradition is composed "not only of the pastness of the past but of its presence." He argues that a person can intuit "a feeling that the whole of the literature of Europe from Homer and within it the whole literature of his country has a simultaneous existence and composes a simultaneous order."[19] Discredited as Eliot remains in some critical circles, his idea of what he called "the historical sense" has become, if anything, more critically acute in recent decades. Indeed, Eliot's historical sense may be seen as explicitly politicized through contemporary theory's broadened awareness of history and its injustices as well as its recognition of cultural and ethnic hybridity. Dislodged from its implicit assumption of European cultural dominance and its air of "ethnic absolutism,"[20] Eliot's ideal order "of existing monuments" may seem more a necropolis to be dismantled than a city of the mind, a tradition that evolves as new talents extend and reconfigure its boundaries. Of course, Eliot's own encompassing interest in non-western cultural traditions ought to mitigate against seeing him as merely a Eurocentric prig. Eliot's idea of tradition may yet survive both the tidal wave of politicized criticism and his own dubious political and racial views, provided such an understanding of tradition can become resilient beyond its original intent in order to become even more worldly, more encompassing—a "traveling tradition" to adapt Paul Gilroy's use of the concept of "traveling cultures" in his book, *The Black Atlantic.*

I raise such intractable issues now, however belatedly and briefly, if only to shift the question of whether there is a tradition of Irish American poetry away from "genetic templates" and clearly identifiable Irish American contexts toward an understanding of tradition that is flexible enough to embrace an inclusiveness and plurality that might keep alive the question of tradition in the ongoing process of seeking to define it. From this perspective, the neglect of explicit Irish American themes in the work of certain prominent Irish American poets becomes an essential part of the story. At the same time, the motifs of travel and exile, often with reference to water, and the recurrent figure of "the west," perhaps constitute an almost unconscious subtext for the theme of dispora in Irish American poetry.

Likewise, the image of Ireland in American poetry as portrayed in the works of poets who are not necessarily Irish American ought to be brought under critical consideration. African American poets like Gwendolyn Brooks have written poems that give us important and challenging images of Irish America. The Irish maid, Patsy Houlihan, in Brooks's "Bronzeville Woman in a Red Hat" offers a sympathetic model of endurance and protest for the African American maid who takes her place in Mrs. Miles's bigoted home. While Gwendolyn Brooks is clearly not an Irish American poet, this is a poem of obvious relevance to Irish America. In any case, to decide whether a poet is Irish American by applying a genetic formula—one quarter Irish makes you eligible for the Irish soccer team—seems equally specious. Indeed, from one perspective the purpose of this anthology is to shift the locus of identification away from genetic templates and toward a cultural nexus so that ethnic claims, while acknowledged and respected, might also enjoin a wider scope of definition and aesthetic expression. For example, "After the Digging" by Jewish American poet, Alan Shapiro, may be the most sustained treatment of the Irish Potato Famine in American poetry, and stands alongside Brendan Galvin's "1847" and James McMichael's "The Begotten" as one of the few lengthy treatments of the subject. By enjoining the work of such non–Irish American poets, Irish American poetry—both conceived of as a product of Irish American poets, and as production itself of social, cultural, and historical forces—may assume an important place alongside other significant traditions within the wider world of American poetry. Indeed, the world opened by such considerations may reveal an imaginative space wherein the many traditions that compose American poetry can be seen in the light of new perspectives. It may also expand our understanding of Irish poetry. If this is true, the tradition of American poetry may itself come to exist as a more self-conscious, complex and evolving whole—a traveling tradition in the richest possible sense. If Eliot is still instructive in such matters it is in his recognition that to remain vital traditions must be attentive to both the past and the present in the attempt to bring into being a future that is not entirely foreseen. However it is constructed, Irish American Poetry will need to reconcile the claims of the individual talent to the evolving standards of just such a living historical sensibility. From such a vantage, within its limits, this anthology seeks to be a testing ground rather than a canonical template for what it means to be Irish American.

In keeping with these assumptions, I have organized the poems historically and in three parts that reflect, as much as possible, general distinctions in the stylistic and thematic orientations of the poets as well as the evolving scope of American poetry. Part One: A Fluent Drift, begins with George Berkeley's "Verses on the Prospect of Planting Arts and Learning in America" and ends with Padraig O'Heigeartaigh's "My Sorrow Donncha" and Paul Laurence Dunbar's "John Boyle O'Reilly." Where Bishop Berkeley's poem looks forward to the rich cultural flowering that was to come over the next three centuries, O'Heigeartaigh's poem, composed in Irish, looks backward toward the Old World and sings out of the tragic sense of exile and loss that so many Irish experienced in making their way to the New. Dunbar's poem acknowledges the centrality of O'Reilly in Irish American poetry. Between them, I have culled a sampling of the best poetry produced by poets who have been lost or ignored by American poetry. These poems mostly fulfill the conventions of nineteenth-century verse, though I have sought to select works both of some artistic merit and that might also communicate a sense of cultural and historical urgency— an engagement with time, place, Ireland and America that precipitates the developments to come. Among these are poems like Thomas Branagan's lost Abolitionist-Homeric epic, "Avenia," and John Boyle O'Reilly's "Crispus Attucks," both of which exemplify an Irish American concern with the plight of African American oppression. Paul Laurence Dunbar's homage to O'Reilly likewise bears witness to a shared belief in freedom, and in the common aspirations of African and Irish Americans. Such poems offer a counter-vision to the racism and mistrust that has historically plagued relations between these two ethnic groups. Similarly, the poetry of Alice Cary, Louise Imogen Guiney, and Kate McPhelim Cleary anticipates the contributions of a plethora of Irish American women to American poetry in the twentieth century.

Appropriately, then, Part Two: Modern Tide begins with Lola Ridge. Like John Boyle O'Reilly, Ridge emigrated from Ireland by way of Australia, though where O'Reilly escaped a Fenian prison term in New South Wales to become one of the most celebrated literary figures of his time, Ridge escaped the lace shackles of a complacent middle-class life to become a powerful voice of the American proletariat. In Lola Ridge's work we find a distinctly modern sensibility expressed in a distinctly modern idiom, and as such the modernist achievements of Marianne Moore, Robinson Jeffers, and Charles Olson find their herald in her, as does the groundbreaking work of Louise Bogan. Moreover, the premature death of Ernest Walsh foreclosed the development of a distinctly Irish American consciousness in modernism. Part Two also includes the second generation of poets whose work traces the shift from modernism to postmodernism, among them John Berryman, Thomas McGrath, and John Montague. Berryman, a supreme literary insider in the mid-century dominated by Robert Lowell, and McGrath, the ultimate literary outsider anathematized in the McCarthy hearings for his radical politics, demonstrate the breadth of the Irish American contribution to American poetry during the period. In turn, William Carlos Williams pervades John Montague's distinctly hybrid Irish American "double consciousness." Following Charles Olson's lead at the Black Mountain School of Poetry, Robert Creeley, Ted Berrigan, and Robert Kelly furthered the experimental tradition in American poetry. Add to them James Liddy's adaptation of Beat Poetry and Frank O'Hara's centrality to The New York School, and Irish American poets begin to reveal themselves as something of a force in the world of American "contrarian" poetics. In contrast, the work of both X. J. Kennedy and Ned O'Gorman locates itself within the formalist tradition of American poetry. In all, Part Two exemplifies the tendency of Irish American poetry to move beyond convenient stylistic categories at the same time as it remains faithful to an abiding preoccupation with history, with other ethnicities and traditions on the American cultural landscape, and with its own evolving consciousness. Like Dunbar's poem from the previous century, Gwendolyn Brooks's "Bronzeville Woman in a Red Hat" demonstrates an intimacy of common cause between African America and Irish America that often has been overlooked.

While on the one hand the sheer variety of voices, as well as the evolving continuities within schools and traditions in the American poetry of the mid-century, mitigates against any clear demarcation between Part Two and Part Three, I have chosen to begin Part Three: Further Harbors with the work of Brendan Galvin. In the poetry of Brendan Galvin, Irish American consciousness manifests itself in a sense of history and culture uniquely its own and, most importantly, that consciousness no longer relies on the immediate experience of the emigrant for articulation but explicitly and consistently inheres in the work of a poet for whom the immigrant experience is a part of a generational awareness. Of course, the work of such poets as Leo Connellan and X. J. Kennedy reveal a distinctly Irish American sense of identity, but the extent of Brendan Galvin's engagement with history is more pervasive—witness "Carrowkeel," "Hearing Irish Spoken," and "1847." At the same time, the tradition of Irish emigrant poetry that begins in the nineteenth-century and continues through modernism and postmodernism finds its continuation in the "New Irish" poets, Greg Delanty and Eamonn Wall. It is a long tradition that begins in the nineteenth century where the major figure is John Boyle O'Reilly, and proceeds through the work of Lola Ridge, Padraic Colum, James Liddy, and Eamon Grennan, before arriving at the New Irish Poets. Noteworthy also are the poets for whom America becomes not only a place of arrival but a point of embarkation back to Ireland, though one that continues to haunt their imaginations. George Berkeley, James Orr, Oliver St. John Gogarty, Padraic Fiacc and, most importantly, John Montague are among this group. Among Irish American poets a generation or more removed from the emigrant experience, we find a wide range of sensibilities extending from the highly experimental to the formal. We also find Irish American poets emigrating back to Ireland and England, such as Chris Agee, Julie O'Callaghan, and Michael Donaghy. Perhaps what binds all of these poets together is an implicit desire to extend the historical consciousness developed over three centuries. In these new poets we find a mix of irreverence and reverence, of popular culture and the sense of tradition, of Irish, American, and global concerns in a multiplicity of idioms that signal still further harbors, new imaginative "landings." From this perspective, the journey metaphor that has underwritten the subtitles of this book intends to speak to the ongoing passage of Irish American poetry within its own evolving traditions, in dialogue with other ethnic American poetries, and within the "traveling" tradition of American poetry as it moves into the twenty-first century.

Finally, this anthology could not have been completed without the generous assistance of Christine Casson, Jane Dorf, Heidi Jugenitz, Justin Kosec, Jenell Forschler, and Jean Preston at Carthage College, and Katie Lehman, Barbara Hanrahan, and Margaret Gloster at the University of Notre Dame Press. The help of a faculty development grant from Carthage College also aided me in the research and organization of the manuscript. I especially thank Jane Dorf for her patience and diligence in securing important and at times rare materials, and Jean Preston and Jenell Forschler for their patience and diligence in enduring my seemingly endless additions, cullings, and revisions. As always, I offer my gratitude to Christine Casson for her love and support. Greg Delanty, Charles

Fanning, James Liddy, and Eamonn Wall supplied essential suggestions for the book as did many of the other poets whose work is represented here. I also want to acknowledge Andrew Carpenter for alerting me to James Orr's "Songs Composed on the Banks of Newfoundland." To these I must add the editors of previous anthologies for their work of collecting poems that might otherwise have been lost. Needless to say, all these "leads" were crucial to my research. To all I owe a debt of gratitude.

—Daniel Tobin
Boston, Massachusetts

An earlier version of this essay appeared in *The Encyclopedia of the Irish in America,* ed. Michael Glazier (Notre Dame, IN: University of Notre Dame Press, 1999), and in *New Hibernia* 3, no. 4 (Winter 1999): 143–54.

1. Charles Fanning, *The Irish Voice in America* (Lexington: University Press of Kentucky, 1998), 4.

2. Ibid., 3.

3. Conor Johnston, " John Boyle O'Reilly as Poet." Unpublished paper given at the Midwest regional meeting of the American Conference for Irish Studies, October 16, 1998.

4. John Boyle O'Reilly, *Selected Poems* (New York: P. J. Kennedy and Sons, 1913), 21.

5. Walt Whitman, *Leaves of Grass,* ed. Sculley Bradley and Harold Blodgett (New York: Norton, 1973), 366.

6. Wallace Stevens, *Collected Poems* (New York: Alfred A. Knopf, 1978), 453, 511. See my essay "The Westwardness of Everything: Irishness in the Poetry of Wallace Stevens," in *The Wallace Stevens Journal* 27, no. 1 (Spring 2003): 27–48.

7. Czeslaw Milosz, *Collected Poems* (New York: Ecco Press, 1988), 224.

8. Marianne Moore, *Collected Poems* (New York: Penguin, 1981), 113.

9. Ibid.

10. Louise Bogan, *The Blue Estuaries* (New York: Ecco Press, 1977), 69.

11. With the exception of the early, difficult to find works of Mathew Carey and Thomas Branagan, I have refrained from including quotations from book-length poems such as those by Thomas McGrath, *Letter to an Imaginary Friend*; Leo Connellan, *The Clear Blue Lobster Water Country*; Brendan Galvin, *Saints in Their Ox-Hide Boat*; and Mary Swander, *Driving the Body Back*, with the hope that the interested reader will seek out these works on their own, and read them in their entirety, as is appropriate.

12. John Berryman, *The Dream Songs* (New York: Farrar, Straus and Giroux, 1982), 334.

13. Alan Dugan, *Poems* (New Haven: Yale University Press, 1961), 28.

14. Robert Creeley, Preface, *Selected Poems* (Berkeley: University of California Press, 1996), xx.

15. Fanning, *The Irish Voice in America*, 4.

16. See *Fifty Years of American Poetry* (New York: Dell, 1984), 6, 20.

17. John Montague, "The Complex Fate of Being Irish American," in *Born in Brooklyn* (Fredonia: White Pine Press, 1991), 32.

18. T. S. Eliot, "Tradition and the Individual Talent," in *Selected Prose* (New York: Harcourt, Brace, Jovanovich, 1975), 38.

19. Ibid.

20. See Paul Gilroy, *The Black Atlantic: Modernity and Double Consciousness* (Cambridge: Harvard University Press, 1993), 143–54.

PART ONE

A Fluent Drift

GEORGE BERKELEY
(1685–1753)

Verses on the Prospect of Planting Arts and Learning in America

The Muse, disgusted at an age and clime
    Barren of every glorious theme,
In distant lands now waits a better time,
    Producing subjects worthy fame:

In happy climes, where from the genial sun
    And virgin earth such scenes ensue,
The force of art by nature seems outdone,
    And fancied beauties by the true:

In happy climes the seat of innocence,
    Where nature guides and virtue rules,
Where men shall not impose for truth and sense,
    The pedantry of courts and schools:

There shall be sung another golden age,
    The rise of empire and of arts,
The good and great inspiring epic rage,
    The wisest heads and noblest hearts.

Not such as Europe breeds in her decay;
    Such as she bred when fresh and young,
When heav'nly flame did animate her clay,
    By future poets shall be sung.

Westward the course of empire takes its way;
    The four first acts already past,
A fifth shall close the drama with the day;
    Time's noblest offspring is the last.

MATHEW CAREY
(1760–1839)

(from) The Porqupiniad

Canto I

Descend, O Muse! my soul inspire;
And fill me with poetic fire,
Rolling in frenzy fine mine eye,
May I with Ward, or Trumbull vie,
While I recite great Cobbett's praise,
In Butler's Hudibrastic lays.
Great Cobbett! wonder of the age,
Whose works for years have been "the rage,"
And made th' enliven'd bosoms glow
Of priest and layman—high and low—
Of male and female—old and young—
Whose praise by grave and gay's been sung;
Whom British Critics celebrate,
And with fulsome praise intoxicate.

From Britain's isle our hero came,
In quest of fortune, pow'r, and fame;
Was hither by the premier sent,
To dictate to our government—
Our state affairs to regulate,
And Britain's cause to advocate:
Columbia's sons to fill with ire,
And all our councils to inspire
Our mother country's wrongs to feel,
In her defence to sharp the steel,
And make to heav'n the last appeal:
Our forces muster against France,

And in the cause of kings advance:
To fight the battles of the Lord,
To propagate his holy word,
And spread the gospel with the sword:
The five-head monster drive away,
Restore the Bourbons *sans* delay;
Who erst, as you may read in story,
Were sworn foes to Britain's glory,
And mark'd for worse than Punic faith
(So e'en our hero, Cobbett, faith)—
Unfeeling despots—tyrants fierce—
To freedom and her sons adverse—
(Whose ev'ry subject was a slave,
Perfidious, vile, frog-eating knave;
'Gainst popery and wooden shoes
What railing in both verse and prose!)—
But now, (what changes a few years
Effectuate, from this appears)
They are become a holy race,
Whose fall indelible disgrace
Casts on this innovating age,
So curst by democratic rage,
(From hell by Belial surely sent
Disorders direful to foment
In every legal government)
Of seventy-five (detested year
When faction's snakes began to rear,
Their baleful heads) accursed fruit
Which in this country first took root,
Transported by Fayette to France,
Where, *malgré* regal vigilance,
King, church, and nobles it destroy'd,
And neighb'ring nations sore annoy'd.
   Why for this scheme was Cobbett chose
Wise Solomon to tell would pose
His Tyburn visage seem'd to speak
That for his neck he'd had a squeak.
All mankind surely must agree
(If by the fruit we judge the tree),

He's 'mongst the worst of human race,
Flint-hearted, cruel, bloody, base—
The cannibal we plainly trace
In all his works. No dev'lish elf,
Nor even Satan's horrid self,
Did e'er breathe more infernal rage
Than he has shewn, through every page
Of his vile writings. A fierce flood
Will pour abroad, of human blood,
In civil war, if this curst knave
Our morals longer can deprave.

    Ne'er pays he least regard to truth—
To lie and swear is "nothing loth."
Illib'ral, rancorous, and vile,
Adept in every fraud and guile—
Possess'd of boundless impudence,
And equal store of insolence—

    As Haman he is vain and proud—
In his own praises ever loud:—
His writings are so base and mean,
So blackguard, stupid, and obscene—
That for this age we can't efface
The dire, th' ineffable disgrace,
Which from his Grub-street works proceeds,
And calculation far exceeds.

    Before our hero wing'd his flight,
His Mentor did his orders write,
To regulate his bold career,
And give the chart by which to steer,
And 'scape the shoal—the hidden rock,
Which might his pinnace rudely shock,
And to the bottom quickly send her
Beyond the skill of man to mend her:

    "Republics and their friends decry,
And monarchy raise to the sky:
Enhance the glories of a court,
Of law—of order—the support—
And eke of church establishment,
That solid prop of government:

Of morals—of obedience too—
Of ev'ry thing that's great or true:
Shew how unfit the people are
To enjoy of government a share-
To anarchy how freedom turns,
And all subjection proudly spurns.
    The Irish "outcasts" vilify,
Paint all their deeds of blackest die—
In Ireland swear, so mild's our sway,
That none our orders disobey,
Save lawless villains, wretched herd!
Unworthy of the least regard,
Wild, vicious, discontented, rude,
A turbulent and factious brood.
Shew how their linen trade we've cherish'd,
Arts, sciences, and commerce nourish'd:
How we have sent them priests and levites,
With judges, viceroys, and their fav'rites:
How for their sons we well provide
In armies and in fleets, our pride,
Which spread our glories far and wide.
How Luther we've 'gainst Calvin, arm'd,
And both with Catholics alarm'd;
Lest they should disobedient be
And madly seek for Liberty—
A strumpet vile and impudent,
Sworn foe to regal government.
And all this purely for their good,
Yet this accurst ungrateful brood:
Unmindful of our ceaseless care
With matchless impudence prepare,
Rebellion's bloody flag to rear.
But of the race we'll purge the land;
None shall our power or force withstand.
    Should e'er the wand'ring wretches dare,
For flight to western world prepare,
With coarse abuse you must o'erwhelm
Each fugitive that leaves the realm;
Them and adherents stigmatise,

By ev'ry fraud you can devise.
   But, mark me well, 'gainst France accurst,
Of all our foes by far the worst,
Your shafts direct with utmost force,
To fraud and falsehood have recourse:
Her crimes, her follies magnify,
Her friends, her leaders villify,
And her opposers justify.
Print Bloody Buoys, the fools to scare,
And cannibalian progress rare:
Let Rapine, Cruelty and Rapes,
With pallid Murder, in all shapes,
Stalk horibly through ev'ry page,
With infamy to blast the age,
When impious man dares raise his hand
Against th' anointed of the land—
Against the holy, sacred few,
To whom *divino jure's* due,
Despotic and unbounded sway;
Whole subjects are their lawful prey,
Created solely for their use.
These sacred maxims introduce,
Vile *"Freedom's leprosy"* to heal,
And to allay her burning zeal.

   "The rebels, too, of seventy-five,
Whether they're dead or still alive,
You must hold up to public scorn,
'Cause they've Columbia from us torn—
A glorious land, which might provide
The means to pamper up the pride
Of all our num'rous kingly race,
St. James's treasure and its grace:
There had they gain'd wealth, titles, pow'r;
But all was lost in luckless hour,
When the redoubted hero, Gage,
'Gan with provincial force engage—
When independence was proclaim'd,
And vile confederation fram'd.

JAMES ORR
(1770 – 1816)

Song Composed on the Banks of Newfoundland

In Ireland 'tis evening. From toil my friends hie all,
    And weary walk home o'er the dew-sprinkled lea;
The shepherd in love tunes his grief-soothing viol,
    Or visits the maid that his partner will be:
The blythe milk-maids trip to the herd that stands lowing,
    The West finely smiles, and the landscape is glowing,
The sad-sounding curfew, the torrent fast-flowing,
    Are heard by my fancy, tho' far, far at sea.

What has my eye seen since I left the green vallies
    But ships as remote as the prospect could be?
Unwieldy huge monsters, as ugly as malice,
    And planks of some wreck, which with sorrow I see?
What's seen but the fowl that his lonely flight urges,
    The light'ning that darts thro' the sky-meeting surges?
And the sad scouling sky, that with bitter rain scourges
    This cheek Care sits drooping on, far, far at sea?

How hideous the hold is!—Here, children are screaming,
    There dames faint thro' thirst, with their babes on their knee:
Here, down ev'ry hatch the big breakers are streaming,
    And, there, with a crash, half the fixtures break free:
Some court—some contend—some sit dull stories telling—
    The mate's mad and drunk, and the tar's task'd and yelling:
What sickness and sorrow, pervade my rude dwelling!—
    A huge floating lazar-house, far, far at sea.

How chang'd all may be when I seek the sweet village!
        A hedge-row may bloom where its street us'd to be;
The floors of my friends may be tortur'd by tillage,
        And the upstart be serv'd by the fallen grandee:
The axe may have humbled the grove that I haunted,
        And shades be my shield that as yet are unplanted;
Nor one comrade live, who repin'd when he wanted
        The sociable suff'rer, that's far, far at sea.

In Ireland 'tis night. On the flow'rs of my setting
        A parent may kneel, fondly praying for me:
The village is smokeless, the red moon is getting
        The hill for a throne, which I yet hope to see:
If innocence thrive many more have to grieve for,
        Success, slow but sure, I'll contentedly live for—
Yes, Sylvia! we'll meet, and your sigh cease to heave for
        The swain, your fine image haunts, far, far at sea.

THOMAS BRANAGAN
(1774 – 1843)

(from) Avenia Book I

Awake my Muse, the inharmonious strain!
I sing of arms on Africa's crimson'd plain:
Of war 'gainst Afric's sons by Christians wag'd,
With all the accursed love of Gold enrag'd.
What pen can half their villanies record!
What tongue can count the slaughters of their sword!
Give me, my muse, my melancholy bard,
Give me to paint their guilt and their reward!
But ere these deeds of carnage I rehearse,
Aid me to trace in less discordant verse
The native virtues of the sable train,
And grandeur of their own paternal plain:
Where fraught with fragrance, crops luxuriant grow,
Where cornels, blushing on the hawthorn glow.
Where with soft tendrils the rich clust'ring vine,
Doth round its friend, the aged elm entwine,
And tow'ring oaks their shadowy branches spread,
O'er the fat herds that on their fruit are fed;
Where stately palm trees form a cool retreat,
To screen the native from the sultry heat;
Where all the various tenants of the wood
Prowl on in safety, and enjoy their food,
Or satiate by the limpid streams abide,
And slumber, as the murmuring waters glide,
Where each harmonious warbler of the grove
Recounts its Maker's wisdom, truth and love,
While the river flow'rets spread their varied dyes,

And from ambrosial groves sweet odours rise:
There Heathens made terrestrial bliss their own,
To Christians, and their bloody arts unknown;
Each humble cottage was a calm retreat,
Ne'er purchas'd by the riches of the great; . . .

    .   .   .

The ships now anchor'd in the winding bay,
As the devoted towns in prospect lay:
The baptiz'd ruffians meet in council join'd,
While dreadful plans engage each hellish mind.
And all in horrid unity conclude
To entrap by fraud, then bathe their swords in blood.
Forth from the ships they send their boats well mann'd;
Which quick disgorge their contents on the land.
Five artful villains now direct their way,
Thro' woodland shades (the rest in ambush lay)
And as by streams with cedars overhung,
Or through the groves they cautious steal along,
Like hungry wolves when clouds involve the day,
Their savage eyeballs glare in quest of prey;
Nor sought in vain—for at his rustic gate,
Unconscious of alarm, old Ango sate,
Around his mansion, in a circle rear'd
With honest toil, a portico appear'd,
Of mud and stone. A fence of native thorn,
Serv'd to defend his hut, and to adorn.

(from) Avenia Book II

Confounded and dismay'd they flee or fall,
Some seek the Ships and some for quarters call;
Some trembling fight, while others pant for breath.
And o'er the wounded stalks gigantic Death.
Onward he speeds, and gloomy as the night,
By deeds, not words, he animates the fight;
Hawkins he seeks, while from his search he flies,
And guilty fear activity supplies:
As doth the hound the fearful lev'ret wind,
Or chase thro' woods obscure the trembling hind;
Now lost, now seen, they intercept his way,
And from the herd still turn the flying prey;
So fast and with such fears, the murd'rer flew,
Thus close and constant did the chief pursue
And many a chief, and many a hero dies,
By fierce *Mondingo's* weapon as he flies . . .
As warring winds in *Sirius* sultry reign,
From different quarters sweep the sandy plain;
On ev'ry side the dusty whirlwinds rise,
And the dry fields are lifted to the skies;
Thus by despair, guilt, rage, together driv'n,
Fly the red troops, and flying darken heaven.
Miller now fell beneath his thirsty dart,
Which pierc'd his satin vest and panting heart.
Brindley and *Everbard* his fate soon shar'd,
And from *Mondingo* met the death they fear'd.
But now his trembling host brave *Lambert* warms,
And by his eloquence inspires to arms,
And fiercely rushing on the sable band,
Drench'd with the natives' blood the thirsty land.
Mingo, Onoko, Bango, Pero fell,
Beneath the dreadful vengeance of his steel:
Rank upon rank the Africans were slain,
And all their former victories were vain:
Meanwhile *Louverture* at a distance fought,
Nor once of *Lambert's* conquest had he thought,

He and *Mondingo*, chiefs of matchless might,
Were absent, the fierce bulwarks of the fight:
Lambert still raging, spread the slaughter round,
And gasping warriors bite the bloody ground.
At one fierce charge three sable chiefs he slew,
And ten that moment from his presence flew.
The trembling *Hawkins* at a distance stood,
And saw the Hero bathe in hostile blood:
On him, and him alone, the natives ran,
With all their darts, an army on a man.
Louverture, now arrived, beholds with woe,
The dreadful carnage for the Christian foe;
And while proud *Hawkins* boasts and vaunts aloud,
He eyes another chief amidst the crowd,
And thus he cries, "Whoe'er thou art, remain,
This jav'lin, else shall fix thee to the plain.
He said, and high in air the weapon cast,
Which whizzing err'd, and o'er his shoulders pass'd,
Then fix'd in earth.—against the quivering wood,
The foe stood propp'd, and trembled as he stood;
A sudden palsy siez'd his turning head,
His loose teeth chatter'd and his colour fled.
The raging prince appoach'd the dastard foe,
And horrible high rising to the blow,
Cleft his proud head with a redoubled wound.
His batter'd brains fell smoking to the ground,
An iron sleep came low'ring o'er his sight,
And wrapp'd the villain in a cloud of night.
Back thro' the cleaving ranks *Mondingo* flies,
That moment, swift as lightning thro' the skies;
He calls his chief by name, exhorts the train,
And with his presence fires the host again:
Soon as the furious Hero came in view,
The dastard *Hawkins* from the combat flew.
Aw'd by no shame, by no reproach controul'd,
Busy in cruelty, in malice bold;
With witty envy studious to defame,
Lust all his joy, and money all his aim;
But chief he gloried with licentious style,

To lash the good, religion to revile;
Potent and rich, in factious councils skill'd,
Proud at the board, a dastard in the field;
His figure such as might his soul proclaim,
One eye was blinking and one leg was lame;
His mountain shoulders half his breast o'erspread,
A long tail'd wig conceal'd his shaven head.
Spleen to mankind his treacherous heart possess'd,
And much he hated all, but most the best,
A hypocrite, a coward dead to fame,
Blood his delight, debauchery his theme.
The chief now foremost in the thickest war,
Harangues his men; dispels their anxious fear;
Clamour, on clamours, tempest all the air,
They shout, they whoop, and thicken to the war
First falls fierce *Picket* at his squadron's head,
The chief was cruel, and the men he led;
The hero wields his sword, the head divides,
The visage parted, fell on equal sides.
His soul he trampled out, his body tore,
And stain'd the verdure with no vulgar gore.
High o'er the scene of death *Mondingo* stood,
All grim with dust, and brains and clotted blood,
He sees young *Lambert*, with his flaming eyes,
And in an instant in pursuit he flies;
Lambert beholds this terror of the plain,
Consents to fly, nor heeds the voice of fame:
Then first the youthful warrior's breast knew fear.
Even then he paused amidst his full career:
As turns the Lion from the nightly fold,
Tho' high in courage and with hunger bold,
When gall'd by herdsmen, and long vex'd by hounds,
Stiff with fatigue and fretted sore with wounds,
Till late reluctant at the dawn of day,
Sour he departs, and quits the untasted prey:
So mov'd fair *Lambert* from his dang'rous place,
With weary limbs, but with unwilling pace;

(from) Avenia Book III

Louverture's steel, unfaithful to his hand,
Broke short, the fragments glitter'd on the sand:
The raging warrior to the lofty skies,
Rais'd his upbraiding voice, and vengeful eyes:
      "Then is it vain in Jove himself to trust,
And is it thus that heav'n assists the just?
When wrongs provoke us, Jove success denies,
The dart falls harmless, and the falchion flies.
If from thy hands the fate of mortals flow,
From whence this favour to an impious foe;
A bloody crew, abandon'd and unjust,
Still breathing rapine, violence and lust?
The best of things, above their measure, cloy,
Sleep's balmy blessing, love's endearing joy,
The feast, the dance, what'er mankind desire,
E'en the sweet warblers in our vallies tire;
But Christians ever reap a dire delight
In thirst for money, and in lust of fight,
Curst gold! how high will daring Christians rise,
In ev'ry guilt, to gain the fleeting prize."
The hero said, and towards the sable crew,
Seiz'd by his belt the panting chieftain drew,
Struggling he follow'd, while th' embroider'd thong
That tied his sword, drag'd the pale chief along.
So when the sov'reign eagle soars on high,
And bears the speckled serpent thro' the sky,
While his sharp talons gripe the bleeding prey,
In many a fold her curling volumes play,
Her starting brazen scales with horror rise;
The sanguine flames flash dreadful from her eyes;
She writhes, she hisses at her foe in vain,
Who wings at ease the wide aereal plain
With her strong hooky beak the captive plies,
And bears the helpless prey triumphant thro' the skies.
Thus had his ruin crown'd *Louverture's* joy,
But lo the foes their old resource employ;

LECLERC had, previous to the single fight,
And while the panting squadrons were in flight,
Employed a man for villany prepar'd
Who dar'd to venture life for a reward;
THOMAS his name, he watch'd with wily art,
The fav'ring moment to discharge his dart:
Where'er the noble prince his steps inclin'd,
The wretch in silence follow'd close behind;
Oft shifted place, ran anxious to and fro,
Flew round the raging chief in act to throw:
And aim'd his lance at the victorious foe;
And while LECLERC he dragg'd o'er come with fear,
Swift from his covert, THOMAS launch'd his spear;
And as the jav'lin sung along the skies,
Al to the champion turn'd their eager eyes:
The prince dragg'd on, regardless of the sound,
Till in his breast he felt the treach'rous wound:
Deep, deep infix'd the ruthless weapon stood,
Transfix'd his heart, and drank the vital blood.
Swift to his succour flew the sable train
And strove their sinking chieftain to sustain;
But far more swift the dastard THOMAS fled,
Trembling with fear, nor turn'd his guilty head.
As when a prowling wolf whose rage has slain,
Some stately heifer, or the guardian swain,
Flies to the mountains with impetuous speed,
Confus'd and conscious of the daring deed,
Claps close his coward tail between his thighs,
Ere yet the peopled country round him rise.
Not less confus'd pale Thomas took his flight,
Shun'd ev'ry eye and mingled in the fight;
The dying prince with agonizing pain,
Tugg'd at the fatal steel, but tugg'd in vain;
Meantime Leclerc the basest of his kind,
Had fled, and thought he left his life behind;
Panting and pale he hast'ned to the main,
And hid him safe within his walls again.
Deep rivetted within, the rankling dart
Heav'd in the prince, as heav'd the lab'ring heart.

He swoon'd he sank and scarcely drew his breath,
His soul now lingering on the brink of death;
As full blown lilies, overcharg'd with rain,
Decline their heads, and drooping kiss the plain,
So sinks the prince-his beauteous head depress'd,
Serene, tho' languid, drops upon his breast;
The vernal splendors languish in his eyes,
The golden sun and all the spangled skies.

(from) Avenia Book IV

Now stern Leclerc with impious *Hawkins* stood,
And saw their soldiers bath in hostile blood,
Embodied close the lab'ring christian train,
The fiercest shock of charging hosts sustain,
Unmov'd and silent, the whole war they wait,
Serenely dreadful, and as fixed as fate.

.   .   .

"Die wretch, none of thy race, nor sex, nor age,
Shall save a negro from our boundless rage;
All, all shall perish, I will butcher all,
Their babes, their infants at the breast shall fall."
And now the soldiers charg'd the foe again,
And fifty warriors gasping, press'd the plain;
Dreadful the show'r of darts by heroes flung,
And arrows, leaping from the bowstrings, sung.
Thick as fog…western clouds o'ercharg'd with rain,
Pours the black storm, and smokes along the plain,
Thick as the gather'd hail tempestuous flies,
O'er the wide main, and rattles down the skies,
When all the frowning heavens are darken'd o'er,
And deep from ev'ry cloud the thunders roar.
Each army now in fierce contention vied.

And crowds of heroes in their anger died.
The sweat and blood descends, while clouds arise,
Of dust, and fields are lifted to the skies.

.   .   .

The monarch tree in flaming ruin lies
Black from the blow, and smokes of sulphur rise;
Stiff with amaze the pale beholders stand,
And own the terrors of th' almighty hand.
Now rushing to the town, the monarch kill'd,
They leave a while the sanguinary field,
In close array to seek the nodding town,
While with their trampling feet the fields resound:
The city now th' advancing host appals,
As with swift pace th' approach the verdant walls,
And from the house-tops, lo! the matrons spy
Their monarch slain, while clamours rend the sky.
He who round Africa sent his commands,
And stretch'd his empire o'er the distant lands,
Now lay a headless carcass on the shore,
The man, the monarch, and the name no more.
Soon as this tragic scene appear'd in view,
Warm'd by their sovereign's love, the women flew,
And from the town a storm of lances threw
With harden'd clubs th' advancing foe they dare,
And with tough staves, repel the rising war;
Old men, boys, maids and dames, with martial fire
Rush on, and for their king with joy and pride expire.
The slaughtering swords of their victorious foes,
In vain the dames and fiery youths oppose;
The troops rush furious thro' the verdant gate,
Nor can the hoary sages shun their fate;
In vain for shelter to each house they fly,
Ev'n there transfix'd in heaps they bleed and die.
Some with closed doors exclude the social train,
Who beg admission to each house in vain;
Here hoary dames, amid the general woe,
Bending with age, are slaughter'd by the foe;

There infants bleed before their parents' eyes,
With piercing shrieks and lamentable cries,
Held by their little feet, and whirl'd around,
They dash their batter'd brains against the ground;
Some pierce children with the ruthless spear,
And whirl the screaming babes aloft in air,
Their weeping mothers hear their screams arise,
And view their darlings quiv'ring in the skies;
Maids, on their bended knees, for mercy call,
Mow'd by the sword their heads yet muttering fall:
Nor age nor youth is spar'd—the pregnant dame
With her untimely infant press the plain.
And all the difference of their fates is here,
That one the sword destroys and one the spear.
Some climb the house to shun the fate below,
And when pursu'd, leap headlong on the foe,
But far within the royal rooms disclose
Scenes far more bloody, yet more direful woes.
Each roof reverberates with female cries,
And the shrill echo strikes the distant skies.
The trembling mothers fly from place to place,
And press their infants in a last embrace;
Th' afrighted babes, amidst the dire alarms,
Now seek for refuge in their mother's arms.
The dome now Hawkins storms with martial fire
The barriers burst, the female guards retire;
The shatter'd doors the thund'ring ruffians ply,
The doors leap back, the sounding hinges fly:
The war breaks in, loud shout the hostile train,
Each house is ransack'd, and it tenants slain.
Rous'd at the deaf'ning peal that roars around,
The sable children listen to the sound:
Thus o'er the corn while furious winds conspire,
Rolls on a wild, devouring flame of fire,
Bursts thro' the forests, gains the mountain's brow,
Then pours and thunders down the vale below;
Consumes the fields, lays waste the golden grain.

.   .   .

And now a thought in *Hawkin's* mind arose,
Most worthy of a demon to disclose,
For, tir'd of slaughter, from the sable train,
Twelve chosen maids he drags along the plain.
Weeping and naked, trembling in their woe,
In tears they follow their relentless foe;
He with their belts, their captive arms constrains,
Late their proud ornaments, but now their chains,
And while the youthful maidens quiv'ring stood,
He stuck their bodies thick with lighted wood,
To which a flaming torch the ruffian threw,
And round the maids the fire congenial flew:
Strait to the town they speed with mad alarms,
And oft they cry for help with outstretch'd arms.
As when in parting spires the flame divides,
And crackling climbs around the caldron's sides,
In the deep womb, grow fierce the hissing streams,
Boil, swell, and foam and bubble o'er the brims;
The mad'ning maids with pain superior stung,
Thus rush'd in flames, amid the astonish'd throng.
Now spread around the dreadful hissing flames,
And fir'd the houses, youths and screaming dames,
While round the town the taunting tyrants flew,
To keep them in, an iron harvest grew,
They poise their threat'ning spears while clamour rise,
And trembling shrieks tumultuous rend the skies.
The curling flames with joy the Christians view'd,
Saw infants with their parents gasp in blood;
Yea, with delight they view'd the flames arise,
And wretched *Congo* mounting to the skies;
The fire rapacious overwhelm it all,
The works of thousands in a moment fall.

(from) Avenia Book V

And now unmoor'd the tyrants launch to sea,
And pale with guilt, commence their wat'ry way
As in her nest within some cavern hung,
The dove sits brooding o'er her callow young,
Till rous'd at last by some impetuous shock,
She starts surpriz'd, and beats around the rock:
Then to the open fields for refuge flies,
And the free bird expatiates in the skies;
Her pinions pois'd thro' liquid air she springs,
And smoothly glides, nor moves her level wings,
So did the vessels their swift course pursue,
And gain'd new force and swiftness as they flew.
Swift as they sail, the waters fly before,
And dash'd beneath the ships the surges roar;
The tars in haste their topsails all unbind
Then sheet them, home, and stretch them to the wind.
High o'er the roaring waves the spacious sails,
Bow the tall masts and swell before the gales,
Each crooked stern the parting surge divides,
And to the stern retreating roil the tides.
They now their flags, their crimson flags unbind,
To tow'r a loft and swell before the wind;
The long proud pendants with the milkwhite sails,
From the high masts, invite the swelling gales;
Past sight of shore, along the surge they bound,
And all above is sky, and ocean all around.

.   .   .

The land approach'd, the slaves with wild affright,
Behold the town and sicken at the sight;
While the proud planters view the ships around,
In haste they rush along the landing ground,
Flush'd at the sight, they haste at early dawn,
Precipitate and bounding o'er the lawn,
To purchase slaves then to the ship repair,
And view the product of the fatal war.

The slaves beheld them in that dreadful hour,
And inly shudder'd at their barb'rous pow'r.
Their cruel trade! who live in heav'ns despite,
Contemning laws, and trampling human right;
Untaught to work, to turn the glebe, or sow,
They all their riches to their neighbours owe.
The tyrants now prepare their slaves to land,
All shorn and trimm'd, upon the yellow sand;
Now forc'd into the boat with wild affright,
A sudden horror struck their aching sight.
The sailors catch the work, their oars they sieze,
And sweep, with equal strokes the smoking seas;
Clear of the ships the impatient longboats fly,
While silent tears flow from each captive's eye.
Within a long recess, a bay there lies,
Edg'd round with clifts, high pointing to the skies;
The jutting shores that swell on either side,
Contract its mouth, and break the rushing tide.
The eager sailors sieze the fair retreat,
And bound within the port the little fleet;
For here retir'd the sinking billows sleep,
And smiling calmness silvers o'er the deep.
With earnest heats the joyful sailors press,
Their friends whose transports glow at their success.
But the sad fate that did their men destroy,
Cool'd ev'ry heart, and damp'd the rising joy.
The shackled captives in their tyrant's sight,
Dejected stand, and shake with wild affright;
Their fate bewail, while to the hated land,
Their masters drive, and range them on the sand,
In droves, unhappy matrons, maids and men,
Are driv'n promiscuous from the imprison'd den.
Like flocks of sheep, alas! they move along,
Scourg'd to the market with the knotted thong.
With red hot irons now they brand the crew,
While from their galled eyes the tears descend anew.
Their sparkling tears the want of words supply,
And the full soul bursts copious from each eye.

They strive their tyrant's pity to command,
The ruffians hear but will not understand.
To what submissions, in what low degree,
Are mortals plac'd, dire avarice, by thee!
They try their suppliant arts, and try again,
To move their pity, but alas in vain.
In body tortur'd, and distress'd in mind,
No hope the poor unhappy creatures find.
They curse their natal and their nuptial hour,
Tears flow amain in one unceasing shower.
And peals of groans in mighty columns rise,
Ascend the heav'ns and echo in the skies.
Pierc'd with the noise the wretch'd babes, in vain,
With tender cries, repeat the sound again,
And at the mournful call the mothers press'd,
Their starting infants screeching to the breast.

.   .   .

Babes to their parents cling with close embrace,
With kisses wander o'er each tearful face;
To separate the hapless, weeping throng,
The cowskin hero wields the knotted thong,
And as he wields, applies the dreadful blow,
While streams of blood in purple torrents flow.
Smit with the sign, which all their fears explain,
The children still embrace, their knees sustain
Their feeble weight no more; their arms alone
Support them, round their bleeding parents thrown.
They faint, they sink, by cruel woes oppress'd,
Each heart weeps blood, and anguish rends each breast.
Now, stain'd with blood, a weeping mother press'd
Her dear, dear trembling infant to her breast,
Then shrieking, to her wretched husband sprang,
A moment snatch'd on his lov'd neck to hang;
Kissing his lips, his cheeks, his swollen eyes,
While tears descend to earth, and groans ascend the skies.
Now furious rage the mournful chief inspires,
And all his soul just indignation fires;

Amid his hapless family he stands,
And lifts to heav'n his eyes and spreading hands.
Oppress'd with grief, and raving with despair,
Groaning he lifts to heav'n his mental pray'r.
Now motionless he stands, in grief profound,
Fixing his eyes with anguish on the ground.
Behold, and blush, ye first born of the skies,
Behold the complicated villanies,
Practis'd by Christian hypocrites, unjust,
Full of rage, rapine, cruelty and lust,
Who, smooth of tongue, in purpose insincere,
Hide fraud in smiles, while death is harbor'd there.
They proffer peace, yet wage unnat'ral war,
From tender husbands, weeping wives they tear:
And still they hope, heav'n winks at their deceit,
And call their cruelties the crimes of fate.
Unjust mankind, whose will's created free,
Charge all their guilt on absolute decree.
The Christian rulers in their ruin join,
And truth is scorn'd by all the perjur'd line.
Their crimes transcend all crimes since Noah's flood
But all their glory soon shall set in blood.
Shall heav'n be false, because revenge is slow?
No-it prepares to strike the fiercer blow,
Sure is its justice. They shall feel their woe.
The day shall come, that great avenging day,
When all their honours in the dust shall lay.
God will himself pour judgments on their land,
Thus hath he said-and what he saith must stand.
Their cruelty for justice daily cries,
And pulls reluctant vengeance from the skies.
Their dreadful end will wing its fatal way,
Nor need their rage anticipate the day.
And tho' they charge on heav'n their own offence,
And call their woes the crimes of providence:
Yet they themselves their misery create,
They perish by their folly, not their fate.
And now th' unhappy exiles mournful stand,

Men, babes and dames, a miserable band,
A wretched train of shrieking mothers bound,
Behold their captive children trembling round.
And oft they strive to ease each other's pain,
But still repeat the moving theme in vain.
Scarce can the whip release the mournful band,
Like sculptur'd monumental grief they stand.

.　　　.　　　.

Now to th' estate the slaves are driv'n like lambs
Bound to the butchers, sever'd from their dams.
With beating hearts, and solemn steps, and slow,
They move along, while tears in torrents flow.
Time here would fail us, did we pause to view,
The various torments of the sable crew,
And as to the plantation they advance,
Take of the hapless drove a transient glance;
Who view, the moment they approach th' estate,
Their countrymen in chains, their own dire fate.
The person who beholds their pains, nor can
Feel pity, is a monster not a man.
No mortal eloquence can paint their woes,
Depict their wrongs, the malice of their foes.
Not *Milton's* pen, not *Shakespear's* tragic lyre,
Not *Homer's* flame, nor *Pope's* poetic fire,
To count their wrongs, demands immortal tongues,
A throat of brass, and adamantine lungs.
Their fate, alas, is dismal and severe,
Their lamentations still assault my ear:
If a poor slave from servitude has run
They lacerate and lop away the man;
When they have caught, they trim with brazen shears
The wretched slave, and rob him of his ears!
And if impell'd by hunger, he should steal,
Or strike his cruel master and rebel,
His arm is sure the vengeful knife to feel.
Nocturnal stars their constant wailings know,
and blushing Phoebus witnesses their woe.

No Christian views them with a tender tear,
They find no mercy, no, nor hope to cheer;
And when their toil is o'er, like hogs repair,
To wretched dens, and far more wretched fare.
All day they tend the canes, and as they grow,
Their tears to water them incessant flow:
Their scanty pittance when their work is done,
Is half devour'd e'er it is well begun;
And while their limbs each hour, are like to fail,
Ah! how they long for ev'n this scanty meal.
Slow seems the sun to move, the hours to roll,
Their native home, deep imag'd in each soul:
As the tir'd plowman spent with stubborn toil,
Whose horses long have torn the furrow'd soil,
Sees with delight the sun's declining ray,
When home with feeble knees he bends his way;
To late repast, the day's sad labour done,
So to the slaves, thus welcome sets the sun.
But he departs to joyful friends and rest,
And these to wretchedness with grief oppress'd.
Their bodies scourg'd, and stiff with clotted gore,
The wounds renew'd that were receiv'd before—
Their lacerated limbs oppress'd with chains,
Their minds, alas! with more than mortal pains.
And when the toil of each sad day is o'er,
They sik to sleep, and wish to wake no more.
Here might I cease, nor further paint their woe,
Too horrid for the sons of men to know.
The pond'rous earth would roll her annual way,
E'er I could half their miseries display:
The woodland monsters would with tears bewail,
And ev'n *Appellyon* shudder at the tale.

JAMES McHENRY
(1785 – 1845)

The Haunts of Larne

Oft as I think on other days,
  When with a blithe light heart I rov'd,
Those haunts which lovely Larne surveys,
  Where first I felt, and first I lov'd;
  What sorrows pierce my bosom's core,
   Since I must sigh,
   Farewell to joy!
Ah! lovely Larne! must I ne'er see, ne'er see thee more?

By Curran's shore I often stray'd,
  And scenes of purest rapture knew,
When there I met the sweetest maid
  That ever blest a lover's view;
  But ah those joyful scenes are o'er,
   And I must sigh,
   Farewell to joy!
Ah! lovely Larne! must I ne'er see, ne'er see thee more?

By Inver's banks, so green and gay,
  I join'd each little warbler's song,
And tuned to love the blithesome lay,
  The fragrant hawthorn shades among.
  Fate ne'er can scenes like these restore,
   For I must sigh,
   Farewell to joy!
Ah! lovely Larne! must I ne'er see, ne'er see thee more?

Oh mem'ry, cease! it gives me pain
    Such recollections dear to wake;
Yet I will think them o'er again,
Although my tortur'd heart should break.
    Yes, still I'll think, and still deplore,
      How I must sigh,
      Farewell to joy!
Ah! lovely Larne! must I ne'er see, ne'er see thee more?

SARAH HELEN WHITMAN
(1813–1878)

Don Isle

Lonely beneath the silent stars
    It stands, a gray and moldering pile,
Wrecked in the wild Cromwellian wars,
    The sea-girt castle of Don Isle.
The wild waves beat the castle wall,
    And bathe the rocks with ceaseless showers;
Dark heaving billows plunge and fall
    In whitening foam beneath the towers.

High beetling o'er the headland's brow,
    All seamed and battle-scarred it stands,
And rents and gaping ruins show
    The ravage of the spoiler's hands.
Two hundred years have rolled away,
    And still, at twilight's haunted hour,
A ghostly lady seems to stray
    By ruined barbacan and tower.

Dauntless within her own domain
    She held at bay her father's foe,
Till faithless followers fired the train
    That laid her feudal fortress low;
Afar her exiled children roam;
    She perished in the smouldering pile,
The last of all her house and home,
    That lonely lady of Don Isle.

The gray moss gathers on the wall,
     And low beneath the crowning stars
The crumbling turrets waste and fall,
     Wrecked in the wild Cromwellian wars:
And peasants round their evening fire
     With many a tale the hours beguile,
Of warrior ghosts and spectres dire,
     That haunt the castle of Don Isle.

HENRY DAVID THOREAU
(1817–1862)

I Am the Little Irish Boy

I am the little Irish boy
    That lives in the shanty
I am four years old today
    And shall soon be one and twenty
    I shall grow up
    And be a great man
    And shovel all day
    As hard as I can.

    Down in the deep cut
    Where the men lived
    Who made the Railroad.
For supper
    I have some potato
    And sometimes some bread
    And then if it's cold
      I go right to bed.

    I lie on some straw
    Under my father's coat

    My mother does not cry
    And my father does not scold
    For I am a little Irish Boy
    And I'm four years old.

Every day I go to school
Along the Railroad
It was so cold it made me cry
The day that it snowed.

And if my feet ache
I do not mind the cold
For I am a little Irish boy
And I'm four years old.

WALT WHITMAN
(1819–1892)

Old Ireland

Far hence amid an isle of wondrous beauty,
Crouching over a grave an ancient sorrowful mother,
Once a queen, now lean and tatter'd seated on the ground,
Her old white hair drooping dishevel'd round her shoulders,
At her feet fallen an unused royal harp,
Long silent, she too long silent, mourning her shrouded hope and heir,
Of all the earth her heart most full of sorrow because most full of love.

Yet a word ancient mother,
You need crouch there no longer on the cold ground
      with forehead between your knees,
O you need not sit there veil'd in your old white hair so dishevel'd,
For know you the one you mourn is not in that grave,
It was an illusion, the son you love was not really dead,
The Lord is not dead, he is risen again young and strong in another
Even while you wept there by your fallen harp by the grave,
What you wept for was translated, pass'd from the grave,
The winds favor'd and the sea sail'd it,
And now with rosy and new blood,
Moves to-day in a new country.

ALICE CARY
(1820–1871)

The Bridal Veil

We're married, they say, and you think
    you have won me,—
Well, take this white veil from my head,
    and look on me;
Here's matter to vex you, and matter
    to grieve you,
Here's doubt to distrust you, and faith
    to believe you,—
I am all as you see, common earth,
    common dew;
Be wary, and mould me to roses,
    not rue!

Ah! shake out the filmy thing, fold
    after fold,
And see if you have me to keep and to
    hold,—
Look close on my heart—see the worst
    of its sinning,—
It is not yours to-day for the yesterday's
    winning—
The past is not mine—I am too proud
    to borrow—
You must go to new heights if I love
    you to-morrow.

We're married! I'm plighted to hold
    up your praises,
As the turf at your feet does its handful
    of daisies;
That way lies my honor,—my pathway
    of pride,
But, mark you, if greener grass grow
    either side,
I shall know it, and keeping the body
    with you,
Shall walk in my spirit with feet on the
    dew!

We're married! Oh, pray that our
    love do not fail!
I have wings flattened down and hid
    under my veil:
They are subtle as light—you can
    never undo them,
And swift in their flight—you can
    never pursue them,
And spite of all clasping, and spite of
    all bands,
I can slip like a shadow, a dream, from
    your hands.

Nay, call me not cruel, and fear not to
    take me,
I am yours for my life-time, to be what
    you make me,—
To wear my white veil for a sign, or a
    cover,
As you shall be proven my lord, or my
    lover;
A cover for peace that is dead, or a
    token
Of bliss that can never be written or
    spoken.

Snowed Under

Come let us talk together,
    While the sunset fades and dies,
And, darling, look into my heart,
    And not into my eyes.

Let us sit and talk together
    In the old, familiar place,
But look deep down into my heart,
    Not up into my face.

And with tender pity shield me—
    I am just a withered bough—
I was used to have your praises,
    And you cannot praise me now.

You would nip the blushing roses;
    They were blighted long ago,
But the precious roots, my darling,
    Are alive beneath the snow.

And in the coming spring-time
    They will all to beauty start—
Oh, look not in my face, beloved,
    But only in my heart!

You will not find the little buds,
    So tender and so bright;
They are snowed so deeply under,
    They will never come to light.

So look, I pray you, in my heart,
    And not into my face,
And think about that coming spring
    Of greenness and of grace,

When from the winter-laden bough
    The weight of snow shall drop away,
And give it strength to spring into
    The life of endless May.

CHARLES G. HALPINE
(1829–1868)

(from) On Raising a Monument to the Irish Legion

To raise a column o'er the dead,
    To strew with flowers the graves of those
Who long ago, in storms of lead,
And where the bolts of battle sped,
    Beside us faced our Southern foes;
To honor these—the unshriven, unhearsed—
    To-day we sad survivors come,
With colors draped, and arms reversed,
    And all our souls in gloom immersed,
With silent fife and muffled drum.

In mournful guise our banners wave,
    Black clouds above the "sun-burst" lower;
We mourn the true, the young, the brave,
Who for this land that shelter gave,
    Drew swords in peril's deadliest hour—
For Irish soldiers, fighting here
    As when Lord Clare was bid advance,
And Cumberland beheld with fear
The old green banner swinging clear
    To shield the broken lines of France.

We mourn them; not because they died
    In battle, for our destined race,
In every field of warlike pride,
From Limerick's wall to India's tide,
    Have borne our flag to foremost place,

As if each sought the soldier's trade,
    While some dim hope within him glows,
Before he dies, in line arrayed,
To see the old green flag displayed
    For final fight with Ireland's foes.

For such a race the soldier's death
        Seems not a cruel death to die,
Around their names a laurel wreath,
A wild cheer as parting breath,
    On which their spirits mount the sky;
Oh, had their hope been only won—
    On Irish soil their final fight,
And had they seen, ere sinking down,
Our Emerald torn from England's crown,
    Each dead face would have flashed with light!

But vain are words to check the tide
    Of widowed grief and orphaned woe;
Again we see them by our side,
As full of youth, and strength, and pride
    They first went forth to meet the foe!
Their kindling eyes, their steps elate,
    Their grief at parting hid in mirth;
Against our foes no spark of hate—
No wish but to preserve the state
    That welcomes all the oppressed of earth.

Not a new Ireland invoke—
    To guard the flag was all they sought;
Not to make others feel the yoke
Of Poland, fell the shot and stroke
    Of those who in the Legion fought;
Upon our great flag's azure field
    To hold unharmed each starry gem—
This cause, on many a bloody field,
Thinned out by death, they would not yield—
    It was the world's last hope to them.

JOHN BOYLE O'REILLY
(1844–1892)

At Fredericksburg

The smooth hill is bare and the cannon are planted,
Like Gorgon fates shading its terrible brow;
The word has been passed that the stormers are wanted,
And Burnside's battalions are mustering now.
The armies stand by to behold the dread meeting;
The work must be done by a desperate few;
The black-mouthéd guns on the height give them greeting—
From gun-mouth to plain every grass blade in view.
Strong earthworks are there, and the rifles behind them
Are Georgia militia—an Irish brigade;
Their caps have green badges, as if to remind them
Of all the brave record their country has made.

The stormers go forward—the Federals cheer them;
The breast the smooth hillside—the black mouths are dumb;
The riflemen lie in the works till they near them,
And cover the stormers as upward they come.
Was ever a death-march so grand and so solemn?
At last the dark summit with flame is enlined;
The great guns belch doom on the sacrificed column,
That reels from the height, leaving hundreds behind;
The armies are hushed—there is no cause for cheering:
The fall of brave men to brave men is a pain.
Again come the stormers! and as they are nearing
The flame-sheeted rifle-lines, reel back again.
And so full noon come the Federal masses,
Flung back from the height as the cliff flings a wave;
Brigade on brigade to the death-struggle passes,
No wavering rank till it steps on the grave.

Then comes a brief lull, and the smoke-pall is lifted,
The green on the hillside no longer is seen;
The dead soldiers lie as the seaweed is drifted,
The earthworks still held by the badges of green.
Have they quailed? is the word. No; again they are forming,
Again comes a column to death and defeat!
What is it in these who shall now do the storming
That makes every Georgian spring to his feet?
"O, God! what a pity!" they cry in their cover,
As rifles are readied and bayonets made tight;
" 'Tis Meagher and his fellows! their caps have green clover;
'Tis Greek to Greek now for the rest of the fight!"

Twelve hundred the column, their rent flag before them,
With Meagher at their head they have dashed at the hill!
Their foremen are proud of the country that bore them,
But Irish in love, they are enemies still.
Out rings the fierce word, "Let them have it!" The rifles
Are emptied point-blank in the hearts of the foe;
It is green against green, but the principle stifles
The Irishman's love in the Georgian's blow.
The column has reeled, but it is not defeated;
In front of the guns they re-form and attack;
Six times they have done it, and six times retreated;
Twelve hundred they came, and two hundred go back.
Two hundred go back with the chivalrous story;
The wild day is closed in the night's solemn shroud;
A thousand lie dead, but their death was a glory
That calls not for tears—the Green Badges are proud.

Bright honor be theirs who for honor were fearless,
Who charged for their flag to the grim cannon's mouth;
But honor to them who were true, though not tearless,
Who bravely that day kept the cause of the South.
The quarrel is done—God avert such another;
The lesson is brought we should evermore heed:
Who loveth the Flag is a man and a brother,
No matter what birth or what race or what creed.

The Exile of the Gael

"What have ye brought to our Nation-building,
    Sons of the Gael?
What is your burden or guerdon from old Innisfail?"

"No treason we bring from Erin—nor bring we shame
    nor guilt!
The sword we hold may be broken, but we have not
    dropped the hilt!
The wreath we bear to Columbia is twisted of thorns,
    not bays,
And the songs we sing are saddened by thoughts of
    desolate days.
But the hearts we bring for Freedom are washed in
    the surge of tears,
    And we claim our right by a People's fight outliving
    a thousand years!"

"What bring ye else to the Building?"

                    "Oh, willing hands to toil;
Strong natures turned to the harvest-song and bound
    to the kindly soil;
Bold pioneers for the wilderness, defenders in the
    field,—
The sons of a race of soldiers who never learned to
    yield.
Young hearts with duty brimming—as faith makes
    sweet the due;
Their truth to me their witness they cannot be false to
    you!"

"What send ye else, old Mother, to raise our mighty
    wall?
For we must build against Kings and Wrongs a fortress
    never to fall."

"I send you in cradle and bosom, wise brain and
      eloquent tongue,
Whose crowns should engild my crowning, whose songs
      for me should be sung.
Oh flowers unblown, from lonely fields, my daughters
      with hearts aglow,
With pulses warm with sympathies, with bosoms pure
      as snow,—
I smile through tears as the clouds unroll—my widening
      river that runs!
My lost ones grown in radiant growth—proud
      mothers of free-born sons."

"It is well, aye well, old Erin! The sons you give
      to me
Are symboled long in flag and song—your Sunburst
      on the Sea.
All mine by the chrism of Freedom, still yours by
      their love's belief;
And truest to me shall the tenderest be in a suffering
      Mother's grief.
Their loss is the change of the wave to the cloud, of
      the dew to the river and main;
Their hope shall perish through the sea and the mist,
      and thy streams shall be filled again.
As the smolt of the salmon go down to the sea, and as
      surely come back to the river,
Their love shall be yours while your sorrow endures,
      for God guardeth His right forever."

Crispus Attucks

Shall we take for sign this Negro-slave
    with unfamiliar name,
With his poor companions, nameless too, till their lives
    leaped forth in flame?
Yea, surely, the verdict is not for us, to render or deny;
We can only interpret the symbol; God chose these
    men to die
As teachers and types that to humble lives may chief
    award be made;
That from lowly ones, and rejected stones, the temple's
    base is laid!

Oh, blood of the people! changeless tide, through
    century, creed, and race!
Still one as the sweet salt sea is one, though tempered
    by sun and place;
The same in the ocean currents, and the same in the
    sheltered seas;
Forever the fountain of common hopes and kindly
    sympathies;
Indian and Negro, Saxon and Celt, Teuton and Latin and
    Gaul,
Mere surface shadow and sunshine, while the sounding
    unifies all!
One love, one hope, one duty theirs! No matter the
    time or ken,
There never was separate heart-beat in all the races
    of men!

But alien is one—of class, not race—he has drawn
    the line for himself;
His roots drink life from inhuman soil, from garbage
    of pomp and pelf;
His heart beats not with the common beat, he has
    changed his life-stream's hue;

He deems his flesh to be finer flesh, he boasts that his
      blood is blue:
Patrician, aristocrat, tory—whatever his age or name,
To the people's rights and liberties a traitor ever the
      same.
The natural crowd is a mob to him, their prayer a
      vulgar rhyme;
The freeman's speech is sedition, and the patriot's
      deed a crime.
Wherever the race, the law, the land, whatever the
      time or throne,
The tory is always a traitor to every class but his own.

Thank God for a land where pride is clipped, where
      arrogance stalks apart;
Where law and song and loathing of wrong are words
      of the common heart;
Where the masses honor straightforward strength, and
      know when veins are bled,
That the bluest blood is putrid blood, that the people's
      blood is red!

And honor to Crispus Attucks, who was leader and
      voice that day;
The first to defy, and the first to die, with Maverick,
      Carr, and Gray.
Call it riot or revolution, or mob or crowd, as you may,
Such deaths have been the seed of nations, such lives
      shall be honored for ay.
They were lawless hinds to the lackeys, but martyrs
      to Paul Revere;
And Otis and Hancock and Warren read spirit and
      meaning clear.

Ye teachers, answer: what shall be done when just
      men stand in the dock;
When the caitiff is robed in ermine, and his sworders
      keep the lock;
When law is a satrap's menace, and order the drill of
      a horde—

Shall the people kneel to be trampled, and bare their
        neck to the sword?
Not so! by this stone of resistance that Boston raises
        here!
By the old North Church's lantern, and the watching
        of Paul Revere!
Not so! by Paris and Ninety-three and Ulster of Ninety-
        eight!
By Toussaint in St. Domingo! by the horror of Dehli's
        gate!
By Adam's word to Hutchinson! by the tea that is
        brewing still!
By the farmers that met the soldiers at Concord and
        Bunker Hill!

There is never legal sin but grows to the law's
        disaster,
The master shall drop the whip, and the slave shall
        enslave the master;
There is only one thing changeless: the earth steals
        from under our feet,
The times and manners are passing moods, and the
        laws are incomplete;
There is only one thing changes not, one word that
        still survives—
The slave is the man who wields the lash, and not the
        man in gyves!

O, Planter of seed in thought and deed has the year
        of right revolved,
And brought the negro patriot's cause with its problem
        to be solved?
His blood streamed first for the building, and through
        all the century's years,
Our growth of story and fame and glory are mixed with
        his blood and tears.
He lived with men like a soul condemned—derided,
        defamed, and mute;
Debased to the brutal level, and instructed to be a brute.

His virtue was shorn of benefit, his industry of
      reward;
His love!—O men, it were mercy to have cut affection's
      cord;
Through the night of his woe, no pity save that of
      his fellow slave;
For the wage of his priceless labor, the scourging block
      and the grave!

Oh, we who have toiled for freedom's law, have we
      sought for freedom's soul?
Have we learned at last that human right is not a
      part but the whole?
That nothing is told while the clinging sin remains
      half unconfessed?
That the health of the nation is periled if one man be
      oppressed?

Has he learned—the slave from the rice swamps,
      whose children were sold—has he
With broken chains on his limbs and the cry in his
      blood, "I am free!"
Has he learned through affliction's teaching what our
      Crispus Attucks knew—
When Right is stricken, the white and black are
      counted as one, not two?
Has he learned that his century of grief was worth a
      thousand years
In blending his life and blood with ours, and that all
      his toils and tears
Were heaped and poured on his suddenly, to give him
      a right to stand
From the gloom of African forests in the blaze of the
      freest land?
That his hundred years have earned for him a place
      in the human van
Which others have fought for and thought for since
      the world of wrong began?

For this shall his vengeance change to love, and his
      retribution burn
Defending the right, the weak, and the poor, when each
      shall have his turn;
For this shall he set his woeful past afloat on the stream
      of night;
For this he forgets, as we all forget, when darkness
      turns to light;
For this he forgives, as we all forgive, when wrong has
      turned to right.

JAMES JEFFREY ROCHE
(1847–1908)

Persepolis

Yellow the sand on the palace floor,
 Heavy the dust on column and wall;
 Without, the jackal's sycophant call
Echoes the lion's angry roar.

Trespassers we on king's domain,
 Who chafes outside in his royal rage:
 Patience, your Majesty, while a page
Of history we pursue again.

Here was a mighty monarch's throne;
 There was the altar men raised to him,
 Where the bones of beats lie white and grim:
How the servile knees have worn the stone!

Netchaieff

(Netchaieff, a Russian Nihilist, was condemned to prison for life. Deprived of writing materials, he allowed his fingernail to grow until he fashioned it into a pen. Wth this he wrote, in his blood, on the margins of a book, the story of his sufferings. . . .)

Netchaieff is dead, your Majesty.
You knew him not. He was a common hind,
Who lived ten years in hell, and then he died—
To seek another hell, as we must think,
Since he was a rebel to your Majesty.
Ten years! The time is long, if only spent
In gilded courts and palaces like thine.
E'en courtiers, courtesans, and gilded moths
That flutter round a throne find weary hours
And days of *ennui*. But Netchaieff
Counted the minutes through ten dragging years
Of pain. His soul was God's; his body man's,
To chain and maim and kill: and he is dead.
Yet something left that you cannot kill,—
The story of his hell, writ in his blood:
Plebian blood, base, ruddy, yet in hue
And substance such blood as once we saw
Baptizing the Ekatrinofsky road:
And *that* blood was your sainted sire's, the same
That fills your veins, and would your face suffuse
Did ever tyrant know the way to blush.

The tale? But to what end repeat
A thrice-told tale? Netchaieff is dead.
Ten thousand others live. Go view their lives:
See the wan captive in his narrow cell;
Mark the shrunk frame and shoulders bowed and bent,
The thin hand trembling, shading blinded eyes
From unaccustomed light; the fettered limbs,
The shuffling tread, and furtive look and start.

Bid the dank walls give up the treasured groans
The proud lips still withheld from mortal ear;
Ask of the slimy stones what they have seen,
And shrank to see, polluted with the blood
Of martyred innocence,—youth linked to age,
And both to death; the matron and the maid
Prey to the slaver's lust and driver's whip;
All gladly welcoming the silent cell
And vermin's company, less vile than man's.

See these and these in twice a score of hells,
And faintly guess what horrors lie behind
That you can never see; and you shall guess
Why we rejoice that Netchaieff is dead:
Kings cannot harm the dead.

DANIEL O'CONNELL
(1848 – ?)

Monterey

In a mantle of old traditions,
    In the rime of a vanished day,
The shrouded and silent city
    Sits by her crescent bay.

The ruined fort on the hill-top,
    Where never a bunting streams,
Looks down, a cannonless fortress,
    On the solemn city of dreams.

Gardens of wonderful roses,
    Climbing o'er roof-tree and wall,
Woodbine and crimson geranium,
    Hollyhocks, purple and tall,

Mingle their odorous breathings
    With the crisp salt breeze from the sands,
Where pebbles and sounding sea-shells
    Are gathered by children's hands.

Women with olive faces
    And the liquid Southern eye,
Dark as the forest berries
    That grace the woods in July,

Tenderly train the roses
　　Gathering here and there
A bud,—the richest and rarest—
　　For a place in their long dark hair.

Feeble and garrulous old men
　　Tell, in the Spanish tongue,
Of the good, grand times at the Mission,
　　And the hymns the Fathers sung;

Of the oil, and the wine, and the plenty,
　　And the dance in the twilight gray;
"Ah, those," and the heads shake sadly,
　　"Were good times in Monterey."

Behind in the march of cities,
　　The last in the eager stride
Of village and town and hamlet,
　　She dreams by the ocean's side.

The Workers

Ours is the earnest strife,
　　Who write and think.
And press the grapes of life
　　That you may drink.
We lay our dearest treasure
　　Before your feet,
Nor pause the gift to measure,
　　So it be sweet.

When we the work have wrought.
    And gained the goal
And wrung the glowing thought
    From burning soul,
To you the key is given
    That we have won;
No need how hearts be riven,
    So it be done.

Our cheeks are pale and wan,—
    Yours flushed with health;
And still we struggle on,
    But not for wealth.
That you may read and learn,
    And gain in mind,—
For this we toil, nor turn
    To look behind.

And if we dream at all,
    Or dare to trust,
The boon is very small:
    That our poor dust
(When weary brain is clam,
    And peace is met,)
The friends we gave the palm
    Shall not forget.

JAMES WHITCOMB RILEY
(1849 – 1916)

John Boyle O'Reilly

Dead? this pearless man of men—
    Patriot, Poet, Citizen!—
Dead? and ye weep where he lies
    Mute, with folded eyes!

Courage! All his tears are done;
Mark him, dauntless, face the sun!
    He hath led you.—Still, as true,
      He is leading you.

Folded eyes and folded hands
Typify divine commands
    He is hearkening to, intent
      Beyond wonderment.

'Tis promotion that has come
Thus upon him. Stricken dumb
    Be your moanings dolorous!
      God knows what He does.

Rather, as your chief, *aspire!*—
Rose and seize his toppling lyre,
    And sing Freedom, Home and Love,
      And the rights thereof!

Ere in selfish grief ye sink,
Come! catch rapturous breath and think—
    Think what sweep of wing hath he
      Loosed in endless liberty.

MAURICE FRANCIS EGAN
(1852 – 1924)

Maurice De Guérin

The old wine filled him, and he saw, with eyes
    Anoint of Nature, fauns and dryads fair
    Unseen by others; to him maidenhair
And waxen lilacs and those birds that rise
A-sudden from tall reeds at slight surprise
    Brought charmed thoughts; and in earth everywhere
    He, like sad Jaques, found unheard music rare
As that of Syrinx to old Grecians wise.
A pagan heart, a Christian soul had he,
    He followed Christ, yet for dead Pan he sighed,
      Till earth and heaven met within his breast:
As if Theocritus in Sicily
    Had come upon the Figure crucified
      And lost his gods in deep, Christ-given rest.

LOUISE IMOGENE GUINEY
(1861–1920)

Gloucester Harbor

North from the beautiful islands,
North from the headlands and highlands,
     The long sea wall,
The white ships flee with the swallow;
The day-beams follow and follow,
     Glitter and fall.

The brown ruddy children that fear not,
Lean over the quay, and they hear not
     Warnings of lips;
For their hearts go a-sailing, a-sailing,
Out from the wharves and the wailing
     After the ships.

Nothing to them is the golden
Curve of the sands, or the olden
     Haunt of the town;
Little they reck of the peaceful
Chiming of bells, or the easeful
     Sport on the down:

The orchards no longer are cherished;
The charm of the meadow has perished:
     Dearer, ay me!
The solitude vast unbefriended,
The magical voice and the splendid
     Fierce will of the sea.

Beyond them, by ridges and narrows
The silver prows speed like the arrows
        Sudden and fair;
Like the hoofs of Al Borak the wondrous,
Lost in the blue and the thund'rous
        Depths of the air;

On to the central Atlantic,
Where passionate, hurrying, frantic
        Elements meet;
To the play and the calm and commotion
Of the treacherous, glorious ocean,
        Cruel and sweet.

In the hearts of the children forever
She fashions their growing endeavor,
        The pitiless sea;
Their sires in her caverns she stayeth,
The spirits that love her she slayeth,
        And laughs in her glee.

Woe, woe, for the old fascination!
The women make deep lamentation
        In starts and in slips;
Here always is hope unavailing,
Here always the dreamers are sailing
        After the ships!

An Epitaph for Wendell Phillips

Of the avengers of the right,
The city's race magnificent,
Here sleeps the last, his splendid light
For lives oppressed benignly spent.
All scorn he dared, all sorrow bore:
Now hang your bays beside his door.

Who shall in simple state endure
Like him, thrice incorruptible?
Who shame his valiant voice and sure,
The strength of all our citadel?
Or turn tyrannic men
That haughty, holy glance again?

Here does he sleep; and hence in grief
We heavily looked toward the sea,
Nor with the passion of belief
Descried one other such as he;
Then shattered his great shield, and knew
The king was dead! the kingdom, too.

Two Irish Peasant Songs

I. In Leinster

I try to knead and spin, but my life is low the while.
Oh, I long to be alone, and walk abroad a mile;
Yet if I walk alone, and think of naught at all,
Why from me that's young should the wild tears fall?

The shower-sodden earth, the earth-coloured streams,
They breathe on me awake, and moan to me in dreams,
And yonder ivy fondling the broke castle-wall,
It pulls upon my heart till the wild tears fall.

The cabin-door looks down a furze-lighted hill,
And far as Leighlin Cross the fields are green and still;
But once I hear the blackbird in Leighlin hedges call,
The foolishness is on me, and the wild tears fall!

II. In Ulster

'Tis the time o' the year, if the quicken-bough be staunch,
The green like a breaker rolls steady up the branch,
And surges in the spaces, and floods the trunk, and heaves
In jets of angry spray that is the under-white of leaves;
And from the thorn in companies the foamy petals fall,
And waves of jolly ivy wink along a windy wall.

'Tis the time o' the year the marsh is full of sound,
And good and glorious it is to smell the living ground.
The crimson-headed catkin shakes above the pasture-bars,
The daisy takes the middle field and spangles it with stars,
And down the hedgerow to the lane the primroses do crowd,
All coloured like the twilight moon, and spreading like a cloud!

'Tis the time o' the year, in early light and glad,
The lark has music to drive a lover mad;
The rocks are dripping nightly, the breathèd damps arise,
Deliciously the freshets cool the grayling's golden eyes,
And lying in a row against the chilly north, the sheep
Inclose a place without a wind for tender lambs to sleep.

'Tis the time o' the year I turn upon the height
To watch from my harrow the dance of going light;
And if before the sun be hid, come slowly up the vale
Honora with her dimpled throat, Honora with her pail,
Hey, but there's many a March for me, and many many a lass!—
I fall to work and song again, and let Honora pass.

The Wild Ride

I hear in my heart, I hear in its ominous pulses
All day, on the road, the hoofs of invisible horses,
All night, from their stalls, the importunate pawing and neighing.

Let cowards and laggards fall back! but alert to the saddle
Weather-worn and abreast, go men of our galloping legion,
With a stirrup-cup each to the lily of women that loves him.

The trail is through dolour and dread, over crags and morasses;
There are shapes by the way, there are things that appal or entice us:
What odds? We are Knights of the Grail, we are vowed to the riding.

Thought's self is a vanishing wing, and joy is a cobweb,
And friendship a flower in the dust, and glory a sunbeam:
Not here is our prize, nor, alas! after these our pursuing.

A dipping of plumes, a tear, a shake of the bridle,
A passing salute to this world and her pitiful beauty:
We hurry with never a word in the track of our fathers.

(I hear in my heart, I hear in its ominous pulses
All day, on the road, the hoofs of invisible horses,
All night, from their stalls, the importunate pawing and neighing.)

We spur to a land of no name, out-racing the storm-wind;
We leap to the infinite dark like sparks from the anvil.
Thou leadest, O God! All's well with Thy troopers that follow.

Monochrome

Shut fast again in Beauty's sheath
Where ancient forms renew,
The round world seems above, beneath,
On wash of faintest blue,

And air and tide so stilly sweet
In nameless union lie,
The little far-off fishing fleet
Goes drifting up the sky.

Secure of neither misted coast
Nor ocean undefined,
Our flagging sail is like the ghost
Of one that served mankind,

Who in the void, as we upon
This melancholy sea,
Finds labour and allegiance done,
And Self begin to be.

KATE McPHELIM CLEARY
(1863–1905)

The Fettered

There's rest for men when day is done,
    For children rest, and many other
Who toil from dawn till set of sun,
But true as truth is, there is none
    For weary wife and tired mother!

Nor cease the tasks to which we wake
    When night to light its way is wending,—
Come calls compelling sleep to shake
Its poppy leaves for their dear sake,
    Whose love is tyranny unending.

"Some day! some day!" we women say,
    But time goes by in all its fleetness,
And we are old, and bent, and grey,
And see the sunlight fade away,
    And life is beggared of its sweetness.

EDWIN ARLINGTON ROBINSON
(1869–1935)

Shadrach O'Leary

O'Leary was a poet—for a while:
He sang of many ladies frail and fair,
The rolling glory of their golden hair,
And emperors extinguished with a smile.
They foiled his years with many an ancient wile,
And if they limped, O'Leary didn't care:
He turned them loose and had them everywhere,
Undoing saints and senates with their guile.

But this was not the end. A year ago
I met him—and to meet was to admire:
Forgotten were the ladies and the lyre,
And the small ink-fed Eros of his dream.
By questioning I found a man to know—
A failure spared, a Shadrach of the Gleam.

A Song at Shannon's

Two men came out of Shannon's, having known
The faces of each other for as long
As they had listened there to an old song,
Sung thinly in a wastrel monotone
By some unhappy night-bird, who had flown
Too many times and with a wing too strong
To save himself, and so done heavy wrong
To more frail elements than his alone.

Slowly away they went, leaving behind
More light than was before them. Neither met
The other's eyes again or said a word.
Each to his loneliness or to his kind,
Went his own way, and with his own regret,
Not knowing what the other may have heard.

The Dark Hills

Dark hills at evening in the west,
Where sunset hovers like a sound
Of golden horns that sang to rest
Old bones of warriors under ground,
Far now from all the bannered ways
Where flash the legions of the sun,
You fade—as if the last of days
Were fading, and all wars were done.

The Sheaves

Where long the shadows of the wind had rolled,
Green wheat was yielding to the change assigned;
And as by some vast magic undivined
The world was turning slowly into gold.
Like nothing that was ever bought or sold
It waited there, the body and the mind;
And with a mighty meaning of a kind
That tells the more the more it is not told.

So in a land where all days are not fair,
Fair days went on till on another day
A thousand golden sheaves were lying there,
Shining and still, but not for long to stay—
As if a thousand girls with golden hair
Might rise from where they slept to go away.

PADRAIG O'HEIGEARTAIGH
(1871–1936)

Ochón! A Dhonncha (My sorrow, Donncha)

Ochón! a Donncha, mo mhíle cogarach, fén bhfód so
    sínte;
fód an doichill 'na luí ar do cholainn bhig, mo
    loma-sceimhle!
Dá mbeadh an codladh so i gCill na Dromad ort
    nó in uaigh san Iarthar
mo bhrón do bhogfadh, cé gur mhór mo dhochar,
    is ní bheinn id' dhiaidh air.

Is feoite caite 'tá na blátha scaipeadh ar do leaba
    chaoilse;
ba bhreá iad tarmall ach thréig a dtaitneamh, níl snas
    ná brí iontu.
'S tá an bláth ba ghile liom dár fhás ar ithir riamh
    ná a fhásfaidh choíche
ag dreo sa talamh, is go deo ní thacfaidh ag cur éirí
    croí orm.

Och, a chumannaigh! nár mhór an scrupall é
    an t-uisce dod' luascadh,
gan neart id' chuisleannaibh ná éinne i ngaire duit
    a thabharfadh fuarthan.
Scéal níor tugadh chúgham ar bhaol mo linbh ná
    ar dhéine a chruatain—
ó! 's raghainn go fonnmhar ar dhoimhin-lic Ifrinn chun
    tú a fhuascailt.

Tá an ré go dorcha, ní fhéadaim codladh, do shéan
    gach só mé.
Garbh doilbh liom an Ghaeilge oscailte—is olc an
    comhartha é.
Fuath liom sealad i gcomhluadar carad, bíonn a
    ngreann dom' chiapadh.
Ón lá go bhfacasa go tláith ar an ngaineamh thú nior
    gheal an ghrian dom.

Och, mo mhairg! cad a dhéanfad feasta 's an saol
    dom' shuathadh,
gan do láimhín chailce mar leoithne i gcrannaibh
    ar mo mhalainn ghruama,
do bhéilín meala mar cheol na n-aingeal go binn
    im' chluasaibh
á rá go cneasta liom: 'Mo ghraidhn m'athair bocht, ná
    bíodh buairt ort!'

Ó, mo chaithis é! is beag do cheapas-sa i dtráth mo
    dhóchais
ná beadh an leanbh so 'na laoch mhear chalma i lár
    na fóirne,
a ghníomhartha gaisce 's a smaointe meanman ar son
    na Fódla—
ach an Té do dhealbhaigh de chré ar an dtalamh sinn,
    ní mar sin d'ordaigh.

(Translated from the Irish)

My sorrow, Donncha, my thousand-cherished
                    under this sod stretched,
this mean sod lying on your little body
                    —my utter fright . . .
If this sleep were on you in Cill na Dromad
                    or some grave in the West
it would ease my sorrow, though great the affliction
                    and I not complain.

Spent and withered are the flowers scattered
                    on your narrow bed.
They were fair a while but their brightness faded,
                    they've no gloss or life.
And my brightest flower that in soil grew ever
                    or will ever grow
rots in the ground, and will come no more
                    to lift my heart.

Alas, beloved, is it not great pity
                    how the water rocked you,
your pulses powerless and no one near you
                    to bring relief?
No news was brought me of my child in peril
                    or his cruel hardship
—O I'd go, and eager, to Hell's deep flag-stones
                    if I could save you.
The moon is dark and I cannot sleep.
                    All ease has left me.
The candid Gaelic seems harsh and gloomy
                    —an evil omen.
I hate the time that I pass with friends,
                    their wit torments me.
Since the day I saw you on the sands so lifeless
                    no sun has shone.

Alas, my sorrow, what can I do now?
                              The world grinds me
—your slight white hand, like a tree-breeze, gone from
                              my frowning brows,
and your little honeymouth, like angel's music
                              sweet in my ears
saying to me softly: 'Dear heart, poor father,
                              do not be troubled.'

And O, my dear one! I little thought
                              in my time of hope
this child would never be a brave swift hero
                              in the midst of glory
with deeds of daring and lively thoughts
                              for the sake of Fódla
—but the One who framed us of clay on earth
                              not so has ordered.

PAUL LAURENCE DUNBAR
(1872–1906)

John Boyle O'Reilly

Of noble minds and noble hearts
     Old Ireland has goodly store;
But thou wert still the noblest son
     That e're the Isle of Erin bore.
A generous race, and strong to dare,
     With hearts as true as purest gold,
With hands to soothe as well as strike,
     As generous as they are bold,—
This is the race thou lovedst so;
     And knowing them, I can but know
The glory thy whole being felt
     To think, to act, to be, the Celt!
Not Celt alone, America
     Her arms about thee hath entwined;
The noblest traits of each grand race
     In thee were happily combined.
As sweet of song as strong of speech,
     Thy great heart beat in every line.
No narrow partisan wert thou;
     The cause of all oppressed was thine!
The world is cruel still and cold,
     But who can doubt thy life has told?
Though wrong and sorrow still are rife
     Old Earth is better for thy life!

PART TWO

Modern Tide

LOLA RIDGE
(1873–1941)

(from) The Ghetto

I

Cool inaccessible air
Is floating in velvety blackness shot with steel-blue lights,
But no breath stirs the heat
Leaning its ponderous bulk upon the Ghetto
And most on Hester street . . .

The heat . . .
Nosing in the body's overflow,
Like a beast pressing its great steaming belly close,
Covering all avenues of air . . .

The heat in Hester street,
Heaped like a dray
With the garbage of the world.

Bodies dangle from the fire escapes
Or sprawl over the stoops . . .
Upturned faces glimmer pallidly—
Herring-yellow faces, spotted as with a mold,
And moist faces of girls
Like dank white lilies,
And infants' faces with open parched mouths
        that suck at the air as at empty teats.

Young women pass in groups,
Converging to the forums and meeting halls,
Surging indomitable, slow
Through the gross underbrush of heat.
Their heads are uncovered to the stars,
And they call to the young men and to one another
With a free camaraderie
Only their eyes are ancient and alone . . .

The street crawls undulant,
Like a river addled
With its hot tide of flesh
That ever thickens.
Heavy surges of flesh
Break over the pavements,
Clavering like a surf—
Flesh of this abiding
Brood of those ancient mothers who saw the dawn
      break over Egypt . . .
And turned their cakes upon the dry hot stones
And went on
Till the gold of the Egyptians
      fell down off their arms . . .
Fasting and athirst . . .
And yet on. . . .

Did they vision—with those eyes darkly clear,
That looked the sun in the face and were not blinded—
Across the centuries
The march of their enduring flesh?
Did they hear—
Under the molten silence
Of the desert like a stopped wheel—
(And the scorpions tick-ticking on the sand . . .)
The infinite procession of those feet?

III

The sturdy Ghetto children
March by the parade,
Waving their toy flags,
Prancing to the bugles—
Lusty, unafraid . . .
Shaking little fire sticks
At the night—
The old blinking night—
Swerving out of the way,
Wrapped in her darkness like a shawl.

But a small girl
Cowers apart.
Her braided head,
Shiny as a black-bird's
In the gleam of the torch-light,
Is poised as for flight.
Her eyes have the glow
Of darkened lights.

She stammers in Yiddish,
But I do not understand,
And there flits across her face
A shadow
As of a drawn blind.
I give her an orange,
Large and golden,
And she looks at it blankly.
I take her little cold hand and try to draw her to me,
But she is stiff . . .
Like a doll . . .

Suddenly she darts through the crowd
Like a little white panic
Blown along the night—
Away from the terror of coming feet . . .
And drums rattling like curses in red roaring mouths . . .
And torches spluttering sliver fire
And lights that nose out hiding-places . . .
To the night—
Squatting like a hunchback
Under the curved stoop—
The old mammy-night
That has outlived beauty and knows the ways of fear—
The night—wide-opening crooked and comforting arms,
Hiding her as in a voluminous skirt.

The sturdy Ghetto children
March by the parade,
Waving their toy flags,
Prancing to the bugles,
Lusty, unafraid.
But I see a white frock
And eyes like hooded lights
Out of the shadow of pogroms
Watching . . . watching . . .

VIII

Lights go out
And the stark trunks of the factories
Melt into the drawn darkness,
Sheathing like a seamless garment.

And mothers take home their babies,
Waxen and delicately curled,
Like little potted flowers closed under the stars.

Lights go out
And the young men shut their eyes,
But life turns in them . . .
Life in the cramped ova
Tearing and rending asunder its living cells . . .
Wars, arts, discoveries, rebellions, travails, immolations,
       cataclysms, hates . . .
Pent in the shut flesh.
And the young men twist on their beds of languor
       and dizziness unsupportable . . .
Their eyes—heavy and dimmed
With dust of long oblivions in the gray pulp behind—
Staring as through a choked glass.
And they gaze at the moon—throwing off a faint heat—
The moon, blond and burning, creeping to their cots
Softly, as on naked feet . . .
Lolling on the coverlet . . . like a woman offering
       her white body.

Nude glory of the moon!
That leaps like an athlete on the bosoms of the young girls
       stripped of their linens;
Stroking their breasts that are smooth and cool
       as mother-of-pearl
Till the nipples tingle and burn as though little lips
       plucked at them.
They shudder and grow faint.
And their ears are filled as with delicious rhapsody,
That Life, like a drunken player,
Strikes out of their clear white bodies
As out of ivory keys.

Lights go out . . .
And the great lovers linger in little groups,
        still passionately debating,
Or one may walk in silence, listening only
        to the still summons of Life—
Like making a great Demand . . .
Calling its new Christs . . .
Till tears come, blurring the stars
That grow tender and comforting like the eyes of comrades;
And the moon rolls behind the Battery
Like a word molten out of the mouth of God.

Lights go out . . .
And colors rush together,
Fusing and floating away . . .
Pale worn gold like the settings of old jewels . . .
Mauves, exquisite, tremulous, and luminous purples
And burning spires in aureoles of light
Like shimmering auras.

They are covering up the pushcarts . . .
Now all have gone save an old man with mirrors—
Little oval mirrors like tiny pools.
He shuffles up a darkened street
And the moon burnishes his mirrors till they shine like
        phosphorus . . .
The moon like a skull,
Staring out of eyeless sockets at the old men trundling
        home the pushcarts.

Brooklyn Bridge

Pythoness body—arching
Over the night like an ecstasy—
I feel your coils tightening . . .
And the world's lessening breath.

The Edge

I thought to die that night in the solitude
    where they would never find me . . .
But there was time . . .
And I lay quietly on the drawn knees of the mountain,
    staring into the abyss . . .
I do not know how long . . .
I could not count the hours, they ran so fast
Like little bare-foot urchins—shaking my hands away . . .
But I remember
Somewhere water tricked like a thin severed vein . . .
And a wind came out of the grass,
Touching me gently, tentatively, like a paw.

As the night grew
The gray cloud that had covered the sky like sackcloth
Fell in ashen folds about the hills,
Like hooded virgins, pulling their cloaks about them . . .
There must have been a spent moon,
For the Tall One's veil held a shimmer of silver . . .

That too I remember . . .
And the tenderly rocking mountain
Silence
And beating stars . . .

Dawn
Lay like a waxen hand upon the world,
And folded hills
Broke into a sudden wonder of peaks, stemming clear
    and cold,
Till the Tall One bloomed like a lily,
Flecked with sun,
Fine as a golden pollen—
It seemed a wind might blow it from the snow.

I smelled the raw sweet essences of things,
And heard spiders in the leaves
And ticking of little feet,
As tiny creatures came out of their doors
To see God pouring light into his star . . .

. . . It seemed life held
No future and no past but this . . .

And I too got up stiffly from the earth,
And held my heart up like a cup . . .

To Larkin

Is it you I see go by the window, Jim Larkin—you not
    looking at me or any one,
And your shadow swaying from East to West?
Strange that you should be walking free—you shut down
    without light,
And your legs tied up with a knot of iron.

One hundred million men and women go inevitably about
    their affairs,
In the somnolent way
Of men before a great drunkenness. . . .
They do not see you go by their windows, Jim Larkin,
With your eyes bloody as the sunset
And your shadow gaunt upon the sky . . .
You, and the like of you, that life
Is crushing for their frantic wines.

(from) Death Ray

There is that in the air, an imminence
Of things that hold the breath still and heart pale;
Nought that the mind affirms, but a fey sense
Illumines, and goes dark. Can it avail
For men to follow what but dreams have had
In high and secret places-the dim torch
That Zarathustra blew on and went mad.

Was this the gleam that Jesus sought by night,
When he walked, veiled . . . in glamorous dim light
Washed, as a white goat before the slaughter . . .
And heard no sound save the soft rhythmic beat
Upon the silken silence of his feet
Beautiful as gulls upon the water.

ROBERT FROST
(1874–1963)

The Cow's in the Corn

A One-Act Irish Play in Rhyme

> A kitchen. Afternoon. Through all O'Toole
> Behind an open paper reads Home Rule.
> His wife irons clothes. She bears the family load.
> A shout is heard from someone on the road.
>
> *Mrs. O'Toole.*
> Johnny, hear that? The cow is in the corn!
>
> *Mr. O'Toole.*
> I hear you say it.
>
> *Mrs. O'Toole.*
>   Well then if you do
> Why don't you go and drive her in the barn?
>
> *Mr. O'Toole.*
> I'm waiting; give me time.
>
> *Mrs. O'Toole.*
> Waiting, says you!
> Waiting for what, God keep you always poor!
> The cow is in the corn, I say again.

Mr. O'Toole.
Whose corn's she in?

Mrs. O'Toole.
               Our own, you may be sure.

Mr. O'Toole.
Go drive her into someone else's then!

     She lifts her flat iron at him. To escape her
He slightly elevates the open paper.
The cow's heard mooing through the window (right).
For curtain let the scene stay on till night.

OLIVER ST. JOHN GOGARTY
(1878–1957)

To a Friend in the Country

(Wyckoff, New Jersey)

You like the country better than the town
And very willingly would dwell therein
Afar from the intolerable din
That makes New York a barbarous Babylon;
But far more willingly would I be gone
From all this mad bombardment of the brain
To fields where still and comely thoughts may reign
Deep in your stately mansion old and brown,
And coloured like a Springtime copper beech:
My God, I would give anything to reach
Your old house standing in the misty rain,
And turn my thought to things that do not pass,
While gazing through a window in the grass
And wet young oak leaves fingering the pane.

WALLACE STEVENS
(1879 – 1955)

Our Stars Come from Ireland

I
Tom McGreevy, in America,
Thinks of Himself as a Boy

Out of him that I loved,
Mal Bay I made,
I made Mal Bay
And him in that water.

Over the top of the Bank of Ireland,
The wind blows quaintly
Its thin-stringed music,
As he heard it in Tarbert.

These things were made of him
And out of myself.
He stayed in Kerry, died there.
I live in Pennsylvania.

Out of him I made Mal Bay
And not a bald and tasselled saint.
What would the water have been,
Without that that he makes of it?

The stars are washing up from Ireland
And through and over the puddles of Swatara
And Schuylkill. The sound of him
Comes from a great distance and is heard.

II
The Westwardness of Everything

These are the ashes of fiery weather,
Of nights full of the green stars from Ireland,
Wet out of the sea, and luminously wet,
Like beautiful and abandoned refugees.

The whole habit of the mind is changed by them,
These Gaeled and fitful-fangled darknesses
Made suddenly luminous, themselves a change,
An east in their compelling westwardness,

Themselves an issue as at an end, as if
There was an end at which in a final change,
When the whole habit of the mind was changed,
The ocean breathed out morning in one breath.

The Irish Cliffs of Moher

Who is my father in this world, in this house,
At the spirit's base?

My father's father, his father's father, his—
Shadows like winds

Go back to a parent before thought, before speech,
At the head of the past.

They go to the cliffs of Moher rising out of the mist,
Above the real,

Rising out of present time and place, above
The wet, green grass.

This is not landscape, full of the somnambulations
Of poetry

And the sea. This is my father or, maybe,
It is as he was,

A likeness, one of the race of fathers: earth
And sea and air.

PADRAIC COLUM
(1881–1972)

Hawaiian

Sandalwood, you say, and your thoughts it chimes
With Tyre and Solomon; to me it rhymes
With places bare upon Pacific mountains,
With spaces empty in the minds of men.

Sandalwood!
The Kings of Hawaii call out their men,
The men go up the mountain in files;
Hands that knew only the stone axe now wield the iron axe:
The sandalwood trees go down.

More sandalwood is called for:
The men who hunt the whale will buy sandalwood;
The Kings would change canoes for ships.
Men come down from the mountains carrying sandalwood
    on their backs;
More and more men are levied;
They go up the mountains in files; they leave their taro-patches
    so that famine comes down on the land.

But this sandalwood grows upon other trees, a parasite;
It needs a growing thing to grow upon;
Its seed and its soil are not enough for it!

Too greedy are the Kings;
Too eager are the men who hunt the whale to sail to Canton
     with fragrant wood to make shrines for the Buddhas;
Too sharp is the iron axe!

Nothing will ever bring together again
The spores and the alien sap that nourished them,
The trees and the trees they would plant themselves upon:
Like the myths of peoples,
Like the faiths of peoples,
Like the speech of peoples,
Like the ancient creation chants,
The sandalwood is gone!

A fragrance in shrines—
But the trees will never live again!

A Rann of Exile

Nor right, nor left, nor any road I see a comrade face,
Nor word to lift the heart in me I hear in any place;
They leave me, who pass by me, to my loneliness and care,
Without a house to draw my step nor a fire that I might share!

Ochone, before our people knew the scatt'ring of the dearth,
Before they saw potatoes rot and melt black in the earth,
I might have stood in Connacht, on the top of Cruchmaelinn,
And all around me I would see the hundreds of my kin.

JOHN GOULD FLETCHER
(1886–1950)

(from) Sand and Spray: A Sea Symphony

The Tide

Con moto ondeggiante

> The tide makes music
> At the foot of the beach;
> The waves sing together
> Rumble of breakers.
> Ships there are swaying,
> Into the distance,
> Thrum of the cordage,
> Slap of the sails.
>
> The tide makes music
> At the foot of the beach;
> Low notes of an organ
> 'Gainst the dull clang of bells.
> The tide's tense purple
> On the untrodden sand:
> Its throat is blue,
> Its hands are gold.
>
> The tide makes music:
> The tide all day
> Catches light from the clouds
> That float over the sky.
>
> Ocean, old serpent,
> Coils up and uncoils;
> With sinuous motion,
> With rustle of scales.

Steamers

Maestoso

Like black plunging dolphins with red bellies,
The steamers in herds
Swim through the choppy breakers
On this day of wind and clouds.
Wallowing and plunging,
They seek their path,
The smoke of their snorting
Hangs in the sky.

Like black plunging dolphins with red bellies,
The steamers pass,
Flapping their propellers
Salt with the spray.
Their iron sides glisten,
Their stays thrash:
Their funnels quiver
With the heat from beneath.

Like black plunging dolphins with red bellies,
The steamers together
Dive and roll through tumult
Of green hissing water.

These are the avid of spoil,
Gleaners of the seas,
They loom on their adventure
Up purple and chrome horizons.

(from) Elegy in a Civil War Graveyard

II
By the clumps of the cedars,
Across the granite ledges,
Whence the smell of the cloverfields came mingled with
    mockingbird' song,
We strolled to see
The ranked bronze tables standing;
Facing each other to speak time's oblivion
A never-ending wrong.

"We will fight in the North,
We will fight in the South;
And the East and the West will gather,
Before our assembled hosts;
Hold up green spears, you cornstalks,
Let the long rains drip down them,
What force can now bring home
Those years too easily lost?"

By the clumps of the cedars,
Across the granite ledges,
Slowly went ranked high clouds, brooding on skies of grey;
And the fields turned wintry and sombre,
Sifted with the snow's white ashes.
Year runs away into year, here; day ebbs to witless day;

"We have lost in the North,
We have lost in the South;
But the East and the West will grow greater
For our unaccomplished dream;
Till the multitude, thoughtless and harried,
The vain breed that succeeds us,—
It too must lose its battle, and pass down time's dark stream."

SHAEMUS O'SHEEL
(1886–1954)

They Went Forth to Battle but They Always Fell

They went forth to battle but they always fell.
Something they saw above the sullen shields.
Nobly they fought and bravely, but not well,
And sank heart-wounded by a subtle spell.
They knew not fear that to the foeman yields,
They were not weak, as one who vainly wields
A faltering weapon; yet the old tales tell
How on the hard-fought field they always fell.

It was a secret music that they heard,
The murmurous voice of pity and of peace,
And that which pierced the heart was but a word,
Though the white breast was red-lipped where the sword
Pressed a fierce cruel kiss and did not cease
Till its hot thirst was surfeited. Ah these
By an unwarlike troubling doubt were stirred,
And died for hearing what no foeman heard.

They went forth to battle but they always fell.
Their might was not the might of lifted spears.
Over the battle-clamor came a spell
Of troubling music, and they fought not well.
Their wreaths are willows and their tribute, tears.
Their names are old sad stories in men's ears.
Yet they will scatter the red hordes of Hell,
Who went to battle forth and always fell.

ROBINSON JEFFERS
(1887–1962)

Continent's End

At the equinox when the earth was veiled in a late rain,
    wreathed with wet poppies, waiting spring,
The ocean swelled for a far storm and beat its boundary, the
    ground-swell shook the beds of granite.

I gazing at the boundaries of granite and spray, the established
    sea-marks, felt behind me
Mountain and plain, the immense breadth of the continent,
    before me the mass and doubled stretch of water.

I said: You yoke the Aleutian seal-rocks with the lava and coral
    sowings that flower the south,
Over your flood the life that sought the sunrise faces ours that
    has followed the evening star.

The long migrations meet across you and it is nothing to you,
    you have forgotten us, mother.
You were much younger when we crawled out of the womb and
    lay in the sun's eye on the tideline.

It was long and long ago; we have grown proud since then and
    you have grown bitter; life retains
Your mobile soft unquiet strength; and envies hardness, the
    insolent quietness of stone.

The tides are in our veins, we still mirror the stars, life is your
    child, but there is in me
Older and harder than life and more impartial, the eye that
    watched before there was an ocean.

They watched you fill your beds out of the condensation of thin
    vapor and watched you change them,
That saw you soft and violent wear your boundaries down, eat
    rock, shift places with the continents.

Mother, though my song's measure is like your surf-beat's ancient
     rhythm I never learned it of you.
Before there was any water there were tides of fire, both our
     tones flow from the older fountain.

Shane O'Neill's Cairn

To U. J.

When you and I on the Palos Verdes cliff
Found life more desperate than dear,
And when we hawked at it on the lake by Seattle,
In the west of the world, where hardly
Anything has died yet: we'd not have been sorry, Una,
But surprised, to foresee this gray
Coast in our days, the gray waters of the Moyle
Below us, and under our feet
The heavy black stones of the cairn of the lord of Ulster.
A man of blood who died bloodily
Four centuries ago: but death's nothing, and life,
From a high death-mark on a headland
Of this dim island of burials, is nothing either.
How beautiful are both these nothings.

The Broadstone

Near Finvoy, County Antrim

We climbed by the old quarries to the wide highland of heath,
On the slope of a swale a giant dolmen,
Three heavy basalt pillars upholding the enormous slab,
Towers and abides as if time were nothing.
The hard stones are hardly dusted with lichen in nobody knows
What ages of autumns in this high solitude

Since a recordless tribe of an unknown race lifted them up
To be the availing hero's memorial,
And temple of his power. They gathered their slighter dead from the biting
Winds of time in his lee, the wide moor
About him is swollen with barrows and breaks upon many stones,
Lean gray guardians of old urned ashes,
In waves on waves of purple heather and blithe spray of its bells.
Here lies the hero, more than half God,
And nobody knows his name nor his race, in the bee-bright necropolis,
With the stone circle and his tribe around him.
Sometimes perhaps (but who'd confess it?) in soft adolescence
We used to wonder at the world, and have wished
To hear some final harmony resolve the discords of life?
—Here they are all perfectly resolved.

Antrim

No spot of earth where men have so fiercely for ages of time
Fought and survived and cancelled each other,
Pict and Gael and Dane, McQuillan, Clandonnel, O'Neill,
Savages, the Scot, the Norman, the English,
Here in the narrow passage and the pitiless north, perpetual
Betrayals, relentless resultless fighting.
A random fury of dirks in the dark: a struggle for survival
Of hungry blind cells of life in the womb.
But now the womb has grown old, her strength has gone forth;
      a few red carts in a fog creak flax to the dubs,
And sheep in the high heather cry hungrily that life is hard; a
      plaintive peace; shepherds and peasants.

We have felt the blades meet in the flesh in a hundred
        ambushes
And the groaning blood bubble in the throat;
In a hundred battles the heavy axes bite the deep bone,
The mountain suddenly stagger and be darkened.
Generation on generation we have seen the blood of boys
And heard the moaning of women massacred,
The passionate flesh and nerves have flamed like pitch-pine and
        fallen
And lain in the earth softly dissolving.
I have lain and been humbled in all these graves, and mixed
        new flesh with the old and filled the hollow of my mouth
With maggots and rotten dust and ages of repose. I lie here and
        plot the agony of resurrection.

Iona: The Graves of the Kings

I wish not to lie here.
There's hardly a plot of earth not blessed for burial, but here
One might dream badly.

In beautiful seas a beautiful
And sainted island, but the dark earth so shallow on the rock
Gorged with bad meat.

Kings buried in the lee of the saint,
Kings of fierce Norway, blood-boltered Scotland, bitterly
        dreaming
Treacherous Ireland.

Imagine what delusions of grandeur,
What suspicion-agonized eyes, what jellies of arrogance and
        terror
This earth has absorbed.

An Irish Headland

Fair head in Antrim, long dark waves of wet heather to the
      black lips of the height
Where the old McDonnel war-chief three days of grief and
      madness raged like a storm on the precipice-head
Watching the massacre that came to Rathlin on ships, helplessly
      seeing
Unavengeable things across the thin sleeve of sea. The old
      man's anguish and burning anger were not
Even in the moment of blood and smoke
Ponderable against the tough and sombre passion of the
      headland; they were nothing; not a gannet-feather's
Weight on the rock; the mood of this black basalt has never
      turned since it cooled.

                  The most beautiful woman
Of the northern world made landfall under this cliff when she
      came to the bitter end that makes the life shine,
But the black towers of the rock were more beautiful than
      Deirdre.
Weep for the pity of lovers and the beauty of bereaved men,
      the beauty of the earth is too great to weep for.

The Stone Axe

Iron rusts, and bronze has its green sickness; while flint, the
      hard stones, flint and chalcedony,
Cut the soft stream of time as if they were made for immortal
      uses. So the two-thousand-year-old
Stone axe that Barney McKaye found in the little field his father
      was ditching kept the clear surfaces

Of having been formed quite lately. He wiped it clean on his
    sleeve, and saw, while he held it to show his father,
Between the knuckled fist on the spade-handle and the brown
    beard spattered with mud, the rounded hill
Toward the Dun River, the bay beyond, all empty of sails, and
    the cliffs of Scotland with yellow sun on them
Between two showers. His father looked at the stone. " 'Tis
    nothing: they do be callin' them thunder-stones,
I think the old people used them when short of iron." It was
    taken home to the cottage, however,
And there was lost at the foot of the mud-chinked wall, in the
    earth floor.

      In 1815
The thatch took fire after a ten-day drought; the ruin was left
    abandoned; beautiful heather
Reclaimed the field. There was a Nora McKaye who married a
    McAuley,
Visited the site of her grandsire's cottage the week before they
    sailed for America. A digging rabbit
Had scratched the flint into view again, and Nora she picked it
    up from between the nettles and took it
To remember Ireland, because it felt fine in the hand and had a
    queer shape. In Michigan it was thrown out
With some cracked cups after she died.

                    There it was taken for a
    Huron tomahawk
By one clearing rubbish to make a garden, who gave it to his
    younger boy, who traded it for bantam eggs;
It wandered from hand to hand and George Townsend had it.
    He moved to California for his son's health
And died there. His son was a hardware merchant in Monterey,
    and displayed the stone axe beside the steel ones
In his window show, but after a time he gave it to the town
    museum. It lay dustily in harbor
Until the new museum was built, and there it lay on a shelf
    under bright glass, mislabelled
But sure of itself, intact and waiting, while storms of time

Shot by outside. The building stood up the hill by the Carmel
      road, and overlooking the city
Beheld strange growths and changes and ghastly fallings. At
      length the glass
Broke from its weary windows, then a wall fell. Young oak and
      pine grew up through the floors; an earthquake
Strewed the other walls. Earth drifted, pine-needles dropped and
      mouldered, the ruin was hidden, and all the city
Below it became a pinewood and sang in the wind.

                        White dawn
      grew over Mount Gabilan and Toro Mountain;
A tall young woman, naked except a deerskin and her sunburnt
      hair, stooped heavily, heavy with child,
To the coals of a hoarded fire in a dry stream-course. She
      awakened them, laying lichen and twigs to catch up the flame,
And crouching found that flint axe, which winter water had
      washed from the gullied bank; she found it with joy
And hastily went up the bank. Dawn like a fruit ripened for
      sunrise;
Monterey Bay was all red and yellow like the flaring sky. The
      woman called down the gully, "Oh, Wolf!
Wolf?" He came up between two pines, saying, "You have
      scared the rabbits." His beautiful naked body
Was as dark as an Indian's, but he had blue eyes. She answered,
      "I had to tell you: I found your axe
You lost yesterday morning; it was lying by the ashes." He took
      it and said, "That's a good thing.
I was greatly afraid I'd lost it, but here it is." She said, "How
      lovely the world beginning again.
Look, dear, there comes the sun. *My* baby be born as quietly as
      that."

Carmel Point

The extraordinary patience of things!
This beautiful place defaced with a crop of suburban houses—
How beautiful when we first beheld it,
Unbroken field of poppy and lupin walled with clean cliffs;
No intrusion but two or three horses pasturing,
Or a few milch cows rubbing their flanks on the outcrop
      rockheads—
Now the spoiler has come: does it care?
Not faintly. It has all time. It knows the people are a tide
That swells and in time will ebb, and all
Their works dissolve. Meanwhile the image of the pristine
      beauty
Lives in the very grain of the granite,
Safe as the endless ocean that climbs our cliff.—As for us:
We must uncenter our minds from ourselves;
We must unhumanize our views a little, and become confident
As the rock and ocean that we were made from.

Patronymic

What ancestor of mine in wet Wales or wild Scotland
Was named Godfrey?—from which by the Anglo-French erosion
Geoffrey, Jeffry's son, Jeffries, Jeffers in Ireland—
A totally undistinguished man; the whirlwinds of history
Passed him and passed him by. They marked him no doubt,
Hurt him or helped him, they rolled over his head
And he I suppose fought back, but entirely unnoticed;
Nothing of him remains.
                I should like to meet him,
And sit beside him, drinking his muddy beer,
Talking about the Norman nobles and parish politics

And the damned foreigners: I think his tales of woe
Would be as queer as ours, and even farther
From reality. His mind was as quick as ours
But perhaps even more credulous.

                                 He was a Christian
No doubt—I am not dreaming back into prehistory—
And christened Godfrey, which means the peace of God.
He never in his life found it, when he died it found him.
He has been dead six or eight centuries,
Mouldering in some forgotten British graveyard, nettles and
      rain-slime.

Nettlebed: I remember a place in Oxfordshire,
That prickly name, I have twisted and turned on a bed of
      nettles
All my life long: an apt name for life: nettlebed.
Deep under it swim the dead, down the dark tides and
      bloodshot eras of time, bathed in God's peace.

MARIANNE MOORE
(1887–1972)

The Fish

wade
through black jade.
    Of the crow-blue mussel-shells, one keeps
    adjusting the ash-heaps;
        opening and shutting itself like

an
injured fan.
    The barnacles which encrust the side
    of the wave, cannot hide
        there for the submerged shafts of the

sun,
split like spun
    glass, move themselves with spotlight swiftness
    into the crevices—
        in and out, illuminating

the
turquoise sea
    of bodies. The water drives a wedge
    of iron through the iron edge
        of the cliff; whereupon the stars,

pink
rice-grains, ink-
        bespattered jelly-fish, crabs like green
        lilies, and submarine
                toadstools, slide each on the other.

All
external
        marks of abuse are present on this
        defiant edifice—
                all the physical features of

ac-
cident—lack
        of cornice, dynamite grooves, burns, and
        hatchet strokes, these things stand
                out on it; the chasm-side is

dead.
Repeated
        evidence has proved that it can live
        on what can not revive
                its youth. The sea grows old in it.

The Pangolin

Another armored animal—scale
    lapping scale with spruce-cone regularity until they
form the uninterrupted central
   tail-row! This near artichoke with head and legs and
                             grit-equipped gizzard,
   the night miniature artist engineer is,
     yes, Leonardo da Vinci's replica—
       impressive animal and toiler of whom we seldom hear.
    Armor seems extra. But for him,
      the closing ear-ridge—
        or bare ear lacking even this small
        eminence and similarly safe

contracting nose and eye apertures
    impenetrably closable, are not; —a true ant-eater,
not cockroach-eater, who endures
   exhausting solitary trips through unfamiliar ground at night,
   returning before sunrise; stepping in the moonlight,
     on the moonlight peculiarly, that the outside
       edges of his hands may bear the weight and save the
                              claws
    for digging. Serpentined about
     the tree, he draws
      away from danger unpugnaciously,
      with no sound but a harmless hiss; keeping

the fragile grace of the Thomas-
   of-Leighton Buzzard Westminster Abbey wrought-iron
                              vine, or
rolls himself into a ball that has
   power to defy all effort to unroll it; strongly intailed, neat
   head for core, on neck not breaking off, with curled-in feet.
    Nevertheless he has sting-proof scales; and nest
      of rocks closed with earth from inside, which he can
                         thus darken.

Sun and moon and day and night and man and beast
　　each with a splendor
　　　　which man in all his vileness cannot
　　　　set aside; each with an excellence!

"Fearful yet to be feared," the armored
　　ant-eater met by the driver-ant does not turn back, but
engulfs what he can, the flattened sword-
　　edged leafpoints on the tail and artichoke set leg- and
　　　　　　　　　　　　　　　　　　　　body-plates
　　quivering violently when it retaliates
　　　　and swarms on him. Compact like the furled fringed frill
　　　　　　on the hat-brim of Gargallo's hollow iron head of a
　　matador, he will drop and will
　　　　then walk away
　　　　　　unhurt, although if unintruded on,
　　　　　　he cautiously works down the tree, helped

by his tail. The giant-pangolin-
　　tail, graceful tool, as prop or hand or broom or ax, tipped like
an elephant's trunk with special skin,
　　is not lost on this ant- and stone-swallowing uninjurable
　　artichoke which simpletons thought a living fable
　　　　whom the stones had nourished, whereas ants had done
　　　　　　so. Pangolins are not aggressive animals, between
　　　　dusk and day they have the not unchain-like machine-like
　　　　　　form and frictionless creep of a thing
　　　　　　made graceful by adversities, con-

versities. To explain grace requires
　　a curious hand. If that which is at all were not forever,
why would those who graced the spires
　　with animals and gathered there to rest, on cold luxurious
　　low stone seats—a monk and monk and monk—between the
　　　　　　　　　　　　　　　　　　　　　　　　thus
　　　　ingenious roof-supports, have slaved to confuse
　　　　　　grace with a kindly manner, time in which to pay a
　　　　　　　　　　　　　　　　　　　　　　　　debt,

the cure for sins, a graceful use
    of what are yet
        approved stone mullions branching out across
        the perpendiculars? A sailboat

was the first machine. Pangolins, made
    for moving quietly also, are models of exactness,
on four legs; on hind feet plantigrade,
  with certain postures of a man. Beneath sun and moon,
                            man slaving
  to make his life more sweet, leaves half the flowers worth
                        having,
    needing to choose wisely how to use his strength;
      a paper-maker like the wasp; a tractor of foodstuffs,
    like the ant; spidering a length
      of web from bluffs
        above a stream; in fighting, mechanicked
        like the pangolin; capsizing in

disheartenment. Bedizened or stark
    naked, man, the self, the being we call human, writing-
master to this world, griffons a dark
  "Like does not like like that is obnoxious"; and writes error
                        with four
  r's. Among animals, *one* has a sense of humor.
    Humor saves a few steps, it saves years. Unignorant,
      modest and unemotional, and all emotion,
    he has everlasting vigor,
      power to grow,
        though there are few creatures who can make one
        breath faster and make one erecter.

Not afraid of anything is he,
    and then goes cowering forth, tread paced to meet an obstacle
at every step. Consistent with the
  formula—warm blood, no gills, two pairs of hands and a few
                    hairs—that

is a mammal; there he sits in his own habitat,
　　serge-clad, strong-shod. The prey of fear, he, always
　　　curtailed, extinguished, thwarted by the dusk, work
　　　　　　　　　　　　　　　　　partly done,
　　says to the alternating blaze,
　　　"Again the sun!
　　　　anew each day; and new and new and new,
　　　　that comes into and steadies my soul."

Spenser's Ireland

has not altered;—
　　a place as kind as it is green
　　the greenest place I've never seen.
Every name is a tune.
Denunciations do not affect
　　　the culprit; nor blows, but it
is torture to him to not be spoken to.
They're natural,—
　　　the coat, like Venus'
mantle lined with stars,
buttoned close at the neck,—the sleeves new from disuse.

If in Ireland
　　they play the harp backward at need,
　　and gather at midday the seed
of the fern, eluding
their "giants all covered with iron," might
　　　there be fern seed for unlearn-
ing obduracy and for reinstating
the enchantment?
　　　Hindered characters
seldom have mothers
in Irish stories, but they all have grandmothers.

It was Irish;
  a match not a marriage was made
  when my great great grandmother'd said
with native genius for
disunion, "Although your suitor be
        perfection, one objection
is enough; he is not
Irish." Outwitting
        the fairies, befriending the furies,
whoever again
and again says, "I'll never give in," never sees

that you're not free
  until you've been made captive by
  supreme belief,—credulity
you say? When large dainty
fingers tremblingly divide the wings
        of the fly for mid-July
with a needle and wrap it with peacock-tail,
or tie wool and
        buzzard's wing, their pride,
like the enchanter's
is in care, not madness. Concurring hands divide

flax for damask
  that when bleached by Irish weather
  has the silvered chamois-leather
water-tightness of a
skin. Twisted torcs and gold new-moon-shaped
        lunulae aren't jewelry
like the purple-coral fuchsia-tree's. Eire—
the guillemot
        so neat and the hen
of the heath and the
linnet spinet-sweet—bespeak relentlessness? Then

they are to me
    like enchanted Earl Gerald who
    changed himself into a stag, to
a great green-eyed cat of
the mountain. Discommodity makes
      them invisible; they've dis-
appeared. The Irish say your trouble is their
trouble and your
      joy their joy? I wish
I could believe it;
I am troubled, I'm dissatisfied, I'm Irish.

ERNEST WALSH
(1895–1926)

Irish

1.

Must I being born Irish
and with black eyes
and black hair
and the white skin of the hot-blooded

be always a mad boy
fighting the wind
coaxing the sun to play
thundering at thunder
spitting at lightning
hitting out with my knuckles
at the rough bark of trees.

And why must I tear past the Sassenachs
who march with steady blue eyes
as if I were a wind that had picked up blood
and wanted to spill it against sharp rock

Why should I being black-browed Irish
Appear like a black moon in the gray dawn
And drive all the white-faced boys into a corner
Into a pale yellow mist as if they had been eaten
and their limbs showed through
                 lumps twisting and shifting

O but the mother of my Jesus never sings nor laughs
And the name Mary will be always a sad name to me
And the thought of dying will be always a sad thought to me
And though the grog warms my bones even
The thought of God is terrible enough
To chill me through and through

2.
I played on the grass with Mary
And I loosened her dress at the throat
And I kissed her young breasts

And with her face whiter than they
She said *I'm a pure girl*
> *Strange to these ways*
> *None but you will touch me*
> *I do love you and trust you.*

And she kissed me
And she trembled and held me so
I could have died with delight and fear
But I kissed her and kissed her
Until her hair was all tumbled down
And her eyes were soft with tears

Then I felt a cold loneliness come over me
As if I had died and she was not there
Holding my head to her breast

She might have been telling a dead man her love
I was that faraway and lonely and sad with an unknown fear

3.

Ah how they called me the white white girls
In Venice they were mist floating close
Suddenly to vanish in a pocket of sunlight
Or they were lights that laughed at me out of the darkness
And left me dreaming in the dark

They were mostly hidden from me in the other cities of Italy
But I knew they were there by the silence of the shutters
And my own footfalls mocking at me as I walked

And they ran all over the hills of Ireland
And out of sight into cool waters bathing
When I was far from them

And the girls of Roumania and Russia were no better
White white parade against the desert
Opening their arms to the dark rider
Unseen by his horse

Saint Patrick's Day, 1926

The oven is getting warm. She sits in her apron with the big
Orange blocks cleaning the birds and I smell the potatoes
On the stove boiling and I see how her face is pale from
My child in her belly. Someone is away who never speaks of
Saint Patrick someone is away as an Irishman is away from
His country. Great people leave their country sooner
Or later. Don't ask me to prove there is a moon in the sky
Tonight, don't ask me to show you where the sun leaves off
And the moon begins. Let us keep some faith in miracles.
Whoever you are I ask you to come running to help me, I am in
Trouble and I need you. Whoever you are I don't need you for I
Am a strong man when I am alone. I am strong enough for all
The strong men to turn to when they are tired of being strong
And want to say to someone anyone that has ears I am tired I
Want to rest. I want to go visit the inn tonight. I want to
Have on my knees the pretty girl who serves me and
Hold her as if she were the moon herself who had mistook
The lights that shine on clear nights in the dark blue sky
For an abundance that rustles the program with polished
Fingers. O damn all this. I could get the pope into
A good humor and say tell me Father because my father is dead
Tell me if Ireland will remember her and if the boys will go
Singing over the hills at dawn in the cold when they think of
Her. I am a son without brothers. A soldier with no friends.

Poem

I wanted to be near her so I took her in my arms
As she lay beside me in my bed but she was not near
I arose and put my head through my window to get
My promised look at the moon because it was so
Near when she had promised it laid two swords
On the cold stone floor and you could see me
Leaning away from them I asked what sound in the
Night was most like her breathing when she goes
From me and I am alone with her pale face
On the pillow beside me and her dark lips have
Nothing for me except kisses which she leaves on
My eyes so I can open them in the morning and
Find her again Yes she wants to be found in the
Morning tonight she has gone from me and hides
Between the tears she does not hide and I
Who am blind know nothing but I know when she
Lies on her back with her knees touching the sky
She holds up the world until it breathes easy
Again. And she is a small woman and her arms
Are not as big as mine when I carry in flowers.
No one says anything. The mailman comes with the
Mail and says goodmorning Madame and then it is
Over until he comes again the next day. There are
Just the trees near the window making soft sounds
And at night they come into the room as if to get
Warm. And she is afraid they will get into bed
With her and she shivers and is very cold until
I hold her near much nearer than the trees can get.
She goes about the house very quiet when I am asleep
But when I am awake the house is full of her in
Every corner. But she is away from me now. She is
Not near enough here in my arms. I cannot sleep in this
Bed. In the mirror my pale face asks me questions I am
Unable to answer. I sang this morning. Why am I silent
Now. Must I always have company when I sing. It is not
The fire, it is not the moon, it is not the far lights of

The city near the sea, it is not the trees looking for
A warm corner in our room, it is not, it is not that
She is twenty-two, it is not that from her toes to her
Head she is curved like a slim willow on white water
It is not that she murmurs in her sleep like
The lake of Killarney when there is no one by.

Poem for a Negro Voice

1.

Honey, I've been thinking up a poem for you.
I've been thinking of them mountains
Hard and rough and not smooth, just white and far
Like your necklace except your necklace
Jangles like the yellow flowers in the grass
When the wind
Goes
By
And doesn't say a word to anybody
'Cause the wind's got a secret it won't tell nobody
And I can't follow the wind, honey.

The trees are fat like grandmas
And they don't move much
'Cause it's summer and the mountains
Are white and far and winter is white and not far.
Honey, I've been thinking up a poem for you
Like my old gray hat that isn't new,
Like your blue earrings it's funny and gay.

Honey, the sheep follow the shepherd
And the sheep are gray, sheep, honey, aren't gay.
And the dog follows the sheep, that dog,
That dog has a notion he's leading the way.
And the sheep jangle like the beads in your necklace
Like the yellow flowers in the grass
When the wind goes by.

2.

The sunset bug licks its paws
And sways on a yellow piece of grass.
The sunset tree shows me
A leg with swollen veins.
The sunset world open a mouth
Pink and fresh calf's mouth and moos.

White houses of peasants
Are sharp teeth no bread to chew.
Houses of the shopkeepers
Are like decayed teeth and for them
The sun goes down like a yellow cake.
There are few flies in this kingdom.

The sunset bug is like a beautiful lady
Opening a green parasol.
Under its shade spiders creep from sight.
The sunset bird sings like a motorcar
Going down hill. The wind is a mule
With floppy ears, the wind is a sleepy mule.

LOUISE BOGAN
(1897–1970)

Medusa

I had come to the house, in a cave of trees,
Facing a sheer sky.
Everything moved,—a bell hung ready to strike,
Sun and reflection wheeled by.

When the bare eyes were before me
And the hissing hair,
Held up at a window, seen through a door.
The stiff bald eyes, the serpents on the forehead
Formed in the air.

This is a dead scene forever now.
Nothing will ever stir.
The end will never brighten it more than this,
Nor the rain blur.

The water will always fall, and will not fall,
And the tipped bell make no sound.
The grass will always be growing for hay
Deep on the ground.

And I shall stand here like a shadow
Under the great balanced day,
My eyes on the yellow dust, that was lifting in the wind,
And does not drift away.

Women

Women have no wilderness in them,
They are provident instead,
Content in the tight hot cell of their hearts
To eat dusty bread.

They do not see cattle cropping red winter grass,
They do not hear
Snow water going down under culverts
Shallow and clear.

They wait, when they should turn to journeys,
They stiffen, when they should bend.
They use against themselves that benevolence
To which no man is friend.

They cannot think of so many crops to a field
Or of clean wood cleft by an axe.
Their love is an eager meaninglessness
Too tense, or too lax.

They hear in every whisper that speaks to them
A shout and a cry.
As like as not, when they take life over their door-sills
They should let it go by.

Cassandra

To me, one silly task is like another.
I bare the shambling tricks of lust and pride.
This flesh will never give a child its mother,—
Song, like a wing, tears through my breast, my side,
And madness chooses out my voice again,
Again. I am the chosen no hand saves:
The shrieking heaven lifted over men,
Not the dumb earth, wherein they set their graves.

Hypocrite Swift

Hypocrite Swift now takes an eldest daughter.
He lifts Vanessa's hand. Cudsho, my dove!
Drink Wexford ale and quaff down Wexford water
But never love.

He buys new caps; he and Lord Stanley ban
Hedge-fellows who have neither wit nor swords.
He turns his coat; Tories are in; Queen Anne
Makes twelve new lords.

The town mows hay in hell; he swims in the river;
His giddiness returns; his head is hot.
Berries are clean, while peaches damn the giver
(Though grapes do not).

Mrs. Vanhomrigh keeps him safe from the weather.
Preferment pulls his periwig askew.
Pox takes belittlers; do the willows feather?
God keep you.

Stella spells ill; Lords Peterborough and Fountain
Talk politics; the Florence wine went sour.
Midnight: two different clocks, here and in Dublin,
Give out the hour.

On walls at court, long gilded mirrors gaze.
The parquet shines; outside the snow falls deep.
Venus, the Muses stare above the maze.
Now sleep.

Dream the mixed, fearsome dream. The satiric word
Dies in its horror. Wake, and live by stealth.
The bitter quatrain forms, is here, is heard,
Is wealth.

What care I; what cares saucy Presto? Stir
The bed-clothes; hearten up the perishing fire.
Hypocrite Swift sent Stella a green apron
And dead desire.

Zone

We have struck the regions wherein we are keel or reef.
The wind breaks over us,
And against high sharp angles almost splits into words,
And these are of fear or grief.

Like a ship, we have struck expected latitudes
Of the universe, in March.
Through one short segment's arch
Of the zodiac's round

We pass,
Thinking: Now we hear
What we heard last year,
And bear the wind's rude touch
And its ugly sound
Equally with so much
We have learned how to bear.

HORACE GREGORY
(1898–1982)

Longface Mahoney Discusses Heaven

If someone said, Escape,
let's get away from here,
you'd see snow mountains thrown
against the sky,
cold, and you'd draw your breath and feel
air like cold water going through your veins,
but you'd be free, up so high,
or you'd see a row of girls dancing on a beach
with tropic trees and a warm moon
and warm air floating under your clothes
and through your hair.
Then you'd think of heaven
where there's peace, away from here
and you'd go some place unreal
where everybody goes after something happens,
set up in the air, safe, a room in a hotel.
A brass bed, military hair brushes,
a couple of coats, trousers, maybe a dress
on a chair or draped on the floor.
This room is not on earth, feel the air,
warm like heaven and far away.

This is a place
where marriage nights are kept
and sometimes here you say, Hello
to a neat girl with you
and sometimes she laughs
because she thinks it's funny to be sitting here
for no reason at all, except perhaps,
she likes you daddy.
Maybe this isn't heaven but near
to something like it,
more like love coming up in elevators
and nothing to think about, except, O God,
you love her now and it makes no difference
if it isn't spring. All seasons are warm
in the warm air
and the brass bed is always there.

If you've done something
and the cops get you afterwards, you
can't remember the place again,
away from cops and streets—
it's all unreal—
the warm air, a dream
that couldn't save you now.
No one would care
to hear about it,
it would be heaven
far away, dark and no music,
not even a girl there.

Among the Shades I Heard My Father's Father

Among the shades I heard my father's father:
"I am a tall man, handsome for my years:
Astute, four score and ten, my six foot three
Mounting to steer horses beggars ride,
Ex-Dubliner, astronomer, engineer
From thick green growing turf where I was born
Where blackbird armies wheeled down from the clouds
Breaking the sky through fractured sunlit rain
Until the violet long archaic twilight
Empties its shadows over hill and plain.
I built my bridges to oblivion
Even here across young lakes, across the sea . . .
Get out of my grave: there is nothing here—
Take your hands away—I want none of you: sons,
Grandsons, cousins and fools.
                                              Put the spade aside,
No treasures here: the inhabitant's gone,
Nor nakedness, nor sins, nor flesh, nor worms,
Nor rings, nor jewels, nor gold.
The grave has a clever way of keeping secrets,
Everything lost in dust and a few odd bones:
And the last pawn-tickets dust,
And long lost ancestors in deeper dust
Under the green-mossed ruins of family pride.
Be careful with that spade. It is made of iron:
It awakes destruction.
If ever there is another resurrection,
I have the great cold strength to stand alone."

(from) Fortune for Mirabel

(3)

Mirabel, the sinful Irish, when they die,
Always return to Eire:
There none is lonely; the cold rain beats
In waves against the soul, and moss-green
Angels in deserted gardens stare through the rain
And slowly lift their wings.
                                        It is where
The sirens, whisky-weeping old women, comb grey hair,
Beg for a penny to curse the world,
To wail, to sing. O it is where
Wandering blue tapers burn through fog
Among frail girls clasping their guilty lovers:
White limbs in the moon's light in an empty house,
Eden's sin in rags by day, and at night
The serpent uncoils his desires.
                                        It is on that dark
Island, Mirabel, where the last wheel turns,
Where cards fly into the wind, good fortune and bad,
Speed into storms that ride behind pale suns.
Mirabel, your eyes are lidless, raise your face:
Look at the birds; the swallows wheel like bats
And have nothing to say
While rooks and ravens circle the cold sky.
Mirabel, the spell is cast, turn where you will,
The purple hills still rise, the blackthorn tree
Tears at your sleeve.
                                This is the place
Where the first sight of heaven is a last look at hell;
Perhaps there is grace before morning, Mirabel.

Seascape at Evening: Cape Ann

What is that sound, what is that blue and golden light
Between the rocks, running through grasses,
And at night walking beneath Orion and the moon?
Its colors are in cornflower and honeysuckle,
And wherever one turns, morning or evening,
It is the sea.

          It is the presence
Everywhere: the invisible weeping face
Between the branches of the trees, the ancient
Wild sound between sun and moon, the Doric
Greek return of rock and island:
Voice of the sisters who walk the tide,
Who speak the fortunes of the dead
In salt wind lifting
The pale arms of the sea.

             Even the innocent
Blue flower at our feet stares at us
Through the bright glass of sea and sky,
Speaks to us of the veined rock and the grey forest
Hidden in roots and moss: what does it say
Of lives that have turned to stone?
I hear their voices in the wind, in the waves, in the cries
Of the white-breasted and great-winged
Birds of the sea.

On a Celtic Mask by Henry Moore

The burnished silver mask hangs in white air,
The eyes struck out, the lips raised in a smile:
Where eyes had been, the hawk-winged Hebrides,
Tall, weeping waves against their friendless shores,

Rain in small knives that cut the flesh away,
And Sun the sword that flashes from the sky:
Sea-lion-headed creatures stalk these islands,
And breed their young to stand before their graves.

A crying Magdalen sings from her grotto,
Precarious life-in-death between the waters—
None see her breasts, flushed limbs and winding hair—
The women hear her in the new moon's madness.

The Saints? That's where they came—Iona!
The burning Saints—charred bones. I saw the green
Grass-heaped and broken naves of a stone abbey,
Graves, graves and salt-cased kings beneath the ruins:

Island of wave-washed islands, as a jewel
Is set in bronze and salt-green blackened silver:
After shipwreck, the lure of peace and haven,
Goat-path and thorn, the walk where once Saint Bridget,

Bride of Mayflowers in a savage pasture,
Turned grey-green eyes to face the swords, the fires,
Spoke in bird-voices and gave grace to poets,
Then sought her Holy Cave, but stepped toward heaven.

Some say that Irish souls turn into lemmings,
And rush the violent seas that guard Iona.

ROBERT FRANCIS
(1901–1987)

The Celt

I heard a voice clang like a brass kettle clanging,
Voice of an Irish bricklayer haranguing
Some lesser bricklayers. His clapper-tongue
Jangled as when a bell is jarred not rung.
Only the tone—but I could understand
The bile and choler of his tragic land,
The Celtic turbulence, wrangling and war—
Things that had been mere history before.

Hermit

Blue frosty stones for eyes.
Bright hairiness for clothing
Except the loins in leather
Burnished with sand and sun.
A voice distant and small
As from across a space.
And no man could tell whether
He worshiped God the One
Or whether stone or fire.
Those who saw his face
Knew not if to call

Him mad or foolish or wise.
He had forgotten fear.
His body knew no loathing.
Warm in his winter cave
He did not shrink from sharing
His body's warmth with serpents
Whose shell-smooth skin is dry,
Whose delicate tongues are fire-points,
Whose ways are subtlety.
And in the hermit's ear
Always the sound of wave,
Always the sound of sea.

Ireland

which the sea refuses
to recognize as bona fide
land, the sea and all her watery clouds

and all her mewing gulls
"white craws as white as snaw"
that sweep, that sweep, that sweep

warm winter into cool summer
"rather cloudy, but with bright
periods in many places this morning"—

Ireland whose weather imitates
bird flightiness, imitates life,
imitates above all the Irish.

Cromwell

After the celebrated carved misericords
And various tombs, the amiable sexton
Shows you by St. Mary's door the stone
Where Cromwell's men sharpened their swords.

Was it not a just, a righteous, war
When indiscriminate Irish blood
Flowed for the greater glory of God
Outside St. Mary's door?

If righteousness be often tipped with steel,
Be rightly tipped, psalm-singing men
Will help themselves to holy stone
To whet their zeal.

So you have both: the mellow misericords
Gracing the choir
And just outside the door
The swords.

St. Brigid's

High
in the open arches
of St. Brigid's belltower

they sit
and contemplate
or if not contemplate

observe
the visible, only
the visible daylight world

the actual
undoctored unindoctrinated
world, the non-theological landscape.

Then
as the spirit moves
and only as the spirit moves

with merely
an initial flap of wings
unfold, detach themselves, take off

and thus
in arcs of perfect confidence
and no less perfect nonchalance descend

to tree
rooftree or grass or wheeling
reascend, float upward, and so gain

again
those welcoming arches
all twelve of them that lure them home.

Doves
who come and go to church
without ever going to church at all

bending
to their own dove devices
that massive immoveable institution.

Below
do the little priests
scheme to dislodge or utterly destroy them?

If so
priestcraft itself
is thwarted for the birds remain.

How
absolute, how beautiful
this dove indifference to Rome

to Brigid
herself whether the saint
or that earlier Irish mother goddess

of fire
fertility, agriculture
household arts and of course wisdom—

also
to mass, confession, Thursday
bingo and to the North Italian style.

Yes
indifferent even to time
and the belltower's hourly counting bell

and if
to time no less
indifferent to eternity.

Ah
serendipitous doves
who lacking wit have all the luck in the world.

KAY BOYLE
(1902–1992)

A Poem of Gratitude

for Caresse Crosby

Now the tide is coming in, each long, low, hastening wave in the cove
Arching a little, barely spuming, but running
Into the salt grass the way a river whispers in.
I see the fluid fingers pass along the shallows
And the scalpel of the jetty probing, and you are far
In ether-sleep, the small door of your heart first swinging wide,
Then closing, opening and closing, hinged not by tissue, but by metal
In their quick, gloved hands. I think of you,
Tender as spring fern in the rain, pliant as seaweed
In man's current. I see the waves ride swiftly in
On the sands, see the weather vane reel on its pole,
Its fluctuating arrow crying: Here, here, there is breath!
And I say: This is good, it must be good, this omen. I have known
The meridian of your heart too long, too long,
To accept any break in it, any crack, any faltering.

Now the far star of the lighthouse shines,
And the moon floats in the trees, rosy and silken. The waves run softly in,
And the nighthawk gives its brief, fierce cry
As you once cried. Where you now lie, the tide of ether ebbs,
And the small door of your heart opens and closes, opens,
But now it is the south wind of your blood that fans it wide.

In the clear dusk, I put my arm around the memory of all we were,
Of all we were not, and I am happy,
Watching the cove hold in its curve the deepening waters of the tide.

The New Emigration

*(On reading a French reporter's account of the clandestine
crossings from Spain)*

They cross the frontier as their names cross your pages,
Dark-eyed, slender-throated, with tongues that have run
As mercury runs to the fever of sun. But now as I read, as
        I write,
They are crossing by moon, traps shut, guitars muted,
Fox-smell on the night, without passport or visa or money
        to ring. So they come
Through the trees. They are young, but they wear
Bleak masks of hunger, coats tight in the armpits, too
        short in the sleeve.
But hope can be cloak, can be shoes on the feet, can be
        lash
Out of bull-hide still tough in the dust when the trumpets
        are done.

The joke of it is they are not in the news. Not Koreans
  who follow torrent and stone
From northward to southward; not Germans who flux
  from east toward the west.
These quick-eyed, these young, who are musical-tongued,
  have blood that is lava
Pursuing the vein from lover to lover, Spaniard to
  Spaniard, dead man to son,
And no milestone to say it is here, the frontier.

  But the dead of wars and hunger rattling in their beds
  Are stilled in the brief, sweet moment that the thin-ribbed come
  Out of the province of Zamora, out of Asturias, Seville,
  Bearing in flight their country, bearing Spain,
  Leaving the soft-voweled names behind to genuflection; not to
    bend
  Elbow or knee again, but to cross before the altars of wild olive
    trees,
  Upright, like men.
  Here France is France, wide open in the dark,
  Who takes them in.

Does history state that all men seek the classical
Grave face of liberty, leave interchangeable footprints as
  they run,
Communicate identical dreams from man to son,
Whatever the continent or century? Listen. Men
Are as different as their climates are. The pride of some
Lies in the passage of firearms from palm to palm,
War after war, along an iron Rhine; in some
The honeycomb has hardened like an artery. But not in
  these
Whose presence states a frontier is that undetermined
  place
One comes upon alone at night, in life, and crosses
Even if afraid.

To America

How shall I come to you with this to say to you,
With soft steps saying hush in the leaves or with anger,
To say that a wind dies down in an old country,
That a storm makes rain grow like white wheat on the sand.

How shall I say there is no desert except beyond him
And that your soil is rich dark banners flying under the plow;
That the clay of his bones is a hard famine
And the taste of his words is strange, strange to the tongue.

To remember is to see goats on the hills with spring in their nostrils,
To see ripples laid sharp as shells at a thin prow;
To cry Now let there be words to come, let there be pillars of song to set
    over him,
Let the rain fall in fresh caverns
And roots weave the earth with trumpets of sound.

There shall be full years and you will not need him,
But in years lean as the locust you shall listen in the crops for him
And he will be there.
He is a full swinging river that has always flowed for you,
His footsteps are wild valleys thundering down under your hills.

He will be a long time in your blood.
He will be a long time coming again to you.
You shall try to gather his seed when it is blown far from the stalk.
If ever you comb the wind for him, or turn the earth for flavor of him,
Night will have fitted a cold armor to him:
There will be flutes of stone and javelins at his fingers
And before him a wild clear sea clanging for war.

ROBERT FITZGERALD
(1902–1985)

Phrase

Sorrowful love passes from transparencies
to transparencies of bitter starlight
between antiquities and antiquities so simply

as in evening a soft bird flies down
and rests on a white railing under leaves

Love thinks in this quietness of falling
leaves birds or rain from the hushes
of summer clouds through luminous centuries

Touch unconsolable love the hands of your ancestors

Atlantic Song

Heaving about Cornwall stone, gold
Combers unfurled from western tempest
Lace the glistering ocean's heel:
Granite, fanned to its speechless rim,
Ringing Merlin's world in azure.
Here through the world's dread shadow
Horsemen in iron bosses rode
Through nightmeadow and savage wood
To the charred tower, the stone pool,
Glared upon by a hairy star.

Whose home was in the wave of the west.

My home is on the smoking billow
With stormboys of the western world,
And their derisive pikemen roaring
Under the swaying and faraway
Foaming ocean of Land's End.
O milkwhite maid the sea rolls over,
Their bitter shrouds unfurled by tempest
Tumble ashore your virgin laces!

See, the old world, its scudding emblems
Fixed on the pale shield of heaven,
Roll in our salty western light—
Bright scuppers and shot buckets, wind
Northeasterly, fair, following
On the long, clear capes of summer
To Caroline and Virginia's shore.
O created world, O maiden world,
See the cold heaven of white cloud
Break out the Admiral's evening star!

Our home is in the wave of the west.

History

It is Leviathan, mountain and world,
Yet in its grandeur we perceive
This flutter of the impalpable arriving
Like moths and heartbeats, flakes of snow
Falling on wool, or clouds of thought
Trailing rain in the mind: some old one's dream
Of hauling canvas, or the joy of swording
Hard rascals with a smack—for lordly blood
Circulates tenderly and will seep away;
And the winds blowing across the day
From quarters numberless, going where words go
And songs go, even the holy songs, or where
Leaves, showering, go with the spindling grasses.
Into this mountain shade everything passes.
The slave lays down his bones here and the hero,
Thrown, goes reeling with blinded face;
The long desired opens her scorched armpits.
A mountain; so a gloom and air of ghosts,
But charged with utter light if this is light,
A feathery mass, where this beholding
Shines among lustrous fiddles and codices,
Or dusky angels painted against gold
With lutes across their knees. Magical grain
Bound up in splay sheaves on an evening field,
And a bawling calf butchered—these feed
The curious coil of man. A man, this man,
Bred among lakes and railway cars and smoke,
The salt of childhood on his wintry lips,
His full heart ebbing toward the new tide
Arriving, arriving, in laughter and cries,
Down the chaotic dawn and eastern drift,
Would hail the unforeseen, and celebrate

On the great mountainside those sprites,
Tongues of delight, that may remember him—
The yet unborn, trembling in the same rooms,
Breakfasting before the same grey windows,
Lying, grieving again; yet all beyond him,
Who knew he lived in rough Jehovah's breath,
And burned, a quiet wick in a wild night,
Loving what he beheld and will behold.

BRIAN COFFEY
(1905 – 1995)

from Missouri Sequence

Nightfall, Midwinter, Missouri

To Thomas McGreevy

> Our children have eaten supper,
> play Follow-my-Leader,
> make songs from room to room
> around and around;
> once each minute
> past my desk they go.
>
> Inside the house is warm.
> Winter outside blows from Canada
> freezing rain to ice our trees
> branch by branch, leaf by leaf.
> The mare shelters in the barn.
>
> On the impassable road no movement.
> Nothing stirs in the sky against the black.
> If memory were an ice-field
> quiet as all outside!
> Tonight the poetry is in the children's game:
> I am distracted by comparisons,
> Ireland across the grey ocean,
> here, across the wide river.
>
> .   .   .

We live far from where
my mother grows very old.
Five miles away, at Byrnesville,
the cemetery is filled with Irish graves,
the priest an old man born near Cork,
his bloss like the day he left the land.

People drifted in here from the river,
Irish, German, Bohemians,
more than one hundred years ago,
come to make homes.

Many Irish souls have gone back to God from Byrnesville,
many are Irish here today
where cedars stand like milestones
on worn Ozark hills
and houses white on bluegrass lawns
house people honest, practical and kind.

All shows to a long love
yet I am charmed
by the hills behind Dublin,
those white stone cottages,
grass green as no other green is green,
my mother's people, their ways.

France one loves with a love apart
like the love of wisdom;
Of England everyday love is the true love;
there is a love of Ireland
withering for Irishmen.

Does it matter where one dies,
supposing one knows how?

Dear Tom, in Ireland,
you have known
the pain between
its fruiting and the early dream
and you will hear me out.

.   .   .

Our children have ended play,
have gone to bed,
left me to face
what I had rather not.

They know nothing of Ireland,
they grow American.
They have chased snakes through the couch-grass
in summer, caught butterflies and beetles
we did not know existed,
fished for the catfish,
slept on an open porch
when Whip-poor-Will and tree-frog
work all night,
observed the pupa of the shrill cicada
surface on dry clay,
disrobe for the short ruinous day.
The older ones have helped a neighbour, farmer,
raise his field of ripe corn
in heat that hurt us to the bone,
paid homage to dead men
with fire-crackers in July,
eaten the turkey in November.
Here now they make their friendships,
learn to love God.

Yet we must leave America,
bitter necessity no monopoly
of Irish soil.
It was pain once to come,
it is pain now to go.

How the will shifts from goal to goal
for who does not freely choose.
Some choose, some are chosen
to go their separate paths.
I would choose, I suppose, yet would be chosen
in some equation between God's will and mine,
rejecting prudence to make of conflict
a monument to celtic self-importance.

The truth is, where the cross is not
the Christian does not go.

.   .   .

Return home takes on while I dream it
the fictive form of heaven on earth,
the child's return to motherly arms
for fright at frogs disturbed among iris leaves.

One poet I admire has written:
wherever the soul gives in to flesh
without a struggle is home.
Would one want home like that,
rest, supine surrender
to oneself alone,
flight from where one is?

There is no heaven on earth,
no facile choice for one
charged with the care of others,
none for one like me
for whom no prospect opens
fairly on clear skies.

It grows late and winter
lays its numbing pall.
Doubts restless like what you see
when you lift a flat damp stone
exasperate my warring wishes
until wrenched apart by desperate extremes
I am back where I started.

Pain it was to come,
Pain it will be to go.

.   .   .

Not just to go,
not just to stay,
but the act done in wisdom's way—
not impossible
if one is wise.

Our William Butler Yeats
made island flowers grow
that need as much
the local rain
as wind from overseas
to reach their prime.
He struggled towards the exact muse
through a sunless day.

No servant, the muse
abides in truth,
permits the use of protest
as a second best
to make clean fields,
exults only in the actual
expression of a love,
love all problem
wisdom lacking.

.   .   .

How near the surface of the pool
sunfish play, distract
us from where down deep
real reasons impose their rule.

The room is filled with children's lives
that fill my cares who turn again
to sudden starting words
like birds in cages.
Without all is silent,
within I have no peace at all,
having failed to choose
with loving-wise choice.

Midnight now.
Deepest winter perfect now.
Tomorrow early we shall make lunches
for the children to take to school,
forgetting while working out the week
our wrestling with the sad flesh
and the only Ireland we love
where in Achill still
the poor praise Christ aloud
when the priest elevates
the Saviour of the world.

Muse, June, Related

To the memory of Denis Devlin

.   .   .

As a dove drives from a rock,
as a seagull rides the shaped air,
June burned searching and accurate.
If once in hours
a wave remembered the cold undersea,
shivers strayed over the fields.

Tides of silk bruised the woman,
the shadow of her eyelashes
lay heavy poplars on her cheeks.
She would sigh for tides,
filling her mind with places where slim weeds
swayed sleeping fish.
If her hand desired her throat,
if her breast strained at a stone,
there was nothing yet,
the valleys yawned hills.

But the locust trilled,
filling neighbouring hearts with lowlands away,
while a sword polished in ice
prepared horizons
white with horses
for winds assembling
broken nations on a balcony.

He stood a statue still,
his shadow growing
through the growing corn,
and stood, his shadow laid
low, the young leaves played
on by the airs moving
like a restless quill.

Blooms such as wither at finger-touch
hid her
while the hawk, blue shark,
prowled the corn.

The cedars had trapped the sun
when he turned
scythe to field
where she bent her head.

Her palms warm strands
for questing ants,
her limbs the forest mounds,
his the silence,
a spring sighed in its depths.

When sun went out
she had been touched
so she lay quiet eyes
whose liner
slips through harbour arms.

If he turned his head
in his course,
he saw her through branches
a slip of light
until the leaves took her.

He went imagining
her tears at morning
spent on the green.
In song he poised her,
lauded victory
over his muse.

What he fancied ended
she smiled at as begun,
knowing him no freeman,
him reginal
astray from the perfect scene.

.   .   .

Missouri, Midsummer, Closure

To Bridget

East our rented field slopes down towards trees,
common Missouri trees rooted in poor soil,
chestnut, walnut, sycamore, elm,
sugar maple, honey locust,
mulberry, persimmon,
willow, cedar, oak,
set by casual fall of seed
near a clear spring.

Roughed by winter, unleaved all but the cedar,
they showed to a pale March sun
lack only, no splendour.
April speeded astonishing rise of sap
to swell with growth the farthest reaching buds.
June summer now and the perfect leaves
compose with boughs and branches
the vivid temple poets contemplate.

Forty-eight years after my birth, tonight,
when faint heart counsels
my concerning me
with family cares and crises
and decline, tonight
I write verses at my desk.

.　　　.　　　.

Once long ago
a girl was crowned
queen of a pale people.

Hers the home of clever ones
scarred with wounds, returned
from droghedas of shame
behind devils of deceit.

It is not new
and they were old.

Their young queen
rose to greet them
like a snowdrop opening
to outface black winter
in a grove of stripped trees.

She was the violet beneath the aged oak,
the promise in April apple bloom
of fruit in the ripe season,
the rose that crimsons June to match
December's white chrysanthemum
in splendour.

Unseen the real action moves
like its currents deepest ocean.
Desert poppies in rare rain,
her people joyed
to meet their woman,
girl, wife, mother and queen.

Who could have refused to wish
that gracious creature well
in her eerie hour?
What, what of decency?
Now even nobody can say:
"I am young today,"
with his best before him,
willing to begin again
with failure for her: "Yes,
I will be queen."

Some are chosen, whereupon they choose
to go their lonely path.
There is the exact relation:
none chooses who were not first chosen
to greet fairly their cross.

The snowdrop rising from the snow,
the violet returned beneath the scarred oak,
the promise of blooming in April and
remedial for lessening strength,
all poor alien symbols these,
they please, they do not temper
the desperate will
like the oath of a young queen.

.   .   .

So, and so,
and what of loving?

Many loves exist,
concur concretely
in this pendant world.
Only in twisted man
does love scatter and disperse.

And is man hopeless?

Never was despair imperative,
never are we grown so old
we cannot start our journey
bound to find
and eternal note of gladness
in loves true for men,
the source whence they flow,
the ocean whither they go.

PHYLLIS McGINLEY
(1905 – 1978)

June in the Suburbs

Not with a whimper but a roar
Of birth and bloom this month commences.
The wren's a gossip at her door.
Roses explode along the fences.

By day the chattering mowers cope
With grass decreed a final winner.
Darkness delays. The skipping rope
Twirls in the driveway after dinner.

Through lupine-lighted borders now
For winter bones Dalmatians forage.
Costly, the spray on apple bough.
The canvas chair comes out of storage;

And rose-red golfers dream of par,
And class-bound children loathe their labors,
While pilgrims, touring gardens, are
Cold to petunias of their neighbors.

Now from damp loafers nightly spills
The sand. Brides lodge their lists with Plummer.
And cooks devise on charcoal grills
The first burnt offerings of summer.

Blues for a Melodeon

A castor's loose on the buttoned chair—
    The one upholstered in shabby coral.
I never noticed, before, that tear
    In the dining-room paper.

When did the rocker cease to rock,
    The fringe sag down on the corner sofa?
All of a sudden the Meissen clock
    Has a cherub missing.

All of a sudden the plaster chips,
    The carpet frays by the morning windows;
Careless, a rod from the curtain slips,
    And the gilt is tarnished.

This is the house that I knew by heart.
    Everything here seemed sound, immortal.
When did this delicate ruin start?
    How did the moth come?

Naked by daylight, the paint is airing
    Its rags and tatters. There's dust on the mantel.
And who is that gray-haired stranger staring
    Out of my mirror?

LOUIS MacNEICE
(1907–1963)

Last before America

A spiral of green hay on the end of a rake:
The moment is sweat and sun-prick—children and old women
Big in a tiny field, midgets against the mountain,
So toy-like yet so purposed you could take
This for the Middle Ages.

At night the accordion melts in the wind from the sea
From the bourne of emigrant uncle and son, a defeated
Music that yearns and abdicates; chimney-smoke and spindrift
Mingle and part as ghosts do. The decree
Of the sea's divorce is final.

Pennsylvania or Boston? It was another name,
A land of a better because an impossible promise
Which split these families; it was to be a journey
Away from death—yet the travellers died the same
As those who stayed in Ireland.

Both myth and seismic history have been long suppressed
Which made and unmade Hy Brasil—now an image
For those who despise charts but find their dream's endorsement
In certain long low islets snouting towards the west
Like cubs that have lost their mother.

JOSEPHINE JACOBSEN
(1908–2003)

Mr. Mahoney

Illicitly, Mr. Mahoney roams.
They have him in a room, but it is not his.
Though he has become confused, it is not in this.
Mr. Mahoney cannot find his room.

A young blond nurse gentles him by the elbow.
I hear her again in the hall: "Mr. Mahoney,
this isn't your room. Let's go back and see
if you've brushed your teeth. Yours is *820*."

Why brushing his teeth is the lure, I cannot say.
Does he prize it so? She darts on white feet
to spear him from strange doors; I hear her repeat
with an angel's patience, "Yours is down *this* way."

But 820 is a swamp, a blasted heath.
A dozen times returned, he knows it is wrong.
There is a room in which he does belong.
He has been to 820; he has brushed his teeth.

Before his biopsy, the harried nurses attest,
Mr. Mahoney was tractable in 820,
though very old and brown. He will have to go;
this is not the hall, not the building for his quest.

Tranquilized, Mr. Mahoney still eludes.
At 2 A.M. in my dark 283
the wide door cracks, and sudden and silently
Mr. Mahoney's nutty face obtrudes.

It is gently snatched back by someone behind it.
"That is someone *else's* room. Yours is this way,
Mr. Mahoney." He could not possibly stay.
He is gone by noon. He did not have time to find it.

First Woman

Do animals expect spring?
Ground hard as rancor,
wind colder than malice.
Do they think that will change?

Sky no color and low;
grass is no color, and trees
jerk in the bitter gust.
In this air nothing flies.

Do they believe it will change,
grass be soft and lustrous,
rigid earth crack
from the push of petals,

sky retreat into blue,
the red wide rose breathe
summer, and the butterfly
err on sweet air?

First woman, Lucy, or another,
did you know it all waited
somewhere to come back?
On the first stripped, iron day

did you believe that?
On this merciless morning
I wake, first woman,
with what belief?

Voyage

Off sand at the edge of bush the ribs
of a fisherman's intentions spring
toward the sea; the old sea shape

stained by rains, gnawed by beach rats,
a copybook illustration, "Aspiration
Versus Attainment." There by the sound of water

the hoarse talk of water, suck and hiss,
this marine intention
more the sea's creature

than that hotel the fathoms float.
Sand's grainy grip tightens
and foliage takes back its wood.

What of the fisherman?
Did he reach the blue glitter?
Are his fingers bone?

The vines are coming.
The vines are coming.
A tendril has touched the keel.

THEODORE ROETHKE
(1908 – 1963)

Gob Music

I do not have a fiddle so
   I get myself a stick,
And then I beat upon a can,
   Or pound upon a brick;
And if the meter needs a change
   I give the cat a kick.

   Ooomph dah doodle dah
   Ooomph dah doodle dah
   Ooomph dah doodle dah do.

Whenever I feel it coming on
   I need a morning drink,
I get a stool and sit and stare
   In the slop-pail by the sink;
I lean my head near the brimming edge
   And do not mind the stink.

   Oh, the slop-pail is the place to think
   On the perils of too early drink,—
   Too early drink, too early drink,
   Can bring a good man down.

I went fishing with a pin
    In the dark of an ould spittoon;
Me handkerchee had fallen in
    With more than half a crown.
I stared into the dented hole
    And what do you think I saw?—
A color pure, O pure as gold,
    A color without flaw,
A color without flaw, flaw, flaw,
    A color without flaw.
I stared and stared, and what do you think?
    My thirst came on, and I had to drink.

Indeed I saw a shimmering lake
    Of slime and shining spit,
And I kneeled down and did partake
    A bit of the likes of it.
And it reminded me—But Oh!
    I'll keep my big mouth shut.

It happened O, in Bofin Town,
    The color, my dears, was Guinness brown,
But it had a flavor all its own,
    As I gulped it down, as I gulped it down.
There on my knees, a man of renown,
    I did partake of it, I did partake of it.

    Oh, the slop-pail is the place to think
    On the perils of too early drink,
    Too early drink, too early drink
    Will bring a good man down.

The Shy Man

The full moon was shining upon the broad sea;
I sang to the one star that looked down at me;
I sang to the white horse that grazed on the quay—
    As I walked by the high sea-wall.
        But my lips they,
        My lips they,
    Said never a word,
    As I moped by the high sea-wall.

The curlew's slow night song came on the water.
That tremble of sweet notes set my heart astir,
As I walked beside her, the O'Connell's daughter,
    I knew that I did love her.
        But my lips they,
        My lips they,
    Said never a word,
    As we walked by the high sea-wall.

The full moon has fallen, the night wind is down
And I lie here thinking in bleak Bofin town
I lie here and thinking, 'I am not alone.'
    For here close beside me is O'Connell's daughter,
        And my lips they, my lips they,
        Say many a word,
    As we embrace by the high sea-wall.
    O! my lips they, my lips they,
    Say many a word,
    As we kiss by the high sea wall.

CHARLES OLSON
(1910 – 1970)

Pacific Lament

In memory of William Hickey, a member of the crew
of the U.S.S. Growler, lost at sea in February, 1944.

Black at that depth
turn, golden boy no more
white bone to bone, turn
hear who bore you weep
hear him who made you
deep there on ocean's floor
turn
as waters stir;
turn, bone of man

Cold as a planet is
cold, beat of blood no more
the salt sea's course
along the bone jaw white
stir, boy, stir
motion without motion
stir, and hear
love come down.

Down as you fell
sidewise, stair to green stair
without breath, down
the tumble of ocean

to find you, bone
cold and new among the ships
and men and fish askew.

You alone o golden boy no more
turn now and sleep
washed white by water
sleep in your black deep
by water out of which man came
to find his legs, arms, love, pain.
Sleep, boy, sleep
in older arms than hers,
rocked by an older father;
toss no more,
love;
sleep.

Enniscorthy Suite

I. The Dry Lot

Atop the down pasture
the wind the wind
incessant in the trees
a shore
pours
a distant sea

One side (the south) is still, then snap, the woods!
craw
bob white bob white
still
huhwheep tzuz, eep eep eep
snap
the woods!

The red road down the north
quiet as a road
lazy in the sun
knowing its own worth

      This is the dry lot, this is the dry lot
      the long slope, sweep, sleep
      up green up green
      green to begin
      green each year anew
      green atop and down
      unceasing green

The long earth the red earth
longer than blood
between the wood and the road
the wind and me

II. Lower Field
The sheep like soldiers
black leggings black face
lie boulders
in the pines' shade
at the field's sharp edge:
ambush and bivouac

A convocation of crows overhead
mucks
in their own mud and squawk
makes of the sky
a sty

A bee is deceived
takes the rot of a stump
for honeycomb

Two black snakes cross
in a flat spiral
the undisciplined path

Report: over all
the sun

III. Bottom Land

The barley's bent beards shine
the oats stand green
spring, it is the spring
green and green

The barley's bent beards shine
the oats a darker green
spring, it is the clover
love and lover

Spring, it is the barley
spring, it is the oats!
Spring, it is the one time,
Sing, springtime!

IV. The Family Plot

Burn the grass as the ground the grave
the sun stays green, the live alive

Turn the soil as the worms the dead
the wind is young, the rain is red

Gray is the stone, dark is the tree

The dead are alone
the live are alone

Alive and alone at Enniscorthy

The Grandfather-Father Poem

rolled in the grass
like an overrun horse
or a poor dog
to cool himself
from his employment
in the South Works
of U S Steel
as an Irish shoveler

>to make their fires hot
>to make ingots above
>by puddlers of
>melted metal

>and my grandfather
>down below
>at the bottom of the
>rung

>stoking
their furnaces
with black
soft
coal soft coal
makes fire
heat higher
sooner,
>beloved
Jack Hines (whose picture
in a devil's
cap—black jack
Hines

>and would come home
>to the little white house
>sitting by itself
>on Mitchell Street
>or was then

Middle River Road
and take off
all his clothes, down to
his full red underwear
the way the story was told

and go out there
on the grass
and roll
and roll

       my
       grandfather

       my Jack Hines
       whose picture
       I have lost

I have also lost
the tin-type
of—was it?—my mother's
mother? a severe face
tight actually

her cheeks
colored false pink

nothing like the
limber
of that harsh
grandfather's
face in the picture

       loving man
       who hated

my father would
'understand'
anyone

and go stupid
when attacked by like
Irish blockheads to
what also conceivably my
grandfather may
have been gave allegiances to
—like the Church I don't know

           was a whisky
             drinker
          but no drunk

             stored barrels
              of apples
            in his cellar
                etc

there was nothing
    that I can honestly recall
wasn't
'strict' about him—that is he wasn't

soft, I don't believe. He would my impression is give up
anything to
anyone or any
thing: (impossible to be

accurate about
'memories' in
that generation
unless

    like one's own parents
they live long enough
    for you yourself
    to be able to

judge: on my father
I'm afraid I am
right, that he did fight
rigidly, the next generation of
'Irish' in the
U S Post Office to

    mon grand
    Père: Paddy Hehir
        "Blocky" Sheehan
    and the Postmaster,
    Healy, ran a travel agency
       Pleasant Street
          Worcester

killed himself
'fighting'
such men (when my grandfather
rolled right over on the rug
when he was leaning over the window seat
getting some magazines say out of the inside
(with the cushions off) when I
came up from behind
and kicked him

        and I went out in the kitchen
      and sd to my mother Grandpa
         is lying on the floor

      he looked out of the tintype
    like a different type
than my pa

                    black walnut
the bed was made of
he put the ridges in
where he missed
when he was giving
my uncle a beating

            my mother used to beg
            to be beaten
            instead

      who knows?
but I make Jack Hines
too mean

   a man and a woman either is only a thing when each
is full of blood

                  This is my poem to my grandfather,
                        John Hines his name was
                        he migrated to the United States
                        from Ireland sometime
                        (my mother was born
                        on this side 1872)
                        before
                        1872

and was employed
so far as I know only
in his lifetime
on this side by
the U S Steel (retired
as such a night watchman

after (I suppose) having

shoveled coal most

of his life

He had been born "in Cork,

brought up

in Galway," and recently

I figured out he must have been

sent 'home' to

Galway during

the potato famine

(the Hines,

as an Irish clan

were reasonably small

and had their center

around Gort

J. V. CUNNINGHAM
(1911 – 1985)

Agnosco Veteris Vestigia Flammae

I have been here. Disperesed in meditation,
I sense the traces of the old surmise—
Passion dense as fatigue, faithful as pain,
As joy foreboding. O my void, my being
In the suspended sources of experience,
Massive in promise, unhistorical
Being of unbeing, of all futures full,
Unrealized in none, how love betrays you,
Turns you to process and a fluid fact
Whose future specifies its past, whose past
Precedes it, and whose history is its being.

"You Have Here No Otherness"

You have here no otherness,
Unaddressed correspondent,
No gaunt clavicles, no hair
Of bushy intimacy.
You are not, and I write here
The name of no signature
To the unsaid—a letter
At midnight, a memorial
And occupation of time.

I'll not summon you, or feel
In the alert dream the give
And stay of flesh, the tactile
Conspiracy.
                    The snow falls
With its inveterate meaning,
And I follow the barberd wire
To trough, to barn, to the house,
To what strangers, what welcome
In the late blizzard of time.

On the highway cars flashing,
Occasional and random
As pain gone without symptom,
And fear drifts with the North wind.
We neither give nor receive:
The unfinishable drink
Left on the table, the sleep
Alcoholic and final
In the mute exile of time.

Montana Fifty Years Ago

Gaunt kept house with her child for the old man,
met at the train, dust-driven as the sink
She came to, the child white as the alkali.
To the West distant mountains, the Big Lake
To the Northeast. Dead trees and almost dead
In the front yard, the front door locked and nailed,
A handpump in the sink. Outside, a land
Of gophers, cottontails, and rattlesnakes,
In good years of alfalfa, oats, and wheat.
Root cellar, blacksmith shop, milk house, and barn,
Granary, corral. And old *World Almanac*
To thumb at night, the child coughing, the lamp smoked,
The chores done. So he came to her one night,
To the front room, now bedroom, and moved in.
Nothing was said, noghting was ever said.
And then the child died and she disappeared.
This was Montana fifty years ago.

CZESLAW MILOSZ
(1911–2005)

To Robinson Jeffers

If you have not read the Slavic poets
so much the better. There's nothing there
for a Scotch-Irish wanderer to seek. They lived in a childhood
prolonged from age to age. For them, the sun
was a farmer's ruddy face, the moon peeped through a cloud
and the Milky Way gladdened them like a birch-lined road.
They longed for the Kingdom which is always near,
always right at hand. Then, under apple trees
angels in homespun linen will come parting the boughs
and at the white kolkhoz tablecloth
cordiality and affection will feast (falling to the ground at times).

And you are from surf-rattled skerries. From the heaths
where burying a warrior they broke his bones
so he could not haunt the living. From the sea night
which your forefathers pulled over themselves, without a word.
Above your head no face, neither the sun's nor the moon's
only the throbbing of galaxies, the immutable
violence of new beginnings, of new destruction.

All your life listening to the ocean. Black dinosaurs
wade where a purple zone of phosphorescent weeds
rises and falls on the waves as in a dream. And Agamemnon
sails the boiling deep to the steps of the palace
to have his blood gush onto marble. Till mankind passes
and the pure and stony earth is pounded by the ocean.

Thin-lipped, blue-eyed, without grace or hope,
before God the Terrible, body of the world.
Prayers are not heard. Basalt and granite.
Above then, a bird of prey. The only beauty.

What have I to do with you? From footpaths in the orchards,
from an untaught choir and shimmers of a monstrance,
from flower beds of rue, hills by the rivers, books
in which a zealous Lithuanian announced brotherhood, I come.
Oh, consolations of mortals, futile creeds.

And yet you did not know what I know. The earth teaches
More than does the nakedness of elements. No one with impunity
gives to himself the eyes of a god. So brave, in a void,
you offered sacrifices to demons: there were Wotan and Thor,
the screech of Erinyes in the air, the terror of dogs
when Hekate with her retinue of the dead draws near.

Better to carve suns and moons on the joints of crosses
as was done in my district. To birches and firs
give feminine names. To implore protection
against the mute and treacherous might
than to proclaim, as you did, an inhuman thing.

JOHN BERRYMAN
(1914 – 1972)

(from) *The Dream Songs*

279

Leaving behind the country of the dead
where he must then return & die himself
he set his tired face due East
where the sun rushes up the North Atlantic
and where had paused a little the war for bread
& the war for status had ceased

forever, and he took with him five books,
a Whitman & a Purgatorio,
a one-volume dictionary,
an Oxford Bible with all its bays & nooks
& bafflements long familiar to Henry
& one other new book-O.

If ever he had crafted in the past—
but only if—he swore now to craft better
which lay in the Hands above.
He said: I'll work on slow, O slow & fast,
if a letter comes I will answer that letter
& my whole year will be tense with love.

290

Why *is* Ireland the wettest place on earth
year-round, beating Calcutta in the monsoon
& the tropical rain-forest?
Clearly the sun has made an exception for Ireland,
the sun growled & shown elsewhere: Iowa,
detestable State.

Adorable country, in its countryside
& persons, & its habits, & its past,
martyrs & heroes,
its noble monks, its wild men of high pride
& poets long ago, Synge, Joyce & Yeats,
and the ranks from which they rose.

Detestable State, made of swine & corn,
rich & ignorant, pastless, with one great tree in it
& doubtless certain souls
perplexed as the Irish whether to shout or mourn
over man's riddling fate: alter, or *stet*:
Fate across all them rolls.

301

Shifted his mind &   was once more full of the great Dean
with his oddities about money & his enigmatic ladies,
the giant presences
chained to St. Patrick's, tumultuous, serene,
their mighty stint done, larger in stone than life,
larger than Henry's belief

who now returns at fifty, conflict-scarred,
to see how they are doing: why, they are doing
just what thirty years ago
he thought they were doing, and it is not hard,
neither in doubt or trouble, neither gaining nor losing,
just being the same O.

His frantic huge mind left him long before the end,
he wandered mad through the apartments but once was seen
to pause by a shelf & look
at a copy of the *Tale of a Tub:* he took it down
& was heard to mutter 'What a genius was mine
when I wrote down that book.'

307

The Irish monk with horns of solid mire
pillaged the countryside: Haw haw they cried
this is our favourite monk
He did them down dirty like a low-down skunk
The Irish sky remained fitful & wide
with clouds bright as fire

Helen or Henry is reborn in this place of the past
The Eighteenth Century lives on & on
Henry is overcome
with this solidity where shall he find a home?
The Irish converse about practical questions
& about finding us a house fast.

Cold & weary sought he a hearth, not just for now
but all the workful months to come, Adrienne
Succor me, be on my side
This is the chief lion-breeding place: I bow
gently to my superiors, being merely men
who have not been denied.

309

Fallen leaves and litter. It is September.
Henry's months now begin. Much to be done
by merry Christmas,
much to be done by the American Thanksgiving
(I hate these English cigarettes), much to be done,
much to be done.

I went shopping today & came back with
a book about the Easter Rising, reality & myth—
all Henry's old heroes,
The O'Rahilly, Plunkett, Connolly, & Pearse,
spring back into action, fatuous campaigners
dewy with phantastic hope.

Phantastic hope rules Henry's war as well,
all these enterprises are doomed, all human pleas
are headed for the night.
Wait the lime-pits for all originators,
wounded propped up to be executed,
afterward known as martyrs.

312
I have moved to Dublin to have it out with you,
majestic Shade, You whom I read so well
so many years ago,
did I read your lesson right? did I see through
your phases to the real? your heaven, your hell
did I enquire properly into?

For years then I forgot you, I put you down,
ingratitude is the necessary curse
of making things new:
I brought my family to see me through,
I brought my homage & my soft remorse,
I brought a book or two

only, including in the end your last
strange poems made under the shadow of death
Your high figures float
again across my mind and all your past
fills my walled garden with your honey breath
wherein I move, a mote.

321

O land of Connolly & Pearse, what have
ever you done to deserve these tragic masters?
You come & go,
free: nothing happens. Nelson's Pillar blows
but the busses still go there: nothing is changed,
for all these disasters O

We fought our freedom out a long while ago
I can't see that it matters, we can't help you
land of ruined abbeys,
discredited Saints & brainless senators,
roofless castles, enemies of Joyce & Swift,
enemies of Synge,

enemies of Yeats & O'Casey, hold your foul ground
your filthy cousins will come around to you,
barely able to read,
friends of Patrick Kavanagh's & Austin Clarke's
those masters who can both read & write,
in the high Irish style.

355
Slattery's, in Ballsbridge

Cling to me & I promise you'll drown too,
this voyage is terminal, I'll take your beauty down
and ruined in sea weed
then it will seem forever. I am you
you are your moan, you are your sexy moan,
we are a 'possum treed.

Difficult at midnight grew our love
as if we could not have enough, enough,
reluctant lady.
Nobody in the world knows where I am.
Your hair drags. You would have made a terrific victim
in one of Henry's thrillers.

Weep for the fate of man, excellent lady.
He comes no near, whereas he is so lost,
a crisis in the ghost
baffles endeavour, so he would lie down.
Attends his sorry perish, excellent lady.
Withhold from him your frown.

RANDALL JARRELL
(1914–1965)

A Rhapsody on Irish Themes

At six in the morning you scratched at my porthole,
Great-grandmother, and looked into my eyes with the eyes
Of a potato, and held out to me—only a dollar—
A handkerchief manufactured with their own hands
By the Little People; a *Post* wet from no earthly press,
Dreamed over the sinking fire
                                    of a pub by a Papal Count.
Look: a kerchief of linen, embroidered cunningly
In the green of Their hearts, in Their own hand:
A SOUVENIR OF OLD IRELAND.

Then you turned into the greatest of the gulls
That brood on the seesaw green
Swells of the nest of the harbor of Cóbh.

All is green, all is small, all is—
It is not; the nuns sailing to Ireland
Disembark, and are dovetailed into the black
Nuns sailing from Ireland: a steady state,
But black. And that patch of the red of blood
On the hillside without any trees, by the topless
Tower, is a Cardinal surely? the steak
This Lady with Cromwell's sword in her suitcase
Wolfs for her lonely supper, with a sigh
Like and empire falling? And the sky is the blue
Of the fat priest's brimmed beret,
Of the figuring and clasps of his new

Accordion (that plays all night, by itself, like the sword
Of a hero, a *Mother Machree*
That'd tear your heart out entirely).

The soft, guileful, incessant speech
Plaits into the smack of the feet
In their dance on the deck, every night in the moonlight;
The smile is, almost, the smile
Of the nuns looking on in delight—
The delight of a schoolgirl at recess, a trouble to no one.
But—blue eyes, gray face—
I was troubled by you.

        The old woman, met in sleep,
Skinned herself of her wrinkles, smiled like a goddess—
Skinned herself of the smile, and said to me softly:
"There's no rest for you, grandson, till you've reached the land
Where, walking the roads with an adding-machine on your shoulder,
You meet no one who knows it."
                Well, I hold nothing
Against you but what you are. One can almost bear
The truth in that soft shameless speech
That everything is a joke—from your Sublime
To your Ridiculous is one false step—
But one settles at birth on that step of the stair
And dislikes being shown that there's nothing there.
But I believe you: the orchestration
Of this world of man is all top or bottom,
And the rest is—
            anything that you say.
To argue longer would be un-Irish,
Unnatural grandson that I am!
               —Great-grandson.

Old sow, old Circe, *I'm* not your farrow.
Yet ah, to be eaten! There honk beside me the Tame Geese
Of the Seven Hills of the City of Dublin,
And it's Stentor I cough like, what with the smoke of peat—
Man is born to Ireland as the sparks fly upward:
A sleepwalker fallen from the edge of Europe,
A goosegirl great among publicans and censors.
—She speaks, smiling, of someone "who felt at home
In whatever was least like home, and fell in love
With the world for not being America"—

                              Old Sibyl!

It's your last leaf . . . Still, play it: it is so;
I'm from nowhere, I'm Nobody. But if I'm to be reminded
By any nobody—

                 Ireland, I've seen your cheeks
The red of dawn: the capillaries are broken.

Long ago, the sun set. These are the Western Isles.

                 —And, waking, I saw on the Irish Sea
Orion, his girdle a cinch, and himself a hunter,
An Irish hunter . . .

              that is to say, a horse.

Great-grandmother, I've dreamed of you till I'm hoarse.
It was all a lie: I take back every word.

                      . . . If your shin *is* speckled,
Your grin, alas! pious—

              still, what a brow-ridge!
You Eden of Paleolithic survivals,
You enclave of Brünn and of Borreby man,
Fold your child home, when—weary of Learning—
He sighs for the Night of the Spirit of Man.

. . . What have I said! Faith, I'm raving entirely:
Your taste is like lotus, you Irish air!
Get the wax out of your ears, you oarsmen,
We sail at six . . . And here's the last lesson
I learned from you, Ireland:

        what it is I've forgotten.

Well, what if it's gone? Here's some verses of Goethe's—
An old upright man, a lover of Ireland—
You Senate of Ireland, to straighten the conduct
Of such of your people as need it: *In peace*
        Keep tidy
        Your little coops.
        In war
        Get along
        With quartered troops.

JAMES LAUGHLIN
(1914–1997)

Martha Graham

Earth and water air
and fire her body

beats the ground it
flows it floats it

seems to burn she
burns herself away

until there is no
body there at all

but only the pure
elements moving as

music moves moving
from her into us.

EUGENE McCARTHY
(1916 – 2005)

No Country for the Young

This is no country for the young.
Vultures prey on living flesh
and eat the skins off kettledrums.
The old refuse to die.

Eyes turn inward, chicken-like,
or stare, unlidded, vague as fish
within a deep and pressuring sea.

At the St. Regis
ice cubes smell of mammoth flesh,
and all the clocks have stopped.
A three-fingered pianist
plays only the black keys
until the dancers fall.
Shadows dare to stand against a sun
veiled by the ash of Hiroshima.

Time is tired of you and me.
It now runs out
like dust
from the broken hourglass.

The young begin too soon
to wait to be the last.
They cover stains of salt and blood
with antimacassars
and watch old curtains disintegrating
from the bottom up.

THOMAS McGRATH
(1916–1990)

Ode for the American Dead in Asia

1.

God love you now, if no one else will ever,
Corpse in the paddy, or dead on a high hill
In the fine and ruinous summer of a war
You never wanted. All your false flags were
Of bravery and ignorance, like grade school maps:
Colors of countries you would never see—
Until that weekend in eternity
When, laughing, well armed, perfectly ready to kill
The world and your brother, the safe commanders sent
You into your future. Oh, dead on a hill,
Dead in a paddy, leeched and tumbled to
A tomb of footnotes. We mourn a changeling: you:
Handselled to poverty and drummed to war
By distinguished masters whom you never knew.

2.

The bee that spins his metal from the sun,
The shy mole drifting like a miner ghost
Through midnight earth—all happy creatures run
As strict as trains on rails the circuits of
Blind instinct. Happy in your summer follies,
You mined a culture that was mined for war:
The state to mold you, church to bless, and always
The elders to confirm you in your ignorance.
No scholar put your thinking cap on nor
Warned that in dead seas fishes died in schools

Before inventing legs to walk the land.
The rulers stuck a tennis racket in your hand,
An Ark against the flood. In time of change
Courage is not enough: the blind mole dies,
And you on your hill, who did not know the rules.

3.

Wet in the windy counties of the dawn
The lone crow skirls his draggled passage home:
And God (whose sparrows fall aslant his gaze,
Like grace or confetti) blinks and he is gone,
And you are gone. Your scarecrow valor grows
And rusts like early lilac while the rose
Blooms in Dakota and the stock exchange
Flowers. Roses, rents, all things conspire
To crown your death with wreaths of living fire.
And the public mourners come: the politic tear
Is cast in the Forum. But, in another year,
We will mourn you, whose fossil courage fills
The limestone histories: brave: ignorant: amazed:
Dead in the rice paddies, dead on the nameless hills.

The End of the World

The end of the world: it was given to me to see it.
Came in the black dark, a bulge in the starless sky,
A trembling at the heart of the night, a twitching of the webby flesh
of the earth.
And out of the bowels of the street one beastly, ungovernable cry.

Came and I recognized it: the end of the world.
And waited for the lightless plunge, the fury splitting the rock.
And waited: a kissing of leaves: a whisper of man-killing ancestral night—
Then: a tinkle of music, laughter from the next block.

Yet waited still: for the awful traditional fire,
Hearing mute thunder, the long collapse of sky.
It falls forever. But no one noticed. The end of the world provoked
Out of the dark a single and melancholy sigh

From my neighbor who sat on his porch drinking beer in the dark.
No: I was not God's prophet. Armageddon was never
And always: this night in a poor street where a careless irreverent laughter
Postpones the end of the world: in which we live forever.

Columbus

Columbus, wearing a night-gown made from a treasure map,
Is sleepwalking on the giant avenues of an invisible sea.

He dreams he had discovered the Isthmus of Compound Interest
In his constant pursuit of the droppings of the One Historical Zero.
Tears fall through the meridians of his hands.
He is sad. His sadness makes the winds blow,

Filling his sails with the algebra of abstract labor.
Birds faint at his passing and the fish turn to stone.
He is looking for gold that breathes and has dark skin
And can be renamed *Slave*. The birds revive, screaming.

In the dungeons of the King the dark zero grows wounds and weapons.
At sea the waves trudge off in search of a new continent.

The Topography of History

All cities are open in the hot season.
Northward or southward the summer gives out
Few telephone numbers but no one in our house sleeps.

Southward that river carries its flood
The dying winter, the spring's nostalgia:
Wisconsin's dead grass beached at Baton Rouge.
Carries the vegetable loves of the young blonde
Going for water by the dikes of Winnetka or Louisville,
Carries its obscure music and its strange humour,
Its own disturbing life, its peculiar ideas of movement.
Two thousand miles, moving from the secret north
It crowds the country apart: at last reaching
The lynch-dreaming, the demon-haunted, the murderous virgin South
Makes its own bargains and says change in its own fashion.
And where the Gulf choirs out its blue hosannas
Carries the drowned men's bones and its buried life:
It is an enormous bell, rung through the country's midnight.

.   .   .

Beyond the corrosive ironies of prairies,
Midnight savannas, open vowels of the flat country,
The moonstruck waters of the Kansas bays
Where the Dakotas bell and nuzzle at the north coast,
The nay-saying desolation where the mind is lost
In the mean acres and the wind comes down for a thousand miles
Smelling of the stars' high pastures, and speaking a strange language—
There is the direct action of mountains, a revolution,
A revelation in stone, the solid decrees of past history,
A soviet of language not yet cooled nor understood clearly:
The voices from underground, the granite vocables.
There shall that voice crying for justice be heard,
But the local colorist, broken on cliffs of laughter,
At the late dew point of pity collect only the irony of serene stars.

.   .   .

Here all questions are mooted. All battles joined.
              No one in our house sleeps.
And the Idealist hunting in the high latitudes of unreason,
By mummy rivers, on the open minds of curst lakes
Mirrors his permanent address; yet suffers from visions
Of spring break-up, the open river of history.
On this the Dreamer sweats in his sound-proof tower:
All towns are taken in the hot season.

How shall that Sentimentalist love the Mississippi?
His love is a trick of mirrors, his spit's abstraction,
Whose blood and guts are filing system for
A single index of the head or heart's statistics.
Living in one time, he shall have no history.
How shall he love change who lives in a static world?
His love is lost tomorrow between Memphis and
              the narrows of Vicksburg.

But kissed unconscious between Medicine Bow and Tombstone
He shall love at the precipice brink who would love these mountains.
Whom this land loves shall be a holy wanderer,
The eyes burned slick with distances between
Kennebunkport and Denver, minted of transience.
For him shall that river run in circles and
The Tetons seismically skipping to their ancient compelling music
Send embassies of young sierras to nibble from his hand.
His leaves familiar with the constant wind,
Give, then, the soils and waters to command.
Latitudinal desires scatter his seed,
And in political climates sprout new freedom.
But curst is the water-wingless foreigner from Boston,
Stumping the country as others no better have done,
Frightened of earthquake, aware of the rising waters,
Calling out "O Love, Love," but finding none.

Love in a Bus

Chicago, 1942

It was born in perhaps the Holland Tunnel,
And in New Jersey opened up its eyes,
Discovered its hands in Pennsylvania and
Later the night came.

The moon burned brighter than the dreams of lechers—
Still, they made love halfway to Pittsburgh,
Disturbing the passengers and sometimes themselves.
Her laughter gamboled in the bus like kittens:
He kissed with his cap on, maybe had no hair.
I kept remembering them even beyond Chicago
Where everyone discovered a personal direction.
She went to Omaha; he went south; and I,
Having nothing better, was thinking of chance—
Which has its mouth open in perpetual surprise—
And love. For even though she was a whore
And he a poor devil wearing built-up heels,
Still, love has light which like an early lamp
Or Hesperus, that star, to the simplest object
Lends a magnificent impersonal radiance,
Human, impermanent and permanently good.

GWENDOLYN BROOKS
(1917 – 2000)

Bronzeville Woman in a Red Hat

hires out to Mrs. Miles

I
They had never had one in the house before.
                The strangeness of it all. Like unleashing
A lion, really. Poised
To pounce. A puma. A panther. A black
Bear.
There it stood in the door,
Under a red hat that was rash, but refreshing—
In a tasteless way, of course—across the dull dare,
The semi-assault of that extraordinary blackness.
The slackness
Of that light pink mouth told little. The eyes told of heavy
        care. . . .
But that was neither here nor there,
And nothing to a wage-paying mistress as should
Be getting her due whether life had been good
For her slave, or bad.
There it stood
In the door. They had never had
One in the house before.

But the Irishwoman had left!
A message had come.
Something about a murder at home.
A daughter's husband—"berserk," that was the phrase:
The dear man had "gone berserk"
And short work—
With a hammer—had been made
Of this daughter and her nights and days.
The Irishwoman (underpaid,
Mrs. Miles remembered with smiles),
Who was a perfect jewel, a red-faced trump,
A good old sort, a baker
Of rum cake, a maker
Of Mustard, would never return.
Mrs. Miles had begged the bewitched woman
To finish, at least, the biscuit blending,
To tarry till the curry was done,
To show some concern
For the burning soup, to attend to the tending
Of the tossed salad. "Inhuman,"
Patsy Houlihan had called Mrs. Miles.
"Inhuman." And "a fool."
And "a cool
One."

The Alert Agency had leafed through its files—
On short notice could offer
Only this dusky duffer
That now made its way to her kitchen and sat on her kitchen
      stool.

II
Her creamy child kissed by the black maid! square on the
      mouth!
World yelled, world writhed, world turned to light and
      rolled
Into her kitchen, nearly knocked her down.

Quotations, of course, from baby books were great
Ready armor; (but her animal distress
Wore, too and under, a subtler metal dress,
Inheritance of approximately hate.)
Say baby shrieked to see his finger bleed,
Wished human humoring—there was a kind
Of unintimate love, a love more of the mind
To order the nebulousness of that need.
—This was the way to put it, this the relief.
This sprayed honey upon marvelous grime.
This told it possible to postpone the reef.
Fashioned a huggable darling out of crime.
Made monster personable in personal sight
By cracking mirrors down the personal night.

Disgust crawled through her as she chased the theme.
She, quite supposing purity despoiled,
Committed to sourness, disordered, soiled,
Went in to pry the ordure from the cream.
Cooing, "Come." (Come out of the cannibal wilderness,
Dirt, dark, into the sun and bloomful air.
Return to freshness of your right world, wear
Sweetness again. Be done with beast, duress.)

Child with continuing cling issued his No in final fire,
            Kissed back the colored maid,
            Not wise enough to freeze or be afraid.
            Conscious of kindness, easy creature bond.
            Love had been handy and rapid to respond.

Heat at the hairline, heat between the bowels,
Examining seeming coarse unnatural scene,
She saw all things except herself serene:
Child, big black woman, pretty kitchen towels.

ROBERT LOWELL
(1917 – 1977)

For Eugene McCarthy

(July, 1968)

I love you so. . . . Gone? Who will swear you wouldn't
have done good to the country, that fulfilment wouldn't
have done good to you—the father, as Freud says:
you? We've so little faith that nayone
ever makes anything better . . . the same and less—
ambition only makes the ambitious great.
The state lifts us, we cannot raise the state. . . . All
was yours though, lining down the balls for hours,
freedom of the hollow bowling-alley,
the thundered strikes, the boys. . . . Picking a quarrel
with you is like picking the petals of the daisy—
the game, the passing crowds, the rapid young
still brand your hand with sunflecks . . . coldly willing
to smash the ball past those who bought the park.

Milgate

Yearly, connubial swallows nest
in the sky-flung gutter and stop its mouth.
It is a natural life. Nettles
subdue the fugitive violet's bed,
a border of thistles hedges the drive;
children dart like minnows. They dangle
over the warm, reedy troutbrook.

It's a crime
to get too little from too much.

In mirage, meadow turns to lawn,
in the dredged cowpond, weed is water,
half-naked children beautify,
feud and frighten the squabbling ducks—
from vacation to vacation,
they broaden out to girls, young ladies,
a nightlife on two telephones.

The elderflower is champagne.

Age goes less noticed in humbler life—
the cedar of Labanon dumbly waves
one defoliated millennial stump;
the yew row, planted under Cromwell
with faith and burnish, keeps its ranks,
unpierceably stolid, young, at ease.

August flames in the rusty sorrel,
a bantam hen hatches wild pheasant chicks,
the dog licks ice cream from a cone;
but mostly the cropped, green, sold-off pastures
give grace to the house, to *Milgate Park,*
its name and service once one in Bearsted,
till uselessness brought privacy,
splendor, extravagance, makeshift
offered at auction for its bricks—
yet for a moment saved by you,
and kept alive for another decade,
by your absentminded love,
your lapwing's instinctive elegance,
the glue of your obdurate Ulster will—
Milgate,
enclosures to sun and space to cool,
one mural varied in fifty windows,
sublime and cozy, stripped of creeper,
its severity a blaze of salmon-pink,
its long year altered by our small . . .
easy to run as things made to run.

REED WHITTEMORE
(1919 –)

The Storing of the Soul

The American soul has been stored under the stairs
In the box with the mittens and scarves
For the longest time. We couldn't think where we had put it.
We looked in the attic and cellar, and in the garage,
And then found it at last, as I say, under the stairs.

Why would anyone store a poor spiritual soul there,
We wondered.
It was ever so slightly creased and deceased but it was
Perfectly safe, we were sure.
We put it back in the box there.

I have been checking it Fridays, just to make sure
It isn't departing,
And see no change in it at all, except in its color,
Which is less.
Of its continuing immortality I have made sure

By adding more mothballs.
But do you think that there is a chance that we will have
    need of it?
I ask because if we will I think I should air it.
A soul is not at its best when it is
Heavy with mothballs.

Let It Blow

Let it blow, said the corp of amalgamated winds,
And let it drip, said the cloud trust.

Where is there an end to it,
The self-interest?
—Whither my feet takest me I find lobbying,
Invented by Joseph Lobby
Who wrote a non-partisan editorial on behalf of his own candidacy
      for alderman in a tiny New England slum housing development
      in 1802.

Now each purple mountain majesty requires a private sunrise.
We pass individually unto grace, cutting each other on the
      thruway,
Singing the brotherhood of one.

Let it blow.
Let the assorted selves drop leaflets against litter,
Picket the morning.

Who will volunteer to park in a bus stop?
Foul the word supply?

—The right of the people to keep and bear arms shall not be
      infringed
Nor other rights of the righteous
So that the pharmaceutical firms may suck forever
On the inner heart of our headache.

How can a nation of smart cookies be so dumb?
Did Washington do it? Jefferson? Thoreau maybe?

—I look into the kindly eyes of my anarchist soul-mate,
She (he) dreaming of a Greek isle with his (her) American Express
      card,
She (he) wanting 400 hp and a water bed
And he (she) a mountain, a guru, and an independent income.

Not an institution in this country is not betrayed by its souls
      in residence.
Who is left to pull the weeds from the Xerox machine?
Where will we find manpower to carry this week's privateering
      to the town dump?

—Let it blow,
And let the associations for the preservation of freedoms publish
      the unexpurgated results
At a profit.

ANN DARR
(1920–)

Gaelic Legacy

1.

Trying to ignore the only thing
I can surely count on, Time,
  as a subject weeded and warted
  by every young twister of words,
  a phase I thought I could slip
  in a slippery apprenticeship
  (Modern Dancing with Miss Muse)
  whose leotard has been replaced
  with ruffled lace before I've reached
  the bottom of the page . . .
which brings me to my subject, space,
  a kind of time.

2.

Having a built-in Irish timing, oblique
as O'Cornered names (dear Great-grandmother
Sally O'Neil has fallen down the O'hill
and died next day with O'Chill and grandpa
was O'sued by his O'widow'O)
  While I knit such
  from a nonsense bush
  time has passed
  in a padded hearse
  with things I meant
  to say aboard.

3.

    Learning that I know
    what I have long known
    gives the effect of
    spending my life
    walking backward.

4.

And dear Great-grandmother Annie Trent
    cornered herself a century
        to become smaller
            and smaller in.
    String saved my life, she said,
    and at the end, For what?

Dear tender Annie Trent,
    le grande experiment.
Your string fenced out the savages
    who meant to do you in.
With exquisite knots you civilized
    your lace, our lives.

5.

Dear Father Hartke,
    How can man escape
        his animality?
          Why
        would he want to?

    Every morning he must
        push it away
          and put on
    his civilized socks.

                Peace.

Flying the Zuni Mountains

Hold death by the heels
and tickle his nose with a feather,
for the wind is our blood
it will blow itself away.
Never a dark red rivulet trickling through the grass
beside the bolts and the pressed-wood props made in
      Camden, New Jersey.

Let the engine drone a funeral dirge,
the sharp staccato when one cylinder plays alone.
The quiet . . . just the wind.
No sound when the ribs crumple,
like the old tree falling in the forest
with no one to hear,
for we are not there.
We stand and lean on a cloud
and call for another beer.

This we know:
we are the wind.
we will come back gently over the lake,
we will lash the waves and bend the trees;
we will lie side by side on the high mountains,
drinking martinis and telling the old jokes over.
Never our wings will crumple with heat or hardness.
This we know.
For the man who draws the blueprints, shapes the wings,
      threads the bolts, pulls the props
is not our faith.
Ours is the wind and the wind is us
and no one shall bury us ever.

We have known space not surrounded by closets and
    cabbages cooking,
we have whirled rainbows over our heads;
we have owned the earth by rising from it,
never again shall we walk with ordinary feet.

The wings were shaped from a woman's weeping . . .
no other tears shall fall.

JAMES SCHEVILL
(1920 –)

For the Old Yeats

The great ripping goes on in all minds,
A tearing of structure, a change;
Piercing through our loves, we find new loves,
Bodies alter in tidal lash of blood,
We are lost, we are found, we are alone.
In that loneliness, a stony center begins,
The hardening of age; lechers of time
We cling to a core of name, ancestral,
But skin changes, stiffens, hair whitens.
Who is that foolish, fond, ridiculous, old man?
Many years ago he was young and ran
His leaping, curving course.
Limping, he enters the noose of time,
Dreaming a fancy of love firm to hold,
And hangs there in his old, ludicrous hope
To the bawdy laughter of the world.

DANIEL BERRIGAN
(1921–)

The Big Wind

Their lives rounded in a backcountry brogue
now to see, at crowd's edge, the fine Athenian profiles
agape, scenting their delicate language like
odor of muscatel or honey:

Peter and John, it is Babel crashing about your ears.
The Spirit, impatient of gross and exquisite tongues, of known
and unknown gods, has riven the abominable tower
The undivided tongues

are abroad, are a wildfire.

You; never again constrained
by scarecrow gestures, by hem or haw. You; to see
agonized at the crowd's edge, the faces emptied of guile,
their human wisdom consumed in a stench of straw.

Dachau Is Now Open for Visitors

The arabesque scrawled by the dead
in their laborious passage,
leaf and flower mould of their spent bodies,
faces frost touches
gently and coldly
to time's geometric—
a multitude of skeletal men
presses forward; such cries
the patient poor speak, whose despair
leaves no man's peace intact, no coin
for death's foreclosing fist.

Immanence

I see You in the world—
venturesome children, their cries and gestures,
the sharp sad whistle at six, the emptying park,
flybitten leaves, embers of the magnificent
weathered candelabra, the poplar lanes.

Yet faith asks, like a shaky woman, some epiphany—
a renaissance cock calling Peter's sin
from the Pantheon roof, shocking the crowd's ease,
sinking the children's fleet

that now make alas, as life does, a silly wayward wake
or none at all; and no one walks waters.

HAYDEN CARRUTH
(1921–)

Her Song

She sings blues in a voice that is partly
Irish. But "music is international." Singing
With her blue eyes open, her auburn hair
Flung back, yes, searching a distant horizon
For a sometime beacon or the first glimmer
Of sunrise. She sings in the dark. Only her own light
Illuminates her, although in the shadows
Are dim shapes, motionless, known to be
The tormented—in the bogs of Ireland, in
The bayous of Louisiana, relics of thousands
Upon thousands who suffered unimaginably
In ancient times. And in her husky contralto
They are suffering still. Knowingly she sings.
Music is anthropological. This is a burden,
For in her song no one can be redeemed.

ALAN DUGAN
(1923 – 2003)

The So-Called Wild Horses of the Water

The so-called wild horses of the water
stumbled all over the boulders
and fell steaming and foaming over
the world's edge down the roaring
white way of the waterfall
into the black pool of the death
of motion at the bottom where
the cold stoned water lay
dense as a diamond of pressure and
the eye of silence stared unmoved
at the world's cavalry falling in
to be the seer not the heard again.

Mockery Against the Irish Censorship

Ireland was better in its dream,
with the oppressor foreign.
Now its art leaves home to keen
and its voice is orange.
It is a sad revolt, for loving's health,
that beats its enemy and then itself.

Now that Irishmen are free
to enslave themselves together
they say that it is better they
do worst to one another
then have the english do them good
in an exchange of joy for blood.

A just as alien pius blacks
their greens of lovers' commerce;
rehearsing victory, they lack
a government to fill its promise.
Worse, law has slacked the silly harp
that was their once and only Ark

out, and I am sorry to be flip
and narrowly disrespectful,
but since I wade at home in it
I stoop and take a mouthful
to splatter the thick wall of their heads
with American insult! Irish sense is dead.

Sailing to Jerusalem

On coming up on deck Palm Sunday morning, oh
we saw the seas the dancy little tourist ship
climbed up and down all night in cabin dreams.
They came along in ridges an horizon wide!
and ran away astern to the Americas we left,
to break on headlands and be called "the surf."
After services below, the pilgrims to the east
carried their processed palm fronds up on deck
and some of them went overboard from children's hands.
So, Christ: there were the palm leaves on the water
as the first fruits of the ocean's promised land.
They promise pilgrims resurrection out at sea,
though sea-sick fasters in their bunks below
cry out for harbor, order, and stability.
This is the place for it! The sky is high
with it, the water deep, the air is union: spray!
We all walk the water just below the decks
too, helplessly dancing to the world's variety
like your Jerusalem, Byzantium, and Rome.

On Voyage

Always getting ready to go out
but never leaving, I looked out
at the developments of the day
from morning up to noon and down
to afternoon and, after that,
night. "To take off," I said,
"always to leave, to begin again,"
but I stayed in my paces and room
always getting ready to go out
but never leaving. Ah how I worked
my youth away to send word out
to the day about my situation. Then
it sent back steamship tickets and
a hammer of images forged by deaths,
the idea of death, and cash, the savior.
"I have broken through," I said
to the window for the last time,
and walked out on to the ocean and
Europe for a closer view of home.

Note: The Sea Grinds Things Up

It's going on now
as these words appear
to you or are heard by you.
A wave slaps down, flat.
Water runs up the beach,
then wheels and slides
back down, leaving a ridge
of sea-foam, weed, and shells.
One thinks: I must
break out of this

horrible cycle, but
the ocean doesn't: it
continues through the thought.
A wave breaks, some
of its water runs up
the beach and down
again, leaving a ridge
of scum and skeletal debris.
One thinks: I must
break out of this
cycle of life and death,
but the ocean doesn't: it
goes past the thought.
A wave breaks on the sand,
water planes up the beach
and wheels back down,
hissing and leaving a ridge
of anything it can leave.
One thinks: I must
run out the life
part of this cycle,
then the death part
of this cycle, and then
go on as the sea
goes on in this cycle
after the last word,
but this is not the last
word unless you think
of this cycle as some
perpetual inventory
of the sea. Remember:
this is just one sea
on one beach on one
planet in one
solar system in one
galaxy. After that
the scale increases, so
this is not the last word,
and nothing else is talking back.
It's a lonely situation.

JOHN LOGAN
(1923 – 1986)

At Drumcliffe Churchyard, County Sligo

1

That great feather the mind's wind drives
over the graves
and which lights
and stays on the tomb of Yeats
is made of skin and of thin stone
akin to cliff, akin to drum.

2

On this ancient monastic spot
I feel the shocks of rhythm underfoot—
gigantic hooves of heaving
Irish horses, their riders weaving
with ecstasy as their long, god-like legs
stretch
      and cleave the tight
breaking up the patterning of light
the brown,
        the black, the roan,
the mottled hides give off
like the sun shining (and then not)
through mist
        in bursts
along Ben Bulben's back. The wild long-
haired men and the wild
long-haired women ride
and merge and are gone.

3

Yeats's grave lifts to heaven
the body of a man, body of a woman—
himself, his wife, his wife, himself,
and his ambiguous epitaph
celebrates his birth forever back into life.
The great "cold eye" now opens
in the soaring brow of Man-Woman.

4

This gravesite is a bridge of sex.
It is a bridge of space
between
            the valley and the mountain—
between the long, free
flanks of the land and the fossil sea.
It is a bridge of time, for the round
stone tower still stands
where the medieval monks hovered
over the church cloths and silver
when the swift, marauding Vikings came.
And the Celtic rock High Cross
(figuring how Christian love
joins Adam and Eve
while
            Cain's hate kills Abel)
is raised along the selfsame
wall where a prehistoric standing stone
covered with its weathered skin
tapers hard toward the moon and sun,
its erect substance teeming full
of the tiny bright seed of shells.

5

Oh, I can feel the mind's wind blow still
over the graves, the church and Ben Bulben hill.
Wait! Touch your cheek!
For this feather breath breathes too
upon you.

(for John Unterecker)

Dublin Suite: Homage to James Joyce

1

The Bridge

It is raining. The child is waiting
for alms on the O'Connell Bridge in
Dublin. An infant cries in her arms.
She stays on the walk morning til night.
The child's eyes are hard. They're almost wild.

Her face is dirty as her dress is.
It is raining. The child is waiting.
The lid of a cardboard box for coins
begins to come apart in the wet.
Many of us pass her by. We fail

to tell how bone thin is her red shawl.
The infant she enwraps weighs heavy
in her small lap, and I tell you they
both lie *here* in the laps of us all.
It is raining. The child is waiting.

Joyce would have watched an epiphany.
His family was constantly poor.
It is Stephen's young sister who sits here.

2

The Library

This massive, carved medieval harp of Irish oak
no longer sounds in the winds from the ancient times gone out
of Celtic towns. It rests in the long, high vaulted room
filled up with one million books whose pages chronicle
the works and ages both in *our* land and in Ireland.
For a hundred years no student has bent here above
those huge, leather volumes that burgeon on the balconies
like matched and staked rows of great pipes
for the unplayed organ of this magnificent place.
But both pipes and harp seem still to come alive and turn
Trinity College Library
into a fantastic temple when we stand over
the twelfth-century Book of Kells,
which James Joyce so loved he carried a facsimile
to Zurich, Rome, Trieste. "It is,"
he said to friends, "the most purely Irish thing we have.
You can compare much of my work
to the intricate illuminations of this book."
Its goatskin pages open up for us under glass
in a wooden case. At this place:
a dog nips its tail in its mouth,
but this dog is of ultramarine, most expensive
pigment after gold, for it was ground out of lapis,
and the tail is of lemon yellow orpiment.
Other figures are verdigris, folium or woad—
the verdigris, made with copper,
was mixed with vinegar, which ate into the vellum
and showed through on the reverse page.
Through the text's pages run constant, colored arabesques
of animated initial
letters—made of the bent bodies
of fabulous, elongated beasts
linked and feeding beautifully upon each other,
or upon themselves. Why, even the indigo-haired
young man gnaws at his own entrails.
The archetypal figure of the uroboros

recurs, as does that the Japanese call *tomoi:*
a circle divided by three arcs from its center.
These illuminations around
the Irish script of the Gospels
are some of them benign and terrible like that
Satan from the four temptations:
the devil is black, a skeleton with flaming hair
and short, crumpled emaciated wings, which appear
to be charred as are the bony feet—
and the reptile with such gentle
eyes is colored kermes (compounded from the dried bodies
of female ants that die bright red).
The covers of jewels and gold are gone from the Book,
stolen for a while from the Kells
Monastery in County Meath
and then found, some of its gorgeous pages cut apart
and the whole stuffed beneath the sod.
These designs were all gestures of the bold minds of monks—
their devils still whirring about their ears while angels
blasted their inner eyes with colors not in any
spectrum, and moaning, primitive Celtic gods still cast
up out of their hermetic interior lives strange figures
which we can all recognize as
fragments of our inhuman dreams:
all this is emblazoned here in the unimagined
and musical colors of a medieval church.
Ah, friend, look how this Book of Kells
pictures all our heavens, all our hells.

3
The Green

Up Grafton Street to Stephen's Green
(which young Dedalus thought his own)
I pass the street named Duke. There two of Joyce's favored
pubs still stand, and one of them holds
in a blank wall the red door of Leopold Bloom's home:
it bears the golden number eight
from the house razed on Eccles Street.

Bloom's and Joyce's friends still lift their glasses of stout.
Two doors down from the Green, Captain America's Inn
offers up burgers and cokes and
those Irish potatoes which once,
boiled, kept the families alive,
but here are prepared like the French.
At the entrance to Stephen's Green
an Irish musician keens
on his pipes that wail like a child,
and the beautiful Irish coins
designed by friends of Yeats (dolphins grace and unplayed harps
adorn) are tossed into his cap,
which matches exactly the scarlet tartan of his kilt.
Gray couples walk or rest on benches and some young men
lounge on the Green with girls who hitch up their skirts and sun
their thighs, while other silent men
go in and out of the latrine again and again.
Students listen to the red-and-gold clad band
play from the raised circular stand
and eat their lunch before heading back across the street
to school. Most go round the corner south to UCD
or back down Grafton Street where Trinity College waits,
but some still stroll across to Newman Hall
where Joyce followed Hopkins and Cardinal Newman too.
Gerald Manley Hopkins (who saw things through drops of blood)
agonized here in this garden
as Christ in his Gethsemane—
he tried to decide even to the eighth of a point
the marks for the students he loved.
(Without high grades the Catholics
could not go to school in England.)
I see him there, lean, at his lecture stand in the hall.
On the Green his and Joyce's and Newman's steps still fall.
They mingle with ours like voices
or like the shouts of the great God-in-the-streets that's Joyce's.

4
The Tower

I stand at the round parapet
of Joyce's Martello Tower.
I look over where the awkward, naked boys holler
and dive in the swimming place called "the forty-foot hole,"
since Joyce's time only for men, though now some militant has scrawled
in chalk at the entrance to the spot a woman's sign:
the Venus Mirror. I wonder
then: did *she* ever think of this?
Imagine Botticelli's figure (with her long, brown
strands) scrambling about those rocks amid angular kids.
How odd that sight. How odd this thought:
this tower was built in the fear of a French onslaught.
And this: Oliver St. John Gogarty paid the rent!
Certainly Joyce somehow did his share. The key's still there.
Huge, bronze, like the key of a king.
With it young Stephen unlocked the secrets of the heart,
but it was Joyce's hand the key
touched and taught. And there, down the long, curving iron stair
is Joyce's cane inside a glass case, and there's his watch,
his eyepatch, the memory of him—head in both hands—
struggling with the blindness of Homer. Or of Milton.
It is as if poets were forced to see inside themselves:
fall out of that insular tower of ignorance.
Tiresias, also blind, held up Venus' Mirror
and the Dart of Mars. Whatever man or woman dared
he did, he knew. There is no poet like that seer
as is Joyce, who was Molly and Leopold too. Jung
wrote him, "You know many things we psychologists don't—
especially about women."
Your cane, Joyce! Your key! The imprint of your foot on stone!
And your folded waistcoat fading there in a closed case.
On it in blue, brown the woven hounds chase the fox.
Or do those hounds that heaved when your body breathed, hunt deer?

I feel the chase inside my chest,
here. Joyce, I feel I wear your vest—
and like you am more than human.
I too have within my self the boy, man and woman.
But your clothes make my heart inflate,
for that is not 'more than human.'
Why, Diana had the hunter that desired her
transformed into a deer, his flesh rent by his own dogs.
How often has the woman punished the man in her?
Or the man the woman in him?
How often have both choked back as they became adult
the boy or girl who wept in them
(although its sight was not the less)?
Joyce, here in this tower with its enigmatic patch
for your omniscient eye, I
see better too. Women have taken up and used with strength
the chalk of men. And those boys have the teats of a girl.
Now from your tower's top, let the pen-
nants of all our humankind unwind.

(for Peter Logan—1977)

JAMES SCHUYLER
(1923–1991)

Our Father

This morning view
is very plain: thou art
in Heaven: modern
brick, plate glass, unhallowèd,
as yet, by time,
yet Thy Name
blesses all: silver tanks
of propane gas, the sky,
Thy will,
is lucent blue, French
gray and cream,
is done: the night
on earth
no longer needs
the one white street globe light
as the light, it is
in heaven.
Give us this day
—and a Friday
13th, August '71,
at that:
our daily bread
and breakfast
(Product 19,
an egg, perchance: the hen-fruit,
food and symbol)
and forgive us our
trespasses

too numerous
to name—as we
forgive our debtors: "pay
me when you can:
I don't take
interest"
how green
the grass! so many
flowering weeds
Your free
will has freely
let us name: dandy-
lion *(pisse-en-lit)*
and, clover
(O Trinity)
it is
a temptation
to list them all.
all I know, that is:
the temptation
to show off—to
make a show
of knowing more,
than, in fact, I
know, is very real:
as real as a twelve
pane window sash
one pane slivered
by a crack, a flash,
a mountain line
that stays
to praise
Thee,
Your Name and Your
   Creation
let me surrender
ever—
poets do: it
is their way
and deliver me

from evil
and the Three
Illusions
of the Will—
for the power
that flows electrically
in me is thine
O glorious central,
O plant,
O dynamo!
and the glory
of this cool a.m.
now
all
silver, blue
and white.

Poem

This beauty that I see
—the sun going down
scours the entangled
and lightly henna
withies and the wind
whips them as it
would ship a cloud—
is passing so swiftly
into night. A moon,
full and flat, and stars
a freight train passing
passing it is the sea

and not a train. This
beauty that collects
dry leaves in pools
and pockets and goes
freezingly, just able
still to swiftly flow
it goes, it goes.

Salute

Past is past, and if one
remembers what one meant
to do and never did, is
not to have thought to do
enough? Like that gather-
ing of one of each I
planned, to gather one
of each kind of clover,
daisy, paintbrush that
grew in that field
the cabin stood in and
study them one afternoon
before they wilted. Past
is past. I salute
that various field.

LOUIS SIMPSON
(1923–)

The Peat-Bog Man

He was one of the consorts of the moon,
and went with the goddess in a cart.

Wherever he went there would be someone,
a few of the last of the old religion.

Here the moon passes behind a cloud.
Fifteen centuries pass,

then one of the bog-peat cutters
digs up the man—with the rope

that ends in a noose at the throat—
a head squashed like a pumpkin.

Yet, there is delicacy in the features
and a peaceful expression . . .

that in Spring the flower comes forth
with a music of pipes and dancing.

The Middleaged Man

There is a middleaged man, Tim Flanagan,
whom everyone calls "Fireball."
Every night he does the rocket-match trick.
"Ten, nine, eight . . ." On zero
p f f t! It flies through the air.

Walking to the subway with Flanagan . . .
He tells me that he lives out in Queens
on Avenue Street, the end of the line.
That he "makes his home" with his sister
who has recently lost her husband.

What is it to me?
Yet I can't help imagining what it would be like
to be Flanagan. Climbing the stairs
and letting himself in . . .
I can see him eating in the kitchen.

He stays up late watching television
From time to time he comes to the window.
At this late hour the streets are deserted.
He looks up and down. He looks right at me,
then he steps back out of sight.

.   .   .

Sometimes I wake in the middle of the night
and I have a vision of Flanagan.
He is wearing an old pair of glasses
with a wire bent around the ear
and fastened to the frame with tape.

He is reading a novel by Morley Callaghan.
Whenever I wake he is still there . . .
with his glasses. I wish he would get them fixed.
I cannot sleep as long as there is wire
running from his eye to his ear.

PHILIP WHALEN
(1923 – 2002)

Homage to St. Patrick, García Lorca,
& the Itinerant Grocer

for M-D Schneider

> A big part of this page (a big part of my head)
> Is missing. That cabin where I expected to sit in the
> Woods and write a novel got sold
> > out from under my imagination
>
> I had it all figured out
> > in the green filter of a vine-maple shade
> The itinerant grocer would arrive every week
> There was no doubt in my mind that I'd have money
> To trade for cabbages and bread
>
> Where did that vision take place—maybe Arizona
> > Or New Mexico, where trees are much appreciated—
>
> I looked forward to having many of my own
> Possessed them in a nonexistent future green world of lovely prose
> Lost them in actual present poems in Berkeley
> All changed, all strange, all new; none green.

PADRAIC FIACC
(1924–)

Our Father

for my sister Mary Galliani

Our father who art a Belfast night
-pub bouncer had to have
A bodyguard, drilled recruits for
The IRA behind the scullery door in
The black back yard,
                              died
In your sleep, in silence like
The peasant you stayed
Never belonging on Wall Street,
Your patience a vice
Catching as a drug!

                    With no hankering
To fly back 'home', the way that you never
Left lifting your feet out of the dung
Of the fields of that crossroad town between
Leitrim, Longford and Cavan, begot
Such a high-strung, tight-knit man, but
For a drinking fit when you vented your spleen
On heaven 'took your woman'
Hissing between nicotined teeth
Collapsing over the 'Hope Chest'

Demolishing the delph closet . . .
Bull-bellowing out in
That hollowing slum subway
'God damn it Christ, why?
That child belonged to me!'
                              Pray
For us now that you and she
Bed together in your American grave
And at what an unnatural price!
The eaten bread is soon forgotten years
Sweltering in the subway—bought
Under Mike Quill nightshift days
Hungering and agitating for
Civil Rights, a living wage
And still, still the injustices,
The evil thing being
That which crushes us . . .

Brendan Gone

for Derek Mahon

    Man seasick with drink
    Steadying himself against a lamp post
    Before he is game to risk: chance
    The long street's precipice brink

    Like a very fleshy ghost
    Doing a St. Vitus dance
    In night's depth, the disappearing
    Act, the deep, death-fearing, lost
    Irish bachelor in a New York flat

After money-making years of waste
Blown up with beer false fat
Losing one's boy taste
For life, woman, or
Enemy encounter during war
At night bolts his apartment door

Alone, window-hurtling to the street

A corpse once young and sweet.

Old Poet

Homage to Padraic Colum

I
Strong as the seedling the clay—
Reared winging bird, bald
But not bent head
The snow thawed on
A yellowing lead from time
(Rattled the lift he took
At night fornenst the park
As time as blood ran
coming home in the dark)
Sings still the single word:

The workhouse and the road
The turf bog, the poplar in Mullingar,
The furze bold as flesh,
The heather weather as blood
The grain from the corn,

The trampling thresh of the existence-limited feet
The vision of futility
As if it did not matter what
It is better not to be than born.

II
The pines stood up as guests about the Hundred and First
    Street Lake,
A table of frozen black glass.
He waved a hand up to the copper beech
To let the greyfaced student strolling with him
A tworthree bit of say

Arguing about El Greco and de Valera
The eye more on the sparrow than the ear on his own
    word
Who strolled the streets of Dublin with James Joyce
and had, like the rest, a bit of tiff with Yeats . . .

Under the iced branches of Central Park West
With a voice could be Daniel Corkery
Said what Yeats said what the best said
'Dig in the garden of Ireland, write of your own.'

When we came to Ninety Sixth Street he
Flung eyes over the old roads
Of the Midlands still looking home,
Blotted out a penthouse here to scan a hill there
Skimmed the snow on the grass as a boythrown stone
Skies the skin of water shyfully . . .

As seasons, passing, the rain
Left on the pavements where the pigeons are
The dead leaves of a summer sun . . .

III

Wind, a wren-wrought silk-for-nesting web
Closed over the havocked to ivory grass.
Smoked ravens with chimneys drifted
Filtered past hunched back silent cats of years
On a wash-line left hanging
Open gates: Unripened
Waiting, crude grain, raw

In the wood, still thriving from
Fermenting childhood's thinning comb
Of wine in time ripening
Truth, a beauty, and a good
Hive-sieve for man, the bee:

His wounds, birdmade, feet-pecked, scar-crowed,
Grin with beaks of panicking gold,
The shuddering wing gasping against the bar of the human
Hand touching the butterfly but not to death
With a green thumb forefinger clutch,
The touch of a mother of a woman

In a lifetime of peace, betrayed or told as a song
The moss winning left on the log,
He girds up his loins and laughs
At the buried bone dug up by the dog
At life, toothless toward night fall.

A. R. AMMONS
(1926 – 2001)

The Pieces of My Voice

The pieces of my voice have been thrown
away I said turning to the hedgerows
and hidden ditches
Where do the pieces of
my voice lie scattered
The cedarcone said you have been ground
down into and whirled

Tomorrow I must go look under the clumps of
marshgrass in wet deserts
and in dry deserts
when the wind falls from the mountain
inquire of the chuckwalla what he saw go by
and what the sidewinder found
risen in the changing sand
I must run down all the pieces
and build the whole silence back

As I look across the fields the sun
big in my eyes I see the hills
the great black unwasting silence and
know I must go out beyond the hills and seek
for I am broken over the earth—
so little remains
for the silent offering of my death

Hymn

I know if I find you I will have to leave the earth
and go on out
      over the sea marshes and the brant in bays
and over the hills of tall hickory
and over the crater lakes and canyons
and on up through the spheres of diminishing air
past the blackset noctilucent clouds
            where one wants to stop and look
way past all the light diffusions and bombardments
up farther than the loss of sight
      into the unseasonal undifferentiated empty stark

And I know if I find you I will have to stay with the earth
inspecting with thin tools and ground eyes
trusting the microvilli sporangia and simplest
      coelenterates
and praying for a nerve cell
with all the soul of my chemical reactions
and going right on down where the eye sees only traces

You are everywhere partial and entire
You are on the inside of everything and on the outside

I walk down the path down the hill where the sweetgum
has begun to ooze spring sap at the cut
and I see how the bark cracks and winds like no other bark
chasmal to my ant-soul running up and down
and if I find you I must go out deep into your
      far resolutions
and if I find you I must stay here with the separate leaves

Expressions of Sea Level

Peripherally the ocean
marks itself
   against the gauging land
it erodes and
builds:

it is hard to name
the changeless:
speech without words,
   silence renders it:
and mid-ocean,

sky sealed unbroken to sea,
   there is no way to know
the ocean's speech,
intervolved and markless,
breaking against

   no boulder-held fingerland:
broken, surf things are expressions:
the sea speaks far from its core,
far from its center relinquishes the
long-held roar:

of any mid-sea
speech, the yielding resistances
of wind and water, spray,
swells, whitecaps, moans,
   it is a dream the sea makes,

an inner problem, a self-deep
dark and private anguish
    revealed in small,
by hints, to
keen watchers on the shore:

only with the staid land
is the level conversation really held:
only in the meeting of rock and
    sea is
hard relevance shattered into light:

upbeach the clam shell
    holds smooth dry sand,
remembrance of tide:
water can go at
least that high: in

    the night, if you stay
to watch, or
if you come tomorrow at the right time,
you can see the shell caught
again in wash, the

sand turbulence changed,
new sand left smooth: if
the shell washes loose,
flops over,
    buries its rim in flux,

it will not be silence for
a shell that spoke: the
    half-buried back will
tell how the ocean dreamed
breakers against the land:

into the salt marshes the water comes fast with rising tide:
an inch of rise spreads by yards
    through tidal creeks, round fingerways of land:
the marsh grasses stem-logged
combine wind and water motions,
    slow from dry trembling
to heavier motions of wind translated through
cushioned stems; tide-held slant of grasses
    bent into the wind:

    is there a point of rest where
    the tide turns: is there one
    infinitely tiny higher touch
on the legs of egrets, the
skin of back, bay-eddy reeds:
    is there an instant when fullness is,
    without loss, complete: is there a
    statement perfect in its speech:

how do you know the moon
is moving: see the dry
casting of the beach worm
    dissolve at the
delicate rising touch:

that is the
    expression of sea level.
the talk of giants,
of ocean, moon, sun, of everything,
spoken in a dampened grain of sand.

Passage

How, through what tube, mechanism,
unreal pass, does
    the past get ahead of us
to become today?

the dead are total mysteries, now:
their radiances,
    unwaxed by flesh, are put out:
disintegrations

occur, the black kingdom separates, loses
way, waters rush,
    gravel pours—
faces loosen, turn, and move:

that fact, that edge to turn around!
senselessly, then,
    celebrant with obscure
causes, unimaginable means, trickles

of possibility, the cull beads
catch centers, round out,
    luminescence stirs,
circulates through dark's depths

and there—all lost still lost—
the wells primed, the springs free,
    tomorrow emerges and
falls back shaped into today.

Easter Morning

I have a life that did not become,
that turned aside and stopped,
astonished:
I hold it in melike a pregnancy or
as on my lap a child
not to grow or grow old but dwell on

it is to his grave I most
frequently return and return
to ask what is wrong, what was
wrong, to see it all by
the light of a different necessity
but the grave will not heal
and the child,
stirring, must share my grave
with me, an old man having
gotten by on what was left

when I go back to my home country in these
fresh far-away days, it's convenient to visit
everybody, aunts and uncles, those who used to say,
look how he's shooting up, and the
trinket aunts who always had a little
something in their pocketbooks, cinnamon bark
or a penny or nickel, and uncles who
were the rumored fathers of cousins
who whispered of them as of great, if
troubled, presences, and school
teachers, just about everybody older
(and some younger) collected in one place
waiting, particularly, but not for
me, mother and father there, too, and others
close, close as burrowing
under skin, all in the graveyard
assembled, done for, the world they
used to wield, have trouble and joy
in, gone

the child in me that could not become
was not ready for others to go,
to go on into change, blessings and
horrors, but stands there by the road
where the mishap occurred, crying out for
help, come and fix this or we
can't get by, but the great ones who
were to return, they could not or did
not hear and went on in a flurry and
now, I say in the graveyard, here
lies the flurry, now it can't come
back with help or helpful asides, now
we all buy the bitter
incompletions, pick up the knots of
horror, silently raving, and go on
crashing into empty ends not
completions, not rondures the fullness
has come into and spent itself from
I stand on the stump
of a child, whether myself
or my little brother who died, and
yell as far as I can, I cannot leave this place, for
for me it is the dearest and the worst,
it is life nearest to life which is
life lost: it is my place where
I must stand and fail,
calling attention with tears
to the branches not lofting
boughs into space, to the barren
air that holds the world that was my world

though the incompletions
(& completions) burn out
standing in the flash high-burn
momentary structure of ash, still it
is a picture-book, letter perfect
Easter morning: I have been for a
walk: the wind is tranquil: the brook
works without flashing in an abundant
tranquility: the birds are lively with

voice: I saw something I had
never seen before: two great birds,
maybe eagles, blackwinged, whitenecked
and -headed, came from the south oaring
the great wings steadily; they went
directly over me, high up, and kept on
due north: but then one bird,
the one behind, veered a little to the
left and the other bird kept on seeming
not to notice for a minute: the first
began to circle as if looking for
something, coasting, resting its wings
on the down side of some of the circles:
the other bird came back and they both
circled, looking perhaps for a draft;
they turned a few more times, possible
rising—at least, clearly resting—
then flew on falling into distance till
they broke across the local bush and
trees: it was a sight of bountiful
majesty and integrity: the having
patterns and routes, breaking
from them to explore other patterns or
better ways to routes, and then the
return: a dance sacred as the sap in
the trees, permanent in its descriptions
as the ripples round the brook's
ripplestone: fresh as this particular
flood of burn breaking across us now
from the sun.

Night Finding

Open and naked under the big snow
the hill cemetery by the falls
looks felled to stump stone

and the rich spray of the summer
falls gathers absent into
glazes of ice wall: here in the

backyard thicket sway-floats
of honeysucklebush brush
(once misted berry red)

bend down to solid touch,
and weed clumps break off
into halfway teepees:

pheasant in the earliest pearl
of dusk bluster in, swirls of
landing and looking, and settled

to the dusk mode, walk under
the snow slants and shelters easing
through brush fox would noticeably jar.

Feel Like Traveling On

Sit down and be patient:
sure, it's a beautiful,
endless, lonely Sunday
afternoon: the old people
are in their graves:
the old places are deserted:
the times of all those
times, faces, flavors
a few minds left hold:
sure, ahead the chief
business is tearing the rest
of the way loose: but by
the empty take the full:
sit down, find something
to read: a grand possibility
was made: who knows
what became of it

ROBERT CREELEY
(1926 – 2005)

Theresa's Friends

From the outset charmed
by the soft, quick speech
of those men and women,
Theresa's friends—and the church

she went to, the "other,"
not the white plain Baptist
I tried to learn God in.
Or, later, in Boston the legend

of "being Irish," the lore, the magic,
the violence, the comfortable
or uncomfortable drunkenness.
But most, that endlessly present talking,

as Mr. Connealy's, the ironmonger,
sat so patient in Cronin's Bar,
and told me sad, emotional stories
with the quiet air of an elder

does talk to a younger man.
Then, when at last I was twenty-one,
my mother finally told me
indeed the name *Creeley* was Irish—

and the heavens opened, birds sang,
and the trees and the ladies spoke
with wondrous voices. The power of the glory
of poetry—was at last mine.

An Irishman's Lament on the Approaching Winter

Hello to you, lady,
who will not stay with me.

And what will you do now for warmth
in a winter's storm . . .

A cold wind take
your mind from its mistake.

Water

The sun's
sky in
form of
blue sky
that

water will
never make
even
in
reflection.

Sing, song,
mind's form
feeling
if
mistaken,

shaken,
broken water's
forms, love's
error
in water.

For Ted Berrigan

After, size of place
you'd filled
in suddenly emptied
world all too apparent

and as if New England
shrank, grew physically
smaller, like Connecticut,
Vermont—all the little

things otherwise unattended
so made real by you,
things to do today,
left empty, waiting

sadly for no one
will come again now.
It's all moved inside,
all that dear world

in mind forever,
as long as one walks
and talks here,
thinking of you.

America

America, you ode for reality!
Give back the people you took.

Let the sun shine again
on the four corners of the world

you thought of first but do not
own, or keep like a convenience.

People are your own word, you
invented that locus and term.

Here, you said and say, is
where we are. Give back

what we are, these people you made,
us, and nowhere but you to be.

For My Mother: Genevieve Jules Creeley

April 8, 1887–October 7, 1972

Tender, semi-
articulate flickers
of your

presence, all
those years
past

now, eighty-
five, impossible to
count them

one by one, like
addition, sub-
traction, missing

not one. The last
curled up, in
on yourself,

position you take
in the bed, hair
wisped up

on your head, a
top knot, body
skeletal, eyes

closed against,
it must be,
further disturbance—

breathing a skim
of time, lightly
kicks the intervals—

days, days and
years of it,
work, changes,

sweet flesh caught
at the edges,
dignity's faded

dilemma. It
is *your* life, oh
no one's

forgotten anything
ever. They want
to make you

happy when
they remember. Walk
a little, get

up, now, die
safely,
easily, into

singleness, too
tired with it
to keep

on and on.
Waves break at
the darkness

under the road, sounds
in the faint
night's softness. Look

at them, catching
the light, white
edge as they turn—

always again
and again. Dead
one, two,

three hours—
all these minutes
pass. Is it,

was it, ever
you alone
again, how

long you kept
at it, your
pride, your

lovely, confusing
discretion. Mother, I
love you—for

whatever that
means,
meant—more

than I know, body
gave me my
own, generous,

inexorable place
of you. I feel
the mouth's sluggish-

ness, slips on
turns of things
said, to you,

too soon, too late,
wants to
go back to beginning,

smells of the hospital
room, the doctor
she responds

to now, the
order—get me
there. "Death's

let you out—"
comes true,
this, that,

endlessly circular
life, and we
came back

to see you one
last
time, this

time? Your head
shuddered,
it seemed, your

eyes wanted,
I thought,
to see

who it was.
I am here,
and will follow.

FRANK O'HARA
(1926 – 1966)

A Note to Harold Fondren

The sky flows over Kentucky and Maryland
like a river of riches and nobility
free as grass. Our thoughts move
steadily over the land of our birth.

Ours is a moral landscape. We
breathe deeply, crowded with values.
We love the world, and it feels a cultivation
like a golden bridle under our touch.

At night the earth gives itself over
into our protecting hands. And the same sun
rises every morning. Our responsibility
is continuous. And painful. But it lingers

just above us and scents everything
like the spoor of a brave animal. We seed
the land and its art without being prodigal
and are ourselves its necessity and flower.

Walking with Larry Rivers

The guts that stream out of the needle's eye
of the pigeon cote where old people rest,
there upon the bird sanctuary the gulled heart
flaps its breezy spieling of nationality.

Praying perhaps for rain and a chess partner
best friends pay off the baby mailman with a bust
and arrest their attention to the feathers falling
from trees that had been in song too long,

oi! prayer, prayer, be mine your lazy latenesses.
And where the path turns its cinders forward in
the face of a jealous trapeze diva, tantamount
glittering in wettest green metal, tzing me,

the west of the passive, upon whose elbow of myrrh
reclines the weight of history, the type who rode
elephants down hillsides into the fray! Those guts
our brains, bashed out in flight against the bridge.

On a Passage in Beckett's Watt & About Geo. Montgomery

There was someone, my life there at that time,
where I'd read this presence out without doubt
and that piercer would quickly overclimb
from what we'd undergone, so blear without,
and what we'd known was in me of our life
and suddenly had trebled and shook clear
at the words' excessive Keatsness. No knife
glancing off both, in hearts, now, even here.
And can I have unburdened me it was?
where must have borne my life beyond all else
who must have knouted feelings as he does
who knells to crime the peasants with his bells.
    I can't remember. No, all, Sinbad, place,
    of clarity, member, redness, or face.

Ode: Salute to the French Negro Poets

From near the sea, like Whitman my great predecessor, I call
to the spirits of other lands to make fecund my existence

do not spare your wrath upon our shores, that trees may grow
upon the sea, mirror of our total mankind in the weather

one who no longer remembers dancing in the heat of the moon may call
across the shifting sands, trying to live in the terrible western world

here where to love at all's to be a politician, as to love a poem
is pretentious, this may sound tendentious but it's lyrical

which shows what lyricism has been brought to by our fabled times
where cowards are shibboleths and one specific love's traduced

by shame for what you love more generally and never would avoid
where reticence is paid for by a poet in his blood or ceasing to be

blood! blood that we have mountains in our veins to stand off jackals
in the pillaging of our desires and allegiances, Aimé Césaire

for if there is fortuity it's in the love we bear each other's differences
in race which is the poetic ground on which we rear our smiles

standing in the sun of marshes as we wade slowly toward the culmination
of a gift which is categorically the most difficult relationship

and should be sought as such because it is our nature, nothing
inspires us but the love we want upon the frozen face of earth

and utter disparagement turns into praise as generations read the message
of our hearts in adolescent closets who once shot at us in doorways

or kept us from living freely because they were too young then to know
what they would ultimately need from a barren and heart-sore life

the beauty of America, neither cool jazz nor devoured Egyptian heroes, lies in
lives in the darkness I inhabit in the midst of sterile millions

the only truth is face to face, the poem whose words become your mouth
and dying in black and white we fight for what we love, not are

The Day Lady Died

It is 12:20 in New York a Friday
three days after Bastille day, yes
it is 1959 and I go get a shoeshine
because I will get off the 4:19 in Easthampton
at 7:15 and then go straight to dinner
and I don't know the people who will feed me

I walk up the muggy street beginning to sun
and have a hamburger and a malted and buy
an ugly NEW WORLD WRITING to see what the poets
in Ghana are doing these days
                        I go to the bank
and Miss Stillwagon (first name Linda I once heard)
doesn't even look up my balance for once in her life
and in the GOLDEN GRIFFIN I get a little Verlaine
for Patsy with drawings by Bonnard although I do
think of Hesiod, trans. Richmond Lattimore or
Brendan Behan's new play or *Le Balcon* or *Les Nègres*
of Genet, but I don't, I stick with Verlaine
after practically going to sleep with quandariness

and for Mike I just stroll into the PARK LANE
Liquor Store and ask for a bottle of Strega and
then I go back where I came from to 6th Avenue
and the tobacconist in the Ziegfeld Theatre and
casually ask for a carton of Gauloises and a carton
of Picayunes, and a NEW YORK POST with her face on it

and I am sweating a lot by now and thinking of
leaning on the john door in the 5 SPOT
while she whispered a song along the keyboard
to Mal Waldron and everyone and I stopped breathing

GALWAY KINNELL
(1927–)

Goodbye

1

My mother, poor woman, lies tonight
in her last bed. It's snowing, for her, in her darkness.
I swallow down the goodbyes I won't get to use,
tasteless, with wretched mouth-water;
whatever we are, she and I, we're nearly cured.

The night years ago when I walked away
from that final class of junior high school students
in Pittsburgh, the youngest of them ran
after me down the dark street. "Goodbye!" she called,
snow swirling across her face, tears falling.

2

Tears have kept on falling. History
has taught them its slanted understanding
of the human face. At each last embrace the dying give,
the snow brings down its disintegrating curtain.
The mind shreds the present, once the past is over.

In the Derry graveyard where only her longings sleep
and armfuls of flowers go out in the drizzle
the bodies not yet risen must lie nearly forever . . .
"Sprouting good Irish grass," the graveskeeper blarneys,
he can't help it, "a sprig of shamrock, if they were young."

3

In Pittsburgh tonight, those who were young
will be less young, those who were old, more old, or more likely
no more; and the street where Syllest,
fleetest of my darlings, caught up with me
and hugged me and said goodbye, will be empty. Well,

one day the streets all over the world will be empty—
already in heaven, listen, the golden cobblestones have fallen still—
everyone's arms will be empty, everyone's mouth, the Derry earth.
It is written in our hearts, the emptiness is all.
That is how we have learned, the embrace is all.

(from) The Avenue Bearing the Initial of Christ into the New World

Was diese kleine Gasse doch für ein Reich an sich war . . .

4

First Sun Day of the year. Tonight,
When the sun will have turned from the earth,
She will appear outside Hy's Luncheonette,
The crone who sells the *News* and the *Mirror*,
The oldest living thing on Avenue C,
Outdating much of its brick and mortar.
If you ask for the *News* she gives you the *Mirror*
And squints long at the nickel in her hand
Despising it, perhaps, for being a nickel,
And stuffs it in her apron pocket
And sucks her lips. Rain or stars, every night
She is there, squatting on the orange crate,
Issuing out only in darkness, like the cucarachas
And strange nightmares in the chambers overhead.

She can't tell one newspaper from another,
She has forgotten how Nain her dead husband looked,
She has forgotten her children's whereabouts
Or how many there were, or what the *News*
And *Mirror* tell about that we buy them with nickels.
She is sure only of the look of a nickel
And that there is a Lord in the sky overhead.
She dwells in a flesh that is of the Lord
And drifts out, therefore, only in darkness
Like the streetlamp outside the Luncheonette
Or the lights in the secret chamber
In the firmament, where Yahweh himself dwells.
Like Magdalene in the Battistero of Saint John
On the carved-up continent, in the land of sun,
She lives shadowed, under a feeble bulb
That lights her face, her crab's hands, her small bulk on the crate.

She is Pulchería mother of murderers and madmen,
She is also Alyona whose neck was a chicken leg.

Mother was it the insufferable wind?
She sucks her lips a little further into the mousehole.
She stares among the stars, and among the streetlamps.

The mystery is hers.

8
The promise was broken too freely
To them and to their fathers, for them to care.
They survive like cedars on a cliff, roots
Hooked in any crevice they can find.
They walk Avenue C in shadows
Neither conciliating its Baalim
Nor whoring after landscapes of the senses,
Tarig bab el Amoud being in the blood
Fumigated by Puerto Rican cooking.

Among women girthed like cedar trees
Other, slender ones appear:
One yellow haired, in August,
Under shooting stars on the lake, who
Believed in promises which broke by themselves—
In a German flower garden in the Bronx
The wedding of a child and a child, one flesh
Divided in the Adirondack spring—
One who found in the desert city of the West
The first happiness, and fled therefore—
And by a southern sea, in the pines, one loved
Until the mist rose blue in the trees
Around the spiderwebs that kept on shining,
Each day of the shortening summer.

And as rubbish burns
And the pushcarts are loaded
With fruits and vegetables and empty crates
And clank away on iron wheels over cobblestones,
And merchants infold their stores
And the carp ride motionlessly sleeplessly
In the dark tank in the fishmarket,
The figures withdraw into chambers overhead—
In the city of the mind, chambers built
Of care an necessity, where, hands lifted to the blinds,
They glimpse in mirrors backed with the blackness of the world
Awkward, cherished rooms containing the familiar selves.

14

Behind the Power Station on 14th, the held breath
Of light, as God is a held breath, withheld,
Spreads the East River, into which fishes leak:
The brown sink or dissolve,
The white float out in shoals and armadas,
Even the gulls pass them up, pale
Bloated socks of riverwater and rotted seed,
That swirl on the tide, punched back
To the Hell Gate narrows, and on the ebb
Steam seaward, seeding the sea.

On the Avenue, through air tinted crimson
By neon over the bars, the rain is falling.
You stood once on Houston, among the panhandlers and winos
Who weave the eastern ranges, learning to be free,
To not care, to be knocked flat and to get up clear-headed
Spitting the curses out. "Now be nice,"
The proprietor threatens; "Be nice," he cajoles.
"Fuck you," the bum shouts as he is hoisted again,
"God fuck your mother." (In the empty doorway,
Hunched on the empty crate, the crone gives no sign.)

That night a wildcat cab whined crosstown on 7th.
You knew even the traffic lights were made by God,
The red splashes growing dimmer the farther away
You looked, and away up at 14th, a few green stars;
And without sequence, and nearly all at once,
The red lights blinked into green,
And just before there was one complete Avenue of green,
The little green stars in the distance blinked.

It is night, and raining. You look down
Toward Houston in the rain, the living streets,
Where instants of transcendence
Drift in oceans of loathing and fear, like lanternfishes,
Or phosphorous flashings in the sea, or the feverish light
Skin is said to give off when the swimmer drowns at night.

From the blind gut Pitt to the East River of Fishes
The Avenue cobbles a swath through the discolored air,
A roadway of refuse from the teeming shores and ghettos
And the Caribbean Paradise, into the new ghetto and new paradise,
This God-forsaken Avenue bearing the initial of Christ
Through the haste and carelessness of the ages,
The sea standing in heaps, which keeps on collapsing,
Where the drowned suffer a C-change,
And remain the common poor.

Since Providence, for the realization of some unknown purpose, has
seen fit to leave this dangerous people on the face of the earth,
and did not destroy it . . .

Listen! the swish of the blood,
The sirens down the bloodpaths of the night,
Bone tapping on the bone, nerve-nets
Singing under the breath of sleep—

We scattered over the lonely seaways,
Over the lonely deserts did we run,
In dark lanes and alleys we did hide ourselves . . .

The heart beats without windows in its night,
The lungs put out the light of the world as they
Heave and collapse, the brain turns and rattles
In its own black axlegrease—
                In the nighttime
Of the blood they are laughing and saying,
Out little lane, what a kingdom it was!

                oi weih, oi weih

The Shoes of Wandering

1

Squatting at the rack
in the Store of the Salvation
Army, putting on, one after one,
these shoes strangers have died from, I discover
the eldershoes of my feet,
that take my feet
as their first feet, clinging
down to the least knuckle and corn.

And I walk out now,
in dead shoes, in the new light,
on the steppingstones
of someone else's wandering,
a twinge
in this foot or that saying
turn or *stay* or *take*
forty-three giant steps
backwards, frightened
I may already have lost
the way: *the first step*, the Crone
who scried the crystal said, *shall be*
to lose the way.

2

Back at the Xvarna Hotel, I leave
unlocked the door jimmied over and over,
I draw the one,
lightning-tracked blind
in the narrow room under the freeway, I put off
the shoes, set them
side by side
by the bedside, curl
up on bedclothes gone stiff
from love-acid, night-sweat, gnash-dust
of tooth, and lapse back
into darkness.

3

A faint,
creaking noise
starts up in the room,
low-passing wing-
beats, or great, labored breath-takings
of somebody lungsore or old.

And the old
footsmells in the shoes, touched
back to life by my footsweats, as by
a child's kisses, rise,
drift up where I lie
self-hugged on the bedclothes, slide
down the flues
of dozed, beating hairs, and I can groan

or wheeze, it will be
the groan or wheeze of another—the elderfoot
of these shoes, the drunk
who died in this room, whose dream-child
might have got a laugh
out of those clenched, corned feet, putting
huge, comical kisses on them
through the socks, or a brother
shipped back burned
from the burning of Asians, sweating
his nightmare out to the end
in some whitewashed warehouse
for dying—the groan
or wheeze of one
who lays bare his errors by a harsher light,
his self-mutterings worse
than the farts, grunts, and belches
of an Oklahoma men's room,
as I shudder down to his nightmare.

4
The witness trees
blaze themselves a last time: the road
trembles as it starts across
swampland streaked with shined water, a lethe-
wind of chill air touches
me all over my body,
certain brain cells crackle like softwood in a great fire
or die,
each step a shock,

a shattering underfoot of mirrors sick of the itch
of our face-bones under their skins,
as memory reaches out
and lays bloody hands on the future, the haunted
shoes rising and falling
through the dust, wings of dust
lifting around them, as they flap
down the brainwaves of the temporal road.

5
Is it the foot,
which rubs the cobblestones
and snakestones all its days, this lowliest
of tongues, whose lick-tracks tell
our history of errors to the dust behind,
which is the last trace in us
of wings?

And is it
the hen's nightmare, or her secret dream,
to scratch the ground forever
eating the minutes out of the grains of sand?

6
On this road
on which I do not know how to ask for bread,
on which I do not know how to ask for water,
this path
inventing itself
through jungles of burnt flesh, ground of ground
bones, crossing itself
at the odor of blood, and stumbling on,

I long for the mantle
of the great wanderers, who lighted
their steps by the lamp
of pure hunger and pure thirst,

and whichever way they lurched was the way.

7

But when the Crone
help up my crystal skull to the moon,
when she passed my shoulder bones
across the Aquarian stars, she said:

You live
under the Sign
of the Bear, who flounders through chaos
in his starry blubber:
poor fool,
poor forked branch
of applewood, you will feel all your bones
break
over the holy waters you will never drink.

LEO CONNELLAN
(1928 – 2001)

York Maine

for Theodore Junkins

Through the Cutty Sark motel room 21 picture windows now
the gray waves coming into York Beach like
an invasion of plows pushing snow. Tomorrow
the sun will scratch its chin and bleed along the skyline
but today everything is gray poached in a steam of fog.
Inedible Sea Gulls, domesticated by human charity,
obliviously peck the land sweeping around like a
sprung fish chowder of rocks of vanished summer
when the outsider empties his pockets here for relief,
fresh salt air, the silence, soothing sleep.
Junkins Country here up the old Berwick road 91
past Mcintyre Garrison built against Abinakis and
Moody's actual church used as a barn now, Junkinses
intermingled with Pines and this earth is Junkins earth.
The Junkinses are spread around the woods here
in little graveyards, beware of hunters if you
try to find their resting places. At Scotland Bridge road the
great stone arch with the name Junkins chiseled out of rock, an
arch of stone all by itself like an entrance to a great
castle but only to a mud rut farm house road with little boys
standing tall and ready to spring if they have to, looking curiously
at you by their swinging tire from a string wondering what
you see in piled rocks they see every day ... hardly! Perhaps they
do know that Moody lies within steps of their yard, Moody of the

shooting accident so he did not wish to show his face to men again.
On a day like this the dead seem to appear. They
were here alright! Blue is overcome by gray
Sepia gray, Umber gray, raw Sienna, burnt Sienna.
Gray seems no color at all. You see it, but how
together? I can come to the under colors.
if I could find it, I could find the answer to life
to what to expect. God's energy, the day's changes,
clouds like a veil, and then the sky clear blue
as if this world has no other color, the sea
just exploding here

Jazz

A groan of brass looking for a note
that sounds like phlegm in a throat
almost giving us lust and the escape of smoke.
The horn has a thing with tin
if tin has a thing with a horn.
We hear what we want to hear
soul moan, not scales, man don't
play scales if you're not Coltrane.
Real horn men risk, when everyone's
playing loud, fast, covering, Miles Davis
blowing slow found us where
we were lost and brings us back.

Oscar Wilde Lament

I **The Grave of Oscar Wilde**
You lie not in England but among the French,
the Epstein Winged Sphinx of your tomb desecrated.
Something gouged the penis and testicles of stone
off the Winged Sphinx. Is it your "exquisite grotesque
half woman, half animal" come in form of English lady
to be certain the stone Sphinx is female? As "she
who loved Anthony and painted pharaohs" reminds
you want "that rare young slave with his pomegranate
mouth," not look to tourists who parade Père Lachaise
like a flying stud leaping through stone to mount any
maiden from the dark earth. No, out of doom, out of
ages something has said "Forever!" to us, to Epstein's
soul, no, you cannot undo what the earth has taken.
Perhaps you wished you were a lover of women, but you
loved the chameleon and the snake with loins and
hurt blue eyes that show pain will snuff them out.
Something, someone who knew well your "bestial sense
that would make you what you would not be," in physical
form of English woman crossed the channel and cut
your stone Sphinx and the way the testicles and penis
are chipped like razor sharp chisel powerfully
driven makes you shudder seeing a Ripper murder
or an ageless female Sphinx you wrote about who will
not let any mortal make her into a man even in stone.
She rides you still who loved Anthony and saw time begin.

II **Reading, Berks**
Just over the wall
of your Reading prison where
you wrote for a man being hung

hanged Hugh Cook Farringdon, Catholic Abbott
where The Holy Brook of The Seven Rivers
of Reading ran

riches to threaten Henry the 8th's
throne, so he hanged
Hugh Farringdon

and now only the shell of ruined walls stands
soon to crumble and vanish forever,
just over the wall of Reading Gaol.

They have made the top
of the wall around Reading Gaol
round now

so that hooks of escape
cannot get a hold to lift
human spirit over.

And just over the wall of Reading Gaol
stands the biggest carved lion
of its kind in the world, yet

the lion's feet point the wrong way.
When this was pointed out to the artist
that no cat stands like that

he went and stood under
his work and
killed himself

where The Holy Brook
runs of The Seven Rivers
Of Reading. . . .

. . . And so you died
of a broken heart, Oscar, yearning for
Westminster Abbey, at least a plaque like
Auden, but he didn't go to prison; your
head cracked by a guard's club in Reading Gaol,
shattering your hearing and your life young
to stumble Paris only a short while far away
from Frank Miles now and the culture your
wit sent chuckling from bedroom, theatre, cricket match.

Dark Horses Rushing

Mathew Brady
        there's an old shack now
                        by the stones
with auto tires hung on nails
        below 7-UP signs and from inside
the nasal adenoid indigestion-giving
                        holla of Bob Dylan.

But I swear, Mat, just as I pulled
        into the Filling Station,
                        Dylan shut off a minute,
and I could hear horses riding hard
        like death in pursuit of itself.

Ages now, Mathew Brady,
        have accomplished Infrared camera
we can point at a group of rocks
        insignificant now alongside
super eight-lane highway
        driving up through the breasts
of Georgia to the moon in her crown.

Near Infrared, closer catching image
                    left by body's heat
will show up a ghost to my great-granddaughter
                    where a corn-haired Confed boy sat
on those stones asleep in the dream of his lady
                    and the blue-coat boy shot him dead
standing up like a despicable Fox hunter
kicked out of the lair for a week
                    in birth of baby fox time,
big wide grin on his face wiped out
                    by a good three-hundred-yard shot
that took measuring the wind by the eye
                    of Confed buddy over yonder
and gunsmoke choked the tears out of leaves.
Then dark horses rushing
        inside thunder
as both sides scattered
        for the life God gives us once.

X. J. KENNEDY
(1928–)

In a Prominent Bar in Secaucus One Day

To the tune of "The Old Orange Flute" or the tune of "Sweet Betsy from Pike"

In a prominent bar in Secaucus one day
Rose a lady in skunk with a topheavy sway,
Raised a knobby red finger—all turned from their beer—
While with eyes bright as snowcrust she sang high and clear:

"Now who of you'd think from an eyeload of me
That I once was a lady as proud as could be?
Oh I'd never sit down by a tumbledown drunk
If it wasn't, my dears, for the high cost of junk.

"All the gents used to swear that the white of my calf
Beat the down of the swan by a length and a half.
In the kerchief of linen I caught to my nose
Ah, there never fell snot, but a little gold rose.

"I had seven gold teeth and a toothpick of gold,
My Virginia cheroot was a leaf of it rolled
And I'd light it each time with a thousand in cash—
Why the bums used to fight if I flicked them an ash.

"Once the toast of the Biltmore, the belle of the Taft,
I would drink bottle beer at the Drake, never draft,
And dine at the Astor on Salisbury steak
With a clean tablecloth for each bite I did take.

"In a car like the Roxy I'd roll to the track,
A steel-guitar trio, a bar in the back,
And the wheels made no noise, they turned over so fast,
Still it took you ten minutes to see me go past.

"When the horses bowed down to me that I might choose,
I bet on them all, for I hated to lose.
Now I'm saddled each night for my butter and eggs
And the broken threads race down the backs of my legs.

"Let you hold in mind, girls, that your beauty must pass
Like a lovely white clover that rusts with its grass.
Keep you bottoms off barstools and marry you young
Or be left—an old barrel with many a bung.

"For when time takes you out for a spin in his car
You'll be hard-pressed to stop him from going too far
And be left by the roadside, for all your good deeds,
Two toadstools for tits and a face full of weeds."

All the house raised a cheer, but the man at the bar
Made a phonecall and up pulled a red patrol car
And she blew us a kiss as they copped her away
From that prominent bar in Secaucus, N.J.

Aunt Rectita's Good Friday

Plate-scraping at her sink, she consecrates
To Christ her Lord the misery in her legs.
Tinges of spring engage the bulbous land.
Packets of dyestuff wait for Easter eggs.

Frail-boned, stooped low as she, forsythia
In its decrepitude yet ventures flowers.
How can He die and how dare life go on?
A beer truck desecrates God's passionate hours.

He died for those who do not give a damn.
Brooding on sorrowful mysteries, she shoves
Into its clean white forehead-fat the ham's
Thorn crown of cloves.

Celebrations After the Death of John Brennan

1

What do they praise, those friends of his who leap
Into a frenzied joy since Brennan died
By his own rifle in his mother's house
Along a rock road on a mountainside?
Do they bring gong and incense, do they stage
Some egocentric homemade Buddhist Mass?

Word stops me as I'm climbing Medford Hill,
Poor East Coast Rocky, ice still in its grass.
I hold on to a railing, dragging steps
Up stepping-planks. Two lines he'd written stare:
Why is it *celebrations often seem*
contrived as war?

2

Churned by the wind, the iceberg of his death
Slowly revolves, a huge stage without act.
A seat bangs like a gunshot—pushbrooms sweep
Litter of paper: poems, scribbled chords
For his guitar. Days earlier he'd climbed
To East Hall, where the litterati live,
And had me get a load of one last song.
Could I have turned him from his blackout phase?
Could anyone? For many must have sensed
A furious desperation in his gaiety.
Chance not to grieve dissolving moons—
An ashen grin of craters on the wane
Emerges and submerges through white waves.

3

Forever looking freshly tumbled out
O a haystack he'd shacked up in, cockeyed grin
Disarming as a swift kick to the chin,
He had a way that put pretense to rout.
That was one hell of an opening
Pedagogue-student conference!—
Cracking rot-gut red in his dorm pad
Till we basked in dippy glows,
Reading aloud his latest hundred poems:
Fragments of mirror ranged along a strand
For sun to rise on, overflow, expose.

4

Teachers and shrinks had pestered him to vow
He'd tread in straight lines—John the circler-by
And lazy wheeler! *Does your infinity
start sooner than mine?* How could he die
From no more than a quarrel with a friend
Or lovers' falling out?
                           Yet he had backpacked
Death telescoped, ready, a hiker's metal cup
Along his mountain path. One day he'd drink.
He'd seen it clear: each poem

A last note scribbled in a hand that shook
I'd been too blind to read. This aftermath
Of snow betrays the walk.

5
Dissolved, those fugitive songs
Blown out of mind: breath from a halted lung—
As though a burst of rain had stricken away
Bright beaded webs the dew had barely strung.

6
Home from his Sligo ramble, skipped sleep nights
Tooling his pen-and-inks, photographs, words.
Self-published his tombstone
In that one cryptic book
And like Huck Finn attended his own rites.

I break it open. Now its message stares,
Plain, that back then had seemed half rained away.
His lens had gorged on thorns, worn timbers, chains,
A ruined abbey, stonework walls a loss
Where one surviving gunslot window yields
A foot-wide view of a constricted cross,
Black children peering through an iron gate—
columbines grow well in boulderfields.

7
Gowned as a clown with greasepaint tears drawn on,
John wraps stunned Seymour Simches six times round
With monkey rope,
Trusses himself up too,
Pratfalls.
The floor implodes. And everyone drops through.

I'd not aspire to be your father, John.
I meant only to copyread your words.
Hard enough now—four blood sons of my own
Trussing me too
In dried umbilical cords.

8

"Well, most of me's still here," my old man said
After the surgeon pared him, hospitaled,
Needing no son's swordthrust where three roads meet:
Eighty-eight, yet guileless as a child,
Still hanging on. John gone. Which one is wise,
A young man worn with age or a wizened boy?
To cling to life with fingerless right hand
Or, with a twitch of a finger, blow it away?

9

Flown from your Rockies, John, did you find home,
Second home on the gaunt cliffs of Moher
Whose face held hide-outs from the Black and Tans,
Men perched in grottoes, cawing out to sea?
Stuck in those crags, did you defy the gale,
Dreaming, a scrap of turfgrass in your fist,
Your long look swooping in an arc to trace
The coastline of a gull?

10

Shank end of spring. A night held in his name.
A full throng waxes. Thin forsythia
Of Medford thrusts indifferent sprigs again.
No prayers, no introductions, no plan,
Yet each knows when to rise and speak in turn
Or do a simple dance, sing, or read lines,
When to join arms, to circle, to return.
Nothing's decreed and yet all present know
The clockstroke when the celebration ends.
The wine stands lower in its gallon jug,
The night grows warm, reluctant to grow late.
It is John Brennan not John Brennan's death
We celebrate.

Ool About to Proclaim a Parable

Plato thought nature but a spume that plays
Upon a ghostly paradigm of things . . .

       —Yeats

One Flash of it within the Tavern caught
Better than in the Temple lost outright.

     —FitzGerald's Khayyám

Pounded the bar. In Mickey's Liffeyside
 All but the muted TV set fell still.
Hands over shuffleboard hung petrified
 While, hoisting high and struggling not to spill

His foam-domed glass, Ool bellowed: "See this fizz?"—
 Siddown, somebody yelled, *you damned old souse*—
"The human race, the head on a draft beer is!"—
 A low guffaw loped houndlike around the house.

"But what's below the suds line? What's he called
 That rides us suckers on his golden breast,
Trickling up bubbles?"—*Ool,* somebody bawled,
 Gas with your ass, man, give your mouth a rest.

Fluorescent lightning prowled each outraged face.
 The pitcher shuddering in his fist, Ool poured
A second glass, blew off the human race,
 And drank deep of the fullness of the Lord.

THOMAS KINSELLA
(1928–)

The Good Fight

A Poem for the 10th Anniversary of the Death of John F. Kennedy

In 1962 people began seriously to calculate that, if the three brothers took the Presidency in succession, it would carry the country to 1984 . . . the succession could then pass to the sons.
—Henry Fairlie, *The Kennedy Promise* (1973)

Those who are imprisoned in the silence of reality always use a gun (or, if they are more fortunate, a pen) to speak for them.
—John Clellon Holmes, 'The Silence of Oswald,' *Playboy* (November 1965)

1

Once upon a time a certain phantom
took to certain red-smelling corridors
in sore need. It met, with a flush of pleasure,
the smell of seed and swallowed
life and doom in the same action.

(Mere substance—our métier.
This is our nature, the human mouth
tasting Justice or a favourite soup
with equal relish.)

He wiped his lips
and leaned tiredly against the window,
flying through the night. The darkened cabin
creaked under a few weak blue lights.
Outside, half seen, the fields of stars
chilled his forehead, their millions centred on
the navigator.

Not commanding. Steering.

Can we believe it possible for anyone
to master the art of steering while he must
at the same time expend his best skill
gaining control of the helm?

                         His hands flexed.
All reasonable things are possible.

All that day, the reporters in the corridor
had pushed closer to the room.
As the hours passed, the press of human beings
—the sweat and smoke—built up
a meaty odour.

Once, he rolled up his sleeve
and looked at the calloused, scratched arm:
'Ohio did that to me.'
(One day in Philadelphia
his hand *burst* with blood.)

He rolled his sleeve down again
and shook his head, not understanding,
then became cool again as ever,
asking: 'Who made that decision?
Who had command decision then?'

.   .   .

Shock-headed, light-footed, he swung
an invisible cloak about him in the uproar
and hunched down from the platform at them,
his hands in his jacket pockets.
A jugular pleasure beat in his throat.

'Ever free and strong
we will march along, going to meet
the harsh bright demands of the West, building
a new City on a New Frontier,
where led and leader bend their wills together
in necessary rule—admit

no limit but the possible, grant
to each endeavour its appointed post,
its opportunity to serve:

our Youth carrying its ideals
into the fettered places of the earth;
our Strength on guard at every door of freedom
around the world; our Art and Music
down from the dark garret—into the sun!
The eyes of the world upon us!'

He held out his inflamed right hand
for the Jaw to grip. The sinews winced.
Crude hand-lettered signs danced in the murk.

'Forward, then, in higher urgency,
adventuring with risk,
raising each other to our moral best,
aspiring to the sublime
in warlike simplicity, our power
justified upon our excellence!

If other nations falter
their people still remain what they were.
But if our country in its call to greatness
falters, we are little but the scum
of other lands. That is our special danger,
our burden and our glory.
The accident that brought our people together
out of blind necessities
—embrace it!—explosive—to our bodies.'

(It sounds as though it could go on for ever,
yet there is a shape to it—Appropriate
Performance. Another almost perfect
working model. But it gets harder.
The concepts jerk and wrestle, back to back.

The finer the idea the harder it is
to assemble lifelike. It adopts hardnesses
and inflexibilities, knots, impossible joints
made possible only by stress,
and good for very little afterward.)

'Welcome challenge, that can stretch
the two sinews of the Soul,
Body and Mind, to a pure pitch,
so we may strike the just note
inside and out . . .'

           'Peace—a process,
a way of solving problems . . .'

               'Leisure—
an opportunity to perfect
those things of which we now despair . . .'

'—Let us make ourselves vessels of decision!
We are not here to curse the darkness.
The old order changes! Men
firm in purpose and clear in thought
channel by their own decisions
forces greater than any man!'

The swaying mass exclaimed
about the great
dream
        steps . . .

(Where is a young man's heart in such a scene?
Who would not be stunned by the beast's opinion?
Nor think wisdom control of the beast's moods?
What schooling will resist, and not be swamped
and swept downstream? What can a young man do?
Especially if he belong to a great city
and be one of her rich and noble citizens
and also fine to look upon, and tall?)

He turned to go, murmuring aside
with a boyish grin:
                              'If anybody calls
say I am
raping the intellectuals.'

Inside, a group of specialists,
chosen for their incomparable dash,
were gathered around
a map of the world's regions
with all kinds of precision instruments.

2
A lonely room.
                    An electric fire
glowing in one corner. He is lying on his side.
It is late. He is at the centre of a city,
awake.

        Above and below him
there are other rooms, with others in them.
He knows nobody as yet, and has
no wish to. Outside the window
the street noises ascend.

His cell hangs in the night.

He could give up.
But there is something he must do.

And though the night passes, and the morning
brings back familiarity, and he goes out
about his business as though nothing had changed
—energyless at his assigned tasks—
and though the evening comes and he discovers
for the first time where to buy bread and tomatoes,
milk and meat, and climbs the dirty stairs
and takes possession for the second time,
and soon discovers how to light the gas

and where to put things, and where to sit
so he can read and eat at the same time,
and reads a long time
with the crumbs hardening and a tawny scum
shrinking on the cold tea, and finally
ventures out for his first night prowl
and takes possession of his neighborhood,

learning at each turn, and turns for home,
and takes possession for the third time,
and reads, and later settles to sleep; and though
next morning he wakes up to a *routine*
for the first time, and goes to work,
repeats his necessary purchases
and manages the routine a little better,
with a less conscious effort; and night begins
to bring familiarity, and finds him
beginning to think at last
of what he is here for; and night follows night
and on a certain evening he puts aside
his cup and plate, and draws his journal to him
and revolves his pen meditatively.

I cannot reach or touch anything.
I cannot lay my hand with normal weight
on anything. It is either nothing
or too much.
                         I have stood out
in the black rain and waited
and concentrated among
those over-lit ruins
irritable and hungry
and not known what city.

I have glided in loveless dream transit
over the shadowy sea floor,
satisfied in the knowledge
that if I once slacken in my savagery
I will drown.

I have watched my own
theatrical eyes narrow
and noted under what stress
and ceaseless changes of mind.
I have seen very few
cut so dull and driven a figure,
masked in scorn or abrupt
impulse, knowing content
nowhere.

        And I have forgotten
what rain and why I waited
what city from room to room
forgotten with father.
                        But not
what hunger as I move
toward some far sum-total,
attacked under others' eyes.

I have seen myself, a 'thing'
in my own eyes, lifting
my hand empty and opening
and closing my mouth
in senseless mimicry
and wondered why I am alive
or why a man can live this way.

I believed once that silence
encloses each one of us.
Now, if that silence does not
enclose *each*, as I am led
more and more to understand
—so that I truly am cut off,
a 'thing' in their eyes also—
I can, if my daydreams are right,
decide to end it.

Soak left wrist in cold water
to numb the pain.
Then slash my wrist and plunge it
into bathtub of hot water.
Somewhere, a violin plays,
as I watch my life whirl away.
I think to myself 'How easy to Die'
and 'A Sweet Death' (to violins).

Or I might reach out and touch.
And he would turn this way
inquiring—Who was that!
What decision was this . . .

and not justice?	*An ambitious man, in a city*
	where honour is the dominant
	principle, is soon broken upon the
	city as a ship is broken on a
	reef.

*Passion, ignorance and concupis-
 cence are obscurities clouding
the soul's natural judgement. They
are the origin of crime.*

	There is none so small or so high
	but that he shall pay the fitting
	penalty, either in this world or in
yet more savage!	*some yet more savage place*
conveyed!	*whither he shall be conveyed . . .*

*Great crimes, that sink into the
abyss . . .*

*Images of evil in a foul
pasture . . .*

*—There are those,
lower still, that seat Greed and*

squat!	*Money on their throne, and make* *Reason and the Spirit squat on* *the floor under it . . .*
	—Democracy cries out for *Tyranny; and the Tyrant becomes* *a wolf instead of a man . . .*
The rest! The whole world but one! An impossible logic-being	*—The rest damned to a constant* *flux of pain and pleasure. They* *struggle greedily for their* *pleasures, and butt and kick with* *horns and hoofs of iron.*

     man   *beast*

    (d)amn

                     best

    mean

                    r i
    team   *b a n s*
                   λ λ

    meat

I wonder what would happen if somebody was to stand up and say
he was utterly opposed not only to the government but to the
people, to the entire land and complete foundation of his society?

3
She was humming to herself
among the heavy-scented magnolia bowers,
chic, with shining eyes, smiling at
Power and its attendant graces,
Aphrodite in Washington,

when all of a sudden a black
shadow or a black ruin
or a cliff of black
crossed at rigid speed
and spoiled everything.

Everybody started throwing themselves down
and picking themselves up and running
around the streets looking in each other's face
and saying 'Catastrophe' and weeping
and saying 'Well! That's that.'

For a few days great numbers of people
couldn't sleep, and lost appetite. Children experienced
alarm at the sight of their parents crying.
There were many who admitted
they expected the President's ghost to appear.

Various forms of castration dreads emerged,
probably out of fear of retribution
for unconscious parricidal wishes.
Anxiety was widespread, with apprehension
of worse things to come.

It was unhealthy—a distortion of normal attitudes.
Things had been exalted
altogether out of proportion. Afterward,
when the shock was over, matters settled down
with surprising swiftness, almost with relief:

shudder
and return
           —a fish, flung back,
that lay stunned, shuddered into consciousness,
then dived back into the depths.

And somewhere in some laughable, echo-chamber, for ever,
a prayer came snarling through devilish electrical smoke,
and, blinded by the light reflecting from

the snow everywhere, Dr Frost tottered forward
scratching his head, and opening his mouth:

4
I am in disarray. Maybe if I
were to fumble through my papers again.
I can no longer, in the face of so much
—so much . . .
                     It is very hard.

But there is nothing for it. On this
everything in me is agreed.

So, weak a thousand ways,
I have come, I have made toward this place,
among wells of profound energy
and monuments to power and tedium.
Not in judgement, and not
in acceptance either.
                     Uncertain.
For if all you wish to do
is curse the world and your place in it
—well then . . .
                     But some appetite
is not satisfied
with that, is dissatisfied unless—

The manipulation, the special pleading,
the cross-weaving of these
'vessels of decision',
the one so 'heroic',
the other so . . .
                     You have to
wear them down against each other
to get any purchase,
and then there is this
strain.
                     That all *un*reasonable things

are possible. *Everything*
that can happen will happen.

My brothers, huddled in wait,
feeble warriors, self-chosen,
in our secondary world . . .
—who can't take our eyes off anything;
who harp on Love and Art and Truth too often:
it is appropriate for us
to proceed now and make our attempts
in private, to shuffle off and disappoint
Plato.
     (His 'philosophic nature'
—balance, you will remember;
apportionment, as between Mind and Body!
Harmony, and proper pitch!
The Dance!)

       Plump and faithless;
cut, as it were, in the sinews
of our souls; each other's worst company;
it is we, letting things *be,*
who might come at understanding.
That is the source of our patience.
Reliable first in the direction
and finally in the particulars of our response,
fumbling from doubt to doubt,
one day we might knock
our papers together, and elevate them
(with a certain self-abasement)
—their gleaming razors
mirroring a primary world
where power also is a source of patience
for a while before the just flesh
falls back in black dissolution in its box.

JOHN MONTAGUE
(1929 –)

The Cage

My father, the least happy
man I have known. His face
retained the pallor
of those who work underground:
the lost years in Brooklyn
listening to a subway
shudder the earth.

But a traditional Irishman
who (released from his grille
in the Clark Street I.R.T.)
drank neat whisky until
he reached the only element
he felt at home in
any longer: brute oblivion.

And yet picked himself
up, most mornings,
to march down the street
extending his smile
to all sides of the good,
(all-white) neighbourhood
belled by St Teresa's church.

When he came back
we walked together
across fields of Garvaghey
to see hawthorn on the summer
hedges, as though
he had never left;
a bend of the road

which still sheltered
primroses. But we
did not smile in
the shared complicity
of a dream, for when
weary Odysseus returns
Telemachus should leave.

Often as I descend
into subway or underground
I see his bald head behind
the bars of the small booth;
the mark of an old car
accident beating on his
ghostly forehead.

A Muddy Cup

My mother,
my mother's memories
of America;
a muddy cup
she refused to drink.

His landlady didn't know
my father was married
so who was the woman
landed on the doorstep
with grown sons

my elder brothers
lonely & lost
Father staggers back
from the speakeasy
for his stage entrance;

the whole scene as
played by Boucicault
or Eugene O'Neill:
the shattering of
that early dream

but that didn't
lessen the anguish,
soften the pain, so
she laid into him
with the frying pan

till he caught her
by the two wrists,
'Molly, my love, if
you go on like this
you'll do yourself harm.'

And warmly under
a crumbling brownstone
roof in Brooklyn
to the clatter of
garbage cans

like a loving man
my father leant
on the joystick
& they were reconciled,
made another child,

a third son who
beats out this song
to celebrate the odours
that bubbled up
so rank & strong

from that muddy cup
my mother refused
to drink but kept
wrinkling her nose
in souvenir of

(cops and robbers,
cigarstore Indians
& coal black niggers,
bathtub gin and
Jewish neighbours).

Decades after
she had returned
to the hilly town
where she had been born,
a mother cat,

intent on safety,
dragging her first
batch of kittens back
to the familiar womb-warm
basket of home

(all but the runt
left to be fostered
in Garvaghey,
seven miles away;
her husband's old home).

A Christmas Card

Christmas in Brooklyn,
the old El flashes by.
A man plods along pulling
his three sons on a sleigh;
soon his whole family
will vanish away.

My long lost father
trudging home through
this strange, cold city,
its whirling snows,
unemployed and angry,
living off charity.

Finding a home only
in brother John's speakeasy.
Beneath the stoup
a flare of revelry.
And yet you found time
to croon to your last son.

Dear Father, a gracenote.
That Christmas, you did
find a job, guarding a
hole in the Navy Yard.
Elated, you celebrated
so well, you fell in.

Not a model father.
'I was only happy
when I was drunk,'
you said, years later,
building a fire in
a room I was working in.

Still, you soldiered on
all those years alone in
a Brooklyn boarding house
without your family
until the job was done;
and then limped home.

A Flowering Absence

How can one make an absence flower,
lure a desert to sudden bloom?
Taut with terror, I rehearse a time
when I was taken from a sick room:
as before from you flayed womb.

And given away to be fostered
wherever charity could afford.
I came back, lichened with sores,
from the care of still poorer
immigrants, new washed from the hold.

I bless their unrecorded names,
whose need was greater than mine,
wet nurses from tenement darkness
giving suck for a time,
because their milk was plentiful

Or their own children gone.
They were the first to succour
that still terrible thirst of mine,
a thirst for love and knowledge,
to learn something of that time

Of confusion, poverty, absence.
Year by year, I track it down
intent for a hint of evidence,
seeking to manage the pain—
how a mother gave away her son.

I took the subway to the hospital
in darkest Brooklyn, to call
on the old nun who nursed you
through the travail of my birth
to come on another cold trail.

'Sister Virgilius, how strange!
She died, just before you came.
She was delirious, rambling of all
her old patients; she could well
have remembered your mother's name.'

Around the bulk of St. Catherine's
another wild, raunchier Brooklyn:
as tough a territory as I've known,
strutting young Puerto Rican hoods,
flash of blade, of bicycle chain.

Mother, my birth was the death
of your love life, the last man
to flutter near your tender womb:
a neonlit bar sign winks off & on,
motherfucka, thass your name.

There is an absence, real as presence.
In the mornings I hear my daughter
chuckle, with runs of sudden joy.
Hurt, she rushes to her mother,
as I never could, a whining boy.

All roads wind backwards to it.
An unwanted child, a primal hurt.
I caught fever on the big boat
that brought us away from America—
away from my lost parents.

Surely my father loved me,
teaching me to croon, *Ragtime Cowboy
Joe, swaying in his saddle
as he sings,* as he did, drunkenly
dropping in from the speakeasy.

So I found myself shipped back
to his home, in an older country,
transported to a previous century,
where his sisters restored me,
natural love flowering around me.

And the hurt ran briefly underground
to break out in a schoolroom
where I was taunted by a mistress
who hunted me publicly down
to near speechlessness.

'So this is our brightest infant?
Where did he get that outlandish accent?
What do you expect, with no parents,
sent back from some American slum:
none of your are to speak like him!'

Stammer, impediment, stutter:
she had found my lode of shame,
and soon I could no longer utter
those magical words I had begun
to love, to dolphin delight in.

And not for two stumbling decades
would I manage to speak straight again.
Grounded for the second time
my tongue became a rusted hinge
until the sweet oils of poetry

eased it and grace flooded in.

The Locket

Sing a last song
for the lady who has gone,
fertile source of guilt and pain.
The worst birth in the annals of Brooklyn,
that was my cue to come on,
my first claim to fame.

Naturally, she longed for a girl,
and all my infant curls of brown
couldn't excuse my double blunder
coming out, both the wrong sex,
and the wrong way around.
Not readily forgiven,

So you never nursed me
and when all my father's songs
couldn't sweeten the lack of money,
'when poverty comes through the door
love flies up the chimney',
your favourite saying,

Then you gave me away,
might never have known me,
if I had not cycled down
to court you like a young man,
teasingly untying your apron,
drinking by the fire, yarning

Of your wild, young days
which didn't last long, for you,
lovely Molly, the belle of your small town,
landed up mournful and chill
as the constant rain that lashes it
wound into your cocoon of pain.

Standing in that same hallway,
'Don't come again,' you say, roughly,
'I start to get fond of you, John,
and then you are up and gone';
the harsh logic of a forlorn woman
resigned to being alone.

And still, mysterious blessing,
I never knew, until you were gone,
that, always around your neck,
you wore an oval locket
with an old picture in it,
of a child in Brooklyn.

All Legendary Obstacles

All legendary obstacles lay between
Us, the long imaginary plain,
The monstrous ruck of mountains
And, swinging across the night,
Flooding the Sacramento, San Joaquin,
The hissing drift of winter rain.

All day I waited, shifting
Nervously from station to bar
As I saw another train sail
By, the San Francisco Chief or
Golden Gate, water dripping
From great flanged wheels.

At midnight you came, pale
Above the negro porter's lamp.
I was too blind with rain
And doubt to speak, but
Reached from the platform
Until our chilled hands met.

You had been traveling for days
With an old lady, who marked
A neat circle on the glass
With her glove, to watch us
Move into the wet darkness
Kissing, still unable to speak.

NED O'GORMAN
(1929–)

Looking Upward at a Waterford Glass Chandelier

for Nora Mathews

When I look upward into that turned sky
of the glass blower's gut, each baked
drop of running heat brings to me
the time I was a boy and woke to find
the world aslant with wickedness.
I walked into the forest and sat on the bank
of a pool where the springs that lay across
the bottom sent up cold rings of peace.
Trees stood on their tops; in the moss that
clasped the banks, ladybugs and red berries
moved like small horns and prickled the
soundless walls of trees. When the sun
had soared to her flaxen perch and fell
into the pool's cast net, a ripe crack
of yellow feathers tapped the power from
my eyes. Turn now, quickly, to the west
window where the sun has moved over the
brick walls of the vegetable garden and hangs
there to salute this sister sun that pours
out above us in a volley of glass wings.
O dear Nora, hear them, how they greet each other
in this coupling of lights.

The Harvesters' Vase

for Sloane Elliott

All things are gods.
            After having accomplished
the embarkation of the lion there was the
unearthing of the orange sarcophagus and the
polished stone gaming board and its tourmaline
counters. And it could not be but a sign of their
desire that they painted fish upon their corpses'
heads and necks.

            The entire world for them
was gods.
            At a harvest festival, fifty men stepped
into a line of march and crossed this black steatite
field on the ripe earth; the wheat shoots were
sharp as crystal on the naked feet of those gleaners
of the Wheat-God's pleasure.
            The wine pouch flew
from man to man. The sheaves' dried seed fell
and stuck to their brows; their skin pulled tight
across their skulls, for the harvest was hard and
winds curled that summer from the air harrowing
their bodies into craters where they stood all day
collecting the ripe lava of the fields.

            When
the temple came in view, cocked on the hill
preened and unconsolable, riot struck the
harvesters in their inner ear. They fell into a
run, belching, clutching at rocks, bleeding,
their bodies bare and black in the sun's mill, and
slammed into the sacred magazines where they upturned
jugs of wine and sacred creams and muted by this
sacral fancy in the steatite thunder of their feast,
they climbed into the precincts of the
Mother Goddess of the Countryside who ran
out of their ears and mouths like a heavy wine.

Wittgenstein Reads Finnegans Wake in Provence: A Pauline Reflection

Take this stone, this word, this flower, this boy.
Take them or not. Set each down somewhere.
I look upward and see the nail that held the net.
Let each be. Each to its own pretension.
Alone. Then how long? Women will come surely:
The gloves, the creature with books, the sacrifice.
The net is no longer above me. The nail only.
I am distracted by the sun. It has folded
across the boy's back, swallowing him. The page
is hot. The boy, the flower, the stone, the word go up in flames.

The Five Seasons of Obsession

I have not, by your instruction, Lord,
learned a rubric of obsession
that will get me out of its crack
and crooning. A cataclysmic drone
of it all day is a hindrance
to thinking and I would be rid of it.

Perhaps it is a fault in the ceding
of the genetic currents.
The galleon sighted, the school
of cool gray fish floating
through the tired waters, late
in summer, a brazier of tulips lit

by their stems—anything will do
it: pushed-over rake and shovel,
a cat behind a bush of laurier roses,
two children on a seesaw, scissors
on a table, blades open, the spine
of a book, a patch of sand hit

by a wave. The four seasons of obsession
come quick, go, return again, repeat,
mirror it all so that it becomes
a feast I no longer unearth the
flacons of wine nor fire the cannon
for. On the stoop I sit

to await the fifth season
when the coded sun, the trickle of blood,
the fissure in my cranium, the
whole assembled platoon of obsession
will face the east wind and in
amazed precision unravel Him whose

mien is the resolution of all contrariness.

DIANA O'HEHIR
(1929–)

Spell for Not Dying Again

So powerful are the two winged open eyes, each with a god in its iris,
The snake on human legs carrying a disk on its head,
The winged three-headed goddess with upright penis
And her fat companion dwarves,
That I, drawing them in wine and myrrh, according to the recipe,
Repeating it with a green stone,
Dipping the bandage in the western lake
And binding your body with their pattern,
Can promise you;
You won't moulder away in the underworld.

Soundness of flesh, roundness of bone are yours,
Like one who doesn't die,
Water from the river, land from a green field,
A star out of the sky, safety against serpents,
All yours, all, forever, beyond the great flood, the fire, the round cloud.

I promise you
That long after I who smoothed cream on your sores,
Cleaned your hinder parts, stopped your nostrils with perfumed
      grease and your stomach cavity with natron,
And now can't pay to have these things done for myself,
Long after I'm dust and shreds, a streak of iron on the desert,
Your sun will keep rising.

You'll be cased in crystal.
Admired by thousands
You'll rest in a hall of safety, wearing your own tough body.

Empty God

The god whose face is blank,
His body blank, his U-shaped head crowned by two straight spires—
No one knows his function.
He bends, arm straight to sow, or pluck, or retrieve a dropped object.
He's god of the empty year,
The year of undoing,
Our records don't say his name.

The year when the heart stopped talking,
You and I flapped like fish,
The blank god led us with his tipped antennae;
I did not satisfy you with what you loved;
You abraded me with harsh questions.

Hail to that god, who grew so powerful.
God of lost battles, of many dead beside a river.

"You should not have let me live," we told each other.

Some of Us Are Exiles from No Land

We march into the suburbs led by a six-year-old kid
Whose only memory is the inside of a cardboard box
Where an electric light shone twenty hours a day.
He is as innocent as a white rock;
His banner carries a fringed open eye.

We don't have memories of white spaces,
Or skies with the right kind of clouds;
Our blood remembers the beat of no better sea.

Living a day at a time is easy, you others say.

You say, I do it the way my Aunty Minna did,
That old lady, crosser than most;
She wears Keds with the sides cut out;
Her nonsense gives life an arrow.

But we must invent it all: relatives out of ads,
Grandfathers shaped into American senators, a lost country
Painted by Dali.

Our army moves in on the hills like picnickers.
Watch out. We will fodder it all.
We can turn rocks into paper;
A bit of sidewalk grass becomes a green, marbled sea,
Opened for us, its chosen jewel.

Our new country will be as artful as Tashkent;
If we get there we will all be real.

KNUTE SKINNER
(1929 –)

The Cold Irish Earth

I shudder thinking
of the cold Irish earth.
The firelighter flares
in the kitchen range,
but a cold rain falls
all around Liscannor.
It scours the Hag's face
on the Cliffs of Moher.
It runs through the bog
and seeps up into mounds
of abandoned turf.
My neighbour's fields are chopped
by the feet of cattle
sinking down to the roots
of winter grass.
That coat hangs drying now
by the kitchen range,
but down at Healy's cross
the Killaspuglonane graveyard
is wet to the bone.

Location

Always your body like a foreign country
seen in a film and partly understood—
in which an elephant destroys a man
who saw it only in his trophy case,
and the man lies helpless, crushed; in which are seen
the broken bones as fragments of the whole,
and the whole is more than is seen and understood
when the elephant charges with noise, the man screams,
and against an exotic background birds fly;
but always in which, on studio location,
a camera functions as an eye, and somewhere
a man behind it knows the way around—
always your body like a foreign country
teases me out beyond its boundaries,
that vague and very strange geography;
and what eye pierces through the allotted time,
these near, immediate thickets where we hide?

The Beautiful White Cow

They came with empty stomachs, pails in their hands,
all the peasants in walking distance of Moher.
You can read about that famine in history books,
about how the blight-prone lumper potato failed
while the rest of Ireland's produce was shipped to England.
Landlords evicted tenants, who dropped by roadsides
with nettle-stained mouths.
One third of the people starved or dyed of typhus,
but briefly there was milk near the Cliffs of Moher,
just at the bay's edge—at Kilconnell, Liscannor—
where the shore rises gradually up to the cliffs.
For one morning a marvellous cow appeared
as if in answer to the people's prayers,
and she gave an inexhaustible supply of milk.
Perhaps the history books don't tell about her,
but there stood this cow, day and night,
for as many to milk as lined the shore with their pails.

I wish this story had a happier ending,
but this is how it was told me.
For a while they had pails of milk to raise to their lips
or to carry off and ladle out to the children,
the boon of the beautiful, white cow.
But if you don't believe in such milk, you may sympathize
with the cynic who came along and ruined it all.
His pail was a pail with a bottom like a sieve,
to prove a point, I suppose, though somewhat obscure.
Perhaps he intended to test the patience of providence.
However that was, the cow disappeared in air,
proving to him the miraculous no doubt
but concluding the milk supply.
And the people who sought the cow went away sadly
to resume their briefly interrupted dying.
The cynic probably starved along with the rest
(take that for cynicism)
or his neighbours may have dealt with him more abruptly.

The beast? She never made a second appearance,
prayers notwithstanding; but she hasn't been forgotten.
And if you're on holiday at Liscannor Bay
on a day when the beach is cold or the golf links crowded,
you may wish to look at the spot where the white cow stood.
Some descendant of those who survived
might show it to you.

JOHN ENGELS
(1931–)

Walking to Cootehill

It has been a long walk to Cootehill
and back again, heel and big toe
blistered, the traffic both ways impetuous
along the narrow lanes.
For a mile or more the journey
stank of ditches, at one point
of a sheep's carcass, three weeks
powerfully dead, already on the way
to almost bones. In Cootehill

at Paddy Boyles's Mens' and Boys'
I purchased for its jauntiness
a new cap, gray wool houndstooth foxhunter,
and on the way back,

in one field spotted an old ram
dangling a hoof. Moved on his account,
I shouted to the farmer, who,
beating dust from his cap against his leg
and wiring shut the gate,
threw over his shoulder *tis only*

a thorn, no more'n a fookin thorn!
making it clear
he believed I had reproved him,
and coming back a little way

let me know I was less by far
than halfway from Cootehill, hinting

I was maybe even losing ground.
Behind me, the lane narrowed
onto distances from which diminished
the monotonous, pained bleatings
of the ram. Whitethorn and wild roses

were in raucous bloom. From everywhere
in the hedges came great chirrupings
and bustle of chaffinches,
cattle lowed, the sky
sputtered with light. I limped
along the dwindling lane,
wary of cars, suspicious of the ditches
out of which some skittish creature, the instant
I least expected it, likely
would flush—as on my way
doves had erupted in wild flight,
hares skidded
on the macadam, and from deep
in the roadside skullcap had come
little angular breakneck skitterings. Now,

at last safely back, and wearing
this new cap, I posture where
my images converge between
the four mirrors of the Music Room,
before and behind and to either hand
grinning and scowling, cocking
the cap over one eye, then the other, alert
for the least anterior glint
of bald spot—in fact, I look,

wearing this cap, my age,
and consider returning it; in fact
I so greatly fail to be pleased
that it rockets up on garish exhausts

of question marks, exclamation points,
asterisks, arrows, stars,
to shudder, hover and bare
to the general mockery
my unbecoming skull.

—Annaghmakerrig, August 1990

Saying the Names

My name: *John. Norbert,*
my father's; my grandfather's, *William,*
David, my brother. *Margaret, Patricia,*
Julie, Euphrasia,
of the women of the family. Uncles,
James, and *Bill,* and *Vincent.*
Laura, Leon, grandparents. My mother,
Eleanor; Arlene, my wife, my

children, *Jessica, David, John,*
Laura and *Matthew;* the dead son,
Philip—all the names
said for the simple saying,
the plain acknowledgment,
always as if my ear were pressed
to the hearts of my people,
my breath warm on their breasts.

And outside, the nameless formulations
waiting for names:
the sun rising, the lakes,
the still fields filling up with snow,
my whole days filling
with the dull syllables of pulse,
the watch in my breast pocket
louder, more regular, than my heart.

Always, more than anything,
I wish to say the names:
even with my dead before me,
I say the names
into the bright, breathable air,
all the names of our uncommon time
beating in my tongue,
myself beyond
that possibility,

myself awakening
in the middle of the night, my breath
regathering, the uncommon breath;
and the last loud syllable
of what I take to be
the one great general name I never hear
just dying in the room, just
whistling backward
to the utterance.

The Storm

I will myself not to despair
when I wait by the sea for good weather.
Even on the brightest of days
the storm has been a continual
awful hanging in the air,
and comes often, and endures,
longer each time, sometimes early

after a windless night that has been calm
with moon and stars, a fog
hanging low and close into the coast, soft
against the window, then
clearing, then

a line of big thunderheads advancing
from the north where last time
I happened to look nothing was, only
the broadest of daylight. And then
the sky breathes deeply,
and before I can think

the whirligig in the yard has spun itself
to pieces, the sea is shuddering
to its floor, and the sea
has flung itself at the window, the window
has bulged inward
and the beach plum and beach roses
have blown flat and seem about
to uproot and fly away,
and it is here, just at this spot
where America stops

thirty feet over the long, unhappy reach
of the ripped Atlantic, that this
is being written—in Maine
looking north from a streaked window
toward some black, savage rock of an island
I have never seen before and swear

wasn't there before, and that seems at this very instant
to have at once fallen from the sky
and boiled up from below, and is being
devoured by its surf and can be reached
only by swimming.

TED BERRIGAN
(1934 – 1983)

Frank O'Hara

Winter in the country, Southampton, pale horse
as the soot rises, then settles, over the pictures
The birds that were singing this morning have shut up
I thought I saw a couple, kissing, but Larry said no
It's a strange bird. He should know. & I think now
"Grandmother divided by monkey equals outer space." Ron
put me in that picture. In another picture, a good-
looking poet is thinking it over; nevertheless, he will
never speak of that it. But, his face is open, his eyes
are clear, and, leaning lightly on an elbow, fist below
his ear, he will never be less than perfectly frank,
listening, completely interested in whatever there may
be to hear. Attentive to me alone here. Between friends,
nothing would seem stranger to me than true intimacy.
What seems genuine, truly real, is thinking of you, how
that makes me feel. You are dead. And you'll never
write again about the country, that's true.
But the people in the sky really love
to have dinner & to take a walk with you.

Heloise

When I search the past for you
Without knowing why
You are the waiting fragments of this sky
Which encases me, and

What about the light that comes in then?
And the heavy spins and the neon buzzing of night-time?
I go on loving you like water, but,
Bouncing a red rubber ball in the veins

In wind without flesh, without bone, and inside
The drowsy melody of languish, silence:
And inside the silence, one ordained to praise
In ordinary places. And inside my head, my brain.

You have made the world so it shall grow, so,
The revolutions not done, I've tucked the earth
       between my legs, to sing.

CATHARINE SAVAGE BROSMAN
(1934–)

Indian Paintbrush

To paint the western steppe, get rabbit-brush
and choose a palette: dusty blue, gray, green,
for sage and grasses, waving in a rush
of jester wind that plays across the scene;

next, yellow, lavender, and prairie white,
for primrose, hopsage, prickly pear in bloom;
and last, apply the brilliant carmine light
of Indian paintbrush, brandishing its plume.

In artistry, each petal, leaf, and bract
provides, by serendipitous design,
enticement—eye and insect drawn to fact
of cunning chemistry incarnadine.

Its flowers fit the tongue of hummingbird
that hovers by invisible decree;
the style and stamens shoot a verdant word
beside the sepals' scarlet poetry.

Resourceful, though a facultative guest,
it takes its beauty from the sagebrush root,
both parasite and ornament. The rest
is sun and rain and Kokopelli's flute,

which whistles from the mesa-tops to lead
imagination past the summer blaze,
and scatters glyphs of memory that bleed
among the playa stones in grief and praise.

Into the Wind

It was Ireland first that nearly killed me,
one of the many boys her green fields bore
but could not feed. My mother's resignation
almost raised the stones; my father's anger
was his hopelessness, shaped into his shouts
and drunken blows; but it helped me leave.
Then there was this war, a way, I thought,
to live, beyond the backwash of the Brooklyn

streets, the iron of struggle in men's eyes;
not that I cared so much about alliances,
an empire strangled for a dissembling czar;
and as for England, only think how Ireland
suffers, blanched of its blood, its honor.
France meant something, though: we couldn't
cross without imagining some glory there—
the wind of chivalry, the immemorial vines;

Paris, women. And perhaps we all love war—
a Celt, at least, whose forebears hammered
bronze to forge their shields and spirits
—fighting for the pleasure, not the gain,
and loving those, above all other causes,
that are lost already. This time, though,
we won—unless you think that tearing Europe
down the seam for fifty months and treading

on the harvest of the human fields is loss.
And as for me, I never did see Paris, just
the trampled land around the lower Somme,
tree stumps and carcasses of wire, artillery
and trenches filthy with the worst that rain
and bodies can produce. And then the gas,
which harrowed the remaining shreds of life
about the countryside and seared our lungs

to cinders. What is left of mine dissolves
among the other signs of war's distempered
feast. I dream of voices waking Ireland. . . .
My son will not go back, I think, to shores
he does not know, and I shall die before I
can. The old world leans into the wind, not
like a dancer to a figure that inhabits her,
but shoulders hunched, awaiting fiery wings.

Sunset, with Red Rain

The sky assumes its grandeur fully, here:
along a canyon, cottonwoods are crushed by space,
and ponderosas lose their majesty
to distances; at the horizon, mesas, pulling
our imagination toward their height,
are merely shallow steps into immensity, purpling

in the mind. Even the thunderheads that led
our way today like angels took up
little room: the sky, so vast, acknowledged
them by deepening, but higher still, a blue capacity
rose heavenwards, its emptiness the predicate
of perfect plenitude. As the dazzling

yellow ball descends, a mass of richer clouds
behind us settles on a ridge, half-dark,
half-light, as rays, inclining, reach its fringes.
Something buzzes—a cicada?—and rustlings
in the desert willow follow the invisible. We wait:
the swollen sun seems motionless,

suspended in the thought of red. The clouds
grow darker . . . denser . . . —then, stained
rose and deep vermilion, pour at last
their molten burden on the mesa tops, the taluses,
the river, as the elements exchange their being—
draperies of water flowing, crimson, down

the shadowed wash, the very flood aflame,
the dust, awakened now and borne
among the raindrops, whirling, incandescent,
in the desiccated wind, the ferrous earth turned
liquid—all the firmament on fire,
streaming with Christ's radiant, dripping blood.

JAMES LIDDY
(1934–)

A White Thought in a White Shade

My poems are never tired
of these long walks in words
that take the turn to the park
to the Northern lights
railed-in trees ice-sky
filtered with pink filaments
a punk snow dazed bleak pink
and creams that are fished out
twig-branch framed
of the lake's ice bucket
dark sounds of a saga passing
black lace with blue behind
a tablecloth out of nature
brain torches yelling out
flames and screams
the painter Bruce Pattison wears
a brown coat half a collar over a
sweater into tree-clouds
into invisible day-stars
poems are invisible day-stars
lain on the edge of the path
whitened leaves want to see them
they rise upon a garden
to low or no-bird dusking
seasonal waving of the clarity
of perfect transition
there can be no going no death

the Northern lights are that pure
so seeing they are god's eyes god's eyes
destinies perfect-shaped white
and we come to the transfiguration
Marilyn Monroe high in her moon
absorbing all earth-ice
or a football-like moon kicked
sailing between tree-posts
berries expanding through cell walls
blood blown on snow cakes
above a yellow and white Virgin
of the Lighthouse fishes for texts
to tie together in a non-fade
to a white thought in a white shade . . .
Bruce at twilight did we look up
and see a man who climbed into a tree
and know him Zachary . . .
what supper can we have after Lake Park
but two sentences of scripture
on plates of grass
and leaves in the lighting-up apartment.

I Hear the Wife of the Governor of Wisconsin Singing

A low note over the water, a moaning
at the bar in two senses, remembrance,
carting, a carrying of the post-licit,

The pure, deluded occupation of all souls.
Activity is divided into two tunes,
shining and moaning.

Sheila, your voice hovers on the shore.
"God knows himself in a garden,
not the water. The garden is foggy
on this side. Facing us a hedge
of dank leaves, birds, and naked
shapes. God is as good as gold
but if he stops too near them
he'll get a cold . . ."

The semi-unexpected happens; the notes
become beautiful, traditional wings.
Pour Erin fever.

"God's garden is full, the kissed
to grief. The woman who
has nothing, who lost her blackhaired,
blueeyed lover to an emigrant boat.
She carries her body in shame and
certainty. Confinement, the dreadful
island laws, the hostile prayers
upon her soul. Impossible to extol
the slavery of the skivvy, expectorate
this from our doom. If we could take
the loveless into fabulous indoor
Februaries, the loveless of a hundred years . . ."
Over the bluff your rock-like song passes,
over soft shade me who
forgets or dislikes most literature.

Lines for Gareth and Janet Dunleavy

I exhort and invoke for you
the little stars over a small place,
the minora sidera writers of this place,
the silence of walkers in the wind of that place.
These are continued. Yes, Wallace Stevens,
our stars come from Ireland and make
doves of fame and trouble in the confined house
of writers. The westwardness of everything
like coffin ships on the horizon.
The music in the sails walks everything,
specially the wind as pen.
The history of Ireland is a script
done in the night of the big pen,
whether in sail dip or in the quiet oar tunes
of the curragh. The westwardness of
sauntering by the light of the heart:
the Galway of the terror of all musical sounds
from the Dublin of the reality of all
verbal tropes. Night of the pens,
verbal long knives never asleep
(the day I was born Ernest Roehm
died and became a movie star).
I was born in English-speaking shoals
and I try to aid the sorcery of that
language, that ashen 18th century woman
whose petticoats explode into English
near-eloquence. History lit few lamps
in modern Ireland and made a dark night.
That is why without looking up we begin with stars.
Minor stars, minor league, on the surface.
We are not known for spelling or dressing well
on any of our walks through battle-
ruined pastures. We do not rebuild,
we listen to your walking. It crunches
on something soft as the heart of doves.
The bones of battle men and women

sleeping in green vestments. By the light
of the grave lamp we'll dig them up.
Why as for weeping, our stars will do that for us.
They do it very well in the dark night.
The reeds in the wind make lament
but there blows a quieter music:
the whole country walking in a silence
that talks like a dried flower.
School and shoal of the coffin and cheap earth
flowers for entwining and winding.
The funeral march of the 18th century
tramping through the nineteen eighties.
Fame flames of the dead saunter out Byzantium.
Then everything clears. The stars become writers,
the writers become walkers who grow silent
as they vanish with knife and pen into
a well-dressed eternal night.

The pastures that thrive under a star-lit dome.
The poison clings to the pens, doves climb on the knives.
Moonlight moved to Brighton Pier but moving
westwards in flower, past the Hartford
Insurance Company buildings, not the fire and life
but the fire folk: real fairies who travel
by big wind of mouth and through ashes
deep lain in grass to exhort us to trouble in
life life in trouble. Brilliance is never being out of trouble,
and the stars have arrived.

*(Written for the Hibernia-Irlande-Eire exhibition at the University
of Wisconsin-Milwaukee's Library)*

Wonderful Tennessee

Middle-aged people in the theatre ran up
to middle-aged failures on stage and said,
"Don't give up, don't panic. I love you so much."
The characters keep weeping to the accordion.

Hundreds in the crowded place berserk
under the lights raising their voices to
six actors, "There's so much love inside you
and us why do you gave to fidget?"

It's on the record. The saint of the island
the fairies and God are the same—are coming back—
are we God-bleeped again and are the fairies trouble
first as Tomás says and happiness afterwards

and what if the saint slides back over the water
in the image of a fairy blessing the dance on
the waves, if a man made by Brian Friel in the image
of Christ is on a pier to tell what to do with stones?

Gold Set Dancing

It's the figures in the set, what they do,
how they execute their wins and weave
they come a little closer than you imagine,
how they start being great friends
thanking / being thanked for attentions.
The walls belong to them and me.

The feeling I had in 1940-something
hurtling out of the Paramount cinema
having heard Delia Murphy singing,
how a whole country could empty its throat.
I would move with boys-in-dreams through
that landscape, shawls, spinning wheels, masts,
a band of soldiers including myself.

For me at the beginning,
never a towered elite hermit,
the gold of Ireland did seduce
then I arrived in gold rush
town San Francisco;
mouths, limbs, kiss-talking,
I replaced home mind,
emigrated to god and play.
I burnt love down to the ground
then we lay there.
Dancing starts again, the ground
is lustrous, all gold leaf.

Happy those stepping on the floor.
If I, woman and man
as my poetry mouth suggests
a sweep from both sides,
take the dancer's hands and kiss them
their ringed fingers turn to gold.
I find now I'm in a set with you
(I'm in love with a man who's just married)
whose movements elaborate. . . .
Your sense of operations your midnight colour
unalterable by heat or moisture.

JERI McCORMICK
(1934–)

The Magpies of Dublin

They have found me, scanned the dirtroads
and turnpikes of two American centuries,
working their way back across the sea
to these worrisome islands, to the crumbling
walls and tenacious moss they never forgot;
I should have known those emigrant women—
the great greats of aunts and grandmothers—
would grow curious about the not-yet-born
they never got to see, demand time out from
eternity for a swoop-forward genealogy.

Life came at them raw, relentless as hunger,
babies and choredom, riding the wagons
to Cumberland Pass and beyond; they staked
hill claims, scratched out hollows with pioneer
urgency, the Shawnee slipping tree-to-tree
bereft of welcomes in that dark and bloody
land. Polly, Hattie, Virgie, all free
of the blurred faces I studied in photogravure,
have come back—sleek-beaked, pecking among

the roof tiles, glaring at the neighbour's
cat, assessing my dusty windows
where lace hangs limp, their own white
aprons spotless. Peering in as I sit
at my writer's desk, they turn to chatter
in the maple, rendering me stiff and wordless;
at last they line up in guttural benediction,
silk heads dipping, weathered wings lifting,
and I rise to watch them choose the West.
Again the West. That gut-jostling passage.

WALT McDONALD
(1934–)

My Father on His Shield

Shiny as wax, the cracked veneer Scotch-taped
and brittle. I can't bring my father back.
Legs crossed, he sits there brash

with a private's stripe, a world away
from the war they would ship him to
within days. Cannons flank his face

and banners above him like the flag
my mother kept on the mantel, folded tight,
white stars sharp-pointed on a field of blue.

I remember his fists, the iron he pounded,
five-pound hammer ringing steel,
the frame he made for a sled that winter

before the war. I remember the rope in his fist
around my chest, his other fist
shoving the snow, the downhill we dived,

his boots by my boots on the tongue,
pines whishing by, ice in my eyes, blinking
and squealing. I remember the troop train,

steam billowing like a smoke screen.
I remember wrecking the sled weeks later
and pounding to beat the iron flat,

but it stayed there bent
and stacked in the barn by the anvil,
and I can't bring him back.

The Waltz We Were Born For

Wind chimes ping and tangle on the patio.
In gusty winds this wild, sparrow hawks hover
and bob—always the crash of indigo
hosannas dangling on strings. My wife ties copper
to turquoise from deserts, and bits of steel
from engines I tear down. She strings them all
like laces of babies' shoes when the squeal
of their play made joyful noise in the hall.

Her voice is more modest than moonlight,
like pearl drops she wears in her lobes.
My hands find the face of my bride.
I stretch her skin smooth and see bone.
Our children bring children to bless her, her face
more weathered than mine. What matters
is timeless, dazzling devotion—not rain,
not Eden gardenias, but cactus in drought,
not just moons of deep sleep, not sunlight or stars,
not the blue, but the darkness beyond.

Heirlooms

We're down to an anvil and conch,
sea shell and useless iron,
not much from four hard years
of war. Mother's grandmother

blew this shell like a horn,
one steady roar to warn
of soldiers scouring Alabama pines,
two blasts to bring him back.

Feel the smooth, curved shell,
taste the dust of the mouth hole.
Touch the knobs like knuckles,
the wavy edges chipped

before we were born. Rub the nicked,
smooth steel of the anvil.
Grandfather felt the smithy's blast,
watched his father pound red iron

until the muscles bulged,
about to burst. Grandfather touched
those fists, the massive biceps.
Hold the pink bowl of the shell,

slide your hand through the spiral
back to the days of Lincoln,
imagine owning ten burned acres
and a leg a Minié ball took off.

Sniff the Alabama pine,
a thousand miles of powder.
Hold it close and hear an ocean
roll near Mobile, blow it long,

now rapid puffs like a hoot owl—
listen to the ringing steel
on the anvil, the clang of hammers
pounding iron to plows.

TED McNULTY
(1934–1998)

Good Sweat

In a Bronx apartment smelling
of legs of lamb roasted years ago
he reads the New York Daily News
trailing a finger of parchment skin
over the ink of the obituary page,
this big man who paid five pound ten
for passage from the other side
in the days when Irish were deloused
on the pier before walking the gangway
of a Cunard White Star Liner.

And he felt the lice hungry on his head
and the weeks of sweat living on him
as he elbowed the kitchen table
at Dinnerty's boarding house in New York City
eating potatoes big as balled fists,
rough carrots, tough beef, in the drench
of Trommers draft beer that came by the bucket
from the River Shannon Saloon.

He had a long back and the spit of youth
but made way with soft humour and slather,
telling of the coarse feel of Katie's stockings
until he came to the holes, and of finding
half-deaf priests to hear confessions
of letting his cock rise like the city
where he bullied crates, slammed pushcarts
over kerbs, the sweat dropping on shoes
black and thick he bought in Mullingar.

The Immigrant

The Yank in me
rides the sound
of loose chippings
on a Cavan road,

a neighbour
taking me along
to the cattle auction
in a shed of wet coats

where I'm the stranger
in a ring of men
but close to the creatures,
smells old as straw.

Driving back, the radio
plays 'California Blue'
as I go in two directions,
neither of them home

While road stones crackle
the hard words of immigrants,
telling me now I must live
in the cut of myself.

GEORGE STANLEY
(1934–)

In Ireland

1 The Dying Cow

My father appeared to me, or rather,
appeared in me, as I was sitting at the bar
in a pub in Wicklow called The Dying Cow.
Appeared in me, shoulders in my shoulders,
lips in my lips, in that attitude
of resignation that marked his old age.

I realized I had long warded him off,
looked in the mirror countless times
& saw my short hair sticking up like his
    from my age-high brow
& quickly brushed it to the side;
felt my lips purse in that small mouth of his
that could not kiss (but admired kissing)
& more & more as he grew old would not
speak, knowing what he had to say would be
of no importance.
                I would be gay, I would
(pretend to) kiss. His anger, in childhood,
    had propelled me outward,
to seek a world where to be what he was not,
whatever that might be, might be wanted—
not learned, because I thought I had it in me—
some secret soul yet daunted by his look,
    by his repeated rebuke,
horrified that I might be that way.

How far I ran from him to discover a place
     (New York)
where I could finally begin. Combed my hair
to let it fall over my brow, widened, with effort
my smile. Especially in snapshots.

I am trying to tell all this too quickly,
as if the right word (that might come to me
as I thought my soul would come to me
as a teenager, breaking away from him) might tell
some truth about us. About him & me.

2   Coolgreany Wood

Thoughts of death walking through old oak wood
much of which had been cut for furniture.
Look at a space between branches: no world,
nothing surrounding, clouds indifferent.

Odd affection for the openness of that sky—
Felt his co-presence sharp again within me—
This time it was the universe's turn
          to say nothing.

Veracruz

In Veracruz, city of breezes & sailors & loud birds,
an old man, I walked the Malecón by the sea,

and I thought of my father, who when a young man
had walked the Malecón in Havana, dreaming of Brazil,

and I wished he had gone to Brazil
& learned magic,

and I wished my father had come back to San Francisco
armed with Brazilian magic, & that he had married
not my mother, but her brother, whom he truly loved.

I wish my father had, like Tiresias, changed himself into a
 woman,
& that he had been impregnated by my uncle, & given birth to me
 as a girl.

I wish that I had grown up in San Francisco as a girl,
a tall, serious girl,
& that eventually I had come to Veracruz,
& walking on the Malecón, I had met a sailor,
a Mexican sailor or a sailor from some other country—
 maybe a Brazilian sailor,
& that he had married me, & I had become pregnant
 by him,
so that I could give birth at last to my son—the boy
 I love.

JEAN VALENTINE
(1934–)

Pilgrims

Standing there they began to grow skins
dappled as trees, alone in the flare
of their own selves: the fire
died down in the open ground

and they made a place for themselves.
It wasn't much good,
they'd fall, and freeze,

some of them said
Well, it was all they could do,

some said it was beautiful, some days,
the way the children took to the water,
and some lay smoking, smoking,

and some burned up for good,
and some waited,
lasting, staring
over each other's merciful shoulders,
listening:
       only high in a sudden January thaw
or safe a second in some unsmiling eyes
they'd known always

whispering
Why are we in this life.

The River at Wolf

Coming east we left the animals
pelican beaver osprey muskrat and snake
their hair and skin and feathers
their eyes in the dark: red and green.
Your finger drawing my mouth.

Blessed are they who remember
that what they now have they once longed for.

A day a year ago last summer
God filled me with himself, like gold, inside,
deeper inside than marrow.

This close to God this close to you:
walking into the river at Wolf with
the animals. The snake's
green skin, lit from inside. Our second life.

To Ireland

By the Granary River
the landlord says,
"All these things—
the lambing—the commonage—
are good—yes—but they are not God."
Looking out over us
with a white and English eye.

Oh yes they are but
by the Granary River
we shut down seven hundred years.
My mother was in it, and hers, and hers,
my great-grandmother, hers died in the black room,
and her mother, mother to mother,
shut down and opened wrong.

Eighteen

Green bookbag full of poems
I leaned with my bicycle
at the black brick edge of the world

What was I, to be lost
or found?

My soul in the corner
stood
watched

.   .   .

Girl and boy
we had given each other
we wanted   breasts
bellies   hair
toenails   fingernails
hair   nipples
foreskin   foreskin
heart

.   .   .

I gave up signing in
to the night book
little notes in time

signing our names
on the train's engine car
gray 19th century Irish men
in our gray stiff clothes

ROBERT KELLY
(1935–)

Haruspex

      Examine the skypatch of sightless birds
drawn by the currents of
           historical
        acts, air, responding to the limits of
any living body, channels of energy.

     Birds, sink down for the food spread here
that auguries be taken from what you pluck & what neglect,
      cold stone, the seed hulls
        shaken down, blown to the ground,
this empty wind.

        I found I had written:
        "Later I watched a river
        that rippled as your flesh did
          or does, the skin of it"

& pecked around for a house for it,
    prepositional,
        putting one thing before another,
            unmerited.

                                The metaphor
walks there, blue tail stiff out behind him, scratching at
    what I put there, not before,
        chasing him away so I could offer,
alienate those seeds
                    & what flows in them.
The birds are in one tree now, neglect, neglect, how many
hours blind here in darkness,
    afraid to turn the lights on,
        not every augury, not any
prophecy worth enduring,

                    but in the sun the bluetail comet walks
& lights the unmerited night with, augury, our common blood,
    what flows
        in us as in them,
            that river I could not
    see without seeing,
                    who?
                        birds,
    spell out the answer to.

A Woman from Connaught

My great-great-great-great-grandmother
on my father's father's father's mother's side
I remember with the curious vividness of all creatures.
She was small

and her perfectly round eyes had not yet
been lost in the big green slit-eyed lewdness of the Kelly eyes.
She travelled once in her long life down
from the north and west where her fathers
had been kings, and their wives and mothers
innocent harlots of sunshine,
paid by green life for all their travail,
wild sex of white-thighed women till she came along.

The exploits stopped then.
A long smouldering
match had reached at last her philosophic powder.
She exploded into a restless stillness,
read books in four languages, wore her round
eyes milky with cataract but still,
even at the last of things, thought she could see
the devoted moon go up
over the rafters of her slatternly house,
all dim spiders and dirt floors she guessed.
But the floors were good oak parquet
and her own bees made the wax that gleamed
high over her mind in the white rooms.

Their echo I still hear, rooms or bees,
song of their summing
all the names and numbers of the flowers
that writhed unseen in her garden. She was not sexy.
She thought things into place and held them there.
She could harldy tell if the candles were lit.

The skirts of her redingote trailed
at times across her feet. She thought them rats
and marvelled at their boldness,
wondered should she not be firmer with the servants,
if indeed those english-speaking shadows
were her servants, not mere ghosts
of all her enemies come back to mock
with unclear whispers at the edge of rooms.

The fields are always blank, she thought,
and autumn rebukes the summer's brashness.
It is empty. They are empty.
So blank there had to be a force somewhere
austere and honest. She called it God
and thought men ought to honor it
by books in many languages, and keeping still,
and sitting in large rooms alone.
                                        Oh God
she prayed, keep the smell of the stables away.
Don't let me hear the wasps yawning all spring long.
Don't let me hear the children singing
or Sarah's petticoat slither on wet grass.
Let me know you in an Irish silence,
sweet dumb heart & clever-mouth & loving.
Let there be nothing but love and then not even that.

But when the gardener mowed the lawns
the smell of the grass came
in the long windows and stood in the room like kings.
From her I have my love of cloudy days,
long pauses in the conversation, silences
at the ends of lines of poetry, thick symphonies,
quiet women and their heavy gods.

Towards the Day of Liberation

It doesnt matter what we see there

(the mouth is full of sense
no taste in listening
no sense to hear
what twists in the shallow water below the tongue)

(and if he says Listen! say
Drink the hearing with
your own ears, a word
is not to hear)

Language? To use language for the sake of communication is
like using a forest of ancient trees to make paper towels and
cardboard boxes from all those years the wind and crows
danced in the up of its slow.

A word is not to hear
and not to say—
what is a word?

The Catechism begins:

Who made you?
Language made me.
Why did It make you?

It made me to confuse the branch with the wind.
Why that?
To hide the root.
Where is the root?
It lies beneath the tongue.
Speak it.
It lies beneath the speech.
Is it a word?
A word is the shadow of a body passing.
Whose body is that?
The shadow's own.

Poem for the Jews

The candles of the Jews are ignited
tallow and paraffin stand tall in the darkness of Friday

In the sabbath lights are created and the Jews regard one another
and their eyes are like rockdoves moving from light to light

The fingers of the Jews dapple in fat from the lovefest
their fingers are white and immaculate stiff with the tendon of kashruth

The gentile walks among them
his heart filled with tolerance and his belly with spoiled meat
his eyes beg for the beginnings of love and dinners
beg for the cup of impossible seders for the endless givings of Jews
beg for the cleansing knife and merciless gestures of fingers

Jews wake up in the sabbath and their stomachs are empty
and there is not a sound of music and they polish their cars
and drive twelve sabbath journeys in sandals to the mountains

Jews rush along highways and see the fields but their eyes look ahead
towards the green lawns and tennis courts and white dresses
the ease of men walking the earth in the cool of the evening

In the sabbaths lights flicker on candles
Jews move quietly through mountains and across lakes
and over bridges and carefully through small streams
and their hands have given everything away and still keep moving
And if you love me take with both hands

At every second the Jews are created
at every second they are newborn and their eyes are filled with
          wings
and their hands have given everything away.

ANNE KENNEDY
(1935 – 1998)

With One Continuous Breath

I have stepped out
onto that same perch of grass
a thousand times,
it is my Heraclitean stream.
You, jingling your car keys,
me, wearing the low-cut lilac dress,
eager for the Italian meal,
unsure, always unsure.
Only your hieratic gestures;
tipping the head waiter,
calling him by name,
assure me you too are uncertain.

Up on the hill our house
dissolving in a sea of lights,
under chaparral, granite decomposing
our oranges slightly sour,
more lemons than we could ever use,
the jacaranda;
life in such profusion.

Again and again I step
out of the car your father gave us,
too posh
too grand for newly marrieds.
The grass springs sere under my lilac sandals,
petal sleeves, beehive, eyes absurdly kohled.

With one continuous breath
I absorb the pungent night air,
never dreaming
that from all our years together
this moment only will sting.

Burial Instructions

I don't want to be cremated,
my clothes sent home in a bag,
my ashes sifted from the furnace grate
for my Claddagh ring
and gold fillings.

No, plant me,
like my Grandmother's blazing dahlias
in the subsuming earth,
where I can be lifted,
where there's a chance of resurrection.

How about the hump-backed hill
beyond Barna
riddled with Celtic crosses,
or the sun-shot meadow on Orcas
facing steaming Mt. Baker.

On second thought
Westwood is best,
beside my mother
where the mocking-bird sang
the night she was buried.

You might know the spot
because that's where they placed
Marilyn's ashes
in a pale marble crypt
looking across at our family plot.

They say it's Joe
provides the perpetual rose,
but no one knows for certain.
Be sure you put me in the ground
where I will have a chance to rise.

JAMES J. McAULEY
(1936–)

A Famine Field

Celbridge will soon reach Maynooth on the road
Along the edge of Speaker Conolly's demesne.
A shopping-center on the one side; on the other, small
Houses, cars bright with dew in the drives.
Across from the shops, a space walled in from the houses:
A little field, that keeps a strange repose
Beside the busy road, a step below
The asphalt. The grass so green.

A few yards in, a Celtic cross, no more
Than a child's height, the kind you'll see on graves
In every cemetery, modest imitations
Of those crosses the early monks raised, shaped
So that the circle of the heathen sun
Embraced the cross of everlasting life,
Golgotha's cross, put here when bones were found
As they began to build the new estate,
What you call, where you are, "development."

Roses and fruit trees leafless, gardens keep
Their backs turned from the field, the sunken grave
Of hundreds who died of what our flesh is heir to—
A few had tried to eat the very dust
Their flesh returned to in this piece of ground.

Sea Writer: Sands

Sand is the history of shell and rock,
The changed word received from our forebears,
How it prevails, headland to headland, dune
To wave. *And* the gulls' mockery!

Sand has every right to arrange its own
Rhetoric, grind it as fine as it likes,
Even to mock it own definitions,
Its fame for taking time's measure with plenty left

To span a beach for the next ice age and more.
We can stand to admire it, or walk off on it.
Even its banality's worth remarking.
Come, walk with me as far as that green cliff.

Make anthologies of its gleams, the means
Glass uses to make metaphors. Its power
Will weave a silky skin round stones,
Although its cruelty may leave you blind.

You will show unlikely mastery
If you can say, precisely, fluently,
Sand, sand, sand, sand, sand.

PART THREE

Further Harbors

BRENDAN GALVIN
(1937–)

My Grandmother Steals Her Last Trout

(Donegal, 1884)

Last night a star followed
the crescent moon, trailing it
west, motif for a journey,
and this morning, skirts tucked,
wading the brook she dammed
with turf, she soothes feet unused to
the boots she's been breaking in
for wear in a Boston kitchen.

All her signs say water.
In its jostling she hears
brothers and sisters
lark in the sleeping loft.
She knows each shallow pool
below her dam, each stone
with a fish in its
shadow. Quick hands
scoop another trout up the bank.
She scrambles after, looks the field
round for the bailiff, slips
it flipping into the fattening
bag: this is demesne land.

F, like the scythe's handle;
T, for the handle of the spade;
Y, the rake's handle:
with the shank of a clay pipe
she has practised her letters
on flagstone. She is Mary Ann,
and she's ready. Below, in the village,
they're baking oaten bread.

Three times to the oven
means loaves for a long sailing.
Last Hallow Eve, blindfolded,
she bypassed the plate heaped with
clay, escaping her death,
and the ring's plate, meaning
marriage, and set her hand
in the plate bearing water.

A Holy Well

I'll drink if I can find it,
but in Ireland now
these springs are unattended,
their wallsteads fallen
into pasturage. Signs
that led me a quarter-mile
beyond the new suburb
leave me here, with the saint's
roofless church open as
a dory to the sky. Outside
and in, centuries of the dead,
mounds and depressions
the sheep are sexton to.
The farmer, almost as modern
as I am, wears a face

passionless as a board
when I climb his wall by
a stair of jutting stones,
one eye out for his bullocks
and one for the minor
penance of their droppings.
Sourney, Boden, Gobnait—these
saints with small-town names
never walked on water. But
the mice trusted them,
and they knew which branch
to tap the ground with
so a spring bubbled up
to plump a child
from a rickle of bones.
Somewhere in this unmown grass
there may be a pagan water hole
that got christianized, where
I'll drink knowing brand names
haven't cured me, loving
the nerve of a common place
that's holy. If this one
isn't muffled in chloroplasm,
if there's a fish circling
its depths like a golden torque,
I'll drink to the miraculous
ordinary: a wren entrusting
an egg to a saint's hand.

Carrowkeel

If I can't be buried
in one of these passage graves,
nameless, without epitaph,
a stone bowl for these bones
instead of some municipal
rectangle, at least let me return
as the raven who watches over
these hills.

Then I could fly
cronking around like God's
only machinery, and roll up
and peel off down Sligo
over green ringforts
untouchable to the men
who plow around them.

These cairns look like
the rubble of roadwork schemes
infinitely postponed. We crawl
under an east-facing lintel
into the earth, and rise in church-cool,
stone-dusted air to admire
in flashlight the corbeled ceiling,
the capstone worked uphill with others
from miles below the mountain.

It would make death
worthwhile if I could hire
the secrets of four old men redfaced
as the sun, their suits worn
from fieldwork, mannerly talkers
who weigh the arts of levering
stones with fire-cured poles.

To have an east-facing door
someone from the future
might crawl into, some winter solstice
in four or five millenia, to wait
long enough for sunrise to strike through.

Hearing Irish Spoken

Later I'd understand how it put
the Atlantic west of them
again, kept places where scraggly grass
prevented the stones from ganging up
the way they did in Boston. On the top
rear porch of a triple-decker,
it tied them to whitewashed farmsteads
splashed with slurry, cowprints
baked in mud by the blue summer air.
All through the distant thwack and roar
of baseball at Glendale Park,
the Saccos voluble at their supper
next door, it ran like water
steady a thousand years from a limestone
lip, plaited itself through bogs
that absorbed roadsigns in English,
ran with watery sunlight after days
of rain. How Anna McCarron rejected
Donal Rua and he went out to Australia;
how a bachelor's money is never lucky.
Time left them to themselves,
left them themselves celebrating
an outlaw tongue. I stood at the twilit
meeting of their knees and voices,
wondering if it meant some failing in me.

1847

1. A Man from Adare, County Limerick

Halfway down Constitution Hill the report of a pistol
was heard. . . . Queen Victoria stood up, and said to the
page accompanying her, "Renwick, what was that?"
"Your Majesty has been shot at," replied Renwick.

It wasn't loaded, or else
loaded wrong, and the man
from Adare was mentally
deficient, maybe
from boiling nettles behind
a bush or begging from inside
a hollow tree while his family
flapped in rags across a field,
hopping barefoot, hunting
row to frozen row
for one glabrous turnip.

Maybe he'd just been skinned
by a passage broker in Liverpool,
and a crimp ran off with
his sea chest while mancatchers
on each arm were trying to pull him
two ways to innkeepers.

Shoveled out, improved off the land,
too poor to be ballast for
a Black Star packet, his fate in
the failed potato, maybe he survived
the season of blackberries
while his children stared
like storybook rabbits
from under a scalpeen: his own
walls thrown on a ditch by
crowbar brigades, the landlord's
payment for rent owed.

Sir Robert Peel has a smile
like the silver plate on a coffin.
Indian corn is his brimstone,
and pokes through a child's
belly like nails through a sack.
When he laughs it's time
to finish the raw cabbage
and start on the seaweed, it's time
for the Dearth and Scarcity Prayer,
for black leg and black fever,
jaundice and the bloody flux,
road fever and typhus.

If Your Majesty pressed her palm
to the hollow of this updrawn
shoulder blade. . . . Heaven tugs
on invisible wings while Hell
drags at the heels,
but there's no tear, only the stare
and muslin pallor, the senile
gape of the man from Limerick's
bald, bearded daughter.

2. Report of the Board of Potato Commissioners

If, because of static electricity
generated by locomotive effluents,
or the mortiferous vapours of
blind volcanoes beneath the earth,
or from the guano of sea fowl
or the potato dropsy or other causes,
your crop is diseased, avail yourself
of a rasp, one square of linen cloth,

one hair sieve or cloth strainer,
two tubs of water and a griddle.
Now grate the unspoiled crop finely
into a tub, wash, strain,
again wash and strain, then dry
resulting pulp on griddle over
slack fire. Milky starch
precipitated in wash water, when
mixed with the dried pulp
of peas-meal, oatmeal, or flour,
makes wholesome bread or
farinaceous spoon meat. Sliced
potatoes soaked in bog water or
oven dried, or spread with lime
and salt, or treated with a mixture
of vitriol, MnO_2, and salt—
said mixture producing chlorine gas—
or baked 18–22 minutes on your cabin fire
at 180° F. . . . All true Irishmen,
we are confident, will exert themselves
to all we recommend, though
there may be a deal of trial and error
at first. If you don't understand
these directions, consult your priest
or landlord.

3. Steerage
If you could set stones on the Atlantic
from Liverpool to Grosse Isle
or New York, some would have graves.

In steerage the luckiest girl
got wedged between her brothers,
and lived despite Holloway's Pills
reputed to cure twenty-three things
worse than the Earl of Aldborough's liver.

Born unlucky, some slipped overboard
weighted with shot and unshriven,
taken by ship's fever
or water bunged in old sperm oil casks.

An orphan could get a customized name
in New York, and One-eyed Daley's
ticket for Detroit could end him
in Albany forever.

Grosse Isle seems to float
its white chapel and fever sheds
on a green shimmer in the St. Lawrence.
Everywhere you step
into the indentations under grass.

Brother Francisco Anthony Eats an Apple

After the first bite watered his thirst,
the bouquet ignited some recall. Was this
second sight, or memory in the cambium
between the flaking bark and heartwood,
where history sticks,
thin as paper yet immortal?

Brother Francisco Anthony, monk
and pomologist, in an Upham orchard,
the trees reverting to wild root stock,
throwing themselves back out of Suffolk
into happenstance. He claimed
in his *Sylva Sylvarum* of 1520
he could taste dispersals in
that golden apple, a hint
of thatch afire, smoke funneling
to the sky, a channel crossing
in a bowman's sack.

He saw a Norman fletcher
pluck it on the road to St.-Milo, 1065,
then tribal palimpsests, migrations,
horsemen, their blades flashing back
across the dark of Europe into
the wild groves of the Caucasus:
Alma Alta, "Father of Apples," its trees
hung with shapes as various as
the faces of those who journeyed there
to twist fruit from the branches
and sugar their bitter lives.

No cider without seasons,
Brother Francisco wrote, *or child*
without a ripeness, no beauty
without flaw, as all rugmakers know
who botch one knot in homage
to the day a lie was told
that brought change to the leaves
and drew down snow. He saw
that apple fallen from a suddenly
fatal hand. The print of perfect teeth
skewed and began to brown
in its flesh, a white mouth whispering
rot among the roots. *Their choice*
was immortality, he said, *or never*
to have tasted this fruit.

RENNY GOLDEN
(1937–)

Letter to Maryknoll

The poor really strip you, pull you,
challenge you, evangelize you, show you God.
                    —Sister Maura Clark

There was no way to imagine this
thirty-five years ago when I walked
away from Pa, from Queens.
What I have of eighteen years
in Nicaragua is:
a habit of surrendering.

Tonight I will hold a four-year-old
while bombs rattle this casita.
Luis will cry, "Mama, oh Mama,"
and I will ask him, the others,
to sing the little chicken song.
They will smile numbly, and,
because they are peasants who treat
terror without the respect it deserves,
and kindness with audacious hunger,
they will sing the little chicken song,
clapping their trembling hands louder
if explosions thump our floor boards.

Pollita chiquitita, pollita chiquitita

Our medicines sit at a checkpoint
near El Paraiso, antibiotics that
could have saved Elena's baby.
Ita argues with them, her voice
thick with constraint,
the force of ocean pounding
in her pulse.

I know the Irish have tempers.
I never did. This is my rage.
Pa was IRA seventy years ago.
I won't say it publicly:
Sure she sympathizes with terrorists,
look at her old man.
I like Jorge, the FMLN commandante,
when he forgets to be intense.
He says we both have vows of fidelity.

The children's eyes seek
protection we can't give.
The ordinary hum of cicadas
lulling the stillness cannot
ease this night's terror.
The children sing Alleluia to the dark.
Alleluia before gun rattle,
Alleluia when a small shadow tiptoes
from the window, whispering:
"Sister, it is over for tonight."

What I have to give and take from this world is
one voice speaking with children who've seen
the dull, infinite stare of corpses.
What I know is that these bones
that once were children, hide something
the world cannot imagine.

Tonight, their small hands take ours,
an act of trust none of us deserve.
I have never felt this fragile.
I have never felt this powerful.
If my voice falls silent,
if this Irish heart stops,
bury it here with children whose singing
burned a hole in the engulfing fire.

SUSAN HOWE
(1937–)

(from) Hinge Picture

Light of our dark is the fruit of my womb

or night falling through the reign of splashes

Liquid light that bathes the landscape in my figure

Clairvoyant Ireland

eras and eras encircled by sea

the barrows of my ancestors have spilled their bones

across the singing ear in hear or shell

as wreck or wrack may be in daring

There were giants on the earth in those days

feasts then on hill and fort

All night the borders of my bed

carve paths across my face

and I always forget to leave my address

frightened by the way that midnight

grips my palm   and tells me that my lines

are slipping out of question

Divorce I manumission round

with a gentle blow the casting branch

my right hand   My covenant

was garment concealed or mask or matron

Proceed with measured step

the field and action of the law

Like day the tables twelve

whip torch and radiate halo

Sky brewing   coming storm

Faraway over the hill

when Hell was harrowed

and earth was brought to heel

how the hills spread away

how the walls crumbled

deathcolored frozen in time

Where was the senate   zone and horizon

Where are the people   mountain of light to the east

Tell them I sail for the deep sea rest

a painless extraction   a joyful day

bird of passage over all I love

Goodbye to all the little fir trees

of the future

Closed Fist Withholding an Open Palm

The great fleet of Unready
floats on the waves

concealed and exposed

all argonauts

soever sweeping

existing dwarf wall one a garden

belligerent

the redcoats land.

Immigrant ship
the hour is late

up from my cabin
my sea-gown scarfed around me in the dark

belly that will bear a child forward into battle

the hieratic night is violent and visible.

Who will bring some pardon?
pushed to the side of the crowd.

Trembling fathers futile in the emptiness of matter
howl "wilderness"

at the waste
a preliminary geste

leap for some spot where a foot may jump

and cease from falling.

Nothing else exists or nothing exists
coming to be

passing away

we go to sea
we build houses

sleep our last sleep in a land of strangers

troops of marble messengers move before our eyes

predecessors

at the vague dawn
where fusion was born

no time, no space, no motion

arrow itself an illusion

fuel to keep from freezing

a sunbeam touches
the austere hymn

of jeopardy

blown through gaps in our community
our lives were wind

the rigor of it
fleece of the lamb of God

torn off

Numerous singularities

slight stutter
a short letter

embrace at departure

body backward
in a tremendous forward direction

house and host

vanished.

SABRA LOOMIS
(1938–)

The Alphabet of Singing

for Achill

I wanted to pronounce
and keep the alphabets alive.
My birds and lambs were the letters,
the lambs standing beside their mothers,
pushing against the mother's ribs
the way alphabet letters lean against each other
in the alphabet of singing.

The birds I was feeding
flocked away, and grew hungrier.
They robbed me—it didn't matter.

I was keeper of the dark green alphabet of woods,
a keeper of sounds, and of arrows. My green sounds
were the words like "moon" and "hunting dog" and "sheep,"
hungry words like "lodging" and "apples."

I pressed *down* with my larynx,
my tongue arched dark
to keep syllables rounded,
the notes and letters moving and alive—

green insect words like "mantis" or "mayfly,"
"house" or "windows" or "caring."

My birds took flight and curved
to the horizon. They grew hungrier
by daylight (what they call the emotions,
which is the sounds always moving within my ribs,
the alternation of sounds—like a sower in fields
casting to left and right, moving his shadow
   across the furrows).

At night, in my hut on the mountainside,
I was keeper of words, and of the ordinary daylight sounds:
the sheep dogs barking, or the clanging shut of a gate.

At night, when I lay down to sleep at the foot of the village,
the apples rolled away from me, down a steep hill in the
   falling light;
the apples rolled silently, intently, down a green hill.

Etruscan

Rain is coming,
bringing cattle
home through the hedges at nightfall.

Hurry to the gate—
to look beyond, to see beyond ourselves:
through a web of roots
uphill, through a gap in the willows.

Wild waters beyond childhood
breathe into the dusk.
They are carried like weight into tree-bark,
and the listening hide of trees.

Forage for the spells
that lie underneath a gate.

Wild waters beyond childhood
breathe us into the dusk.
Bringing cattle to the edges of fields;
to push their heads forward
and drink beneath the wires
in hedgerows, at the corners of fields.

They breathe in the dusk
behind a field-gate.
With wide, Etruscan eyes
and with a ragged breath, at nightfall.

The Ship

When they had climbed up the high pine hill, they saw a cloud rapidly approaching. As it flew near and skirted around them, they saw it was a ship. It was drawing streamers, hundreds of colorful streamers after it; like a bird coming to rest on a hill top, or a rainbow breathing the air. Down it came, the shrouds and halyards rattling, and they held to the gunwales and climbed aboard. As the ship moved away from land, they saw farther than they had ever seen before. The skies were every shade of blue, until far out on the horizon. They held tight to the gunwales, which were also of blue, and along with the exploring, the hunger of waves, came a calm deeper than they had known. *Come shrouds, come flowering of a shipboard hunger* . . . Drawing near the sun, they were themselves again, with the great salt stars, tasting of grief. They saw the girth, the far edges of childhood, and labored to draw in the sky like a sail. They held on into the blue, in spite of words and a murmuring of voices, and night, and the turning of the waves.

MICHAEL COADY
(1939–)

The Letter

for James Coady, lost father of my grandfather

1
If there can be some
redemption in the word
then let this telling reach
across the silence
of a hundred years
in Oven Lane.

About your feet upon the earthen floor
let me find the child who will
out of the slow unravelling
become my grandfather
and in the curtained room
your young wife Mary Ager
still beside an infant
bound with her in rituals
of laying-out and prayer.

This dark hour's nativity
will shape and scar your destiny
and in the unformed future
cast its shadow over hearts
that will engender me;
in time it will call up

this impulse
and these words.

Let me try to know you
in the anguish of that hour

a man of no importance
trapped in a narrow place,
enmeshed in desperate circumstance
as at the whim of some
malignant puppeteer.

The image holds the lane,
its stench, the fetid hovels
crowding down toward
the quayside of the Suir
where kinship and compassion
resurrect in time upon the page
the murmured solidarity
and flickering of candles
about the human face
of piteous travail.

2
A hundred years and I will come
to try the lane for echoes

the coughing and the crying
of children in the dark,
the nameless incarnations
of love and grief and hunger
where the river flows
coldly past.

These broken walls were witness
to your leaving, whether
in morning sun or rain,
your firstborn child still sleeping
when you left him,
the dark-shawled blessings
from the doorways of a lane
you'd never see again.

3
What I know has come to me
out of dead mouths:
through the barefoot child
left with your father,
the old boatman, and from
the mouth of my own father,
that child's son.

A life I'll never know
is buried with you
in a place I'll never find:

a generation turned before
the morning of the letter
sent to find your son
become a man
with children of his own.

Out of the maze of circumstance,
the ravelled tangle of effect and cause,
something impelled you,
brought you finally
to bend above
the unmarked page—

an old man
in some room in Philadelphia
reaching for words to bridge
the ocean of his silence,
pleading forgiveness of the child
of Oven Lane.

4
Silence was the bitter
answer you were given
every empty day
until you died:

by a breakfast table
my child father
watched your son unseal
his darkest pain,

saw the pages torn and cast
in mortal grief and anger
out of an abandoned child's
unspeakable heart-hunger
into the brute finality
of flame.

5
Now all of these
have gone into the dark
and I would try again
to reconcile the hearts
of which my heart's compounded
with words upon a page.

I send this telling out
to meet the ghosts
of its begetting,
to release it from stone mouths
of Oven Lane.

PHILIP DACEY
(1939–)

Inheriting the Gift of Blarney

My mother kissed the inconvenient stone
by hanging upside down at Blarney Castle.
She went back every summer
and kissed the Irish air.

Her father, a Cork man, recited poetry
to captive relatives at holidays
and once chased his son down the street
for snickering at a solemn line.

I grew up inside the word,
though I did not know it then.
My place was green with vowels,
and waves against the cliffs of Moher

were consonants. Blind to maps,
I wandered the hills and valleys
of a sentence, cooled in the shadow
of a pause like a ravine.

I think of this now because today
I talked a man out of a gun,
with my words pried his fingers loose
from the loaded anger.

Because he was no fool, I even
warned him of my words, their undeniable
design. But I didn't warn him of
my warning, which was, of course,

in words, all honest ones, of course,
yet kissed with something like music
to enchant the will, no force but that
of the tongue, its tender insinuation.

O, may I always hang so upside down,
beside my mother, my lips pressed
to whatever's slab-cold
and a bit of a reach, perfect

precondition for speech, and may
I live out all my days in Blarney,
hometown for the ear, the mouth,
so that when I die I'll translate

wholly into it, a story to tell.
Make me up well, Friends,
and say Death's the biggest
load of blarney there is.

Why Jesus Was Crucified

I thought they were Georgia O'Keefe's flowers, or
struggling pencil imitations of them,
but then I saw the mirror under the bed,
where I'd found the artist's pad, and knew my wife
had been drawing herself between the legs.
Soon-to-be-ex-, that is. I was moving out,
divorce a certainty, but not before
she'd started pursuing what her therapist,
I came to learn, had recommended, this
study, a way to begin anew, I guess,
sight, insight, a long overdue and deep-
rinsed apprehension of her central self.
I imagined her on her back, head sharply
propped by pillows, nightgown pulled belly-high

out of the way, knees flexed as in birthing,
one hand holding the long-handled mirror
flashing between her legs as she tipped it—
I think now of a dentist maneuvering
to get right the angle of his own in a
mouth, and vagina dentata—the other
against the pad that lay flat on the bed,
eyes concentrating as they wove between
the image and the moving point of lead.
Imagining all that, the awkwardness,
I thought how lucky we are, men, the obvious
ones, ours always in plain view, with not the
slightest intention of hiding away.
You want to see it? There it is. So what's new?
But there she lay, working at acquiring
a vision we take for granted. Is that
what husbands are for, to act as reflectors
for wives' self-knowledge? And our marriage failed
because I was only a cracked, dim mirror?
The perfect world a perfectly polished
surface. I slid the equipment back to where
I'd found it and kept packing, wondering
as I did what dear dead Grandma McGinn
would say. Irish immigrant, she never
missed a daily rosary. And bore nine kids,
a religious duty, no questions asked.
I knew what: "Jesus, Mary, and Joseph," as
she made the sign of the cross, "what in the
good name of God is this world coming to?"
But only one of those three invoked might know,
who found the feathers of the holy ghost
between her legs soft but a dull mirror.
But maybe Jesus, too. Maybe Jesus
held the mirror there for Mary Magdalene
as she drew, knowing he had the angle right
by her smile. And maybe that's why the Romans
killed Jesus, for assisting at one of
those births, where a woman emerges out
of herself, onto a glass, onto paper,
with nothing renderable to Caesar.

Portrait, with Lightning Rod

My daughter hates the sun and loves the rain.
She likes it overcast, a touch of pain

on everything. The leaves have such a gloss
when wet, it makes a shining of our loss.

She's drawn to coastal fog or low-slung clouds
that bring the sky down to its knees, and shrouds

the wind blows in to drape across the day
comfort her, promising the dark will stay.

Seattle, London, Ireland's west coast—these
are magic places guaranteed to please

because the air is silk enough to wear.
She dreams of growing up and moving there.

I don't know when it was inclemency
first touched her so: the night she came to be,

most likely: I drove her mother through a storm
of snow, and birth made falling skies the norm.

In fact, we'd thought of making "Storm" her name,
but then she slept, and made the storm go tame.

She wishes now we'd named her so. I think
she'd like it as a bridge across the brink

between the outside and inside worlds she knows
are facing mirrors. At least, each year she grows

more natural to me: she moves like air
when change is coming in, her plunging hair

a cataract beneath which lovers stand,
her eyes a center quickening the land.

SUSAN DONNELLY
(1939–)

The House of My Birth

A flotilla of ceilings
moves like gulls over the drowned

faces of ancestors. In a garden of shells,
Kitty, my great-grandmother,

plays a coral pianoforte.
Her black curls, "beau-catchers,"

flutter with every current.
The carpets give up their ghosts.

All the eccentric corners
hold uncles, ginger-haired, twisting

pouches of tobacco. The sachet aunts
are tucked into oak and cherry.

Missals lie heaped on the hall table,
their silk snake tongues

marking penance and Pentecost.
The weighted grandfather

clock descends through each week
with his gold burdens. I hear an

alto-soprano of daughters
doing the Sunday dishes:

"Over the Ocean Columbus Came."
They plunge their hands wrist-deep

into suds like trousseau lace.
A flicker of nightfall

darkens their faces. I see the glow
behind skin as it waits

with a candle. Then each sister
enters her own castle. One is hidden

by sea urchins. One trails
her long green hair

like moss from a window. A third,
my namesake,

climbs to the tower of bone.
What is darkness?

What is light? she sings. And above her
the family motto:

Amor et silentium.

The Tile Setter

John P. Donnelly
1901–1995

I

When he heard that the others
were planning to tar and feather
the Protestant neighbor girl
who loved a Black and Tan soldier,
he ran, because of who he was
and would be for ninety-four years,
over the back fields to warn her.
He was the quiet brother, a camouflaged
gunrunner during the civil war,
who passed messages along the deep hedge lanes,
left notes in the crook of a tree.
Everything local, personal. He'd show
his American grandchildren the IRA medal
kept in a desk drawer, then talk of how,
outside his childhood door,
was the "biggest field in the world."

II

For one who had learned,
in a new country, to set
tile, learned how to fit
corners, cut each smooth square
into place, round the whole
with the curved border tile; to a man
with his own thoughts doing this,
his dreams and absorbed calculations:
bank account, house, first child
a daughter who fit his arms,
for such a person, what of the crash
of the big, strange country, the Thirties'
great downslide, harsh shattering, loss
of customers, house gone, second child coming,

wife's stony eyes, all the tiles
rubbling down and the tile dust blinding?

III
When his daughter-in-law first met him
he was coming in from his shift
at the Railway Express,
where he'd labored for twenty-five years.
He stumped off his boots
in the back hall—it was December, and snowing.
"You can come right in, John,"
his wife called, "She's a regular girl."
He came in, wearing workclothes, his face drawn,
very pale, held out his hand in welcome.
He was all bent inward in those years,
as though tons of boxes and parcels
had been lowered, one by one,
onto his shoulders at the station.
Like the medieval Celtic trials
to prove poets: that they bore
in a pit, under a testing of stones.

IV
Then, in early old age, he finds
the falling-down little house he can fix over.
Rooms that, once cleaned, cry out
for tile, tile everywhere:
above kitchen counters, up the stairs,
a riot in the bathroom, lining the basement shower.
Once that's all set, he goes out
on early spring mornings—he's retired now—
to yard sales, brings back
small tables of every shape, just waiting
to be tile-covered. Blue, cream, brown-speckled,
dusted with gold, they fly off
as wedding presents, gifts to nieces.
There are always new patterns.
Under each table he paints
a huge shamrock, "John P. Donnelly," the date.

V

"Maureen," his whispered protest, "I'm still not dead . . ."
He's off-schedule, impatient. He told his daughter
yesterday he'd not live past midnight.
Now here's the city sun, filled with haze,
coming through dull hospital curtains.
Down Cloone's main street it would pour
clear honey till ten at night . . .
He's let so much go:
the hard marriage, little house, apartment
full of trailing plants and Irish tea towels,
big TV for watching Notre Dame.
He's left his zinnia garden,
planted along the parking lot. That design
of colors. Left his canopy bed.

The Gospel Singer Testifies

When she spoke, I looked down
the way I would if she'd begun undressing
before everyone, not to entertain
but to show things about ourselves
we knew to cover. So aware that beside me
a Jewish friend listened—or didn't—
to her praise of Jesus.
I wanted to signal, "We're not all like that."
But my friend is, we are, all like that:
having something we'd get naked for
before a whole group of people.
That is, if we're lucky. So my body heard
before I did, with tears at the corners of my eyes,
as the words that had begun in song *Thank you, Jesus!*
dissolved back into song, or a finer
distillation, and the singer closed her eyes,
Thank you! bent like a bowstring
shot forth her nakedness to save me.

STEPHEN DUNN
(1939–)

Regardless

Once, my father took me to the Rockaways
    during a hurricane
to see how the ocean was behaving,

which made my mother furious, whose love
    was correct, protective.
We saw a wooden jetty crumble. We saw water

rise to the boardwalk, felt the wildness
    of its spray.
That night: silence at dinner, a storm

born of cooler, more familiar air.
    My father
always rode his delightful errors

into trouble. Mother waited for them, alertly,
    the way the oppressed
wait for their historical moment.

Weekdays, after six, I'd point my bicycle
    toward the Fleet Street Inn
to fetch him for dinner. All his friends

were there, high-spirited lonelies, Irish,
    full of laughter.
It was a shame that he was there, a shame

to urge him home. Who was I then but a boy
    who had learned to love
the wind, the wind that would go its own way,

regardless. I must have thought damage
    is just what happens.

The Resurrection

In the converted stable where I work,
after the kerosene warmed the room,
one deadened fly rose to life—
a phenomenon that could turn a boy
from street crime to science
or, if less bright, to the church.
Lucky such a boy wasn't present.
I watched that fly push against the window
as if it had just learned something
about the locomotion of its wings
and its little fly heart. Perhaps
it wanted to foul whatever it could reach,
an act, no doubt, of temperament and taste.
I was beginning, no, deciding,
to be the poet of this fly, didn't every thing
in the world need its poet?
and I would tell of its resurrection
in a deceptive room with temporary heat
and illusory glass. To be a fly
was to fly in the face
of all that could defeat it,
and there was the pleasure of shit
to look forward to, the pleasure of bothering
cows and people, the pleasure of pure speed.
Another fly rose and pushed

against the window, two flies now,
and suddenly I was poet of flies in winter
as they sought the other side
of the glass, which was death,
victims of having once risen, ignorant
buggers, happy on bad evidence, warm, abuzz.

Oklahoma City

The accused chose to plead innocent
because he was guilty. We allowed such a thing;
it was one of our greatnesses, nutty, protective.
On the car radio a survivor's ordeal, her leg
amputated without anesthesia while trapped

under a steel girder. Simply, no big words—
that's how people tell their horror stories.
I was elsewhere, on my way to a party.
On arrival, everyone was sure to be carrying
a piece of the awful world with him.

Not one of us wouldn't be smiling.
There'd be drinks, irony, hidden animosities.
Something large would be missing.
But most of us would understand
something large always would be missing.

Oklahoma City was America reduced
to McVeigh's half-thought-out thoughts.
Did he know anything about suffering?
It's the naïve among us who are guilty
of wondering if we're moral agents or madmen

or merely, as one scientist said,
a fortuitous collocation of atoms.
Some mysteries can be solved by ampersands.
Ands not *ors;* that was my latest answer.
At the party two women were talking

about how strange it is that they still like men.
They were young and unavailable, and their lovely faces
evoked a world not wholly incongruent
with the world I know. I had no illusions, not even hopes,
that their beauty had anything to do with goodness.

Something Like Happiness

Last night Joan Sutherland was nuancing
the stratosphere on my fine-tuned tape deck,
and there was my dog Buster with a flea rash,
his head in his privates. Even for Buster
this was something like happiness. Elsewhere
I knew what people were doing to other people,
the terrible hurts, the pleasures of hurting.
I repudiated Zen because it doesn't provide
for forgiveness, repudiated my friend X
who had gotten "in touch with his feelings,"
which were spiteful and aggressive. *Repudiate*
felt good in my mouth, like someone else's tongue
during the sweet combat of love.
I said out loud, *I repudiate,* adding words
like *sincerity, correctness, common sense.*
I remembered how tired I'd grown of mountaintops
and their thin, unheavenly air,
had grown tired, really, of how I spoke of them,
the exaggerated glamor, the false equation between

ascent and importance. I looked at the vase
and its one red flower, then the table
which Zennists would say existed
in its *thisness*, and realized how wrong it was
to reject appearances. How much more difficult
to accept them! I repudiated myself, citing my name.
The phone rang. It was my overly serious friend
from Syracuse saying *Foucault, Foucault,*
like some lost prayer of the tenured.
Advocates of revolution, I agreed with him, poor,
screwed for years, angry—who can begrudge them
weapons and victory? But people like us,
Joan Sutherland on our tapes and enough fine time
to enjoy her, I said, let's be careful
how we link thought and action,
careful about deaths we won't experience.
I repudiated him and Foucault, told him
that if Descartes were alive and wildly in love
he himself would repudiate his famous dictum.
I felt something like happiness when he hung up,
and Buster put his head on my lap,
and without admiration stared at me.
I would not repudiate Buster, not even his fleas.
How could I? Once a day, the flea travels
to the eye of the dog for a sip of water.
Imagine! The journey, the delicacy of the arrival.

Afterlife

There've been times I've thought worms
        might be beneficent, speeding up,
as they do, the dissolution of the body,

I've imagined myself streamlined, all bone
        and severity,
pure mind, free to contemplate the startling

absence of any useful metaphysics, any final
    punishment or reward.
Indulgences, no doubt. Romances I've allowed myself

when nothing ached, and the long diminishment
    seemed far off.
Today I want my body to keep making its sloppy

requests. I'm out among the wayward dazzle
    of the countryside,
which is its own afterlife, wild, repeatable.

There's no lesson in it for me. I just like
    its ignorant thrust,
it's sure way back, after months without desire.

Are wildflowers holy? Are weeds?
    There's infinite hope
if both are, but perhaps not for us.

To skirt the woods, to walk deeply like this
    into the high grass,
is to invoke the phantasms of sense

and importance. I think I'm smelling the rain
    we can smell before it rains.
It's the odor of another world, I'm convinced,

and means nothing, yet here it is, and here
    sweetly it comes
from the gray sky into the small openings.

IRENE McKINNEY
(1939–)

Twilight in West Virginia: Six O'Clock Mine Report

Bergoo Mine No. 3 will work: Bergoo Mine
No. 3 will work tomorrow. Consol. No. 2
will not work: Consol. No. 2 will not
work tomorrow.

Green soaks into the dark trees.
The hills go clumped and heavy
over the foxfire veins
at Clinchfield, One-Go, Greenbrier.

At Hardtack and Amity the grit
abrades the skin. The air is thick
above the black leaves, the open mouth
of the shaft. A man with a burning

carbide lamp on his forehead
swings a pick in a narrow corridor
beneath the earth. His eyes flare
white like a horse's, his teeth glint.

From his sleeves of coal, fingers
with black half-moons: he leans
into the tipple, over the coke oven
staining the air red, over the glow

from the rows of fiery eyes at Swago.
Above Slipjohn a six-ton lumbers down
the grade, its windows curtained with soot.
No one is driving.

The roads get lost in the clotted hills,
in the Blue Spruce maze, the red cough,
the Allegheny marl, the sulphur ooze.

The hill-cuts drain; the roads get lost
and drop at the edge of the strip job.
The fires in the mines do not stop burning.

Visiting My Gravesite: Talbott Churchyard, West Virginia

Maybe because I was married and felt secure and dead
at once, I listened to my father's urgings about "the future"

and bought this double plot on the hillside with a view
of the bare white church, the old elms, and the creek below.

I plan now to use both plots, luxuriantly spreading out
in the middle of a big double bed. —But no,

finally, my burial has nothing to do with my marriage, this lying here
in these same bones will be as real as anything I can imagine

for who I'll be then, as real as anything undergone, going back
and forth to "the world" out there, and here to this one spot

on earth I really know. Once I came in fast and low
in a little plane and when I looked down at the church,

the trees I've felt with my hands, the neighbors' houses
and the family farm, and I saw how tiny what I loved or knew was,

it was like my children going on with their plans and griefs
at a distance and nothing I could do about it. But I wanted

to reach down and pat it, while letting it know
I wouldn't interfere for the world, the world being

everything this isn't, this unknown buried in the known.

JAMES McMICHAEL
(1939–)

(from) The Begotten

> Until given out later as what has been
risen from,

origin has not happened.
It cannot be returned to, having
never yet been.
Able to be longed for

rearward through forgottenness are

kin willed whole.
These are the originals,
the participant

young among one's people who had
not yet bred.
Inseparable in them from what could
not have been that was
is what was not that

could have been.
Remembered as
phantasms only,
their bodies' members are

assigned them anew.
There had been

drugget to wear, and worsteds,

flax.
Their fathers were tenant farmers.
The ground they lived from was
not theirs by law.
Its statute acres in the straths and leas were

wanted for grass. Subject to
rack-rent, tithes and cesses,
in arrears,

they were sent away so as to be

shut of.
They were the expelled.
Modesty would have had them give up being seen
anywhere at all.
Not in keeping with the prevalent due

measure was it of them
to outlast on other
poorer ground
the riddances ordained.

The bogs were left them.
Leached and stony
hillsides were left,

the moors and marches. Up from bare
rock on the islands out of layered

kelp-bed cuttings and sand
they built
soil for their husbanded seed-tubers,
all roots the axes for new
second-order shoots,

new third-.

Around the sink each
bud is in its loading of starches,
there is by enough

more there for it than it needs
that the canopy

too can grow. The tuber draws down
into it through its stalks its assimilate carbons.
When shading at last starves it inside,
such are its

root dry matter stores that any refuse
keeps it from frost.
Replicate,
the bulbs were of their element
if just as patently

not it.

The sheer spread of them in their sets
repeated them as items.
They were sown wherever.
Taking up more and

more again nearby
an earth that in itself
could not be eaten,

they gave
bone and sinew cheap.

Potatoes were the one food. So

peopled did they let it be
that heritable plots kept being halved.
Marriage was to the ground.
The young were often not

seen by one another until
joined in their match.
So they could live with someone they chose,

daughters engineered their own abductions.
Landless sons were either

buried or so they left.
Among the still unwed there were no longer
strips to share out.
Land promised that when
dug for across a straggle of

waste and upland holdings,
its bulbs could be fit wards
for some few only

only for a time.
Digging was in the fall.
With the stock of them
low by late summer,

the aftermost were taken

raw nearly.
This slowed their transfer through the body.
It let them last.
The new ones were still of too little bulk.
They were looked toward with the more

care this time. Covered
one by one, each plant had

fastened to it by airborne
spores at their tips
a down of long threadlike fibers.
These would not whisk away.

It was all
one for the plants
that the infestation was theirs.
Their leaves turned black. They withered.
When loosed by

hand at last from under their
inches of soil lid,
the potatoes were black too. Their skins

scraped at
made the tissue inside

collapse to a pulp.

There was no drying them out that they might be food.
Some foraged
inland for a while on

cresses, herbs, wild cabbage,
silverweed,
young furze.
Put off their plots by bailiffs,

some cornered
cattle where they could and bled them.

Plover and

grouse were caught,
as on the grounds of the estates,
in thickets,
bramble-covered
mantraps caught the ones who poached.

Itinerants at the shores took sand-eel,
periwinkle, dulse and limpet.
Ropes lowered them to the cliffs for
seabirds' eggs. They tramped for fluke.

There were no

songs for these labors. . . .

PETER COOLEY
(1940–)

Ararat

This is the room where summer ends.
This is the view, a single window
opening to evening: banks of clouds,
shivering to be called down quickly,
step forward, naked, to greet me.

How beautiful each is, assuming
animal form on the lawn
never known before, with beaks & tusks
silver, their feathers, fluttering gold.
Quivering, they pair off, pair off

till I wonder if the ark has docked tonight
for me. I am not ready yet
though darkness falls from the air
& I have dreamed of this. I've got to pack,
I've got to be wished well by somebody

familiar. The animals are darkening,
calling. They are wading the dark, thrashing.
And now their ivory fetlocks, their horns,
demand an answer going down, *Are you coming*
before the waves close over us, are you.

So. This is my night to leave
carrying nothing, the wind between my eyes,
no one to clear the room of me
or to lie down with me even once.
No one saying the dark is not enough.

The Soul

In their ascent from the pavement
the ten white fingers of my soul
should be drumming out their thanksgiving
I'm still alive. But they're too scraped, shaking.
I stand up. Now my feet, too, prove it:
I'm here, the alley of the downtown Y.
On the rooftops of the tenements around me
it is the same night coming down
I've always known, though this time
the arm which reaches for my gym bag
could be a phantom limb, not mine,
while the full figure of myself against a wall
dances skeletal, dances, a wild man in the cave.
As if for the first time I am a man standing up. . . .
notice the stars I count on have begun to pulse
since I lay down, belly-flat, crying
at his command while he stood over me
while he cried back, you Mother, Mother,
repeating it as he tore my wallet for ten bucks,
all I had, and left the credit cards
while the pistol in his fist shook like his voice
and then decided I will sit down to dinner
this evening at the table whose edges I can grip
that the wine, the bread, my wife and children
be seen above water when I rise to them,
my vision rinsed in a white light
I never asked for from a man, weeping,
putting his finger on nothing he could name
until he turned and ran and chose to spare me.

For Jay Gatsby

Once it was the pulse of the green light
where Daisy throbs on and off

at the end of the dock, her promise
the new world stretched out before us—

yes, I believed in that and more than Nick
longed to be your sidekick at parties in the blue dark,

in love with myself and my reflections
inventing a story of myself each step,

the moonlight transfiguring our faces, uplifted,
assuring both of us we would keep this going forever,

no moment ever the same myth.
Now that young man is dead as you are,

face down in the pool's black shallows.
Now it's the scene with the shirts I love

and re-live whenever I need a small bright place
charged, no matter how false, with expectation.

Each time I come here Daisy is weeping, fingering
their pastel splendors: alone with herself

in Gatsby's dressing room, beside the lover
who dressed himself in the most essential of disguises

that he come upon no one he could recognize himself,
no matter what vision he follow of that man: lavender,

apple-green, orange, coral, the palette of jungle birds
too gorgeous to be killed for meat or feather—

these, the gods we turn to without question,
assuring us the beauties of the world are all there is,

and the divine human and survives the metaphor.

JOHN DONOGHUE
(1940–)

Revision

In Rwanda she gave her victims a choice: *Buy the bullet*
I will soon put through your head, or be hacked to death.
And here in this river, she doesn't raise that blue heron
from the shallows, she is the rising heron,
as she is the mother of napalm, destroyer
of the ozone, as she is my eyes that see this glass light
lapping at my feet: I've come to search the bottom
for things magical, and I have a pailfull,

but I am sick to death of praising her, and sick
of her illusions—*language, consciousness.*
Look at me, she says, *and see yourself as separate*
and responsible: I'll *make your body,* you
drop the bomb—then act as if you came from someplace else.
See that desert's beauty?—I dried a sea for it.

Space

Space knocks on my red door
answering the ad for the empty room: stooped, tired,
collapsed down to a point,
it talks of nothing but everything at once
in the same place. I argue for differences—
summer shade, ocean voyages—I stall for time,
space touching my face with hands
drained of heat. *No room!* I say,

space dragging me down
to the floor. *Once I was a seed,*
I sing, *once filled nothing at all.*
Through the window—a black sky,
dense with stars,
where light moves freely.

FANNY HOWE
(1940–)

Seven Poems

Now a night long
longed for is over.

Now windows onto water's
windows and a corridor to an elevator
have closed and come apart.

The summer is expanding its handful of hours.

But there's just enough dark to depart.

Remember Columcille crossing the sea
in a coracle carrying poetry?

He turned his back on his country
to look for the miracle
place where east becomes west.

Where he could be as circumspect
as the stars on a whirling glass telescope.
Where the longing resurrects.

.   .   .

The dim interior of a dumb bubble
is how it felt in the middle. Now only the weather
is that grim along with a certain shading
to super 8 film. Things are grayer than they were
before this century began.

Let red iodine remind me of
my interior so I can learn how to spit the poison out
without ingesting it. Swallow instead
the image of uncontaminated things
like moonlight of ether sniffed in childhood fevers.

.   .   .

I was sick of my wits like the kids
in "Landscape in the Mist."

Everyone lacks reassurance.

Hammered down into a sequence
like climbing onto a train
and sitting down

I had to keep moving the books around.

.   .   .

The life I will never lead
has me on a farm
by the sea with a donkey,
a dog, my same children and friends
in a garden tucked in honeysuckle shoots
and smells like tomato vines.

But what is a birthright?
Does it help me write poems and live in a shoe?
Or are those the effects of wishing too?

.   .   .

Heaven has been my nation-state,
safe sanctuary from the law
or else the production of hate and bread is not increasing.
At least I know my tradition is among the contradictions.

And rests "upon a time"
and just above the vale of war and peace
as close to never-was as anything can be.

But still a story of something that almost came to be—
the never-quite-but-hinted-at
attention of a Thee.

.   .   .

One black wing was blowing down the road.
(Rain-washed road).

In the old days horses wearing green shoes
would trot on that grass.

Our caravan has sought a remedy for memory
by moving over the same path.

.   .   .

In November the men push barrels around
collecting leaves though flowers are still up coloring.

I erase all the files and carry my work
in a handbasket back to Block 8
on a birdless dock, before the tender goes down
and I re-embark.

Oh man, I've done the world
and the work and something motherly
is being banned. They're leaving home.
I'm being split into the longitude of one.

FRED MARCHANT
(1940–)

Directions Down

First, you will have to cross
a talus slope, stretches of
sphagnum and low growth fern,
a purple cluster of lupine.

Then down through the dwarfed
evergreens, moss-shrouded,
miraculous to the touch,
the bark smooth as new flesh.

Hold onto whatever offers itself.
Be thankful for the roots rising
like knuckles and fists, and
for the deadfall which will stop

you should you trip. You might
feel the impulse to linger awhile,
maybe to listen to the wood thrush,
but the light will be dimming,

and there will be the knife-
edge, the sheer drop, the stones
unwilling to stand still and
pass you on gently to the next.

When you smell our cooking fires
and hear our prayers mingling,
we will know you are near.
We may be feeling ashamed

of the flaws you will find in us,
of the mistakes we have made,
of the crude place we have built
for you to live among us.

But we are part of who you are,
and we have been waiting a long time.
We are glad now to see you.
Oh, angel, landed, stay.

The Afterlife on Squaw Peak

No matter the machines
with their silent flywheels
and strange swinging on cables
that helped you get here.
No matter the masts of measurement
and reason which the earnest
have strapped to the summit.
There is still the terrible loneliness
of the next valley over
to convince you with its quartz
and granite flashing like ice
and its meadow emptied of the human.
Flower blossoms—little trumpets
of delight—shudder at your feet.
The shale you stand on is splattered
with bright lichens. You join them
by laying low out of the wind
to look up the flower's name—
scarlet penstemon—and you have
that small, but significant human
pleasure of finally knowing.
This high, you have trouble breathing,
and feeling sleepy, you find

a place without thorns. Your eyelids
tighten, and the wind carries voices
that seem shaken, as if assembled
at your sickbed.

                    When you wake,
you note how little seems changed.
You perhaps wonder where you came from
and why. You want to take off
your clothes and mark where you have
lain. Now the wind sounds out clearly
and says this is the mountain
of forgiveness, and that the work
will be to traverse the empty spaces
with meaning. If those you love
glimpse you, it will be in the form
of a red-tailed fox crossing at dusk
into the wood stand, and because they
have loved you, they will watch
as long as you let them. They will not
harm you, so swears the wind,
not this close to heaven.

St. John's Point

Donegal

After supper, we pedalled to a sandstone cove,
watched the tidepool dramas, the opal periwinkles,

waving sea lettuce, hermit crabs nibbling.
We wondered together what it might mean to depend

on the flat, warmed rocks slipping under the tide.
When we started back, it was pitch black everywhere,

and I asked if you'd ever heard of night vision,
how the iris will stretch to gather in ambient

light from stars, moon, and the distant city.
But there was none or little that night.

There was internment in the North, and imaginary
gunmen hiding in the ditches. A fine gravel

on the road made the wheels slip. On our faces
we could feel moisture from the ocean, hear

the thump of surf, and all the little mechanical
sounds of gear-teeth, sprockets, oily axles,

the squeak of saddle springs when we hit the ruts,
the metal of handlebars that sometimes touched.

SEAN O'DWYER
(1940–)

The Big House

The Georgians knew how to make windows
sometimes with a graceful arch.
You feel better sitting at their windows
looking out, then later looking at others
seated where you were, measuring the delay
between now and your previous chair
where your surrogate ponders—
Windows are sometimes dangerous, adjudicating
inside and outside so insistently
they ask to be broken, though most of us seem
never to get over respecting windows,
drawing with the finger as the room exhales
its mist on the panes—stick figures, smiles,
zig-zags, balloons—random thoughts evaporating
even as you sign your name.
Yes, you can mislay yourself at windows
pleasurably chewing the cud of years
you do not understand, laying the grid
of window panes across the untidy past
hoping for a better fit.
Everything here is in proportion.
That was the gift they gave us. They knew,
those Georgians, how to arrange windows
diminishing serially upward from vertical
masters with their feet on the ground floor
to squatting servants bending to peer out
as the ceiling lowers and oppresses—a perfectly
designed social echelon, subject of course

to revisions. Cast your eye on
that window. It has a defective memory
and makes no judgements. It turns a blind
eye on much that it observes.
In that, no different from most of us.
That's why we are here, to remember for it,
for glass is slippery, the finger squeaks
and the teeth curdle—that, short
of violence, is all you can do to it
unless your thoughts are gathered
to a point hard as a diamond.

Someone is stirring outside behind
the monkey-puzzle on the ancestral lawn.
Is that your grandfather's father, touching
his cap, going round to the backdoor
where the youngest maid, his brother's child,
has her hands on some food in a bitter time.
As he disappears to the left the Master
on his high horse canters in from the right
as if the two were counter-weighed on a balance
around the fulcrum of the 18th century.
What a horse! A white stallion dipping
his head and lifting his hooves as if
the ground were charged with electricity
(that's one for the old painter dying above
the canal). Are you waiting for the old man
to appear again? He never will, no matter
how long you wait time will not vomit him up.
Maybe he's gone back another way
through the fields of rotting stalks
to the windowless cabin with the thatch
ready for burning (what you see
from the front door is another order of things
than what you see from the back).
The sounds behind you are perfectly moulded:
a civil murmur of voices, a distant
piano, the intimate whisper of silk,
and the partial eclipse of doors quietly
closing, each sound in its place.

Through the window is an enormous convulsion
a shudder like a great eye blinking
everything still looks the same but isn't—
That's when you know the rules have changed
dividing those who know and those
who don't. This happens from time to time
and the window can't do much about it
—it's merely a transparent quarter inch
hospitable to light, a fragile abyss
between inside and outside, having and not
having, between two categories of desire.
Things are changed utterly when a vagueness
deep in the bowels names itself,
that feeling becomes a notion, then
an idea, an abstraction pitiless in its
conviction, passing through everything as if
the world were transparent, burning the flesh
as it becomes flesh and thus more
dangerous, then on again draped
in curtains of blood. It is out there
now, in apparitional faces as the light
is leached from the sky, and a sediment of clouds
drops to the horizon. The exclusive acres
sitting in the house's lap, traversed
by the sigmoid curve of the avenue, judiciously
interrupted by beeches and elms which have
insolently agreed to stay where they are,
are infested with trespassers on whose backs
the great house was built, stone by stone.
They had the patience of stones, but their
mineral density is split by an idea.
Outside, flirting with trees like spies,
they do not want the house to see them
until the lawns are alive with enough
of their company (one of them in the torchlight
has your grandfather's young face).
It's getting dark enough to see
developing in the glass's double exposure
a transparent face, a face you know well

now pocked with torches lighting up
fifty faces like glittering shillings,
hidden feet are trampling the distances
between nose and chin, forehead and cheek—
No, not his Lordship's face, he
is currently across the water where
they think his accent a little peculiar—
not a bad man at all as they go (and by God
they are going!). He wasn't evil, but evil
chose him for company. He never noticed—
how could he?—for the medium is always
unaware of its intimates. The voices
shouting and cursing outside in the dark
sound like his Lordship's pack at the kill—
cacophony of yelps, snarls, growls
seeking a single voice which they
will inevitably find to recreate the familiar
beast, born out of hatred's dry womb.
The glass goes first with its image, and you
are out there howling with the others,
rushing to the transcendent fusion, the ecstasy—
rejoicing in the burning Chippendale, there
go the Reynolds and Guardis, the Meissen,
the Gobelin—good riddance. No one there
but the servants fleeing the back door.
What a good ruin it makes, exhaling its afterbreath
of smoke, settling down with cracks
and sighs like an old dame going to bed.
Now you can walk in the privileged spaces
newly secularized, the ceiling
underfoot, the etiquette of drawing
and dining rooms exploded like the bottles
of Chambertin in the cellar. Look up beyond
the absent bedrooms to the lightening sky
sending a convenient ray through
a bulbous lump of fused glass
that with some license you may say
was your window. Standing over it,
the animalcule curved in its depth

stares back at you, changing its shape
as you move your head from side to side.

It musn't have been too bad a ruin
because the developer saw its capabilities.
You can sit at the window again and look out
at the golf course, and the guests from America
arriving in their Hertz rentals, excavating
huge bags and tennis racquets from the boots.
Some young ones may snort a few hits before
coming down for dinner. The old ones
may be looking for ancestors as they shuffle
towards the exit.

Céad míle fáilte,
God bless those who help the economy,
Not a beggar in sight. The monkey puzzle
has a few more branches. After last night's rain
there are patches of blue in the sky.
It looks like it will be a good day.

TOM SEXTON
(1940–)

The Alaska Range

All morning we climb through deep snow
above a maze of alders
where a black bear might be sleeping.
In the last stand of spruce
before the summit, pine grosbeak
fly from tree to tree,
their feathers tinged a delicate rouge.
We climb for nothing more important
than to see the mountains
in the fading winter light.
It is almost night when we go down,
the wind rising.
Every so often in the woods
beyond the marsh, a fierce whiteness
of snow falls from a branch,
and who is to say that this is not
the turning pages of a sacred book?

Homecoming

On the Irish coast, a rutted road
traced a winding track along the wind-
scored face of a limestone bluff.
Rock flowers cascaded to the surf.
Where the road began its long descent
a ruined church sheltered only wind,
and a great tree drained what light was left.
When we were younger, I would have brooded,
even in this ancestral place, on my fate
and Cuchulain's battle with the sea.
You would have talked of Aphrodite.
Now after we've drunk our pint of bitter,
I limp, like that crippled smith, in your wake
back to our turf fire lifting its small wings.

RICHARD TILLINGHAST
(1940–)

A Quiet Pint in Kinvara

for Jeff O'Connell

Salt-stung, rain-cleared air, deepened as always
By a smudge of turf smoke. Overhead the white glide
Of seagulls, and in the convent beeches above the road,
Hoarse croak of rooks, throaty chatter of jackdaws.
High tide pounds stone wall.
I shut the door behind me and head downhill,

Gait steadied by the broad-shouldered gravity
Of houses from the eighteenth or nineteenth century—
Limestone, three storeys, their slate roofs rain-slick,
Aglow with creeper and the green brilliance of mosses.
No force off the Atlantic
Could threaten their angles or budge their masses.

They rise unhurriedly from the strong cellar
And hold a fleshy hand, palm outward, against the sea,
Saying "Land starts here. Go peddle your salt airs elsewhere."
From farms down lanes the meat and milk of pasture,
Root crops and loads of hay,
By hoof or wagon, come down to Kinvara quay.

And so do I—to drink in the presence
Of these presences, these ideas give substance,
Solid as your father's signature
On a letter you unfold sometimes from a quiet drawer,
Yet semi-detached, half free,
Like the road that follows the sea down from Galway,

Curving like a decorated S
Drizzled through a monk's quill plucked from the goose,
Spelling *Sanctus* onto vellum newly missed by the herd,
In a cell where the soul's damp candle flared—
Roofless now to the weather's
Inundations, while ravens walk the cloisters.

A Backward Glance at Galway

for Thomas Lynch

I can almost predict what it would be like
If I should ever go back: The medieval
Streets aswarm with German tourists in Aran
Sweaters, piling off coaches, in town for Race Week;
I'd be craning up at the façade of Lynch's Castle
Studying an anachronistic bartizan,
Getting jostled and elbowed and breathed on by every
Member of the European Community.

But I had my innings there, hitching the coast road
Through salt meadows saturated and green,
Then walking up from the quays—a wind at my back
With the North Atlantic behind it, that thinned the coalsmoke
And refreshed with raindrops the chiseled limestone.
I would hole up in Naughton's pub with my notebook
Ferreting words from a secondhand thesaurus,
Sounding out rhymes in a snug with a pint of Guinness.

From those raptures all I have to show is a snapshot
That I took last December from Nuns' Island
Of the crumbling city walls and quayside quarter.
In the frosty air the slate roofs show up white,
The chimney-pots sooty and Dickensian.
The river pushes downstream glistening with power.
And nothing stands between the lens and the sky
But clarity and salt and a breeze off the sea.

KAREN BRENNAN
(1941–)

My Mother and the Shepherdess

The lamp is a woman
who is a shepherdess
who coyly gazes at my
mother who is sewing
with a white thread
the white hem of a dress.

The tiny veil is ringed
with lily-of-the-valley.
On the table
a prayer book, a silver
rosary, white cotton
gloves.
      She pulls the
needle through and it's
as if the dress itself
were breathing,

the stitches bringing
the dress to life
or the mother
or the girl whose
dress is breathing or

whose dress will bring
life to the girl who
holds her breath.
                    Who
looking at the shepherdess
feels the affinity
one feels with the merely
beautiful:

Under a tree
which is the lamp-post
and a sun which is only a lightbulb,
the little sheep by her shoes
sleep on
like nothing in this world
and nothing out of it.

Grandfather

What can I say to you, in your fat grave
your body no longer inside itself?
Here is a mound, remarkable
form of a wave, which
in its momentary lapses
is simply gathering what has been lost
and repeating it.
Here, then, you are.
Your skin, closer to angels, your
large generous hands resting, as was their custom,
and the interlocking gold ring
from which memory will finally engrave
itself with your initials is present

and absent at the same time.
We are growing apart
as distance is beleaguered by silence
whiter than carnations; and closer
as the mind adjusts to your memory:
As we cannot do.
For there you were, sitting on the green
bench, eyes even then wandering beyond
as if toward some future and arresting
landscape. And we, the objects of the real world,
colorfully arranged, as we are bound to be.

TOM CLARK
(1941–)

The Black Weir

To woo the heathen priests he healed with a leaf
Of shamrock, symbol of the three-headed god.
Under his heel, the serpent powers objected,
Were tricked into the black weir anyway.
He chased out the weird supernatural
Residuum, some crusty old creatures
Who hung around cave mouths, smoking, tippling.
Still my wearing of the green to the Chinese
Jawbreaker proved less than lucky. Pity.
You can't build clouds. Futures you shape in dreams self
Erase. You came in here for mercy and grace
After your measure, found darkness, confusion,
Mystery, blank space. St. Paddy's Day,
You lose your last teeth: an Irish commonplace.

Prolepsis

Melodious liquid warble in the plum
Tree tells the sinking year how to feel
Its recession into grief as if a thorn
Poked a nester in an old wounded heart
Of stone from which slowly drips recognition

All breathing human passion far above
These days atonal as white noise
Through bare branches cotton clouds drift by
Last yellowed leaves catch lone rays of sun
Going down into the motherless ocean
A light plane buzzes off toward brown hills
As shade drops over the next urban plot
To prepare the air for what the dead don't know
How swiftly we are coming to join them

BILLY COLLINS
(1941–)

Tourist: Dromahair, Co. Sligo

After dinner you stroll from the hotel
through this village that could be an allegory
with its single barbershop, single laundry,
its one-of-each simplicity, free of duplication.
Everything here begins with a capital letter.

The evening hangs in the air like lace
which stirs with river breeze as you cross the bridge,
walking the length of the one street
until it broadens at each end into outbound roads
which channel cars through the darkness
and empty them into the light of other towns.

You pass the Garage, Butchershop, Milliner's,
a place for every nameable need, taste, whimsy,
then the Library stacked with complication
and the Church housing its single idea.

The inhabitants could pose for a group photograph
that could be called Humanity, babies included,
you think as you head for the one pub.

You, of course, would be the photographer—
head and shoulders shrouded by the black cloth,
palm raised to tell them to hold still and smile—
not in the picture, but still a part of all
that your lens and mirrors turn upside down.

Afternoon with Irish Cows

There were a few dozen who occupied the field
across the road from where we lived,
stepping all day from tuft to tuft,
their big heads down in the soft grass,
thought I would sometimes pass a window
and look out to see the field suddenly empty
as if they had taken wing, flown off to another country.

Then later, I would open the blue front door,
and again the field would be full of their munching,
or they would be lying down
on the black and white maps of their sides,
facing in all directions, waiting for rain.
How mysterious, how patient and dumbfounded
they appeared in the long quiet of the afternoons.

But every once in a while, one of them
would let out a sound so phenomenal
that I would put down the paper
or the knife I was cutting an apple with
and walk across the road to the stone wall
to see which one of them was being torched
or pierced through the side with a long spear.

Yes, it sounded like pain until I could see
the noisy one, anchored there on all fours,
her neck outstretched, her bellowing head
laboring upward as she gave voice
to the rising, full-bodied cry
that began in the darkness of her belly
and echoed up through her bowed ribs into her gaping mouth.

Then I knew that she was only announcing
the large, unadulterated cowness of herself,
pouring out the ancient apologia of her kind
to all the green fields and the gray clouds,
to the limestone hills and the inlet of the blue bay,
while she regarded my head and shoulders
above the wall with one wild, shocking eye.

Home Again

The black porcelain lamp
painted with boughs of cherry blossoms
still stands on its end table,
unlit, the little chain untouched,
just the way I left it,

just the way it remained while I was off
leaning into the prow of a boat,
doused with spray, heading for a limestone island,
or sitting at the base of a high Celtic cross
eating a green apple.

While I balanced a pan of hot water on a stone wall
and shaved outside a cottage
overlooking the Irish Sea,
this stack of books, this chair, and paperweight
were utterly still, as they are now.

And you, red box of matches on the floor,
you waited here too, faithful as Penelope,
while I saw the tiny fields
disappear under the wing of my plane,
or swam up and down the flowing Corrib River.

As I lay in a meadow near Ballyvaughan,
ankles crossed, arms behind my head,
watching clouds as they rolled in—
billowing, massive, Atlantic-fresh—

you all held your places in these rooms,
stuck to your knitting,
waited for me to stand here again,
bags at my feet, house key still in hand,
admiring your constancy,
your silent fealty, your steadfast repose.

Design

I pour a coating of salt on the table
and make a circle in it with my finger.
This is the cycle of life
I say to no one.
This is the wheel of fortune,
the Arctic Circle.
This is the ring of Kerry
and the white rose of Tralee
I say to the ghosts of my family,
the dead fathers,
the aunt who drowned,
my unborn brothers and sisters,
my unborn children.
This is the sun with its glittering spokes
and the bitter moon.
This is the absolute circle of geometry
I say to the crack in the wall,
to the birds who cross the window.
This is the wheel I just invented
to roll through the rest of my life
I say
touching my finger to my tongue.

Questions About Angels

Of all the questions you might want to ask
about angels, the only one you ever hear
is how many can dance on the head of a pin.

No curiosity about how they pass the eternal time
besides circling the Throne chanting in Latin
or delivering a crust of bread to a hermit on earth
or guiding a boy and girl across a rickety wooden bridge.

Do they fly through God's body and come out singing?
Do they swing like children from the hinges
of the spirit world saying their names backwards and forwards?
Do they sit alone in little gardens changing colors?

What about their sleeping habits, the fabric of their robes,
their diet of unfiltered divine light?
What goes on inside their luminous heads? Is there a wall
these tall presences can look over and see hell?

If an angel fell off a cloud would he leave a hole
in a river and would the hole float along endlessly
filled with the silent letters of every angelic word?

If an angel delivered the mail would he arrive
in a blinding rush of wings or would he just assume
the appearance of the regular mailman and
whistle up the driveway reading the postcards?

No, the medieval theologians control the court.
The only question you ever hear is about
the little dance floor on the head of a pin
where halos are meant to converge and drift invisibly.

It is designed to make us think in millions,
billions, to make us run out of numbers and collapse
into infinity, but perhaps the answer is simply one:
one female angel dancing alone in her stocking feet,
a small jazz combo working in the background.

She sways like a branch in the wind, her beautiful
eyes closed, and the tall thin bassist leans over
to glance at his watch because she has been dancing
forever, and now it is very late, even for musicians.

The Afterlife

While you are preparing for sleep, brushing your teeth,
or riffling through a magazine in bed,
the dead of the day are setting out on their journey.

They are moving off in all imaginable directions,
each according to his own private belief,
and this is the secret that silent Lazarus would not reveal:
that everyone is right, as it turns out.
You go to the place you always thought you would go,
the place you kept lit in an alcove in your head.

Some are being shot up a funnel of flashing colors
into a zone of light, white as a January sun.
Others are standing naked before a forbidding judge who sits
with a golden ladder on one side, a coal chute on the other.

Some have already joined the celestial choir
and are singing as if they have been doing this forever,
while the less inventive find themselves stuck
in a big air-conditioned room full of food and chorus girls.

Some are approaching the apartment of the female God,
a woman in her forties with short wiry hair
and glasses hanging from her neck by a string.
With one eye she regards the dead through a hole in her door.

There are those who are squeezing into the bodies
of animals—eagles and leopards—and one trying on
the skin of a monkey like a tight suit,
ready to begin another life in a more simple key,
while others float off into some benign vagueness,
little units of energy heading for the ultimate elsewhere.

There are even a few classicists being led to an underworld
by a mythological creature with a beard and hooves.
He will bring them to the mouth of a furious cave
guarded over by Edith Hamilton and her three-headed dog.

The rest just lie on their backs in their coffins
wishing they could return so they could learn Italian
or see the pyramids, or play some golf in a light rain.
They wish they could wake in the morning like you
and stand at a window examining the winter trees,
every branch traced with the ghost writing of snow.

EAMON GRENNAN
(1941–)

Traveller

He's ten, travelling alone for the first time—
by bus to the city. He settles an empty seat
and waves out at where I stand on the footpath
waiting for him to be taken, barely a shadow
grinning behind smoked glass. To his eyes
I'm a dim figure far off, smiling and waving
in a sea of traffic. Behind me, the blinding sun
melts down the black back of hills
across the Hudson. For all there is to say
we are deaf to one another
and despatch our love in shrugs and pantomime
until he gives thumbs-up and the bus
sighs shut, shuddering away from me. He mouths
words I can't understand; I smile back
regardless, blowing a kiss through the air that
starts to stretch and empty between us. Alone,
he stares out a while, admiring his height
and speed, then reads two chapters of *The Dark
Is Rising*. When the real dark leaches in
he sees nothing but the huge loom
of a hill, the trees' hooded bulk and
come-hithering shadow. He tries to curl up
in sleep, but sleep won't come, so he presses
one cheek flat against the cold black glass
and peers past his own faint ghost
up at the sky, as any night-time traveller
would—as Henry Hudson must have, sailing

his *Half Moon* past Poughkeepsie, already
smelling the Pacific. My son seeks the stars
he knows: Orion's belt, his sword, his dog
fall into place, make sense of the dark
above his voyaging. *When I found him,* he says,
I felt at home, and fell asleep. I imagine
him asleep in his rocky seat there,
like that wet sea-boy dozing at mast-head,
whose lullaby the whole Atlantic hums
in the lull between storms, the brief
peace between battles, no land in sight.

Men Roofing

for Seamus Heaney

Bright burnished day, they are laying fresh roof down
on Chicago Hall. Tight cylinders of tarred felt-paper
lean against one another on the cracked black shingles
that shroud those undulant ridges. Two squat drums
of tar-mix catch the light. A fat canister of gas
gleams between a heap of old tyres and a paunchy
plastic sack, beer-bottle green. A TV dish-antenna
stands propped to one side, a harvest moon, cocked
to passing satellites and steadfast stars. Gutters
overflow with starlings, lit wings and whistling throats
going like crazy. A plume of blue smoke feathers up
from a pitch-black cauldron, making the air fragrant
and medicinal, as my childhood's was, with tar. Overhead,
against the gentian sky, a sudden first flock whirls
of amber leaves and saffron, quick as breath, fine
as origami birds. Watching from a window opposite,
I see a man in a string vest glance up at these

exalted leaves, kneel to roll a roll of tar-felt flat; another
tilts a drum of tar-mix till a slow bolt of black silk
oozes, spreads. One points a silver hose and conjures
from its nozzle a fretted trembling orange lick
of fire. The fourth one dips to the wrist in the green sack
and scatters two brimming fistfuls of granite grit:
broadcast, the bright grain dazzles on black. They pause,
straighten, study one another: a segment done. I can see
the way the red-bearded one in the string vest grins and
slowly whets his two stained palms along his jeans; I see
the one who cast the grit walk to the roof-edge, look over,
then, with a little lilt of the head, spit contemplatively
down. What a sight between earth and air they are, drenched
in sweat and sunlight, relaxed masters for a moment
of all our elements. Here is my image, given, of the world
at peace: men roofing, taking pains to keep the weather
out, simmering in ripe Indian-summer light, winter
on their deadline minds. Briefly they stand balanced
between our common ground and nobody's sky, then move
again to their appointed tasks and stations, as if they were
amazing strangers, come to visit for a brief spell
our familiar shifty climate of blown leaves, birdspin. Odorous,
their lazuli column of smoke loops up from the dark
heart of their mystery; and they ply, they intercede.

Walk, Night Falling, Memory of My Father

Downhill into town
between the flaring azaleas
of neighbour gardens: a cairn of fresh-cut logs
gives off a glow
of broken but transfigured flesh.

My father, meeting me years ago
off a train at Kingsbridge: greenish
tweed cap, tan gaberdine, leaning
on a rolled umbrella, the sun
in his eyes, the brown planes of his face
in shadow, and all of a sudden
old. The distance between us
closes to an awkward, stumbling,
short embrace. Little left

but bits and pieces: pints in Healy's
before tea; a drive with visitors
to Sally Gap; my daughter making
game with his glasses; the transatlantic calls
for an anniversary, birthday,
or to the hospital
before his operations. Moments
during those last days
in the ward, under the big window
where the clouds over the golf course
would break or darken: his unexpected
rise to high spirits, my hand
helping his hand
hold the glass of water. And one memory
he kept coming back to,
of being a child in a white frock,
watching his mother and another woman
in long white dresses and broad straw hats
recline in a rowing-boat on the Boyne
near Navan: how the boat rocked
side to side, the women smiling and
talking in low voices, and him
sitting by himself on the bank
in a pool of sunshine, his little feet
barely reaching the cool water. I remember
how the nurses swaddled his
thin legs in elastic bandages, keeping him
together for a day or two.

Uphill again, the dark now down
and the night voices
at their prayers and panicky conjurations,
one thrush still bravely
shaping in song
the air around him. Fireflies
wink on and off
in lovers' Morse, my own head
floating among them, seeing—
as each opens its heart in silence
and in silence closes—
just how large the dark is. Now,
cold moonglow casts
across this shaking summer world
a thin translucent skin
of snow; tall tree shapes
thicken, whispering; and on ghostly wings
white moths brush by. Indoors again,
I watch them—fallen angels
the size and shade of communion wafers—
beat dusted wings against the screen,
flinging themselves
at this impossible light.

Levitations

(after Chagall)

Airborne as they are, his lovers are solid as we are,
although we too drift between these walls of glass
as if we'd lost our moorings and might any minute
vanish through the skylight. They've lifted each other up
above the furniture with a single kiss, pointing themselves

in a westerly direction like two primed torpedoes,
or held together as halves of the one body, not yet
blown open and apart, their horizontal faces calm
and taking us in with little interest where we stare
from a net of blackbirds that pay no attention to how
we've stepped into the blue like this, hang-gliding
on our own updraft or doing the advanced backstroke
in our sleep. Coming back, we're groundlings, earthbound,
or you're upstream in a salmon jacket, me treading water
and snapping at the lure. Later, we held each other
in the palms of our hands and said, *Are we not*
light as feathers now, lying down? Here, then,
is the very self in all its cubist shreds and patches,
planted next to *The Poet at Half Past Three*, who is
a thing of stubble and vodka, cranberry atmospherics,
a crude rooster crowing in the corner of his eye
while his other half lies on grass, parcelled up in himself
like a secondhand violin and chewing a pointed leaf
of field sorrel, that cures thirst and putrefaction. Like us,
he is interested in the resurrection of the body,
wrapped as he is around a dream as hard as a barn door
through which the blue horse has just bolted. And now
we are coming in by the window again, bringing
my shoulders, your breasts and hips, a fan of black feathers
and a glass filled with, spilling, wine. Meanwhile an angel
on loan from Tintoretto makes a crash-landing
somewhere east of Kiev, translating the way the light
sits on things, all the realms of the lucid turned inside out
by this apparition of wings. His dog, it is true, barks
at the lilac tree, but the ground we think is steady under us
isn't, but spins its heartless wheel, while those savvy
whitebreasted swallows or sandmartins standing on the wind
like idle things, are all the time working their hearts out
to stay in the one place, still as we are, and go on holding.

DEREK MAHON
(1941–)

Global Village

The reader need only . . . separate in his own thoughts
the being of a sensible thing from its being perceived.
                                    —George Berkeley,
                                    The Principles of Human Knowledge

This morning, from beyond abandoned piers
where the great liners docked in former years,
a fog-horn echoes in deserted sheds
known to Hart Crane, and in our vigilant beds.
No liners now, nothing but ice and sleet,
a late flame flickering on Brodsky St.
News-time in the global village—Bosnia, famine, drought,
whole nations, races, evicted even yet,
rape victim and blind beggar at the gate—
the images forming which will be screened tonight
on CNN and *The McNeil-Lehrer News Hour,*
the sense of being right there on the spot
—a sense I get right here that Gansevoort
has no 'existence, natural or real, apart
from its being perceived by the understanding'. Not
that I seriously doubt the reality of the Hudson Bar
and Diner; but the skills of Venturi, Thompson, Rowse
that can make post-modern a 19th-century warehouse
and those of Hollywood *film noir* have combined
to create virtual realities in the mind
so the real thing tells us what we already know:
American Gothic. Obviously I don't mean

to pen yet one more craven European
paean to the States, nor would you expect me to,
not being a yuppie in a pinstripe suit
but an Irish Bohemian even as you are too
though far from the original 'Ballroom of Romance',
far too from your posh convent school in France.
Out here, in the clear existential light,
I miss the half-tones I'm accustomed to:
an amateur immigrant, sure I like the corny
humanism and car-stickers—'I ♥ NY'
—and yet remain sardonic and un-*chic,*
an undesirable 'resident alien' on this shore,
a face in the crowd in this 'off-shore boutique'
inscribed with the ubiquitous comic-strip blob-speak
—LOVE ONE ANOTHER, RESIST INSIPID RHYME—
exposed in thunderstorms, as once before,
and hoping to draw some voltage one more time
or at least not die of spiritual cowardice.
'After so many deaths I live and write'
cried, once, Geo. Herbert in his Wiltshire plot:
does lightning ever strike in the same place twice?

Beauty and the Beast

'I don't know any stories; none of the lost boys
know any stories.'
'How perfectly awful,' said Wendy.
                    —J. M. Barrie, *Peter Pan*

I go nightshopping like Frank O'Hara I go bopping
up Bleecker for juice, croissants, Perrier, ice-cream
and Gitanes *filtre,* pick up the laundry, get back
to five (5!) messages on the answering machine
from Mary K. and Eliza, Louis, Barry and Jack,

and on TV sixty channels of mind-polluting yuck.
Thank God for the VCR. Now at last I can screen
the old movies I haven't seen since I was 'young'—
A Night to Remember, Rear Window, High Noon,
The Man Who Never Was, A King in New York . . .
Tonight, for example, tickled to bits, I stick on
the 'original, uncut' version of *King Kong*:
childish, perhaps, but a cultural critic's dream.
I re-wind, fast-forward, and replay the scene
where Kong instals Fay Wray screaming on the high rock
where he lives, and she's attacked by a gryphon, roc,
velociraptor, hoopoe, some such creation,
a thousand feet above the Indian Ocean,
wherever, and you can see the little freighter
sitting far out there on the sparkling water.
Sensitive Kong doesn't interfere with her sexually
though he does *paw* and sniff his fingers, actually,
eyes bright with curiosity; then the entire cast
come tough-talking through the primaeval rain-forest,
chivalrous Robert Armstrong sets her free
and they run off together down to the shore,
indignant Kong chasing them with a roar
because the poor sap really loves her, do you see—
and how exciting it must have been in the heyday
of Prohibition, 40% unemployment and the WPA!
—for that matter, it's still thrilling even today.
I sit here like an old child with a new toy
or a creature from outer space, Saturn perhaps,
inventorying the resources of the planet of the apes
when (look!) the huge gorilla, the size of a fly
('Eighth Wonder of the World', says the publicity),
climbs up, like Batman later, the sheer side of the Empire State,
a black speck outlined against the morning sky
clutching Fay, said Noël Coward, 'like a suppository'.
It's all inconsistent, of course, and disproportionate,
he's too small there and too big on the street, *I know*,
but it makes no difference, it's a magnificent show.
. . . The little bi-planes come gunning for him now
and Kong, by Jove, knocks one of them out of the sky
with a hairy hand. They wear him out, of course,

and he falls to extinction among the crowds below.
And Fay??? She screams but she's safe; it might've been worse.
I breathe again and zap, lord of the universe,
the credits. Semiotician, couch potato,
I've had them all here in my room on video—
Leigh, Grahame, Taylor, Kelly and Monroe;
but why so few poems for the women I know?
Because these things used to be open to innuendo?
Fay, born in Alberta, you were also in *Dirigible*
and 'existed most forcefully when faced with terror'
says *Video Guide*—like most of us, probably. Well,
Kong and I dedicate this one to you, old girl,
wherever you are; pushing 90 and hanging in there,
we want you to know we love you and root for you still.

(for Fay Wray)

Key West

our little wooden northern houses
            —Elizabeth Bishop

Somewhere along Route 1—Plantation, Tavernier—
cloud-splitting Angie broke over the Keys last year
in June, the earliest ever, bringing torrential rains,
though it wasn't one of those really *terrible* hurricanes
you hear about, that wreck 'homes' and wreak atrocities
on isolated farms, snug harbours, close communities,
but a swift cloud-stream of premonitory showers
that waltzed off, 'mad lutanist', in the direction of New Orleans
irrigating pine and cedar, lemon groves and sand-bars
while the 'still-vex'd' Bahamas heaved in still-turbulent seas.
The outskirts of Key West, when we got there,
you driving, a white bandana round your hair
and Satchmo's 'Wonderful World' on the car radio,
were still where they were supposed to be, and calm

between downpours red poinciana, jasmine, 'royal' palm
and the white frame-houses built a century ago
by tough skippers against cyclone and tornado
whistling in off the Gulf of Mexico.
The town gasped in a tropical heat-wave
and I recalled old Mr. Temple's narrative
in *Key Largo,* the great nameless storm of 1935
that killed 800 people (it did too) and blew
the East Coast Railroad into the ocean—true,
the bridges are still standing, but that was the last train.
Suave, mari magno turbulantis aequora ventis,
e terra magnum alterius spectare laborem:
it's cool, when gale-force winds trouble the waters,
to watch from shore the tribulations of others!
. . . Uh-oh, before dawn it came around again,
fat drops hitting on storm lanterns, demented budgies
screeching beyond the pool and the churning trees;
and I pictured the vast turmoil undersea,
a mute universe of sponge and anemone,
of conch and snapper, octopus and algae,
odd fish of every stripe in their coral conservatories,
while counting the stiff electric chimes of St. Mary's,
    Star of the Sea.
Later, exhausted hens on the telephone lines,
disheveled dogs in the flooded Bahamian lanes:
chaos, *triste tropique*—till, mauve and rose,
flecked with pistachio cloud, a new kind of day arose
and I saw why once to these shores came *other* cold
solitaries down from the north in search of love and poetry
—the mad sailor, the stuffed bullfinch blue and gold,
the shy perfectionist with her painter's eye—
to sing in the crashing, galaxy-lit sea-porches.
It was one of those far-out, raw mornings, the beaches
littered with dreck, and a derelict dawn moon,
mountains and craters in visible cameo, yearned
close to the Earth as if murmuring to return,
milk of what heavenly breast, dew drenching the skin—
a wreckers' morning, with everyone a bit lost
as if landed from Senegal or the Ivory Coast.
Why so soon in the season? Newspapers and TV

spoke of 'El Niño', the fabulous, hot tide-thrust
born in December off Peru like the infant Christ
sea-changing *all* with its rough magic; and advised
of hurricanes to come, so that one feared not only
for the Cuban cabin and the gimcrack condominium
but for the 'sleek and effortless vacation home'
featured in the current issue of *Key Design,*
the 'storm-resistant' dream house with its 'vinyl membrane',
a bait-fridge and 'teak sailfish-fighting chair';
for roads and bridges, lighthouses, any structure
presumed permanent; towns and cities everywhere
vulnerable to a trickle of sand, to a breath of fresh air;
and thought of the fragility of all architecture,
the provisional nature even of aerospace.
I keep on my desk here a coarse handful of Florida sea-moss
and remember, this wintry night, that summery place—
how we strolled out there on the still-quaking docks
shaken but exhilarated, turned to retrace
our steps up Caroline St., and sat in Pepe's
drinking (rum and) Coke with retired hippies
who long ago gave up on the land and settled among the rocks.

'To Mrs. Moore at Inishannon'

The statue's sculptor, Frédéric-Auguste Bartholdi, reacted
with horror to the prospect of immigrants landing near
his masterpiece; he called it 'a monstrous plan'. So much
for Emma Lazarus . . . I wanted to do homage to the ghosts.
          —Mary Gordon, *Good Boys and Dead Girls*

No. 1, Fifth Avenue, New York City, Sept. 14th, 1895
—and Mother, dear, I'm glad to be alive
after a whole week on the crowded *Oceanic*—
tho' I got here all right without being sick.
We boarded in the rain, St. Colman's spire

shrinking ashore, a few lamps glimm'ring there
('*Will the last to leave please put out the lights?*'),
and slept behind the engines for six nights.
A big gull sat at the masthead all the way
from Roche's Point to Montock, till one day
it stagger'd up and vanish'd with the breeze
in the mass'd rigging by the Hudson quays . . .
Downtown, dear God, is like a glimpse of Hell
in a 'hot wave': drunken men, the roaring 'El',
the noise and squalour indescribable.
(Manners are rough and speech indelicate;
more teeming shore than you cd. shake a stick at.)
However, the Kellys' guest-house; church and tram;
now, thanks to Mrs. O'Brien, here I am
at last, install'd amid the kitchenware
in a fine house a short step from Washington Square.
Protestants, mind you, and a bit serious
much like the Bandon sort, not fun like us,
the older children too big for their britches
tho' Sam, the 4-yr.-old, has me in stitches:
in any case, the whole country's under age.
I get each Sunday off and use the privilege
to explore Broadway, the new Brooklyn Bridge
or the Statue of Liberty, copper torch on top
which, wd. you believe it, actually lights up,
and look at the Jersey shore-line, blue and gold:
it's all fire and sunlight here in the New World.
Eagles and bugles! Curious their simple faith
that stars and stripes are all of life and death—
as if Earth's centre lay in Central Park
when we both know it runs thro' Co. Cork.
Sometimes at night, in my imagination,
I hear you calling me across the ocean;
but the money's good, tho' I've had to buy new clothes
for the equatorial climate. I enclose
ten dollars, more to come (here, for God's sake,
they fling the stuff around like snuff at a wake).
'Bye now; and Mother, dear, you may be sure
I remain
        yr. loving daughter,
                —Bridget Moore

WESLEY McNAIR
(1941–   )

To My Father, Dying in a Supermarket

At first it is difficult
to see you
are dropping dead—

you seem lost
in thought, adjusting your tie
as if to rehearse

some imaginary speech
though of course beginning
to fall,

your mouth opening wider
than I have ever seen
a mouth,

your hands deep
in your shirt,
going down

into the cheeses, making the sound
that is not
my name,

that explains nothing
over and over,
going away

into your hands
into your face,
leaving this great body

on its knees,
the father
of my body

which holds me
in this world,
watching you go

on falling
through the Musak,
making the sound

that is not my name,
that will never
explain anything, oh father,

stranger, all dressed up
and deserting me
for the last time.

Blame

Now my mother has a new man
to sit with, only the back
of a head from my angle
in the rear seat, with curly hair
I've never seen in our family
before. Everything seems new,
even the rummage-sale shirts
my brothers and I are wearing, even

the old Ford he's spent so long
fixing and shining for this ride
on the superhighway. I'm
the one who notices the trace
of blue above us, beautiful at first
as it gathers into a wide, long
ribbon. Then it transforms
into a haze my older brother
calls smoke in a loud voice,
and we are all suddenly opening
the doors and standing outside
the car in the breakdown lane.
Who is to blame for this misfortune
in my family's uncertain,
hopeful life? Not my mother,
so pleased seconds ago to have us
traveling together, not my brothers
and I, looking forward to our trip
into America's future, not
my stepfather, who, having no one
to accuse for the bad luck
he cannot change, goes around
and around the billowing car,
blaming each tire with his foot.

History by George B. Yeaton

Notes left by George B. Yeaton for a town history of Epsom, New Hampshire

Once, above the fading and
blotted loops of his antique
calligraphy,

the man who wrote it sat entering
the date and signing his name, George B.
Yeaton, relieved

to have written these words in time:
"With the death of Ernest M. Green
last Thursday

August 30 there are only three men left
from the crew that worked with me at the mill
in 1905." Which mill,

we cannot ask George B., now vanished
from the crew himself, nor ask the names
of the men

he somehow chose to designate in another
note as Mr. L., Mr. B., and Mr. W.,
some of whom

would not speak to each other
one afternoon on a farm
somewhere

while threshing, but who had a conversation
anyway: "Mr. L. talked to Mr. W., Mr. W.
talked to me,

Mr. W. talked to Mr. L., Mr. B. talked
to me, I talked to all three. George
B. Yeaton."

What can the patient reader
do, not even having a motive
for why,

in still another entry, the poor first-
nameless wife of Daniel W. Pierce
hanged herself

from one of the largest
apple trees "in her husband's
orchard"—

what, but think of history
as the facts that are arranged
and lost

by one whose reasons for telling it
aren't always clear? Yet clarity
might obscure

George B.'s unwitting point about the lack of it
in history, whether or not the version's
contained in loopy notes

like those of his long, dateless story
recalled from childhood about Aunts Nabby
and Molly singing

in the darkness on a sleigh ride, ignoring
the widely known adage that it was dreadful
to sing outdoors

at night and frightening him to tears.
"I will never forget that music," he wrote,
and signed his name

and took the memory of which song it was
along with the world that believed in this
odd adage

with him, where most of what we love
or fear or vow always to remember
finally goes,

mysterious in spite of us, beyond the power
of history, George Yeaton's or anyone's,
to sum up or explain.

GIBBONS RUARK
(1941–)

Words for Unaccompanied Voice at Dunmore Head

One old friend who never writes me tells another:
The boy has need of lyrical friends around him.
Don't ask me how I ever found that out,

Given as I am to these fugitive headlands
Where not so long ago the news from Dublin
Arrived washed up with driftwood from the States,

Where the gulls rehearse the local word for weather
And then free-fall through ragged clouds to the sea wrack.
The bar at the end of the world is three miles east.

Last night the music there ascended with the smoke
From a turf fire and showered down in dying sparks
That fell on lovers and the lonely ones alike

Where they cycled the dark roads home or lingered
By a bridge till every cottage light was out—
Fell silent from the night as innocent as milkweed.

All night those soft stars burned in my watchful sleep.
At dawn I abandoned my rackety faithless car
To its own persuasions, took up a stick

And leaned uphill into the wind for the summit.
No music here but the raw alarms of seabirds
And the tireless water high against the cliff face.

No more the flute and the whiskeyed tenor rising,
The chorus of faces in the drift of smoke.
This is the rock where solitude scrapes its keel

And listens into the light for an echo.
This has to be good practice for that last
Cold wave of emptiness on whatever shore,

But why do the reckoners in my nightmares
Never ask me what I said to the speechless
Assembly of whitecaps instead of was

There anyone arm-in-arm with me as I spoke?

Working the Rain Shift at Flanagan's

for Ben Kiely

When Dublin is a mist the quays are lost
To the river, even you could be lost,
A boy from Omagh after forty years
Sounding the Liberties dim as I was
When that grave policeman touching my elbow

Headed me toward this salutary glass.
The town is grim all right, but these premises
Have all the air of a blessed corner
West of the westernmost pub in Galway,
Where whatever the light tries daily to say

The faces argue with, believing rain.
Outside an acceptable rain is falling
Easy as you predicted it would fall,
Though all your Dublin savvy could not gauge
The moment the rain shift would begin to sing.

They are hoisting barrels out of the cellar
And clanging them into an open van,
Gamely ignoring as if no matter
Whatever is falling on their coats and caps,
Though the fat one singing tenor has shrugged

Almost invisibly and hailed his fellow
Underground: "A shower of rain up here,"
He says with the rain, "It'll bring up the grass."
Then, befriending a moan from the darkness,
"Easy there now, lie back down, why won't you,"

As if the man were stirring in his grave
and needed a word to level him again.
His baffled answer rising to the rainfall
Could have been laughter or tears or maybe
Some musical lie he was telling the rain.

This if a far corner from your beat these days,
But why not walk on over anyway
And settle in with me to watch the rain.
You can tell me a story if you feel
Like it, and then you can tell me another.

The rain in the door will fall so softly
It might be rising for all we can know
Where we sit inscribing its vague margin
With words, oddly at ease with our shadows
As if we had died and gone to Dublin.

With Thanks for a Shard from Sandycove

for Seamus Heaney

Late afternoon we idled on a bench
In memory of the man from Inniskeen,
The slow green water fluent beside us,

High clouds figured among leaves on the surface.
Then down along the strand to Sandycove
And the late-lit water, the sun emigrating

After a parting glance, the distant ferry
Disappearing soundlessly toward Holyhead.
We were laughing, riding the crest of company,

Your beautiful laughing wife and you and I,
When suddenly you tired of hammering
With a pebble at a stubborn boulder

And lifted it and dropped it on another
And handed me the chip that broke away.
I thought of the brute possibilities

In those farmer's hands, the place they came from,
What they might have done instead of simply
Dropping one stone on another to give

This pilgrim a shard of where he'd been.
You lifted that heaviness handily,
Keeping it briefly elevated in the air

As if more nearly the weight of a bowl
Of sacramental lather than the capstone
Of a dolmen in some field near Ballyvaughan.

Guilty as charged with a faithless penchant
For the elegiac, shy of the quick-drawn line
In the schoolyard dust, we prayed for nothing

Less than calm in the predawn hours and the laughter
Of disarming women when the hangman comes.
The sea grew dark, and then the dark was general

Over the suburbs, the window where I slept
Thrown open on the moon picking out the angle
Of a spade left leaning in a kitchen garden,

Shining like something prized from underground.

The Enniskillen Bombing

Remembrance Day, 1987

"Showery with bright periods," said the forecast,
The way it does so many days in Ireland,
And indeed the arrowy soft rain fell

And the clouds parted more often than not
Above that watery parish, and the farmer
Walked in collarless from Derrygore,

The butcher left his awning snug against the lintel,
Two boys forgot their caps on the orchard wall.
Nobody looking at the sky or listening

To the weather would ever have predicted
That thunder would erupt before the lightning,
Blow the whole end gable of St. Michael's out

And bring the roof spars raining piecemeal down—
Not the slow-tempered grocer gone open-mouthed
With or without a cry as the windows roared,

Not the stooped pharmacist red-faced with grief,
Not the veteran of two World Wars in all
His ribbons, scrabbling with his raw bare hands

Through the choking dust for anybody's heartbeat,
Not the father wandering almost blindly,
Eyebrows seared from his face, who found his son

Still breathing only to knock the tip of his stick
Against his daughter's wedding ring, her splintered
Hand upturned in the rubble incarnadine

As the fuchsia banking a rain-swept roadside.

Before It Happened

One afternoon a friend from the Falls and I
Drove out from Sligo into Enniskillen
For a quiet drink among old lamps and mirrors,

The glancing talk conspiratorial
As wives at the half-doors, silences freighted,
Lamplight pooled with sunlight on the polished bar,

The street outside a cleared-out Control Zone.
Across the street and up the narrow stair,
In a room with spring light swimming in the windows,

Fine as lace and firm as Blake's engravings,
The paintings of a dozen Irish wildflowers,
One after one, hung cleanly on the wall.

My friend in country walker, botanizer
Reared in the gutted streets of West Belfast,
Called every one by name from memory.

Bogbean, pipewort, grass of Parnassus,
Harebell looking so fragile it might tatter
In a breeze, yet stubborn as the stone ones

High on the capitals at Corcomroe.
We came downstairs into the slant of evening
And drove away in the unmolesting dark.

As we left behind the small lights of the town,
The voice at the wheel was naming constellations,
Orion, Cassiopeia, where they wavered

At first, then spread their nets of stars in the night wind.

Miles from Newgrange at the Winter Solstice

The long-lit landscape of the summer solstice
Just over our heads, we stood in a seamless
Darkness. I touched your hand to the carved stone
Like some deep negative of Braille, each crevice

The whorl of a mind now wordless and flown.
Outside, the long shine on the river ran,
Shadows mingled, and a sudden fish leapt
And fell back scattering its reflection.

I heard the tenderness of your taken breath,
Felt for your hand again, and out we crept
Into the smell of mown hay and daylight,
Those stones left weighing the silence they kept.

Summer ended. Leaves fell. Now the window's white
With flurries or the full moonlight of late
December, we're too fleshed with desire to tell.
Beyond the waters, beyond the dark, light

Makes its once-a-year move down a channel
Intelligence left in the tumulus wall,
And while we lie together close as a fever
On childish limbs, it glosses for a still

Second a text as fine as a feather.
After long love, we should let dawn discover
The crevices between us, so we might not lie
Underground unread and dark forever.

MICHAEL HEFFERNAN
(1942–)

Kennedy

One late afternoon I hitched from Galway down to Kinvara on the edge of the Burren, one of those long midsummer days when the sun labors at last out of all day rain and sets very late in the evening. In dark pubs all up and down the street, the townsmen hunched to their pints, silent and tentative as monks at supper. Thinking to take my daily Guinness, I stopped, and Kennedy was there, his picture on the mantel behind the bar.

A black-headed citizen half in his cups sidled over and smiled. Ah Kennedy Kennedy, a lovely man, he said and bought me a Guinness. Ah yes, a lovely man, I said, and thank you very much. Yes Kennedy, and they slaughtered him in his youth the filthy communists, he said, and will you want another. Yes, slaughtered him in his youth, I said and thanked him very much.

All night till closing time we drank to Kennedy and cursed the communists—all night, pint after pint of sour black lovely stout. And when it came Time, I and my skin and the soul inside my skin, all sour and lovely, strode where the sun still washed the evening, and the fields lay roundabout, and Kinvara slept in the sunlight, and Holy Ireland, all all asleep, while the grand brave light of day held darkness back like the whole Atlantic.

To Cathleen at Patricktide

. . . I saw a young girl,
and she had the walk of a queen
>   —Yeats

If you'd come back I'd make a rime of it.
I'd say, It took you long enough. This place
got lonesome and then lonesomer night by night
until we all gave up, or almost did.
One of us stood and hollered at the moon
begging for nothing but the moon's regard,
but all that happened was the moon went down
and it got so dark that the man said, God,
there's nobody out here but me and stones
and hunger from some raging demiurge's
worst intentions toward the likes of me.
I'm going in before the cold comes on
and nighttime fills the middle of my bones
with fire's own opposite, the dearth of fire.
Then in he went, and nothing came about
out in the bogland where he said these things,
though nobody could show it to a child
or any simpler creature wanting comfort.
If you'd come back at such a time as that
I would have said the moon had taken form
and risen in the face of woman now
and given reason for the souls of men
to climb amongst a merriment of suns
bearing no burdens but the ones they love.

The Atonement

On into spring, around St. Anselm's day,
I take another look at the Redemption,
and first I ask, What is there to redeem?

What have I done but fall into this flesh
which is the way it is because it is
and not because of something someone did

to That-Than-Which-None-Greater-Can-Be-Conceived—
which is a phraseology I admired,
and admired Professor Quinn for saying it

the spring of '62 in that lecture hall
with casement windows hung on the musky breeze
bloody and bosomy and rank with love

and not God's love but Beverly Doherty's,
who drove men mad on her front porch in the lamplight
to be at one with parts of her she kept

untouchable behind her father's door,
shutting out all but the last smell of her
under the nostril in the sweet night air.

A Rhetoric Upon the Window

Since it is open and the world is blue,
I want to know why God's face can't be there,
watching me from the yard beyond the window.
Brothers and sisters, I have been trying hard
to find him, and I know you say you know

precisely where it happens we should look,
which isn't anywhere near my backyard.
I can't help asking why he can't be there,
unless he is and I'm not seeing him
for something in my eye that's in the way
or something in my brain that makes him fade
as soon as what I see goes through the nerve
and comes out on the other end a blur,
a scrambled message that the brain can't keep
because of what I put there in the way.
The mind goes blind as surely as the eye—
but what if suddenly I am proven wrong
and there he is, an enormous hummingbird,
gathering the air around him as he raises
his winged face and everything else with him,
taking me through the window into light
as quickly as he came, and there I am,
rapt in the radiance with nothing left
but blue as blue as all there is of blue—
what if that happened and this poem came true?—
with the blank space or the stillness afterward
like daylight emptied of the one hummingbird.

A Highway Brook in Dingle

Traveling the coast road from Ventry to Slea Head,
    we came to a place where the blacktop
stops by a brook rushing down from the mountain
    over stones replacing the highway,
providing us both miracle and hazard,
    with a thought for the County Council
and how they could countenance such a marvel—

as well as a thought for the cliff's edge just there
    to one side of us, frighteningly
hidden by the roadside wall and swollen turf.
    We scarcely thanked God for good weather.
Mist would at least obscure the terrible plunge.
    We had no choice but to go on through.
Halfway over, we stopped and opened the doors

to pick up glistening stones for souvenirs.
    The water rattling from above us
purled and winked and murmured underneath. Below,
    the ocean spoke in tones oceans use.
Old gods might be staring from behind the light
    at this intersection of known worlds,
while the human roadway rose to carry us.

Merciless Beauty

Look to the blue above the neighborhood,
and nothing there gives any help at all.
We have seen the fuchsia, and it doesn't work.
Time flows away. The mystery it fills
with our undoing moves aside awhile
and brings a new reality into play,
apparently—and here is the main idea:
the wind of time appears to blow through here,
the periwinkle and the mayapple
trembling in wind that is of their own kind,
a gorgeous color of a clarity
that fills our eyes with brightness to see through,
for all the good it does us, and to tell
the morning glory from the glory of God.

MICHAEL LALLY
(1942–)

(from) The South Orange Sonnets

2

My brother brought the moon back from
Okinawa. I mean, there they learned of
the surrender three days late and then
they danced all night. My brother played
the saxophone. Junkman Willy did a one
step that most girls didnt want to do.
They called him that for all the old cars
he worked on til he was old enough to
drive. He was a paddy cat like me and we
lived on Cabbage Hill til we were old
enough to live anywhere. We believed
Italians and Jews ran *THE SYNDICATE*
maybe the world. In West Orange a man
hung himself higher than he could reach.

9

When my mother died two Irish great aunts
came over from New York. The brassy one
wore her hat tilted and always sat with
her legs wide apart. At the wake she told
me loud You look like your grandfather
the cop if you ever get like him shoot
yourself. The other one waited til after
the funeral to pull my ear down to her
level and whisper Youre a good looking
young man but if you dont shave off them

side boards people will mistake you for
a Puerto Rican. We had so many cousins
in our neighborhood everybody called my
mother Aunt Irene. Even the Italians.

10

My uncle shot himself before I was born.
My grandfather who carried and old petri-
fied potato in his pocket for his arthr-
itis got up and walked out of the funeral.
His sons slipped out of their pews as
piously as they knew how and went to find
him. He was buttoning up his fly as they
came through the big oak doors of the
church and caught the reflection of the
sunlight on his piss. He used to open the
door of a fast moving vehicle which the
driver would hysterically beg him to a stop
squeezing everything. He'd say It's time
to shake a little water off the potatoes.

20

My father lost the store, we all went to
work when I was ten. Then he became a
ward healer. My grandfather was dead before
I knew he spoke Gaelic. My father could
remember when they had mules instead of
automobiles and you had to remove your cap
and step to the curb to let the rich walk
by. My grandfather was glad to die in the
USA. He'd say if you cant find a job within
thirty miles of New York City there arent
any jobs to be found. My father would say
You can write all the poetry you want to
when youre a millionaire. Eddie would say
You got to try a shoe on before you buy it.

KATHY CALLAWAY
(1943–)

Love in the Western World

Think of family, Ulster Irish
run out on a ram's horn,
our first real move.
The same square hands
ploughing through Missouri
and Iowa and Minnesota,
where we learned to muffle
the cavities of the body,
batten the heart down
on loneliness. Still it beats
family, family, as if the pulse
of our one-to-a-body rivers
ever ran singular. And if nothing
continues—the body ending
in this fist, everything short
of the mark—what do we want?
Don't give me history. No bridges
from my heart to your heart
to all of them stringing back
like dark berries: only
open my hand, press it
for the feel of the river,
the old fishline unreeling again.

TESS GALLAGHER
(1943–)

Still Moment at Dún Laoghaire

for my sister, Stevie

You cross the ramp, its sure suspension
above the blue rope net
that means water not seen
for this nearness of ship to dock.
Now it is below you, a channel
you will think of as an ocean
where we met once and talked back
into a lost continent, childhood,
and a single house that keeps us sisters.

You were right to call it a language,
the way I will know that tree
blocking the view of the peninsula
and the bluff dropping away each year
so the house must stand with conviction
flanked by the blue spruce, the swing set
waiting for our brothers' children.

Already we are more together
for how the house looks back on us.
Through the glass your face will float away
like a ship of its own
over the boundary that knows with us
the world is steady
in another view.

Look back. There is a woman
beside me, younger, older, waving
as you are waving yet,
with your blonde hair
wound and pinned, into this distance.

Second Language

for Ciarán

Outside, the night is glowing
with earth and rain, and you
in the next room take up
your first language.
All day it has waited
like a young girl in a field.
Now she has stood up
from the straw-flattened circle
and you have taken her glance
from the hills.

The words come back.
You are with yourself again
as that child who gave up the spoon,
the bed, the horse to its colors
and uses. There is yet no hint
they would answer to anything else
and your tongue does not multiply the wrong,
the stammer calling them back
and back.

You have started the one word
again, again as though it had to be made
a letter at a time
until it mends itself into saying.
The girl is beside you as lover or mother or
the aunt who visited you with a kindly face
and the story of your mother
as a girl in a life before you.

She leads you across that field
to where the cows put down their wet lips
to the rust-dry trough.
But before you can get there
it will have changed. The water
will have two names
in and out of the ground. The song
you are singing, its familiar words and measures,
will be shadowed and bridged.

Remember the tune for the words.
Remember the cows for the field, those
in their sacred look who return
their great heads to the centuries of grass.

Out of sleep you are glad
for this rain, are steadied by my staying awake.
The trough will fill
and it will seem as though the dream
completes its far side.

To speak is to be robbed and clothed,
this language always mine
because so partly yours. Each word
has a crack in it to show the strain
of all it holds, all that leaks
away. Silent now, as when another
would think you sullen or
absent, you smoke after a meal, the sign
of food still on the plate, the two
chairs drawn away and angled again
into the room.

The rain enters, repeating its single word
until our bodies in their store-bought clothes
make a sound against us, the dangerous visit
of the flesh perfecting its fears
and celebrations, drinking us in
by the slow unspeakable syllables.

I have forced up the screen
and put out the palm of my hand past the rush
of the eaves. In the circular glow of the porch
the lighted rain is still, is falling.

Disappearances in the Guarded Sector

for Ciarán Carson

When we stop where you lived, the house
has thickened, the entry
level to the wall with bricks, as though
it could keep you out.

Again the dream has fooled you into waking
and we have walked out
past ourselves, through the windows
to be remembered in the light
of closed rooms
as a series of impositions
across the arms of a chair, that woman's face
startled out of us so it lingers
along a brick front.

You are leading me back to the burned arcade
where you said I stood with you
in your childhood last night, your childhood
which includes me now
as surely as the look of that missing face
between the rows of houses.

We have gone so far into your past
that nothing reflects us.
No sun gleams from the glassless frame
where a room burned,
though the house stayed whole. There
is your school, your church,
the place you drank cider at lunch time.
New rows of houses are going up.
Children play quietly in a stairwell.

Walking back, you tell the story
of the sniper's bullet
making two clean holes in the taxi, how
the driver ducked and drove on
like nothing happened. No pain
passed through you; it
did not even stop the car
or make you live more
carefully. Near the check point we
stop talking, you let the hands
rub your clothes
against your body. You seem to be
there, all there.

Watching, I am more apart
for the sign of dismissal they will give me,
thinking a woman would not conceal,
as I have, the perfect map
of this return where I have met
and lost you willingly
in a dead and living place.

Now when you find me next in the dream,
this boundary will move with us.
We will both come back.

(Belfast, Winter 1976)

487

The Ballad of Ballymote

We stopped at her hut
on the road to Ballymote
but she did not look up
and her head was on her knee.

What is it, we asked.
As from the dreams of the dead
her voice came up.

My father, they shot him
as he looked up from his plate
and again as he stood and again
as he fell against the stove
and like a thrush his breath
bruised the room
and was gone.

A traveller would have asked directions
but saw she would not lift her face.
What is it, he asked.

My husband sits all day in a pub
and all night and I may as well
be a widow for the way he beats me
to prove he's alive.

What is it, asked the traveller's wife,
just come up to look.

My son's lost both eyes in a fight
to keep himself a man
and there he sits behind the door
where there is no door
and he sees by the stumps
of his hands.

And have you no daughters for comfort?

Two there are and gone to nuns
and a third to the North
with a fisherman.

What are you cooking?

Cabbage and bones, she said. Cabbage
and bones.

Lie Down with the Lamb

and rise with the bird—
an old Irish saying meant to keep
the riverbank of the day: David's lambs
are grazing the lush green
of Ballindoon, green fortified
with limestone. When the man
is late a week to carry them
to market, I decide to save one.
For eighty Euro I buy her back
from the slaughter house. "*She*
is white with a black head,"
Josie writes, "and sixteen mothers
are looking after her." While
my country makes war, one lamb
is saved in the West of Ireland,
a sign to what oppresses, but a sign
of what? That we survive degrading
times through the emblematic?
The old saw of saving one saves
all? That in helplessness before
atrocities any innocence is oasis?

I drink from you, my lamb,
although I have never seen you.
But hearing they held you back,
how account for the white funnel
of joy you make on a bank of green
for no one's sake? My dusk
lies down with you a continent,
an ocean away. You are my army
of one, though your brothers and sisters
are gone to table. So are we all
bought and sold in the coin of the realm.

Lie down, my lamb, with the piteous
cries of your mothers. You are saved,
as surely as the bird will rise.
Saved and with no use
except to run free on a hillside,
peaceful and far from the horrors
of war, where sacrifice is shamed
by terms other than its own
pure gift. Lamb, I wish it were
otherwise, and my wish
is your life.
I've done the next-to-nothing I could.
As surely as that, we rise
with the bird.

KATHLEEN LYNCH
(1943–)

Hanging Family Photographs

This is the wall for ancestors
 and we will include ourselves
around the edges, though we are still
 in the world of color.
But we have been told there was rain,
 centuries of it, and so many weathers
between the first spoon of soup
 and last suck of tea between teeth
there was no choice but to believe
 in God and other gods.

Before the stones of the walls
 dissembled, before horses
came blooming smoke and riders,
 who were not part of the dream,
we were thick with dreams
 and songs and mistakes.

No one knows what will be
 asked of them. Bellies of ships
growled in the harbor.

Always when an outside thing
 rages, an inside thing sifts
information, and a voice within
 says Forget what you wish for.
Get up and go. Now.

Grasses in the new place waved
and bent without wanting us
and we went without knowing.
Everyone leaned toward the impossible.
No wonder that great dark haul
of water can never be still.

LINDA McCARRISTON
(1943–)

To Judge Faolain, Dead Long Enough: A Summons

Your Honor, when my mother stood
before you, with her routine
domestic plea, after weeks
of waiting for speech to return
to her body, with her homemade
forties hairdo, her face purple still
under pancake, her jaw off just a little,
her *holy of holies* healing,
her breast wrung, her heart
the bursting heart of someone
snagged among rocks deep
in a sharkpool—no, not "someone,"

but a woman there, snagged
with her babies, *by* them,
in one of hope's pedestrian
brutal turns—when, in the tones
of parlors overlooking the harbor,
you admonished that, for the sake
of the family, the wife
must take the husband back to her bed,
what you willed not to see before you
was a woman risen clean to the surface,
a woman who, with one arm flailing,
held up with the other her actual

burdens of flesh. When you clamped
to her leg the chain of *justice,*
you ferried us back down to *the law,*
the black ice eye, the maw, the mako
that circles the kitchen table nightly.
What did you make of the words
she told you, not to have heard her,
not to have seen her there? Almost-
forgiveable ignorance, you were not
the fist, the boot, or the blade,
but the jaded, corrective ear and eye
at the limits of her world. Now

I will you to see her as she was, to ride
your own words back into light: I call
your spirit home again, divesting you
of robe and bench, the fine white hand
and half-lit Irish eye. Tonight, put on
a body in the trailer down the road
where your father, when he can't
get it up, makes love to your mother
with a rifle. Let your name be
Eva-Mary. Let your hour of birth
be dawn. Let your life be long
and common, and your flesh endure.

October 1913

for my father, William

In the story it is Philadelphia,
two years since they fled Dromore,
the fire and oil of Presbyterian/Catholic
Ulster near Civil War, of Scottish
and Irish, whole families *turning coat,*
as they say, of Patrick, your father,
and Margaret, your mother, who was
to become a scrapper on the streets
of Lynn, fighting, fist-fighting, the men,
getting knocked to the roadside by
the bosses as she battled for her shoe-factory
union. And what she could not get with her fists
—a big woman, beautiful and vain, crazy
when she drank, often displaying her beautiful
breasts—she got by taking them home,
the men, the way women properly did
to get what they needed.

But in Philadelphia still, it was John.
He came into the kitchen, where you
were the new, fifth baby, the first since him
who was to have been the end, and crying.
It was America, and she could see from the window
a road—not *this* road or *that* road, or road
to here or road to there, but *road,*
way, path, for the first time. Her milk
was still coming in. Her breasts were swollen
and throbbing. It was your fifth day of living,
unnamed, who was to become the minder of fire
in boilers bigger than public buildings
—stories high—crisscrossed
with catwalks of waffled metal, the thick
steel faces roaring your whole shift long
like a bank of hurricanes, the gauges leaping

and trembling toward red, and in each face
a single dense glass lens where the flame stroked
and pried like a living finger. Was she drunk?
Was she raging? Or did she press you
to her shoulder where she stood at the cookstove

lifting the lids off the firebox
with the other hand? Common measures
she had carried in her heart in steerage
aboard the SS Parisian, brutal tools
accustomed to safe-keeping there. One,
two, the crosspiece between, and the whole
rectangle glowed open below you
as John your brother came in,
John the child, with already the child
lost to knowing. She was about
to solve a problem as problems had been solved
crossing back and forth in flight over
the Channel. She was about to undo you,

the way she'd undone a religion
in order to live, the way she'd undone a home
and a country, a name, and a table of faces
lined up where there was no food. Seeing him

see her, she stopped. She crushed the flames
back under the black lids. She would have
nursed you then. She would have sat down
to do it, unbuttoning the bodice on her
scalding breasts. We do not know if,
as she nursed you, she wept.

She wept.

Local

In an Irish pub, vatican
of stout and *fags,* I travel back
a family generation, to the land
of *an honest man's failing.* With such

no other island is so richly
endowed. I myself was many years
inclined to honesty but now deceive
myself perhaps and others, having come

a decade—more—ago to the crossroad
where the pure refusal of a drunk's
grave meets the compromise of walking
the crooked lane conscious.

I cannot bear to watch the man
who so delights them in a parody
of dance but watch them watch him
with smiles that shine communal and

benign, whose brother, just months past,
himself was swept—like an ill-advised
explorer in the ocean-caves below
this Fisher Street bar—away

in the gay and honest waves of drink
turned savage in the innerworld, turned
toothed and clawed in the changeless
village tide that always turns.

MAUREEN OWEN
(1943–)

She had her socks   rolled up over her pants
like an Irish brat.

                    Anonymous

Until I heard Kay Boyle say   "You know that quality the
Irish have   of being somewhere else   the mind   far
away . . . ."   I had assumed mine was   an individual   a
personal insanity   Forgetting!   to include   How
my grandmother ordered the desk   out of the house   when he
died   pronouncing it haunted   banishing it   to the
granary   under bushels of oats   year after year   the
mice nibbling the ledgers   & bills of lading   Forgetting!
the rollicking stories   bad tempers   red hair
Forgetting blue eyes & umberous   & the whiskey   holier   than
holy water
          Forgetting how I always loved the phrase

          "Three sheets to the wind!"
          O   uncommon sails
               & Aunt Nell   who was so lavender   lavender

"Can I Still Love You   & Hate the Word Husband?"

is it any wonder   when you've taken caffeine   sugar
red meat   & butter   out of your diet   you feel
something is missing . . . . or your dentist   checking
out your x-rays asks   "Is there anything that's bothering
you?"   & a terrible   silence falls . . . .   On Tuesday
a little fit arrived on a postcard saying   "Science
has ruined   all my sunsets"   as when he   hired a skywriter
to draw a   giant stem   & leaves around the sun   making it
the largest sunflower of all time!   it lasted less
than a minute   but So many people   are happy   in love
with lovers   sassy with idiosyncrasies of their children
relentless! to their daily tasks   & those
irritating harmonies!
                        as in absent-minded   Kyran dropped
the washcloth into the toilet   just as he flushed.   blueterry
in a whirling   but according to her   color scheme
my name is brown, red, gray, orange-red   green, green, gray
White, light brown, green   & gray   & I wish to mention
the trees   in this blue terry air   it's autumn   I
should have invited everyone   to give a Chinese honor
to a season   autumn viewing on the veranda   if we
had a veranda   but tea is possible   in the deepest blue
teapot   whose embossed bulges   tell us the myths   & their
names   one more time
                        Instead I woke into   the melancholy
of departure   where the wrong clock sentinels from a
balcony   or raised floor   supported by a series of pillars
some slit-wide flags blow sideways   but the train's steam
stops   in the immense pigment   & the road
could be   completely out of whack   it seems of wrong
perspective   & mistaken for a tower   with a train at the top
suggested flight   proves nothing   the train's not passing
through   & two   figures are flanked by insect shadows   they

got so small   from standing on the road to look even more so
out   of proportion   we know they have strolled   ¾'s of it
but   not to catch the train   they don't know they are so small
to know what they're doing   At least they have time to yawn
& be part   of the painter's enigma!   & I am merely crushed! by
Fall's dark beauty   whose trees are full of pterodactyls!

"It's impossible to get out of Ireland"   was what he said to
me driving home last night.

EAVAN BOLAND
(1944–)

The Emigrant Irish

Like oil lamps we put them out the back,

of our houses, of our minds. We had lights
better than, newer than and then

a time came, this time and now
we need them. Their dread, makeshift example.

They would have thrived on our necessities.
What they survived we could not even live.
By their lights now it is time to
imagine how they stood there, what they stood with,
that their possessions may become our power.

Cardboard. Iron. Their hardships parceled in them.
Patience. Fortitude. Long-suffering
in the bruise-colored dusk of the New World.

And all the old songs. And nothing to lose.

In a Bad Light

This is St. Louis. Where the rivers meet.
    The Illinois. The Mississippi. The Missouri.
The light is in its element of Autumn.
    Clear. With yellow Gingko leaves falling.
There is always a nightmare. Even in such light.

    The weather must be cold now in Dublin.
And when skies are clear, frosts come
    down on the mountains and the first
inklings of winter will be underfoot in
    the crisp iron of a fern at dawn.

I stand in a room in the Museum.
    In one glass case a plastic figure
represents a woman in a dress,
    with crepe sleeves and a satin apron.
And feet laced neatly into suede.

    She stands in a replica of a cabin
on a steamboat bound for New Orleans.
    The year is 1860. Nearly war.
A notice says no comforts were spared. The silk
    is French. The seamstresses are Irish.

I see them in the oil-lit parlours.
    I am in the gas-lit backrooms.
We make in the apron front and from
    the papery appearance and crushable
look of crepe, a sign. We are bent over

    in a bad light. We are sewing a last
sight of shore. We are sewing coffin ships.
    And the salt of exile. And our own
death in it. For history's abandonment
    we are doing this. And this. And

this is a button hole. This is a stitch.
   Fury enters them as frost follows
every arabesque and curl of a fern: this is
   the nightmare. See how you perceive it.
We sleep the sleep of exhaustion.

   We dream a woman on a steamboat
parading in sunshine in a dress we know
   we made. She laughs off rumours of war.
She turns and traps light on the skirt.
   It is, for that moment, beautiful.

Home

for Jody Allen-Randolph

   Off a side road in southern California
   is a grove of eucalyptus.
   It looks as if
   someone once came here with a handful

   of shadows not seeds and planted them.
   And they turned into trees.
   But the leaves
   have a tell-tale blueness and deepness.

   Up a slope to the left is a creek.
   Across it lies a cut-down tree trunk.
   Further back again is the faraway,
   filtered-out glitter of the Pacific.

   I went there one morning with a friend
   in mid-October
   when the monarch butterflies
   arrive from their westward migration:

thousands of them. Hundreds of thousands
collecting in a single location.

I climbed to the creek and looked up.
Every leaf was covered and ended in
a fluttering struggle.

Atmosphere. Ocean. Oxygen and dust
were altered by their purposes:
They had changed the trees to iron.
They were rust.

I looked at my watch. It was early.
But my mind was ready
for the evening
they were darkening into overhead:

Every inch and atom of daylight
was filled with their beating and flitting,
their rising and flying at the hour
when dusk falls on a coastal city

where I had my hands full of shadows.
Once. And planted them.
And they became
a suburb and a house and a doorway
entered by and open to an evening
every room was lighted to offset.

I once thought that a single word
had the power to change.
To transform.

But these had not been changed.
And I would not be changed by it again.

If I could not say the word *home.*
If I could not breathe the Irish night
air and inference of rain coming from the east,

I could at least be sure—
far below them and unmoved by movement—
of one house with its window, making

an oblong of wheat out of light.

In Exile

The German girls who came to us that winter and
the winter after and who helped my mother fuel
the iron stove and arranged our clothes in wet
thicknesses the wooden rail after tea was over,

spoke no English, understood no French. They were
sisters from a ruined city and they spoke rapidly
in their own tongue: syllables in which pain was
radical, integral; and with what sense of injury

the language angled for an unhurt kingdom—for
the rise, curve, kill and swift return to the wrist,
to the hood—I never knew. To me they were the sounds
of evening only, of the cold, of the Irish dark and

continuous with all such recurrences: the drizzle in
the lilac, the dusk always at the back door, like
the tinkers I was threatened with, the cat inching
closer to the fire with its screen of clothes, where

I am standing in the stone-flagged kitchen; there are
bleached rags, perhaps, and a pot of tea on the stove.
And I see myself, four years of age and looking up,
storing such music—guttural, hurt to the quick—

as I hear now, forty years on and far from where
I heard it first. Among these saltboxes, marshes and
the glove-tanned colors of the sugar maples, in
this New England town at the start of winter, I am

so much south of it: the soft wet, the light and
those early darks which strengthen the assassin's
hand; and hide the wound. Here, in this scalding air,
my speech will not heal. I do not want it to heal.

KATHRYN STRIPLING BYER
(1944–)

Lineage

This red hair
I braid while she
sits by the cookstove
amazes her. Where
did she get hair the color
of wildfire, she wants to know,
pulling at strands of it
tangled in boar-bristles.
I say from Sister, God knows
where she is, and before
her my grandmother you
can't remember because
she was dead by the time
you were born, though you hear
her whenever I sing,
every song handed down
from those sleepless nights
she liked to sing through
till she had no time
left for lying awake
in the darkness and talking
to none save herself.
And yet, that night
I sat at her deathbed
expecting pure silence,
she talked until dawn
when at last her voice

failed her. She thumbed out
the candle between us
and lifted her hand
to her hair as if what
blazed a lifetime might still
burn her fingers. Yes,
I keep a cinder of it
in my locket I'll show you
as soon as I'm done telling
how she brought up from
the deep of her bedclothes
that hairbrush you're holding
and whispered, "You
might as well take it."

Alma

Two dead leaves
on the table and ice

floats on milk like the ashes
of leaves. Oak
twigs kindle
and fire leaps like a prayer, "Give us

breath." When I open
the door and breathe deeply
the cold air inflames me.
The fire seizes log after log.

In the garden my husband burns
dead stalks of squash and potatoes.
I sweep my dust into the coals
and our smoke mingles over the orchard.

In autumn I sweep the floor gladly.
I gather the crumbs from the cupboard,
and the rinds of the apples.
When my dustbin grows heavy,
I give what it holds to the fire
and the fire sings its song:

raise your dead
from the earth, make a fire
of their bones,
set them free

to be sky,
to be nothing at all.

The Ballad Singers

They had no use
for such romance as clings
like the stubbornest

ivy. Those gypsy-black boots
in the stirrups,
those gay golden rings left

behind on a pillow, what good
to them, nursing their babies
and watching the gangplanks beginning

to rise on the ships named *Prosperity,*
Rainbow, Glorious
Memory? Having no say

in their journey, they came
here. They stood
on the high ridges, listening

into the ceaseless
wind sounding the bedrock
of what lay beyond them.

At nightfall they pulled shut
the doors of their cabins
and blew out their lanterns.

They waited.
What else could they do?
But when they sang

their solitude into
those old songs of love
and betrayal, each verse

must have called like a path
to them, braving the laurel
hells, rockslides

and bottomless chasms.
How else journey
into those distances

where they heard night
after night in the new world
the dark itself howl

like a woman cast into
the wilderness? One by
one, I see them open their mouths.

Here I am,
they sing,
having become their own voices.

Backwater

Over frozen weeds,
I let my shawl drag its black fringes,
hauling up spent leaves

and husks like a net
in which I've become tangled.
To wind its length all the way

round me, I cast
its warp wide as the span
of a raptor's wings.

I used to see
myself fierce as the gleam
in an unblinking eagle's eye.

Now I see only an old
woman hunched over cold
hoecake crumbs in my lap

while I take stock
of what I still know,
over which stone

my wet garments lay
and from which limb my fleece lifted
out of the dye pot dripped

indigo, rose
madder, brightest
of hickory-bark yellow.

With which bucket did
I draw up from the well's silence
water and more water?

Granny they call me.
When they think I can't hear them, hag.
The hag of Blood Mountain.

My real name?
A fiddle string snapped in the course
of a slip jig, the sound of no more left,

go home now, the fun's
over. Wind spins the leaves
round my feet like a tide

shifting. Sail away,
I used to sing, in the swim
of things. Even then

I could feel deep water
tugging my buck-and-wing
I loved to dance

on the wooden floor.
Soon it will carry
me out, past the offing

and into that yonder
sea. Blue nothing
I call it. Calling me.

JAMES CHAPSON
(1944–)

Farewell to My Protestant Cousins at Inch

Around the little grey church at Inch
warped stone slabs big as doors cover the graves
ready to open at the end of time
so "William Kerfeot who Departed this Life
May the 13th 1775 Aged 27 years"
can wake up with a new body
golden like Adam's
and toot a trumpet feeling good after his long nap:
gloomy Inch become a Paradise with robins, picnic baskets,
families playing croquet around the Tree of Life.

Now the doors only close after them as Mr. Henry
and Miss Moore enter the earth
which keeps them as a chrysalis.
My cousins in this little Protestant churchyard
nearly abandoned to the weeds
beside the big curve of a euro highway
carrying tourists to Dublin from Rosslare,
though dust and exhaust soot settle on your stones
and vandals break the church's diamond windowpanes
patient underground you are being transformed in time.

Wilton Castle, County Wexford

Blue-green dragonflies rise from the bracken;
a river winds through the demesne

where certainties of privilege and responsibility
raised noble trees and a fabulous 19th century "castle."

Only the walls remain, torched by other certainties:
liberty, equality, revenge.

On featherbed or pallet they slept soundly,
men without doubt.

Their ruined mansions haunt the countryside.
Their rebel songs echo in the pubs.

They learned nothing from the mist obscuring hedgrows,
the soft, evasive fog.

Bullocks grazing under the elms
eye nervously the tourist reconnoitering the ruins;

dragonflies—now blue, now green—
hover over the river's shifting banks.

THOMAS DILLON REDSHAW
(1944–)

Rowen

Into a snow-flecked hollow, below the dam
and sluice-gate of the Sangamon, we walked out
a December afternoon threatening more snow.
Above withered heal-all and wintergreen
that soft silence lay near in spidery limbs
of oak or maple still holding paper leaves.
Only our shoes had made this serried track
down the narrow causeway to the far channel
where the river we seek runs on, out of sight.
A sunken field lies behind, rimed with ice.

Grey stalks of St. John's wort, burdock,
reedy water parsnip lie prone and collared
in white crystal the momentary sun captures,
releases brightly, to show every stem bent
or brushed over, mowed in one last harvest,
by a secret flood silence and night loosed
and let ebb to leave scattered, like old coin
or wafers of finest silver, little fishes.
Trails and currents of them lie treasured up
where the last water gathered to sink away.

And under these thick brown cottonwoods
whose bare root and knee hold back a bank
of rich soil, we look under leaning branches,
some bridging the dark swirl of water that
clears golden sand at the low shore.
The further west we look, this stream turns

steely like our sky, then mercurial, then
blue where briefly clouds break to illuminate
teal, black duck, or mallard flying, swimming
where their two elements of water and air meet.

We alone hear them call one to another
in that distant space, not solitary at all,
unlike the tapping flicker hidden, hidden
above our heads. All fly up slowly in pairs.
Two snow geese flash their white wings last,
linked in life as by some golden thread,
invisible but there, like the sunlight
they whitely climb. Open water they circle
in free air as if to declare this present life
theirs, . . . and we only dim intruders on it.

Liús

Where an omnibus idles in lucent July, Japanese couples
come from the nuns' tearoom past postcard racks & snap,
redundantly, themselves before a blue boat beached in the rushes.

There are two Hinde sights of Kylemore Abbey—the Gothick chapel
& this lakeside pastoral, but no Polaroid can develop
the long bronzy thrash of the pike sawing the line
at an oaken oarlock &

                    plunging deep from the light.
The instinctual hunter betrays the serene Latin
of these Irish Dames of Ypres, Benedictines all,
a crucifix in each varnished room of the robber baron's castle.

But the sign foresight makes is not the chalk or charcoal
fish of the catacombs, but the real ravener—slick, toothy,
Y-boned, haunting the glacial chill of Pollacappul—
implacable & ancient, myopic, deaf to human prayer.

Yarrow Charm

Smooth yarrow
will I cut

that my figure
be sweeter,

that my lips
be warmer,

that my voice
be gladder.

May my voice be
juice of the strawberry.

May I be one island
in this sea,

one hill
in this land.

May I be a star
in the dark time,

a staff
to the weak one.

Every man
shall I wound

& no man
shall harm me.

BEN HOWARD
(1945–)

(from) The Mother Tongue

II

What is a mother tongue if not a vessel,
Impervious to rain but vulnerable
To ruin? Here in the *Gaeltacht,* smashed and scattered
Over the rocky fields of western counties,
The mother tongue resembles nothing more
Than bits and pieces of an ancient vase,
Whose sturdy clay reliably contained
The truths of saga, balladry, and song,
The cold ferocity of poets' curses,
The seacoast dirges and the *sean-nós* cries
And crazy Sweeney warbling in his tree.
And though each shard retain the history
And half-remembered grandeur of the whole,
The whole has vanished into empty air,
Condensing here and there in mound or dolmen,
In passage-graves and rings of standing stones.
But while I'm thinking of the mother tongue
I can't help adding that apostrophe
Which bears the freight and onus of possession
And makes the mother tongue a mother's tongue—
That tablespoon and weapon of destruction,
So fit for nurturing or rendering,
For feeding open minds and trusting eyes
Or ripping infant psyches, limb from limb.
All of this by way of introducing
That savage moment from my childhood

When Mother, having heard of my affection,
My childish crush on someone else's daughter,
And having heard from me the prototype
Of all my later lovesick declarations,
Retailed my story to her next-door neighbours
And spilled my innocent, untried desires
Over the coffee cups and playing cards,
The chocolate wafers and the word Canasta.
In a small corner of that living room,
Recoiling from the blow of that explosion,
I listened to the voice of an announcer
And heard in low, authoritative tones
That I could be sure if it was Westinghouse.
For a long time, I curled up on a cushion
Repeating that insinuating phrase.
But decades on, I'm sure of very little,
Except that in the passing of a moment
And the passing of my words across the table,
I learned the bitter truth of violation,
The first invasion of the private heart,
And learned against a child's deepest wish
That I could love but never trust my mother.
Walking the sandy beach at Brandon Bay,
Its warmth a solace to my calloused feet,
I call upon those waters to remove
The last contusions of that primal hurt
And speak across an arc of forty years
The words of peace and the phrases of forgiveness.

(from) The Holy Alls

The Burren, County Clare, 1950

II
No silence ever came more suddenly
Than what I happened on in mid-July,
Having bestirred myself to take a walk
Across the most intransigent of landscapes,
A coastal stretch comprised of creviced rock.
A *boulder-meadow,* someone might have called it,
Were not its contours quite the opposite
Of anything hospitable or kind
To lost sheep or ramblers like myself.
Call it, if you like, a sandless desert
In tones of gray, its western edge converging
With bands of shifting, pewter cumuli,
Its eastern border reaching out to sea.
Within the cavities between the rocks
The colonies of violet lobelia
Sent up their quiet message of survival,
As if to contradict a larger voice
Which spoke of poverty and stark extinction.
What am I doing here? I asked myself,
Feeling the bumps of stone beneath my feet
And picturing myself, if only briefly,
As a Methodist's impression of a pilgrim,
A thick-heeled parody of penitence
In search of something not unlike atonement.
I might have made a tale of that vignette,
A fantasy replete with pieties,
My infant spirit nursed on paps of stone
And succored by the silence of the place—
A silence even I, a connoisseur
Of quietude and dank monastic places,
Had never quiet experienced before.
As it happened, that unbroken silence,
So rich in resonance if poor in speech,

So redolent of absence and abstention,
Was soon to be dismantled by the advent
Of startling company. At first a scarfed
Silhouette, a set of toiling shoulders
Moving across a monochrome of stone,
Her presence soon took on its full proportions.
"A cold day," she said, as if the shawl
Wrapped securely round her coiled arms
Weren't evidence enough. Across its folds
Her black hair fell in runnels, flecked with gray.
"It is indeed," I said, and from that small
Aperture there flowed the usual
Banalities and customary phrases,
A stream of speech that widened as we walked,
Bearing in its waters bits of old
Biographies, the sticks if not the stones,
The stories that accompany a self
Over the boundaries of state and nation
And stay afloat through winding ways and decades.
From her I heard the story of a husband
Returned from war, his mind an aching muscle,
His heart a ghost. "A canister for drink,"
His well-wrought body swelled into a carcass
With which she lived, bruised but not disloyal,
But which at last she left, finding the stony
Soil of Co. Clare, where she was born,
A refuge from the dirty streets of Boston.
From me she heard the story of a wife
Gone off the rails—a noisy locomotive
Careening down a pebble-strewn embankment
And taking as its train the rumbling freight
Which her uncommon lust for acquisition
Had packed and lengthened, year by struggling year,
Its clanking boxcars bordered at the front
By her, and at the trailing end, by me.
"You were the red caboose?" my present consort
Made bold to ask. "I was indeed," I said,
"Though at the start I'd thought I was the tender."
Out of such assertions and exchanges,

Colored, to be sure, by overtones
Of self-conceit and self-exoneration,
We fashioned something wider than ourselves
And less distinct—a fluid atmosphere
Within whose ambience those well-defined
Conglomerations called identities
Mingled in a shapeless, shifting wash
Which neither she nor I could call our own.
Over the course of many stony miles,
Accompanied by gulls and crashing surf,
We clambered over knee-high fieldstone walls
And helped each other over crevices,
Talking all the while. But only hours
Later, when the temperature was falling
As surely as the sun into the water,
Did we compare our first, erroneous
Impressions. "You know," said she, "when I first heard
Your voice, I could have sworn that you were Irish."
And that, she added, was the honest truth,
Or as they say, "the holy alls of it."
I, in turn, confessed that in her speech
I'd heard the tones of an American,
Retuned, or so I'd thought, by County Clare
And tempered by the wear of Irish weather.
Was it the joint force of those disclosures
That parted us—or merely the signs of rain?
I couldn't say. But in their aftermath,
We went our ways, promising to meet
Again on some fortuitous occasion,
As though by meeting we had made the sign
Of infinity or cut a figure-eight
On water no more stable than ourselves,
On ice no less resurgent than our lives.

V

    Call it an indefinite courante,
Whose formal pattern changes by the second,
Revealing to the world and to oneself
The vagaries and checks, the graceful turns

And not-so-graceful lurchings of the spirit,
Which, had it never ventured such a caper,
Had never known itself. To that bold dance,
Which once was called the making of a soul
And now is called the finding of a self,
I pay the homage of an ardent mind.
Am I no more than that imagined man
Whom I've invented, not to spare myself
The old constraints of county, state, and country
But merely to be free of those compulsions
Which come with being what you've always been
Or think you've been—a being twice defined
By place and parentage, its image stamped
And dated? *There you go,* that coin declares
To all who have an interest in the matter.
But am I not entitled to envision
A being neither struck nor carved on stone
By accidents of lineage, place, and nation?
Call it the energy of generation,
That stirring at the center of the heart,
Where sometimes in the evenings I repair,
As eager for the heart's arcane reportage
As for the suet of the evening news.
Warming my damp feet before the fire,
I sometimes suffer glimpses of a self
Beholden not to eastern Iowa
Nor to the wild stones of County Clare
Nor even to its own unbounded nature
But wandering from spring to plain to delta,
Itself a wave in swift, unending water.
And sometimes in my reveries I'm joined
By my astute companion from the Burren,
Whose name, if I may speak it now, is Maire.
Hearing, as I often do, her stories
Of Irish hardships, dreams, and peccadilloes—
A brutal hiring fair in Monaghan,
A statue shimmering in Castleblaney,
A shady rendezvous in Lisdoonvarna—
I sometimes travel freely to those places

Of which she speaks, becoming now a farmer
And now a priest, and now an Irish lover.
From time to time, our conversation turns
To that imponderable mystery
Of who we are, or were, or might become
Were circumstance consistent with desire.
And when she asks me, as she sometimes does,
To tell her in a nutshell what I *want,*
Or what, if I could have it, I would *have,*
I find myself adopting in my speech,
As in my turn of thought, her own inflections.
The holy alls of it, I want to say,
Referring to a self I've yet to see
But have, on certain nights, intuited—
A self without the usual partitions
Dividing it from leaf and lake and stone,
As from its neighboring inhabitants
And any color other than its own.
To think of such a self, as thin as silk
And no less porous, is to entertain
A solemn mystery, though not the kind
Accompanied by thurible or cantor
Or pondered mightily from lofty pulpits.
I see it rather as a stormy day
Without the storm, the treetops undulant,
The hillsides ready for a blast of rain.
And when I think of it, it's not a sacred
Text that comes to mind, nor yet a vision
Of angels loitering around an altar
But something altogether natural—
A sky where clouds are forming and unforming
Even as they pass. And add to that
The flight of the indomitable kestrel
In search of prey, its attitude as clear
And purposeful as any sculpted form,
Its veerings no less strange for being familiar,
Its cry no less remote for being known.

J. D. McCLATCHY
(1945–)

Irish Prospects

I. *Spenser's Tower*
Kilcolman, Co. Cork

There is nothing left. The monument's a ruin
His poem was to be, its allegory broken off
Like a partizan. He sat inside this tower,
Or walked beside the Awbeg's illuminated
Page on which a sweep of sky's reversed,
And under these alders' small-branched virtues,
Putting a fantasy back together. The kingdom's
Come to nothing, too, his poem was to celebrate,
Its sovereign power a vellum-scaled garrison
Disguised as law. From this tower he looked
Down on the shawls and glibs of the vagrant poor,
Anatomies of death who made their meal
Of other corpses cut down from the English gallows.
The evill that is of itselfe evill
Will never come to any goode for us, he wrote
Before the rebels—in our sense, the underground—
Their faces slurred with dirt and long concealed
In the leafy oakblind, drove him out,
Set fire to his tower, his tour of duty,
And to his infant son, the unfinished account
Of a life spent trying to be somewhere else.

To whom do they belong now, this safehold,
The poem conceived as an empire's emblem,
The burning baby boy? Here in the field
Nobody's about. No historical marker.
Surrender or advance, I cannot tell which
The bog cotton's ragged pennants are signaling.
A mare, though, looks all at once my way,
As if to ask by what right do I threaten
The splayed, unsteady colt nuzzling her flank.
Is that how history looks, mutely accusing?
Minutes go by before she turns away and stares
At a foxglove's comb of honeyed canticles
Two bees are pouring over. There's a story
In the morning newspaper under my arm
Of two policemen shot to death in Belfast
As they sat in a patrol car reading the paper.
Why should that be called a "story"? Does whatever
We read happen to us symbolically? Or to others?
Here in the kingdom of time and place
There are no beasts and bowers, no *whilom,*
No *wights.* Here is a country of ruins,
Vine-propped facing stone pushed back to clay,
The dead eating the dead down there,
And up here, where so many paths, so many
Turnings are to be seen that all is in doubt,
The way here and back again, a stair
That rises now into the murderous air.

II. *After an Old Text*

Handfuls of brookwash and watercress, the steam
Of breath bitter on my hands. The wolves watch
Until I run again with a stag across the plain
And each night sleep in the oak's spiring crotch.
But the wind devours me whole, body and dream,
Like twigs in heaven's own fire. How explain
The wind? Even the stars are blown this way
And that, and snow on the gorse, and grief.
It leaves a man full of emptiness and beliefs,
Making a home for himself, day by day.

III. *Achill Island*

High-piled haycocks edge to the cliffs, like beehive
Huts with long views seaward, a dozen fledgling
Monks all perched there, settled in under storm cowls,
        Watching the ocean's

Prayers ascend and fall onto deafened slab rocks.
Eyebright's underfoot, and the square-sprigged self-heal.
Tufts of white sea campion fleck the cliff face,
        Shrugging off danger.

Plunging through their hesitant peaks, the breakers
Rush at seal caves, empty now, pups and cows gone
Down the coast, the echo inside a second
        Emptiness sounding

Out the quartz-gashed precipice, past which black-backed
Gulls will swoop young rabbits to drown them. Listen. Mewing
Cries—of predator now or victim?—
        Drift on the currents,

Spouts of air that curlews and petrels spiral
Up and down on, motionless concentration,
Backgrounds shifting toward the prevailing head wind.
        Awkwardly landing,

One by one they crowd in with thousands roosting
There already, tiers of old pilgrims ranged on
Inch-wide, limed, precarious ledges, waiting,
        Waiting for something

New to happen, silvering shoal or swollen
Cloud to break near land, on this island off an
Island. How the isolate soul will cling to
        Anything solid—

Seeming, sandstone, updraft, the gurge of seatides,
Faith of sorts and shelter against the rain that
Starts at last, a darkening wing they tuck their
        Heads under, wary.

G. E. MURRAY
(1945–)

Caitlin's Poem

for my daughter

> Lifting now to voices,
> shifting shapes, tendrils
> of air, you join
>
> an essay of people.
> You join, and renew again,
> old women from Dingle,
>
> Kerry, washboard America—
> your provincial mothers
> wrapped like skirts,
>
> bundled under earth,
> each fertilizing a time.
> Some begged for drink,
>
> laughter, for a kindness,
> all reciting poetics
> of kitchen, street, church.
>
> They direct you somehow,
> their ancient ways sweeping
> through new blood—

your soft, sweet edges,
your first body
wrinkled like a peach stone.

There is this haystack
of eyes, daughter,
the menace of affection

told in visits,
gravy kisses, gifts
of silver and wood block.

Kate, beware and rejoice
in the same breath,
but don't hold it too long.

Wear us like a raincoat,
my love, then shed us
in a flush of sunlight.

We'll call it love,
call it order, our hearts.
Consider mechanics,

law, a life in medicine,
the everlasting fix
of your mother's fine face.

Baby, woman—it snows.
We are ignorant
of snow, its perfect

lurking promise. No matter.
We're snow beings,
ice dolls, figures of mind,

ripe for sunstroke.
Far off, wild as lightning
and marshgrass,

you will own all your own
blind possibilities.
No brooding ever helps

sell fatherly strategies—
save little things,
like you, or a blessing

of weeds, wind that tunes
us like pianos,
a legacy of blood's wine

and vinegar. It's this,
babe: a haul of high waters,
with or without oars.

On Laying Keel

As if this wound was nearing completion,
The brawn of it, the brain of it. . . .

I would power into pine
Until I became pine-edged,
A spasm spent by moonlight,
Then I would buck and shudder
To the instructions of pine
Becoming backbone for us both.

Out on the Ways,
Working on the wombstone
Of what will be lost eventually
To ocean's thrift,
I set another trendline,
Extend appendage,
Defy what's cockeyed
To set courses straight.

All the black winter
This bitch of a wind punches holes
Up river and me.
It's the wind's participation
In process. It's my content.

I rely upon the shipbuilder's dominion
For all my cunning stunts.
I thaw as well when spring stalls,
The blood running again,
Corrosion in the air,
The sudden pulse of pine
Whipsawed and tamed, cradled alive,
So blessed, far and away,

As if this healing was never ending.

MICHAEL D. RILEY
(1945–)

Passage Graves

for Seamus Heaney

Early on he felt the fatal itch
for the right word, arched syllable and fit.

The ground of sense always giving way
he felt in boot and fingertip, and so

built on rock the rhythms and lines
of a house worth living in:

Until the sun slid beneath the windows
so often the paint blackened with shadows,

his eyes sore from failing, dumb with work.
All the while the crooked footers, skulled brick,

bent nails and weaving plywood hung on,
he hardly knew how. Except the muscles and bone,

those old ropes and scaffolds, clung
still. And still the mortar sang

as it hardened, the plaster set free
in whisperings, clods that flew

to powder and graced each window.
Then the moon rebuilt the lawn of snow,

refracting the dying hour, shaking night
from his rooms into a choir of light,

the winter solstice dawn at Newgrange,
most sacred of the ancient passage graves.

The glow, one thousand seconds saved, floods
the passages with light, redeems each rib of mud.

In the Garden

"The important thing is not to think much
but to love much and so do that which best
stirs you to love."
                    —St. Teresa of Avila

Each day the old man clipped a leaf,
held it first among its neighbors
on the tree or shrub, comparing
without judgment, picturing the whole.

Then a closer look in the sun.
Margins, leaf base, and stem.
Lobes by number and size.
Midrib to main and secondary veins.

April through October he would lose
whole afternoons above a pinoak,
red maple, bigtooth aspen,
herringboned hawthorn or sweetgum.

Slow fingerings in his darkened room,
plastic spring into autumn leather,
parsing sound, odor, texture
as he rubbed and bent them tenderly,

waxy cuticle moistening his thumb,
scent filling his fingerprints.
Then on to the radiant lights
of his worktable, hand-held lens

and microscope crowding the stage
with personality in strands
of spider web, insect egg,
drought burn, tooth mark of caterpillar

or gypsy moth, each particularity
sung now in chorus with sense
and memory, a life fallen leaf by leaf
into the garden of humility.

(for Bobbie Kevelson)

BETSY SHOLL
(1945–)

Sweeney at Prayer

" . . . he was filled with a restless tottering unquiet and with
a disgust for the places that he knew and with a desire to be
where he never was, . . . from the curse of Ronan bird-quick in craze
and madness from the battle."
　　　　　—Flann O'Brien, At Swim-Two-Birds

> Why Sweeney haunts me while I wait outside
> the ICU has something to do with wind-blown
> pigeons on the sill, the family gathered
> in one house, filling every bed, and snow
> falling for days, blustery winds, sleet on glass.
>
> Sweeney, who couldn't keep his battles
> to himself, or wait for the appointed time,
> but had to spear chuck the priest's cleric—
> till din of battle or Father Ronan's curse
> drove him to the woods in skittish fright,
>
> all stumble and thrash, lurching into liftoff,
> huffing himself up like a lumpy dove.
> Down here, the bypass surgeon tells the truth
> when he says he'll do some damage.
> Face blackened, body pierced with tubes,
>
> her monitors pulse, but no mother's there,
> she's flown off, roosting somewhere in the room,
> and no one knows how soon she'll come back,
> if she's strong enough to press against
> whatever rubs out kings and aging women,

those nettles within and without, divided
loyalties, mental unmoorings. Better
to be mad, perched in scruffy boughs, griping
about the cold or some thorny bed—Sweeney,
all groan and grief, but still in song after song

loving grouse, gull, stag cry, and every kind
of tree—except the human family's.
In her room we coo, smooth pillows,
hover helpless against this violent cure.
Did they operate with bats and chains?

She's broken enough, impossible to lure
back from her woods. Rub forehead or hand,
and her lids flutter, but off she flits,
refusing to land, as if baited by Sweeney,
leap after leap, till they're so far out

on a limb, it buckles and chucks them
to the ground, giving what reason didn't.
Reason, with its monitors and tubes.
There are prayers it's a terror to say,
it's snow hurl, wind bite, ice dam on roof,

plaster and sky howling down, as if you
had begged: make my mistakes worse,
prayers you say bent over with your face
in your hands, feeling the cheekbones, knuckles
and knees you will one day become,

lice-ridden prayers, nothing to do with
what you wanted, with *sorry* or *please*—
they clabber the mouth with nettles,
with longing and muck, hurling you
heart-sore and hoarse into the flimsiest trees.

Two Worlds

I
Good fortune when a dream speaks—
as when after years of poverty, Rabbi Eizik,
son of Yekel, of Krakow, dreams a voice
tells him to look for treasure in Prague

under a bridge leading to the king's palace.
Three nights, the same, so off he sets.
But there are guards, and he dare not dig.
Better fortune when two dreamers meet

on a real bridge, water running beneath them,
reflecting turrets, steeples, domes, roofs made
of thatch: two worlds, one above, one below,
one solid, one fluid. Eizik paces for a week

until the captain finally asks, what or who
he is looking for, and when the Rabbi explains,
the captain laughs, *Ha! To please a dream,*
you wear out your shoes. If I had faith

in dreams, I'd have to go to Krakow
and dig under the stove in the room of a Jew—
Eizik, son of Yekel! A duck squawks,
a fish leaps in the river, a hay wagon

rumbles by, wooden wheels on the cobbled bridge.
Eizik bows, he thanks the laughing captain,
hurries home and with what he finds
under his own stove, builds a house of prayer.

So, there is something you cannot find
anywhere in the world, the rabbis
who tell this story like to add, *and yet*
there is a place where you can find it.

II

Good fortune when a dream speaks, two dreamers
or two startled madmen meet, when Sweeney,
that bird-jumpy Irish king, wild with flight,
hears moaning in the trees, and it's Alan,

poor fellow, who loved his chief so much,
when a battle was planned he ran through the realm
demanding no one show up unless dressed
in fine silk . . . Of course, the other king arrives

with burlap banners, men in mended wool, rags
on their feet, three thousand strong, while Alan's
beloved sire stands alone. *What traitor,*
the chief cries, *has done this to me?* As if shot,

Alan teeters, takes off, jumping at every twig
snap, partridge flush, himself the traitor chasing
himself, or waiting in thickets to pounce,
himself the monster looking up from pools.

And the point of such stories? Isn't it
always simple until applied to ourselves,
our own two worlds—*something you cannot find,
and yet there is a place* . . . Even Alan,

arrives at that place where what the day gives—
bird cry or berries—is enough. No more
groaning through woods, he sings from tree to tree
with Sweeney, and when his end comes—

it's a waterfall's dense spray, small slippery
rocks, wind so strong it knocks him over
the edge of that wild unraveling
into the pure silk of ruffles and cuffs below.

The Past

I love hanging out laundry, bright linens,
billowy tables of air, and how when the pins slip,
wind like a mad lover tumbles a sheet
up gusty ladders, over treetops and roofs.

Birds flitting from branch to branch,
bright leaves, smoke from the neighbor's roof—
everything rises. Why should smoke hesitate
on the chimney's edge? Why should it

stiffen and fear sheet-fall, dog-snap, rag-rot,
the fire roaring below? In the book of Acts
our mother read to us, there's a chapter
where if you circled the words *rise, stand, get up*

those whisper-thin pages would be full of eyes.
And if those words did what they said, there'd be holes
to see through, like stepping into brightness,
the sidewalk glittering outside of church,

or getting our cards back when Sunday is over,
the game my sisters and I loved to play,
its object to cheat and get caught, accuse
and roar with laughter. I like to think

there are rules in the Bible like that, God
shuffles the deck with great leaping arcs, deals in
the one standing on the edge sucking her lip.
Maybe we get aces slipped off the bottom,

and the game shifts so fast, everything's wild,
loser takes all. What was our mother thinking
when she put away those cards, took our matches
and pennies, called everything she didn't want us to be,

common? In her Bible with its dog-eared pages,
isn't it hustlers and cheats who fall on their knees?
I used to pray for another childhood, and here it is,
my son's, here's the dog I never had, a sweet one,

we name *Stray* for the way she came to us,
loping out of nowhere, worm-ridden, mangy,
tearing sheets off the line, and every time my son
calls her in from the fields, we can almost hear

God calling the used, the thrown out, the scolded,
a child with her head down, hands twisted
around a wad of blue dress, who ought
to just hush now, who ought to be ashamed

for the way she slammed into those wet sheets
with her dirty hands, whooping it up, pretending
they were walls she could pass through—
but that is the past now, now she has to let go.

TERENCE WINCH
(1945–)

A Short History of 20th-Century Irish Music in America

The Flanagan Brothers prospered, picking out tune after tune
in the bright light of New York, back when everyone could dance
the Stack of Barley and sing "the Old Bog Road" at the same time.
They strode into the Yorkville Casino, where their money
was no good. They took out their instruments, chose a key
(probably D), and tore into a paradise of jigs and reels.

The Clancy Brothers and Tommy Makem played no reels.
They dwelt within the universe of song, where no mere tune
held sway. Decked out in tuxedos, they lived on stage, the key
to the city in their pockets, sin in their hearts, the dance
of love in their beds. Ed Sullivan controlled all the money
till they made him give some up: "C'mon, Ed, it's time."

Where were the McNultys by then, but shrouded in the mists of time,
Pete and Ma dead, Eileen in exile, Rockaway just an old newsreel
in her memory, the glory days long over, applause gone, the money
spent, Ma's old accordions in a closet somewhere, no more tunes
from them. Pete living on in the hearts of the people—O, to see him dance
once more, his mother on the box, Eileen warbling slightly out of key!

Others took the stage. Mickey and Ruthie, each of them a key
contributor, reconstituted the cosmos in three-four time,
so that every Bingo hall in New York every weekend held a dance,
and it was the waltzes versus the foxtrots versus the reels,
and anybody in the parish who could remotely carry a tune
sang "Danny Boy," and the Monsignor left last with all the money.

You could sense the pace quicken by then, antennae out for the big money
the music could make. The Dubliners, the Chieftains, stuck the key
in and unlocked the loot, and suddenly at every turn the great tunes
took root—fiddles, flutes, accordions blazing, bodhrans marking time
in smoke-filled pubs, drunken pipers copulating with a set of reels
in the after-hours street, while feet entreated feet: let's dance!

Who can say what happened next? We are in Circuit City and "Riverdance"
is playing on seventy-five monitors, and the cold smell of money
is in the air. The ghost of the great sean-nos master Joe Heaney reels
around in confusion. Fat record-label moguls sport scary key
board size smiles. We hear spooky New Age confections every time
we turn around, hoping always to catch someone cantering out a real tune.

So we rant and rave about money and decline, berating everything,
    fumbling for the car key
when the dance is done, the century nearly at an end, our fragile sense of
    time
bolloxed up and reeling, when suddenly we hear—listen!—some distant,
    lovely tune.

Shadow Grammar

If there were a road to the horizon,
if the surface of the water were a staircase
to the rising sun, if I could stand in
the breeze and balance two feathers
on a saxophone, then I would come into the dark
bedroom and lie down with you. We would sing
together and fall asleep and have nightmares
about real estate agents.

Let me tell you about the farm houses
of my past. They stood upon a hill
overlooking a slum. Everyday more
animals were born and we gave them names:
Jocopone, Oswald, Florence, Leo. Good
animal names. We loved it there.
We were happy.

But we had to sell, because the market
grew ominous, and move away. We traveled
to this spot to watch the smokestacks
along the shoreline. There is a war
going on between fundamentalists
and drug lords. I hate it, but still
I lie on the beach and sleep with barbarians,
who are everywhere here. There is no escape.
My glass is empty. The clocks stopped
ticking long ago. When I'm drunk
I look for interesting rocks along the shore.

Noise Under Glass

An old man arrived at my door with light bulbs.
I opened the door a crack
and asked what he wanted. He said he wanted
to tell me that when a man dies,
his body is placed in the middle
of the men's lavatory, with two urinals side by side.
I had never heard this before, and was happy to get
the word. I stood in the hallway with him,
hoping my friends couldn't hear him. Finally, he departed.

The old man crept through the mysterious grass
of the bush and put the coffee right here
on this table. We sat on French chairs
in the middle of the hut while the bodyguards
walked around the body sprinkling milk and murmuring
"I'll have some coffee too, I'll have some coffee too."
Nobody said anything about the funeral.

I am restless, now that the old man is gone.
My entourage yeses me to death.
I am bored. As the soul of my mother was taken
into that greater territory of the self, I lay
on the bed watching "Entertainment Tonight"
with the sound off, trying to remember
something, anything, about her.

CHRISTOPHER JANE CORKERY
(1946–)

The Annunciation

The angel of the Lord came unto me
carrying a dove with curious, blinking eyes.
The angel said to me in an accent I had heard
This is the spirit of the word. And then,
You are the one who shall bear it.
The words hung there, like inedible fruit,
while the angel stiffly cleared his throat.
Yet I rejoiced greatly, not knowing why,
but sensing that my pleasure,
once caught inside this room,
was suddenly boundless and that it let me see
beyond the dust in the fly-thick road
and the cankered chickens pecking at the door,
beyond my neighbor Isa whose sobs cut the air,
beyond the web of Father's swollen hands.
I am chosen? I asked again, as if I could be sure.
And the angel pointed. *See the dove? It stays.*
And indeed it had found a little perch
in the deepest slit of our one white wall.
You are blessed among women, a mellow tone now,
and all will rejoice when you bear your fruit.
The angel paused here and began to smile
and amazed, I understood, exactly, what was meant,
as if another voice were speaking inside me.
So I took the tally board that Father made for market
and the pot of nettle liquor, pulling out the cork.
Then I plucked and cleaned a quill from that quiet bird.
The angel seemed disturbed.
I began to write.

Magdalen's Song

I am a portal. Men pass through.
No one gives me blessing.
Uncle was first, when I was twelve.
The black bees kept on humming.

When I gave Jesus food and drink
I did not say my name.
Simon would tell him later, I knew.
By then I would be gone.

I only wanted to bring him the figs,
two fat ones, just at their peak.
And a pitcher of water from Levi's well,
where only the holy walk.

I did it, and ran away through the crowd.
Simon's shouts filled the air.
But what are a fisherman's taunts to me,
or the fat little taxman's jeer?

I am a lintel, flower-hung.
Nobody knows but me.
I understand how his life ends.
Leaves. Then wind. A tree.

Water

We cannot be as water always.
Cannot fall graceful
over treacherous rocks
continuous to the pool below,
always heading home, always
having arrived there, no space
between the changes and the self.

I want to ask the child who tunnels
up from your dim past:
your eyes, how did you come by them
that trace the lineaments of love
in the remotest longing?
Your ears that hear the sound
of footfall far away
intimating oh what is it
coming soon to round the corners of your blood?
Your hands that tell me what the child could not,
how did you find them in that deafmute's country?

We cannot be as water always
but only on occasion,
the graceless hands turned up,
revealing grace, the tongue
one mute, released,
and yielding for a moment
what the heart had always felt.

ED COX
(1946–1992)

The Other Side

From sleep, the much-desired nap,
undershirt wet, I return, slowly move.
The blanket forms a body from the dream,
heard a muddled voice across the wide,
turbulent river and I asked, repeatedly,
for what was said from the beginning
to the man beside who could not hear.

My grandmother dreamed she witnessed
her mother ascend the clouded Cork sky.
She ran, sought to touch the dress hem
and saw herself in the white lace gown.
Her large arms were smooth, almost clear
of needle marks, patches of bruises.
Bedridden, she spoke of heaven's journey,
day and night visions. "I was twelve,"
my mother said, "the day my older sister
found her turned toward the open window."

As she stood on deck, hands at the rail,
my grandmother watched her father shake
his fist from the pier and loudly damn her
for leaving Ireland to work as a maid
for the British, earn passage to America.
Obedient, she vowed, as he bellowed anger,
to obey his command to never again return.

The ship steamed from port, the wake wide
in the morning fog. Grandmother covered
her face, stared to the obscured shore:
O Ireland, Ireland.

DENNIS FINNELL
(1946–)

The Irish Wilderness

Tonight I sit up with Ursa Major, telling him the story
Of the cultured pearl of our loneliness.

The eighteen-wheelers in this rest stop idle like dozing animals,
The kind that sleep, eyes wide, standing up in the pasture,
And each trucker, coiled up asleep in his cab,
Is the genii of his truck, dead tired.

The sky wants my head, of course,
In its maw, between a pair of twinkling canines.

Who, after all, understands desire's tongue
O sibilants and fricatives, much less speaks it, if not
The one standing in her distant grotto of common sea shells,
Feeding a sparrow in her outstretched palm?

The one whose skin I love chafing against mine, whose soul
Is the blue-headed flame of a pilot light,
Has looked at me, more than once, the way a small cloud will,
And said, "Explain that one more time."

Long ago one Father Hogan on his mule into these Ozarks
Led a clan of Irish families, homesteaders
Pulling on their handcarts the Old World's carcasses
Of children and seed potatoes into the New World.

Now locals call it the Irish Wilderness, that plateau
Of limestone and scrub oak and freshwater springs mumbling insanely,
And today in broad daylight I hiked into it,
The chert gravel under my boots, coerced to speak,
Reciting its few choice consonants, and I repeat them for you two,
Great Bear who will eat me, woman with her tongue in my mouth:

One morning they disappeared, just like that,
Like a bowl of water in August, a plate of millet for sparrows,
They disappeared without trace, without logic,
The sustenance of the wilderness, an enactment of faith,

And today in broad daylight I hiked into it,
As I rounded a stand of scrub oak and their knotted gargoyles,
And I nearly disturbed the flock of vultures
Forming a black rose around a dead thing,

And you who house your tongue in my mouth
Don't see the beautiful wound.

Tongue. *The End of the World Is Roadless.* Exile

The Danube has a mouth. Out of it the tongues
    Of Europe pour in a polyglot stream,
And the Friendly Sea is the continent's black thesaurus.
    Near the mouth I live in a noun,
Exile, with stick walls for consonants,
    My own mouth open round as a vowel.
I have a name, and in Rome my old friends excuse
    Themselves, bringing it up in public.
A new coin says in Latin and with the Emperor's
    Face, it's year xxxvii of Augustus.
To get to the end of the world I could not march
    On a stone road radiating from Rome,

Worn smooth by the Legions. To get to this town
    Called Tomis (named after a man
Butchered here by his wife) I paced Rome's un-
    Forgettable streets weeks on the ship's deck,
On legs I ended up naming *taedium* and *terror.*
    I kept my back to home, to avoid my wife's
Face on the sea's wake. I offered her my back.
    And from the wooden Nereid of a bowsprit
I looked into the three Seas and vomited
    To their accompaniment, even into
The *pax* of the Bosporus and the friendly Black Sea,
    Even my ration of Rome's hard bread
Exiled. The end is one large mouth and a score
    Of smaller ones, none speaking the mother
Tongue. The end of the world is roadless. *Exile*
    Means I hold my face and walk around
Inside the stockade, displaying it like
    A baby held up at eye level—
Look, my face is wailing, it is innocent.
    Nevertheless, the minutes parade by
Like Legions, and the natives treat me like a dog
    They know, seeing it gnaw itself,
And let be. *Exile* means the red-haired
    Girl I have put lips on me and breathe
As I sit on the riverbank, I call *Erato,*
    After the muse. *Inspire me now,*
Beauty, betrayer. It means my ears thirst
    For Latin, that the native tongue is dice
And the clack of dice, that with my own tongue
    Nowhere, every unheard word of Latin
Is an ideal world—a stillborn Atlantis.
    Out here, I am Rome.
I wear the skins of animals just like
    A native and run helter-skelter inside
The stockade, dodging the barbarians' poisoned arrows—
    Taedium, terror, taedium, terror . . .
What I do with my stick walls and open
    Mouth is write epistles in verse,

Tristia, and send each year a book
     Of these "Sorrows" to Rome. What I do is
What the red-haired girl does, posing
     As letters of the alphabet. Her mouth
Opens for *O.* Legs spread for *V.* I grow erect for *I* . . .
     Most air is liberated as it expires
At my mouth, and it walks off, sometimes limping.
     It will walk up to the sky and say
Nothing. The air going into *Tristia* for Rome
     Wears a long white toga. It lies
Face down at the feet of the First Citizen Augustus.
     This air says everything. It says,
I was wrong. Forgive me my dirty
     Book about love. Please at least ship
Me where our tongue is spoken, where
     An ear exists for my mouth. My real
Crime was to imagine love. My real sentence
     Is to imagine Rome here by the
Danube's mouth. Out here, I am Rome.
     My alphabet turns its head, gazing
Back at me, a vowel in a bearskin. Inside some
     Sticks I push a bowl of ink
Nearer a candle. The stockade is an *O* around
     Me, an *O* on a page of the steppe.
My friend in Rome wears my likeness in gold
     On his finger, my friend holds it to his ear—
Believe Pythagoras. The soul follows the body,
     Haunts its place of rest. I am
The steppe and the river delta, I am the Friendly Sea.
     The months melted away like sherbets.

The Cloud of Unknowing

Took off on time, and over the Gold Coast
saw Lake Michigan evaporating
in veils of fog, and the fog similarly
ascending into clouds. We're in the clouds

now, United Flight 406, and a large man is consumed
by reciprocal trade, —"Our soybeans,
their labor!" Isn't electricity
running inside others, this animal fear

alternating with awe? We are flying
inside mother-of-pearl clouds, and our iced drinks
do not tremble. Big Jim is laughing
open-mouthed, silent to what we hope

are a comedian's words inside his headphones.
Somewhere someone must be spinning a prayer wheel,
and we fly on into a cloud, a stately
pleasure dome. "What keeps us here?" the Khan asks.

Lake Michigan flashes sunlight from its face,
and a long ore boat pulls the widening
V of its wake, floating on nothing
but water, and all of the words for water.

VICKI HEARNE
(1946 – 2001)

Soliloquy of the Irish Poet

My singing moves the wind, the seeking of swift horses
Does not thrill the earth so, I wear the six
Colors in my coat. The seventh, for king's death,
Encumbers all but me. The drumming of wild hooves,
The fright of all who have been spared by the great
Mild mercy of horses, the flimsy call of flat birds
Against the summer thunder, the thunder itself,
And earthquakes, the earth trembling to knowledge
As the huge harps tremble to the light fingers
Of girls, the invocations of priests like sweet oil
Scenting the stones of churches, and the great bells'
Reverberations are but flax for my linen and forms
For my flight. I wear the six colors, the last,
Scarlet for the king's death, is hid in cunning
Threads inside the seams, binding him, freeing me.

The American Dream

for Jim Weaver

It happens in the daytime, requires
Magnificent vistas that argue
A careful focus near to but not

Exactly on the point where beauty
Does her famous acrobatic flip,
Flinging terror loose. And whether "frightened"

Means betrayed by picturesque cages
Built flimsily by workmen who knew
Better, or by the ordinary

Mechanics of seeing, matters less
Than the technologies we invent,
Trying for love, standing on a rock

And speaking to the rock, or praying
For entry, praying for horses that
Break it, open poems, word for word,

From which we get a view of the sea.
It is our rock, built by our full hearts.
The rock is all we have to stand on.

Listen to the song it fails to sing.

JOAN HOULIHAN
(1946–)

Somnambulist

Arose from bed as if incompletely burned.
Only unsteady, not a golem.
Not much of a talker, either.
Just mumbled through a cloth.

It must have been bred in the blood,
this hypnogogy, as much family
as my pouch of paltry things, my scruples.
Coming early from a last compassion

as soon as I had a mind to make
I'd go stand on high places: the altar's ledge,
the head of a saint. Not safe, a fanatic
without faith, a voice going through me:

Give me your winged and injured;
all the expiring breeds. I was so charmed
by the damaged. So difficult to reach.
Whatever it was that struck me came from beneath.

Waked by wind, sea talk

Waked by wind, sea-talk, the sound of the hurt horse walking,
us kept to the lying and lower, wound into a cover,

knees tucked up. As it shrilled on the cliff, clacked
on the rocks, stopped at ours door then passed—

us crept to the wind-holes, spied through cracks and eye to the dark
saw the bent-down walk, the way it stopped at a farther hut,

lifted its head and went in.

Morning, that hut, smoke-dead, no sound, had a quiet spread out
from the wind-holes and us knew to leave it alone.

Only the sen would enter and speak for what were took:
food-holes emptied, clothing tore, ours kindred stamped and killed.

Carried heavy and swaying, holding fast to arms and legs,
us hove ours dead over the cliff, down to where it lived.

Shaked later in sleep by wind crying up and sea as it fought
on the rocks, us lay awake in dark, could not turn or talk.

PATRICIA MONAGHAN
(1946–)

What the Wind Said

There was nothing but bog and sky.
Shallow lakes, and scrub grass,
and the gray distant mountains.

And rock. Bones of the bog,
jutting from the thin blanket
of grass and shining water.

I stood on one of those rocks,
staring into the blue sky.
Clouds formed and reformed.

On the open bog, the wind
was fierce and cold. I stood
open and cold, in the wind.

After a time, the wind spoke.
It spoke the way the wind speaks.
And for once, I understood.

I spoke back to the wind.
I breathed the wind. I sang
the wind. I became the wind.

The bog stirred, shaking its
grassy head, and the sky stirred,
tossing its cloudy head, and

I was nothing now except
the wind, and it was I who
stirred the clouds and grass,

it was I who sang that wordless
song, it was I who pushed
against the gray mountains

and tore them slowly down,
and it was I who carried the bee
fertilizing the gorse and heather,

and even now, I know the wind
lives in me, and this is its song,
but sung this time with words.

Kevin Barry Gave His Young Life

In the grandmother's front closet,
packed away among the winter coats,

was a picture of him, hanging from
the gallows tree, somewhere in Ireland,

sometime in the past, during one
of the revolutions they sang about

at the picnics and parties. Kevin
Barry gave his young life for the cause

of liberty, and wasn't his execution
at Tuam, near Grandpa's Mayo home,

or was that Roddy McCorley, who went
to die on the bridge that day, not Kevin

hanging there like another martyr
for the cause in the front closet. Grandpa

knew all the songs, and the uncles did
too, and they drank to old Ireland and

to Father Murphy from old Kilcormick
who spurred up the rocks with a warning

cry, and Kelly the Boy from Killane, and
Dauntless Red Hugh, and Connaught and

Gallowglasses thronged from the mountain
passes and quietly, so quietly, Kevin Barry

hung there in the front closet, just
exactly the size of a standing child,

a child who might open the closet
to get a winter coat and see—his eyes

bulging, his head skewed painfully
to the side—how painful rebellion

was, how hopeless, how useless,
while in the kitchen the uncles

sang rebel liturgies, sang and drank
in the long evenings, and nobody

ever knew the way the children
pushed each other into the closet

yelling, Kevin Barry, Kevin Barry,
while the trapped child screamed.

MICHAEL RYAN
(1946–)

The Pure Loneliness

Late at night, when you're so lonely,
your shoulders curl toward the center of your body,
you call no one and you don't call out.

This is dignity. This is the pure loneliness
that made Christ think he was God.
This is why lunatics smile at their thoughts.

Even the best moment, as you slip
half-a-foot deep into someone you like,
sinks through the loneliness in it
to the loneliness that's not.

If you believe in Christ hanging on the cross,
his arms spread as if to embrace
the Father he calls who is somewhere else,

you still might hear your own voice
at your next great embrace, thinking
loneliness in another can't be touched,

like Christ's voice at death answering Himself.

The Past

It shows up one summer in a greatcoat,
storms through the house confiscating,
says it must be paid and quickly,
says it must take everything.

Your children stare into their cornflakes,
your wife whispers only once to stop it,
because she loves you and she sees it
darken the room suddenly like a stain.

What did you do to deserve it,
ruining breakfast on a balmy day?
Kiss your loved ones. Night is coming.
There was no life without it anyway.

God Hunger

When the innumerable accidents of birth—
parentage, hometown, all the rest—
no longer anchor this fiction of the self
and its incessant *I me mine,*

then words won't be like nerves in a stump
crackling with messages that end up nowhere,
and I'll put on the wind like a gown of light linen
and go be a king in a field of weeds.

Switchblade

Most of the past is lost,
and I'm glad mine has vanished
into blackness or space or whatever nowhere
what we feel and do goes,
but there were a few cool Sunday afternoons
when my father wasn't sick with hangover
and the air in the house wasn't foul with anger
and the best china had been cleared after the week's best meal
so he could place on the table his violins
to polish with their special cloth and oil.
Three violins he'd arrange
side by side in their velvet-lined cases
with enough room between for the lids to lie open.
They looked like children in coffins,
three infant sisters whose hearts had stopped for no reason,
but after he rubbed up their scrolls and waists
along the lines of the grain to the highest sheen,
they took on the knowing postures of women in silk gowns
in magazine ads for new cars and ocean voyages,
and, as if a violin were a car in storage
that needed a spin around the block every so often,
for fifteen minutes he'd play each one—
though not until each horsehair bow was precisely tightened,
and coated with rosin, and we had undergone an eon of tuning.
When he played, no one was allowed to speak to him.
He seemed to see something drastic across the room
or feel it through his handkerchief padding the chin board.
So we'd hop in front of him waving or making pig noses
the way kids do to guards at Buckingham Palace,
and after he had finished playing and had returned to himself,
he'd softly curse the idiocy of his children
beneath my mother's voice yelling to him from the kitchen
That was beautiful, Paul, play it again.

He never did, and I always hoped he wouldn't,
because the whole time I was waiting for his switchblade
to appear, and the new stories he'd tell me
for the scar thin as a seam
up the white underside of his forearm,
for the chunks of proud flesh on his back and belly,
scarlet souvenirs of East St. Louis dance halls in the Twenties,
cornered in men's rooms, ganged in blind alleys,
always slashing out alone with this knife.
First the violins had to be snug again
inside their black cases
for who knew how many more months or years or lifetimes;
then he had to pretend to have forgotten
why I was sitting there wide-eyed across from him
long after my sister and brother had gone off with friends.
Every time, as if only an afterthought,
he'd sneak into his pocket and ease the switchblade
onto the bare table between us,
its thumb-button jutting from the pearl-and-silver plating
like the eye of some sleek prehistoric fish.
I must have known it wouldn't come to life
and slither toward me by itself,
but when he'd finally nod to me to take it
its touch was still warm with his body heat
and I could feel the blade inside aching
to flash open with the terrible click
that sounds now like just a *tsk* of disappointment,
it has become so sweet and quiet.

A Version of Happiness

for Ellen Bryant Voigt

Tonight the band's Nigerian—
Afro-Cuban, last week; next week, Cajun:
the summer multicultural concert series
in the San Juan Capistrano library courtyard;
two hundred of us, all ages, in the audience;
Edenic evening air and stars: tickets six bucks.
You'd love this music, this place:
the musicians are like poets (they have day jobs)
and they're *good:* they play this music
because they love it, love making it,
love being able to make it—together
(unlike poets?). The sound
each is part of and takes part in
feeds through their collective body
into the next chord and phrase—
into fingers, lips, lungs, even elbows
in the case of the maniac-god on the congas
when guitars and horns cease
and lead singers politely step aside
that we may witness his five-minute solo
and feel, as they do, the triumph of prowess
over human clumsiness, and notice
who's drumming us into this happy trance.
Now they give us this chance: to notice.
They eye us like parents watching children
unwrap gifts. He sweats not only for us
but for what against all reason he can do
with whapping palms and shuttling elbows
that engender exponentially beyond his allotted
two of each, because how can one man do this?
Ancient our amazement and this power
that has caused sane men to run point-blank into fusillades
or shuttle themselves, their wives, and their postmarital

566

extra twenty pounds behind a column of the courtyard portico
to dance beside an eleven-year-old and her mom.
All evening these two have been a joy to notice:
the girl goofing with her dancing, freckled, gangly,
her mom I imagine still her best friend
before the teenage hormonal tsunami sweeps her away
like a beach shack. Mom's late-thirtyish,
bespectacled, frumpy, doing dorky disco moves (like me)
she probably learned riding *her* tsunami
in front of a mirror to Bee Gees songs
with an inconsolable crush on John Travolta
and no clue that happiness might come
someday from a parental talent for pleasure
in what a child can do. I know
your father thought your playing piano for the choir
in Baptist churches in rural Virginia
the pinnacle of achievement.
He love music but couldn't play it,
so he wanted you to, and you did.
How extreme a child's love is. I guess
we'll do anything to make our parents love us
even if they can't. The ones who can
though . . . —ludicrous of me
to try to put in words what it does to be loved
like that, but it's still visible
in you, my dear friend. This frumpy mom
shows it, too, as does her girl
despite trials, heartbreaks, and disasters
she may have already and certainly will suffer.
Nobody gets out alive, except in spirit
(the lucky ones), which as you know
can grow through music that couldn't be more
bodily, but translates beautifully.

God

Maybe you're a verb, or some
lost part of speech
that would let us talk sense
instead of monkey-screech

when we try to explain you
to our loved ones and ourselves
when we most need to.
Who knows why someone dies

in the thick of happiness,
his true love finally found,
the world showering success
as if the world were only a cloud

that floated in a dream
above a perfect day?
Are you also dreaming our words?
Give us something to say.

(for D. B.)

MAURA STANTON
(1946 –)

Elegy for Snow

My grandmother dreamed
of horses with red flanks
moving in a cloud through the village.
The riders changed into swans,
she said, & beat turbulent
over her young girl's head—
It meant travel, snow.
                                She emigrated.
My own dreams are blind, without
prophecy . . .
Sometimes she floats across them,
staring furiously with the oiled
irresponsible eyes of the dead.
I once rode the Rock Island Line
north at Christmas, watching
snow vanish ghostlike into dark.
My face rose on the window
in white fragments, disfigured with breath
freezing across the glass.
I was really a snowmaiden
melting down to strange rock
even then, kissing my grandmother
who dripped at the heart, her snowflakes
packed, designless . . .
Sometimes I light candles
for the old Irish who fiercely
outlive their bodies, insisting

on a resurrection in the hot
mouths of their children's children.
All I want is her dream, though—
those red horses signaling
movement over a continent, home
through the Illinois snow
to an imprisoned memory, not her,
by myself, myself, myself.

The Tidal Wave

Today the window pane is starred with ice.
The map of Ireland glitters in the frost
And from my bed I watch the sun dissolve
The little flakes I call the western coast.
I walked there as a boy, my life a dream,
Ungraspable as clouds, a mystery
I thought I'd pass into as I grew up
Like a boat on course gliding into fog.
One day I sailed out to America
In darned socks, and my father's mended suit.
My arm ached in the socket as I waved
Goodbye to every disappearing face.
Now my past is a cloud, faint and shapeless—
The packed-in feathers of my old pillow
Are all I feel beneath my heavy head.
My birthdate's carved into polished granite
Next to the name and death date of my wife.

A caretaker will give my son a map
To find our graves if he forgets the place.
A mower, taking off his sweaty shirt,
May cool his back against the grey headstone,
May read my name aloud, and speculate
About the man from Ireland buried here

So far from home, in view of skyscrapers.
And what will be the difference to me?
When I was ten I loved a neighbor girl.
We used to climb a hillside where sheep grazed,
Sit on a stone wall, and stare at the sea,
Talking shyly. She used to bite her nails,
Or comb the tangles out of her black hair.
Sometimes we shut our eyes against the wind.
Our lives were equal then. We'd both grow up.

That spring her family drove to Castlebar.
The blackest storm old men had ever known
Rose from the sea when they were almost home.
The horse could hardly step. The baby cried.
I used to dream of what I never saw,
The mother with her shawl, the little girl
Grabbing her father's arm as the horse reared.
It was too dark to see the wave curl up
And cross the beach, the low dunes, and the road,
To smash them like an iron battering-ram.
Deep-sea fish writhed in the farmers' fields
Next day, but no one found the cart or horse.
The whole family had been dragged to sea.

For years I walked the beach, wondering
If she might wash ashore. I was afraid
Of dark seaweed floating under the surf.
Then I forgot, and sailed above her grave,
Thinking about New York, jobs, and money.
She was a tale I told, an old story.
She has no monument, no name in stone.
She's undistinguished, nothing more than foam.
But who am I? My life has vanished, too.
My son will choose one of my baggy suits
To bury my corpse in, give the rest away.
A granddaughter may someday speak of me,
Then comes oblivion. I'll melt like ice.
Already on the sunny windowpane
My map of Ireland has begun to run
In speeding droplets down the empty glass.

Ode to Berryman

"Fame is the spur . . ."
   —Milton

  I opened your book today, John Berryman,
And gasped to see you, a "majestic shade,"
Towering over my desk in this cramped room
As if it were your tomb
And you'd returned to make me feel afraid
That I'd forgotten all the poems you made.
When I was twenty-two I watched you loom
Above a hundred students in the lecture hall.
We fidgeted in January gloom

  As you balanced there, back against the wall,
Wishing we'd disappear. Who could take notes
About the valiant poets
Of the Renaissance, when ink froze in pens?
Swaddled in coats and hats, our noses red,
We puffed our steamy breath into our scarves,
Half-numb from bus rides, or stalled-out cars.
You stared, I think, in horror,
Exiled, like Ovid, where barbarians roared.

  That's when you grasped the heavy podium
And leaned against it with your trembling weight,
Making it rattle. Then nodding your head
Involuntarily like a puppet,
You rattled it some more and started humming,
Involved in your debate
With inner voices that wanted you dead.
We sat there cowering in our bolted chairs,
Afraid of your unmanageable despair.
For five minutes you wobbled before us
And when you stopped there was a gaping hush.
At last you cleared your throat,
And like an ordinary teacher assigned days,
Said who to read, and what to know by rote.

  Because I longed to be a poet, too,

I sidled up to you once after class.
You twitched around so I could smell the booze
Flaming on your breath, removed your glasses,
And scrutinized me while I stammered out:
"I'm reading your poems, Mr. Berryman."
"Good for you, dear. Louise Bogan
Rejected me at *The New Yorker* again.
Do you know why?" I shook my head in doubt
As you pulled out her letter.
"John," you mimicked, "You're not getting better."
You laughed, your forehead clenching up with pain.
"This century sickens me. So am I worse?
Does Vietnam require sublime verse?"

    Two years later at an Iowa party,
You smiled to hear me flatter your ego,
And stroked your veined hand across my knee
In front of your wife, who stared straight ahead
As she perched, shoulders clenched, by the piano,
Her back to the shut keys, her face red.
I knew your value then as a celebrity
Though your strange, anguished lyrics meant little
As I wrote alone in winter, the tea kettle
Boiling dry to silence while I thought
Of my own words and images, and wrought
Poems out of nothing. When I heard you'd jumped
Off that bridge into the Mississippi
One cold January, my throat lumped:
I knew the attraction of the frozen waves,
Had felt that stomach-thrilling vertigo
As I brushed against the rail in flying snow
On my way to a detested job that began
At nightfall when the prairie wind saves
And hardens the grey slush.
Then I dismissed you, raving old man
With your theatrical failure and sour lust.

    Today, restless in middle-age,
I paced my empty house, then glimpsed my face
Reflected in a saucepan and felt caged
Inside my wrinkling body's narrow space.

So I was stunned to open this old book
Your *Dream Songs,* and see you yearn and flash
Out of the meter and fast, talky rhyme
Just like some fabulous crook
Imprisoned for life, who wished his pals in crime
Could find the loot he stashed.
   "Action in the midst of thought," you wrote
Picking up two chairs, then tossing them down
Before the undergraduates you hoped
Might somehow preserve your personality
In scribbled diaries
As you played the role of sage or desperate clown.
Our blank looks must have troubled your pose
As you strove for fame even in awkward prose
Written by students with pale memories.
And so I conjure you, John Berryman—
Stand again on that stage
Laboring to vindicate your poems
Through gesture and rage,
And force the world to hear your mortal howl
Though you are far beyond your fading groans
And have become your old friend, Mr. Bones.

Croagh Patrick

"This holy ground
No place for litter"

I watched him pour his tea
into his saucer to cool
as he talked about the curse
on our family for drowning a landlord

in the lough behind Toureen,
and the Big Storm of 1881
that had drowned his own grandparents
on the Ballinrobe road.

He kept his gun and holster
next to the Infant of Prague
on the dresser. Once he pinned
his silver badge on my collar

and I danced around the kitchen
while he sang about Finnegan
sitting up in his coffin,
and praised the rose of Tralee.

He said he'd climbed Croagh Patrick
barefoot, his feet bleeding
to get a plenary indulgence
and cancel years in Purgatory

before he sailed to America.
He'd named my father Patrick—
my father, nostalgic for Ireland
all his life in the Midwest,

too busy raising nine children
to come here until he was sick,
his heart too weak to climb
this hill. So I'm doing it

for him. Panting, I turn
but Clew Bay's vanished in mist.
Below me a few hikers
toil up the steep scree

in slickers, nylon hoods,
but no one's barefoot, or kneeling
humbly on the windy summit,
pelted by gusts of sleet,

and my own hands, cold claws,
do not fold in prayer
though father and grandfather
clutched rosaries in their coffins;

but as I dig in my pocket
for my last piece of chocolate,
a tissue goes flying off.
A believer in holy ground,

I scramble after it,
startling mountain sheep
who run on thin black legs
down the same pilgrim track

my grandfather hobbled up
that far off day, his sins
absolved, his offspring
charged inside him like ions

inside a sudden, violent cloud.
Here's thunder, here's lightning,
here's me on the mountain
like a strike from his brain.

SUSAN WOOD
(1946–)

Geography

Summer afternoon, Henry James said,
the most beautiful words in the language.
It's what I think of when I think of summer afternoons

in California when the fog
swaggers in like a man with something
to hide. Sometimes he stays the night, sometimes

he's gone by dusk, the guilty lover who takes
his hands from a woman's face just in time
to get home for supper, though he's forgotten

the telltale signs, that he's left behind
a scarf, a glove, wisps of himself
for her to remember. Climbing a foggy hill

I thought the lover must be Japanese
he'd left such elegant drawings—a bridge,
the long hair of willows, a garden of black ink

traced on a lavender sky. He might have been
a lover I had once, a continent away. Each day
he'd face the red persimmon of the rising sun and dream

of home, though he went on making music
in his head. Each night he played a Chopin nocturne,
the passage where the music wavers like a face

mirrored in water and the composer sees,
just for a moment, his own death.
Think of Henry James in the Orient! That's how wrong

it felt to be apart from everything
he loved. It's what I feel sometimes when I think
of hills, who grew up in flat country.

I've been told, and believe, we carry inside us
a past we've never seen. I've never been
to Ireland, but sometimes, summer afternoons,

a girl stands on a hill above the harbor at Galway,
the emerald grass kissing the dewy hem of her skirt.
It is the nineteenth century and far away

she sees sailors loading crates of barley
on a ship. Here everyone is starving. Soon
she'll be going to America. A little in love

with her own recklessness, she imagines herself
on the deck, at night, in fog, a few possessions—
the rosary her mother gave her, a black-haired boy's

tortoiseshell comb—stuffed in her pockets,
wisps of themselves for her to remember,
everything before her facing home.

KEVIN BOWEN
(1947–)

Inchemekinna

I never asked how it was that when the Hunger came
they all went to the island;
or how they could survive on that small slip
of broken rock and green,
only a quarter mile across, a half mile long.
Never a good place to land a boat;
no sure footing.
Southwest, looking to the Arans, the single high point,
no more than twenty feet above the tide.
A few low, sloping trees.
But all around the island's waist
the kelps' rocky harvest, the razor necks,
shells rising up like white, speckled hands
to draw the gulls and birds
whose leavings made the beds deep and safe,
sent the flowers crawling up in terraces
the whole eastern side of the island.
The houses abandoned now,
chimneys crushed,
five, counting the one I stand in.
The shadow of its fires still black
against the back room wall,
the room where Bríd, the last to die here, was waked,
long lines of men and women
sailing in from Gorumna, Lettermore, and Spiddal,
wet scarves dripping up the path all afternoon.

A Granite Stairway: St. Joseph's School for Boys

So many lives pressed into stone.
No vacant moments but always the praying,
praying for the right words to come.
For forgiveness. Always, the Nine am
rush of cassocks along the rails,
boys off to mass and funerals.
Afternoons, air raid drills,
cold dark walls against legs,
dreaming the flash of the bomb,
the heavy tomb like quiet,
a litany of names called into darkness:
Jackman, Kussy, Macaroni,
Bedugnis, Fitzgibbon, Pienisuski,
Salvator Bordinaro.
Boys whose fathers
worked at the post office,
bakery, track, the shoe store.
Boys down on their knees
praying for the war not to come,
for Russia's conversion.
Boys stepping off into a grey mist
to lead the procession each spring,
listening one more time
to the story of a girl in France,
and three children in Portugal,
who'd seen the Virgin;
and of one who carried a message to the Pope
who had yet to reveal its secret.

Sailing to Thai Binh

Who would have thought so much cold
this far south? Early morning, we drive
Route Five, the great wide mouth
of the Red River opening out before us.
Dark brown fields hang in the mist,
stretch to the vanishing point.
The farmers who work them have bent
their thin bodies already for hours to earth.
They wear red bandannas around their necks,
bundle for warmth in the rhythm
of flood and mud and rain,
planting the last winter rice.
Three centuries since men and women
cut out a road from here to drag
a new bell for Keo Pagoda.
They laboured so hard to set it
gently in the wooden tower
high above the lily pond,
last carved their names in bronze, then turned,
foot by foot to cover the road over again.
Thirty nine stones in the temple well,
each one knocked hollow hammering
grain to feed the workers.
From here the French hung bodies
as warnings by the side of the road,
lifted whole villages to the mountains.
From here, Bui Vien picked up his small bundle,
walked the long road south,
sailed a year around the world,
to step into Tyler's office,
beg him to send the French away.
From here a boy crossed from a buffalo's back,
looked down at his fields from the moon.

MICHAEL CASEY
(1947–)

A Bummer

We were going single file
Through his rice paddies
And the farmer
Started hitting the lead track
With a rake
He wouldn't stop
The TC went to talk to him
And the farmer
Tried to hit him too
So the tracks went sideways
Side by side
Through the guy's fields
Instead of single file
Hard On, Proud Mary
Bummer, Wallace, Rosemary's Baby
The Rutgers Road Runner
And
Go Get Em—Done Got Em
Went side by side
Through the fields
   If you have a farm in Vietnam
And a house in hell
Sell the farm
And go home

Learning

I like learning useless things
Like Latin
I really enjoyed Latin
Caesar and the Gallic Wars
Enjoyed his fighting
The Helvetians and Germans
And Gauls
I enjoyed Vietnamese too
The language
Its five intonations
Its no conjugations
A good language to learn
Vietnam is divided in
Three parts too
It makes me wonder
Who will write their book

GERALDINE CONNOLLY
(1947–)

Our Mother Tongue

My aunts held it behind their lips,
and would spit out the flames
at each other when they needed
to keep secrets from the children.
And my grandmother had it but kept it
hidden. She was the quiet one,
of great sadness. Language slept
inside her like a sleeping map
of the old country until it was
passed to my mother whose pen
skittered over creamy sheets
like a tall ship carrying messages
over the ocean to those who were left
in the cities of straw and cathedrals.
The trumpet notes travelled
the thin air in blizzards
of sons and daughters forgetting
even their names in the sharp winds
of Pittsburgh and Chicago, the words
melting as they touched
the hard ground of a new land.

Procession of All Souls

Gnarled and blessed
be the hour of autumn when
spotted pears sink
into wet sod, and blessed be
the songs of virgins rising
into hunchbacked trees.

November dawn.
Down damp stone stairs
we followed the priest,
past leaf-choked wells
and jagged trees,
past a red rage of dogwood
ringing a black lake.

Dies Irae, he intoned,
Dies Illae, day of wrath.
We followed his swinging
censer, trail of smoke:
schoolgirls in gray, novices
in white veils, nuns in ragged black
tapping tortoise canes.

What joy to bear the fear,
smell orbs of incense
perfuming the rot of leaves,
to cross the stubbled field
as crows rushed and whirled,

pecking at windfall seeds.
We arrived, rainsoaked, awed
to watch young nun-brides
kneel, and spread their thin bodies
across green doors of graves.

JOHN MALONEY
(1947–)

Steady Dreamers

Almost everywhere they are silent, even
their eyes do not tell. If you joke, they
laugh; turn, they wait, for they have learned
not to compete with feeling. They choose

to love—they know you will not believe
them. This resistance calms them, they bring
what they can, remember everything
they once revered. They do not teach you.

They do not take you places. They do not want
your money or your good looks. They are not
afraid. Not afraid of being alone, they are
not afraid of being wrong, they are not afraid

that it's not worth it. They just continue living
in your expanding universe. They listen,
they hear you object to ambiguities, discredit
the ridiculous. They watch your face fade

in the room like innocence, but they are not
fooled. They deny nothing, admit nothing.
They are walking the back streets, lifting
belief from ruined worlds, taking the odds.

Lace Stone Walls

for Mitchell Posin

Mud and clay caked
in cold crevices of
their scraped hands—

Two bending men placing
a stone in the hollow
of two stones, one rock

on two rocks the length
of the wall—there's strength
in movement. Lace wall

or farmer's, they leveled
with the land, building wide
as stone to stone allowed;

lace walls for hilltops,
leaving uneven spaces,
holes for the wind—

No art, just the ordinary
lifting up of what's
deepest, stiles to climb—

Chattered slate of sky
through a loose knit
of weathered stone.

MAUREEN SEATON
(1947–)

Vows of Chastity and Indulgence

When I was born my mother said she had prayed so long I must be a
   miracle.
There was only one way to go with a reputation like that—very bad
   or very good.

I chose good and admired the quiet Mary who sat at Jesus' feet and
   drank him in,
content to be there with her hair on his arches, oil dripping down his
   toes.

Jesus was the only boyfriend I ever wanted. I could be the Virgin Mary
   one day, Mary
Magdalen the next—but most of the time I preferred to be his girl, not
   his mom.

Thus I chose bad to round myself out and relate to humans, radical
   notoriety and
fluent glossolalia at the same time so I could see who was right: Galileo
   or the Pope.

Now here I am clumped in a circle of roses red, white, and bittersweet.
   All the girls
melting and cohesive, our flames tonguing the walls, banked on universal
   principles.

Come all ye faith-filled, goals pre-empted and useless as menstrual blood.
Some think this is the better way, some say we better stop now and get
   saved.

Forty-four maidens in a boat and one big mother. Pop!—a leak of sea-
   water sprouting
beneath five acres, across the tops of trees. Some women welcome the
   same

diversions as men yet need to stay put, we can't help it, we require faith-
   fulness.
Now I'm surrounded by Christian memorabilia, some of it pink, some
   purple—

Lenten grief and circumstance. A man puts on his special clothes, swal-
   lows the bones
of Christ, the eighty-proof claret, lifts the wafer up and brings down
   blood and fruit.

There is turbulence in the room, hypervigilance. Never mind the show-off
   in the corner,
the wracking cough—proceed to any holy place, the sweet marrow
   of your own amen.

There is nothing here to mourn, you pretty, the ocean flows over your
   right lobe,
everything you expected flows in: succulence, salt, the dark raw deep.

Saved

The great grandmother who blossomed
at the foot of our meals like a huge mushroom,
who had offspring all over the east and always
near the sea as if she'd been thinking *home,*
as if great grandfather had pursued her
with a hunger so radical, catholic,
it couldn't be contained in one civilized city—

Newport News, Chester, P.A., Elizabethport—
that great grandmother never budged
from the foot of the dining room table
even after the head of all those dead baby boys
died himself and left her to raise Baptista,
the Sister of Charity who taught
two-thousand kids in the same classroom;
Mary, the great listless aunt in her upstairs
bed over thirty years; and Frances
who married Franklin and mothered Frank
in a deliberate design to appropriate
his first-born girl. Time is tricky,
like the Irish. It flips into one child's
life-view stolen from family archives
while everyone else, cousins, aunts,
all those inter-marriages, all those
folks go about their own lives making soup,
selling books, horticulturing—all those
lumps removed from the same small inherited
breasts. And still some of the children
are *born again* in special Christian schools
where Catholics are unsaved afterall. Time
does all that and then distorts and magnifies
and wrestles with reality—the cousins
successful, monied; the siblings
not talking to each other. My great grandmother
loved Parlay Bars and mashed potatoes.
She gave me Frances who, widowed,
drank four quarts of warm beer every night,
smoked half a pack of Viceroy Kings
in bed while reading the news and listening
to the dreams of a granddaughter religious
with the sins of possibility.

After Sinéad O'Connor Appears on Saturday Night Live, the Pope

for Janet Bloch

The night we baptize the sidewalk outside Our Lady of Sorrows
across from Nelson's Funeral Home where the Neo-Futurists
spray-paint *Too Much Light Makes the Baby Go Blind,*

the only soul in sight is a woman with black eyes and bruises
staining her chin like grape juice. Perplexed, she leans
above a small figure stenciled on pavement and frowns.

Barb and Van and I are moving away from the church like clouds
up Clark toward Thybony Paints, which I always call "Thy bony,"
and we're stunned to hear her voice behind us say: "What's that?"

That is our simple rendering of a fifteenth-century criminal—
incantatrix, fascinatrix, malefica, sortilega, the one
who gathers herbs, charms, boxes of gooey sacred ointments.

When an old woman begins to doat and grow chargeable to a Parish,
she is generally turned into . . . a stick-rider, poisoner,
magus, hag, kasaph, evil eye, screech owl, night monster.

When a young woman goes *surfing* on a river in Essex, *to and fro,*
on a board standing firm bolt upright, turning and winding it
which way she pleases . . . , she is a strix, curandera, hocus-pocus.

When she heals a cold, braids her hair, unbraids it, breathes, dis-
respects a pope, has freckles, pockmarks, insect bites, cysts,
she's charged, raped, starved, robbed, beaten, drowned, burned.

"It's a woman," I say as our interloper gets close enough to touch.
The neighborhood looks so bloodless on a Wednesday night, its
citizens washed in TV, snug in bungalows and two-flats—

a ma-and-pa world, hard-working-hard-playing-fear-of-the-Lord
on a turquoise lake in the middle of turkey foot grass
and cornfields. Redeemed. Three witches embracing a fourth.

R. T. SMITH
(1947–)

Waterford

County Cavan

Lifted down from the guest parlor's
shelf, Mrs. Lane's pitcher is
light and ice, a gleam

of cut facets
that makes me tremble. Not
the leafy Lismore

pattern, nor Aisling's lotus frond,
it is the simpler Clare,
upswept wheat recalling

the artisan's blown stalk, its bell
of stillness. All
Irish, stressed from fluted rim

to medallion base and sharp
at every edge, it
centers the collection—Maeve

decanter to the reed-seeming
vase of Kildare—as if
to whisper, *Forget famine,*

assassination, Derry saracens,
and the dole: beauty harbors
here. While my hostess fetches tea

from the kitchen, I study
the flawless polish with immigrant
glee and give it

all my reverence for skill
and a pilgrim's mixed envy,
till I hear the kettle's

whistle and the hall
clock gongs four. Almost calm
but finding I have nicked my

finger on one corner,
I long still, here on the northern
border, for the wintry

clarity of this Irish
vessel, fragile and dazzling
in my trespassing hands.

Leabai

Ravenstones, I'd call them,
but the Celtic tongue says
leabai means these slab beds
above the graves. Was it
Saint Breachain whose lair
this was, Ne Seacht Teampall,
the Seven Churches, where now
the black birds perch on
penitential stones? Inis
Mor's north knuckle holds
them, and I climbed over hare
terraces and stiles to reach

this place by twilight,
to touch the high crosses
and lie on pocked limestone,
to ask for secrets the clover
keeps, answers deep in bone
and crozier, a red-letter
Gospel gone to dust. I want
the fallen walls and lintel
to teach me solitude's
ceremony, a foxed prophecy
to coax a wayward soul home.
I want cairn kin and moss
wraiths from the holy well
to shake and parch me, and when
I have been wrung to a dry
seed, the clapstone inside
a sea bell, I want some
god's boundless love
to swallow my sins
and wind to find me
on a saint's ravenstone
and pick me clean.

Passage to Kilronin

On the morning boat from Rossveal
I listened to the outboard's knock
behind our dory creaking like coffinwood
and tugged my borrowed slicker snug
as a monk's storm cowl. As sea chop
and the odors of oil and salmon stunned
me, the boatman offered a flask
of brandy, saying it was a big day

for the Irish, World Cup soccer match,
the Republic against the North, but
a boy off one of the local trawlers had
been missing since dawn. I was dazzled
by sun flashing off the bow cleat
and every wavelet. I was out to study
vowels and isolation, the Gaelic
nouns not even Cromwell's henchmen
nor TV could root out. I was riding
the swell and luster to the ruins
of a language, walls and hedges
honeycombing the limestone in obsolete
syntax, but the sea's pitch and wind
said grief is the only dialect that
endures. I breathed shallow and
chatted about penalties and corner
kicks as the Arans rose like loaves
in the distance. Then we struck a zone
so calm we were spellbound to silence.
On the shore where water was unsinging
itself in the old tongue the boy's
soft body waited, wedged fast amid
the still and eloquent island stones.

Road Fever

Before I was born the evicted
Irish walked this road,
with no notion where to aim
their anger. What was left

of their households bruised
their shoulders. What remained
was a broken gate and the reek
of spoiled potatoes.

They boiled tack leather.
They sipped rain from ivy.
Beyond a ditch where the weary
sought shelter, in pennyroyal

and weeds I discover
the memorial cut to a boundary
stone: *1848/Sorrow/Our Mother.*
Typhus struck them—sister, child,

farmer—lice-borne, or carried
by touch. The word in Greek
means *mist* like the brothy
fog bewitching the evening

air. What I have read
is this: their brows burned
and skin speckled like buckshot
as they fell. I should stop

everything to kiss the ground
that a roof in nearby Kilmurry
waits for me, that the downy
fringe of blight no longer

infests the food.
I should push my hand
wrist-deep into the healthy
earth and press my ear

to the road for its story:
they walked here, they wept,
they haunt the wind.
But the night will be soft,

and I will find a stuffed fox
in the parlor, and lavender.
A girl will bring me a dash
of whiskey against the sleet

chill. A table will be set
before me with oat farls
and berry jams as faces
from Gort or Ennis flower

in kettle steam and tenant
the starless evening air.

NATHALIE ANDERSON
(1948–)

Slow Airs

The bow burrs on the hoarse string, a husky whisper
whiskey-throated in the stillness: tune-up, warm-up,
try-out, space-out, that sweet moment's hesitation
before the melody begins. Then the bow turns
and the note thickens, heartens, tarries, swells, extends,
cautiously cranes its neck out, tinges, verges, bends.
No false start: here's the song itself, maybe even
a song you love well, "Carrickfergus" or "Salley
Gardens," but played now so lingeringly, you hear
every unfolding pocket-handkerchief of sound,
every quivering hair's-breadth stair-step of a trill,
every unexpected sweep and sprawl. The bow burrs

and the air slows, smolders, smokes up rosin-hazy,
burrs out at the flute's mouth, blues, billows, blurs. Easy
as breathing tawny autumn, the banked leaves chafing,
their little blue tongues loosening and flickering,
the fevers raised by their trembling skirling up blue,
the sky softening, night coming early. The bow
burrs on the hoarse string, the breath burrs at the flute's mouth,
the air eases, rises, slows. Between the bracelet
and the arm, between the finger and the ring, you're
putting on that air, you're easing it in and through
the weave of your skirt, the savannah of fine hairs
on your thigh. Open your lips, that air's on your tongue.

That air's on your tongue, that air's slow on your tongue, slow
in your throat, sweet and slow in your opening lungs.
Airs and graces: hold a thing that lingeringly,
it starts to turn—chaff buttering into sunlight,
the black berry of juniper slipping its skin,
still waters deepening into wine. The bow burrs
and the air slows, curtsies and meanders, tracing
within the long-held breath the quaver at the heart
of any whole note. Deep in your chest the blue tongues
are flickering, grace notes skirling up blue, husky
whispers fluttering. An air that slow can only
quicken. Play it again: even the dust will stir.

Féis

How long since you last gazed into a face
this beautiful, since a face this beautiful
opened its gaze for you? A full moon couldn't
loom any larger, rising late and low
in hazy autumn, couldn't fill any
lake or pool more full than your eye is full,
holy water rising in the holy well.

You can't follow a third of what he's saying,
his lips moving slow, then fast, then slow, tilting
his face from seduction into friendliness
and back again, the words flying fast, birds
surprised from hedges, the lashes raising
and lowering their heavy wings, the hair
a dense cloud stroking and unravelling

over the hill's brow, the shirt washed to a
pale soft heft. Behind him in the pub, two
pipers, one's lean head shaved down to a shadow,
self-absorbed, arrogantly serious;
one curly-haired, wind-blown, gregarious
and gap-toothed. This one's different, looks at you,
at you only, your search-light. Is there danger?

There's always danger. The pipers pack their
sticks and bags, the guitarists click shut the doors
of their cases, the fiddlers raise their bows
precisely together, the lights go up
without your seeing. So this is what they once
called glamour: leave him so much as a ribbon,
your world can age without you. Water rising in the well.

Country Night, County Donegal

Meanwhile, in the pub at the Foreland Heights Hotel
a weathered man in a western shirt straps himself
to a rhythm machine: giddy up, giddy up,
giddy uppity up—it's that dreadful: poky
cowpoke choking a lame colt. He spurs it, reins it,
stops and starts a dozen times before he gets it
not right, exactly, but so it suits him, one-man
swing band, tone-deaf and mush-mouthed, the words and the tune
lost in his lazy gallop, one song much the same
as any other. Oh Bob Wills, oh Patsy Cline—
        Time changes everything.

Now you've seen it, how the Irish love their country
and western—the young bucks at the bar, backs turned but
toes tapping; the older couples straining to hear
above the clink of pints, each other's bulk; elders,
women mostly, settled on the settees, widows
or spinsters out for the night, impeccably groomed,
each with her pearls, her proper handbag, snowy hair
crisped and lofted by spray. Eight at the next table,
none of them minding what passes for the music
any more than you. Oh Bill Monroe, oh, Johnny Cash—
          Time changes everything.

Three songs in and you've had enough, you're up to go,
so it's no surprise when they rise too, six of them,
double-knits, pleats, stack heels and hose, proper ladies
headed surely for the ladies' room. Six ladies
standing up together, two guarding their bags, who
step firmly now into formal embraces—arm
circling waist, hand pressed to shoulder—and—purposeful,
sensible, comfortable, practiced, and pleased—canter
away, riding the rollicking beat, smiling their
Saturday smiles. Oh Charlie Pride, oh k d lang—
          Time changes everything.

SUSAN FIRER
(1948–)

My Mothers' Rosaries

Rosaries of night breath,
rosaries of woman smell,
rosaries of dream, spoon
rosaries blue, rosaries of yarn
knots greed rosaries, dandelion
rosaries, dough rosaries,
crystal Slovac rosaries,
baked potato rosaries, cock
hot rosaries, sunflower
yellow rosaries, phone line
rosaries, human hair
rosaries, butterfly blue
rosaries, snow rosaries,
dark cherry red burn rosaries,
say lead rosaries, flour
white first communion rosaries,
lemon rosaries, cold-cock punch
rosaries, confessional dark
water holy rosaries, sweet apple
red rosaries, concertina sweet rosaries,
before bed rosaries, wild
asparagus rosaries, smooth
wood beaded rosaries, see
all the way to heaven rosaries.
Keep me sighted rosaries,
don't let me be pregnant rosaries,
don't let anyone die rosaries,

bring him here rosaries,
keep me sane rosaries,
keep him off me rosaries,
My mothers' rosaries fill
my mouth with dark prayer names:
My name is Susan the Baptist,
daughter of Ruth Lorraine Brophy
whose mother Katherine Boussart
came from Alsace-Lorraine
with an immigrant's trunk
full of women's lost names,
and prayers, rosaries, Maypoles, and angels.

The Lives of the Saints

Wildgoose the boy dies over and over in the autumn
leaves. Each Apache death
louder and more disorganized than the previous.
His sister, my daughter, plays Mozart's
"Divertimento No. 2" in our driveway-parked car.
Behind the windshield she looks like a silent
movie star, her mouth forming silent words:
pizzicato, allegretto, arco. Her violin bent
arm and tilted chin no longer look strange
behind the dashboard where she has insisted
on practicing this summer and fall.
"A room of my own," she calls from the front seat.
Autumn's boxelder bug black and orange colors, beets'
reds. (Is there any vegetable that tastes more
like the ground it grows in than beets?)
Every season has its own taste and smell:
autumn is extreme unction. The Dairyland Twirlers
practice on the Shorewood high school football
field, their tossed and spinning batons turn to stars,

their tossed and split-legged-costumed bodies
a lovely throw of sequins on twilight. All
early evening under my not yet closed autumn
windows, people hurry walk home through
the confetti, purple-loud leaves. Soon it will be
snow shovel scrape, harps, communion white, and
salters with their orange light topped trucks
spilling blue. But sweet now is this
relic tent of leaves, lighted with all the saints:
Saint Agnes breasts in hand, Saint Antony
ringing bells and riding pigs, my son
and daughter dreaming the wild autumn children
dreams that become their bodies, become the overtures
of their holy, tumultuous, leaf blessed lives.

RICHARD KENNEY
(1948–)

The Uilleann Pipes

Connemara
"I was a boy, and didn't mind his bottle,
see, so the doctor walked with me, finger
out over the Connemara hills. *Rotten*
with tuberculosis, he'd say. *Cottages like lungs*
themselves. There was a dying woman, and her daughter
beside her, he said. The son-in-law was a drinker.
Weak as she was, she held one hand closed
taut, white as lime, so shrunk it might
have been the skull of a bird. Inside was her last
coins, kept for the daughter, see. She died
though, and the son-in-law broke open the fist.
Those infected houses are burned now, like mad
animals, destroyed. Not so many live now in the west
of Ireland. How could they live? Good God. . . ."

The British Museum
"Paleolithic man was presumed in the southern
British peninsula during interglacial times,
a half-million years before the final turning
of the ice-sheets, in the tenth millennium B.C. The primary
migrations to the north came in the Boreal climatic
phase, when the land was warming, and the great deciduous
forests beginning to spread elm, lime, and oak.
The Dover Strait had formed, and the old land bridges
closed for good. The North Sea flooded the salt-
marshes and lagoons—already crossed by small savage

groups, moving west from Denmark with a mesolithic culture
A sea-loch filled the flat land north of Stirling
and in the tidal shallows, hunters killed
sand-birds, and huge beached breathing whales. . . ."

Dublin
Room dark, a rifled souterrain, this land—
Peat blankets this land; fall heather flames
like leaking backlight from Old Ireland, the Lamp
of the West. In cigarette light I listen, refrains,
old reels, slip-jigs, and a piper's love lament:
*Do bhi bean uasal—I wish I had you in Carrig
Fergus, only for nights in Ballygrant. . . .*
The sea is dark, a lover's love growing vague
with drink, with drink—*I wish I met with a handy
boatman*—he cradles his breathing pipes like a bag
of blood, loosens airs old as moonlight,
bright as wildflowers thawing on the tongue
of a mammoth ice-kept carcass, his wild mourning
deep in this deep skin of uilleann pipes—

(from) The Invention of the Zero

West
X-rays leaking from a black hole, let's say, limn
these bones, Dear Reader: soft and stirring, embryos
blown forward through all time to come, like a sudden aria
of soap bubbles, dozens at a breath, or an hour's exposure
of the moon's eclipse: *ring, ring, ring,* lamplight
flaring on the lens—

            The sun's the real plot-
line here, of course. My role—Apollo's chariot
and all (a Chrysler), in reverse: first tincture
of the photochemical response: aurora

oriented west, once, and the world changed . . .
                                        Withershins:
begin, accelerating eastward through foreshortened
headlight, dim at ninety miles an hour, land tec-
tonic, slipping past at either side, torn chintz
in ragged folds in the middle ground, and earth-
shine silver overhead—
                        Ahead, the far shore
draws the mind on the neap outflow of frail Atlantic
tide, let's say, where stars will slip back in
again—
            Gone West we say, following the ortho-
doxy of the sun's own hemisphere,
its track and disappearance there, the stone's throw
off the California coast, where I began
this drive (as once before, some years the other
way)—and what's to come? As if the sun might misfire,
fail to rise one day! What do I know? *M* is for
mass, and *E* the awful energy that beckons
from inside it (oh, and flickers in our leaders'
eyes!) like firelight through a stone scrim . . . the speed
of light's another thing. Night now. The semaphore
of starlight winking overhead while the nearer beacon's
blacked out, blinked out, filtered through the zillion liters
of liquid stone yolk and granite mantle and broken
crust where the planet's come between—
                                        Protective disk,
the veil of film held up to each mundane, parochial
eclipse, called *night.* Imagine this: a slight bleed
of shadows through it, oil-drop through the flat statistics-
sheet this quantum world is said to be—blank keyhole,
tumblers, *tic, tic,* all space itself in pleats
and folds, and light sucked back around a flat accretion
disk such singularity attracts, all axes
bent to pretzels—what a world! Why not an X-
ray of the earth, then, pinned beside the Pleiades
at night, like so, a black hole *here,* a gauzy creche
here, where stars still reproduce their subtle lattice-
works of ones and zeros, lacing blue creation
into form—

MARY LEADER
(1948 –)

Among Things Held at Arm's Length

They planted cedars around the farmhouses in those days:
Homeplace. Cedars are fast growers, and they mass, they're thick:
Windbreak. So when a thunderstorm would rant and rave and spew,
The cedars would take it, would wrestle the thing, stop it

At the windows. The people would be lying there a yard away
In nice dry bedclothes. The dog's eyes would be open, waiting.
And in the afternoon, which is the calm, why then the cedars

Would shift a little in the breeze, and their shadows
Would move all dappley on the windows, on the white windowsills.
This is a permanent thing, seen from cradles, seen from deathbeds.

.   .   .

A woman, for example, one of whose names was Muriel, had
Her window, her branch, her bird, her hour for the watch. Free,
Because she'd draped the dish towel over the dishes to dry; free,
Because she had a cocker spaniel pup on her lap, his head silky

To stroke; free, because by then she had mostly quit talking.
That a name means matters. What the name *is* doesn't, or, varies.
Pawnee County, Oklahoma. Place shows the difference between

Anywhere, which it can be, and *arbitrary,* which it can't. A time
All people find, a joint time, a time certain, not known,
Ordinarily, in advance. A time came and a Muriel died.

.   .   .

And when she was a bride, and even a young wife, her red-haired
Husband would come in from the field his energy scarcely
Diminished and he would pick her up around the waist and whirl
Her around in the dusty yard until her stockings would cowl

The tops of her laced-up shoes. She would laugh and he would
Smile. The first child was a daughter and they named her Armand,
A girl more somber than either parent, a girl with auburn hair;

Then a boy with clay red hair, Bryce, soon nicknamed "Brick";
Then a boy with hair the color of a new penny, Joe; then Rex,
With hair the color of an old penny; finally, a dark-haired girl,

   .   .   .

Hair dark as Muriel's own, a joyous child, called Claudie Ann.
And the sodbuster's name, not to be omitted, was Arnold,
Which only Muriel ever voiced. To everyone else he was "Red."
His brother, whose real name even I don't know, was "Blue,"

On account of his coal black hair. The time came and the time
Came and the time came; the time will come and come and come
And come, for the littlest daughter, will come likewise.

With luck: a cedar branch, a wind, with luck a cardinal bird.
Hazel eyes, or blue or brown, or gray or green, the same for one
Whole lifetime. The pre-sunrise light is daily. Today

   .   .   .

I just happened to see it. I aligned my palm with the horizon.

Madrigal

How the tenor warbles in April!
He thrushes, he nightingales, O he's a lark.
He cuts the cinquefoil air into snippets
With his love's scissors in the shape of a stork.

Hear the alto's glissando, October.
She drapes blue air on her love's shoulders,
On his velvet jerkin the color of crows.
Her cape of felt & old pearls enfolds her.

How the baritone roots out in May!
His depths reach even the silence inside
The worms moving level, the worms moving up,
The pike plunging under the noisy tide.

Hear the soprano's vibrato, November,
Water surface trembles, cold in the troughs.
She transforms blowing hedges into fences,
She transforms scarlet leaves into moths.

THOMAS LYNCH
(1948–)

The Moveen Notebook

In memory of Nora Lynch
(1902–1992)

> When I first came, the old dog barked me back,
> all fang and bristle and feigned attack.
> I stood frozen in the road. The taxi man,
> counting his crisp punt notes from Shannon said,
> "Go on boy. That's your people now." I went.
> Sambo, the dog, went quiet as a bluff called.
> Curtains parted in the house across the road.
> The momentary sun gave way to rain.
> *3 February 1970—*
> the oval welcome in my first passport.
> What kind of Yank comes in the dead of winter?
> Nora stood in the doorway, figuring.
>
> My grandfather's grandfather, Patrick Lynch—
> her father's father, thus, our common man—
> was given this cottage as a wedding gift
> when he first brought Honora Curry here
> from somewhere eastern of Kilrush. Well met,
> I imagine, at a cattle mart
> or ceilidh dance or kinsman's wedding;
> and she the grandniece of Eugene O'Curry
> whose name's on the college in Carrigaholt,
> accounting, according to Nora, for
> any latter genius in the gene pool.
> "The O'Curry breed" she would always call it
> when the answer was clever, or the correct one.

As for the newlyweds, they made children:
birthed a sickly daughter and five sons here
in the first spare decade after the famines.
The names repeat themselves down generations now of
Mary Ellens, Michaels, Sinons, Dans, Pats, Toms.
And pity little: what I know of them.

Michael, the eldest boy, impregnated
one of the McMahons from across the road.
(Maybe an aunt or grandaunt of old John Joe
who was aged when I first came here. He's dead
the Lord've mercy on him, ten years now.)
But Michael and his pregnant neighbor wed
and moved beyond the range of gossip here
and prospered and were happy it is said
in spite of the shame of that beginning.
And Dan died young and Mary Ellen, swept
from the ledgerocks at Doonlicky by
a freak wave when they were picking sea grass
to green the haggards with. As for Pat, the son,
he sailed to Melbourne and was never heard from
except for the tail end of a story of how
he sang from one end of the voyage
to another. "But for Lynch, we'd all do!"
it's said was said about him, his lovely tenor.
And Sinon married Mary Cunningham
and stayed here in the land—the first freehold
after centuries of British landlords.
And after Sinon died, 'twas Nora sold
eggs and new potatoes till the debt was paid
and kept her widowed mother into her age
and thereby let her own chances grow cold
for a life of men and motherhood. She stayed.
And her brother Tommy stayed and worked the land—
and loyal if withered and spinsterly end
of the line until, as Nora said, I came.

My great-grandfather sailed for Michigan—
Tomas O'Loinsigh, Nora's Uncle Tom—
and married Ellen Ryan there and worked
as a guard at Jackson Prison, pin-striped
Studebakers and lied about his age
for the warden or the factory boss or wife.
The parish house in Clare records his baptism
in 1861. The stone in Jackson's cut
1870. Either way, he died
in 1930 of the heart attack
that killed his son and killed my father after that.
And Nora, twisting these relations round once said:
"'Twas Tom that went and Tom that would come back."

All of which might seem unnecessary now
at the end of yet another century
on the brink of a brand-new millennium
trying to set these lives and times into
Life and Time in the much larger sense:
those ineluctable modalities
that joyous man said we were given to:
how we repeat ourselves, like stars in the dark night,
and after Darwin, Freud and popes and worlds at war,
we are still our father's sons and daughters
still our mother's darling girls and boys,
aging first, then aged then ageless.
We bury our dead and then become them.

What kind comes in the dead of winter then?
The kind that keeps a record, names names
says what happened, remembers certain things,
wakes the dead, leaves a witness for them after him.

So gospel or gossip, chitchat or my party piece:
a gift for my children, if they want it, this
membrance of the visit and revisiting
the stones, the fire, and the sod from which
we came, somehow, and must return again.

That first month in Moveen was wet and cold;
a fire on the floor, an open hearth,
the turf reddening against the wind that roared
up unencumbered out of Goleen bay.
And warmed likewise against the rising damp—
that pelting daylong nightlong driven rain
that fed the puddle underneath the land.
Nora hung huge pots and kettles from the crane
and settled them into the fire coals
to boil chicken, cabbage, potatoes
or bake the soda bread or steep the tea.
Or boil water for the cow that calved,
or mare that foaled or whatever hatched
in what seemed to me endless nativity
presided over by my distant cousins:
the chaste and childless aging siblings
Tommy and Nora Lynch of Moveen West
County Clare, "on the banks of the Shannon"
my grandfather always told us—"don't forget"—
after grace was said over turkey dinners.

Tommy died in March of seventy-one.
I still can see him laid out in his bed
a rosary laced among his fingers, thumbs
curled, the purple shroud, bright coppers on his eyelids,
the Missal propped between his chest and chin
as if to keep your man from giving out
with whatever the dead know that the living don't—
a tidy West Clare corpse in readiness.
Sean Collins brought the oaken coffin in
and Sonny Carmody and J. J. McMahon
and Sergeant and Tommy Hedderman
bore him on their shoulders through the yard
and out into the road where Collins' funeral car
waited with the neighbors' cars lined up behind it.
To Carrigaholt then into the cold church
where Fr. Duffy waited with his beads
and gave poor Tommy one glorious mystery
before returning to his tea and paper work.
Next morning, Mass, then down to Pearce Fennel's
where boozy eulogists recalled the way

that Tommy would stand among his cattle
and speak to them. He called them by their names.
Or how he sang "The Boys of Kilmichael"
whenever his turn came around those nights
of talk and song and dance and old stories,
more common in the townlands years ago.
And then the slow cortege to Moyarta
beneath sufficient rain to make us quote:
"Happy is the grave the rain falls on," of course
a paltry omen in those soggy parishes.
And he was buried there among the stones,
illegible with weather, worn by wind,
his mother's bones, his brother Mikey's bones—
a tidy pile beside the grave's backfill—
together again, interred, commingled,
on the banks of the River Shannon. "Don't forget."

Thus, "don't forget" becomes the prayer we pray
against the moment of our leave-taking—
the whispered pleadings to our intimates,
the infant held, the lover after lovemaking,
the child who ages, the elder who
returns to childhood again. "Gone west"
is what the Clare folks call it when some old
client on the brink of dying sees
a long-dead mother in a daughter's eyes
or hears God's voice Himself in the free advice
some churchman mutters among final sacraments.
"Be stingy with the lord and the lord will be
stingy with you" is what Fr. Kenny said,
which was his careful way of putting forth
the theory that you get what you pay for.

So do the dead pray for remembrance as
the living do? Are these the voices that we hear
those Marchy darknesses when the whitethorn limbs
tick along the eves and window ledges?
Or the wind hums in chimneys overhead:
or whispers to us underneath the door,
old names, old stories, old bits of wisdom?

"All winter we watch the fire" Nora said.
"All summer we watch the sea." Then she would sit
for hours hunched over, elbows to knees,
warming the palms of her hands to the fire
smoking the cigarettes from the duty-free
shop in Kennedy I would always bring her.

"Whatever happened 'twas a freak wave took them,
above in Doonlicky and a grand fine day
and they were swept away, all Lynches and O'Dea's
two out of this house—a boy and a girl—
and one out of Carmody's house above—
an uncle I suppose of old Kant Lynch's.

And where was the God in that I wonder?"

Then rising up amid her wonderments
she'd look out westwards past the windowpane
past Sean Maloney's house gone derelict
in half a dozen winters of disuse
over hedgerow after hedgerow until her gaze
would fix on Newtown and P. J. Roche's lights
where the lap of land rose upwards to the sea.

"I wonder if there's anything at all.
I wonder if He hears us when we pray."

Then chilled by her inquiries she'd sit
to stir her coals and hum *Amazing Grace,*
or give out with the names she kept alive
in the cold heaven of her memory
that tallied all but ten years of the century
the rest of us kept track of by the wars
but Nora measured by the ones she'd known:
who'd lived where, who'd married whom, who died.
And after that, who was left to grieve them.
Who waited in the land, who moved away.
Who sent home dollars. Who sent home pounds.
Who sang, who danced, who played, who drank too much.
"The cross off of an ass!" is what she'd say.

Who could be trusted, who couldn't be, who lied,
and who, though dead and buried still survived
in the talk of men in public houses
or the talk of women in shops and market stalls
or the talk of neighbors at stoves or fires:
the mention of the name that keeps the name alive
and what it was they did or didn't do
to win the race or save the day or just survive—
the extraordinary moment we attribute to
them alone, irrevocably. Them only.

As, for example, how Mary Maloney,
once kicked by a cow when she was a child
would work circles well around any man,
the limp notwithstanding. Or how she smiled.
Or the way her eyes unfailingly moistened
whenever she spoke of her dead mother.
Or how her brother Sean danced like a bull—
wide eyed and red faced when the music played.
Or how Dan Gorman, the Lord have mercy,
was mad for the drink and games of chance.
Or the way Kant Lynch's blinded eye
bore through me when I told him how I had
nearly been swept off the cliff at Doonlicky
by a wave that came up from the rocks behind—
a freak wave really like the hand of God—
that knocked me flat out inches from the edge.
"Mind yourself now boy," the old man said,
"the sea's ever hungry for Lynches there."
I can still see it now, near thirty years since—
the milky cataract, the thick brow arched,
the slim red warning in his good eye's squint.

As I see Johnny Hickey with his fiddle and
Denny Tubridy and his tin-whistle and
the pink Collins sisters, Bridie and Mae,
swooning in the corner to the music made
or that song Ann and Lourda Carmody sang—
Dow-n by th-e Sal-l-y gar-dens
M-y love a-nd I did meet . . .

when they were little more than little girls
singing of true romance before their time
for their elders whose moments had come and gone:
Maloneys and Murrays, Deloughreys and Downeses,
McMahons and Carmodys, Curtins and Keanes,
Burnses and Clancys, Walshes and Lynches—
old names that fit like hand-me-downs: too loose
at times, at times too snug, sometimes all too well.
Like Theresa Murray and her sister Anne,
good neighbors who would call in on their rounds
to trade the current news, the talk in town
for Nora's ancient recollections of
the dead, the dying and the grown or gone.

And I see Nora in the years I knew her
astride her Raleigh bike enroute to town,
(One time an old dog, barking, knocked her down.
She wore the cast a week then cut it off and
holding her hand up for inspection scoffed
"That wrist is right as paint. Three weeks? I'm healed.")
or walking with me up the coast road to
fish the mackerel or take the air or
ponder the imponderable expanse—
No parish between here and America.
We'd walk back then, with fresh fish and hunger.
Or how she battled with the Land Commission
to keep her thirty-acre heritance,
when certain neighbors had put in for it.
"Grabbers," she called them. "They want it for nothing."

"A cousin in America," she wrote
"a young and able man is coming soon"
ten months before this unknown cousin showed
up—twenty-ish, unwittingly, a sign from God.
No farmer, still, I kept it in the courts
for twenty years and Nora let the land
to P. J. Roche, from Newtown, a young man
with a wife and child and a resemblance to
Tommy, the brother who had died before.
And once over pints in Mary Hickie's bar

P. J. asked me would I ever sell, if
God forbid, something should ever happen.
Take care of Nora is the thing I told him,
and I'll take care of you. The deal was cut.
So that recurring dream I'd always had
of Nora dying some night in the dark,
alone, unmissed by anyone for days,
was put to rest. P. J. and Breda kept their part
and doted over Nora like their own.
I often thought of P. J.'s evenings there—
after saving hay or dosing cattle
or maybe on the way home from the bar
he'd stop for tea, she'd put down the kettle.
He'd organize himself then go home to Breda.
And knowing how it was, I envied that—
the quiet in the room, the way the light
went golden just before it died. The tune
she seemed always on the brink of singing,
the tiny rattle of the cups and saucers dried,
the talk between a young man and a fierce old woman.

And Nora outlived the Land Commission
and most of those who'd tried to take her land.
(One was found, fell off his tractor in a ditch
and no few thought that maybe Nora's ban
was the thing that brought him to that hapless end.)
Two weeks before she died I had her will
the land outright to P. J. and his wife.
I kept the house, the haggards, and the yards,
I kept the cow-cabins, out-offices,
I kept her name in Moveen where it'd been
as far back as anyone remembered,
because I think that's what she had in mind.
And I dream you, my darling Nora, now
free of great stone vault at Moyarta
restored to the soft chair by the fire,
a kettle on, the kitten sleeping still
among the papers on the window ledge
and, maybe April, the one you never
lived to see, greening out of doors. And we

are talking in the old way, talking still,
of how the cuckoo's due here any day,
or how to count the magpies for a sign.
"A great life if you do not weaken!
And if you do . . ." you say. You turn and smile.

You approve of the hearth I had your P. J. build
of smooth gray stones drawn up from Shannonside
and how the flagstone floor was raised and thick
dampcourse put down and sand poured under it,
a window opened in the northern side,
the bathroom tiled like a French bordello
and every wall repainted *apricot*
on Mrs. Carmody's own good counsel.
You approve, likewise, of how I stir the coals
and add the sods and stare into the fire.

Is what I see there what makes me reckon
the lives we live in counterclockwise turns,
better at elegy than commencement,
better at what was done than what's to do?
To bury the dead must we first unearth them,
to see the bones still brittle in the dust,
the poor kite-work on which the poorer flesh
was hung? Is it afterwards their voices
return to us in the words of others?
In the call of blackbirds or the noise of
wind and rainfall at the window sash?
Is it in their silence that the noisome
truth is spoken, the body's hunger hushed,
as last night's reddened coals turn whitened ash?
Is not the grave's first utterance, "enough, enough"?

A Rhetoric Upon Brother Michael's
Rhetoric Upon the Window

Like you, I wonder why the face of God
is any more hidden from us than a neighbor's
beaming over the back fence with his gab
and gossip. Why all this cloak-and-dagger
ritual of blood, these scriptural intrigues,
these hocus-pocuses, hide-and-seeks
by which the blind are given leave to lead the blind.
And you, out in Arkansas with your wife
and boys and bosom friends who drop around
to keep that vigil with you that you keep
at the window, waiting for a Sign.
You say you're waiting for a bird this time?
A hummingbird, no less, its wings a-blur
with furious deity, to appear
in all its majesty and take you up
into that rapture where the light is blue
and you become a hummingbird yourself.
Whereupon you pose the Eternal Question:
what if after that there's only space
and silence, once the hummingbirds are through—
the bright vision vanished without a trace?
What if, after everything, there's only you
and your imagination of that light?
What if we find that image and likeness
gazing back at us behind the eyes
of our darling sons and daughters or the eyes
in the faces of women we sleep with
or the timely friend with time to kill enough
to listen to us while we spill our guts
about our latest heartbreak or our sins?
What if the window is for looking in—
where we abide with our personal saviors
who save us from ourselves? Are they gods enough?
The lovers and children and the heart's neighbors
who turn the words to flesh and dwell with us?

HEATHER McHUGH
(1948–)

Faith

Electric lines are ripped from trees,
the blinds and bathtubs dangle,
chalk blooms high into the air
and dozers scrounge in the exposed
rubbish of interiors.

A letter's dated half a century ago
to someone in the penitentiary.
You got to have a faith unshakeable, she wrote.

And now from morning until dusk
the workers rip and roar, they
pound and they resound until
translucent air becomes a thick
acoustic medium, breathable air a test of dust,
and one whole streetful of amazing residences,
intricate with human life, inscribed
with human history, becomes

a vacant lot. This is the nothing
someone so emphatically wanted.
I stood for hours at a nearby window
and I could see a hundred years undone;

but there remains untouched a space they never made,
the kind of space they could not fill.
There is a sky they cannot deconstruct,
a clarity that moves to its own tune.
We may not hear, the sun is deafening, our lives
a din of disregards, but don't let worldly
meanings shake your faith:
there is a moon.

Message at Sunset for Bishop Berkeley

How could nothing turn so gold?
You say my eyelid shuts the sky;
in solid dark I see stars
as perforations, loneliness
as blues, what isn't
as a heavy weight, what is
as nothing if it's not ephemeral.

But still the winter world
could turn your corneas to ice.
Let sense be made. The summer sun
will drive its splinters straight
into your brain. Let sense be made.
I'm saying vision isn't insight,
buried at last in the first
person's eye. You

should see it: the sky
is really something.

A Physics

When you get down to it, Earth
has our own great ranges
of feeling—Rocky, Smoky, Blue—
and a heart that can melt stones.

The still pools fill with sky,
as if aloof, and we have eyes
for all of this—and more, for Earth's
reminding moon. We too are ruled

by such attractions—spun and swaddled,
rocked and lent a light. We run
our clocks on wheels, our trains
on time. But all the while we want

to love each other endlessly—not only for
a hundred years, not only six feet up and down.
We want the suns and moons of silver
in ourselves, not only counted coins in a cup. The whole

idea of love was not to fall. And neither was
the whole idea of God. We put him well
above ourselves, because we meant,
in time, to measure up.

Nano-Knowledge

There, a little right
of Ursus Major, is
the Milky Way:
a man can point it out,
the biggest billionfold of all
predicaments he's in:
his planet's street address.

What gives? What looks
a stripe a hundred million
miles away from here

is where we live.

. . .

Let's keep it clear. The Northern Lights
are not the North Star. Being but
a blur, they cannot reassure us.
They keep moving—I think far
too easily. September spills

some glimmers of
the boreals to come:
they're modest pools
of horizontal haze, where later

they'll appear as foldings in the vertical,
a work of curtains, throbbing dim
or bright. (One wonders at
one's eyes.) The very sight
will angle off in glances or in shoots
of something brilliant, something
bigger than we know, its hints uncatchable
in shifts of mind . . . So there

it is again, the mind, with its
old bluster, its self-centered
question: what

is dimming, what is bright?
The spirit sinks and swells, which cannot tell
itself from any little luster.

RICHARD BRODERICK
(1949 –)

Johnny Broderick

for my great-grandfather

Tonight, the ship that brought
you here still rocks at dockside.
The gangways are crowded,
emigrants spill on board and huddle
into steerage, the hawsers moan
and twist against the breeze, and the pilot
boat prowls the end of the slip.

Just before going below, you
pause again to press your cap
down on your head and stare off
into darkness. Behind you
the lights of Cahirciveen
bank themselves against the hills;
beyond them lies everything you know.

If you could see far enough ahead,
see the hard times, your death on the docks
of Hell's Kitchen, would you turn
around and stay at home?
The whistle sounds twice.
Even in steerage, you can feel
the swell lift the ship and begin
to carry you from the harbor. It's

night on both sides of the ocean.
The wind picks up. Stars toss and roll
above the deck. And somewhere
out there I am waiting to catch
the first glimpse of your
dark hull hoving into view.

LARRY LEVIS
(1949–)

Irish Music

Now in middle age, my blood like a thief who
Got away, unslain, & the trees hung again in the grim,
Cheap embroidery of leaves, I come back to the white roads,
The intersections in their sleeves of dust,
And vines like woodwinds twisted into shapes
For playing different kinds of silence.
Just when my hearing was getting perfect, singular
As an orphan's shard of mirror, they
Change the music into something I
No longer follow.
But how like them to welcome me home this way:
The house with its doorstep finally rotted away,
And carted off for a stranger's firewood,
And yet, behind the window there,
A woman bent over a map of her childhood, but still
A real map, that shows her people's
Ireland like a bonnet for the mad on top of
Plenty of ocean.
Hunger kept those poor relations traveling until
They almost touched the sea again,
And settled.
And there have been changes, even here.
In Parlier, California,
The band in the park still plays the same song,
But with a fresher strain of hopelessness.
This, too, will pass.
That is the message, always, of its threadbare refrain,

The message, too, of what one chooses to forget
About this place: the Swedish tailgunner who,
After twenty missions in the Pacific, chopped off
His own left hand
To get back home. No one thinks of him;
Not even I believe he found another reason, maybe,
For all left hands. So memory sires
Oblivion—this settlement of sheds, & weeds,
Where the last exile which the bloodstream always sang
Comes down to a matter of a few sparrows hopping
On & off a broken rain gutter, or downspout, & behind them,
A barn set up on a hill & meant to stay there,
Ignoring the sky
With the certainty they bolted into the crossbeams—
The whole thing
Towering over the long silent
Farmer & his wife; & that still house
Where their fingers have remembered, for fifty years,
Just where to touch the bannister; & then the steps,
That, one day, led up to me. Come home,
Say the blackened, still standing chimneys, & the missing bell
Above the three-room schoolhouse—
You've inherited all there is: the ironic,
Rueful smile of a peasant who's extinct,
Who nods, understanding, too well, the traveler,
And who orders another shot of schnapps
While his wife, pregnant, angry, puts both hands
Under her chin, & waits up.

And always, I pack the car, I answer no. . . .
When my own son was next to nothing,
He, too, would wait up with us,
Awake with hands already wholly formed,
And no larger than twin question marks in the book I closed,
One day, in a meadow,
When I reached for her—above the silent town,
Above the gray, decaying smoke of the vineyards.
A stranger who saw us there might have said:
I saw two people naked on your land.

But afterward, our pulses
Already lulling & growing singular, my eyes
Closed on that hill, I saw
A playground, mothers chatting; water falling because
It was right to *be* falling, over a cliff; & the way
Time & the lights of all home towns grew still
In that tense shape of water just before it fell . . .
I watched it a long time,
And, for no reason I could name, turned away from it,
To take that frail path along a mountainside—
Then passed through alder, spruce, & stunted pine,
Stone & a cold wind,
Up to the empty summit.

Bunny Mayo in the New World

We brought the shape of the angel with us
In the shapes of women and in the shapes
of ships because we trusted only what we

Could feel by hand, beneath us and above us.
And sure some among us had seen angels,
In the blacksmith's empty fire in the street

With no one there. And sure someone felt an angel
In the shape of the mad daisy the hammer
In his hand became before he was emancipated

From his troubles and his flesh was left hanging
From limbs of trees and little gateposts
In the rain—as a lesson to us all—

The kind of thing the British made us memorize,
Generation after generation after generation
Until it was knowledge not worth the knowing.

Larry Doyle touched an angel once, he said,
In the woods, and said its back was thick,
Thick and fat and flat. And look at what

Happened to your Larry Doyle at the end,
Gone to hell in an Easter Basket with
Your permission, Mrs. Munna Mayo.

We was just two tents of flesh over bones.
Still, it was a surprise how easy it was
To leave the place on a warm spring afternoon,

And clatter over these long planks into
The ship with its hull shaped like famine itself,
Angel and woman and famine taking the same shape

And crowding one another in and out of it.
To follow the path those shapes kept
Disappearing on, I knew where that led,

I'd seen asylums grazing the sides of hills.
More of 'em around the City every day.
You see an angel in a bar in North Beach Love

You keep your cake hole shut about it.
Remember, a lie here and there is a veniality,
Forgettable and necessary as sin unless

You've become overattached to your state
of unemployment and think there's a sandwich
Under every pillow; otherwise, where it says

Experience on the application, you're better off
Letting your imagination fill in the blank.
But seeing things is another matter altogether.

Here in the Sunset it is. It's not allowed.

MICHAEL WATERS
(1949–)

The Mystery of the Caves

I don't remember the name of the story,
but the hero, a boy, was lost,
wandering a labyrinth of caverns
filling stratum by stratum with water.

I was wondering what might happen:
would he float upward toward light?
Or would he somersault forever
in an underground black river?

I couldn't stop reading the book
because I had to know the answer,
because my mother was leaving again—
the lid of the trunk thrown open,

blouses torn from their hangers,
the crazy shouting among rooms.
The boy found it impossible to see
which passage led to safety.

One yellow finger of flame
wavered on his last match.
There was a blur of perfume—
mother breaking miniature bottles,

then my father gripping her,
but too tightly, by both arms.
The boy wasn't able to breathe.
I think he wanted me to help,

but I was small, and it was late.
And my mother was sobbing now,
no longer cursing her life,
repeating my father's name

among the bright islands of skirts
circling the rim of the bed.
I can't recall the whole story,
what happened at the end . . .

Sometimes I worry that the boy
is still searching below the earth
for a thin pencil of light,
that I can almost hear him

through great volumes of water,
through centuries of stone,
crying my name among blind fish,
wanting so much to come home.

Mythology

Because no one has ever asked,
because the task is incumbent upon me,
I want to reveal the secret
gathering place of heroes:

we scaled the rough, stucco wall
of a row of one-story garages
and loitered on the tar roof,
staring down the weakening sun—

Tommy O'Brien, Glenn Marshall,
everyone's girl, Rosemarie Angelastro,
and the dumb kid, Gregory Galunas,
who let ants walk on his tongue.

We smoked butts and told no one.
Once Billy McAssey jumped
and stove the canvas top
of a cream-and-blue convertible.

At five o'clock the mothers
groaned their chorus from the curb,
each name shouted like a warning
to the worn men leaving work.

But I remained on the roof
till lights blinked on in tenements,
the smell of fish oiled the air,
and radios sent forth tiny polkas . . .

and through a tinted wing of glass
began to read the heavens,
the bright syllables of stars,
as words took shape, lyrical prose,

a whole story
filled with heroes, their great names,
their impending deaths praised
on the darkening pages of the sky.

A smart kid,
when I asked my spiritless father,
"Where do the dead go?"
I already knew the answer.

Brooklyn Waterfall

for Stephen Dunn

Water where you least expect it:
    swelling every closet,
        tumbling down stairwells,

raining through light
    fixtures onto night tables . . .
        my good aunt Beatrice,

ever forgetful, had twisted
    the faucet handle fully,
        plugging the drain

with a red rubber stopper,
    then set off to shop.
        If water can be joyous,

imagine the unfettered
    revelry: no one home,
        the glorious, porcelain

plashing from the third
    story so loud, abandoned,
        anticipatory.

By the time she piddled
    Saturday morning away,
        the water had traveled

miles—no slow, molten
    flow, but unabashed
        raveling, elemental motion.

So when my aunt looked up
        from her swollen mop,
                my father stormed back out,

the water trailing him
        to the local tavern.
                He swilled it with bourbon.

How far he managed to float away
        from his fearful, weeping family,
                or for how many hours,

I don't remember, but
        he swayed home later,
                muttered *what the hell,*

and joined the communal
        sweeping, work that keeps
                a family together, water

still seeping into the earth
        where it waits for us,
                not needing forgiveness.

Christic at the Apollo, 1962

"Even in religious fervor there is a touch of animal heat."
—Walt Whitman

Despite the grisly wounds portrayed in prints,
the ropy prongs of blood stapling His eyes
or holes like burnt half-dollars in His feet,
the purple gash a coked teenybopper's
lipsticked mouth in His side, Christ's suffering
seemed less divine than the doubling-over
pain possessing "the hardest working man."
I still don't know whose wounds were worse: Christ's brow
thumbtacked with thorns, humped crowns of feet spike-split—
or James Brown's shattered knees. It's blasphemy
to equate such ravers in their lonesome
afflictions, but when James collapsed on stage
and whispered *please please please*, I rocked with cold,
forsaken Jesus in Gethsemane
and, for the first time, grasped His agony.
Both rose, Christ in His unbleached muslin gown
to assume His rightful, heavenly throne,
James wrapped in his cape, pussy-pink satin,
to ecstatic whoops of fans in Harlem.
When resurrection tugs, I'd rather let
The Famous Flames clasp my hand to guide me
than proud Mary or angelic orders
still befuddled by unbridled passion.
Pale sisters foistered relics upon me,
charred splinter from that chatty thief's cross and
snipped thread from the shroud that xeroxed Christ's corpse,
so I can't help but fashion the future—
soul-struck pilgrims prostrate at the altar
that preserves our Godfather's three-inch heels
or, under glass, like St. Catherine's skull, *please,*
his wicked, marcelled conk, his tortured knees.

CAROLYNE WRIGHT
(1949 –)

Ancestress

(Ballsbridge, Dublin, circa 1900)

She climbs the stairs slowly,
a grand old lady, stares out
stained windows at the frozen
garden, ties edged ribbons
in the stray hairs of the day.

Not much is left of the old ways.
After the children moved out,
the secret halls and corridors
seemed to go on forever
in all directions, a forgotten maze.

The many-generationed family
had learned perfectly the art
of discreet evasion. Every time
a butler passed, a door jamb
offered itself, or a Persian drapery,

or a deep bay window. *Hide here,*
they whispered. *The others never look,*
never imagine anything foreign
creeping in. It's always afternoon
here, always prosperous and between wars,

always dust-free where the sun falls.
Alone, her life runs down, clock left
in a vacant room, her mind reshelving
each thought, librarian at closing.
Forgotten questions pay their calls

as the afternoon sinks to its knees
and light leans toward the far edge
of the fields like a child over a ledge.
"What does the blood say?" *Silence, please.*
"The breath, bird's voice?" *The trees, the trees!*

(*for my paternal grandmother, Eva Madeline Ball*)

In the Yeats Class, Summer Term

"She stood in desperate music wound . . ."

The young professor squeaks the chalk across
the blackboard. The blind girl, all her senses rapt,
punches her notebook paper with a stylus,
translating his drawl to the pointillist's *Ur*-script

of Braille. The rest of us are bored. The gray
wind from the crowded, muggy street: more real
than "Hades' bobbin-cloth unwinding from the soul"
or "shadows of birds on a sea-starved, hungry sea."

And I? I've lost my hard-won second sight
since that young married professor beat
his heart on mine. What vision will complete
the cries I stifled in his arms all night?

I gaze out the window, take automatic notes,
while mid-day breaks the songs from birds' throats.
In its own fuel, the lamp's wick drowns. I open
an ancient Chinese book, and throw three coins.

(in memory of my aunt, Eileen Wright Carey)

Clairvoyant's Reading

Unlock the Sphinx, she tells me, there's
a yellow scent for miles.
Roman sculptures cluster on the hills.
The Archer draws his crossbow
over the observatory dome.
At the field's edge, an Arab pony
paws the mustard flowers. Pyramids
glisten in blood-begotten light.

Mustard flowers at the field's edge,
centaur over the observatory dome.
Sandalpaste and turmeric, she tells me,
from the sacrifice of fire. Pyramids
glisten in blood-begotten light
where the Archer draws his crossbow.
And the woman you once were
poises at the casement, listening

for the Arab pony's neigh, a message
from the sacrifice of fire.
Where are the sculptures that crowned
the Palatine? The Bronze Age guides
who walked among us with their javelins,
their granite, anachronistic lions?
Their yellow scent clings, their blood-
begotten mustard flowers glisten.

Listen: the woman you once were
hands you keys to unfamiliar doors.
The guide to the Bronze Age leads you
to the waterline mirrored in hemlocks'
downward shadows, where the Centaur
and the Arab pony graze. Sandalpaste
and turmeric—runes on the observatory
dome, foretellings from the sacrifice of fire.

Stone lions on the steps, the Alexandrian
Library burns to the waterline, weathervanes
stop spinning. The woman poises at the casement,
hands you her keys and parasol. A mustard sun
sets over the Adriatic. Have you been reading
Plutarch's *Lives*? The Bronze Age hemlocks
wrap you in their shadows. What is behind you
is forgiven. Now go, unlock the Sphinx.

(for Julia Rowe Hooper Ball,
my great-grandmother, County Wicklow)

THEODORE DEPPE
(1950 –)

Translations from the Irish

for Cathal

> Ó Searcaigh, granted one wish by the fairy youth,
> wants nothing but one dropdead kiss from that youth,
> so help me, but how can he forget Jack Nolan
>
> who wished away Death for us all, Gortahork's own Jack Nolan
> whose uncharacteristically generous wish
> trapped Death in his fisherman's duffel, a large-hearted wish
>
> though it ended poorly, leaving the old with perpetual suffering
> and the young to put up with those everlasting sufferers.
> So Jack Nolan reluctantly released Death
>
> from the duffel, returned to the people their longed-for deaths.
> Something smaller, then, thinks Ó Searcaigh, maybe a single day
> in which everyone is happy, just one day
>
> in which each of us gets what we've most desired—
> why not unite all separated lovers in a Feast Day of Desire?
> But even this wish gives pause: mightn't we get what we want
>
> and ruin our lives, never again holding those we want?
> The fairy agrees: life can be fucked-up if the wrong prayer's satisfied.
> Better, says Ó Searcaigh, one moment when we're all satisfied,

one instant when everyone everywhere tastes
joy's full measure, sunlight on our backs or the taste
of Cloughaneely honey, oh anything, anything

that lets us know the tang of bliss, anything
that quickens gratitude. Ó Searcaigh wishes this, and it comes to pass.
For one girl, it's a twilight of thrushes near a mountain pass;

for a boy fishing near Errigal, it's his made-up song;
for his mother, picking loosestrife, it's hearing her son sing;
for one, home at last, water from the family well. At that moment

the fairy flies to Ó Searcaigh, wild with kisses. Oh, shared moment
when we all enjoy together this heaven of earthly delights—it can't last,
can it? No. No, it can't last longer than heaven ever lasts.

Midsummer's Night, Cape Clear

Eight miles out, on this island without police,
the music starts at midnight. By one you say
"Let's forget the rest of the hike and stay here."
Free pints from Clare, applauding our lack
of ambition: "The Deppes aren't going anywhere!"

It's Maggie Breen's twenty-first birthday
so twenty-one men line up to kiss her.
Fiddlers strike up a stately version
of "Margaret's Waltz" that soon turns rowdy
and set-dancers swirl and meet together

with hoots and shouts while a border collie
makes its rounds, flops down finally
by the seeing-eye dog of Cormac the fiddler.
I walk the last two hundred miles of the trip
in my mind, Mizen Head and Sheep's Head,

then Allihies by way of Bantry,
each mountainous peninsula conjured
and let go. Buying the next round I hear
Maggie's laughter rise above the hooley
after she breaks her glasses dancing.

All the songs, my love, are celebrating love.
Soon it will be the morning after the night before
and we'll hike across the heather home, spend
the year's longest day in bed. For now
let's linger in this moment, suspended

in darkness as earth swings near the sun,
listen as long as tonight's music lasts. Maggie's
standing in the doorway, pale features glowing
as she gazes at blurred stars, singing and sung
against the side of kiss number twenty-one.

MARIE HOWE
(1950–)

The Dream

I had a dream in the day:
I laid my father's body down in a narrow boat

and sent him off along the riverbank with its cattails and grasses.
And the boat—it was made of bark and wood bent when it was wet—

took him to his burial finally.
But a day or two later I realized it was my self I wanted

to lay down, hands crossed, eyes closed. . . .
Oh, the light coming up from down there,

the sweet smell of the water—and finally, the sense of being carried
by a current I could not name or change.

From Nowhere

I think the sea is a useless teacher, pitching and falling
no matter the weather, when our lives are rather lakes

unlocking in a constant and bewildering spring. Listen,
a day comes, when you say what all winter

I've been meaning to ask, and a crack booms and echoes
where ice had seemed solid, scattering ducks

and scaring us half to death. In Vermont, you dreamed
from the crown of a hill and across a ravine

you saw lights so familiar they might have been ours
shining back from the future.

And waking, you walked there, to the real place,
and when you saw only trees, came back bleak

with a foreknowledge we have both come to believe in.
But this morning, a kind day has descended, from nowhere,

and making coffee in the usual way, measuring grounds
with the wooden spoon, I remembered,

this is how things happen, cup by cup, familiar gesture
after gesture, what else can we know of safety

or of fruitfulness? We walk with mincing steps within
a thaw as slow as February, wading through currents

that surprise us with their sudden warmth. Remember,
last week you woke still whistling for a bird

that had miraculously escaped its cage, and look, today,
a swallow has come to settle behind this rented rain gutter,

gripping a twig twice his size in his beak, staggering
under its weight, so delicately, so precariously, it seems

from here, holding all he knows of hope in his mouth.

Encounter

First, the little cuts, then the bigger ones,
the biggest, the burns. This is what God did
when he wanted to love you.

She didn't expect to meet him on the stairway
no one used but she did, because she was
afraid of the elevator, the locked room.

She didn't expect him to look like that, to be
so patient, first the little ones, then
the big ones. Everything

in due time, he said, I've got all the time
in the world. She didn't imagine it would take
so long, the breaking.

He did it three times before he did it. Love?
She had imagined it differently, something
coming home to her,

an end to waiting. And she did stop, when
the big cuts came. It was all there was,
the burning, and that's what God was

everywhere at once. Someone had already
told her that, only not in his voice. He was
inside her now—

the bigger ones, then the burning—and gone,
then back again. This was eternity, when
nothing happened that wasn't

already happening. She couldn't remember.
After the burning, even the light went quiet.
She didn't think God would be so

specific, so delicate—inside her elbow, under
her arm, the back of her neck
and her knees.

It's true, she struggled at first, until after
the breaking. Then God was with her, and she
was with him.

MEKEEL McBRIDE
(1950 –)

Metaphor for the Past

The sugared, powdered bride stumps
slowly through the white mud of a baker's making.

Her ankle catches in a blue rosette
and when she finally shakes her foot loose,
she loses one oyster-colored shoe.
A curl of her shellaced hair

shakes free, so that already she resembles
a sailor's widow, watching for something
that cannot return. Hours

later she reaches the edge
of the confectioner's miracle,
but she does not mean to jump and couldn't anyway

half cemented as she is in a beautiful
quicksand of sugar and vanilla.

Below, on the holiday plateau,
she watches children spill champagne;
a golden rain of congratulations
wash over the happy crowd

as now the groom, twenty times her size
appears in white seersucker.

The crowd stands,
cut-glass crystal raised in praise
of continuity, or ritual. Shyly the groom accepts
the heavy silver knife

and moves toward the shining cake,
thinking of how he must cut evenly,

thinking only of the hunger which must
be appeased, the need to keep
the crowd of his inviting loyal, pleased;

the tiny bride on cake-heaven:
a lighthouse in a snow of roses
showing him exactly where to place
the knife's first quiet slice.

Transmigration

The lingering scripture of bleach
praised itself in each towel and sheet
while insect-starred roses
stitched the red thread of sweet
July into the collars and stiff cuffs
of our well-worn summer clothes.

Coarse rope, tied from elm to elm,
like the line of white a child
will sometimes draw for heaven,
held us all bodiless and pure
in that distant air. My mother's pastel dresses,
inhabited by wind, swayed, almost danced
as she danced in the kitchen alone

and the sleeves of my father's weekday shirts
pointed to a day moon, tree stump,
the white wheelbarrow,
as if looking were lesson enough to cure
for the slight ache at the shoulder
where the colorless V of clothespin

kept with soldierly pinches
the float and swell of drying clothes
in place. And so a day might pass, give way
to the setting sun through a backyard tree,
making a foreign lace, a frail brocade
of nightgowns, blouses, handkerchieves

and wind invaded them with such levity
that I could guess at their escape;
ghost clothes blue in the evening air
like odd birds or aliens migrating slowly
over houses, trees, a whole tribe
of cloud-grazing nomads. Then one blouse

drops, the white one my mother wore on holidays,
the one with rhinestones at the collar
and the sleeves; each replica gem
silly with star glitter, the gossip of comets.
All of this to be claimed, taken in, submitted
to the hissing oracle of the small flat iron,

then blessed away into the dark kingdoms
of wardrobe and drawer—
like souls who believe nothing
can be lost, nothing dies—waiting
in windless dark, in summer sleep
to be taken out again and worn.

(for my mother)

Strauss and the Cows of Ireland

From my room at dusk I watch
the cows in their late graze.
Great clouds of gnats hang over
them, gauzy as a bride's bouquet.
Downstairs, a radio.
Soprano's aria swells
so delicate and pure
it must be unrequited love
but just what the opera is
I can't tell from here,
though later learn: Strauss,
Der Rosenkavalier.
Cows continue to drift
the dusky pasture, luminous,
as if fed on candle-light
instead of grass. They pass
with heavy gentleness, now
and then stopping to lean toward
our windows with little regard
for human arias that reach them
though it conducts
through me a sweetness:
distant opera and the wandering
of star-tiaraed cows in darkness.

ROBERT McNAMARA
(1950 –)

Sati, Seventh Month, By the Sea

Unlike the sea, she turns
slowly on shoulder and hip, the round
and tide of her belly rising
and setting with a star's grace, a small
thing asleep on the beach, down

from the trees and sea grass, through
the hot windblown sand. Beyond
her camp, the tip
of the tide's tongue, with its
rudely burgled clams, and a huff

of feathers around the gristled
bones' nest. In the swash
a seagull grapewalks, stirring up lunch.
The sea makes
the sound she sleeps to, the intimate

indiscriminate roar against which
birds call from the trees, the *krik* and *scratch*
of a mimic jay, the sweet
clear baroquerie of a fox sparrow.
The rising sea hurls itself

indifferently, scouring what it chiselled,
receding, with its hundred hands.
Sand does not surround her
any more than
the sea, though she is jar-round

and full. Even
her book is lost in it, a sand
dollar, invested as the tide
recedes, in drying
sand. The sea's cry is like footsteps

in the bleached grass, driftwood, sea-
rounded stone, that the child hears, turning
in water toward air
like orca or porpoise not quite breaching
the tessellate mirror of the sea.

On the '7' Train

I'm in Seattle and not, if you know what I mean,
he says from his hospital bed—or is it the war—
struggling to disentangle *is* from *seems*—

Can the real be the ICU, IVs, morphine,
the blinding post-op pain? *And you, Bob, you're . . . ?*
Yes, I'm in Seattle. And I know what he means,

halfway to New York already with needing to see him.
How through a transcontinental snarl of wire
to begin to untangle *is* from *seems,*

when he's in Africa and I'm on the 7 train
with him rattling our way to the '64 World's Fair.
I'm in Seattle and not, if you know what I mean

he says. Or I say, who can say? The *I*'s a dream
uncircumferenced, its center everywhere.
Whatever the yarn of *is* and *seems*

we're in it like kittens. One voice between
reveries testing the threads, the other in nightmare—
I'm in Seattle and not, if you know what I mean—
needing a knife for the knot of *is* and *seems.*

653

MARY SWANDER
(1950–)

Lynch's Window

1

There is a son kneeling
on a stone floor,
a father standing
at the window,

a priest beside him.
This is a last confession.
There is a son
telling his story.

He stabbed the man
three times in the heart
then floated the body
out into the bay.

And now it has all
come back to this: a rope
tied from the ceiling beam,
a cloud at the window,

blocking the light,
beads of rain just
beginning to form
on the castle wall,

the son's features
a blur, his eyes closed,
as a cloth falls
over his face,

as his father draws
him close against
his chest, the priest's
hands opening in a final

blessing over this:
a single cell:
house of the father,
flesh of the son.

2

There is a plumed hat
lying on a stone floor,
its feathers arching
toward the window,

a small skull
beneath the window
freshly chiseled
into stone.

It's beginning to rain,
There is the rope,
the ceiling beam,
the plumed hat

found near the body
washed from the bay,
the sword left
in the sand,

the crystal rosary
sent by the pope
to give the father strength.
And there is the father

standing in the room,
the rosary in his hand.
Its dark amber beads
shine in the dim light.

They swing down, tighten,
become heavy with weight.
They swing down, snap
and break, falling

through the air,
falling like feathers,
dissolving in the rain,
into lead, into sand.

For Mary Lynch

The white cement walls, thatched roof,
the rose bush blooming just outside, the small table
inside next to your rocker—it all looked so familiar.

And over the hearth, the picture of the Virgin's heart,
the layers of flesh torn away, the bramble
of thorns twisted around the fist-shaped muscle.

And the picture of your father, his fields
dried up, the potatoes shriveled to the size
of your fingers, then curled back into the earth,

everyone else gone and relatives
there at the tip of Inishmore, "the isle of tears,"
taking one last look at the ships leaving.

That night I found you in the old church
kneeling alone, hands folded, your white hair
wet with rain, pressed under a woolen scarf,

the soft light of the votive candle blurring
your face, and I could feel the weight of your body,
of a whole family, fall away, dissolve as if a thin wafer.

The next morning we ate breakfast together:
eggs, scones, tea, brown bread and strawberry jam.
Then half way down the road, I turned and waved,

the ship's bell clanging. You stood there by the bush,
the sun shining into the house, your one hand
raised, the fingers, blossoms, curled open.

Scales

I slide the weights to the right,
the bar suspends in air,
then once again you are
in the room, dust in your sleeves,
your shoes covered with sand,
your black bag opening,
filling like a pool,
the only hint of water
in this dry summer.
The scales tip and I slide
down through the bag,
the floor, the cracked ground.
My body floats into a bay,
the waves lapping the rocks,
the gulls circling. A man
kneels, kisses the sand,
kisses the damp stones
of a castle room, a rope
tied from the ceiling beam.
He stands, teeters from one leg
to the other and the veins
in the stones flow together
forming the lines of a map.
He holds a compass in his hand.

The rope breaks and the room
floats west. The scales tip
back and I stand before the window,
your bag in my hand. Grandfather,
this is what you brought;
this is what you left:
scales, rags, needles,
your rosary, plumed hat and sword.
I stand before the window,
the light blaring, almost
blinding, the clouds folding,
shriveling to small metal balls.

Swift

Now it is loose in the room, ashes falling
from its wings, falling from the ceiling,
the large black flakes, the large black
wings pressed against the cold window glass,
my grandmother waving a long yellow broom.

Now it comes down again and again,
moves inside the pipes of the house, flutters,
knocks, pounds, the water rising around it,
its head down, body bent down, mouth open,
now closed, trailing a long streamer of paper.

Now there are twenty, thirty piled by the chimney.
I lie down and they come out of my skin,
cover me completely. I pick them up and they dissolve
in my hands—feather and bone, a splinter,
one thin wafer the size of the moon filling the room.

Then they are gone. December, my grandmother
and I sit before the fire and drink tea.
She smoothes the napkin over her thigh,
rattles her saucer, brings the cup to her lips.
This is lovely, I say, *lovely*, a huge white bird in my arms.

Succession

It doesn't matter if the light fails.
Tonight, my fingers move automatically
Along the rows, each stitch
As familiar as a bead of the rosary.

I simply follow the family pattern
My Irish grandmothers knit into sweaters
For their sons, the fine threads
Spun off the skulls of Nordic sailors.

And when I stop to raise my hands,
It will be in the way of a priest
Blessing boats. I'll poke my arms
Through the dark and listen

For the clack of needles, oars.
I'll prostrate myself on the floor,
Let down the nets, the great walls
Of the house, and float out,

The tides, the full moon, a tangle
Of yarn, pulling me in, cell by cell,
My flesh unraveling, all revealing
Marks gone: scars, face, fingerprints,

My whole body the shore by dawn.

EDWARD BYRNE
(1951–)

Homecoming

I have a feeling for those ships
Each worn and ancient one . . .
        —Herman Melville

> Often I think of those lost and luring
>   evenings I'd walk along the wharves
>
> where the charter ships were rooted:
>   *Virginia II, Susanna B, Princess Ellen. . . .*
>
> The workers would still be there, hosing
>   down the decks, storing supplies, sometimes
>
> scraping paint from the blistered hulls.
>   After a while I knew their names too.
>
> Slattery was my favorite. He understood
>   what a boy wanted to hear, wanted to see.
>
> Once, pointing to a lagoon where scows
>   lay at anchor in the offshore shallows,
>
> each darkening the green water-light
>   like a brush stroke too thickly applied,

he spoke of their owners, men he'd known
   since he was a boy, and how they lived

the way their fathers had before them,
   unchanged, like the long, straight skyline

of the sea. Daily, in all weather,
   they cruised those waters, indistinguishable

as driftwood. In the pre-dawn they'd cross
   against the slow pull of the tide,

their lamps burning through the frost-smoke
   that rose over the black bay, then linger

along the point in the first wink of sun.
   When the ships returned in the late afternoon,

each with an elongated shadow trailing
   beside the whiteness of its wake, I'd watch

until I could see every man's face,
   each one sun-puffed, imprinted with squint marks.

Overhead, the flowering sky would clutter
   with gulls following indiscernible clouds

of fish scent, as if in a homecoming.
   Soon, the constellations, too, would collect

far above the darkened harbor, and I,
   too young to know any better, would leave

for home, believing everything would remain
   the same, that even I would never change.

Listening to Lester Young

. . . regrets are always late, too late!
                    —John Ashbery

Late at night, I'm listening to one of Lester Young's
          slower solos again, and although I know he's playing

those same notes I've heard over and over, as the tone
          of his tenor saxophone turns toward a lower register,

even that patter of cold drizzle now pasting shadowy
          leaves against my window seems to follow his lead.

I wonder what you would be doing tonight, and I want
          to write a few lines in my notebook about how blue

and ivory skies gave way to rain today after you left,
          or how coming home from the train station, I thought

I saw something, a large and ominous animal suddenly
          outlined by lightning on that sparsely wooded hillside

beside the deserted highway we always drive to save
          a little bit of time. As you travel farther away, hurrying

through the muted darkness still surrounding everything,
          so that you cannot even see the land tilting at the sea

or the gulls slanting overhead when you approach
          the coastline, I imagine you beginning a new book

in the dim light of that passenger car, reading another
          long novel about characters not so unlike ourselves,

each chapter titled and numbered as if to indicate life
          is merely a neat progression of unpredictable episodes.

By tomorrow evening you will be at that old hotel
          where we once stayed for days in a room overlooking

plaza monuments deformed and whitened like marble
        by a winter storm, while its foot of snowfall closed

the city down as though no one there had ever known
        such weather in their lives. If you were still here,

you'd be able to hear Lester backing Billie Holiday
        on another ballad recorded more than six decades ago,

but years before the two of them finally knew the truth
        about that high cost of living they would have to pay.

I'm beginning to believe their duets of lost love,
        the ways they phrase each line of lyric or melody,

create images in the mind as vivid as any photo
        or poem we might have seen, evoke those places

Prez and Lady Day played in their earlier days—
        Harlem cabarets and the late-night cafés downtown,

or those small neighborhood halls with bare walls
        and a gray haze of smoke above the stage, the ebony

and violet glow of an angled piano lid under indigo
        lights, and a congregation of friendly faces gradually

fading into the black background with a persistent
        chatter and clatter of glasses that lets everyone know

they are not alone. In the half hour before your
        departure, when we sat silently on that station

platform bench, as though any attempt at conversation
        would be hopeless and in fear someone around us

might overhear what we had to say, I tried somehow
        to take into account how far apart we already were:

even then, I felt regrets are all we had left in common.

DAVID CAVANAGH
(1951–)

It's So Much Like Missiles

One day you hear they've been fired—
the missiles I mean—you imagine them
curving like so many Golden Gates
between a hundred cities, serene vapour trails
with some message you cannot imagine,
and don't have to, for you know
you have one half of one hour.

And everything's suddenly simple,
like the time you heard your father had died,
long-distance the phone clicking
softly as a heart while you felt everything
freeze in your tiny kitchen, altered,
and impossibly unchanged.

And the funny thing is not that they've gone
up—the missiles I mean—but that they remind
you of something you didn't do, some words
you didn't say, just didn't take the trouble
to say, like the time you were leaving town,
and a friend, and you never told her how much
she meant to you, and you never saw her again.

Now missiles are flying, and it's just
like when your father died, and the visit
you'd put off became a dream-train you lived
on nightly, dark train pounding on smoothest
rails of guilt, and never ever arriving.

The thing about what's unsaid is
you can never take it back.
If you had made that final visit
you'd have fought with him, most probably,
over Trudeau, or disarmament, something
not too close. And it would have been
furious and futile till it hit you
that this time he was dying,
and you'd have stopped, and so would he,
both of you sheepish, feeling
each other sheepish, awkwardness
your last strange sharing.

But the thing about not visiting, not
loving enough to say or fight or apologize
or see something new between you—
the thing about not saying is
it's so much like those missiles
up there, on the way, on the final way,
so undone, so unsaid, and so impossible
to take back.

The Middleman

Legs stretched out in a delicious sort of traction,
I lounge in the blue-green, low-slung beach chair

planted on the backyard lawn in the bright
slack middle of the last full day of summer.

Equinox. *Aequinoctium.* Half light, half dark,
the shift of seasons seeming suspended, neither

here nor there. And for reasons only half known
I hover between comfort and terror. Purple

petunias wave like dignitaries from the lavender
picnic table. The oddest thing—one minute

I feel tucked inside a dead-end safety zone, middle
of a middling life, pleasant home, decent

income, fenced backyard, a long good love.
The next I'm strung out on the thinnest

of taut high wires, the balancing act of a lifetime,
the crowd hushed below. Without ever

making a stir, I've stepped right off the platform—
a mid-life Flying Wallenda, cat-walking high

above ground. Look down beyond the tip of slipper
or think too hard of one side or the other

and I'm gone. Dead meat. Splayed on the seething
dump of career, TV, pumped-up media sex,

the smother love of stuff . . . or else the cold bare
locker of denial. Never mind—even to think

of sad diversions slides a foot sideways
off the wire. Tonight a half moon will rise

over this wedge of middle America; I'll sip
a toast to that silky moon, especially the dark half

I can't see, shadowed by our world. But now,
in the lawn chair, on the equinox, working

the crowd of purple petunias, I'm right where I
have to be. Take another sip. Keep the balance,

kiss my wife, keep moving, bucko. I'm high
on my own thin wire, gamely stringing myself

along, half wanting to look down, half blinded
by midday glare, stretching for who knows where.

PETER FALLON
(1951–)

from The Deerfield Series

Bloody Brook

1675

Eastwards the Pale.
Westwards scowls
a thicket, crouched
hinterlands, abode of owls

the whole way to the Hudson.
September light transmutes
leaf and vine, and they
who count among the fruits

and profits of the place
fresh water and wild grapes
dally a while
as a train of grain carts scrapes

behind, the 'flower of Essex county',
Captain Lathrop's choice brigade,
at ease until enticed
into an ambuscade

of Indians who, as if
in broken English, mistook,
and blushed, and changed
the name of the Muddy Brook.

Mehuman Hinsdale

1709

Consider the case of the man
whose people came to settle and stay,
whose shares broke ground
in 1669
four years before he became
the first white baby born
in the shade of Beaver Ridge,
whose father, uncles, and grandfathers
were killed that noon at Bloody Brook,
whose own new son was slaughtered
in the Leap Year massacre,
who with his wife was captured
and held two years in Canada
before his first redemption.

Consider him on an April morning,
1709,
driving north from Northampton
a team of horses
and a cart of apple-trees;
how he was carried off again,
west through the woods
and overland again to Kahnawake,
to Quebec, and overseas to France and England,
until after more than forty months
he came home, home here,
the horses older,
those apples planted in the ground
and new fruit on their branches.

Strength of Heart

Who knows what sorrows pierced our souls.
The human heart admits a choice
by way of suffering and grief. Rejoice
in the prudence of a place as it extolls

the election of a spirit to grow
instead of wilt. What were they waiting for
that winter of the massacre, of want and war?
Deliverance? What came? The past is also

ours in all its ways: the quiet boy in his heyday
cut down by his own hand, the public mystery
of the smiling boy soaring over Lockerbie,
and a later boy swept away

from all of us one evening on the Lower Level . . .
Time weaves loose threads into a pattern.
The ghosts of Charter Day, they are not taciturn;
they resonate and revel

in their legacy, a promise which unfurled
like the flag of liberty. That promise kept.
It said there are uncarved commandments to accept.
Be worthy of this life. And, Love the world.

JAMES GALVIN
(1951–)

Navigation

Evergreens have reasons
For stopping where they do,
At timberline or the clean edge
Of sage and prairie grass.
There are quantities of wind
They know they cannot cross.

They come down from the tundra
On waves of ridges and stop,
Staring out over open country,
Like pilgrims on the shore
Of an unexpected ocean.
The sky is still the sky, they know;
It won't understand ordinary language.

Meet my mother, twice removed,
Who could tell the time from stars.
She said everything is its own reward,
Grief, poverty, the last word.
Evening was her favorite time
And she walked along the shore of trees,
Carrying herself as if afraid
She might give herself away.
She called this being quiet.

Just inside the treeline, out of the wind,
Father built a handrail along the path.
She'd stand there like a sailor's wife
And stare at the high plains as dark came on.
She said mountains might be islands
But the sky is still the sky.

She'd wait for the ranch lights
On the prairie to come out
Like a fallen constellation.
She said watching is its own reward,
The lights are only reasons.

For Our Better Graces

God loves
the rain, not us.
Ours is
what spills over,
what we look for
that finds us:
innocence
by association.
Cloud shadows
feel their way,
rapid and blind,
over the face
of the prairie.
Pine trees
atop the ridge
row the world
into the dampblack sky.
God's mistress
rides by
on a feather of water.
After she is gone
her fragrance
is everywhere.

Misericord

Out at the end of a high promontory
above the dim, oceanic prairie,
we built a little fire for warmth.

Who ever doubted that the earth fell from the sky?
As though it had traveled a great distance to reach us

and still could not reach us,

though we held our hands out to it,
some vague intention, some apprehension
occurred between us.

That night we slept in the snow
by a half-frozen lake.
I could smell the woodsmoke in your hair.

We heard the earth cloud over, clear again,
the low voltage of granite and ice,
and everlastingness

let fall the moment
like a girl slipping out of her silk chemise.

But forget all that.
I wanted to tell you, the girl,
that when I woke in the morning

small frogs were singing from the lake as if
we had become transparent in our sleep.

Materialism

If things aren't things
So much as happenings,
Or a confluence even
More complex,
Then there's no such thing
As sky, though sky
Is real, and we
Have not imagined it.
The everlasting
Never began.
Everything, then,
Is the direction everything
Moves in, seeming
Not to move.
I am waiting
For something very
Nice to happen,
And then it happens:
Your long dark
Hair sweeps
Across my chest
Like sweeps of prairie
Rain. Loveliest
Of motion's possessions,
Hold me still.

BRIGIT PEGEEN KELLY
(1951–)

The Place of Trumpets

To the place of trumpets,
To the place where the sun sets,
To the place where peace sits,

We are going. By twos
Or threes, going to choose
New weather and new clothes,

The new sound of words walking
As trees among the winging
Fields, the fields on herons' wings;

Where all who wake, wake undone,
Back beyond their fragile bones,
Back to where the self is song,

Where the unmade hands are wheels,
The arms newest prayer shawls,
And the heart the child that kneels

And never tires, and never
Fails to watch at the door
The sun plucking its poor

Chest open and scattering
Its blood out, dropping
Down its bloody lasting blessing.

To the place of trumpets
We are going. To the sweet
Beggar's pipes blowing and wet

Winds unwinding the last
Winding sheets on streets where past
And present meet, where West

Marries East, and trust turns
To betrayal as its friend,
Where days and moon and sins are one

Blessed wind passing over
The passing plains, over
The sea, the comforter,

Full of salt so sweet it fills
The hollow tongue until
It splits as time will

Split and spill its tattered toys,
Fixed by the merest gaze
Or longing in the place

Where quiet ways grow,
Where the wound loves the arrow,
Where ankle and adder know

Accord, where the lion's lamb
Leads him to the grasses down,
Leads him with her little song,

Lay us here, lay us long,
Let us in this grass as one
Sleep now where we first began,

Here on the sand where we first met,
Under the trees before His seat,
Out of the cold, out of the heat,

In the place of trumpets.

Of Ancient Origins and War

And briefly stay, the junketing sparrows, briefly,
Briefly, their flurries like small wine spills,

While the one divides into two: the heart and its shadow,
The world and its threat, the crow back of the sparrow.

Near the surface, beneath the soft penetrable mask—
The paste of white blossoms slurring the broken ground—
Alarm begins its troubled shoot: *the fruit tree*

Beareth its fruit: a load of old fruit tricked out
By the scattershot light, figured gold by the furious light.

The will given early to the dream of pleasure falters,
In a slurry of scent, in a posture of doubled-over gold,
And then there is the rift, the sound of cloth tearing

As the crow shoots up—fast with apparent purpose—
Splitting wide the leaves of a tree we cannot name,
Growing by a gate made from another tree, a gate

That cries as it swings, the cry of the broken safety.
The world and its haste, the world and its threat,
The here where we will die coming closer. All the sorrow

Of it, sparrow trouble, sparrow blow, our hands
These sparrows, quick and quick, but tippling now,

Toppling, bellies full of the bad seed the hair spilled
When it broke from the last comb it was locked into.
The will given early to the dream of pleasure falters.

And now, in the dark, listen, in the dark
The tulip poplar is singing, the leaves are singing,
The clear high green of a boy's imperilled soprano.

The moon is rising, the sound like wine spilling.
The boy will grow a beard, the boy will be bearded.
The bird will dive back down in perfect execution.

The damaged will can only watch and wonder
Through a surface alarmed with dust. . . . And so now.
An so that now. We are in the trouble of a sleep

We did not dream of. And the shadows of the trees
Are breaking. The shadows of the world's broken vessels.

Song

Listen: there was a goat's head hanging by ropes in a tree.
All night it hung there and sang. And those who heard it
Felt a hurt in their hearts and thought they were hearing
The song of a night bird. They sat up in their beds, and then
They lay back down again. In the night wind, the goat's head
Swayed back and forth, and from far off it shone faintly
The way the moonlight shone on the train track miles away
Beside which the goat's headless body lay. Some boys
Had hacked its head off. It was harder work than they had imagined.
The goat cried like a man and struggled hard. But they
Finished the job. They hung the bleeding head by the school
And then ran off into the darkness that seems to hide everything.
The head hung in the tree. The body lay by the tracks.
The head called to the body. The body to the head.
They missed each other. The missing grew large between them,
Until it pulled the heart right out of the body, until
The drawn heart flew toward the head, flew as a bird flies
Back to its cage and the familiar perch from which it trills.
Then the heart sang in the head, softly at first and then louder,
Sang long and low until the morning light came up over
The school and over the tree, and then the singing stopped. . . .
The goat had belonged to a small girl. She named
The goat Broken Thorn Sweet Blackberry, named it after
The night's bush of stars, because the goat's silky hair
Was dark as well water, because it had eyes like wild fruit.
The girl lived by a high railroad track. At night

She heard the trains passing, the sweet sound of the train's horn
Pouring softly over her bed, and each morning she woke
To give the bleating goat his pail of warm milk. She sang
Him songs about girls with ropes and cooks in boats.
She brushed him with a stiff brush. She dreamed daily
That he grew bigger, and he did. She thought her dreaming
Made it so. But one night the girl didn't hear the train's horn,
And the next morning she woke to an empty yard. The goat
Was gone. Everything looked strange. It was as if a storm
Had passed through while she slept, wind and stones, rain
Stripping the branches of fruit. She knew that someone
Had stolen the goat and that he had come to harm. She called
To him. All morning and into the afternoon, she called
And called. She walked and walked. In her chest a bad feeling
Like the feeling of the stones gouging the soft undersides
Of her bare feet. Then somebody found the goat's body
By the high tracks, the flies already filling their soft bottles
At the goat's torn neck. Then somebody found the head
Hanging in a tree by the school. They hurried to take
These things away so that the girl would not see them.
They hurried to raise money to buy the girl another goat.
They hurried to find the boys who had done this, to hear
Them say it was a joke, a joke, it was nothing but a joke. . . .
But listen: here is the point. The boys thought to have
Their fun and be done with it. It was harder work than they
Had imagined, this silly sacrifice, but they finished the job,
Whistling as they washed their large hands in the dark.
What they didn't know was that the goat's head was already
Singing behind them in the tree. What they didn't know
Was that the goat's head would go on singing, just for them,
Long after the ropes were down, and that they would learn to listen,
Pail after pail, stroke after patient stroke. They would
Wake in the night thinking they heard the wind in the trees
Or a night bird, but their hearts beating harder. There
Would be a whistle, a hum, a high murmur, and, at last, a song,
The low song a lost boy sings remembering his mother's call.
Not a cruel song, no, no, not cruel at all. This song
Is sweet. It is sweet. The heart dies of this sweetness.

ETHNA McKIERNAN
(1951–)

Céilí Mór

Half daft with music,
flushed with drink,
sweaty as cows at yesterday's market

we spun all night in giddy step
and stamped our neighbors' toes
three inches to the left.

The bank played reels and waltzes
till the breathless crowd had stopped;
the arms around waists were prizes carried off.

And hours afterward, just this—
two bodies in an empty room
still circling in around desire

toward the prize not given yet,
that final dance
into the liquid elegance of sex.

To Inishmore

The boat engines whir and hum
and the gangplank scrapes shut.
Cold sounds, final languages.

Someone is always leaving, leaving—

In Mexico, the child cries to his mother
as the train pulls away, while somewhere else,
perhaps, events and bodies gladly break apart.

Above the ship, gulls are thrashing the air
to bits. Their high calls
slice the air like knives, a Greek chorus.

Did the woman in the black dress there
leaning toward the wind,
fall, last night,

before she closed her eyes,
to that old lie
of softness in dark?

Remote, awkward today,
empty of promises
as the grey Galway sky,

we'll part strangers again,
blank as the creamy surf
that rings the shipsides

as your boat glides out into the distance.

Driving the Coast Road to Dingle

for John Sweetser 1919–1998

The light was thinning. Dusk fell
in soft haphazard clumps on the sheep,
the hills, the long streak of sea
below, the boys sprawled across
the back seat, their smell of wet wool,
of child-musk and sleep.

Ahead, two horse-trailers took the curves
slow and their brake-lights deepened
on-off, on-off, a red glow. Who
could hear me singing on this road
above the sea, who could hear
the leaps and dives my heart made
on-off, on-off, as I drove?

We headed west into dark
toward the harbour-town
whose name repeated in my brain
like rain sweeping now
across the windshield. The Volvo
skimmed the hedgerows to the left
and my hands gripped the steering wheel
a few times before the boys woke up.

At that moment
stars began to push
their white necks through
the shawled sky above.
I knew then there was no
inch of earth, no
other world than this
I loved.

LYNNE McMAHON
(1951–)

Wedding Ring

Common all over Ireland, unknown to me,
    (tell me again the name of this thing?)
it's a claddagh, a sweetheart ring,
    silver hands clasping a rounded heart,
an apple, I had mistakenly thought,
    topped by a crown.
I still think of it as my regnant pomme
    because it's French, and wrong,
and invented etymologies pass the time
    those days you're gone.
Irish cliches, like certain songs,
    wring from me
a momentary recognition that trash
    sent bowling down the street
by sudden wind, or showery smoke trees
    whipsawing across the path
their fine debris, means heimat,
    means home, and however
long estranged we've been, or silvered over
    by borrowed themes,
these homely things make meaning of us.
    I feel it just as much as you—
that near-empty diner in Sligo
    where you found the ring
wedged in the cushioned booth,
    rejected, perhaps, or lost,

hidden while the lover nervously rehearsed
     his lines, then abruptly interrupted,
who knows how, and now distraught,
     had no more thought for such
sentiment as this. I never take it off.

We Take Our Children to Ireland

What will they remember best? The barbed wire
still looped around the Belfast airport,
the building-high Ulster murals—
but those were fleeting, car window sights,
more likely the turf fires lit each night,
the cups of tea their father brought
and the buttered soda farls, the sea wall
where they leaped shrieking into the Irish Sea
and emerged, purpling, to applause;
perhaps the green castle at Carrickfergus,
but more likely the candy store
with its alien crisps—vinegar? they ask,
prawn cocktail? Worcestershire leek?
More certainly still the sleekly syllabled
odd new words, gleet and shite,
and grand responses to everyday events:
How was your breakfast? Brilliant.
How's your crust? Gorgeous.
Everything after that was gorgeous,
brilliant. How's your gleeted shite?
And the polite indictment from parents
everywhere, the nicely dressed matrons
pushing prams, brushing away their older kids
with a Fuck off, will ye? Which stopped
our children cold. Is the water cold,

they asked Damian, before they dared it.
No, he said, it's not cold, it's
fooking cold, ye idjits.
And the mundane hyperbole of rebuke—
you little puke, I'll tear your arm off
and beat you with it, I'll row you out to sea
and drop you, I'll bury you in sand
and top you off with rocks—
to which the toddler would contentedly nod
and continue to drill his shovel
into the sill. All this will play on
long past the fisherman's cottage and farmer's
slurry, the tall hedgerows lining the narrow
drive up the coast, the most beautiful
of Irish landscapes indelibly fixed
in the smeared face of two year old Jack—
Would you look at that, his father said
to Ben and Zach, shite everywhere, brilliant.
Gorgeous, they replied. And meant it.

Glasnevin

"To seem the stranger lies my lot"—this written
in estranging Ireland among estranged priests
conspiring against his native skies, Hopkins,
at three removes from hope, could not foresee
a happy ending. England, wife to his creating thought,
had dropped once-beautiful Dublin and left her
to her own decline, sooty, shabby, and foul,
too poor to put in adequate drains,
the Liffey now the chief public sewer
for the entire mains. Smelly metaphor indeed
for the fastidious Hopkins, who did finally come to see
that Home Rule was right, but at what price?

The Church split between those who thought
religion and education could transcend petty
nationalism (but petty is an English word),
and those who would perpetuate what was steadfastly Irish,
could not be mended. All discussion ended,
the Troubles mounted the shoulders of the priests,
and climbed the worn steps at 86 Stephen's Green
whose familiar worn tablet famously records
the famous feet passing up and down the stairs:
John Henry Newman, Gerard Manley Hopkins,
James Joyce, the choice spot for pilgrims of all sorts
to linger, tracing the stone remains of those names.
A century later Dublin displays her writers on
ten pound notes, spending poetry for food,
electricity, mission work (or dope, abortions,
rifle sights—money, like words, reinvents its context
with each new partnership) and thus does honor
to such bitterness, heartache, ambivalence and despair
as soul can commit to paper. What prayers Joyce wrote,
once called obscene, still lift heavenward in college texts,
and Hopkins' cries to him who lives, alas, away
still echo in the cemetery wind at Glasnevin
where he lies, amid the bones of his fellow priests,
far from his own poem-freighted Hampstead Heath.
"To seem the stranger lies my lot," and in the anonymity
of the Jesuit space, where no one bears a particular plot,
just a designation on the general plinth, the strangeness
is ground down to dust, indistinguishable from the dust
above or below, one holy bone pile in the bony house
from which, as he once wrote, the skylark is released,
thieving its song from all the other birds, whose
currency lies beyond the reach of words.

In Love With It, If It Requires No Tending

Adam's curse was work, but his gift for naming, given first,
endured beyond the field's exigencies, or slain and slaying sons,
the history of thirst that worsened diasporas and enclosure acts
and land-grabs of the ruling parties, sorties sent out
to annex neighbors, favors bestowed and sown in earth,
reversing owners and disputing births
till each untilled but worthy plot was parceled out
and border wars were made eternal. Property
is theft, William Godwin said. But Wordsworth disagreed.
A scrap of land confers a dignity on man, not to be had
by any other means. O the greater fleabane, Patrick Kavanagh
exclaimed, that grew at the back of the potato-pit! He knew it
was unremitting toil. But loved the language it employed:
Autumn gentian. Bitterroot. Love-lies-bleeding. Adam's fruit.

JAMES McMANUS
(1951–)

Two Songs for Hendrix

1 **"The Star-Spangled Banner"**
The national anthem at sunrise,
August 17, '69—summer of Manson,
Nixon's halfhearted troop withdrawal
and Neil Armstrong's walk on the moon—
this on a dairy farm outside Bethel,
New York. Without words, in this context,
it takes a few bars to make out the melody
through the visceral haze of distortion, of
scattering quarks and dislodged muoniums
oscillating at zero-point energy
toward 130 Db, but as soon as we do
we're locked into it. James Marshall
Hendrix, all business. The Kid.
Jamestown. The Acid King. Lefty.
A red bandanna bisects his these days
barely medium-sized afro, this to go
with a white buckskin Navajo surplice
and blue velvet bellbottoms: *Damn!*
The backward and upside down white-
on-white Stratocaster is going ballistic,
balls-out. No showboating dental
or behind-the-back picking. No muscle shirts,
somersaults, processed hair, spotlights, chartreuse
feather boas, or ritual lighter fluid. No
amp-humping, either, this morning.
Except for the ten-inch fringe on his sleeves

flapping like albino hawk's wings, or eagle's,
he may as well be standing at attention
as the notes whang and toggle, feeding back hard
through the Marshalls. He's making it talk with a
vengeance. The air cavalry's "rockets' red glare"
gets warped into painterly screeches,
onomatopoeia at Mach 1.7;
"bombs bursting in air" becomes blistering
napalm cacophony, hyperincendiary payloads
arcing down into inhabited jungle—as Beethoven
under these circumstances might have rendered
this hijacked, unwonderful hymn to Anacreon,
inventing outlandish contrapuntal alignments
and vertical tone combinations, hammering away
through a Fuzz Face on a Rickenbacher twelve-string
or a Synclavier II suitably retooled by Rog Mayer. . . .
As "proof through the night that our flag was still there,"
Hendrix, deadpan, interpolates George M. Cohan's
"Over There," flashing us back to another Great War's
gung-ho vigor and shrapneled, Jim-dandy aftermaths,
then continues the martial motif on "the land
of the free and the home of the brave"
by making the Strat trill like bagpipes.

Couple more reverb-charged chords and it's over.
There's nothing much, really, to say. We're agog.
We've all of us by now heard hundreds of covers
—by marching bands, pianists, Arditti and barbershop
quartets, altos and tenors, even baritones, pop
stars (Whitney Houston stooping to lip-sync
at Joe Robbie as flags waved and fighters screamed
over her wig, Roseanne at Jack Murphy, Linda Ronstadt
at Dodger, even Wynton Marsalis going a little flat
in the Superdome, Mariah Carey forgetting the words
but still ripping sweetly through four or five octaves
in the Madhouse on Madison, Marvin Gaye toning it up
for all time in the Forum), but nothing remotely like this.
And no one's got clue number one how he does it.
"Hey, all I do is play it," he says a week or so later

on Cavett. I'm American so I played it. They made me
sing it in school, so it's sort of a flashback."
Cavett, flashing us forward to his slick Nineties self
as a middlebrow pitchman, waxes sarcastic:
"This man was in the 101st Airborne,
so when you write your nasty letters in—"
Hendrix, baffled, says, "Nasty letters? How come?"
Cavett: "When you mention the national anthem
played in any unorthodox way, it never fails.
You get a guaranteed percentage of hate mail
from people who say, 'How dare he?'" Hendrix,
still baffled: "Unorthodox? It wasn't unorthodox."
Cavett: "It wasn't unorthodox?" Hendrix: "No.
I thought it was beautiful, but there you go."
He shoots the camera a rightside up, then
upside down, not unbelligerent, peace sign.

The upshot? Whenever we hear the national anthem
because a war is about to get started, fought
by soldiers in camouflage or surrogate warriors
in eyecatching uniforms, we have to think of Jimi.

2 "Purple Haze"
On the evening of January 19, 1991, seventy five
hours in Operation Desert Storm, four bands I know of
played "Purple Haze": Shrimp Boat at Metro; the Kronos Quartet
at Park West; violinist Nigel Kennedy, while conducting the St.
Paul Chamber Orchestra, between the Fall and Winter movements
of *The Four Seasons;* and Sting, as both host and musical guest
on *Saturday Night Live.* Another dozen ensembles, in concert
halls, studios, heated garages, or stadia may have covered it sometime
that evening, but no one keeps very close track of these things
anymore. In any event, the invocations of Hendrix's spirit
were welcome gestures of reproach as the Cubist F-117's
and Futurist Tomahawks went about their grim business,
even when we remembered that it was the well-oiled jihad
machinery of an undereducated dipshit like Saddam Hussein
they were obliterating, not Ho Chi Minh's barefoot minions.

Throughout the evening CNN cameras show Tel Aviv
bracing for Scud attacks, F-15's taking off from carriers
and the president speaking with cool determination, with Dana
Carvey's flawless blend of John Wayne and Fred Rogers.
Weekend Update included a skit in which a Tomahawk missile
made a direct hit on a reporter in Baghdad—homage, perhaps, to
the first scene of *Gravity's Rainbow*, in which Pirate Prentice
imagines himself being brained by the tip of a German V-2.
Then again, perhaps not. By this point Der Stinglehoffer
had already played "Mad About You," the latest hit single
in his ongoing McCartneyization, and appeared in four skits,
including one as an arch combination of 'Enry 'Iggins
and Victor Frankenstein, another as an awkward college boy
introducing his loony fiancee to his parents. But why did he
(and Shrimp Boat and Kronos and Kennedy) play "Purple Haze"?
(My daughter and wife would happily, both of them, kill
to be able to ask him.) The song's a succinct acid blues
with an adequate rhythm section, spacey but straightforward
enough lyrics, and a jaggedly incendiary guitar line.
It apparently functions as well as a NutraSweet jingle
or all-purpose garage-band fodder as it does as "arrangement
for three pianos" for the out-there ensemble Ensemble.
But its connotative power as a sometime anti-war anthem
has mainly to do with its emergence during the summer
of 1967, on millions of record players and hundreds of
millions of radios from Selma to Da Nang, Port Huron to London
and Paris to Saigon as the baddest and catchiest licks
on the soundtrack to "Vietnam"—to the roiling matrix
of dope, civil rights, rock and roll, loud clothes, lame
politics, the war in Southeast Asia and the protests of same
in cities, politburos and on campuses all over the planet.
Just as Herman Hupfeld's "As Time Goes By," a haunting
but thoroughly apolitical love song, has become ineluctably
associated with *la Resistance,* or Mozart's G minor quintet
will remind you you're going to die but won't make it seem
all that terrible. Hardly. The fact is, we've come
in the last quarter century to read Jimi Hendrix
as a braid-weaving common denominator: simultaneously

Western, African and Native American; urban and cosmic,
subversive and patriotic, combative and peaceloving;
as bluesy, metallic, serious, pop, avant garde. His music
took mindbending, uncorporate risks—and paid off.
His swagger and verve, both with and without his guitar,
were an unignorable dis to the corporate
mentality then emerging as the pop music industry
began to achieve blue-chip-scale profitability,
and Hendrix paid for that attitude big-time, with
humiliating royalty percentages, circumscribed airplay
on black *and* white radio stations, getting relentlessly
hassled to front for some well nigh extravagantly racist
and/or naively pacifist rhetorics—plus we let the guy die
far from home, in the megalopolis, London, that launched
and revered him, by suffocating on his own vomit.

However. To the extent that wars tend to be organized
by unbent, religio-corporate interests, any song he recorded
still can effectively stand as a shorthand gesture of reproach:
thumbs down, a raised middle finger, a peace sign. You pick.
Because even in a lyrics-intensive little ditty like "Purple Haze"
Jimi, true to his words, let his fingers do most of the talking.

The Unnamable

This defiantly ugly *Prelude in A Minor*—four
ever steeper descents; crazed, irresolvable chords—
inspired in Gide an almost physical terror.

Me too—okay? Of things I have never had words,
even thoughts, for. To turn *up* my Discman, inhale
the canal's dank black coolth. The two-thirds-

time lecturer paid millions of lire to roll
and ignite our untwisting blue cigarettes blinks
away smoke nylons wafting from one sightly nostril.

Because just as a fiftyish chair from the Bronx
via Lisle and Winnetka's like, "Whoa! He went off
for fifty-five *there?*" "Now that shit is dope" or "Jinx

us why don't you," I gulp down my *ombra* and cough
while Tzimon Barto hammers and measures as Chopin
himself might've: extra slentando, precisely enough

sostenuto, what's left of the pulse all but gone.
I take hold of mauve nipples and smudge them, *buh-bing
buh-duh boom,* sw-swaying along with old Tzimon

until the final statement stabilizes the thing,
at least for a moment. It's time. *You must go on
playing!* And yanking off earphones. And trembling.

PAUL MULDOON
(1951–)

Immrama

I, too, have trailed my father's spirit
From the mud-walled cabin behind the mountain
Where he was born and bred,
TB and scarlatina,
The farm where he was first hired out,
To Wigan, to Crewe junction,
A building-site from which he disappeared
And took passage, almost, for Argentina.

The mountain is coming down with hazel,
The building-site a slum,
While he has gone no further than Brazil.

That's him on the verandah, drinking rum
With a man who might be a Nazi,
His children asleep under their mosquito-nets.

Promises, Promises

I am stretched out under the lean-to
Of an old tobacco-shed
On a farm in North Carolina.
A cardinal sings from the dogwood
For the love of marijuana.
His song goes over my head.
There is such splendour in the grass
I might be the picture of happiness.
Yet I am utterly bereft
Of the low hills, the open-ended sky,
The wave upon wave of pasture
Rolling in, and just as surely
Falling short of my bare feet.
Whatever is passing is passing me by.

I am with Raleigh, near the Atlantic,
Where we have built a stockade
Around our little colony.
Give him his scallop-shell of quiet,
His staff of faith to walk upon,
His scrip of joy, immortal diet—
We are some eighty souls
On whom Raleigh will hoist his sails.
He will return, years afterwards,
To wonder where and why
We might have altogether disappeared,
Only to glimpse us here and there
As one fair strand in her braid,
The blue in an Indian girl's dead eye.

I am stretched out under the lean-to
Of an old tobacco-shed
On a farm in North Carolina,
When someone or other, warm, naked,
Stirs within my own skeleton
And stands on tip-toe to look out
Over the horizon,
Through the zones, across the ocean.
The cardinal sings from a redbud
For the love of one slender and shy,
The flight after flight of stairs
To her room in Bayswater,
The damson freckle on her throat
That I kissed when we kissed Goodbye.

(from) 7, Middagh Street

GYPSY

Save thou, my rose; in it thou art my all.
In Mother's dream my sister, June,
was dressed in her usual cal-
ico but whistling an unfamiliar tune
when a needlecord
dea ex machina
came hoofing it across the boards—
a Texan moo-cow
with a red flannel tongue,
a Madamish leer
and a way with the song
it insinuated into Mother's ear;
'You've only to put me in the act
to be sure of the Orpheum contract.'

She did. We followed that corduroy cow
through Michigan, Kansas,
Idaho.
But the vaudeville audiences
were dwindling. Mack Sennett's
Bathing Beauties
had seen to that. Shakespeare's Sonnets,
Das Kapital, Boethius,
Dainty June and her Newsboy Songsters—
all would succumb to Prohibition,
G-men, gangsters,
bathtub gin.
June went legit. In Minneapolis
I spirit-gummed pink gauze on my nipples.

And suddenly I was waiting in the wings
for the big production-routine
to end. I was wearing a swanky
gaberdine
over my costume of sherbet-green tulle.
I watched two girl-Pawnees
in little else but pony-tails
ride two paint ponies
on a carousel. They loosed mock arrows
into the crowd, then hung
on for dear life when the first five rows
were showered with horse-dung.
I've rarely felt so close to nature
as in Billy Minsky's Burlesque Theatre.

This was Brooklyn, 1931. I was an under-age
sixteen. Abbott and Costello
were sent out front while the stage
was hosed down and the ponies hustled
back to the *Ben Hur* stables.
By the time I came on
the customers were standing on the tables,
snapping like caymans
and booing even the fancy cyclorama

depicting the garden of Eden.
Gradually the clamour
faded as I shed
all but three of my green taffeta fig-leaves
and stood naked as Eve.

'I loved the act. Maybe you'd wanna buy
Sam?" asked Nudina, over a drink.
Nudina danced with a boa
constrictor that lived under the sink
in the women's room. 'He's a dear.'
'So *this* is a speakeasy,'
Mother whispered. We'd ordered beer
and pizza.
'Don't look now,' said Nudina, 'but Waxey's
just come in.' 'Waxey?' 'A friend of mine
from Jersey. Runs applejack
through special pipelines
in the sewers. Never even been subpoenaed.
But let's get back to discussing the serpent.'

I've no time for any of that unladylike stuff.
An off-the-shoulder shoulder-strap,
the removal of one glove—
it's knowing exactly when to stop
that matters,
what to hold back, some sweet disorder . . .
The same goes for the world of letters.
When I met George Davis in Detroit
he managed the Seven Arts
bookstore. I was on the Orpheum circuit.
Never, he says, give all thy heart;
there's more enterprise in walking not quite
naked. Now he has me confined to quarters
while we try to solve *The G-String Murders*.

We were looking over my scrapbook entries
from the *New Yorker,*
Fortune, Town and Country,

when I came on this from the *Daily Worker:*
'Striptease is a capitalistic cancer,
a product of the profit system.'
Perhaps we cannot tell the dancer
from the dance. Though I've grown accustomed
to returning the stare
of a life-size-cut-out of Gypsy Rose Lee
from the World's Fair
or the Ziegfeld Follies
I keep that papier-mâché cow's head packed
just in case vaudeville does come back.

Milkweed and Monarch

.   .   .

As he knelt by the grave of his mother and father
the taste of dill, or tarragon—
he could barely tell one from the other—

filled his mouth. It seemed as if he might smother.
Why should he be stricken
with grief, not for his mother and father,

but a woman slinking from the fur of a sea-otter
in Portland, Maine, or, yes, Portland, Oregon—
he could barely tell one from the other—

and why should he now savour
the tang of her, her little pickled gherkin,
as he knelt by the grave of his mother and father?

.   .   .

He looked about. He remembered her palaver
on how both earth and sky would darken—
'You could barely tell one from the other'—

while the Monarch butterflies passed over
in their milkweed-hunger: 'A wing-beat, some reckon,
may trigger off the mother and father

of all storms, striking your Irish Cliffs of Moher
with the force of a hurricane.'
Then: 'Milkweed and Monarch "invented" each other.'

.   .   .

He looked about. Cow's-parsley in a samovar.
He'd mistaken his mother's name, 'Regan', for 'Anger':
as he knelt by the grave of his mother and father
he could barely tell one from the other.

HARRY CLIFTON
(1952–)

Euclid Avenue

after Hart Crane

The blazing stanchions and the corporate lights—
Manhattan over the bridge, from Brooklyn Heights—
Were energies like yours, without a home,
That would not be condensed inside a poem

But endlessly dispersed, and went to work
For time and money, hovering over the masses
Like terrible angels. . . . Now, I stand in New York
And watch those energies sweat themselves out, like gases

Through a subway grille, to keep the derelicts warm
In a new depression. Or, at station bookstalls,
Calm at the eye of the electric storm
I drink your words, like prohibition alcohol

Capital hides from itself. On soundless trains
Through Middle America, citizens fishing in creeks
That rise and flow nowhere, disappear again
In a private wilderness you were born to seek

And lose yourself in. But none of them will thank you—
They, nor the desolate children that they raised
On a thousand streets called Euclid Avenue
For travelling inwards, damning with faint praise

The forces that they freed, to blast through gravity
Into a loveless, extraterrestrial space
Like night bus stations, galaxies of strays—
The sons and daughters of the human race.

Absinthe at New Orleans

America, your poisons and elixirs
    I drink by the glass
On Bourbon Street, and watch the winter pass.
An hour before dinner, the temperature hovers at sixty
Like perfection, neither hot nor cold,
And the tapdancers, thinking on their feet,
Are back on their beats. A child of Europe, I drink
The essence of wormwood, greenish, bittersweet,
And look at yesterday's slaves, the bought and sold,
And wonder at this freedom to travel and think

The State Department pays for. *Feeling alone?*
    You can always telephone
Our special number in Washington, free of charge.
We know you're out there somewhere, a conscience at large
In the privileged states. For you, distinguished guest,
Hotels are booked, there are alter egos to meet
Among the civil servants, disarmingly nice,
Who show you Death Row, agreeing when you protest.
About your dark side, too, we can be discreet
And omni-tolerant. Everyone has a price

In the cities we've raised. . . . A week ago
    I saw them shovelling snow
Off Omaha Pavements, in an arctic breeze—
The disinherited negroes, the wizened Vietnamese
In coldweather clothing. As he paid the toll
And drove me to the airport, from my graduate class
In the politics of modern poetry,
Kurt Helmut Schroeder, working in Riot Control,
Looked at them coldly, and then looked at me,
'There is no poverty here—only laziness!'

Approaching Denver, gradually losing height,
    I imagined a city
Out of green smog and buildings, a hundred miles away
As we made our descent. I would sleep that night
With the Void for company, sirens, breaking glass,
And shouts below of illegal Spanish and blacks
Who left their souls behind, at the point of entry,
To be officially no one here, to hustle on East Colfax—
And businessmen, from Hiltons of steel and glass,
Who hurried in groups towards the invisible centre

Of a town with no after hours. . . . They had booked me through,
    The government, on the silver and blue
Amtrak, through to the Pacific side
Of whatever was missing here. On the Great Divide
Were failed utopias, desolate heavens on earth
A soldier on leave got down at, met by a girl—
And blizzards fumed under station lamps in the cold,
And voices of porters, urgent as death and birth,
Recalled me from the platform, where I strolled
Examining snowflakes, tiny, complete as worlds

At midnight in Salt Lake City. *Lie on the bed*
    The negro steward prepares
At body temperature. Know the government cares
Beyond space and time, as you sleep through watersheds
And wake to a conscienceless desert, replacing the dark
With auto wreckage, chapels for divorcées.
Nevada bombsites—all the fossilised fishes
Of a prehistoric sea. Change before Reno, at Sparks,
And cross the stateline. Quickly, forget all these,
For the bed we have made for you now, fulfills all wishes

In San Francisco. . . . Yes, I see what you mean
    About everyone having a side.
In blue December, the month of suicides,
I saw the drugged in doorways, the sadness of queens,
From an old Chinese hotel on Geary Street,
And mornings brought me unofficial news
That pulsed like pleasure, through the affective centres—
Blonde Saskatchewan girl, between my sheets,
Who never told me who it was had sent her
To compromise me, and to be my Muse.

America, the electric cablecars
    Along Saint Charles
Will carry me back, in another hour or two,
To the last hotel before Europe. . . . Meanwhile, the blues
And Dixieland jazz, the salesmen of joy and despair
At every corner—like me, *poètes maudits,*
Imbibing essence of wormwood, bittersweet—
And the steady Trades, the temperate gulf air
Emancipating crowds onto the streets
And winter, going unnoticed, everywhere.

ALICE FULTON
(1952 –)

Everyone Knows the World Is Ending

Everyone knows the world is ending.
Everyone always thought so, yet
here's the world. Where fundamentalists flick slideshows
in darkened gyms, flash endtime mess-
ages of bliss, tribulation
through the trembling bleachers: Christ will come
by satellite TV, bearing millennial weather
before plagues of false prophets and real locusts
botch the cosmic climate—which ecologists predict
is already withering from the green-
house effect as fossil fuels seal in
the sun's heat and acid rains
give lakes the cyanotic blues.

When talk turns this way, my mother speaks in memories,
each thought a focused mote in the apocalypse's
iridescent fizz. She is trying to restore a world
to glory, but the facts shift with each telling
of her probable gospel. Some stories have been
trinkets in my mind since childhood, yet what clings is not
how she couldn't go near the sink
for months without tears when her mother died,
or how she feared she wouldn't get her own
beribboned kindergarten chair, but the grief
in the skull like radium
in lead, and the visible dumb love like water
in crystal, at one with what holds it. The triumph

of worlds beyond words. Memory entices because ending is
its antonym. We're here to learn
the earth by heart and everything is crying
mind me, mind me! Yet the brain selects and shimmers
to a hand on skin while numbing the constant
stroke of clothes. Thoughts frame and flash
before the dark snaps back: The dress with lace tiers
she adored and the girl with one just like it,
the night she woke to see my father
walk down the drive and the second she remembered
he had died. So long as we keep chanting the words
those worlds will live, but just
so long, so long, so long. Each instant waves
through our nature and is nothing.
But in the love, the grief, under and above
the mother tongue, a permanence
hums: the steady mysterious
the coherent starlight.

Days Through Starch and Bluing

In Memoriam: Catherine Callahan, "Katey," my Grandmother

Mondays, sweating the flat smell
of boiled cloth, Octagon soap,
washday moves in. Stirring work-
clothes with a stick,
chafing grime against the washboard's crimp,
labor-splurging to coddle the particular
Mrs. Westover's preference for blue and white paper-
ruled pinafores done just so, she knots
cubes of Rickett's bluing in small
knapsacks, swirls them through rinse water
till the tub mirrors a periwinkle
sky for her dingy whites.

Steam and lye.
The wringer chews things dry.

Collars and cuffs are dipped in the hot
icing of starch: crisp wings, crackable
as willowware. She tacks the scrapping
armfuls on five lines: shirts, bloomers,
livelier than when worn,
doubledare the wind. They'll freeze soon enough—
her fingers are stiff as clothespins.
She sings. The sound forms quick clouds
that mark the time: "Take me out to the ball-
game, take me out to the . . ." After dark, she'll drag in
the tough sheets. They'll score the snow toward home.

Tuesdays, uncurling linens,
towel-rolled, water-sprinkled
for slick ironing, she'll iron. Now she counts
her kids back from school. In the kitchen
they're spilling tea on their dresses.
Goodwhite, Proudblue. This happened
every week. She sits to think
of tonight's dinner. Tomorrow's pressing.

Maidenhead

In the closet, the dress lives, a deep white in its vinyl
bag, its crepe ivoried, tartared
like a tooth, feeding on what leaks through
the zipper's fervent mesh, an unmentionable,
unworn, waiting, immortally in mind. Open

a window, please, I'm feeling faint. On the bus home
from school, I'm reading Dickinson, living on her

aptitude for inwardness and godlessness, thinking
of the terror she could tell to none
that almost split her mind.
She made solitude honorable. But how hard
it would be to keep ink off a white dress
or keep black cake crumbs or lily pollen off,

how difficult to have only one dress and that one
white. Unlikely really, likely

to be a myth. But don't tell me that at seventeen.
I wear the same harsh uniform each day.
Narrow choices seem natural, strictures
more common than their opposite,
and I am always famished, crushed
on the bottom stair, the door closing
its rubber lips on my hair, trapping
lengths of it outside—

Last one in is an old maid. Your aunt is
mental, some kid says. There is a lace

of nerves, I've learned, a nest of lobe and limbic
tissue around the hippocampus, which on magnetic resonance
imaging resembles a negative of moth.
She felt a funeral in her brain. Somehow I get the fear
of living in the world's unlove forever
better than I get the cheerleaders' braced grins.
I understand my aunt's mind as the opposite of
Dickinson's, though Dickinson also was unnormal, her white
matter more sparkingly aware.

You understand the dress in stanza one is mine,
my one white dress, in which I'll never

shine at graduation, in whose chaste V
the nuns won't stuff linty lumps of Kleenex
to keep covertness whole. In winter in upstate
New York, the snow is too bright on the bus window,
too crusted with singular crystals that toss
sun around inside them the way diamonds pitch
the light between their facets,

gloss to gloss. My aunt lived alone, as you do,
and if that sounds presumptuous, I meant it

in the sense that your head is mostly cloistered
though symptoms of your innerness leak out.
You know, the blush of a pink diamond
is caused by structural strain.
But her aloneness was deeper, I think,
than your own. Hers extended miles below
the surface, down, deep down
into pleats where no interfering rays
can reach and thought is not veiled

so much as sealed. A cap of lead.
Not veiled

since a veil's a mediatrix, at least in the West,
negotiating sun and glance. Veils screen
a virginal reserve = = the mind, I mean, or maidenhead,
a crimp at the threshold, figured as door ajar or slip
knot now, once thought to be homogenous,
a membrane nervous and dispersed
throughout the body, more human than female,
both linkage and severance, the heart and brain
sheathed in its film of flesh and pearled
palladium effect. It is the year the nuns change

their habits at Catholic High, while senior girls
spend recess studying *Modern Bride,* learning

how Honiton = = a bone lace
favored for Victorian veils = = was rolled
rather than folded for storage, sprinkled
with magnesia to remove the oily substance
which gathered after contact with the hair,
cleaned by being covered
with muslin and the muslin lathered
and rubbed until the lace below was soaked,
at which time it was rinsed, dried betwixt

the folds of a towel and sunned
for twelve hours till it looked new

and had no smell. If anything has no smell, it's a gem
and gems are seldom, the rare results
of deviance beneath earth's skin, of
flukey stresses that get carbon to exalt into
the flicker of a pre-engagement ring, a baby diamond,
as solid and as spectral as
a long white dress flaunted by a
girl with nothing else. There's an optical effect,
interference, I think it's called, that puts the best
light on a gem's flaws, transhimmering
its fissures into vivid = = Your flaws
are the best part of you, Marianne Moore wrote,
the best of me too, though as I write it, I recognize
an obvious misquote. Stet and stet again,

place dots under material marked for deletion
and let it stay, let the starved crystal raise

its hackles across the gap inside the gem = =
the trapped drop become a liquid momento,
let wave trains of light collide
from aberrations and give the thing a spooky glow.
Prove—like a Pearl. The paranormal glow

or "orient" of pearls exists between
the nacre shingles, and nacre begins, as is

well known, with injury, a dirt that must be
slathered with the same emollient
used to line the inside of the shell. Solitude deepens,
quickening, whether hidden or exposed as those girls
sunbathing by the gym at noon in the thick of winter,

Janelle, the only black girl in the school,
who covers the white album with foil

and buries her face in the blinding book it makes
so that, as she explains, her skin might reach
the shiny jet of certain Niger tribes
or the saturated blue-black of subdural bleeding.
Her transistor, meanwhile, plays a blues that goes

I got a soundproof room, baby, all you got to say is
you'll be mine. I visited

Dickinson's white dress in Amherst where
it stands in her room, looking so alive it might be
but for the missing head. The phantom pains,
escaping diagnosis, led to bolts of shock—
and tines of shudder—volting through
her mind, my aunt's, that is—stricken into

strange, her language out of scale to what
she must have felt, and Dickinson's metaphors—

And then a Plank in Reason broke—no help.
The doors are locked
to her little house, she has removed
the knobs, leaving deflorations you can peek through
once your eyes adjust, up the stairs and to the left

beyond the thresholds' velvet ropes you'll glimpse
the shell pink walls and hope chest full of failed

trousseau beside the single bed.
Look in upon that sunburst clock, the china creature
on a leash, some pearls unstrung, convulsions of—
the Frigidaire and oilcloth and radiator's
blistered pleats, the slot in which
we slip our fare—

"I sweat blood over this," the dressmaker sighs
at the final fitting, and I can believe it,

the pattern—imported, the seams—so deep,
the stitches—so uncatholic and so—
made for me. *Snap out of it*
someone says as we gain traction and wind
parts my hair, parts the comfort drops
my lenses float on, and I lean against
the door, the white lines vanishing
beneath us = = the measure rolling on the floor = =

Industrial Lace

The city had such pretty clotheslines.
Women aired their intimate apparel

in the emery haze:
membranes of lingerie—
pearl, ruby, copper slips—
their somehow intestinal quivering in the wind.

And Freihofer's spread the chaste, apron scent
of baking, a sensual net
over a few yards of North Troy.

The city had Niagara
Mohawk bearing down with power and light
and members of the Local
shifting on the line.

They worked on fabrics made from wood and acid,
synthetics that won't vent.

They pieced the tropics into housecoats
when big prints were the rage.
Dacron gardens twisted on the line

over lots of Queen Anne's lace.
Sackdresses dyed the sun
as sun passed through, making a brash stained glass
against the leading of the tenements,

the warehouse holding medical supplies.
I waited for my bus by that window of trusses
in Caucasian beige, trying to forget
the pathological inside.
I was thinking of being alive.

I was waiting to open
the amber envelopes of mail at home.
Just as food service workers, counter women,
maybe my Aunt Fran, waited to undo
their perms from the delicate insect meshes
required by The Board of Health.

Aunt Alice wasn't on this route.
She made brushes and plastics at Tek Hughes—
milk crates of orange
industrial lace
the cartons could drip through.

Once we boarded, the girls from Behr-Manning
put their veins up
and sawed their nails to dust
on files from the plant.
All day, they made abrasives. Garnet paper.
Yes, and rags covered with crushed gems called
garnet cloth.

It was dusk—when aunts and mothers formed
their larval curls
and wrapped their heads in thick brown webs.

It was yesterday—twenty years after
my father's death,
I found something he had kept.
A packet of lightning-

cut sanding discs, still sealed.
I guess he meant to open the finish,
strip the paint stalled on some grain
and groom the primal gold.

The discs are the rough size
of those cookies the franchises call Homestyle
and label Best Before.

The old cellophane was tough.
But I ripped until I touched

their harsh done crust.

JULIE KANE
(1952–)

Connemara

The sky here
is as low as thatch.
Stone walls hug the earth
like old men's prayers.
The sons are grown,
and gone to Belfast.

Only the sheep
can survive on such beauty,
but their wool is
wronged terribly with dye,
like the hair of the daughters
who have gone to the cities
after men. This is done
so that a man may tell
his sheep from his neighbor's.

The rage of
The Twelve Fierce Tribes
has seeped
back to the earth
through bone, and the sheep
are the colors of nightmares.

The young
learn the faces of lambs
and forget.

Ode to the Big Muddy

1.

Because I grew up a half hour's drive
from the North Atlantic, always within reach
of the dried-blood-colored cranberry bogs,
the ice bucket water, the desolate beach
with its circular rhythms, I looked down
on linear things, so like an erection
straining against a blue-jeans zipper,
always pushing in the same direction,
spine for brains. But I have learned to mimic,
quick for a girl, the river's predilection.

2.

The first time I saw the Mississippi,
under the curving wing of a jet plane,
it lay there listless as a garden slug:
glistening, oozing, brown. Surely Mark Twain's
paddlewheel visions, Hart Crane's hosannas
to the Gulf, Muddy Waters's delta blues
hadn't sprung forth from a drainage canal?
"Fasten your seatbelts for descent into
New Orleans. Looking to the left, you'll see
the Mississippi River"—so it was true.

3.

Unlike the ocean, the river's life is
right on the surface, bobbing there like turds:
a load of tourists on the *Delta Queen*
drunkenly singing half-remembered words
to showtunes played on steam calliope;
the push-boats nudging at oil tankers;
and nothing underneath but chicken necks
in crawfish nets, and our own dropped anchors.
The sea is our collective unconscious;
the river our blank slate, growing blanker.

4.

And yet the river gathers memories:
the ugliest things grow numinous
over time—the trail of a garden slug
crystalline, opaline, luminous
when the garden slug itself has gone
as the river itself will one day go,
already trying to change its course—
an afternoon we watched the ferryboat
go back and forth until the sun went down,
skimming the water like a skipping stone.

5.

Or the morning we gave back Everette's ashes:
homeless alocholic poet-prince.
A cold March wind was ruffling the water.
Wouldn't you know, the ashes wouldn't sink;
so someone jumped in to wrestle them under.
It hit me then: I didn't want to die.
And so I made a choice, against my nature,
to throw my lot in with that moving line:
abstract, rational, conscious, sober—
cutting a path through human time.

MARY LOGUE
(1952–)

Song in Killeshandra

Toward the end they ask Seamus to sing.
An old man lifts a wee girl
to his knee and gives her a taste of
foamy Guiness. The rain teems
through the night. We are safe.

Seamus lifts the shoulders of his shirt,
runs a finger down his thin nose and then,
like a wren, throws his head back and begins
to sing the song that we all know,
the words little changed, of loss and love

and loss and luck and we hope so much and get
so little. Something settles on us as we
breathe in the smoke-plumed air.
His voice flies in circles
and we watch as the bird batters his wings.

If only a window would open, the sky
would break, releasing his voice of trills
and valleys. Seamus sings the song
that our mothers taught us and our fathers
hummed coming home in the dark.

JAMES SILAS ROGERS
(1952–)

Three Things Remembered from a Life of Georgia O'Keeffe

I.
She tells her friends
she has begun to think
in colors instead of words.

Not so hard to imagine;
no more than to admit
of invented codes between twins,

or even to accept that a dog,
ears cocked and back
bristled by a scent

is in that moment alert,
as much or more in the world
as any of us.

Or to think about
Blake's blade of grass:
color coextensive

with the life
that brings the color forth,
a pulse, a current in green.

Sixty years among paints,
she and her work
fall into their own language

or, rather, find a language
already there
outside the eyes of the world.

II.
At eighty-five or so this cross
and often selfish old lady
said she could live in prison
if she had a window
through which to see the sky;

the bursting buzzing world
reduced to the breeze above it,
pared down to that.
Just light, falling through
the thousand strata of the air.

III.
We hiked the dry riverbeds
evaluating stones,
holding them in our palms
and asking if geology and time
had brought about perfection.

You found a faultless stone,
or so you thought.
I found it again on your coffee table.

You tested me by turning your back,
invited me to whisk it into my pocket
like a hungry man stealing a loaf.

You seemed to think this differed.

I say,
when Satan stretched out his arm
to unfurl the whole world
as a jeweler might roll out a cloth,
where was the temptation?
It was already Christ's in the first place.

ALAN SHAPIRO
(1952–)

from After the Digging

(A Sequence of Poems on the Irish Famine 1846–1849)

Randolf Routh to Charles Trevelyan

—*September 6, 1846*

> Dear Sir, the harvest, such as it will be,
> will be here soon. Yet we know it is Summer
> only by the calendar. The rain
> falls in unebbing tides, making each day
> a darkness that the light illuminates.
> Sir, the reports which come in every day
> are not, as you suggest, exaggerations:
> from Giant's Causeway to Cape Clear, from Dublin
> to Galway Bay, the cold fires of disaster
> burn through the green fields and each black plant blooms
> luxuriant as an abundant harvest.
>
> The people do starve
>   peaceably, as yet.
> But how much longer, how much longer?
>   Armed
> with spades, a horde of paupers entered Cork—
> 'So thin,' the officer in charge has written,
> 'I could not tell which ones were men, and which
> were spades, except the spades looked sturdier.'
> They demanded food, and work. And when dispersed,

'Would that the government would send us food
instead of troops,' one of them muttered, while
the rest like phantoms in an eerie silence
went off.
    Last week, outside of Erris where
the poor like crows swarm, combing the black fields,
living on nettles, weeds, and cabbage leaves,
women and children plundered a meal cart,
fifteen of them tearing at the sacks;
enlivened rags, numb to the drivers' whips,
too weak to drag the sacks off, or to scream,
they hobbled away, clutching to themselves
only small handfuls of the precious stuff.

Please do not think me impudent. Like you
I feel no great affection for the Irish.
But it is not enough that 'we should tell them
they suffer from the providence of God';
or that 'in terms of economic law
it's beneficial that the price of grain
should rise in proportion to the drop in wage'.
We can no longer answer cries of want
with quoting economics, or with prayer.
Ireland is not, and never can be, Whitehall.
And while they starve, no Englishman is safe.

Sir, you have said yourself, 'The evil here
with which we must contend is not the famine,
but their turbulent and selfish character,'
which I half think Nature herself condemns:
today, as if from the Old Testament—
with thunder beating on the iron clouds
which do not bend—the electricity
strikes with the bright and jagged edge of judgment,
while over each blighted field a dense fog falls
cold and damp and close, without any wind.

MEMORANDUM: On the Selling and Preparing of Indian Corn To the Officers of the Relief Commission From Charles Trevelyan

—*November 12, 1846*

Supplies have now been purchased to relieve
those whose distress derives exclusively
from the potato blight, and not to those
whose suffering is but ordinary want.
This distinction must be clearly kept.

> When our own food grew scarce as gold
> > They sold at no cheap rate
> Indian Corn to the penniless.
> > So gold was what we ate—

> A flint-hard gold that would carve fire
> > As it entered our insides;
> The lucky ones would vomit it;
> > The ones who didn't, died.

The proper method is to grind it twice.
Yet we should not give more than wholesome food.
Depending on our charity is not
to be made an agreeable way of life.
Unground, it can afford a decent diet.

> We ate it while long lines of ships
> > Of barley, oats, and wheat
> Floated in convoy down the Shannon
> > Guarded by our Queen's fleet.

> When children ate, an alchemy
> > Which left want unassauged
> Transformed them right before our eyes
> > To the angels of old age—

It can be soaked all night, uncrushed, in warm water,
then boiled for at least an hour and a half,
and eaten with some salt, or milk, if at hand.
Ten pounds of meal prepared this way
should feed a laboring man for seven days.

Their yellowed, rickety, small hands;
      Hair growing on their chins;
While they fed on each golden blade
      Each gold blade fed on them.

Then from our bones, the parched skin swelled
      Past human form, with heat,
And we became pure forms of pain-
      Who could only starve, not eat.

The Dublin Evening Mail

—*December 6, 1846*

CLARE
This afternoon a gruesome incident,
not unfamiliar in these parts, occurred:
Captain Wynne's Inspector of the Works,
a Mr Pearson Hennessey, incurred
near fatal wounds as he approached Clare Abbey.
He was accompanied by his chief clerk
and five foot soldiers—three in front of him
and two behind—when a man dressed in a skirt,
with blackened face, walked slowly from a ditch
and fired his blunderbuss at Hennessey,
who fell back in great torture.
                  The man bowed,
or rather as the clerk reports, curtsied
telling the others, 'I mean *ye* no harm.'

Shocked by his monstrous crime, and almost gay,
disarmingly good manners, no one tried
to apprehend him as he walked away.
Yet, fearing to be shot themselves, they ran
while Mr Hennessey, without assistance,
with eighty shots lodged in his body, crawled
into the village.

        And the peasants danced
as if it were a circus that approached,
aplauding the poor man like fiends in hell,
and, when he pleaded for a doctor, joked
'Sure, now ye are a beggar like ourselves.'

(from) Passage Out

(The log of Thomas Preston, captain of the brig Temperance
carrying Irish emigrants to Canada in the year of 1847)

JUNE 1
This good wind which has not let up
makes reaching Canada in six
or seven weeks conceivable.
And for our tattered Irish cargo
I pray we do. Our food will not
last any longer. As it is,
each person gets but seven pounds
of meal a week, which I have had
to ration daily. For I fear
these passengers, already being
in such a wretched state, would surely
consume at once all their provisions.

Almost none of them seem fit
for any travel. Most were sick
when we embarked, and some were starving.
Yet all were medically examined,
if one can call it that. They filed
one by one in quick succession
before a window, from which a doctor
glanced at their tongues, and took their money.
So frightened were they, filing past
with their tongues out and eyes shut tight,
it almost seemed they were receiving
communion and not passage out.
And yet so destitute perhaps
the only grace they now expect
is passage out.
                    The brig itself
seemed like the new world they were seeking
as they climbed slowly up the planks,
up to the deck and, from the railing,
waved triumphant to their loved ones
whose cries rose up as much from fear
as grief, because they stayed behind
to turn back, exiled, to their homes.

JULY 30
Gross Isle, Canada
The foul mattresses, huge barrels
of vilest matter, the rags and clothes
dumped from the ships that came before us,
dumped in this river that is now
undrinkable, this water we
for weeks have dreamed of.
                    When we anchored
the doctor came on board and said,
'Ha, there is fever here,' and left.
And since then, now almost a week,
only the dead are brought to shore.
The rest must wait until there is room
for quarantine.

So from the brig
we watch while large and graceful ships
from Germany glide past with ease
bearing the robust passengers
on to their precious days. Cruel
the way they sing, the girls who laugh—
their blond hair shining in the sun—
laughing as they blow kisses to
these blighted shades who stagger out
of the dark hold, pained by the light.

AUGUST 10
After the digging, Sean McGuire,
his skin too papery to sweat,
drove two shovels into the ground
making a cross, and said, 'By this,
Mary, I swear I will go back
as soon as I earn passage home
and murder him that murdered you,
our landlord, Palmerston.'
                              And went,
like all the rest, like living refuse
half naked, maimed, to Montreal,
to Boston, to New York; the seeds
of typhus already blossoming.

And blossoming those other seeds
as virulent as a disease,
that grief which suffering can't feel,
that will return as surely as
the seasons when the flesh returns.
Who have endured must now endure
a healing no less unbearable,
must be consoled by hate's cold feel
fixing all their memories
into a purpose stronger than life,
immutable as loss.
                         They go,
and may God go with them who bring
into the new world nothing else
but epitaphs for legacies.

ELIZABETH SPIRES
(1952–)

The Travellers

We have black teeth but we dream just the
same as people who live in houses.
> —Janine Wiedel and Martina O'Fearadhaigh,
>   *Irish Tinkers*

When the lake lies still as a mirror,
giving the sky back every star it has stolen,
when the moon bleaches our nightclothes
white as the shirts that flutter in store windows,
when fog erases the walls you have built,
stone by stone, to keep us out,
                              then we will come,
driving our wagons through your painted dreams,
entering your houses on tiptoe.
We've brought the tin cup
you never bought from us, a penny
for your tongue since you like the taste
of money. We've brought our daughters and sons,
the dead ones, who whisper and sing
as they go through your children's playthings.
They beg us to stay awhile, they say
they are cold and want to drink all the milk
they can hold. But we are travellers.
We know it's bad luck taking the dead on the road.
We'll leave them here, stopping again
in a year or a week or tomorrow.

You wake up sweating, feverish.
Your blankets are gone, all the windows
in your house are open.
You will never catch us.
We have taken the crooked road
to the next county, the trees hurrying
us along, pointing *this way, this way,*
with their crooked arms.
But the little ghosteens stay on,
hiding in closets and cupboards, whispering:
We are the rag and bone.
We are the summer walkers of the long acre.
We've come to pick the potato eyes
out of the quality folk,
to comb the gristle out of the meat
of the country men.

KILLARNEY CLARY
(1953–)

(from) Who Whispered Near Me

White Sand, Tall Grass

White sand, tall grass. This strip of ocean is a thin bit of
deep blue as if the earth bends suddenly out there, beneath
the dark storm moving, pushing shadows on the surface of
the sea which presses in close and rushes away. A cold
wind feels impatient, too, as it returns in force with each
break, again. And the sky that splits is a surprise, sending
a straight shaft of silver to claim its town of luck. Doors
blow open with a crash, close gently a ways away. They
would close.

The sun is faith and will be for so many months of empty
houses, linen closets, shelves of cold glasses, while the un-
ending sand in the undying wind heckles the clapboards,
blasts the paint.

Sometimes everything is all right except my ears are cold.
I think, if only my ears were warm again. If only again,
want. Away. A whistle in the wind. If something changed
it all forever . . . It is all changing always forever. Cer-
tainly the fish must swim deeper and birds leave for a
while. In the back of a school desk a scrap of paper learns
its folds until they are weak, and the penciled joke is lost in
the creases, graphite dust.

There is no imitating the weather, no remembering but a dullness I think is near my heart. And when I am asked to carry out the one fine thing from the burning house, I'll know what reflects me is arbitrary; I am invisible. Won't my habits be undercut while the paces across a familiar room are smoke and ash, distance no more? I don't know myself without these clothes—the buttoned coat of answers and shoes of home.

(from) By Common Salt

Only the Size of a Hand

Only the size of a hand, a pounded gold boat was disrupted from the bog by the coulter of a plow. Oars no larger than sandwich picks. A mast of bent gold wire.

For two thousand years it sailed an airless voyage, filled and surrounded by black peat. Dark comfort of its secret, the way each part, each piece was suspended and blind. . . .

If there were messages they vibrated and garbled across hammered strap benches; there was no space through which to shout. In perfect sleep. No rocking. No song.

What beauty and what prince, apple or thorn? Was it such trouble to shine empty in daylight? Darker still was that inclination to tip forward and take on heaviness, sigh, "I don't remember." "Don't remember me."

Clear of Oak Groves

Clear of oak groves, sunrise stretched a
thin reach deep into the chamber, tripping the setting of fires
on hilltops: signals relayed to the quarters. A day to plant or
hunt, enter women or agreements.

Night skies were laid on fields in perfect orientation before the
plates opened, wandered, collided; they continue and will. There
is so much to take into account. It may be impossible to choose
for myself; all pleasures might hand me loneliness.

I'll find the dark room, tip the white table to catch a shaft bent
by a mirror, shot through a pin hole, and I'll watch the ocean
upside down. Foam churns at the edge of a vision. It is time to
do something in particular.

Their Boat Was Lost in the Surf

Their boat was lost in the surf. She keened
for it; her husband urged her away. They walked together over
the storm beach; she didn't hold on to him, but to what he car-
ried: net or rope, his pack of woven straw.

He'd been unable to land the curragh; she was sorry and he,
blameless. I can't watch their mix of pardon and disappoint-
ment; I turn it off. The world must break.

ROBERT McDOWELL
(1953–)

The Islander

*After Tomás O'Crohán, chronicler of the Great Blasket Island,
whose last human residents were removed in 1953.*

When I move off my island
Winter will go with me,
Our names in the sand
Disfigured by the sea.
The wind will blow
Where my people go.

Great storms bull through our houses,
Time flattens the seawall.
A songbird browses
In the ass-deserted stall.
How could we know
Where our world would go?

Like rags for the poor we're gathered,
Like crockery we break.
Who among us bothered
To prepare for this heartache,
This final blow
On the world we know?

No Blasket man is free
Of the politician's scheme.
What trick of cruelty
Makes me the last to dream?
May my curragh repair,
Never sailing from there.

Give us this day our portion,
Which is salty, small, and dry.
The pride of our nation
Is water in the eye.
The wind will blow
Where my people go.

The Banshee, riding a cloud,
Gathers my thoughts tonight
In her winding shroud.
May stories told by firelight
Survive in the air,
An echo there.

The wind will blow
Through the world we know,
Where my people go.

Prayers That Open Heaven

Of a declaration of faith proclaimed among many,
The congregation rising up in song;
Of a lonesome walk around a muddy pasture,
A lullaby boating children to sleep;
Of the bond between your dog and you,
Of forgiveness for those who burn fields
And break promises, who use their power
To lord it over others; of the ditch you dig
With a neighbor, the piles of leaves you rake,
The barn's sure bridge to the past;
Of Our Father and Hail Mary,
Of the sight of a solitary rider
In late afternoon sun on the Cascade range,
The horse moving like the motion of God;
Of a sky so full of stars you know you are not alone.
What are the prayers that open Heaven, where
Are the words and guides you should follow?
No one answers, no one lifts up your heart but you.

KEVIN BOYLE
(1954–)

The Lullaby of History

I put the bookmark in the page after Lincoln's
silence during the 1860 campaign, after no one
in the Gulf States cast a single vote for him,
then march off to the car, carseat in tow, drive on
cruise, mainly, to the site in Durham where Sherman
coaxed the Southern general—Johnston—
to submit twice, sign twice. The six hundred thousand
dead were like the shucks inside the reconstructed
bed, the smoke the chimney slewed, the clayish mud.
In the museum, name-tagged women watch our daughter,
four months here, while we investigate the flags
with gunshot holes, the uniforms with gunshot holes,
the shells of the Union Army with three rings, the shells
of the Confederate's with two. We take our daughter
to the filmstrip where she sleeps through
the stills of uniformed corpses in ditches, and cries
at war's end, one flag for all these states. We ride,
strapped, to the Greek restaurant known for its sauces
and lamb, stroll inside the tobacco warehouse transformed
into a mall, each glass pane so large a truck
could drive through and pick up brightleaf to ship.
They say this section profited when South met North
and troops took in the smoke of this leaf, spreading
by word of mouth the flavor, until the profits
were so large owners began to donate. In the antique store
we happen upon a map my father might love
of Ireland before division, just as it appeared

when he was born, the north a section, not another country,
Ulster's counties awash in the orange the mapmakers
stained it. But we can't commit to buy for this price,
or prevent our daughter from falling asleep as we discuss
facts the map makes clear: battles marked in bold,
our side losing again and again, the Flight of the Earls,
Vinegar Hill, the Battle of the Boyne, and we donate
a moment during the ride home to feel
the weight of the centuries' dead, almost cry for all
those men who gave their skin to the ground so young,
so young brought their lips to earth and let their mouths
cave in, accept the soil as their voice. We did not wake
our girl through this. *Let her sleep,* we said.

MICAHEL CAREY
(1954–)

The Islandman

If he could,
he would live
on an island,

the soft waters
of nothingness lapping
forever at his shores.

So many of the old ones:
the Skelligs, the Blaskets,
the Aran Islands

are silent now
or barely breathing
with human consciousness.

Who or what
were they fleeing,
those crazy men

who settled
them so many
years ago

when the world
was vast and its people
so few in number?

This farm will have
to do, he figures, his children
his only exotic beauties.

What his hands
find to do, he does
and he calls it meditation.

He'll never know
why he was put here
on this island

in a sea of islands,
his nothing in the
middle of the world.

Aubade for Allihies, County Cork

One dark morning you awake far from here
on a foggy cliff overlooking the Atlantic.
A strange dog stares at you
as you stare back and the wind
buffets you both. You can't help feeling
rugged and lyrically independent
in all this mist. It is so much like the movies.
Something important is going to happen.
At any moment you will be called on
to act. But the Armada does not wreck;
German guns and barrels of French rum
do not wash up on the foam below,
although the sea is tumultuous enough
to dissolve anything, even the light
as it falls, almost, between you and the dog.

In the two-room schoolhouse
that you intend to enter, the village
is still dancing. Fishermen share their catch
while their wives bake bread and break it.
This is the center of what matters. Everyone
on this spot on the spinning earth
spins beautifully, as they have all night,
in gentle interweaving patterns
as the music curls and curls back on itself
like time, time that even now is taking you
back to your morning chores, the here and now
of Iowa farm life, light-years from
whatever planet you were on when you
first heard the sweet screams of the
fiddle and the pipes and the whistles
fading into the ocean's turbulence,
and millions upon millions of lives away
from the passionate pagan hearts
that first decided to pass them on.

MICHAEL COFFEY
(1954–)

Mid-life, Looking North

Tendering motes in falls of light
siftingly, like soft flakes of soap,
drift in a column of space
over Fifth Avenue.

The steady solid forms of the street—
architectures deeply footed, high, broad-
shouldered stones faced in gallant glass:
mixture of air and lives.

Stood on pavement, one eye in a slow storm,
a motion tracing what is life, a pastime;
the persistent erasing is it
of disarticulated spaces, other's spices?

A long Wednesday, anyway, getting longer.
Struck like Yeats in a London shop,
not with blessing or the blessed, but torso-stocked,
iron-lunged, a soul turning into things.

The Saranac River

I look so much better
in the mirror of home
since I left—
a kind of sumac grows at its edges.

Light like a liquid
or a wind stream
over me—a father's word
yields a red berry in the fall.

Their tumbling shapes,
a mother's graces rippling past
burnishing my face—
notions bouldering down the gorge.

I stand in the current
my eyes have opened,
and when they close
the Algonkians walk down from Canada.

I remember
a poem by Theodore Roethke
but vaguely-it is far upstream—
they crushed the red berries for war paint.

Mouthing a torrent of images
a mentor read it to us aloud:
Where the mind can go in poetry, he said.
The river isn't moving, I am.

I'll see them when they come,
dark bent bodies intent in the dawn.
And there's no hurry—
they are chanting the unknown French.

Miles from home like them,
ranked against a warm building,
a poem wades in riverlight,
guessing how a river got its name.

MICHAEL DONAGHY
(1954–)

City of God

When he failed the seminary he came back home
to the Bronx and sat in the back pew
of St. Mary's every night reciting the Mass
from memory—quietly, continually—
into his deranged overcoat.
He knew the local phone book off by heart.
He had a system, he'd explain,
perfected by Dominicans in the Renaissance.

To every notion they assigned a saint,
to every saint an altar in a transept of the church.
Glancing up, column by column, altar by altar,
they could remember any prayer they chose.
He'd used it for exams, but the room went wrong—
a strip-lit box exploding slowly as he fainted.
They found his closet papered floor to ceiling
with razored passages from St. Augustine.

He needed a perfect cathedral in his head,
he'd whisper, so that by careful scrutiny
the mind inside the cathedral inside the mind
could find the secret order of the world
and remember every drop on every face
in every summer thunderstorm.
And that, he'd insist, looking beyond you,
is why he came home.

I walked him back one evening as the snow
hushed the precincts of his vast invisible temple.
Here was Bruno Street where Bernadette
collapsed, bleeding through her skirt
and died, he had heard, in a state of mortal sin;
here, the site of the bakery fire where Peter stood
screaming on the red-hot fire escape,
his bare feet blistering before he jumped;
and here the storefront voodoo church beneath the el
where the Cuban *bruja* bought black candles,
its window strange with plaster saints and seashells.

The Classics

I remember it like it was last night,
Chicago, the back room of Flanagan's
malignant with accordions and cigarettes,
Joe Cooley bent above his Paolo Soprani,
its asthmatic bellows pumping as if to revive
the half-corpse strapped about it.
It's five a.m. Everyone's packed up.
His brother Seamus grabs Joe's elbow mid-arpeggio,
'Wake up man. We have to catch a train.'
His eyelids fluttering, opening. The astonishment . . .

I saw this happen. Or heard it told so well
I've staged the whole drunk memory:
What does it matter now? It's ancient history.
Who can name them? Where lie their bones and armour?

Pentecost

The neighbours hammered on the walls all night,
Outraged by the noise we made in bed.
Still, we kept it up until by first light
We'd said everything that could be said.

Undaunted, we began to mewl and roar
As if desire had stripped itself of words.
Remember when we made those sounds before?
When we built a tower heavenwards
They were our reward for blasphemy.
And then again, two thousand years ago,
We huddled in a room in Galilee
Speaking languages we didn't know,
While amethyst uraeuses of flame
Hissed above us. We recalled the tower
And the tongues. We knew this was the same,
But love had turned the curse into a power.

See? It's something that we've always known:
Though we command the language of desire,
The voice of ecstasy is not our own.
We long to lose ourselves amid the choir
Of the salmon twilight and the mackerel sky,
The very air we take into our lungs,
And the rhododendron's cry.

And when you lick the sweat along my thigh,
Dearest, we renew the gift of tongues.

Reliquary

The robot camera enters the *Titanic*
And we see her fish-cold nurseries on the news;
The toys of Pompeii trampled in the panic;
The death camp barrel of babyshoes;

The snow that covered up the lost girl's tracks;
The scapular she wore about her neck;
The broken doll the photojournalist packs
To toss into the foreground of the wreck.

Caliban's Books

Hair oil, boiled sweets, chalk dust, squid's ink . . .
Bear with me. I'm trying to conjure my father,
age fourteen, as Caliban—picked by Mr. Quinn
for the role he was born to play because
'I was the handsomest boy at school'
he'll say, straight-faced, at fifty.
This isn't easy. I've only half the spell,
and I won't be born for twenty-eight years.
I'm trying for rainlight on Belfast Lough
and listening for a small, blunt accent
barking over the hiss of a stove getting louder like surf.
But how can I read when the schoolroom's gone
black as the hold of a ship? Start again.

Hair oil, boiled sweets . . .
But his paperbacks are crumbling in my hands,
seachanged bouquets, each brown page
scribbled on, underlined, memorized,
forgotten like used pornography:
The Pocket Treasury of English Verse,
How to Win Friends and Influence People,
Thirty Days To a More Powerful Vocabulary.

Fish stink, pitch stink, seaspray, cedarwood . . .
I seem to have brought us to the port of Naples,
midnight, to a shadow below deck
dreaming of a distant island.
So many years, so many ports ago!
The moment comes. It slips from the hold
and knucklewalks across the dark piazza
sobbing *maestro! maestro!* But the duke's long dead
and all his magic books are drowned.

Exile's End

You will do the very last thing.
Wait then for a noise in the chest,
between depth charge and gong,
like the seadoors slamming on the car deck.
Wait for the white noise and then cold astern.

Gaze down over the rim of the enormous lamp.
Observe the skilled frenzy of the physicians,
a nurse's bald patch, blood. These will blur,
as sure as you've forgotten the voices
of your childhood friends, or your toys.

Or, you may note with mild surprise,
your name. For the face they now cover
is a stranger's and it always has been.
Turn away. We commend you to the light,
Where all reliable accounts conclude.

MICHAEL McFEE
(1954–)

Family Reunion Near Grape Creek Church,
Four Miles West of Murphy, N.C., 1880

Everybody moved. Only that background shed
is focused, its roof a black hat for the ladies
clustered toward the rear of this sober choir
behind the bearded blurs in Confederate dress,
the infants and the witch-like matriarch.

And nobody smiled, unwilling to suffer
minutes of breathless muscle before a camera
omniscient as the Lord or a ready predator,
forgetting that the involuntary subtle pulse
of simply being human and alive would erase

this effort at a record, sure as the weather
would wash its hands on their soapstone graves
until no text was left, sure as bitter years
would blight their genealogy with stillbirths,
death in the service, "bean lodged in throat."

Even the trees above moved. This might as well
be any family, Adam's fallen clan, regathered
outside Paradise for their farewell picnic.
What curse or promise do they bear, these men
with radiant chests and women brightly buttoned,

that tall unbiblical couple near the border,
her birdlike hands poised in some peculiar sign,
his right hand not sheathed over the starchy heart
but pressed to his temple, sharp index finger
cocked in some elaborate parody of suicide?

Vague old ghosts, "four miles west of Murphy"
might as well be four miles east of Manteo:
the dumbfounded verge of nowhere, a landscape
lost to heaven's shutter since the deluge
or buried for decades now under dammed water.

The Family Laugh

for Miriam Marty Clark

On my way from the kitchen to the living room,
I heard you laugh while cooking and your mother
laugh while telling a story to the dinner guests

and it was uncanny, precisely the same sound,
an identical inarticulate explosion of delight
at some absurd turn in the recipe or narrative.

I stood frozen between your matching happiness
just like the time I heard my cousin's cackle—
its gentle unforced tone, its melodious cheer—

and shivered because it was just like Messalina,
my favorite fun-loving aunt, dead for many years
yet alive in the genuine mirth of her daughter.

What better legacy to leave my son than this?—
the family laugh, a manner of taking pleasure,
an antidote to poisonous genetics or habits,

the lethal words and looks and offhand guilt
I've given him without thinking; so that, one day,
somebody might hear him and his son laughing

in exactly the same way, at exactly the same time,
and hear a perfect echo of me and my parents
and all the unlikely generations of laughter

back up the Appalachians, across the dour ocean
to a place where joy was as precious as food,
all the way back to the original couple who saw

something in the garden that made them feel odd,
that inspired a sweet illogical noise, the first laugh.
It baffled the animals, but God saw that it was good.

The All-Dog Siren Choir

Their ears can smell trouble coming
miles away, its painful scent:

even the faintest ambulance
triggers unconditional keening

for the firestruck and crimeridden,
for all the sick and injured and dead,

a ghastly polyphonic sobbing
shocking our neighborhood's sober air

with the hackle-raising grief
of blink cockers, half-cocked dachsunds,

sentimental crapulous Irish tenors,
the lab's black baritone.

Under their hysterical blues
the siren's orchestra builds to crescendo

and flashes by, but the mournful dogs
continue to make lamentation,

answering wail for wail for wail for wail
long after Emergency has passed,

their grief ludicrous to the cats
sharpening their claws, keeping out of it,

but pleasing somehow to the tone-deaf angels
and their dyslexic god.

JANICE FITZPATRICK SIMMONS
(1954–)

The Sirens

We are in the Sirens hotel on the Liffey
and through the open window the dense,
autumn air carries Handel's *Water Music* —
'that flow endearing flow over skin, limbs . . .'
A candle-like light glows on the dark water
and repeats and repeats in the living body
of the river—the water is round, striated
with light. Tinfoil eyes glare gold then green.
Newly returned to the half-clean water
salmon and trout are in the flux of survival.
People are here, occasional shouts
rise from the quays.

Rivers of stars move on the fluid body
of the Liffey. The river is so dark
that the granite banks are light beside it.
These stars in the varying dome of Dublin sky
mean only light and are all light.
The night unfolds around us like a river
past the Ormond Hotel, lit with the candle's
first flicker, candles I light in memory
of each year I endured without love. There will be more,
more feasts and flesh—the silver and rose
of salmon slipping quietly like this nation
into the silken thread of my spine.

Where the Roads Lead

for Mary Reid

1. At Beltony
The sun of early November bears down
on the stone circle causing the mist to rise
from the sodden ground of a year
with no summer and early gales.
At Beltony, set on a small green hill between green hills,
my sight is aimed through the bare branches
to Barnesmore Gap and the sea.

Behind me there are hills too,
covered with leaveless trees
of Columbcille's foretelling—
evergreens block the sight line from here
to Grianan of Aileach. Shadows fall
and steam rises from the half-buried
male and female marking stones,
and from the finger stone
that marks the journey's way.

I walk the descending path
through the darkness of pines
and the brief wet glitter of twigs and moss.

2. St. Patrick's Purgatory
The ferryman steering St. Bridgid is old and dark.
Yeats's giant bird of the lake is in a dreaming underwater
November hibernation communing with generations
who have made their way up this riven valley
to the lough and sulphurous island's Basilica,
at one with knights and poets,
shopkeepers and maids, traditions echo.

Derg water slaps and foams
about the solid boat, and the sun is aching
and bright on a Heron's wing as it rises
from a dark rock in the lake.
To step on the receiving dock in the emptiness of winter
is to hear only the sounding of belief
and half-belief through the old chapel,
round and round the stones of the station,
in the tired wind clanging the penitents' bell—
Mea culpa, Mea culpa, Mea culpa.

Blame me too for my physical nature
for what I liked the most was the wide window
in the new hostel where I could look out across
the water and fields and watch the procession
of myself projected there—
that dream-like country of the past
unreeling, making its way toward me
in blazing autumn light, travelling the path
that led to this valley, this lake, this island.

NUALA ARCHER
(1955–)

Emigrant

A migrant
I know return

is impossible
the sea sieves

our unmakings
no place

can center such
only the whole

earth can vibrate
to such vagrancies

of home such reaches
of abandonment

released into
our evolving names

I now live out
the longings of this

century
the astonishing

communing
through us

Between Swilly and Sewanee

for Naomi

Who is the mother of these words? Nonsense syllables
leaping up between Swilly and Sewanee. Three-
thousand miles of ocean: *O, bring back, bring*

back: Lovers crossing over: winging the never-
forever gap, the Atlantic assemblage: her mother
and my mother and myself: *Make me as I am—*

make me beautiful. Each with the wind of watery
trees in our faces and faith in the following dolphins—
bowing and breathing in dawn's opal brilliance,

the colostrum of our comings. Barking like Blueticks
for the sun, curling into the Q.E. II, the dolphins are
the clouds at my window, nuzzling the green stillness

of flight—as if the third leave-taking were a coda,
another Rosetta story—finally cracked. In the wavering
hyphens—a home between homes—a liquid blossoming of

bones—a zany confluence: the Darién and Dublin—
made flesh in a matinée of sheer quiet. Pine and palm tracks
merging. A life glowing in mots of otherly swayings.

JULIE O'CALLAGHAN
(1955–)

The Long Room Gallery

Trinity College Dublin

There is nothing to breathe
here in the Gallery
except old years.
The air from today
goes in one lung
and 1783 comes out the other.
As for spirits,
stand perfectly still
and you will feel them
carousing near your ear.
Tourists down below
think they've seen a ghost
when they spot you
floating through bookcases
over their heads.
On a creaky wooden balcony
you tunnel through centuries,
mountains of books
rising into the cumulus.
You could scale a ladder
up the rockface of knowledge
or search the little white slips
stuck in books
for a personal message
from Swift.

Ancient oxygen,
antique dust particles,
petrified wood …
Who are you kidding?
You belong down there:
baseball caps, chewing gum, videos.

The Great Blasket Island

Six men born on this island
have come back after twenty-one years.
They climb up the overgrown roads
to their family houses
and come out shaking their heads.
The roofs have fallen in
and birds have nested in the rafters.
All the white-washed rooms
all the nagging and praying
and scolding and giggling
and crying and gossiping
are scattered in the memories of these men.
One says, 'Ten of us, blown to the winds—
some in England, some in America, some in Dublin.
Our whole way of life—extinct.'
He blinks back the tears
and looks across the island
past the ruined houses, the cliffs
and out to the horizon.

Listen, mister, most of us cry sooner or later
over a Great Blasket Island of our own.

Home

The Illinois sunrise demonstrates
exactly what an alien you are
in your car on the prairie
heading north to Chicago
where some Irish guy
aimed a hundred years ago.
That's why you're going there
instead of somewhere else.

He is controlling your life
and the direction of you auto.
If he had decided on Boston—
you'd be driving there instead.
Funny how we let this geezer
place us here and give us an accent,
expecting us to live surrounded
by corn and soybean fields.

In a booth at the Dixie Truck Stop
you drink your bottomless coffee
and figure how the rustics to your left
and the military personnel to the rear
were similarly plonked down
in the middle of nowhere.
Simple souls that we are
we now call this region 'Home'.

EAMONN WALL
(1955–)

Hart Crane's Bridge

Rows of immigrants facing west
behind, the Bridge
city onto itself, world
within world, poem
of boats, steel, sailors;
Amen to seagulls, shifting
riverbeds hold this nest
of cars. Submarines to
Brooklyn come up for air
Thomas Wolfe's dead, body electric
of America. To the right
a lady of the harbour
swathed in centennial
Band Aid. The paper says
the French repairmen will not
go home when the work's done.
What does Whitman mean?
What have our bodies built for,
definitions through paper or
sunsets in familiar places?
Where in the forest grows
the Green Card?
Is it what surrounds the primrose
on the Wexford road?
Sit under a pine
with food and open lips,
hold this child of ours

upwards to the sky
to bronze his skin
any sky, any where
only the Irish pines and primroses
are mine.
America,
how she deals the cards.

At the Edges of the Nerve: Song for the Americas

At the edges sand and rocks lap the sea
body of a continent
relentless
but always this wondrous skin
of blue and grey

whatever I can imagine
is here

Rockaway Beach to
a roadway in California,
Alaska to Patagonia
to Darwin's bird lands

this skin of give and stone
holds it all
and freckled faces

and our griefs and possibilities
after all are nothing
there are no forms to fill

airplanes, sporting fields, trains,
these sturdy buildings where we live

in an instant I may walk another road
or watch the dust and sage brush grow

the skin of the human form
bathed in limes or mud,
but the blood flows

and morning comes in,

each day a door opens to street or field
edges survive their wind and water

and there is a belly of softness
beyond the apartment door to get used to,

I alight from the train in a new town
to change my clothes, and eat breakfast.

Song at Lake Michigan

I walked to Lake Michigan
with thoughts of a sea nearer home
where we swam under clouds of departure
Maria, my father, and me.

I walked towards Wisconsin's waters
to take wind of some boats and the rocks
a child of the green on the waterfront
faces of the past in my eyes.

This country is drinking itself
working by day for the right not to sleep
galloping along without comment or thought
content that some time is at hand.

But here I can sing to myself
unbound by traditions of death
I'm not working for brothers or nuns
I'm drinking slowly at the wild neon bar.

Four Stern Faces / South Dakota

I was living in a bedsit in Donnybrook
when John Lennon was shot outside the
Dakota apartment building in New York City
and that's what I'm thinking this morning
piloting my family through the hollow
darkness on Iron Mountain Road, trespassing
on the holy ground of the Lakota nation.

Four stern faces in the distance address
me and when I get stuck after rattling off
Washington & Lincoln I call on Matthew to
fill in the blanks and wonder how the hell
will I pass the civics test when I apply
for citizenship. I could tell you all
about Allen Ginsberg and Adrienne Rich
but presidents, state capitols and amendments
to the constitution would snooker me, and
I get the feeling the I.N.S. doesn't care
too much for postmodern American poetry.
Caitlin belongs to the woods—mosses,
pine needles, slow moving light and shade,
a bright face in the back of the car
breathing a fantastic language, this
slow mid-morning pilgrimage I drive
my loved ones forward and climbing.

When Lennon was dying I was typing
the forms to come to America: on this
journey through the Sandhills—Irish sand
dunes without the sea—to the Black Hills
to wild flowers with names so gorgeous
I cannot bear to hear you say them.
Native people, 'Strawberry Fields Forever,'
Ryan White dying in Indiana. My children
craving this just as the matchsticks and
cats' eyes on the Gorey road mesmerized them,
howling now for lunch. Here the light is
different, the evenings shorter, Gods are weeping.

And there's no escape from caring or
from history: to lie on high plains,
prairie grasses, and Black Hills is to
be blown into their stories, drowned in
their summer rains. Just when I think I've
lost the Irish rings around the tree, I open
the door and find red clay stuck on the
tyres, the whole earth screaming, my children
breathing on the electric hairs above my collar.

Being woken one ordinary workday to Lennon
being dead, 'Imagine' on the radio, remembering
the grown-ups weeping in late November '63,
one morning in Dublin when it finally struck
that heroes are flowers constantly dying on
these black and holy hills we spend the years
wandering towards till light reveals a universe
beyond stony victorious faces bolted to a rock.

The Westward Journey

Setting out on the westward journey
with eight suitcases and two cats.
On this last night we sleep at the
La Guardia Marriott to swim in the pool,
and begin the busy work of forgetting
Mr. Pedro's large hands stuck in the
till as his fingers float among the
pennies. 'You are leaving New York
to live in America,' he says. 'I would
be afraid of that, and the little ones
will lose their Spanish.' At the end of
the street each Sunday morning bright
speedboats race for the early shadows
under the George Washington Bridge.

I have stored away your cries of
being born: from these ugly streets,
red paint on the old benches in
Payson Playground, to the sweet
brown eyes of an immigrant from
Galicia fumbling and cursing quietly
about for our change. My own childhood
unimaginable without the Slaney humming
'Son, you breath' as I read the clock
each morning above Louis Kerr's shop.
Impossible that there was another life.

Tonight, my children are singing in the
water at the prospect of a plane ride to
another life, but someone must remember,
there must be someone to write this down.

CHRIS AGEE
(1956–)

Thistledown

in memoriam the dead of Omagh

> A gnomon falls a shade past XII on the Hospital's
> Sun-dial at Kilmainham. How far am I now? Maybe
> *Nel mezzo del cammin*—this noon at least,
>
> Still fit at forty-two? Above it Anglican gold
> Numbering our own clock's linear round. And higher still
> The steeple-vane's golden Cockerel and Four Directions
>
> Capped by the sailing white leviathans of a bright day
> Whose sweeping windrushes shadow
> In and out over the hot plaque of the Courtyard's sunstrapped
>
> Dust and gravel like pages turned now and then
> In a book of light—or a white road at night gleaming
> Polarized in an old vineyard of *la France profonde.* Past
>
> The aluminum flagpole whose stick shadow right-angles
> The jib of an invisible dhow: past the de Chirico arcade
> Whose shadowland cuts light out of shade: Jake gallops again
>
> Towards the Great Hall's façade—staffed by Crimean redcoats—
> In some endless enchanted Alamo of the spendthrift
> Imagination. Strange how I never noticed the numerals

Descend on the right from VI to I
But ascend on the left from XII to VII
As if the ornate curlicues of the gnomon's idea

Topping my son were parallel lives of light and dark
Unfolding and folding. For a moment the moment
Revives a crystalline June evening at the Giant's Ring

Where Jake ran wild on Indian paths through silage
Thick with buttercups and the purplish tinge of timothy-ears;
Then, upstairs in the old wards where he might have caught an eye,

The five green pears around a white plate in Scott's
Stilled zen-lifes of colour and form. As he runs on into new memory
Between the West Gate and the East, scuffing up dustiness,

Ghostly glints of the field-lint of thistledown
Sail around him like a tumbleweed of souls fleeing from
The child massacre at Omagh already happening three hours later.

(Note: *The Royal Hospital Kilmainham, which
once housed military pensioners, is now the Irish Musuem
of Modern Art, where a William Scott restrospective was
on show. The Omagh massacre took place at 3:10 p.m. on
Saturday, August 15, 1998.*)

Offing

That sun, a moon almost: I remember it like a bindi
On the cool brow of a porcelain buddha, a red spot

In the mist of dusk. That place, that microcosmos,
The clean lines of clapboard, the crimson cupola,

Summers in New England, light in August,
What can I say? What can you say of life?

That I was there, that it was here. That place
I first felt its deep offing, that porch I walked from,

The gingerbread of the spartan Cottage,
The shuffleboard, the lawn's two iron deer

Asperged with dew, a Wednesday's sixties line-dance,
Deck rockers under the trestle of stars, gin rummy

In the Sun Room. On down the hill rippling through
To the swans on the Spring House pond,

A teardrop on the brow of the Bluffs,
Deep in cornflowers and Queen Anne's lace.

That place I still return to, fresh as ever,
The clatter of dishes, the old Polish cook

With his broken English and wild eyes,
The waitresses in white, meals *al fresco*

On the laundry landing, *circa* '71.
Sails in the offing, our Shack and psychedelic Barn

Out back towards the wall-quilt and grasses
Sprinkled with cornflowers and Queen Anne's lace.

Out for a break from the dinner din.
In stillness, the empty Annex, a red disc sinking

Like the buoy of crepuscule. That time. That place
I spent some misspent youth. That porch. That dew.

By the HARP Brewery

Hearing *Dundalk* he remembers, he says, the hour
Waiting for the train: the orange at Loughran's,
The sill's padded red-leather seat where he sat perched
In the lounge window, the station's ten-to-five clock

Stopped like Chirico's. Will he still, when I'm as shadowy
As our two shadows together on the dusty pavement—
Golden light, empty hour—as we passed a church chock-full
For Saturday night mass, the walk in the bog

Already a dead dream of bog-asphodel and buttercup,
Birch and turf-banks, a pine-stump like a Shiva in rushes,
Behind us kegs in shadow, old lettering and an open door
To time's strangeness, as if he had stepped into the past, or out of it?

First Light

One begins not knowing
what the mind will beachcomb from the radiant flux
of things in the intertidal zone, what the combers

have left at first light:
a sawn stump with three worn nodes,
a buoy in wrack, a corncob, a dead ray:

the subtle patinas of the bluffs
beetled by bay and bittersweet,
riddled by the cliff-dwellings of swallows:

dark glistening surf
occasioned by trails of mackerel-cloud:
the vast abstraction

of dry smooth shingle-stones infinitely variable
under foot. Or, finally, brilliant indigo-and-seagreen
under a clearing sky. You have quickstepped thus

in spirit, from stepping-stone to stepping-stone
as if some surefooted Chinese boatman
leaping nimbly athwart junk-to-junk at a mooring—

though unable to say, looking back,
should you ask yourself, how exactly you traversed
that hour's crescent of foaming sand and shingle-bank.

PATRICK DONNELLY
(1956 –)

I am a virus

I am a virus
        probably
I am no plant
        or animal
I am no vegetable
        or mineral
I may not even
        be alive
I do not eat
        or need to eat
I only know
        how to increase
I make your cells
        my brothel
I make your life
        my toilet
I give you time
        if I care to
Or bite your head off
        this very night
I have no king
        or kingdom
I have your life
        and your breath
between my teeth.

How the Age of Iron Turned to Gold

My death makes her way to me
carrying green leaves.

I hear my prayer coming
behind illness, romantic noise,

urgent telephone messages,
alchemical lab results,

like a brook weaving
through thicket.

Water knows the way,
it isn't lost.

My teacher comes to me
by the western gates,

her eyes gone violet
as the peal of a bell

as she bends to gather
all her tender puppies by the neck.

MARY JANE NEALON
(1956–)

Heirlooms Not Relinquished in the Great Depression

Coal, as a black shiny reminder of birth-place,
was left in Christmas stockings or carried in a scuttle,
whose wide-lipped mouth spit dust. The lack of heat
sent us scurrying, in our fleece-feet, to the parlor
floor, where the player-Baby Grand shone oily black,
two tons of wire and wood hammer on the Chinese rug.

We ran, collecting static from the deep blue rug,
and circling the wool, we stood in stoic place,
electric shocks from the brass lamp, whose blue-black
currents spurned us. Spinning in arcs, we'd scuttle
through the roaring-twenties cocktail parlor
where our great aunts smoked, stoked heat

and fine cigars in the smoking room, fashionable heat
and marble table top. The blue sculpted Oriental rug
was in the sectioned-off and stuffy French parlor,
hidden in our rowhouse in Jersey City, out-of-place
in a town of railroads and alley cats. They would scuttle
the yard, tufted hair, foreheads pointy black,

they'd paw the sorry square of our hilly, black
back-yard: their shrill cries were a reminder of heat
matched only by the load we carried in our scuttle
from the coal-basement. The dusty hearth: a stone rug
that warmed our headboards, scapulas hung in their place
on the wooden swirls of our bedposts: a holy parlor.

So we welcomed into the satined parlor,
the whole neighborhood: the Polish tailor, the Black
flat-tire marvel, even the deaf ice-man had a place
in the frigid January gathering for heat
where we spun for near-death on a rug
whose shock was as mean as the sharp-lipped scuttle.

We carried the barrels to the cellar, dropped the scuttle
into the shute and filled it with coal to warm the parlor.
We felt fire rise through the thick blue rug
while we washed off excess ash: dusty black,
and as radiators whistled up their heat
we rinsed the dark surplus into its porcelain place

and felt the scuttle's satisfaction, it's nightly black
reminder of the parlor's desperate need for heat
exposing, in the maze of the exotic rug, our true inherited place.

THOMAS O'GRADY
(1956–)

East Side Story

for Brendon

I
Holding at forearm's length
an old recording, its coalhard burnish
sheer as pearls of jet, I can almost divine
that 'thirties world of East Side
walkups: lace-ruffled curtains,
heavyset sofas, doilies,
dark veneer—

my father's place and time.

Like a prayer (or like a charm)
a thumb-rubbed label—*Miss McLeod's,
The Bard of Armagh*, Bing's *Without a Song*—
can almost conjure up his father
ushering Sunday-collared countrymen
to square-backed chairs half-circled
in a line.

II

It lent the parlor focus,
like a shrine. Or like a hearth.

Or like the gilded ark from *Exodus*.
Though common as a steamer trunk upended deep
in steerage, taking space, that Edison Victrola
seemed a cubit-measured casket for plates
of black shellac encased in upright
shelves below the crank-wound works.
Tempered tablets etched in finespun
whorls like fingerprinted code, those
waxen disks composed a tabernacled
covenant for homesick exiles
fixed in heartsore hope before
the upraised lid.

That phonograph: its corner
was the center of the room when
my father, from the doorway, watched
in wonder as his father touched the stylus
to a well-worn groove. Then how
those sea-crossed bodies moved!
Delivered by the lilt or swing
of John McCormack, Michael Coleman—
Goodman's *Sing, Sing, Sing*—
transplanted neighbors, cousins,
friends all linked uplifted hands
to bind their newfound land of promise
with one now left behind.

III

Witness to that test (or testament)
of trust, my father told this story less
like memoir than like myth, as if familial
fact meant more as tribal lore of rustic rites.
And yet the tableau that he sketched
seemed so temporal at heart: not epic

but nostalgic, his self-effacing art
restored to truest life the moment
when-between two worlds—a father
turned toward his son as if familiar
tunes and tones could summon
the spirit of longlost
place and time.

Holding at forearm's length an old recording,
I can almost feel my father's father link
his hand with mine.

As in Wild Earth a Grecian Vase

—Colum

I
Still forlorn after weeks,
still reeling from exile's
first slap, the sting of salt-
licked rain off Dublin Bay

across my sorrowful cheeks,
I sickened at how all
near to me, oceans away,
slept on while I—as if

dead to that world—walked
thronging foreign streets
& dreamt of swift return:
if only for one day.

II

"It's only for a year,"
I wrote to lessen longing.
My mother wrote of weather
in reply until lost in the ache

of being neither here
nor there, I almost broke
with hunger for the scent
of line-dried laundry starched

by early frost—so real
& yet so unreachably far
from where I spent each
waking, or wakeful, hour.

III

How I lived for letters
filled even with old scraps
of news—page after transporting
foolscap page of local names,

familiar places . . . *life*
in short, until that morning,
my sloven's hair grown
long by monkish self-

neglect, I read that word
my mother's mother's
mother used to tease
a sheepishly untonsured son:

IV

streelish, she spelled it—
from *straoille* (I had learned)
in the native Doric
meaning "untidy crone."

O what would I give
now—unfathomable depths
& graying decades hence—
for how those doubly crossing

syllables lifted me, freshly
shorn & fit for the fold,
from an *An Lár* barber's throne?
O to feel so suddenly at home.

Exile

Sometimes, exile makes the heart
grow harder than the iron edge,
exposed at last, of a long-discarded
cartwheel in the sand. The calloused
sole of absence, distance dulls
all but the phantom pain of taking
leave until I walk this stony
foreign shore.

At home the russet strand gives way
beneath soft feet except
where knuckly knots of mussels
barnacle themselves to salt-brushed
shelves of shale. Encrusted
so, not hardened to the core,
I suffer once more that surging bone-
deep hurt of parting. *At home. . . .*
Washed by that tide, my brittle bedrock
heart erodes.

MICHAEL CHITWOOD
(1958–)

The Great Wagon Road, or How History Knocked the
Professor Cold, or A Storyteller's Story, or Why
Appalachians Are Mountains and a People

Scotch-Irish, by way of Ulster, Philadelphia,
the Valley of the Shenandoah,

generous, clannish, violent, kind-hearted,
they walked in (the Germans rode)

and stayed mostly out of county records
and the backs of Bibles, unlettered.

Their only correspondence with me,
son of their children's children's great grandchildren,

is this ditch, these nearly healed wheel cuts,
the line they traced in the earth.

.   .   .

Locally, it took its name from where it was going,
the potent away-from-here, the better place,

the how-it-could-be, not wintering on beans,
the infant not dead with the flux,

the ground not snagged with roots
that sang from the plow's cut and welted the shins.

Yonder. Chewed with scratch biscuits,
smoked in the porch shade,

something to be believed
when believing was the only solace.

.   .   .

"Fortunately, only Single Brothers
made this trip. This trail

at times is impassable and these folk
are wild, unpredictable.

Unlike our brethren,
they came not seeking but fleeing,

the almshouse, the sheriff,
a shamed woman or her brothers.

We sought the freedom to worship.
They worshipped freedom from seeking."

.   .   .

"I don't know now, though I knew. . . ."
Her palsied hand goes to her forehead

as if to draw memory with a touch.
My past grows dim,

illiterate, abandoned,
free for the taking.

.   .   .

A boy of four, he killed
one of the King's overlords

for casting a desirous eye on his mother,
and stowed away to sail the whale road.

Saving the crew and cargo from storm,
he was rewarded in Philadelphia

with a seventeen-hand stallion
and road out of the city stench

to the Blue Ridge which reminded him of home.
There he killed and married Cherokee,

fathered seven sons and seven daughters,
coaxed Highland pipes from fiddle's catgut,

distilled moonlight, slaughtered hogs,
lost fingers in sawmills,

hoed, suckered, topped and primed tobacco,
discarded washing machines in creekbeds,

learned to read the Bible, believe obituaries
and recite where he was and what he was doing

when the first Ford, radio, television
and news of JFK's death arrived.

He put on a tie, conditioned the air
and forgot the song of the whippoorwill.

.   .   .

"There is no history, but histories."
His shoes aren't right for this rough ground.

The sapling branches whip his back
as he backs into where we're going.

Educated, tenured, he hopes to publish
a study of The Great Wagon Road.

"Until documented the facts are in flux."
He is lecturing backward into the understory

where a honeysuckle vine catches his heel.
He barks his bald spot on a sweet gum

and is silenced into the fact of himself.
Out cold, he's received his dissertation's introduction.

.   .   .

Count Casimir Pulaski, Bishop
Francis Asbury, Lorenzo Dow,

the Moravian Single Brother who wrote
"We had to watch our horses closely. . . ."

They crossed Maggodee, Blackwater,
and Pigg, scribbled down some thoughts

that I'm stealing outright,
keeping an eye on their horses, too.

Warrior's Trace, gospel road, going now
into sumac, scrub pine and brooks.

I take your dirt in my hand.
Yonder. Yes, I'm coming.

NICOLE COOLEY
(1958–)

Drinking: A Suite

1. *Gin Palace*

The olive floats in the glass like a moon.
Dark red center I thought was rot
or an eye, watching my father.

Glass pearled with cold in his hand,
Martini's Holy Trinity in a triangular glass,
gin, vermouth, the twist, recipe

he taught us in childhood. Now
he has already left me to find the drink's pure
dry taste like the skin of a woman

who feels nothing when you touch her,
a woman in a white dress, choker of ice
circling her neck, the real happiness.

On the other side of the room, alone,
I build a castle of glasses, crystal
skyline. The tower a silver canister, the children's

rooms a shot glass. Inside, the family is all
reflections. Multiplied a thousand times
they can't recognize each other. If you touch

your tongue to the roof, your mouth fills with bitterness.

2. *The King's Daughter*

Older than the photograph
the cocktail is a drink with a history.
A father named it.
Conjure up a story:
the princess Coctel is twelve, mixing drinks
for her father's guests, a feather
stuck in every glass.
Tray in her hand, she curtsies
spreading the skirt of her white dress.

Conjure up a story:
the King's voice is slurred.
His daughter is terrified.
In the twentieth century other fathers invent drink names:
American Beauty. Maiden's Prayer.
Fallen Angel. Philomela. Mary Pickford.
White Witch.

3. *Your Bride*

When she opens her dress inside
she is all glass, bottle after bottle hung from her neck,
her breasts, shimmering.
In the half-dark of your room, she is your angel,
her body a hall of mirrors.
Where is the dark red heart in the center of her chest?
Run your hands over her skin, constellation of smooth surfaces.
Where is her sadness?
She'll pour you anything you want.
She'll lead you outside to a garden of olives and lemon peel,
row of toothpicks flaring into flame.

4. *Prohibition Recipe 1920*

Take three chorus girls and three men. Soak in champagne till midnight.
Squeeze into an automobile. Shake well. Serve at 70 miles an hour.

Enter the Speakeasy from the telephone booth. Whisper the password
and the trapdoor swings open to the stairs.

5. *Shirley Temple*

At twelve my sister pours witch hazel on ice.
I fill a shot glass to the top with turpentine.

We toast to the future we do not believe in.

Years ago we refused the small cup of grape juice,
Christ's blood, sweet and thick, swallowed at the altar,

to drink the way soldiers drank during the war:
blood red mercurochrome, Aqua Velva, Mr. Clean.

Anything bitter, burning the tongue, anything dangerous.

Years ago we named the family of dolls after
cocktails—Fallen Angel, White Witch—and gave up

the parasol stuck in the glass, the children's drink
with its bells of ice, pink and filtered with sugar.

Give American Beauty a medicine dropper of vermouth.
Her glass eyes roll closed as we hold her head still.

Force her to swallow. Force the happiness down her throat.

6. *Ramos Gin Fizz*

The drink named for the man whose house we lived in
in New Orleans
named for the house
where my father stepped through
the glass door shattering the panes

1 1/2 ounces gin
1 tablespoon powdered sugar
3-4 drops orange flower water
juice of 1/2 lime
juice of 1/2 lemon
1 egg white
1 1/2 ounces cream
1 squirt seltzer

the house where cream pooled on the table
the orange flower water
too sweet to drink it should be perfume coating the tongue
with white   like a sickness

house where a key cranked the ice machine
to foam the silver pitcher
with a magic potion I believed in
I was not allowed to taste it

Burn the twist of lemon over the drink's surface
till you're left with an oily slick of lemon
Burn the recipe   Burn the house

7. *Diorama*
Here is a matchbox bed where we slept,
draped with a remnant of red,
my sister's Sunday dress.
Here is a kitchen, a row of china
thimbles of vegetable soup and gin
lined up on a table,

where a miniature bottle has rolled
under my father's chair, hidden
in darkness.

The cardboard door leads nowhere
and the window casements open
onto nothing.

Drifting world, held still as a photograph,
forced into the box—
the dolls are drunk now, the dolls live here.

8. *Icehouse*
of memory where I remember that world, where I sit
freezing on a block of crystal, dull

white mirror. I could take up the pick,
the mallet, to crack the past,

crush the family in their box to pieces,
break the bottles.

When I go back my hands ache with cold,
my hands are shaking,

and I can do nothing to stop any of it.
All reflections

in the white room where my sister and I wait,
side by side on the ice bed.

Oh, Memory Palace I can't burn down
where American Beauty

is already numb and anesthetized and blank.
Turn the key to fill

the pitcher, whisper the password and the trapdoor
swings open to the new world,

world beyond childhood, world none of us can enter.

GREG DELANTY
(1958–)

We Will Not Play the Harp Backward Now, No

> *If in Ireland*
> > *they play the harp backward at need*
> > > —Marianne Moore,
> > > "Spenser's Ireland"

We, a bunch of greencard Irish,
   vamp it under the cathedral arches
   of Brooklyn Bridge that's strung like a harp.
But we'll not play
the harp backward now, harping on
    about those Micks who fashioned
this American wind lyre
and about the scores
    who landed on Ellis Island
or, like us, at Kennedy and dispersed
through this open sesame land

in different directions like the rays
   of Liberty's crown, each ray set
   against the other, forming a wedge or caret.
We'll refrain from inserting
how any of us craved for the old country
    and in our longing, composed a harp,
pipe, porter and colleen Tir na nOg.
And if we play
    the harp right way around now
we'll reveal another side of the story
told like the secret of Labraid the Exile: how

some, at least, found a native genius for union
    here and where like the Earl Gerald,
    who turned himself into a stag
and a green-eyed cat
of the mountain, many of us
    learned the trick
of turning ourselves into ourselves,
free in the fe fiada anonymity
            of America. Here
we could flap the horse's ears
of our singularity and not have to fear,

nor hide from the all-seeing Irish
    small town, blinking evil eyes—
    Nor does this landscape play that unheard,
but distinctly audible
mizzling slow air
            that strickens us with the plaintive notes
of the drawn-out tragedy
of the old country's sorry history.
            No, we'll not play the harp backward
anymore, keeping in mind the little people's harp
and how those who hear it never live long afterward.

(Note: The epigraph of 'We Will Not Play the Harp Backward Now, No'
            was taken from Marianne Moore's 'Spenser's Ireland.'
            The editors of the Norton Anthology of Modern Poetry
annotated these lines of Moore: 'The harp is the symbol of Ireland.
            To play it backward is to be sentimental about the past.')

On the Renovation of Ellis Island

What is even worse than if the walls wept
like a mythical character trapped in wood
or stone is that the walls give off nothing:
nothing of all those who were chalk-branded
for a limp, bedraggled look or vacant brow;
nothing of the man who thought Liberty

wore a crown of thorns; nothing of boys
who believed that each foot of anyone
who wore pointed shoes had only one toe;
nothing of mothers clutching tattered shawls
& belt-strapped cases like Old World beliefs;
nothing of petticoated women who turned flapper . . .
Surely if we stripped the coats of fresh paint
as anxiously as those women undid petticoats,
walls would weep, but for nothing now, for ever.

The Shrinking World

to Mary & Niall on Catherine's first summer

Reading how the European long-tailed tit
builds a perfect domed nest, gathering lichen
for camouflage, feathers to line it
& cobwebs as binding so the nest can

stretch while chicks grow, I thought of you
rushing to crying Catherine, as if her mouth shone
like those of finchlings guiding parents through
darkness. If only chainsaw-armed men,

felling whole forests by the minute,
could have seen you hover around your fledgling,
they would have immediately cut
engines & listened to your lullabying.

But their lumbering motors drone on
in the distance & perhaps approach us.
And what about all those other Catherines,
imperial woodpeckers and birds of paradise?

I sing now like the North American brown thrasher,
who at one point in its song orchestrates
four different notes: one grieves, another
frets, a third prays, but a fourth celebrates.

Homage to the God of Pollution in Brooklyn

The gravid gray sky, languor made visible,
    threatens rain, but holds back to keep us
on edge, wind-whispering if clouds could really whisper
    what in vain we can't catch; call them
intimations of, call it the old country.
    But what's odd about this drear déjà vu is
what was once laden with melancholia, heebie-jeebies,
    willies, now seeps with comforting familiarity.

But this emigrant nostalgia run amok
    has far less to do with the drab welkin
than the concomitant grey-green water of Brooklyn
    drifting into Buttermilk Channel and the waters
surrounding Ms. Liberty, befouling the hem of her dress.

Like so many I grew up with in a town with a belovèd river
    the colour of slime
I took for the natural colour of all waterways.
    I couldn't fathom why teachers made us paint
the waters of our colourbooks blue, and ever since,
    passing through cities,
I hardly think twice about why I've never beheld
    a winding blue streak even on sunny days.

And as much as I'm over the moon about rumors of this
    mire's clean up
and concur with the protesters crying for the waters
    —O Aqua Mundi; as much
as I want to see the waters swell like the fish-surging
    biblical sea of the miraculous catch,
a story I loved as a kid; as much as I'd give my writing
    arm to witness trees along the banks
shake off their sickly hue, and to hear returning birds
    of the resurrected world
hosanna the airways, I admit to a silent prayer perverse.

I confess to the god of pollution in Brooklyn that if
    ever this blue
that frightens me to dwell on can be retrieved I'll be
    lonesome
for the iniquity of fishless water slouching towards the
    putrid shore. But heaven
on earth, I don't suppose I need worry on that score.

(from) The Hellbox

All I want is not simply to parrot American voices,
    reminding me of how immigrants learned
a new tongue from mimicking gramophone songs
    and following theatre stars from show to show,
pronouncing actors' lines, rhythms, always a fraction behind,
    till they knew every word, so much so, according to
Ondaatje, that when Wayne Burnett dropped dead
    on stage a Sicilian butcher in the audience took over.

No siree, I eschew such mimicry and want to be poetry's
    Temelcoff, who so desperately learned a new tongue
that he had translation dreams where trees not just changed
    their names, but their looks and character,
men answered in falsetto and dogs spoke in the street.
    More than anything I want my utterance to become the stuff
of such dreams, while remaining always human, open, up front.

I'm the cocky young cleric coming to St Brendan's door
    refusing to leave till I've played the music of the world:
more pleasing to me any day than the saint's dazzling angel
    who, from the altar on high, drew the bow from its beak
across the harp of its wing and played a tricksy, highbrow
    lay that was so ethereal, Brendan forever afterwards plugged
his ears to any human harp. A pox on such angelic harping.
    Let my fingers pluck the common note of an open harp.

But who am I kidding? Where is that down-to-earth angel
    who Mossy, fellow agent of the muse, swore is sooner rather
than later going to turn up to give poetry the kiss of life
    and 'blow us all out of the water' as we mused
one night about our own strains and how the general state
    of poesy is at a low ebb. So where are you, you human angel,
or whatever you are? Give us a stave, a melody, an air.
    Who are we bluffing with our efforts? Oh come on out.
We love you Buster. Blow us all out of the water.

KATHY FAGAN
(1958–)

Migration

You say it is extraordinary
to have heard the migration of geese at night,
to have left my bed,
run into the yard naked,
and watched them go, dozens of pumping moons
over the homes of neighbors.

But I tell you, they were there.
And there was another also who saw—
a child at a window,
her hair lit by a small lamp
somewhere in that warm room.
She watched quietly and with no wonder
to speak of; just her small hand,
palm up against the pane, the fingers
loosely arched as if she
had released those great white birds
and ordered their going herself.

It was the sight of me that surprised her.
The sight of a woman standing
straight up in moonlight,
straight up with no clothes
and hair that blew uncontrollably.

Of the geese, I am sure.
Of the child's small fingers reaching,
in silhouette, to her lips in a kiss,
I am uncertain.
What I did know,
when the light in the window
went suddenly out, was
that the child would remember nothing.
Or if she did she would not tell,
because she knew, even at that age
when one is expected to believe every lie,
that no one would believe her.

So she slept
just as I slept again that night,
just as everyone slept that night,
letting the stars pin our eyes shut
and prick at the landscape
of our dreams.

Tympani

Pomegranate beads loose
bracelets of them & under the skins
the small pink juices
a weight that drums as it falls to the table

Not the kettledrums of telethons drummed up drummed
out but tympani nonetheless

Like the difference between the Woolworth Building &
the 5 & 10 my grandparents ate breakfast in
sopping their tea up the Irish way
the way the word
martyr carries its own cross and the garter
snake wears them but whose leg not his
the way the offertory bells lifted
like the lid off a platter lamb
of god fisher of men prince of peace doorbell & phone
rung & the way we pretended Hello, Jesus?

Bells & drums lights & whistles
Blow flash & blossom

In 1906 the owners of Luna Park
decided Coney Island's electrical plant could do more
than light an amusement park and successfully
electrocuted one of their herd of working elephants.
It took ten seconds.
In silent footage Topsy is alive,
then a long stillness,
then the crumpling mass of her body,

& after
& after that

glitter tremble

Here are the seeds
they are ripe to bursting
they are ripe to bursting the drums of their bodies
this is my body
tympani toteboard reprise &
the hour chiming
& then the curtain (deus) rises—

or does it part?

LAURA MULLEN
(1958 –)

The Surface

Sudden cold or the sudden sense of having been cold for a long time
He said he was getting back some things that had been lost like what
Love oh great looking out across the river he wouldn't meet my eyes either
Something flashed up and fell back down into the water there look no
I told him about the time I saw them feeding the crowd up out
Of the dark water of paler mouths opening closing like what
Getting the strength to say lost he was beautiful the play
Of that muscle I make you tense don't I just under the tan skin of his jaw
I keep coming back to the surface that river your wrist I must have
Pressing my mouth I can't look at your hands thinking of how you
Touched me hurt you a lot love like what those memories
Saying you're wearing mallard colors after I chased to frighten
For no reason the ducks because I can't stand still enough if I could
I would be so still you would think I would never hurt you
Screaming what was her last name what was her name
The wind-scarred surface of the water
What I'm not allowed to feel what I'm not allowed to say pressing up
As though feeding my heart is everywhere under my skin
And rising up to the surface of the water clenching and unclenching
The thick grey muscle the dense shoal of fish brought to just beneath
The surface the grotesque bouquet of their rapidly blossoming and
Shutting the crowd but as if behind glass so there was no sound
Of people screaming I feel helpless and cold saying please believe
I did not mean to hurt you you could say that to me too in *Orphée*
The poet presses against the mirror which wavers like water which lets him in

Long Coat

I was letting the lining wear out

I was willing to let the sleeves
Rip to open
To show to the empty
Air all the places
The body in time
Tries to break
Out

The pockets were already useless

Admitting I couldn't stop

The collar fraying
Where we turned to look
For what
Failed to appear
Or vanished
In our vast
Disappointment

In the cavernous
Library's draft

You leapt up
You grabbed the coat
And flinging it on flung yourself
Out into the night

Thin where it moves against
The body opening
Where the satchel full
Of books rides and the body
Tries to compensate

Worn transparent

I thought it was time

Letting the threadbare
Cuffs leave themselves
On the tables
They swept
Turning pages the wind
Shifting the leaves
Of notes

Daylight
A ragged hole
Left
In black silk

DANIEL TOBIN
(1958–)

Double Life

The Sky Road
To have been born on the very edge of things
in a whitewashed hut with blonde bangs of thatch
and an unlatched gate that leads into the open,
sky and sky beyond the window onto land's end,
everything blending and the ocean shattered with light

and not to be this strange face peering through a hedge
your dead once walked beside, earrings of fuschia
astride the rock wall: it is no nostalgia,
but the plain air of things, the very curb of exile,
this dwelling on the edge where you are born.

Headlands
To have driven along blue levitating roads
this far into land's end, golden, rumpled,
these humps that could be the goddess's bedclothes,
and that red broach of a bridge pinning the continent
together; it is all ample and errant

like this wind and the garrulous ocean below
bellowing on in the voice of Whitman
Death, Death, Death, Death, Death on the wrong shore,
the horizon as much behind us as before,
always our eyes rising to the sky's imprint on tar.

A Mosque in Brooklyn

There is no prayer that can abolish history,
though in this basement mosque the muezzin's history

gathers in his throat like a tenor's aria
and he calls to God to put an end to history.

From my courtyard room I hear his song ascending,
the divine name whirling its rebuke to history—

Allah, Allah—above the crowded rowhouse roofs.
Their rusted antennas, stalled arrows of history,

would transmit a daily riot of talk and news,
the world boxed inside a glowing square of history.

I've seen them on the street, the faithful in their robes
walking along store-fronts, a different history

clothing them, like me, in our separate skins,
though here we are at the scope-end of history:

Goodness is timeless, the great English poet wrote,
and not just for himself—the crime is history.

But as if to prove the old Sufi fable true
these prayers are lifted on the thermals of history,

and sound strangely like that congregation of birds;
no, the remnant who survived a blighted history,

having stayed their quest into the final valley
where a Great Tree rose, its branches thick as history.

And there they lost themselves, flourishing into the One
without division, without names, without history.

St. John

*St Mary's (Cemetery) is located at the crest of a windswept knoll,
on the south side of Loch Lommond Road, in East Saint-John.
There are no markers or fences to define its actual parameters . . .*
—Mary Kilfoil McDevitt, *We Hardly Knew Ye*

On these shores
the ocean slides like a veil from the continent,
rocking tides from half a world away
withdraw
in a froth of seething dulse
where the bay's laid bare to slosh and wrackline.
Terns print momentary braille
on the sea-bed shiny as shellac, and cast-up
islands appear lost Atlantises
outlasting
the incredulity of the stunned explorer,
or whale-backs for some new Brendan to mistake
before his quest resumes.
On these shores
the old city, hasped by modern bridges, stares
at itself across a river flowing
in reverse

against the Fundy as though against
          itself—scale after scale of whirlpools—
     and years of tourists
marveling at the gorge. Cruise ships
     glide sleek hulls into the harbor,
moor at quays
          along Water Street, the crowds
emptying into shops on Prince William, St. Germaine,
     gentrified gargoyles
          hovering like geniuses
over steam-blasted facades of the varnished wards.
          On these shores
   time swirls
backwards in a dream of race memory. The shipyards
                    brim with "shovel-fisted Irish,"
rag-heaped slovens wheeled by the remnant
          of gutted townlands.
   They gather
outside the waterfront's slop-bucket tenements
     —Flagor's Alley, York Point—
King's Ward, Duke's Ward, Sydney Ward, Portland;
   riot through the cholera-strafed streets
                against Loyalist bunting and Orange drums.
   On these shores
ghosts speak the lingo of lost tongues and shipwrights,
   of keel and keelson,
                of reamer, hauser, fid, and maul,
dead-strap, dead-eye, straker, oakum, sawpit.
          On these shores
the scribers notched their signatures in timber
   Brayons axed in the Micmac forests
     for Cunard to fill with conifer and trade,
to return again with their starving human ballast.
     The Alms House
   purveyed its "fine healthy children,
     bound out
to proper persons on immediate application"—
          orphan charges
     discharged like slaves at auction.

On these shores
the Guatamalan restauranteur adorns his shop-front
    with rainbow displays of home.
Trees canopy the Loyalist Burial Ground
            in century's-old growth,
    while the immigrant cemetery beside the refinery
      rots in its shower of acid rain.
  On these shores
the *ceilidh* still thunders on late into the night
      in backroom pubs
          where the latest heirs
of history recede into their undreamt futures.
  Lovers make love
      in trashed gun-emplacements,
and the new Museum rises astride the new Hilton.
          But on these shores
there is no sea-road to that island off the coast
      with its quarantine stations
    and graveyards
where coffin ships emptied their wasted holds
      —*Aeolus* and *Swan*—
        the light-bearing names;
and salt winds off the Great Banks lick the Cross
    raised in remembrance,
        while the lighthouse signals its golden door
          to an offing
that levies its apocalypse of fog over the town
    from High Point to the breakwaters.
          On these shores
where tombstones recede into earth like shells
      below the tide,
I riffle through remains of dig books
            to find my own past,
then drive with my love to the bare knoll's crest,
      the stone gateposts gateless,
    no walls, no boundary,
and walk among the footstones, lost avenues,
      currents of grass, still ponds
    of moss

fast rising to erase the names.
    On these shores
I kneel inside the empty townland of the dead
        for James and the others,
            travelers
who left no trace but this code in my bones,
    an unmarked grave, the tern's trail
        of history,
and the tide coming in with a screech of seabirds
            on these shores.

JEAN MONAHAN
(1959 –)

Woman Falls Asleep Doing the Sunday Crossword

Too tired to rout the words
hidden behind the clues, you
paused on the stair joining
ogham and *owl,* and bowed
before the puzzle's paper tyranny,
an uncapped pen brandished

in your fist. Good soldier,
it stood guard all through
your dreams, trailing your
thoughts along one arm,
then dashed between ear,
eye and mouth, bleeding

itself dry with so many
messages. By daybreak,
you were your own
manuscript. Whatever stumps
us—leaves us at a loss for
words—folds over our sleep

like a flimsy tent, a matrix
of nouns, adjectives and verbs
we labor to connect. Last
night, your oracle sat, as
usual, at the intersection
where three routes meet.

Imagine her delight at
the pen in your hand,
a slim sword to cut the cord
between your two minds,
the one that sees, hears,
and says, and the one that

denies, denies, denies.
Learn to trust her inklings,
her scrawl, her stab
in the dark when all
else fails. Learn to read
what the blind hand writes.

GERARD DONOVAN
(1960–)

(from) Columbus Rides Again

White
Columbus refuses to act white.
He hangs around the alleys and smokes. The Italian
smokes. He likes to wear suspenders and play blues guitar
and push cues in the blue halls. That is not why
Columbus is now at the docks boarding this ship.
He is being sent back
because he has not kept his promise
to stay away from the harbour and the sailing ships.
He was caught making drawings and selling them.
He denies that he drew inferences
or intended ingratitude. The canvas showed white sky,
rolling blue underneath, and a stick floating.
We roast primitive myth from the earth,
we thank God for our confinement in the States of Eden,
and this man keeps insisting that there is no edge out there,
that we can travel in a straight line
and return without turning back. We found him
breathless behind a trash can holding a torn idea.

Columbus is nearing the horizon
because we have enough mythology now.
Let him disappear in the pinprick of a sail
and contend to others that he saw another land
where there were riches and high buildings.
But Columbus doesn't know the name of the race: how it navigates
through his veins—how it will
read the maps to every part of him,
then set up a frontier camp in his heart.
They will sit in their poverty and hear the shouts of a man
gesticulating by a campfire, his words
as meaningless as the shadows. When the natives
turn away from his words,
he will slaughter them.

They Write

Show me your verse, I'll show you mine,
and if you say you hail from *here* or *there*
or that *all poems are national,*
I'll show you a medieval drawing of a head on a stick
whose owner fought for one general's idea
and now sees the world but can't put it into any order.
Our verse is fish
navigating an ocean of glass bowls
painted with big glistening faces;
we are the centre of our own attention,
we gobble what sky breaks down.

No poems are national,
no poet is dead from a single line.
Let's detect the remains of this country you declare
(fill in something here) and write your delirium:
some local genocide deletes a face,
some posture, some tranquilized beauty out of place
remembered without passion, without grace.

Who writes any country?
Rub your hands. Conjure all the reliables.
This may be the way to write:
to say nothing extremely well,
as one whose head pops into the basket
and sees the sky and its fallen body
and says, *I see the sky.*
Can you see it?
Hey, can you see it?

On a Trawler to the Mainland

A stormy crossing.
With one hand on the pole
I blow in the air like a flag,
claiming no territory these days
but journeys, no colours but white.

To be uncultured: impossible of course
to undo an idea—the place you shine—
since you can be gone but not quite.
The empty shot glass smells.

Still, blood carries its own bags,
lugging its light to new roads;
the infantry called instinct
straggles with stolen paintings,
prods you along from the known siege
of streets, faces you sow. Gunfire grows distant
yet delays on the air; smoke
balloons the horizon, won't completely clear.

Your steps grow groundless, mud the sun.
Towns wear down to one place.
If return is the question, the question returns:
Did you ever leave? And what's the residue
of any travelling, and of none?

JOHN FLYNN
(1960–)

Pow Wow at Greenbriar

Numbers may be small
Nipmuc, Algonquin, Abenaki
but they're all here
to fight off extinction
with a wedding on stolen land
where wild sons picked wild grapes
and pickerel chased silver pines
before state engineers drained the streams.

Parking and admission 99 cents
under skies of sunny early autumn
bride and groom inside the circle,
the fire smoldering as chief and best man
in English first, then relaxed native syllables
pray for animal spirit unions,
holding in a circle each other's hand.
After the maid of honor wraps the couple
in a blanket of tears,
the chief invites his nation to dance.

Inside the beat of the drum
their faces striped in blues and vermillion,
in feather fur and leather adornments
to honor the heart of a living earth.
No certainties without loss
no deeper innocent woods
than the mesmeric fires in a bride
calling her groom to the stars
over paradise.

NICK FLYNN
(1960 –)

The ocean is always looking for a way into your boat

A woman stands before us   her poem about a man drowning

she reads   *I'm tired of writing about fishermen*

a man in front fights sleep   his arms folded his eyes

a doll's eyes   slowly closing   until his head

whiplashes the air   rousing he

focuses on one word   the word *salt*

until his chin drops again to his chest   I think

this is how my father moves through life

drifting off   then righting himself   a few lucid moments

maybe a week   standing outside a building he once lived in

searching his pockets for the key   The poet whispers

the ocean is always looking for a way into your boat

the sea lifts itself   everyone   thrown overboard

the man's head breaks the surface   just long enough for a mouthful

then back under   *the overwhelming silence beneath the waves*

It could be me   up there   my father drowning in his chair

I could stand before him all night   trying to find one

word   precise   a rock slipped into his open mouth

to weigh him under   away

Father Outside

A black river flows down the center
of each page

& on either side the banks
are wrapped in snow. My father is ink falling

in tiny blossoms, a bottle
wrapped in a paperbag. I want to believe
that if I get the story right

we will rise, newly-formed,

that I will stand over him again
as he sleeps outside under the church halogen
only this time I will know

what to say. It is night &
it's snowing & starlings
fill the trees above us, so many it seems

the leaves sing. I can't see them
until they rise together at some hidden signal

& hold the shape of the tree for a moment
before scattering. I wait for his breath
to lift his blanket

so I know he's alive, letting the story settle

into the shape of this city. Three girls in the park
begin to sing something holy, a song
with a lost room inside it

as their prayerbook comes unglued

& scatters. I'll bend
each finger back, until the bottle

falls, until the bone snaps, save him

by destroying his hands. With the thaw
the river will rise & he will be forced
to higher ground. No one

will have to tell him. From my roof I can see
the East River, it looks blackened with oil

but it's only the light. Even now
my father is asleep somewhere. If I followed

the river north I could still
reach him.

CHRIS FORHAN
(1960 –)

Family History

Out of the womb of God, she ran off. We,
conceived in the muck the rain and her
wake-dust made, her eight score children,
rubbed our eyelids, licked the birth blood
off each other's faces, stood
and split into equal tribes to find her.

Over the goat-strewn hills we wandered,
over the dawn-lit cliffs and meadows,
along the marshes dotted with sedge,
begetting in gardens of larkspur and jasmine,
begetting in damp caves, boat bottoms, back
of some crumbling castle, our fall night's fire low.

Now we are many, and stumble often
across each other in drugstore lines
or hunched on separate barstools, wolf's hair
slicked down, eyeing each other sideways,
each of us hugging the narrow cage
of his body, guarding his own lost cause.

The Vastness. The Distant Twinkling

When the Great Unknowable One shook out
the immaculate tablecloth of the stars,
concealing all the while the sight
of his own magnificence, we applauded.
We kept this up for some time. What else

could we do? What words could we speak
in reply? Oh, it was past all comprehension.
The vastness. The distant twinkling. The simple
inexplicableness of the trick. Ourselves there
to witness. A wonder, we told each other, to be sure,

but with something a little sad about it.
At last, our hands numb from clapping,
each of us slipped his hat on, waved so long,
and went his solitary way. We were hungry
and we had a few things to think about.

The Fidgeting

Easy to make prayers to the darkness, to break bread
with the inconceivable. Harder to love

the moon—dusty dead-white relic
in the star museum, bald and obvious

as a drunken uncle. Hard to find worth
in the crooked pine that creaks

outside the kitchen window, every twig
a wagging finger as it lectures

on the miracle of the physical world.
Any day is the same day—the hours

writhe like worms in a bucket.
One can be an astonished infant

for only so long before the fidgeting,
before a flock of blackbirds bursting

from poplars, or a sodden collection
of fallen leaves blown against a fence,

is wearisome. Even the stiff, bloated opossum
by the roadside is only a brief diversion

before one longs to follow the opossum-soul,
to know where it goes and how it fares

in the province it scuttles off to,
the who-knows-where, anywhere but here.

CLAUDIA KEELAN
(1960 –)

The Secularist

I know the staggering
    lights from the Hancock Tower
searing the river's face
    were the end of the story.

But in that light, stripped of candescence,
    sinking into the river's crawl,
I almost believed
    again, candle's flicker

spreading, in the underwater church,
    across the feet of the stewards,
across the money box
    where they dropped their love, across

the stone robes, and what we call *answers,*
    kept hidden there. In after
-thought: the light brushed finally
    the feet of the kind, dearly dead god.

I stood there often,
    fingering absence at the Charles'
edge. I considered
    my choices. There in that place

—what was it you called it?—
  "the spirit of matter"
raised its divining finger
  toward me. What do you do

with light you can't be quit
  of, throwing its gleam
on you from a holy grave
  you thought you'd dreamed

clear out of your sleep
  years ago? I'm trying to say
I didn't want that touch
  there in that imagined place,

couldn't want that touch
  here on the nearly ruined shore.
Behind me, in the real city,
  the coal muffles the birth
-cry of the woman

  cutting her own umbilici
in a single room. She wraps
  the slippery string around
the child's neck, kisses

it once on the forehead,
  and tightens. Do you hear
her prayers mumbled rapid
  fire? The spirit of matter

scratches its ass against
  a brick wall. I know
if I stay here
  let the light drift

slowly across me
    I could feel love.
But, I'm going to go home.
    I'm waking up in my own bed.

Ave Verum Corpus

It occurred in the spaces the community choir left in the new concert
hall. The body the composer was trying to make, I mean. In those
four minutes, hovering, but finally only *there* as they left, American
and amateur in the black clothes required. My people leaving
on crutches, in columns, single file, until their absence, the thing
he must have wanted, stark against the farthest sandalwood wall.
By comparison, the next, busy violin, gratuitous applause.

We'd been finally West, our figures in the old building's light
projecting from the cliff onto the ocean, unappeased. So far from
our bodies there, weren't we so far, I believed we might gladly touch
there, until I recalled how touch looked in the painting, the century's
comment on intimacy, our spotlight's hypodermic, a clarifying virus.
Gone, though we looked all through the museum for it. I'd known where
it was but even its wall was gone and I was afraid for the theft.

Between vision and love, too much beauty. A woman miscarrying
in a high hotel room and each time she opens her eyes again
the people in the building across the street, opening windows, smiling
out into the brick face, each time a new body and its morning.
And then the possibilities of the traffic jam, the bridge a harp
thick with not speaking. The American choir singing our body.

CAMPBELL McGRATH
(1960 –)

Four Clouds Like the Irish in Memory

First memory of school: sitting in the grass beneath a blossoming
dogwood tree while the teacher explains how to write a poem.

Boisterous sun, orbital crab apples, isn't the springtime
beautiful? What do the clouds look like? Butterfly, banana split,
polar bear, clown. What does the dogwood look like, its bracts
and tiers and white cascades of flowers? Snowflakes. A birthday
cake. Good, good. Like going to New York for the holidays, like
heaven or the George Washington Bridge at night, its titanium
spans and whirligigs, garlands of popcorn, garlands of
cranberries, baked ham and my grandfather's accordion, my
mother and sisters trying out their old Shirley Temple
routines amidst an Irish stew of relatives and well-wishers
immersed for the day in the nostalgic mist and manners of the
old sod.

Shamrock, whiskey bottle, subway train, diaspora.

One year my grandfather drove with us back to Washington after
Christmas. I remember him chiefly for that matchless
accordion, the hats and boats he made from newspaper, the
senility that claimed him like an early snowfall—

as I remember my father's father for the crafty wooden puzzles
he assembled at the kitchen table with a box of Ritz crackers and
a quart of Rheingold beer—

but this was my mother's father, a countryman from Donegal, famous for long strolls in Riverside Park collecting weeds for home remedies, for walking the bridge to save a penny on a pack of cigarettes. He worked forty years as a ticket taker in the subway, pent too long 'mid cloisters dim, and somewhere in southern New Jersey, in the backseat of the station wagon looking out past the turnpike traffic, he said, in his thick brogue, to no one in particular, *goodness,*

I had no idea there were such great forests left.

Angels and the Bars of Manhattan

for Bruce

What I miss most about the city are the angels
and the bars of Manhattan: faithful Cannon's and the Night Cafe;
the Corner Bistro and the infamous White Horse;
McKenna's maniacal hockey fans; the waitresses at Live Bait;
lounges and taverns, taps and pubs;
joints, dives, spots, clubs; all the Blarney
Stones and Roses full of Irish boozers eating brisket
stacked on kaiser rolls with frothing mugs of Ballantine.
How many nights we marked the stations of that cross,
axial or transverse, uptown or down to the East Village
where there's two in every block we'd stop to check,
hoisting McSorleys, shooting tequila and 8-ball
with hipsters and bikers and crazy Ukrainians,
all the black-clad chicks lined up like vodka bottles on Avenue B,
because we liked to drink and talk and argue,
and then at four or five when the whiskey soured
we'd walk the streets for breakfast at some diner,
Daisy's, The Olympia, La Perla del Sur,

deciphering the avenues' hazy lexicon over coffee and eggs,
snow beginning to fall, steam on the windows blurring the film
until the trussed-up sidewalk Christmas trees
resembled something out of Mandelstam,
Russian soldiers bundled in their greatcoats,
honor guard for the republic of salt. Those were the days
of revolutionary zeal. Haughty as dictators, we railed
against the formal elite, certain as Moses or Roger Williams
of our errand into the wilderness. Truly,
there was something almost noble
in the depth of our self-satisfaction, young poets in New York,
how cool. Possessors of absolute knowledge,
we willingly shared it in unmetered verse,
scavenging inspiration from Whitman and history and Hüsker Dü,
from the very bums and benches of Broadway,
precisely the way that the homeless
who lived in the Parks Department garage at 79th Street
jacked in to the fixtures to run their appliances
off the city's live current. Volt pirates;
electrical vampires. But what I can't fully fathom
is the nature of the muse that drew us to begin with,
bound us over to those tenements of rage
as surely as the fractured words scrawled across the stoops
and shuttered windows. Whatever compelled us
to suspend the body of our dreams from poetry's slender reed
when any electric guitar would do? Who did we think was listening?
Who, as we cried out, as we shook, rattled and rolled,
would ever hear us among the blue multitudes of Christmas lights
strung as celestial hierarchies from the ceiling? Who
among the analphabetical ranks and orders
of warped records and second-hand books on our shelves,
the quarterlies and *Silver Surfer* comics, velvet Elvises,
candles burned in homage to *Las Siete Potencias Africanas*
as we sat basking in the half-blue glimmer,
tossing the torn foam basketball nigh the invisible hoop,
listening in our pitiless way to two kinds of music,
loud and louder, anarchy and roar, rock and roll
buckling the fundamental with pure, delirious noise.

It welled up in us, huge as snowflakes, as manifold,
the way ice devours the reservoir in Central Park.
Like angels or the Silver Surfer we thought we could
kick free of the stars to steer by dead reckoning.
But whose stars were they? And whose angels
if not Rilke's, or Milton's, even Abraham Lincoln's,
"the better angels of our nature" he hoped would emerge,
air-swimmers descending in apple-green light.
We worshiped the anonymous neon apostles of the city,
cuchifrito cherubs, polystyrene seraphim,
thrones and dominions of linoleum and asphalt:
abandoned barges on the Hudson mudflats;
Bowery jukes oozing sepia and plum-colored light;
headless dolls and eviscerated teddy bears
chained to the grilles of a thousand garbage trucks; the elms
that bear the wailing skins of plastic bags in their arms all winter,
throttled and grotesque, so that we sometimes wondered
walking Riverside Drive in February or March
why not just put up cement trees with plastic leaves
and get it over with? There was no limit to our capacity for awe
at the city's miraculous icons and instances,
the frenzied cacophony, the democratic whirlwind.
Drunk on thunder, we believed in vision
and the convocation of heavenly presences summoned
to the chorus. Are they with us still? Are they
listening? Spirit of the tiny lights, ghost beneath the words,
numinous and blue, inhaler of bourbon fumes and errant shots,
are you there? I don't know. Somehow I doubt we'll ever know
which song was ours and which the siren
call of the city. More and more, it seems our errand
is to face the music, bring the noise, scour the rocks
to salvage grace notes and fragmented harmonies,
diving for pearls in the beautiful ruins,
walking all night through the pigeon-haunted streets
as fresh snow softly fills the imprint of our steps.
OK, I'm repeating myself, forgive me, I'm sure brevity
is a virtue. It's just this melody keeps begging to be hummed:
McCarthy's, on 14th Street, where the regulars drink

beer on the rocks and the TV shows "Police Woman"
twenty-four hours a day; the quiet, almost tender way
they let the local derelicts in to sleep it off
in the back booths of the Blue & Gold after closing;
and that sign behind the bar at the Marlin, you know
the one, hand-lettered, scribbled with slogans of love and abuse,
shopworn but still bearing its indomitable message
to the thirsty, smoke-fingered, mood-enhanced masses—
"Ice Cold Six Packs To Go." Now that's a poem.

Sunrise and Moonfall, Rosarito Beach

What I remember of Mexico
is how the glass apple of mescal glowed
and exploded like a globe of seeds
or something we couldn't pronounce
or know the secret name of, never,
and even when the federales shook us down for twenty bucks
as they must, to save face,
I couldn't loose the curve and rupture
of that sphere—half-full, hand-blown, imperfect
as our planet. Sure, everything is blowing open
now, all the freeways and skinheads, the music
invisibly blasting, radio waves invading the spines and craniums
of all this. San Diego, Tijuana, the Beach of Dead Dogs
where we slept in the cold, local kids incredulous
of Ed up early for no reason
driving golf balls out into the restlessly pounding surf.
Jesus, we're always hitting golf balls. It seems to be
some irreducible trait. There's Rob smashing the plaster icons,
all the bleeding martyrs and aqua pigs
and pink squinting Virgins the radiant chapel of candles
induced us to need. Jesus, let me ask, please,

before he decapitates you also with a wicked six-iron slice,
why are we always the last ones on the beach
as dawn sucks the last drops from mescaline shards,
the ones who beat the sacred iguanas to death
as the sun comes right up
and the shadow-globe finally dances off stage,
the moon, I mean,
that other white world of men
driving golf balls to seas of dust and oblivion—
chrome-headed, flag-waving, violent, American.

ELIZABETH ONESS
(1960 –)

Belleek

I am troubled, I'm dissatisfied, I'm Irish.
                    —Marianne Moore

For years I resisted it, the only
shatterable part of my inheritance

china sprinkled with insipid shamrocks,
two tones of green, the sweetly clustered leaves

bordering the plates in an Irish ring-a-rosy,
unfurling from the teapot's stalk

like a fairy invention, a porcelain version of
a time that never was.

There was no blarney in the house where I grew up.
We were tight-lipped, silent;
                                        superfluity was sin.

Nothing to do? I'll give you something to do.
You want something to cry about? I'll give you something . . .

My grandmother cried leaving Ireland the last time.
I sat beside her on the plane

staring down at the Cliffs of Moher,
water breaking over the wrack-mired stone.

She had shown me the house where she grew up,
the nettled fields, the barn

where her father locked her in a stall
and she stayed all night afraid
                                    and no one let her out.

A vine of angry fathers, mothers porcelain pale.

When I left my father's house
I too knew it would be my final visit.

But I left without tears, shook the dust from my feet,
the only nostalgia a wordless music.

I was as guilty as anyone. I knew it.

Every time I opened my mouth there was drama,
accusation, but my words fell on whiskey

dissolved in that distillate warmth.

And still this problem with the china—
unadorned it would be lovely,

translucent weave of white on white,
the palest gloss of yellow

tipped inside the teapot's stem.
It's the sentiment that spoils it,

as if the unembellished can't be pleasing.
I want a teapot bearing

each denial of the body, bitterness and bad teeth.

But even the blemished past isn't
unblemished truth.

The darker truth

is what's confided. Her whisper

whispers through me now: *Come here little one. . . .*
Come here 'till I tell you.

First Frost

in memory of Ed Cox

Unexpected, it wings the smallest spears
so lightly, the touch of cold like the touch
of a new hand which asks the tentative body
to ache into a flowering that leaves the earth behind.
This is the season of darkness increasing,
of silence pressed against the panes. This is the first
bright chill of morning, the heat not yet turned on,
there is no refuge. There is only sunlight
silvered in pale tufts of grass,
this stinging alive in a season's turning,
like the moment after the news of your death,
when the flame-leafed tree outside my door
grew distinct in a terrible clarity,
the way some things are most
bright before their passing.

CHRISTINE CASSON
(1961–)

Learning Death

Another morning's mouth yawns wide as a cat's.
I break eggs into a bowl. Each white clings
to its shell. Nothing entices. It all just sits,
like me. The gleam's gone out of the silver,
wood floors hooded with dust. Books lie,
mute stones on tabletops and shelves.
Breakfast done, I wash my plate: my thumbnail
scrapes the hardened yolk.

                  You bring red roses,
and as the days pass each opens in concert
with the rest, a perfect choreography of petals.
My father, in his last month, unable
to rise and walk, would crawl about the house,
hands and knees icy from the bare floors.
In her twelfth year, my niece's underwear
are brightly stained. She scrubs them hard
to whiten them. Her mother, face flushed, fiftyish,
stands near an open window, flaps her skirts.

Your mother will not eat: she sits with head
to knees or goes to bed to lie, unmoving,
until dark. The Irish call it *"ag foghlaim
an Glais,"*—learning the river—tell stories
of those who'd walk to hospital Christmas Eve,
demand to be alone, then face the wall to die.
His body chill and weighty on the sheets,
I watched my father skip one painful breath,
and in the next, master that lesson.

ANN TOWNSEND
(1962–)

Pattern for a Sweater

I am banished outside to smoke an evening cigarette;
drink in hand I sit on a concrete step to watch
the smoke twirl away. Such banishment
may not be bad. My grandmother smokes this way,
annexed from her husband on the screened-in balcony.
She watches western Florida ten stories
below her, its bays and bridges filtered
in an evening light, cars stitched across
suspended twin wires. And how she thinks about
such patterns, as the smoke weaves through her body
at a regular pace, might echo her hands' movements
when she knits, the steady labor of intricate form
I wear as her mark. Below my feet the porch
struggles outward in bricks laid into a similar
fastidious mesh. Each clay form curves close
against the next. The sky above me clouds
against the cold; sparks drift down from my hand.
Alone, she may stub out her smoke and take up her work.
She may wander inside. She may sit still
in the twilight and listen for the night-voices
to kindle below her, to drift among her tropical trees,
cool voices mingling without definition,
like a kind of static electricity.

Irish

Candles lit to St. Augustine's life-thirst,
to his battle over the body,
pepper the room, glowing incandescent. The dreamy

strength of my Irish and their shrines comes to life
around Cousin O'Leary's bed. Flowers
sicken the stale air. The perfume of wax settles

into the wood, dark shutters drowning in light:
I sit alone with a sleeping body, taking my turn
in a formal death-watch. When it is over, as it must be,

we will kiss her waxy face and abandon her.
In the green kitchen, my aunts drink tea, their dour
murmurs floating up in scraps. Boy cousins play tackle

football in the side yard, dodging outflung arms,
swerving and leaping for each other. Why
do the saint's eyes reach to heaven for redemption

here? What is to redeem? The human world opens up
in laughter, even in this room, pressing
its suffering outwardly toward grace.

Evening Burning

      Vapor trails unfurl in the north sky,
dissolving as they slide,

      but the rain approaches—
cool, a sueded glove brushing,

      finger by finger,
across his forehead. The old leaf-smell hovers,

broken-down wet rot
cupped in the curves

of hillsides. Behind the house
the perpetual fire burns

and he pushes leaves and twigs
into the dugout pit,

its comforting red mouth.
Smoke divides around him—

burning leaves leap up,
bright sparks, a cloud of fireflies.

The church bells toll in town,
calling the wind

to evening mass.
If he works slowly,

it will burn all night
while the rake-flattened grass slowly

unbends, and the starlings
step in formation

to mine the grounds for grubs.
In the grove of trees,

the raised rough skin of the trunks
pebbles and shines

as the last light
catches hold of the bark, its grooves

and indentations, the pockmarks
of woodpeckers, the natural

abrasions. He leans a hand there,
in support, and the living skin

is so cold, so slick with moss,
it's wet before the rain comes down.

ED MADDEN
(1963–)

Sacrifice

When my father bound me, I submitted,

closed my eyes to the lifted knife in his fist.
Even now, the cords still hold my wrists,

rough ropes of love. My chest is bare,
my heart lies open. He loves his god more

than me. I open my eyes, watch my father
raise his fist against a bright and bitter

sky, no angel there to stay his hand.

Aisling

for Margot

The narrow streets of Sligo thickened with secrets,
melodramas of fog. Cigarettes and cider
on Helen's lips. We kissed in the darkened room
empty bunks around us, the other boys
having coffee in the adjoining kitchen,
listening. . . . And then he came to me,
walking down Markiewicz, his red hair
and white hands, his knee against mine
under the table at tea one afternoon.
He was fresh off the ferry from France,
an attorney on tour, Australian, of Irish descent,
his green eyes glossed with a blue sky's
brightness. The day he left his key and caught me
in the street, asked me to let him in,

we rushed back to find company gathered
in the house. Two loves had I of comfort
and deception: Helen's tiny fingers
on my hand, his knee against my knee,
rubbing indetectably, that summer
of masks and lies, a man's eyes bright
with revelation—summer of Helen, summer
of a man whose name I can't recall,
just a face, the knee, shoulders broad
in dreams, and my vacillation, refusing
to admit quite yet that I was waiting
for this vision, this deliverance, years
before I would lament the nameless men,
the years lost, what might have been.

STEPHEN McNALLY
(1963–)

Snow

Someone outside is scraping the immigrant snow, making a red sound.
This sound clears sidewalks, gathers itself up,
escapes the feet of children running past
and hides under the umbrellas
of gentlemen, amid the steam of a railway station where the tired
figures await the brooding, filthy, weightless engine. They climb aboard
like pilgrims hungry for passage, for nightfall.

Now it mingles with the whistle of the train, the howl cascading
through the iron fences downtown. A man in a blue suit sits
alone in a diner. A bald man serves him, and they both hear it,
this voice that trembles fishermen adrift in their ragged boat, finds
the drunken farmers by a mill who throw dead bottles
into a stream pushing past, and follows the water through a tangle
   of weeds.
toward the lumberyard where the old men in denim shirts
pound an anvil into the shape of the world, the shape
of a red sound cracking the center of a stone.

The Adventure

We loaded the ship and set off with white sails swelling in the wind,
the brown cliffs to our left.
We had left their wars, their golden temples, their women prophesying
behind curtains of scented smoke.
One of us took his shield and hurled it into the sea.
He spat after it. "Never again," he said. "I won't worship their gods or kill
for them. Those promises of salvation were empty. Every word they
spoke was a lie."
He spoke for us all. Our sweat glistened in the sun as circling birds dipped
their wings.
At last we were free. We had no country, no home.
But if we died now, our deaths would be our own.

JENNIFER O'GRADY
(1963–)

The Miraculous Draft of Fishes

In one boat, two men are hauling up nets,
the sculpted columns of their arms unceasingly
brightened by the afternoon light.
In another, three haloed figures float
over water so still, it might not exist
but for the pale bodily parts
it reflects. One can only imagine
the fluid red of Christ's robe, its generous folds
now dulled a milky pink, or the heightened coloring
of Peter looking up with pure wonder
at the unmoving face of God
or Andrew, standing, his arms wide open
and perfect in perspective.
Somehow the skiffs' thick pilings of fish,
frozen mouths aghast, seem to have been there
longer than the hungry crowd
darkening a far shore.
Closer, a trio of cranes strains upward
as if remembering how to fly.

If what we want most is what's forever
lost, then there's something mournful about
this loosening and dissolution of pigments
pressed from once-living things.
If only faith were this easy, its forms
this visible, as Raphael might have believed
they were, believed in the lasting life
of white lead, azurite, red lake, vermilion,

smooth shells of muscle, and the definition
shading lends to light. Not knowing
how quietly his featherstrokes
of birds above the thinning horizon
would fade until they were mere suggestions,
like shadows, or the sudden dying of a wind
before it has fully arisen.

Blue Heron

All through that dim, uncertain summer
    we'd glimpse him, sometimes jutting from a rock
        near the uninhabited shore
or perched on a concrete barrier
    at the pond's shallow end. How confidently
        out-of-place he seemed—

ash-blue, the belly white as snow
    and thickly fledged, the question-mark neck
        elegantly held in an attitude
of tense rest, reminding us
    of angels in Renaissance paintings:
        humble, still, expectant.

After a while, we came to believe
    we would always find him, just beyond a bend
        or at dawn, like a carved figure
at the edge of our borrowed lawn-
    lonesome, remote, almost godlike,
        surveying the opposite shore.

What was he waiting for? Or did it
    merely seem to us (creatures
        so deeply immersed in each other)
that he must have wanted something more
    than the constant sum of himself?
        With the first early dark, he was gone

as suddenly as he'd arrived
    and the pond again flattened into
      its hushed, unmiraculous state.
While already, leaves showed the transient gold
    that signals the very end of life,
      the beginning of lives to come.

MEG KEARNEY
(1964–)

The Prodigal Father

It's too late—he can't go back, gas up the old Ford
Fairlane and head for Midland Avenue, frosted mugs
and football at Sullivans or buckets of beer with all
the Smiths and the McErlanes down at Sandy Point
Beach. No more Scotch and tube steaks at the King's

Park drive-in, the Everly Brothers and Elvis and his
hands on a girl's hips in the smoky dim of Shady's
or the Golden Nugget. *You're my piece of gold*, he
murmured into that last girl's ear, *Hell, I must be
at the rainbow's end*, and the way she looked at him—

well, he doesn't want to think about her or what
he said later in the Fairlane's back seat. She should
have known better—she was one of those good
girls—as he knew better than to call, or be seen
in the Nugget for a while, though soon he'd heard

she'd moved, maybe Arizona, maybe New Mexico.
It took nine or ten pints at Sullivans to convince
himself the other half of that rumor wasn't true—
or if it was, she could have been knocked-up by
anybody. Another couple of pints and he knew

he was moving, too, taking the wife and kids north
to New England and a new life. But it took more
than a shot of whiskey to quiet that song, that
wordless ballad moaning in his head, something
with a fiddle, something with a pipe, a mandolin.

Gin

She came to sex as she'd come to gin. Five
years in the convent, what did she know
about gin? Sister Emmanuel said the Devil
himself was suckled on it, and after her
third drink in the Red Kilt she knew he was
inside her like a crazed Wizard of Oz,
pushing and pumping her levers and gears.
Each time she brought the glass to her lips,
Sister's voice whispered, "You couldn't
lift one finger, not one pinky of one hand
if not for the Love of God." But she was
twenty-five and didn't know anything about
love. She knew she wasn't holy, or chaste, or
even sorry. And she knew she was alone when
the man called her beautiful, when the gin
said *Baby, relax, enjoy it while you can.*

CHRISTOPHER CAHILL
(1965–)

Sandalwood

for Ada Marcella

> The one peacock we didn't find cries from a bed of ivy under an eave
>   of the rector's Dutch roof
> As is it the fifth grade shouts by on its way back to class. And I sit
>   beneath a pergola on a bench
> In the biblical garden by a stunted judas tree (Matthew 27:5) between
>   the blackened apse
> Of the cathedral with its green angel trumpeting towards Harlem, its
>   lost evangelists,
> And a wearied wooden colonnade, once white, like the porch at Vyra
>   or Rozhdestveno,
> And as you harry the margins with a sprig of juniper for a pigeon and
>   a rabbit you've lost
> (Or is it a hound, a bay horse, and a turtledove?—either way I'll never
>   know if you find them)
> I'm dipping into *The Ghost Orchid* by Michael Longley and between
>   wondering if sandalwood
> Is biblical and in this garden and even what it is I begin these lines for
>   you, ink on envelope,
> Seeing no reason not to imitate his poems written with a fennel brush
>   on Japanese air.

Lamplighting

The curfew tolls the death of Little Nell.
Nearby a dog barks at a rival dog
Barking nearby, and if not for these alarms
There would be more to call us out from thought,
From work, the eyes desperate to rest
Against the blue evening air we missed
The onslaught of, stars in place
Before the ink has dried, urging us
To kill the lights and let the night take hold
Of us along with the museum's battlements,
The trees' branches rooted in the sky,
The lonely passengers drifting home
After one more day of unrecorded longing.

The message of the night is simple and familiar.
The moon spells it out in marble hieroglyphs.
It is asking us to recollect the love
Made, by us as well, on beds and couches
Spaced throughout the empty house:
It is letting us know how soon that vanishes,
How quick the come dries on the flesh
She wiped it on that once, then flakes away,
Words we thought had meaning gone
The unremembered way of words.

Tonight Nell dies again, it says, little or not,
Attended by her dying father, attending him,
He dies. The heart of stone laughs, cries,
Stops and is forgotten. Out in the air
A colorless wind is rubbing its eraser
Slowly over the visible world.
Nothing seems to vanish but it does.

AIDAN ROONEY
(1965–)

Safe Haven

The things you find when you drive a pick beneath the lawn's thick turf,
then prise it off—a rusted nest of tools, a boot's uppers, a brittle cloth,

and an old fork, its tines and nape still parallel and arched. And then again,
the things you're glad you don't. Earthmovers turn up bones and stall

the *Big Dig* in what could be Srebrenica; but there's no mother here to claim
a tibia in a hightop is her son's, and point to a hole in the skull. Or Ballinakill,

this fume of rain the same that helped the sods take; but no one's here
with a chrisom child in a wooden box, leaning in to a headland wind.

Here, ghosts dream they wake from quarantined sleep to this, a choice view
of Boston, too late or too soon for asylum, but for long enough to glimpse

that other boat from China or Haiti, anchored off Deer Island. Wasn't it there
their ship dumped keep? And there too, a young man snatched from dream

stirs in a coop. Tomorrow we'll dig again, a new highway put underground
to relieve congestion. And I'll fling gravel where the sod was, tell a neighbour

what I'd found, conjecture a narrative, as we savour the sound, scrape
then racket, of each crushed stone sent off the shovel and finding a place to rest.

Holy Water

I

Three sparrows swoop in to the window's rectangle to bathe in the garden.
Backpedal of wing, as their kindling legs catch the smooth rim of the stone font.
A quick genuflect and they're in, scattering diamonds from the gathered rain
like benevolent aristocrats. Spruced up for the day, they shuffle and jaunt
in fledgling ostentation, and wink at themselves in the fractured basin,
till suddenly, a vision of grain spills an idea to the eye's glint.
A cocked moment, and before you know it, in unison, they're up and gone.

II

The plastic bottle warms on the sill, where you left it before you flew back
from your benediction visit. What was it anyway?—the unblessed house,
conception, the mixed marriage? Is it Lourdes, Knock, or bubbled in before mass
in the fragrant dark at the back of a church, the bottle submerged in moss-cool
stone? The priest strides up the aisle with a frond of palm and sprinkles his flock.
A mental patient from St. Davnet's thumps his heart with a fist, like a clock-
work soldier seized in confirmation, his mind aflutter, beyond egress.

The cool sparks fly, livened with candle flicker, and a wayward drop beads
on the tea-gold glow of an empty pew. The vaults are catapulted down
into its minute, shuddering world, the stained daylight filtering its shards
of errant dust, buoyant and silver in the glittering air, through the dome
of its dazed meniscus. It could be the single shed tear of a bold child,
caught etching in the wood's wax, on the wrong page of his communion missal,
or the frozen moment of a candle's drip before it freezes to bone-white pearl.

Like a landed bubble, bruised and desperate, it swirls around its embers
of coloured glass in the vitreous swell of its empty liquid, refused what
every happy bubble wants, a laying on of children's hands, their fingers
fused, exalting in the air, begging their weightless worlds not to burst, blink out
to motes that spark a moment and are gone, caught between knowledge and desire,
captive and liberative, wanting nothing but for one of them to stay,
to spin and sing a while, or drift off intact, winging it, up and away.

The Island of Women

She all but withdrew when I came
to, splayed on her damp shingle, licked
of grime, reporters gathered round
to experience this fishy bird
of a man she'll loophole in, pleading,
'we will not throw him back; he's come
so far,' then (and this is where they
were had), '. . . he did make it to shore';
well-versed in the delivery
of saying nothing, I squinted
at the wide, sun-glittering sea
that just a while ago they'd carved
up with their powerboats, hoses
raining down on our make-shift skiff,
my more worldly-wise companions
hauled to safety but whisked
away back home, agreeably
love-sick, as I, husbanding smiles
to the elders, make to get up.

JOSEPH LENNON
(1967–)

(from) 29th Birthday

(Co. Kerry, August 5th, 1997)

Cords

Arriving in Kenmare, grease under my nails,
over soup and brown bread in the Horseshoe pub,
Dennis, bass-player and publican, leans over:
"There's the man who succeeded Haughey,
Bertie, the leader of our country, just there,
not trailed by guards, cameras, or crowds,
just lunching with the wife and daughter."
With six elbows and flowers on the table,
the politician on holiday sits like any old man:
aloof, stupefied, buttering his bread.

No one minds him-with-the-reins-of-Éire-
in-his-hands. Everyone seems occupied
by their own affairs, upsets, goings-on,
their own slippery lives. We all track
our bloodless revolutions every year,
ticking off days of local bothers,
family squabbles, money troubles,
rarely marking a day of witness.
But today, I make myself a present,
to watch the photo-ready family having tea.

I think, I could join them that first family
and be the silent son to the silent father,
to the Taoiseach, just through tea-time,
just till the car was ready. Perhaps,
they need a quiet brother for the silent sister,
a dumb son for the dumb mother.
We could chart our anamnesis during the lulls—
one to reconnoiter on this day
when my cord was cut
and I was spanked into breath.

But I stay on my stool, chewing bread
in thought. I decide I'll stay
wherever I go today,
to take my boots off the roads,
unlace my mind from my lessons,
go back to trace my living
in the contours of my day.

Walnuts
In Illinois whenever my family built a bonfire, after we tossed
the brush, limbs, leaves, logs, branches, briar bundles, mown
grass, dead clippings, garden weeds, stiff feral, flattened
pumpkins, apple-orchard prunings, rotten boards,
railroad ties, broken chairs, and wooden rubbish
onto the heap, I'd gather up in my newspaper-
delivery satchel a horde of lemony
walnut fruit & drop them
one by one
into the burning pile.

I longed then to hear of mysteries to learn
of tribal wrongs that could sear me;
to know how whites set upon the Sangamon,
and how the river flowed before;
to resurrect the Illini and hear
stories of the fields that lashed out
from piles of flaming light;
to hear what walnuts roasted in dying
embers could cure or curse; to know
why this flatland was one way

and not another.
But we are from places we do not know.

BETH ANN FENNELLY
(1971–)

The Names of Things

1.

Why? asks the Sears' security guard, but she can't
tell him about the names of colors in the lip gloss sampler
she's slipped inside her tote. She has no words to say
that the name *Ballerina Pink* is scruffed toe-shoes
stuffed with lambs woll and bleeding feet,
that *Boysenberry* draws boys to lips of ripening spring.

Soon she will be taken home, climb the long stairway
to her mother lying in the sick room of the girl's
entire childhood, because of the tragic Missed Carriage.
Sometimes the girl imagines a baby brother
held through the carriage window by sequined gloves.
Sometimes the school nuns produce the boy,
finger their heavy crosses before signaling the driver
to crunch on through the gravel. She can't ask why
her mother was late, or if this too was her father's fault—
her mother is "not to be pestered by precocious little girls.
You're a queer one," says the nurse. "Mind your p's and q's,"
the girl would have retorted if every day her father
didn't put three fingers to his lips and twist, throw the key
over his shoulder, like you do with spilt salt, no bad luck.

2.

The names of things will never lose their hold on her.
By now, her parents have surrendered. She knows
nothing of her history, must rediscover everything.
She starts with her name. From the Gaelic, "Fennelly"
means "fair warrior." Her mother's "McNamara":
"son of the hound of the sea." And there in the book:
"These two clans have been warring for centuries . . ."
The names, making it happen. Within, she is chanting
Tawny Peach, Passionfruit, smearing her lips *Cotton Candy,*
Black Coffee, staining her *Scarlet, Burnt Clay,*
and *Blood Red*—lubricants, but still a lip-locked girl.

JILL McDONNAGH
(1972–)

(from) The Execution Sonnets

June 28, 1895: Michael McDonough
Columbus, Ohio

> Say he's my great great grandfather. Or say
> he's yours. *Cleveland Press—FRESH OHIO NEWS—*
> put our grandfather's hanging on the sports page,
> after *THE DEADLY CIGARET* and *soon*
> *C. Grimes will start in business, giving baths.*
> McDonough's headline's hard to find, and then
> it's *SICKENING. Awful Scene at the Gallows. As*
> *Shocking* and *Gory as a Guillotine.*
> *He'd stabbed his wife to death on a dark bridge,* lost
> his case and spent a year in prison where
> he *had grown heavy, his flesh and muscles soft:*
> his head came off. *Blood spurted* in the air,
> *upon the spectators, executioners.*
> And on *the prison physicians, bloody as butchers.*

June 11, 2001: Timothy McVeigh
Terre Haute, Indiana

Victims' loved ones in Oklahoma City
gathered to watch on closed circuit TV;
security kept *hackers from stealing the signal.*
His lawyer said McVeigh *was able to see*
the moon in the sky on the way to the death house, and that
meant something to him. Viewers saw his *face*
hard as stone, face of evil. His eyes looked black.
He stared at the camera, jaw clenched, *the face of hate.*
His eyes *rolled back when his heart stopped* and he died.
Most saw *The Devil,* back *in hell,* which caused
one man to say *He's not a monster, guys,*
not when you're looking him in the face. He paused.
There's no facial expressions on him, so there's
no way of knowing exactly what he is.

BRENDA SHAUGHNESSY
(1972–)

The Question and Its Mark

May I cast a spell on the many swans of Leda,
making at last one spastic blizzard in spring
with only enough divine mania to take one
blinding day from her?

The godbirds and their scopophilia
keep her open for view and review, with ever
new speculum and never the elegant jewelry
of stigmata or a heart of quartz.

May I give her only one death? Can we live if she
lies closed in a single final pose, no syphilitic
autopsy or cygnet interrogation?
May I mark her prophecy,

her presence in the very air, with a single
gargoyle on the streetside wall on a place
of worship, finally allowed inside if only by
disappearing into the stones?

Leda possessed a pair of knees that also bent
in prayer. I ask of you only what she asked for there.

TYLER FARRELL
(1973–)

Letter from Madeline Island

If I were sick once again, I would think of long lighted days
stuck with you on the island opening can after can of Miller High Life
to tell stories of the frozen ponds at the back of your house,
the stumbling uncle from your wedding reception, an old friend
whom you no longer talk to. You played old tunes on a jukebox
and stood around waiting to be asked to dance, rotten odd
moments like complaints or fly by night religions or talk of the weather—
chill outside, last year's frozen spout on top of the water treatment tank
with strange stains on its balled feet and rounded silver and
bulging primer coat layered in the thickness from a young boy's
heavy shaken hands. There is an old motel on Bayfield peninsula.
It smells of trout and aged whiskey. The owner is a merciless
women with holes in her slippers and a cigarette hanging
from a half opened mouth, lipstick on the filter, nicotine stains
on her knuckles. She hobbles to our room with glasses of ice,
seltzer water, a bucket with extra pillow cases, more dry towels.
She once played trombone with the Sweethearts of Rhythm
and married the owner of this land. He built her a motel, told her
to run it while he flew around the continent creating new ways
for her to hate him. I scrawl a note on a napkin and tape it to
my leg. It is an outline of a plan to meet you again on the island,
a dream of long distance swimmers struggling toward the sand
and rock of its southern tip where the post office sits with white
painted boards as the small plot of land it rests on erodes further
into the lake. Maybe I will bitterly move away from here. The loss

from back home, the cabin sunsets, the isolation even for birds.
There is a staggered wind, a reminder to crouching farmers.
There is no rest from a wicked life. Even this small land fastened
to the lake could never float away like a piece of driftwood caught
on a heavy wind and northern wave. We are the stationary ones.
We are like islands, free from the mainland, still tethered to the earth.

KATHLEEN ROONEY
(1980–)

Hometown

It's the last place you'd want your ghost to haunt:
the first house, first street, first life you knew well;

the hand you were dealt and how it felt
to play the spots off those crooked cards;

kissing the shadow of your own rough mouth
on the yellowed paper of the bedroom wall;

anyone, surfacing like a corpse in a millpond,
who still recalls your unglamorous youth.

It's your pentimento; your palimpsest.
It's the mirror you break your nose against.

COLLEEN ABEL
(1980–)

On Touring the U.N. with My Mother-in-Law

Behind glass are the remnants of war:
helmets, uniforms, tatters of clothing
from civilian casualties. Maps locate concentrations
of poverty, disease; hundreds of flags
hang their heads, defeated. You've fallen
behind the group by several feet to chat with me
about the latest book you've read, your last
vacation. I strain to pay attention
in the cavernous assembly room to the workings
of world order. Standing stiffly beside you,
I can sympathize with the tiny countries
that gather here, hoping to influence giants.
Your eyes wander; there's not much
you wouldn't know about wielding power
and money, you who conceded me one thing only:
your son. And that just barely.
Entering the chamber of the security council,
you analyze the mural over the guide's talking
and point out the phoenix—huge and golden—sputtering
up from ash. It's all wrong, of course,
as a symbol for us, unless perhaps
it represents the hope that years will kill
our old selves to each other, and we will come
out on the other side, not golden, but whole.

GENERAL HISTORICAL CHRONOLOGY

2500 BCE:	Building of passage graves, Newgrange, in Ireland
680 BCE:	Emain Macha (Navan Fort near Armagh)
500 BCE–500 CE:	Adena and Hopewell mounds in North America
1–500:	La Tene culture in Ireland
432:	Traditional date of St. Patrick's arrival in Ireland
524:	Death of St. Brigit
530:	St. Brendan explores the Atlantic in a curragh and, legend has it, reaches America
563:	Monastery at Iona founded by Columcille
622:	Death of St. Kevin of Glendalough
637:	Battle of Moira, basis for the legend of Buile Suibhne (Mad Sweeney)
795:	Viking raids begin in Ireland
841:	Dublin founded by Vikings
1000:	Norse settlement at L'Anse aux Meadow in Newfoundland
1014:	Brian Boru killed at the Battle of Clontarf
1066:	William the Conqueror victorious in the Battle of Hastings, setting stage for Norman invasion of Ireland
1210:	Submission of the Irish kings to King John of England
1492:	Columbus lands on Guanahani Island in the Bahamas, renames it San Salvador; Poyning's Law makes Dublin's parliament subservient to London
1497:	The Cabots land in North America
1534:	Act of Supremacy makes Henry VIII head of the Church of England
1541:	Henry VIII proclaimed King of Ireland
1561–1567:	Shane O'Neill's Rebellion
1562:	John Hawkins, an English navigator, leads the first slave-trading expedition to the Caribbean via Guinea, Africa
1583:	Munster Plantations begin
1587:	Hugh O'Neill proclaimed Earl of Tyrone
1588:	Spanish Armada wrecked on the Ulster Coast; Edmund Spenser at Kilcolman Castle in County Cork
1600–1630:	Irish Catholics begin emigration to North America as indentured servants
1601:	O'Neill's defeat at the Battle of Kinsale
1603:	Death of Queen Elizabeth
1607:	Flight of the Irish Earls; English settlement in Jamestown, Virginia
1608–1610:	Ulster Plantations
1619:	First Africans in North America arrive in Virginia as indentured servants
1620:	Pilgrim emigrants reach Provincetown on Cape Cod; found New Plymouth settlement
1625:	Dutch colony of New Amsterdam founded on Manhattan Island
1628:	Company of New France begins trade in Canada
1630:	Great emigration to Massachusetts
1643:	New England Confederation founded

1649:	Oliver Cromwell arrives in Ireland as civil and military governor; massacres in Drogheda and Wexford
1651:	Transportation of Irish Catholics as slaves to Virginia and the West Indies under Cromwell
1654:	First Jewish settlers in North America arrive in New Amsterdam
1660–1678:	Irish Catholics comprise one third of the free population of the Leeward Islands (Barbados)
1664:	English capture New Amsterdam and rename New York
1688–1689:	The Siege of Derry
1690:	William III defeats James II at the Battle of the Boyne
1691:	Williamite plantations begin in Ireland
1695:	Penal legislation against Catholics begins in Ireland
1704:	Irish Penal Codes enforced
1713:	Jonathan Swift becomes Dean of St. Patrick's Cathedral in Dublin
1718:	Scots-Irish emigration to New England, Maryland, and Pennsylvania
1730:	German and Scots-Irish colonization of Carolina back country
1756–1763:	French Indian War in North America
1760:	Whiteboy movement begins in Tipperary and Waterford
1762:	First British settlement in New Brunswick
1770–1775:	Ulster emigration of mostly Scots Presbyterians to North America
1770:	British troops fire on protesters in the "Boston Massacre"; African American seaman Crispus Attucks killed
1771–1773:	Crop failures and depression in the Ulster linen trade lead to Ulster Scots emigration to America
1773:	Bostonians protest against East India Company's monopoly on tea by throwing 342 crates overboard in the "Boston Tea Party"
1775:	Revolutionary War begins in Concord, Massachusetts
1776:	American Declaration of Independence approved by the Continental Congress
1780:	Irish politician Henry Grattan demands Home Rule for Ireland
1783:	Massachusetts bans slavery; Revolutionary War ends in the Peace of Paris
1784:	Irish Catholics comprise seven eighths of the population of St. John's, Newfoundland
1787:	United States Constitution ratified
1789:	United States Congress meets for the first time in New York; the French Revolution begins
1791:	The French Revolution ends; foundation of United Irishmen in Belfast; British North America divided into Ontario and Quebec under the Canadian Constitution Act; slave revolt in Santo Domingo led by Tousaint L'Ouverture
1792:	Partridge Island off St. John, New Brunswick, opens, North America's first immigrant receiving station
1798:	Rebellion in Wexford, Battle of Vinegar Hill; Henry Joy McCracken hanged; Wolfe Tone commits suicide; rebels forced to emigrate to the United States; others follow
1801:	Philadelphia bookseller, Mathew Carey, helps establish the American company of Booksellers in New York; Act of Union creates the United Kingdom of Great Britain and Ireland
1803:	Napoleonic Wars begin; Robert Emmett executed after aborted rebellion in Ireland; Louisiana Purchase

1805–1807:	Lewis and Clark expedition
1812:	Anglo-American War begins
1815:	Napoleonic Wars end with defeat at Waterloo; Anglo-American War ends
1818:	Seminole War
1819:	First steamship, the *Savannah,* crosses the Atlantic
1820:	The United States Congress decides on the "Missouri Compromise" permitting Missouri to enter the Union as a slave state, Maine as a free state
1825:	Erie Canal completed under Robert Fulton's direction
1828:	Daniel O'Connell elected MP for Clare
1829:	Andrew Jackson, the son of Ulster-Scots immigrants, is elected the seventh President of the United States; Catholic Emancipation in Ireland
1831:	The Trail of Tears
1834:	Department of Indian Affairs established
1835–1842:	Second Seminole War
1838:	English Poor Laws extended to Ireland
1845–1848:	Mexican-American War; conquest of California
1845–1850:	The Great Famine in Ireland; Robert Peel, Prime Minister, Charles Trevelyan, Assistant Secretary to the Treasury; over one million die and two million emigrate, most to the United States and Canada on so called "coffin ships"
1847:	"Black '47"; thousands of Irish die of disease upon arriving at Grosse Isle, Quebec; Daniel O'Connell dies
1855:	Castle Garden immigrant receiving station opens in New York; the anti-immigrant Know Nothing Party reaches its peak of influence with forty-eight seats in the House of Representatives
1857:	The Dred Scott decision reverses the Missouri Compromise, setting the Stage for the Civil War
1858:	Irish Republican Brotherhood established in Ireland
1859:	Abolitionist John Brown leads an unsuccessful raid on Harper's Ferry to spark a slave revolution; Fenian Brotherhood established in the United States
1861–1865:	The American Civil War; Irish American legions fight for both the Union and the Confederacy
1862:	Union general Thomas Meagher leads the Irish Brigade at the Battle of Fredericksburg
1863:	The Emancipation Proclamation frees slaves in the Confederacy; Irish protesters kill hundreds of African Americans in the New York Draft Riots
1867:	Clan na Gael revolutionary society established in New York; The Molly Maguires, a secret labor society, reportedly agitating in Pennsylvania coal mines; purchase of Alaska; Canadian Confederation established
1869:	The first United States transcontinental railroad completed
1870:	Queenstown and Moville replace Liverpool as major embarkation points for Irish emigrants bound for the United States and Canada
1873:	Home Rule League established in Ireland
1876–1877:	Sioux Wars for the Black Hills; Custer defeated at Little Big Horn
1877:	Charles Stewart Parnell elected president of the Home Rule Confederation
1879:	Land League founded by Michael Davitt
1880:	Parnell addresses United States House of Representatives in the Irish situation
1882:	Oscar Wilde tours North America

1885:	Irish Mine Workers of America established
1889:	Jane Addams founds Hull House for white immigrants in Chicago
1890:	United States troops massacre 350 Sioux Indians at Wounded Knee; North American Women's Suffrage Association founded; Parnell dies; Castle Garden closes
1890–1900:	African Americans denied the right to vote in the South
1892:	Ellis Island immigrant station opens in New York; Annie Moore, a fifteen-year-old Irish immigrant, is the first to pass through the gates
1893:	The Gaelic League founded in Ireland
1894:	The Pullman Strike; miners riot in Pennsylvania and Ohio
1898:	The Spanish American War
1904:	The Abbey Theatre opens
1907:	James Larkin organizes dock strikes in Belfast
1913:	James Larkin and James Connolly organize ITGWU (Irish Transport and General Workers' Union) strike in Ireland
1914–1918:	World War I
1916:	Padraic Pearse leads the Easter Rebellion in Ireland
1920:	19th Amendment grants Women's Suffrage; Black and Tans recruited; Kevin Barry executed in Mountjoy Jail
1921:	Anglo-Irish Treaty; Irish Free State established
1922:	Civil War in Ireland; death of Michael Collins; James Joyce's *Ulysses* published in Paris by Shakespeare and Company
1929:	The Stock Market crashes on Wall Street; the Great Depression begins
1932:	Eamonn de Valera elected president of the Irish Free State
1933:	Adolph Hitler rises to power in Germany; persecution of Jews intensifies leading to the Holocaust
1939:	World War II begins; Ireland declares neutrality
1941:	America enters World War II after the Japanese attack Pearl Harbor
1945:	World War II ends
1948:	Republic of Ireland established
1950–1953:	The Korean War
1954:	Army-McCarthy Un-American Activities Committee Hearings; Ellis Island closes
1955:	AFL-CIO (American Federation of Labor and Congress of Industrial Organizations) established
1956:	Montgomery Bus Boycott; Civil Rights Movement begins
1961-1975:	The Vietnam War
1962:	The Cuban Missile Crisis
1963:	President John F. Kennedy assassinated
1964:	President Johnson signs Civil Rights Act
1967:	Daniel and Philip Berrigan raid the Catonsville, Maryland, secret service office in protest over the war in Vietnam; foundation of the Northern Ireland Civil Rights Association
1968:	Martin Luther King, Jr. assassinated; Robert Kennedy assassinated
1969:	Astronauts walk on the moon
1972:	"Bloody Sunday" massacre in Derry; United States withdraws from Vietnam
1973:	*Roe v. Wade* gives women the right to reproductive choice
1979:	The Shah of Iran flees to Egypt
1980–1990:	The "New Irish" emigration to America

1980:	Maura Clark, an Irish American Maryknoll stationed in Nicaragua, is murdered with another nun by government troops in San Salvador
1981:	United States hostages freed by Iran
1985:	The Iran-Contra Conspiracy comes to light
1985:	Anglo-Irish Agreement signed
1987:	The Remembrance Day Enniskillen bombing kills eleven people
1989:	Fall of the Berlin Wall
1990–1991:	The Gulf War (Operation Desert Storm)
1993:	Islamic extremists bomb the World Trade Center in New York; six killed; European Union established; Timothy McVeigh bombs the federal building in Oklahoma City; hundreds killed
1994:	IRA ceasefire
1998:	The Omagh bombing; the Good Friday Agreement signed
2001:	Islamic extremists hijack commercial airliners and fly them into the Pentagon in Washington and into the World Trade Center in New York; World Trade Center destroyed; over 2,500 killed; in Northern Ireland, the IRA agrees to decommission arms
2002:	U.S. and Afghan troops launch Operation Anaconda against remaining al-Qaeda and Taliban fighters in Afghanistan; the IRA issues its first apology to the families of the 650 civilians killed by the IRA since the late 1960s
2003:	U.S. and Britain launch war against Iraq
2004:	Tsunami devastates Asia; 200,000 killed
2005:	Pope John Paul II dies (April 2); Benedict XVI becomes pope; London hit by Islamic terrorist bombings; the Irish Republican Army announces it is officially ending its violent campaign for a united Ireland and will instead pursue its goals politically; earthquake in the Pakistani-controlled part of the Kashmir region kills more than 80,000; Hurricane Katrina hits U.S. Gulf Coast
2006:	United States supports a June 29 statement by British Prime Minister Tony Blair and Irish Prime Minister Bertie Ahern outlining the steps needed to restore Northern Ireland's government by November 24, ending years of political deadlock

BIOGRAPHICAL
AND EXPLANATORY NOTES

George Berkeley (1685–1753): philosopher and bishop of Cloyne; wrote this his only known poem after he had sailed to Rhode Island to establish a missionary college. He returned two years later after he realized the funding promised by the British Government would not be forthcoming.

Mathew Carey (1760–1839): born in Dublin, settled in Philadelphia in 1784. Chiefly a publisher and journalist, he was one of the most prolific and influential book publishers in the early years following the Revolution. William Cobbet was a famous detractor of the American experiment and wrote under the pen name, "Porcupine."

James Orr (1770–1816): a poor weaver poet, born in country Antrim, who went to America briefly after fighting in the Battle of Antrim. For a more extensive note see *Verse in English from Eighteenth-Century Ireland.* Andrew Carpenter, ed. (Cork: Cork University Press, 1999), 542.

Thomas Branagan (1774–1843): born in Dublin, in 1790 he sailed from Liverpool to Africa on a slave ship, traveled with its cargo to the West Indies, and eventually settled in Philadelphia. Eschewing his part in the slave trade, Branagan became an abolitionist. Written in 1805, *Avenia: A Tragical Poem on the Oppression of the Human Species and Infringement of the Rights of Man*, aspires to be a distinctly American epic in the Homeric tradition in which historical figures like the slave trader Hawkins and the heroic African Louverture are fictionalized. For a more extensive account of Branagan's life see Noel Ignatiev, *How the Irish Became White* (New York: Routledge, 1995), 51–58.

James McHenry (1785–1845): Protestant immigrant from Ulster; one of the first Irish American novelists. "The Haunts of Larne" appears in his first novel, *The Wilderness*. See Charles Fanning, ed. *The Exiles of Erin* (Notre Dame, IN: University of Notre Dame Press, 1997), 84–95.

Sarah Helen Whitman (1813–1878): born in Providence, Rhode Island of Irish American lineage, daughter of Nicholas Power, Whitman also wrote a biography of Edgar Alan Poe; Oliver Cromwell (1599–1658), ruled Britain and Ireland as Lord Protector from 1649–1658 during which time Catholic Ireland underwent ruthless suppression and the destruction of the traditional Irish social order.

Henry David Thoreau (1817–1862): in addition to the poem included here, Thoreau's reflections on Irish Americans may be found in *Walden* as well as his short piece, "The Shipwreck."

Walt Whitman (1819–1892): for an extended analysis of Whitman's connection to the Irish see Joann Kreig's *Whitman and the Irish* (Iowa City: University of Iowa Press, 2000).

Alice Cary (1820–1871): poet and novelist, born near Cincinnati, Ohio; moved to New York with her sister, Phoebe, where she hosted one of the mid-nineteenth century's most famous literary salons.

Charles G. Halpine (1829–1868): born in County Meath, son of a Church of Ireland clergyman, came to America in 1850. "On Raising a Monument to the Irish Legion" memorializes the legendary "Fighting 69th" organized by General Thomas Meagher (1823–1867) in New York. The poem speaks to the role of Irish soldiers on both sides of the Civil War, but in particular it commemorates the extensive losses suffered by the brigade at the Battle of Fredericksburg in 1862.

John Boyle O'Reilly (1844–1892): born in County Meath, Fenian, journalist, and the most significant Irish American poet of the nineteenth century. In "The Exile of the Gael," "Innisfail" refers to the traditional literary name for Ireland. Crispus Attucks, an African American killed at the Battle of Lexington (1775), was the first casualty of the American Revolution. For note of "At Fredericksburg" see note under Charles G. Halpine (1829–1868).

James Jeffrey Roche (1847–1908): born in Ireland, Roche emigrated to Prince Edward Island before becoming editor of the Boston *Pilot.*

Daniel O'Connell (1848–?): born in Liscanor, County Clare; arrived in New York in 1867 and subsequently moved to San Francisco where he worked as a journalist.

James Whitcomb Riley (1849–1916): born in Indiana and known as the "Hoosier poet," Riley was one of the most popular poets of the nineteenth century. See note under John Boyle O'Reilly (1844–1892).

Maurice Francis Egan (1852–1924): born to a prosperous Philadelphia Catholic family; professor, journalist, diplomat under Theodore Roosevelt. Maurice De Guérin (1810–1839) is a French Romantic poet and writer.

Louise Imogene Guiney (1861–1920): born in Massachusetts of Irish parents, Guiney published over thirty books of poetry as well as essays.

Kate McPhelim Cleary (1863–1905): best known for her fiction detailing lives of Irish Americans in Chicago or rural Nebraska; for a fuller account of her work and history see Charles Fanning's *The Exiles of Erin.*

Edwin Arlington Robinson (1869–1935): born in Maine of Irish ancestry, Robinson is an essential American poet whose poems depicting the inhabitants of his fictional Tilbury Town ("Luke Havergal," "Mr Flood's Party," "Eros Turanos") constitute a permanent contribution to American literature. I have chosen only those poems that carry some explicit Irish or Irish American reference, or seem to resonate thematically with other works included in this volume.

Padraig O'Heigeartaigh (1871–1936): Thomas Kinsella notes in *The New Oxford Book of Irish Verse* that O'Heigeartaigh "emigrated from County Kerry to Springfield, Massachusetts, as a child. He sent this lament on his son's death to Patrick Pease's paper *An Claid-heamh Solus* (The Sword of Light) at the turn of the century; a number of phrases out of Pearse's translation are included" (p. 407).

Paul Laurence Dunbar (1872–1906): It is, perhaps, appropriate to end this section with a poem on the most prominent Irish American poet of his time by one of the notable African American poets of the late nineteenth and early twentieth centuries.

Part Two. Modern Tide

Lola Ridge (1873–1941): born in Dublin, raised in Australia, Ridge emigrated to America and settled on New York's Lower East Side where she found a place among the left-wing and ex-perimental artists and writers of the day, among them Alfred Kreymbourg, William Carlos Williams, Marianne Moore, and Hart Crane. Almost entirely neglected, her work combines a passionate sense of social justice with an equally passionate religious sensibility. She won the Shelley Memorial Award before she died in 1941. James Larkin (1874–1947) was an Irish Communist and labor leader.

Robert Frost (1874–1963): Frost's whimsical side, rarely seen, presents itself in this piece of "Irish American" light verse.

Oliver St. John Gogarty (1878–1957): born in Dublin, Gogarty was a fiction writer, play-wright, and poet. He moved to America in 1939.

Wallace Stevens (1879–1955): In the last decade of his life, Stevens carried on an extended correspondence with the Irish poet Thomas McGreevy (1893–1967). Stevens found his in-spiration for "The Irish Cliffs of Moher" in a postcard—he never traveled to Ireland.

Padraic Colum (1881–1972): born in Longford, playwright, novelist, and poet of some stature in the generation succeeding Yeats, Colum emigrated to America in 1912 and traveled extensively over the course of his long life.

John Gould Fletcher (1886–1950): southern poet born of Scots Irish ancestry; his early work was influenced by Amy Lowell and the Imagists, though his best work evinces not only a strong impressionist bent but a deep awareness of history.

Shaemus O'Sheel (1886–1954): American poet who took the early Yeats as his exemplar. His "They Went Forth to Battle but They Always Fell" constitutes a belated American version of the Celtic twilight.

Robinson Jeffers (1887–1962): born of Scots Irish ancestry, Jeffers is a neglected though nonetheless essential figure in American poetry. I have included a sampling of those poems that best represent both the stark sensibility behind his work as well as his ardent historical consciousness. Shane O'Neill, Earl of Tyrone, was murdered by the McDonnells in 1561. Rathlin is a remote island off the Northern Irish coast. Deirdre refers to the figure in Irish myth, Deirdre of the Sorrows, also significant for Yeats's plays and poetry.

Marianne Moore (1887–1972): born in St. Louis, Moore is an essential figure of American modernist poetry. I have chosen poems representative of her intricate style, as well as

"Spenser's Ireland" which meditates in her own idiosyncratic way on her ancestry and the nature of being Irish.

Ernest Walsh (1895–1926): World War I aviator, poet, and member of The Lost Generation; he died in France at the age of thirty-one. For an account of his life see Kay Boyle and Robert McAlmon, *Being Geniuses Together* (New York: Doubleday, 1968), 194–215.

Louise Bogan (1897–1970): born in Maine of Irish American ancestry, Bogan is a crucial figure in American poetry, and particularly American women's poetry. Medusa and Cassandra are figures from Greek mythology, "Hypocrite Swift" refers to Jonathan Swift (1667–1745), the great Irish satirist.

Horace Gregory (1898–1982): born in Wisconsin, Gregory became a member of The Lost Generation and later a critic of some influence. Largely neglected, his poetry evinces a strong awareness of its Irish American context. Henry Moore (1898–1986) is one of the most important of twentieth century sculptors.

Robert Francis (1901–1987): born in Massachusetts, Francis's poetry comes out of Frost's exploration of the New England locale, but with a particularly Irish American sensitivity. St. Brigid refers to the legendary Irish saint. For a note on Cromwell see Sarah Helen Whitman (1813–1878).

Kay Boyle (1902–1992): famous more for her novels, short stories, and memoirs, Boyle's poetry reveals an ardent social consciousness similar to that of Lola Ridge, her early exemplar when she joined the group of artists and writers on convening in the 1920's on Manhattan's Lower East Side.

Robert Fitzgerald (1902–1985): famous for his translations of Homer's *Iliad* and *The Odyssy*, his own poetry reveals an abiding interest in classical forms.

Brian Coffey (1905–1995): born in Dublin, from 1947–1952 Coffey taught at St. Louis, Missouri, during which time he wrote "Missouri Sequence." Thomas McGreevy (1893–1967) and Denis Devlin (1908–1959) are Irish poets.

Phyllis McGinley (1905–1978): born in Oregon, McGinley moved to New York and eventually became one of America's most widely read poets. She won the Pulitzer Prize in 1961.

Louis MacNeice (1907–1963): born in Belfast, and a member of the group of poets that included Auden, Spender, and Day-Lewis, McNiece is one of the most important Irish poets to emerge after the turn of the century. His poem "Last before America" beautifully portrays the tradition of emigration from the other side.

Josephine Jacobsen (1908–2003): born Josephine Boylan, before her death Jacobsen had a long and distinguished career as a poet, short story writer, and critic. Former poetry consultant to the Library of Congress (now the post of poet laureate), Jacobsen won the Fellowship from the Academy of American Poets, the Shelley Memorial Award, and the Lenore Marshall Prize, among her other honors.

Theodore Roethke (1908–1963): These poems are two of Reothke's "pub songs." O'Connell's daughter refers to Roethke's wife, Beatrice Heath O'Connell.

Charles Olson (1910–1970): senior figure in the Black Mountain College group of poets that included, among them, Robert Creeley, Olson stands as one of the pillars of post-modern

American poetry. Born in Worchester, Massachusetts, Olson was deeply influenced by Pound and William Carlos Williams. Like Pound's *Cantos*, his *Maximus Poems* attempt an epic synthesis of culture and history. The selections offered here focus on the Irish side of his heritage.

J. V. Cunningham (1911–1985): born to Irish working class parents, Cunningham lived his early years in Billings, Montana where his father worked fro the railroads. A renowned Shakespeare scholar and poet, Cunningham is widely regarded as an elegant formal poet and epigramist. Agnosco Veteris Vertigia Flammae translates "I recognize the traces of the old flame (of love)" (see *The Poems of J. V. Cunningham*, 152).

Czeslaw Milosz (1911–2005): one of the greatest poets of this century, Milosz won of the Nobel Prize for literature in 1980.

John Berryman (1914–1972): born John Smith in McAlester, Oklahoma, John Berryman claims Irish ancestry on his mother's side. His *Dream Songs*, from which these poems are gleaned, are a monument of the confessional school of American poetry and won for him numerous awards, including the Pulitzer Prize.

Randall Jarrell (1914–1965): a major poet of the generation of Lowell and Berryman, Randall Jarrell is assured of a permanent place in American Literature for his acclaimed books of poetry and criticism. He was also a novelist, translator, and children's writer.

James Laughlin (1914–1997): a student of Ezra Pound, Laughlin founded New Directions, one of America's premier avant-guard publishing houses. Martha Graham refers to the famous dancer and choreographer.

Eugene McCarthy (1916–2005): long time senator and anti-war candidate for President of the United States in 1968. The St. Regis Hotel is in New York City.

Thomas McGrath (1916–1990): black-listed during the McCarthy era, McGrath stands prominently alongside those Irish American poets of acute social conscience, especially his fellow communist, Lola Ridge.

Gwendolyn Brooks (1917–2000): this poem, drawing together Irish American and African American contexts, appears in her Pulitzer prize winning *Selected Poems*.

Robert Lowell (1917–1977): Lowell moved to Northern Ireland with his last wife, Lady Caroline Blackwell, shortly before his death in 1977.

Reed Whittemore (1919–): taught for many years at Carleton College and at the University of Maryland; in addition to many books of poetry he has also published a collection of short biographies, *Six Literary Lives*.

Ann Darr (1920–): born Ann Russell, Darr has published eight poetry collections, including *Flying the Zuni Mountains*, inspired by her experiences as a WASP pilot during World War II.

James Schevill (1920–): is the author of *New and Selected Poems* (Swallow Press, 2000). He taught for many years at Brown University.

Daniel Berrigan (1921–): is Jesuit priest and social activist.

Hayden Carruth (1921–): has published twenty-three books of poetry, a novel, four books of criticism, and two anthologies. Among his awards are National Book Awards, and the National Book Critics Award, The Lenore Marshall/*The Nation* Award, the Paterson Poetry Prize, the Vermont Governor's Medal, the Carl Sandburg Award, the Whiting Award, and the Ruth Lily Prize, as well as fellowships from the Bollingen, Guggenheim, and Lannan Foundations.

Alan Dugan (1923–2003): born in Brooklyn, before his death Dugan produced sardonic, hard-bitten poems for nearly fifty years. His work won the Pulitzer Prize and two National Book Awards.

John Logan (1923–1986): born in Iowa, Logan was a poet affiliated marginally with the Beats. Uroboros refers to the figure of a snake eating its own tail. UCD is the acronym for University College Dublin. John Henry Cardinal Newman (1801–1890 was an English theologian, author of *Apologia Pro Via Sua*, and mentor to Gerard Manley Hopkins (1844–1889). Carl Gustav Jung (1875–1961) was a psychologist who championed the idea of archetypes and the collective unconscious.

James Schuyler (1923–1991): along with Frank O'Hara, a prominent member of the New York School of poets. His long poem, *The Morning of the Poem*, won the Pulitzer Prize.

Louis Simpson (1923–): a Jewish American poet, Simpson's "The Peat Bog Man" ought to be compared with Seamus Heaney's bog poems in *Wintering Out* and *North*.

Philip Whalen (1923–2002): was a Beat generation poet and Zen monk.

Padraic Fiacc (1924–): pseudonym for Joe O'Connor, born in the Bronx, New York, Fiacc returned with his family to Belfast. El Greco (1541–1614) is the famous Spanish painter. Eamonn De Valera (1882–1975) was a revolutionary and a dominant figure in Irish politics. Daniel Corkery (1878–1964) was a senator, man of letters, and author of *The Hidden Ireland*.

A.R. Ammons (1926–2001): born in North Carolina and for many years Goldwin smith Professor of Poetry at Cornell University, Ammons was of Scots Irish ancestry on his father's side, his great grandmother having come to this country during the Great Famine. Winner of two National Book Awards, the National Book Critics Circle Award, The Bollingen Prize, the Levenson Prize, and the Robert Frost Medal, as well as fellowships from the Guggenheim and: Lannan Foundations and the National Institute of Arts and Letters, Ammons is an essential American poet of the twentieth century. I have chosen only a few poems from his prolific output that resonate with the themes of the present volume.

Robert Creeley (1926–2005): was a central figure among the Black Mountain poets, and an important exemplar and mentor for an emerging counter-tradition in American poetry. Creeley published more than sixty books of poetry and more than a dozen books of prose before his death in 2005. His awards included the Lannan Lifetime Achievement Award, The Frost Medal, the Shelley Memorial Award, and fellowships from the National Endowment for the Arts, The Rockefeller Foundation, and the Guggenheim Foundation. He was elected a Chancellor of the Academy of American Poets in 1999.

Frank O'Hara (1926–1966): luminary figure in the New York School until his untimely death. Harold Fondren and Larry Rivers are both prominent New York artists and friends of the poet. The title of "The Day Lady Died" refers to the Jazz singer Billie Holiday.

Galway Kinnell (1927–): one of the central figures among American poets rising to prominence during the 1960's and winner of the Pulitzer Prize. The selections from "The Avenue Bearing the Initial of Christ into the New World" are intended to revisit, as it were, the locale depicted in Lola Ridge's "The Ghetto" nearly fifty years before. "Oi weh" is a Yiddish expression of exasperation.

Leo Connellan (1928–2001): born in Maine and for many years a businessman in New York City, before his death Connellan was named poet laureate of Connecticut. His long poem *The Clear Blue Lobster Water Country* examines his Irish American ancestry. The Abinaki's were the Native American inhabitants of Maine and surrounding areas before the Europeans. Miles Davis (1926) is the great Jazz trumpeter.

X. J. Kennedy (1928–): born in New Jersey, Kennedy is a prominent poet in the "formalist" tradition of American poetry, and an exemplar for the next generation of "New Formalist" American poets. His many awards include the Lamont Poetry Prize.

Thomas Kinsella (1928–): along with Seamus Heaney and John Montague, he is one of the principal Irish poets of his generation. Kinsella taught for many years at Temple University in Philadelphia. "The Good Fight" is written in memory of John F. Kennedy.

John Montague (1929–): born in Brooklyn, along with Thomas Kinsella and Seamus Heaney Montague is one of the dominant figures of Irish poetry after Kavanagh. His *The Rough Field* constitutes one of the essential long poems written in the English language in the second half of the century. The selections here focus on his American connection, some of which are taken from *The Rough Field* and others from *The Dead Kingdom*, his other major long sequence. The "El" refers to the elevated train in New York City.

Ned O'Gorman (1929–): was born in New York City in 1929. In 1966 he founded the Children's Storefront School in Harlem, which he directed until 1998 (and of which he wrote in his nonfiction book *The Storefront*). He has published six collections of poetry and four books of prose, and has received two Guggenheim Fellowships, and Ingram Merrill Award, a Rothko Chapel Award for Commitment to Truth and Freedom, and four honorary doctorates. In 1998, he founded the Ricardo O'Gorman Library in Harlem, which he continues to direct.

Diana O'Hehir (1929–): neglected among the prominent poets of her generation, O'Hehir's work demonstrates a strong Native American influence. Tashkent is the capital of Uzbekistan.

Knute Skinner (1929–): born in St. Louis, Missouri. Though not Irish American by ancestry, Skinner has lived off and on for forty years in Killaspuglonane, County Clare. Giacamo Leopardi (1798–1837) is the greatest Italian poet of his century.

John Engels (1931–): a long-time professor at St. Michael's College in Burlington, Vermont, Engels is the author of twelve books of poems, most recently a collected works, *Recounting the Seaons: Poems, 1958–2005*. He has won awards from the National Endowment for the Arts, the Rockefeller Foundation, the American Poetry Series, and the Fulbright Foundation. *Weather-Fear: New and Selected Poems*, was a finalist for the Pulitzer Prize. Cootehill is outside Anaghmakerrig in Northern Ireland.

Ted Berrigan (1934–1983): was the leading figure in the second generation of the New York School of poets.

Catharine Savage Brosman (1934–): lives in New Orleans, was born in Colorado but also claims West Texas as a girlhood home. She is Professor Emerita of French at Tulane University and Honorary Research Professor at the University of Sheffield (UK). A scholar as well as a poet, she is the author or editor of eighteen volumes and numerous articles dealing with modern French literature.

James Liddy (1934–): key figure whose work links the Irish parish of Patrick Kavanagh with American Whitman tradition and the Beats. He is an exemplar and advocate for many "New Irish" poets. Creighton University Press published his *Collected Poems*, and Salmon Press his most recent collection, *Gold Set Dancing*. Brian Friel (1929–) is Irish dramatist and short story writer.

Jeri McCormick (1934–): Wisconsin poet whose work reflects insightfully on her Appalachian and Irish ancestry.

Walt McDonald (1934–): a prolific poet who has published nineteen collections and director of the writing program at Texas Tech University, McDonald is also a former Air Force pilot. His books have won four Western Heritage Awards from the Cowboy Hall of Fame.

Ted McNulty (1934–1998): born in the United States, McNulty moved to Ireland after his retirement and began to write poetry. He published two books of poems before his death in 1998.

George Stanley (1934–): Canadian poet, living in Vancouver, who with James Liddy was a part of the San Francisco Renaissance in the 1960s. He has published ten books of poems.

Jean Valentine (1934–): author of several books of poems, Valentine moved to Ireland in the mid-1990s. Her *Door in the Mountain: New and Collected Poems* won the National Book Award for 2004.

Robert Kelly (1935–): another prominent figure affiliated with members of the Black Mountain School, though for years he has been poet in residence at Bard College in New York. "Haruspex" is one of a class on ancient Roman diviners who based predictions on animal entrails.

James J. McAuley (1936–): born in Dublin, McAuley taught for many years in the United States while writing several books of poems.

PART THREE.   FURTHER HARBORS

Brendan Galvin (1937–): author of twelve books of poems, and most recently *Habitat: New Selected Poems*. His honors include the O. B. Hardison, Jr. Poetry Prize and the Iowa Poetry

Prize, among his many honors. Galvin's work in many respects constitutes a sustained investigation of his identity as an Irish American. Robert Peel was the British statesman in charge of famine relief. The quarantine station at Grosse Isle, Quebec, saw the deaths of thousands of famine Irish. It is now the location of a memorial Park; Carrowkeel, Newgrange, and many Ireland's other passage graves, date from 2500 B.C.E.

Renny Golden (1937–): founded the Chicago Religious Task Force on Central America; Maura Clark, a Maryknoll missionary in El Salvador, was raped and murdered with two other sisters in 1980.

Susan Howe (1937–): emigrated from Ireland to the United States as a child. Finding examples in the work of Emily Dickinson and Charles Olson, Howe is an important figure affiliated with L=A=N=G=U=A=G=E poetry whose work investigates the more brutal legacies of history and culture.

Sabra Loomis (1938–): lives in New York City and on Achill Island in County Mayo. She is the author of three books of poems.

Michael Coady (1939–): born in Carrick-on-Suir, County Tipperary, Michael Coady is the author of three books of poems and prose, *Oven Lane* (1987), *All Souls* (1997), and *One Another* (2003). His poetry and fiction have earned a number of literary prizes and distinctions, including the Patrick Kavanaugh Award for poems in his first collection, *Two for a Woman, Three for a Man* (1980), and the O'Shaughnessy Poetry Award (2004). In 1998 he was elected to Aosdána.

Philip Dacey (1939–): is the author of seven books of poems, most recently *The Death Bed Playboy*. He teaches at Minnesota State University.

Susan Donnelly (1939–): was born and raised near Boston, in a large Irish-American family with strong literary traditions. She graduated from Mount Holyoke College. Her first book of poetry, *Eve Names the Animals* (1985), won a Samuel French Morse Prize from Northeastern University Press. Her second book, *Transit*, was published in 2001 by Iris Press. She has also written two chapbooks: *Tenderly Pressed, A Memoir in Poetry* (1993) and *The Ether Dome* (2000) from Every Other Thursday Press. She lives in Cambridge, Massachusetts where she writes and teaches poetry. She has a daughter Rachel, a physician, and a son Patrick, an actor.

Stephen Dunn (1939–): author of eleven widely acclaimed collections of poems including *Different Hours*, which won the Pulitzer Prize. Timothy McVeigh was convicted of the terrorist bombing of the federal building in Oklahoma City. Rene Descartes (1596–1650) and Michel Foucault (1926–1984) are French philosophers.

Irene McKinney (1939–): born in West Virginia, McKinney has published five books of poems, *The Girl with the Stone in Her Lap*, *Wasps at the Blue Hexagons*, *Quick Fire and Slow Fire*, *Six O'Clock Mine Report*, and *Vivid Companion*. She has won a fellowship from the National Endowment for the Arts.

James McMichael (1939–): is the author of six books of poetry, including *The World at Large: New and Selected Poems, 1971–1996* and *Capacity*. He has also written two critical volumes, *The Style of the Short Poem* and *"Ulysses" and Justice.* Among his awards are a Guggenheim Fellowship, a Whiting Writers' Award, and the Shelley Memorial Prize.

Peter Cooley (1940–): teaches at the Loyola University in New Orleans and has published six books of poems. Among his awards are a Yaddo Foundation Fellowship, a Mellon Foundation grant, a Louisiana Creative Writing Fellowship, and the Robert Frost Fellowship. Ararat is a mountain in eastern Turkey traditionally considered to be the landing place of Noah's ark. Jay Gatsby is the protagonist in F. Scott Fitzgerald's novel, *The Great Gatsby.*

John Donoghue (1940–): in addition to being a poet, Donoghue is professor of Electrical and Computer Engineering at Cleveland State University.

Fanny Howe (1940–): is the author of over twenty books of poetry and prose. Her most recent collection of poems include *On the Ground* (2004) and *Gone* (2003). The recipient of the 2001 Lenore Marshall Poetry Prize for *Selected Poems* (2000), she has also won awards from the National Endowment for the Arts, the National Poetry Foundation, the California Council for the Arts and the Village Voice, as well as fellowships from the Bunting Institute and the MacArthur Colony. Howe was shortlisted for the Griffin Poetry Prize in 2001 and 2005. She is Professor Emerita of American Literature and Writing at the Unviersity of California, San Diego. St. Columbcille (c. 540 C.E.) founded monasteries at Derry and Iona.

Fred Marchant (1940–): is the author of *Tipping Point,* winner of the Washington Poetry Prize, and two other books of poems, *Full Moon Boat* and *House on Water, House in Air,* the latter published by Dedalus Press in Ireland. He directs the Suffolk University Writing Program in Boston.

Sean O'Dwyer (1940–): born in County Wexford, O'Dwyer emigrated to the United States and worked for many years with the United States Postal Service. He lives in New York City and writes poetry "when the spirit moves him."

Tom Sexton (1940–): born in Lowell, Massachusetts, Sexton has been Alaska's poet laureate since 1995. His book of poems, *Autumn in the Alaska Range,* was published in Ireland by Salmon Publishing. Cuchulain is the legendary hero of *The Tain.*

Richard Tillinghast (1940–): is the author of several books of poems, published in the United States as well as Ireland. He teaches at the University of Michigan.

Karen Brennan (1941–): born in New Rochelle, New York, Brennan is the author of *Here on Earth* and *Wild Desire,* as well as a memoir, *Being with Rachel.* She has won the AWP Award In Fiction and a fellowship from the National Endowment for the Arts. She teaches at the University of Utah and the MFA Program for Writers at Warren Wilson College.

Tom Clark (1941–): born in Chicago and educated at the University of Michigan and Cambridge, he is associated with the New York School of poets. He is the author of many volumes of poetry, most recently, *Light & Shade: New and Selected Poems* (2006) as well as fiction and criticism. Clark is also author of several biographical works on poets such as Charles Olson, Ted Berrigan, Robert Creeley and others.

Billy Collins (1941–): has published seven widely acclaimed books of poems and was named poet laureate of the United States in 2001. His awards include the Oscar Blumenthal Prize, the Bess Hokin Prize, the Frederick Bock Prize, the Levinson Prize as well as fellowships from the New York Foundation for the Arts, the National Endowment for the Arts, and the Guggenheim Foundation. Edith Hamilton (1867–1963 was a classical scholar and writer of books on Greek mythology.

Eamon Grennan (1941–): an Irish citizen who has lived in the United States since the sixties, Grennan teaches at Vassar College and has published several lauded books of poems. Marc Chagall (1887–1985), Russian painter; Tintoretto (1518–1594), Venetian painter.

Derek Mahon (1941–): one of the essential poets of his generation in Ireland, these poems were written during Mahon's extended stay in New York City during the final years of the twentieth century.

Wesley McNair (1941–): is the author of five books of poems and recipient of fellowships from the Rockefeller, Fulbright, and Guggenheim foundations, as well as from the National Endowment for the Arts and the National Endowment for the Humanities. Other honors include the Devins Award and an Emmy Award.

Gibbons Ruark (1941–): author of four widely praised books of poems, and professor of English at the University of Delaware; The Liberties, a traditionally poor area of Dublin near St. Patrick's Cathedral; Sandycove, an area a few miles south of Dublin where Joyce lived in the Martello Tower evoked at the beginning of *Ulysses*; Enniskillen, a town in Northern Ireland, famed for the Remembrance Day bombing in 1987 that killed eleven people; The Falls Road, traditional Irish Catholic area in Belfast.

Michael Heffernan (1942–): teaches in the MFA Program for Writing at the University of Arkansas, Fayetteville. Winner of the Iowa Poetry Prize as well as three fellowships from the National Endowment for the Arts, Heffernan has published widely in both the United States and Ireland. His family emigrated from Tipperary and County Cork.

Michael Lally (1942–): born in Orange, New Jersey, Lally has published twenty-four books of poetry and has won the PEN Oakland Josephine Miles Award, the American Book Award, as well as fellowships from the National Endowment for the Arts, the Poets Foundation, and the Pacificus Foundation. He is also an actor in film and television.

Kathy Callaway (1943–): is the author of several books of poems the first of which, *Heart of the Garfish*, won the Agnes Lynch Starrett Poetry Prize.

Tess Gallagher (1943–): born in Washington state, in addition to her widely praised poems, Gallagher has published short stories and essays. *Dear Ghosts,* her most recent poetry collection, was published by Graywolf Press in 2006.

Kathleen Lynch (1943–): lives in California and is the author of *Hinge*, which won the 2006 Black Zinnias National Poetry Award. Her other collections include *How to Build an Owl,* which won the Select Poet Series Award from Small Poetry Press and *No Spring Chicken,* which won the White Eagle Coffee Store Press Award. She is also the author of *Alterations of Rising* published by Small Poetry Press in its Select Poet Series.

Linda McCarriston (1943–): grew up in Massachusetts and has published three books of poems, the second of which, *Eva-Mary,* was a finalist for the National Book Critics Circle Award. *Little River: New and Selected Poems,* was published in 2000 by Salmon Publishing and in 2002 by Northwestern University Press.

Maureen Owen (1943–): born in Minnesota, Owen is a poet whose work experiments with line and structure. She has published several books of poems, including *Erosion's Pull* and *American Rush: Selected Poems,* and has won the Before Columbus American Book Award, as well as fellowships from the National Endowment for the Arts and the Foundation for Contemporary Performance Arts.

Eavan Boland (1944–): one of the most important Irish poets of her generation, for years Boland has been poet in residence at Stanford University.

Kathryn Stripling Byer (1944–): born in North Carolina, Byer's work explores her Scots Irish ancestry through the lives of Appalachian women. She has published four books of poems, and has won the Lamont Poetry Prize, the Brockman Campbell Award, a fellowship from the national Endowment for the Arts, and the North Carolina Arts Council.

James Chapson (1944–): born in Hawaii, Chapson is the author of the poetry collection *Sentimental Journey.* He lives in Milwaukee, Wisconsin.

Thomas Dillon Redshaw (1944–): poet, scholar, and editor, Redshaw teaches at the University of St. Thomas in St. Paul, Minnesota. He has published three collections of poems and edited two collections of essays on the poetry of John Montague.

Ben Howard (1945–): poet and critic, Howard teaches at Alfred University in New York; Sweeney is the legendary protagonist of *Buile Suibhne* (The Madness of Sweeney), a medieval work of poetry and prose most recently translated by Seamus Heaney as *Sweeney Astray.*

J. D. McClatchy (1945–): of Scots lineage, McClatchy is one of the most respected poets of his generation.

G. E. Murray (1945–): is the author of six books of poems and winner of the Devins Award, as well as co-editor of *Illinois Voices: Illinois Poetry in the Twentieth Century.* He also has been poet critic for the *Chicago Tribune* and *Chicago Magazine.*

Michael D. Riley (1945–): teaches at Penn State University—Wilkes-Barre, and has published one full-length collection of poems entitled, *Circling the Stones.* He has won grants from the Institute for Arts and Humanistic Studies and a verse fellowship from the University of Washington and Poetry Ireland. See note on passage graves under Brendan Galvin (1937–).

Betsy Sholl (1945–): has published five books of poetry and teaches at the University of Southern Maine. Her awards include an Associated Writing Program Prize, the Felix Polack Prize, and a fellowship from the national Endowment for the Arts. See note on Sweeney under Ben Howard (1945–); Flann O'Brien was the pseudonym for Brian O'Nolan (1911–1966) under which he wrote *At Swim-Two-Birds,* a novel based upon the legend of Mad Sweeney.

Terence Winch (1945–): a poet and musician, Winch is also director of publications at the National Museum of the American Indian. Born in the Bronx, New York, he has won the American Book Award and the Columbia Book Award, and has recorded three albums with his band, Celtic Thunder. In addition, "A Short History of Irish Music in America" appears in *New Perspectives on the Irish Diaspora,* ed. Charles Fanning (Southern Illinois University Press, 2000). "Shadow Grammar" first appeared in *The World* (#50; ed. Lewis Warsh) magazine (which comes out of the St. Mark's Poetry Project in NYC) and was later included in *Best American Poetry 1997* (Scribner, ed. James Tate; series ed. David Lehman). "Noise Under Glass" first appeared in *The World* (#54; ed. Ed Friedman).

Christopher Jane Corkery (1946–): is the author of *Blessing* (Princeton University Press, Ex Libris). A member of the English Department of the College of the Holy Cross, she did her graduate studies in Anglo-Irish Literature at Trinity College Dublin. Recipient of a Pushcart Prize, as well as of fellowships from the Ingram Merrill Foundation, the Massachusetts Artists Foundation, the St. Botolph Club Foundation, the MacDowell Colony, and Yaddo, Corkery lives in Concord, Massachusetts.

Ed Cox (1946–1992): lived in Washington, D.C. until his death in 1992. In addition to being a poet, Cox was also a social activist and teacher. He won the Lyndhurst Prize in Poetry in 1989.

Dennis Finnell (1946–): won the 1990 Juniper Prize for his first book of poems, *Red Cottage.* The University of Georgia Press published his second book of poems, *Belovèd Beast.* He has also won a fellowship from the Ludwig Vogelstein Foundation.

Vicki Hearne (1946–2001): an animal trainer, before her death Hearne published several books of poems and books on dogs. She taught at Princeton University.

Joan Houlihan (1946–): is the author of *Hand-Held Executions: Poems & Essays* (2003) and winner of the Green Rose Award from New Issues Press for *The Mending Worm.* She is founder and executive director of the Concord Poetry Center in Concord, Massachusetts.

Patricia Monaghan (1946–): born in New York and reared in Alaska, Monaghan is the author of three books of poems and has also written on ancient Celtic spirituality and mythology. She teaches at DePaul University.

Michael Ryan (1946–): winner of the Yale Younger Poets Award, the National Poetry Series, the Whiting Writers Award, as well as fellowships from the National Endowment for the Arts and the John Simon Guggenheim Foundation, Ryan is also the author of the award-winning memoir, *Secret Life.* His *Selected Poems* won the 2004 Kingsley Tufts Award.

Maura Stanton (1946–): winner of the Yale Younger Poets Award, Stanton is the author of several books of poems as well as a novel, *Molly Companion.* She teaches in the M.F.A. Program at Indiana University in Bloomington. Croagh Patrick is the mountain in Mayo near Westport where, according to legend, St. Patrick fasted and prayed.

Susan Wood (1946–): is the author of three books of poems, *Bazaar, Campo Santo,* and *Asunder,* which won the National Poetry Series. Her awards include fellowships from the Fine Arts Work Center in Provincetown, the National Endowment for the Arts, the Guggenheim Foundation, the Lamont Poetry Prize, and a Pushcart Prize. She teaches at Rice University in Houston, Texas.

Kevin Bowen (1947–): is director of the William Joiner Center for the Study of War and Social Consequences at the University of Massachusetts—Boston. His collections of poetry include *Playing Basketball with the Viet Cong, Forms of Prayer at the Hotel Edison,* and *In*

Search of Grace O'Malley, all from Curbstone Press, as well as *Eight True Maps of the West*, from Dedalus Press, in Ireland. Bowen is the recipient of the Pushcart Prize and awards from the National Endowment for the Arts and the Massachusetts Cultural Council. He has also edited several anthologies of Vietnamese literature, and shares a house with poet, Sabra Loomis on Achill Island. "Bird" was the nickname for Charlie Parker (1920–1955), Jazz saxophonist and composer.

Michael Casey (1947–): winner of the Yale Younger Poets Award for his first book, *Obscenities*, Casey's work included here carries forward the tradition of war poems (and anti-war poems) written by Irish American poets into the context of Vietnam. He is also the author of two other collections, *Millrat* and *The Million Dollar Hole*.

Geraldine Connolly (1947–): has published two full-length collections of poems, and has won fellowships from the National Endowment for the Arts, the Maryland Arts Council, and Yaddo. Her other honors include the Margaret Bridgeman Fellowship of the Bread Loaf Writers Conference.

John Maloney (1947–): worked as a stonemason for over twenty years as well as an artist in the schools and lives in Massachusetts. *Proposal* is his first collection of poems. His family emigrated from County Clare and Tipperary.

Maureen Seaton (1947–): winner of the Copernicus Award, the Midland Authors Award, the Iowa Prize, as well as fellowships from the National Endowment for the Arts. Sinéad O'Connor is an Irish rock singer.

R. T. Smith (1947–): is the author of four books of poems as well as a book of short stories, and is the editor of *Shenandoah*. He has received fellowships from the National Endowment for the Arts, the Virginia Commission for the Arts, and Arts International.

Nathalie Anderson (1948–): born in South Carolina, Anderson teaches at Swarthmore College; she has won a Pew Foundation Fellowship and a Washington Poetry Prize. Bob Wills and Patsy Cline are American county/folk singers. Altan is an Irish traditional band.

Susan Firer (1948–): author of three books of poems, Firer has won the Cleveland State Poetry Center Prize. She lives in Milwaukee, Wisconsin.

Richard Kenney (1948–): winner of the Yale Younger Poets Award, Kenney is the author of three highly praised collections of poetry.

Mary Leader (1948–): born in Oklahoma, Leader now teaches at the University of Memphis. She has won the National Poetry Series and the Iowa Poetry Prize.

Thomas Lynch (1948–): has published three highly acclaimed books of poems. His nonfiction book, *The Undertaking: Life Studies from a Dismal Trade*, was a finalist for the National Book Award and won the American Book Award. Under British rule, the Land Commission decided the fate of many land-owning Irish families.

Heather McHugh (1948–): winner of the O. B. Hardison, Jr. Poetry Prize among her many honors, McHugh is Milliman distinguished Writer in Residence at the University of Washington and a Chancellor of the Academy of American Poets.

Larry Levis (1949–): winner of numerous awards, Levis was a major American poet of his generation until his death in 1996. The poems included here reveal the influence on his work of Irish American experience.

Richard Broderick (1949–): is the author of *Woman Lake,* published by New Rivers Press. Nominated for the Pushcart Prize, his work has also received the International Merit Award from the *Atlantic Review.* His poems appear in *Prairie Schooner, The Laurel Review, Notre Dame Review, Poetry East, Slant, Smartish Pace,* and elsewhere. The recipient of a Minnesota State Arts Board fellowship, he co-edits the *Great River Review.*

Michael Waters (1949–): born in Brooklyn, Waters has published seven collections of poems and teaches at the University of Salisbury in Maryland. He has won fellowships from the National Endowment for the Arts, the Maryland Arts Council, as well as the Pushcart Prize.

Carolyne Wright (1949–): is a second-generation Anglo-Irish American, with nine generations of (Anglican) Church of Ireland clergy on her father's side. She has four collections of poetry and has won the Blue Lynx Prize, the Oklahoma Book Award in Poetry, and an American Book Award from the Before Columbus Foundation, the Witter Bynner Poery Prize and a fellowship from the National Endowment for the Arts.

Theodore Deppe (1950–): born in Minnesota, Deppe has won a Pushcart Prize and a fellowship from the National Endowment for the Arts. Cathal O'Searcaigh (1956–), born in Donegal, is one of the finest Irish language poets of his generation.

Marie Howe (1950–): Howe's first book of poems, *The Good Thief,* won the National Poetry Series. She has won a fellowship from the National Endowment for the Arts, and teaches at New York University.

Mekeel McBride (1950–): lives in New Hampshire and has published several collections of poems.

Robert McNamara (1950–): teaches at the University of Washington and has published one book of poems, *Second Messengers.* He has won fellowships from the Fulbright Foundation and the National Endowment for the Arts.

Mary Swander (1950–): has published three books of poetry as well as books essays and a memoir. He many awards include The Discovery / *The Nation* Award, a Whiting Writers Award, a fellowship from the National Endowment for the Arts, the Carl Sandburg Award, and awards from the Ingram Merrill Foundation.

Edward Byrne (1951–): is a professor of American Literature and creative writing in the English Department at Valparaiso University. He has published five collections of poetry, most recently *Words Spoken, Words Unspoken* (Chimney Hill Press, 1995), *East of Omaha* (Pecan Grove Press, 1998), and *Tidal Air* (Pecan Grove Press, 2002).

David Cavanagh (1951–): a Canadian-born poet, Cavanagh's *The Middleman* was published in Ireland by Salmon Press. He is Dean of Johnson State College in Vermont. The Flying Wallendas were a troupe of circus aerialists.

Peter Fallon (1951–): Irish poet and founder of Gallery Press, Fallon composed *The Deerfield Series* while he was poet in residence at the Deerfield Academy in Massachusetts.

James Galvin (1951–): *Resurrection Update*, Galvin's collected poems, is available from Copper Canyon Press, as well as his book of poems entitled *X*. He has also published several prose books available from Henry Holt. He teaches at the University of Iowa Writer's Workshop.

Brigit Pegeen Kelly (1951–): winner of the Yale Younger Poets Award and the Lamont Poetry Award, Kelly teaches at the University of Illinois at Urbana-Champaign.

Ethna McKiernan (1951–): born in New York, McKiernan now manages Irish Books and Media in Minneapolis, Minnesota where she has won arts grants for her poetry. Her latest book of poems is *The One Who Swears You Can't Start Over* (Salmon Publishing, 2002).

Lynne McMahon (1951–): has published three books of poetry and has won awards from the Ingram Merill Foundation and the John Simon Guggenheim Foundation. She teaches at the University of Missouri—Columbia. Gerard Manley Hopkins is buried in Glasnevin Cemetery in Dublin. John Henry Cardinal Newman (1801–1890) was a British theologian and authors, as well as Hopkins' mentor; William Godwin (1756–1856), British political philosopher and writer, and husband of Mary Wolstonecraft.

James McManus (1951–): in addition to his award-winning poetry, McManus has published four novels the most recent of which, *Going to the Sun*, won the Carl Sandburg Prize. Jimmy Hendrix was a famous rock guitarist and icon; Dick Cavett and Dana Carvey are American television personalities; Operation Desert Storm is the military name for the American forces who waged The Gulf War (1991); *The Unnamable* is a novel by Samuel Beckett.

Paul Muldoon (1951–): born in Northern Ireland, Muldoon is now a citizen of the United States and Howard G.B. Clark Professor at Princeton University. He has won the *Irish Times* Prize for Poetry and the T. S. Eliot Prize. Muldoon is widely regarded as the most influential poet of his generation in Ireland and the United Kingdom. The term "imrama" refers to the mythological voyages of Irish legend; Walter Raleigh (1552–1618), the English explorer and writer; Gypsy Rose Lee was an American burlesque queen who went on to become a television personality; Abbott and Costello are the famous comedy team of the 1940s and 1950s.

Harry Clifton (1952–): born in Dublin, Clifton's most recent book of poems is *God in France: A Paris Sequence 1994–1998*. Gallery Press has published five collections of his poems: *The Walls of Carthage* (1977), *Office of the Salt Merchant* (1979), *Comparative Lives* (1982), *The Liberal Cage* (1988) and *The Desert Route: Selected Poems, 1973–1988* (1992), a Poetry Book Society Recommendation. His chronicle of a year in the Abruzzo Mountains, *On the Spine of Italy,* was published in 1999, and his stories are collected as *Berkeley's Telephone and Other Fictions* (2000). He is the recipient of the Patrick Kavanagh Award for poetry.

Alice Fulton (1952–): author of six highly praised books of poems, Fulton's honors include a fellowship from the John D. and Catherine T. MacArthur Foundation; Emily Dickinson (1830–1886), the great American poet.

Julie Kane (1952–): is the author of two books of poems, *Body and Soul* and *Rhythm and Booze*, which won the National Poetry Series. She teaches at Northwestern State University in Natchitoches, Louisiana.

Mary Logue (1952–): born in Minnesota, Logue's first book of poems won the Mid-List Press Award. In addition to two books of poetry, Logue is also the author of three novels.

James Silas Rogers (1952–): was born in Minnesota in 1952. A longtime employee of the Irish American Cultural Institute, in 1996 he became managing director of the University of St. Thomas Center for Irish Studies. He has published a number of articles on Irish-American authors, including Edwin O'Connor and Joseph Mitchell.

Alan Shapiro (1952–): a Jewish American poet whose honors include the O.B. Hardison, Jr. Poetry Prize, Shapiro's "After the Digging" is one of the most extensive treatments of the Irish Potato Famine (1845–1852) in poetic form; Charles Edward Trevelyan was Assistant Secretary to the British Treasury from 1840–1859. His strict application of Malthusian economic policies contributed to the devastation of The Great Famine.

Elizabeth Spires (1952–): author of four widely praised books of poems, as well as books for children, Spires has won the Witter Byner Poetry Prize, a Guggenheim Fellowship, and a Whiting Writers Award. She teaches at Goucher College in Baltimore, Maryland.

Killarney Clary (1953–): has written two highly praised books of prose poems and has won a fellowship from the Lannan Foundation.

Robert McDowell (1953–): in addition to writing several books of poems and books on poetry, McDowell is also the founding editor of Story Line Press. His family emigrated to Virginia after the rebellion of 1798.

Kevin Boyle (1954–): teaches at Elon College in North Carolina. His first book, *The Lullaby of History*, won the Green Rose Poetry Prize. lity in 1607; Vinegar Hill in Wexford was the location of the final defeat of the Irish in the uprising of 1798; at the Battle of the Boyne (1690) the forces of William of Orange defeated those of James II.

Michael Carey (1954–): farms in southwest Iowa. He has published four books of poems as well as plays and books of non-fiction. In 1588 the Spanish Armada was wrecked off the coast of Ireland.

Michael Coffey (1954–): in addition to being the author of two books of poems, Coffey is also managing editor at *Publisher's Weekly* as well as editor of *The Irish in America.*

Michael Donaghy (1954–2004): born in The Bronx, New York, Donaghy moved to England where he has published two books of poems. His work has won the Whitbred Prize, the Geoffrey Faber Memorial Prize, and fellowships from the Arts Council of England and the Ingram-Merrill Foundation.

Michael McFee (1954–): born in North Carolina, McFee has published six collections of poetry and edited two anthologies of North Carolina poems.

Janice Fitzpatarick Simmons (1954–): born in the United States, Simmons has published two books of poems with Salmon Publishing in Ireland where she moved and where she co-founded The Poet's House in County Donegal with her late husband, James Simmons.

Nuala Archer (1955–): has lived on and off in Ireland and the United States and has published several collections of poems with Gallery Press and Salmon Press in Ireland.

Julie O'Callaghan (1955–): born in Chicago, O'Callaghan has lived in Dublin since 1974. She has published four books of poems, all of which were recommended by the Book Society. She won awards from the Ireland Bursaries and most recently the Patrick Kavanagh Award. She has also published two collections of children's poems.

Eamonn Wall (1955–): born in Enniscorthy, County Wexford, Wall is a leading poet of the New Irish emigration to America. He has published four books of poems with Salmon Press in Ireland—*Dyckman–200th Street, Iron Mountain Road, The Crosses*, and *Refuge at DeSoto Bend*—and his non fiction book, *From the Siné Café to the Black Hills*, won the Paul Durkan Prize. He is the Smurfit Professor of Irish Studies at the University of Missouri—St. Louis. Hart Crane (1899–1932), American poet who wrote an epic poem using the Brooklyn Bridge as its underlying conceit; Thomas Wolfe (1900–1938), American novelist; John Lennon (1940–1980), member of "The Beatles" and rock icon killed by an assassin in New York City.

Chris Agee (1956–): born in San Francisco, Agee has lived in Belfast for over twenty years. In addition to publishing two books of poems with Dedalus Press in Ireland, he has been on the Board of Directors at Poetry Ireland as well as its editor, and has also edited *Scar on the Stone: Contemporary Poetry from Bosnia*, a Poetry Society Choice. He is currently editor in chief of *Irish Pages*. The Omagh bombing occurred in 1998 and precipitated the Good Friday Agreement. Kilmaingham is the jail in Dublin where the leaders of the Easter Rising of 1916 were held before being executed.

Patrick Donnelly (1956–): is an Associate Editor at Four Way Books and the author of one book of poems, *The Charge*. His writing has appeared in *American Poetry Review, Yale Review, Virginia Quarterly Review, Marlboro Review, Quarterly West, Beloit Poetry Journal*, and *Barrow Street*. He lives in Brooklyn, NY.

Mary Jane Nealon (1956–): has won fellowships from the Fine Arts Work Center in Provincetown, Massachusetts, the New Jersey State Council on the Arts as well as the mid-Atlantic Arts foundation, as well as the Amy Lowell Traveling Fellowship. She is the author of two books of poems, *Rogue Apostle* and *Immacualte Fuel*, and has worked as a registered nurse and works with the poor in New York City.

Thomas O'Grady (1956–): born on Prince Edward Island, and author of one highly praised book of poems, O'Grady directs the Irish Studies Program at the University of Massachusetts—Boston. Bing Crosby (1904–1977), the popular American crooner and film actor.

Michael Chitwood (1958–): born in Virginia, Chitwood has published three collections of poems and a collection of essays in addition to being a radio commentator. He currently lives in North Carolina.

Nicole Cooley (1958–): won The Discovery / *The Nation* Award in Poetry as well as the Walt Whitman Award for her first book of poems, *Resurrection*. She teaches at the City University of New York, and is the daughter of Peter Cooley whose work is also included in this volume. Mary Pickford was a famous silent film actor.

Greg Delanty (1958–): born in Cork, Delanty is a leading poet of the New Irish emigration to America. He is the author of seven books of poems, including *Collected Poems*. He has also edited (with Nuala Ni Dhomhnaill) *Jumping Off Shadows: Selected Irish Poetry*, and is consultant editor for *The History of the Irish Book*. His numerous awards include the Patrick Kavanagh Award, the Allen Dowling Poetry Fellowship, the Wolfers-O'Neill Award, the Austin Clarke Award, the National Poetry Competition Prize from the Poetry Society of England, the Arts Council of Ireland Bursary, and an award from the Royal Literary Fund. He lives in Burlington, Vermont and teaches at St. Michael's College in Burlington, Vermont. Tir na nOg refers to the Land of the Young in Irish myth and legend. The legend of Earl Gerald is referenced in Marianne Moore's "Spenser's Ireland," to which Delanty's poem pays homage.

Kathy Fagan (1958–): is the author of three books of poems, *The Raft, Moving and St. Rage*, and *The Charm*. She has won the National Poetry Series and the Vassar Miller Award. She teaches at the Ohio State University where she also co-edits *The Journal*.

Laura Mullen (1958–): is the author of four collections of poetry and a verse novel. She has won the Rona Jaffe Prize and a fellowship from the National Endowment for the Arts.

Daniel Tobin (1958–): born in Brooklyn, New York, Tobin is the editor of the present volume. Awards for his poetry include The Discovery / *The Nation* Award, The Robert Frost Fellowship from the Bread Loaf Writers Conference, the Donn Godwin Poetry Prize, a fellowship from the National Endowment for the Arts, and the Katharine Bakeless Nason Poetry Prize. He is the author of four books of poems. St. John, New Brunswick, was one of the primary ports of entry for the famine Irish; bryons are lumberjacks; the island referred to is Partridge Island in the Bay of Fundy; Hy-bresil is a mythological island of the young in Irish legend.

Jean Monahan (1959–): is the author of *Hands* (Anhinga Press Prize, 1992), *Believe It or Not* (Orchises Press, 1999), and *Mauled Illusionist*. She currently lives in Salem, Massachusetts.

Gerard Donovan (1960–): born in Wexford, Donovan is the author of three collections of poetry. He has been a fellow at the Bread Loaf Writers Conference and has been nominated for the Irish Times Poetry Award. He teaches at Southampton College in New York.

John Flynn (1960–): born in Boston, Flynn is a former Peace Corps volunteer who won the RPCV Writers and Readers Award for Poetry, the H.G. Roberts Award, and the Erika Mumford Award from the New England Poetry Club.

Nick Flynn (1960–): winner of The Discovery / *The Nation* Award and the Pen/Joyce Osterweil Award for Poetry, as well as fellowships from the Guggenheim Foundation and the Provincetown Arts Work Center, among others.

Chris Forhan (1960–): born in Seattle, Washington, Forhan won the Katherine Bakeless Nason Poetry Prize for his first book of poems, *Forgive Us Our Happiness*, as well as fellowships from Yaddo and Bread Loaf. His second book of poems, *The Actual Moon, the Actual Stars*, won the Samuel French Morse Poeetry Prize. He has also published two chapbooks, *x* and *Crumbs of Bread*. He teaches at Auburn University.

Claudia Keelan (1960–): has written four books of poems and teaches at the University of Nevada—Las Vegas. Among her honors is the Beatrice Hawley Poetry Award. The Hancock Tower is a skyscraper in Boston; *Ave Verum Corpus* is Latin for "Hail the True Body."

Campbell McGrath (1960–): teaches at Florida International University. He has published six highly praised books of poems, *Capitalism, American Noise, Spring Comes to Chicago, Road Atlas, Florida Poems* and *Pax Atomica*. Among his wards are the Kingsley Tufts Prize, the Witter Byner Prize, as well as fellowships from the Guggenheim Foundation and John D. and Catherine T. MacArthur Foundation. His maternal grandparents originated in Donegal, and his paternal grandparents in Limerick. Roger Williams was a country singer whose most famous song was "King of the Road."

Elizabeth Oness (1960–): has published two chapbooks of poems. Her collection of short stories, *Articles of Faith*, won the Iowa Short Fiction Award.

Christine Casson (1961–): is Scholar / Writer in Residence at Emerson College. Her poems have been publshined in *The Alabama Literary Review, Natural Bridge, Fashioned Pleasures, Never Before*, and other venues.

Ann Townsend (1962–): lives in Granville, Ohio and teaches at Dennison University. Her first book of poems, *Dimestore Erotics*, won the Gerald Cable Award for Poetry. Her other honors include The Discovery / *The Nation* Award, The Staley Hawkins Poetry Prize, and a Pushcart Prize.

Ed Madden (1963–): is associate professor of English at the University of South Carolina, and poet in residence at the Riverbanks Botanical Gardens in Columbia, SC. He is co-editor of *Men Emerge into the 21st Century*, a collection of writings about masculinity and male experience.

Stephen McNally (1963–): McNally's first book of poems won the Juniper Prize from the University of Massachusetts Press. He lives in Dallas, Texas.

Jennifer O'Grady (1963–): lives in New York City. *White*, her first book, won the Mid-list Press Poetry Prize. Raphael (1483–1520) is a famous Italian painter.

Meg Kearney (1964–): is the Associate Director of the National Book Foundation and the author of one book of poems, *An Unkindness of Ravens*. Her awards include an Artist's Fellowship from the State of New York.

Christopher Cahill (1965–): in addition to being a poet, Cahill is editor of *The Recorder*, the publication of the American Irish Historical Society. He lives in New York City.

Aidan Rooney (1965–): grew up in Monaghan, and presently lives and teaches in Massachusetts. He has won the Guinness Award for Poetry as well as a poetry award from the Yeats Society and the Hennessy Cognac New Irish Writing Award. The "Big Dig" refers to an ongoing public works project in Boston.

Joseph Lennon (1967–): writes and lives in New York City, where he teaches literature and creative writing at Manhattan College in the Bronx. He has published poetry and essays in a number of journals, magazines, and essay collections in the U.S. and Ireland. His book, *The Oriental and the Celt: Ireland and Empire* was published by Syracuse University Press in 2004; he has recently completed a poetry manuscript, *Every Call, An Answer*.

Beth Ann Fennelly (1971–): has published two books of poems, *Open House* and *Tender Hooks*. Her awards include the Kenyon Review Prize and a fellowship from the National Endowment for the Arts. She teaches at the University of Mississippi, Oxford.

Jill McDonnagh (1972–): is the recipient of fellowships from the Fine Arts Work Center, the National Endowment for the Arts, and the Dorothy and Lewis B. Cullman Center for Scholars and Writers at the New York Public Library.

Brenda Shaughnessy (1972–): has published one book of poems, *Interior with Sudden Joy*. She lives in New York City.

Tyler Farrell (1973–): is an Assistant Professor of English at the University of Dubuque in Dubuque, IA. He is currently the book review editor for *An Sionnach* and has articles and poetry published in *The New Hibernia Review, The Recorder, Natural Bridge, The Cream City Review, Nebraska English Journal, Jabberwock, Front Range Review, Yemassee,* and *The Blue Canary*. His first book of poetry, entitled *Tethered to the Earth,* is forthcoming from Salmon Press in 2007.

Kathleen Rooney (1980–): teaches at Emerson College in Boston where as a graduate student she won the Ruth Lilly Poetry Prize. She is the author of *Reading with Oprah: The Book Club that Changed America*.

Colleen Abel (1980–): Her work has appeared in *Bluesap Magazine, Branches Quarterly, Bellevue Literary Review* and in the anthology *Best of Branches 2002*. She is fellow at the Wisconsin Institute for Creative Writing at UW–Madison.

BIBLIOGRAPHY

Agee, Chris. *First Light*. Dublin: Dedalus Press, 2003.

———. *In the New Hampshire Woods*. Dublin: Dedalus Press, 1992.

Ammons, A. R. *Bosh and Flapdoodle*. New York: W. W. Norton, 2005.

———. *A Coast of Trees*. New York: W. W. Norton, 1981.

———. *Collected Poems, 1951–1971*. New York: W. W. Norton, 1972.

Anderson, Nathalie. *Following Fred Astaire*. Washington, D.C.: Word Works, 1998.

Archer, Nuala. *From a Mobile Home*. Galway: Salmon Publishing, 1995.

Berkeley, George. *The Works of George Berkeley, D.D.* Edited by Alexander C. Fraser. Oxford: Oxford University Press, 1901.

———. "Verses on the Prospect of Planting Arts and Learning in America" in *The Oxford Book of English Verse*. Edited by Christopher Ricks. Oxford: Oxford University Press, 1999.

Berrigan, Daniel. *Selected and New Poems*. New York: Doubleday, 1973.

Berrigan, Ted. *Collected Poems*. Berkeley: University of California Press, 2005.

Berryman, John. *The Dream Songs*. New York: Farrar, Straus and Giroux, 1982.

Bogan, Louise. *The Blue Estuaries: Poems, 1923–1968*. New York: Ecco Press, 1977.

Boland, Eavan. *In a Time of Violence*. New York: W. W. Norton, 1994.

———. *The Lost Land*. New York: W. W. Norton, 1998.

———. *An Origin Like Water: Collected Poems 1967–1987*. New York: W. W. Norton, 1996.

———. *Outside History: Selected Poems, 1980–1990*. New York: W. W. Norton, 1990.

Bowen, Kevin. *Eight True Maps of the West*. Dublin: Dedalus Press, 2003.

———. *In Search of Grace O'Malley*. Dorchester, MA: West Cedar Street Press, 1997.

Boyle, Kay. *Collected Poems*. Port Townsend, WA: Copper Canyon Press, 1991.

Boyle, Kay, and Robert McAlcom. *Being Geniuses Together, 1920–1930*. Garden City, NY: Doubleday, 1968.

Boyle, Kevin. *A Home for Wayward Girls*. Kalamazoo, MI: New Issues Press, 2005.

Branagan, Thomas. *Avenia, or, A Tragical Poem, on the Oppression of the Human Species; and Infringement on the Rights of Man. In Five Books. With Notes Explanatory and Miscellaneous. Written in Imitation of Homer's Iliad*. Philadelphia: J. Cline, 1810.

Brennan, Karen. *Here on Earth*. Middletown, CT: Wesleyan University Press, 1988.

Broderick, Richard. *Woman Lake*. Minneapolis, MN: New Rivers Press, 2000.

Brooks, Gwendolyn. *Selected Poems*. New York: Harper and Row, 1963.

Brosman, Catharine Savage. *Finding Higher Ground*. Reno: University of Nevada Press, 2003.

———. *Journeying to Canyon de Chelly*. Baton Rouge: Louisiana State University Press, 1994.

———. *The Muscled Truce*. Baton Rouge: Louisiana State University Press, 2003.

———. *Passages*. Baton Rouge: Louisiana State University Press, 1996.

———. *Places in Mind*. Baton Rouge: Louisisana State University Press, 2000.

———. *The Shimmering Maya and Other Essays*. Baton Rouge: Louisiana State University Press, 1994.

———. "Indian Paintbrush" in *Chronicles: A Magazine of American Culture* 30 (April 2006).

Byer, Kathryn Stripling. *Black Shawl*. Baton Rouge: Louisiana State University Press, 1998.

———. *The Girl in the Midst of the Harvest*. Lubbock, TX: Texas Tech University Press, 1986.

———. *Wildwood Flower*. Baton Rouge: Louisiana State University Press, 1992.

Byrne, Edward. *East of Omaha*. San Antonio, TX: Pecan Grove Press, 1998.

———. *Tidal Air*. San Antonio, TX: Pecan Grove Press, 2002.

———. *Words Spoken, Words Unspoken*. Indianapolis, IN: Chimney Hill Press, 1995.

———. "Listening to Lester Young" in *Crab Orchard Review* 5, no. 2 (Spring/Summer 2000): 47.

Callaway, Kathy. *Heart of the Garfish*. Pittsburgh, PA: University of Pittsburgh Press, 1982.

Carey, Mathew. *The Porcupiniad: A Hudibrastic Poem in Four Cantos: Addressed to William Corbett*. Philadelphia: Mathew Carey, 1799.

Carey, Michael. *Honest Effort*. Duluth, MN: Holy Cow Press, 1991.

Carruth, Hayden. *Doctor Jazz*. Port Townsend, WA: Copper Canyon Press, 2001.

Cary, Alice. *The Poetical Works of Alice and Phoebe Cary*. Boston: Houghton Mifflin, 1865.

Casey, Michael. *Obscenities*. New Haven, CT: Yale University Press, 1972.

Cavanagh, David. *The Middleman*. Cliffs of Moher, Co. Clare, Ireland: Salmon Publishing, 2003.

Chapson, James. *Sentimental Journey*. Berkeley: Hit and Run Press, 1985.

Chitwood, Michael. *Gospel Road Going*. Chapel Hill, NC: Tryon Publishing, 2002.

———. *Hitting Below the Bible Belt: Baptist Voodoo, Blood Kin, Grandma's Teeth and Other Stories from the South*. Ashboro, NC: Down Home Press, 1998.

———. *Salt Works*. Athens, OH: Ohio Review Books, 1992.

———. *The Weave Room*. Chicago: University of Chicago Press, 1998.

———. *Whet*. Athens, OH: Ohio Review Books, 1995.

Clark, Tom. *Light & Shade: New and Selected Poems*. Minneapolis, MN: Coffee House Press, 2006.

Clary, Killarney. *By Common Salt*. Oberlin, OH: Oberlin College Press, 1996.

———. *Who Whispered Near Me*. Newcastle-upon-Tyne: Bloodaxe Books, 1993.

Cleary, Kate McPhelim. *Poems*. Chicago: Vera Valentine Cleary, et. al., 1922.

Clifton, Harry. *The Desert Route: Selected Poems 1973–1988*. Loughcrew, Ireland: Gallery Press, 1992.

Coady, Michael. *All Souls*. Loughcrew, Ireland: Gallery Press, 1997.

Coffey, Brian. *Selected Poems*. Dublin: Raven Arts Press, 1971.

Coffey, Michael. *87 North*. Minneapolis, MN: Coffee House Press, 1998.

Collins, Billy. *The Apple that Astonished Paris*. Fayetteville: University of Arkansas Press, 1988.

———. *The Art of Drowning*. Pittsburgh, PA: University of Pittsburgh Press, 1995

———. *Picnic, Lightning*. Pittsburgh, PA: University of Pittsburgh Press, 1998.

———. *Questions About Angels*. Pittsburgh, PA: University of Pittsburgh Press, 1999.

———. *The Trouble with Poetry and Other Poems*. New York: Random House, 2005.

Colum, Padraic. *The Collected Poems of Padraic Colum*. New York: Devin-Adair, 1953.

Connellan, Leo. *The Clear Blue Lobster Water Country*. San Diego, CA: Harcourt Brace Jovanovich, 1985.

———. *New and Collected Poems*. New York: Paragon House, 1989.

———. *Provincetown*. Willimantic, CT: Curbstone Press, 1995.

———. *Short Poems, City Poems 1944–1998*. Willimantic, CT: Curbstone Press, 1999.

Connolly, Geraldine. *Food for the Winter*. West Lafayette, IN: Purdue University Press, 1990.

———. *Province of Fire*. Washington, D.C.: Iris Press, 1998.

Cooley, Nicole. "Drinking: A Suite" in *Chelsea* 70/71 (2001): 245–49.

Cooley, Peter. *The Astonished Hours*. Pittsburgh, PA: Carnegie Mellon University Press, 1992.

———. *The Room Where Summer Ends*. Pittsburgh, PA: Carnegie Mellon University Press, 1979.

———. *Sacred Conversations*. Pittsburgh, PA: Carnegie Mellon, 1998.

Corkery, Christopher Jane. *Blessing*. Princeton, NJ: Princeton University Press, 1985.

Cox, Ed. *Collected Poems*. Arlington, VA: Paycock Press, 2001.

Creeley, Robert. *Collected Poems: 1945–1975*. Berkeley: University of California Press, 1975.

———. *Later*. New York: New Directions, 1979.

———. *Selected Poems*. Berkeley: University of California Press, 1996.

Cunningham, J. V. *The Poems of J. V. Cunningham*. Edited by Timothy Steele. Athens, OH: Swallow Press, 1997.

Dacey, Philip. *The Deathbed Playboy*. Cheney, WA: Eastern Washington University Press, 1999

———. *The Paramour of the Moving Air*. Princeton, NJ: Quarterly Review of Literature, 1999.

Darr, Ann. *Flying the Zuni Mountains*. Washington, D.C.: Forest Woods Media Productions, 1994.

———. *St Ann's Gut*. New York: William Morrow and Company, 1971.

Delanty, Greg. *American Wake*. Belfast: Blackstaff Press, 1995.

———. *The Blind Stitch*. Baton Rouge: Louisiana State University Press, 2002.

———. *Collected Poems, 1986–2006*. Manchester: Carcanet Press, 2006.

———. *The Hellbox*. Oxford: Oxford University Press, 1998.

Deppe, Theodore. *Cape Clear: New and Selected Poems*. Cliffs of Moher, Co. Clare, Ireland: Salmon Publishing, 2003.

Donaghy, Michael. *Conjure*. London: Picador, 2000.

———. *Dances Learned Last Night: Poems 1975–1995*. London: Picador, 2000.

———. *Safest*. London: Picador, 2005.

Donnelly, Patrick. *The Charge*. Keene, NY: Ausable Press, 2003.

———. "I am a virus" in *The Four Way Reader 2: Poetry/Fiction/Memoir*. Edited by Carlen Arnett, Jane Brox, Dzvinia Orlowsky, and Martha Rhodes. Hanover, NH: University Press of New England, 2001.

Donnelly, Susan. *Eve Names the Animals*. Boston: Northeastern University Press, 1985.

———. *Transit*. Boston: Iris Press, 2001.

Donoghue, John. *Precipice*. New York: Four Way Books, 2000.

Donovan, Gerard. *Columbus Rides Again*. Galway, Ireland: Salmon Publishing, 1992.

———. *Kings and Bicycles*. Galway, Ireland: Salmon Publishing, 1995.

———. *The Lighthouse*. Cliffs of Moher, Co. Clare, Ireland: Salmon Publishing, 2000.

Dugan, Alan. *Poem Seven: New and Complete Poetry*. New York: Seven Stories Press, 2001.

———. *Poems*. New Haven, CT: Yale University Press, 1961.

Dunbar, Paul Laurence. *The Complete Poems of Paul Laurence Dunbar*. New York: Dodd, Mead and Company 1913.

———. "John Boyle O'Reilly" in *Irish Americans: A Versified Company*. Edited by Richard Demeter. Pasadena, CA: Cranford Press, 1999.

Dunn, Stephen. *Different Hours*. New York: W. W. Norton, 2000.

———. *New and Selected Poems, 1974–1994*. New York: W. W. Norton, 1994.

Egan, Maurice Francis. *Songs and Sonnets*. London: Kegan Paul, Trench and Company, 1885.

Eliot, T. S. "Tradition and the Individual Talent." In *Selected Prose of T. S. Eliot*. New York: Harcourt, Brace, Jovanovich, 1975.

Engels, John. *Big Water.* New York: Lyons and Burford, 1995.

———. *Recounting the Seasons: Poems, 1958–2005.* Notre Dame, IN: University of Notre Dame Press, 2005.

———. *Walking to Cootehill: New and Selected Poems, 1958–1992.* Hanover, NH: University Press of New England, 1993.

Fagan, Kathy. *The Charm.* Lincoln, NE: Zoo Press, 2002.

———. *Moving and St. Rage.* Denton, TX: University of North Texas Press, 1999.

———. *The Raft.* New York: Dutton, 1985.

———. "Tympani" in *The Progressive* 65, no. 7 (July 2001): 40.

Fallon, Peter. *Eye to Eye.* Loughcrew, Oldcastle, Co. Meath, Ireland: Gallery Press, 1992.

———. *News of the World: Selected and New Poems.* Oldcastle, Co. Meath, Ireland: Gallery Press, 1998.

Fennelly, Beth Ann. *Open House.* Lincoln, NE: Zoo Press, 2001.

———. *Tender Hooks.* New York: W. W. Norton, 2004.

Fiacc, Padraic. *Ruined Pages: Selected Poems.* Belfast: Blackstaff Press, 1994.

Fifty Years of American Poetry. Academy of American Poets. New York: Dell Publishing, 1984.

Finnell, Dennis. *Belovèd Beast.* Athens: University of Georgia Press, 1995.

———. *Red Cottage.* Amherst: University of Massachusetts Press, 1991.

Firer, Susan. *The Lives of the Saints and Everything.* Cleveland, OH: Cleveland State University Poetry Center, 1993.

Fitzgerald, Robert. *Spring Shade: Poems 1931–1970.* New York: New Directions, 1971.

Fletcher, John Gould. *Selected Poems of John Gould Fletcher.* Fayetteville: University of Arkansas Press, 1988.

Flynn, John. *Moments Between Cities.* Lewiston, NY: Mellen Poetry Press, 1997.

———. *Washing Apples in Streams.* Los Angleles: So-Called Press, 2000.

Flynn, Nick. *Blind Huber.* St. Paul, MN: Graywolf Press, 2002.

———. *Some Ether.* St. Paul, MN: Graywolf Press, 2000.

Forhan, Chris. *The Actual Moon, the Actual Stars.* Boston: Northeastern University Press, 2003.

———. *Forgive Us Our Happiness.* Hanover, NH: University Press of New England, 1999.

Francis, Robert. *Collected Poems 1936–1976.* Amherst: University of Massachusetts Press, 1976.

Frost, Robert. *Collected Poems, Prose and Plays.* New York: Library of America, 1995.

Fulton, Alice. *Cascade Experiment: Selected Poems.* New York: W. W. Norton, 2004.

———. *Palladium.* Chicago: University of Illinois Press, 1986.

———. *Sensual Math.* New York: W. W. Norton, 1995.

Gallagher, Tess. *Amplitude: New and Selected Poems.* St. Paul, MN: Graywolf Press, 1987.

———. *Dear Ghosts.* St. Paul, MN: Graywolf Press, 2006.

———. *My Black Horse: New and Selected Poems.* London: Bloodaxe Books, 1995.

Galvin, Brendan. *Great Blue: New and Selected Poems.* Urbana: University of Illinois Press, 1990.

———. *Habitat: New and Selected Poems, 1965–2005.* Baton Rouge: Louisiana State University Press, 2005.

———. *Saints in Their Ox-hide Boat.* Baton Rouge: Louisiana State University Press, 1992.

Galvin, James. *Resurrection Update: Collected Poems, 1975–1997.* Port Townsend, WA: Copper Canyon Press, 1997.

Gogarty, Oliver St. John. *The Collected Poems of Oliver St. John Gogarty.* New York: Devin-Adair, 1954.

Golden, Renny. *The Hour of the Furnaces.* Minneapolis, MN: Mid-List Press, 2000.

Gregory, Horace. *Collected Poems.* New York: Holt, Rinehart and Winston, 1964.

Grennan, Eamon. *The Quick of It*. St. Paul, MN: Graywolf Press, 2005.

———. *Relations: New and Selected Poems*. St. Paul, MN: Graywolf Press, 1998.

———. *Selected and New Poems*. Loughcrew, Ireland: Gallery Press, 2000.

———. *Still Life with Waterfall*. St. Paul, MN: Graywolf Press, 2002.

Guiney, Louise Imogen. *Happy Ending: The Collected Lyrics of Louise Imogen Guiney*. Boston: Houghton Mifflin, 1927.

Halpine, Charles G. *Poetical works of Charles G. Halpine (Miles O'Reilly). Consisting of Odes, Poems, Sonnets, Epics, and Lyrical Effusions, Which Have Not Heretofore Been Collected Together*. New York: Harper and Brothers, 1869.

———. "On Raising a Monument to the Irish Legion" in *The Household Library of Ireland's Poets with Full and Choice Selection from the Irish American Poets*. Edited by Daniel Connolly. New York: Daniel Connolly, 1887.

Hearne, Vicki. *In the Absence of Horses*. Princeton, NJ: Princeton University Press, 1983.

———. *The Parts of Light*. Baltimore, MD: Johns Hopkins University Press, 1994.

Heffernan, Michael. *The Cry of Oliver Hardy*. Athens: University of Georgia Press, 1979.

———. *Love's Answer*. Iowa City: University of Iowa Press, 1994.

———. *To the Wreakers of Havoc*. Athens: University of Georgia Press, 1984.

Houlihan, Joan. *Hand-Held Executions: Poems & Essays*. Washington, D.C.: Del Sol Press, 2003.

———. *The Mending Worm*. Kalamazoo, MI: New Issues Press, 2006.

Howard, Ben. *Dark Pool*. Cliffs of Moher, Co. Clare, Ireland: Salmon Publishing, 2004.

———. *Midcentury*. Cliffs of Moher, Co. Clare, Ireland: Salmon Publishing, 1997.

Howe, Fanny. *Gone*. Berkeley: University of California Press, 2003.

———. *On the Ground*. St. Paul, MN: Graywolf Press, 2004.

———. *Selected Poems*. Berkeley: University of California Press, 2000.

———. *The Wedding Dress: Meditations on Work and Life*. Berkeley: University of California Press, 2003.

———. "Seven Poems" in *Conjunctions* 26 (Spring 1996): 327–29.

Howe, Marie. *The Good Thief*. New York: Persea Books, 1988.

———. *What the Living Do*. New York: W. W. Norton, 1998.

Howe, Susan. *The Europe of Trusts*. New York: New Directions, 2002.

———. *Frame Structures: Early Poems 1974–1979*. New York: New Directions, 1996.

———. *The Midnight*. New York: New Directions, 2003.

Jacobsen, Josephine. *The Crevice of Time: New and Selected Poems*. Baltimore, MD: Johns Hopkins University Press, 1995.

———. *The Instant of Knowing*. Ann Arbor: University of Michigan Press, 1997.

Jarrell, Randall. *The Complete Poems*. New York: Farrar, Straus and Giroux, 1969.

Jeffers, Robinson. *Rock and Hawk*. Edited by Robert Hass. New York: Random House, 1987.

———. *The Selected Poetry of Robinson Jeffers*. Edited by Tim Hunt. Stanford, CA: Stanford University Press, 2001.

Johnston, Conor. "John Boyle O'Reilly as Poet." *American Conference for Irish Studies*. Unpublished paper given at Mid-west regional meeting, October 16, 1998.

Kane, Julie. *Body and Soul*. Paradis, LA: Pirogue Publishing, 1987.

———. *Rhythm and Booze*. Urbana: University of Illinois Press, 2002.

Kearney, Meg. *An Unkindness of Ravens*. Rochester, NY: BOA Editions, 2001.

Keelan, Claudia. *The Secularist*. Athens: University of Georgia Press, 1997.

Kelly, Brigit Pegeen. *Song*. New York: BOA Editions, 1995.

———. *To the Place of Trumpets*. New Haven, CT: Yale University Press, 1988.

Kelly, Robert. *Lapis*. Boston: D. R. Godine, 2005.

———. *Red Actions: Selected Poems 1960–1993*. Santa Rosa, CA: Black Sparrow Books, 1995.

———. *The Time of Voice: Poems, 1994–1996*. Santa Rosa, CA: Black Sparrow Books, 1998.

Kennedy, Anne. *The Dog Kubla Dreams My Life*. Dublin: Salmon Publishing, 1994.

Kennedy, X. J. *Cross Ties: Selected Poems*. Athens: University of Georgia Press, 1985.

———. *The Lords of Misrule: Poems, 1992–2001*. Baltimore, MD: John Hopkins University Press, 2002.

Kenney, Richard. *The Evolution of the Flightless Bird*. New Haven, CT: Yale University Press, 1984.

———. *The Invention of the Zero*. New York: Alfred A. Knopf, 1993.

Kinnell, Galway. *The Avenue Bearing the Initial of Christ into the New World: Poems, 1953–1964*. Boston: Houghton Mifflin, 2002.

———. *The Book of Nightmares*. Boston: Houghton Mifflin, 1971.

———. *Mortal Acts, Mortal Words*. Boston: Houghton Mifflin, 1980.

———. *A New Selected Poems*. Boston: Houghton Mifflin, 2000.

———. *Strong Is Your Hold*. Boston: Houghton Mifflin, 2006.

———. *What a Kingdom It Was*. Boston: Houghton Mifflin, 1960.

Kinsella, Thomas. *Citizen of the World*. Dublin: Dedalus Press, 2000.

———. *Collected Poems: 1956–1994*. Oxford: Oxford University Press, 1996.

———. *Collected Poems: 1956–2001*. Winston-Salem, NC: Wake Forest University Press, 2006.

———. *Marginal Economy*. Dublin: Dedalus Press, 2006.

———. ed., *The New Oxford Book of Irish Verse*. Oxford: Oxford University Press, 1989.

Lally, Michael. *Catch My Breath*. Portland, OR: Salt Lick Press, 1995.

———. *It's Not Nostalgia: Poetry and Prose*. Santa Rosa, CA: Black Sparrow Press, 1999.

Laughlin, James. *Poems: New and Selected*. Introduction by Charles Tomlinson. New York: New Directions, 1998

Leader, Mary. *The Penultimate Suitor*. Iowa City: University of Iowa Press, 2001.

———. *Red Signature*. St. Paul, MN: Graywolf Press, 1997.

Lennon, Joseph. "29th Birthday" in *Foilsiú* 4 (Spring 2005): 76.

Levis, Larry. *Elegy*. Pittsburgh, PA: Pittsburgh University Press, 1997.

———. *Winter Stars*. Pittsburgh, PA: University of Pittsburgh Press, 1985.

Liddy, James. *Collected Poems*. Omaha, NE: Creighton University Press, 1994.

———. *Gold Set Dancing*. Cliffs of Moher, Co. Clare, Ireland: Salmon Publishing, 2000.

———. "Lines for Gareth and Janet Dunleavy" in *The Legend of Being Irish*. Edited by David Lampe. Buffalo, NY: White Pine Press, 1989.

Logan, John. *The Collected Poems*. New York: BOA Editions, 1989.

Logue, Mary. *Discriminating Evidence*. Denver, CO: Mid-List Press, 1990.

Loomis, Sabra. *Travelling on Blue*. Cliffs of Moher, Co. Clare, Ireland: Salmon Publishing, 2000.

Lowell, Robert. *Collected Poems*. Edited by Frank Bidart and David Gewanter. New York: Farrar, Straus and Giroux, 2003.

Lynch, Kathleen. *Hinge*. Palo Alto, CA: Black Zinnias Press, 2006.

Lynch, Thomas. *Still Life in Milford*. New York: W. W. Norton, 1998.

Macneice, Louis. *Collected Poems, 1925–1948*. London: Faber and Faber, 1949.

Mahon, Derek. *The Hudson Letter*. Loughcrew, Ireland: Gallery Press, 1995.

Maloney, John. *Proposal*. Cambridge, MA: Zoland Books, 1999.

Marchant, Fred. *Full Moon Boat*. St. Paul, MN: Graywolf Press, 2000.

———. *House on Water, House in Air*. Dublin: Dedalus Press, 2002.

———. *Tipping Point*. Washington, D.C.: Word Works, 1994.

McAuley, James J. *Meditations, With Distractions: Poems, 1988–1998*. Fayetteville: University of Arkansas Press, 2001.

McBride, Mekeel. *The Going Under of the Evening Land*. Pittsburgh, PA: Carnegie Mellon University Press, 1983.

———. *Red Letter Days*. Pittsburgh, PA: Carnegie Mellon University Press, 1988.

———. *Wind of the White Dresses*. Pittsburgh, PA: Carnegie Mellon University Press, 2001.

McCarriston, Linda. *Eva-Mary*. Evanston: TriQuarterly/Northwestern University Press, 1991.

———. *Little River: New and Selected Poems*. Cliffs of Moher, Co. Clare, Ireland: Salmon Publishing, 2000.

McCarthy, Eugene J. *Selected Poems*. Rochester, MN: Lone Oak Press, 1997.

McClatchy, J. D. *Hazmat*. New York: Alfred A. Knopf, 2002.

———. *The Rest of the Way*. New York: Alfred A. Knopf, 1990.

McCormick, Jeri. *When It Came Time*. Cliffs of Moher, Co. Clare, Ireland: Salmon Publishing, 1998.

McDonald, Walter. *Blessings the Body Gave*. Columbus: Ohio State University Press, 1998

———. *Counting Survivors*. Pittsburgh, PA: University of Pittsburgh Press, 1995.

McDowell, Robert. *On Foot, In Flames*. Pittsburgh, PA: University of Pittsburgh Press, 2002.

McFee, Michael. *Colander*. Pittsburgh, PA: Carnegie Mellon University Press, 1996.

———. *Earthly*. Pittsburgh, PA: Carnegie Mellon University Press, 2001.

———. *Vanishing Acts*. Frankfort, KY: Gnomon Press, 1989.

McGinley, Phyllis. *Times Three: Selected Verse from Three Decades, with Seventy New Poems*. Foreword by W. H. Auden. New York: Viking, 1961.

McGrath, Campbell. *American Noise*. New York: Ecco Press, 1993.

———. *Capitalism*. Hanover, NH:Wesleyan University Press, 1990.

———. *Road Atlas*. New York: Ecco Press, 1999.

McGrath, Thomas. *Letter to an Imaginary Friend*. Port Townsend, WA: Copper Canyon Press, 1985.

———. *The Movie at the End of the World*. Swallow Press, 1980.

———. *Selected Poems 1938–1998*. Port Townsend, WA: Copper Canyon Press, 1988.

McHenry, James. "Don Isle" and "The Haunts of Larne" in *Exiles of Erin*. Edited by Charles Fanning. Notre Dame, IN: University of Notre Dame Press, 1996.

McHugh, Heather. *Eyeshot*. Middletown, CT: Wesleyan University Press, 2003.

———. *The Father of the Predicaments*. Hanover, NH: University Press of New England, 1999.

———. *Hinge and Sign: Poems, 1968–1993*. Middletown, CT: Wesleyan University Press, 1994.

McKiernan, Ethna. *Caravan*. Dublin: Dedalus Press, 1989.

———. *The One Who Swears You Can't Start Over*. Cliffs of Moher, Co. Clare, Ireland, Salmon Publishing, 2002.

McKinney, Irene. *Six O'Clock Mine Report*. Pittsburgh, PA: University of Pittsburgh Press, 1989.

———. *Vivid Companion*. Morgantown, WVA: Vandalia Press, 2004.

McMahon, Lynne. *Devolution of the Nude*. Boston: D. R. Godine, 1993.

———. *The House of Entertaining Science*. Boston: D. R. Godine, 1999.

———. *Sentimental Standards*. Boston: D. R. Godine, 2004.

McManus, James. *Great America*. New York: Harper and Row, 1993.

McMichael, James. *Capacity*. New York: Farrar, Straus and Giroux, 2006.

McNair, Wesley. *Faces of Americans in 1953*. Columbia: University of Missouri Press, 1983.

———. *Talking in the Dark*. Boston: D. R. Godine, 1998.

———. *The Town of No; & My Brother Running*. Boston: D. R. Godine, 1996.

McNally, Stephen. *Child in Amber*. Amherst: University of Massachusetts Press, 1993.

McNamara, Robert. *Second Messengers* Middletown, CT: Wesleyan University Press, 1990.

McNulty, Ted. *On the Block*. Galway, Ireland: Salmon Publishing, 1995.

———. *Rough Landings*. Galway, Ireland: Salmon Publishing, 1992.

Milosz, Czeslaw. *Collected Poems: 1931–1987*. New York: Ecco Press, 1988.

Monaghan, Patricia. *Homefront*. Cincinnati, OH: Word Tech Press, 2005.

Monahan, Jean. *Believe It Or Not*. Washington. D.C.: Orchises Press, 1999.

———. *Hands*. Tallahassee, FL: Anhinga Press, 1992.

———. *Mauled Illusionist*. Washington, D.C.: Orchises Press, 2006.

Montague, John. "The Complex Fate of Being Irish American." In *Born in Brooklyn: John Montague's America*. Edited by David Lampe. Fredonia, NY: White Pine Press, 1991.

———. *Collected Poems*. Loughcrew: Gallery Press, 1995.

Moore, Marianne. *The Collected Poems of Marianne Moore*. New York: MacMillan, 1951.

Muldoon, Paul. *The Annals of Chile*. New York: Farrar, Straus and Giroux, 1994.

———. *Selected Poems: 1968–1998*. New York: Farrar, Straus and Giroux, 2001.

Mullen, Laura. *The Surface*. Urbana: Univeristy of Illinois Press, 1991.

———. "Long Coat" in *The Alembic* (Spring 1996): 19–20.

Murray, G. E. *Repairs*. Columbia: University of Missouri Press, 1980.

———. *Walking the Blind Dog*. Urbana: University of Illinois Press, 1992.

Nealon, Mary Jane. *Immaculate Fuel*. New York: Four Way Books, 2004.

———. *Rogue Apostle*. New York: Four Way Books, 2001.

O'Brien, Michael. *Sills*. Cambridge, MA: Zoland Books, 2000.

O'Callaghan, Julie. *The Long Room Galley*. Dublin: Trinity Closet Press, 1994.

———. *No Can Do*. Newcastle-upon-Tyne: Bloodaxe Books, 2000.

———. *Two Barks*. London: Bloodaxe Books, 1998.

———. *What's What*. Newcastle-upon-Tyne: Bloodaxe Books, 1991.

O'Connell, Daniel. "Monterey" and "The Workers" in *The Household Library of Ireland's Poets with Full and Choice Selection from the Irish American Poets*. Edited by Daniel Connolly. New York: Daniel Connolly, 1887.

O'Dwyer, Sean. "The Big House" in *The Recorder: The Journal of the American Irish Historical Association* 10, nos. 1 and 2 (Spring and Fall 1997): 206.

O'Gorman, Ned. *Adam Before His Mirror*. New York: Harcourt, Brace and World, 1961.

———. *Five Seasons of Obsession: New and Selected Poems*. Chappaqua, NY: Turtle Point Press, 2001.

———. *The Harvesters' Vase*. New York: Harcourt, Brace and World, 1968.

O'Grady, Jennifer. *White*. Minneapolis, MN: Mid-List Press, 1999.

O'Grady, Thomas. *What Really Matters*. Montreal: McGill-Queen University Press, 2000.

O'Hara, Frank. *The Collected Poems of Frank O'Hara*. Edited by Donald Merriam Allen. Berkeley: University of California Press, 1995.

O'Hehir, Diane. *Spells for Not Dying Again*. Cheney, WA: Eastern Washington University Press, 1996.

———. *Summoned*. Columbia: University of Missouri Press, 1976.

O'Heigeartaigh, Padraig. "Ochón! My Donncha (My Sorrow, Donncha)" in *An Duanaire 1600–1900: Poems of the Dispossessed*. Edited by Seán ÓTuama. Trans. by Thomas Kinsella. Mountrath, Portlaoise, Ireland: Dolmen Press, 1990.

Olson, Charles. *The Collected Poems of Charles Olson: Excluding the Maximus Poems*. Edited by George Buttrick. Berkeley: University of California Press, 1987.

Oness, Elizabeth. *Sure Knowledge*. Madison, WI: Parallel Press, 1999.

O'Reilly, John Boyle. *Selected Poems*. New York: P. J. Kennedy and Sons, 1913.

Orr, James. "Song on the Coast of Newfoundland" in *Verse in English from Eighteenth-Century Ireland*. Edited by Andrew Carpenter. Cork: Cork University Press, 1999.

O'Sheel, Shaemus. *Jealous of Dead Leaves: Selected Verse of Shaemus O'Sheel*. New York: Boni and Liveright, 1928.

Owen, Maureen. *American Rush: Selected Poems*. Jersey City, NJ: Talisman House Publishers, 1998.

———. *Erosion's Pull*. Minneapolis, MN: Coffee House Press, 2006.

———. *Zombie Notes*. New York: SUN Press, 1985.

Redshaw, Thomas Dillon. *The Floating World*. St. Paul, MN: Aquila Rose, 1979.

———. *Heimaey*. Dublin: Dolmen Press, 1974.

———. *Such a Heart Dances Out*. Dublin: New Writer's Press, 1971.

Ridge, Lola. *Dance of Fire*. New York, H. Smith and R. Haas, 1935.

———. *The Ghetto and Other Poems*. New York: B. W. Huebsch, 1918.

———. *Sun-Up and Other Poems*. New York: B. W. Huebsch, 1920.

Riley, James Whitcomb. *The Complete Works of James Whitcomb Riley*. Indianapolis, IN: The Bobbs-Merrill Company, 1913.

Riley, Michael D. *Circling the Stones*. Omaha, NE: Creighton University Press, 2000.

———. "In the Garden" in *Cumberland Poetry Review* 18, no. 2 (Spring 1999): 57–58.

Robinson, Edwin Arlington. *Selected Poems*. New York: MacMillan, 1965.

Roche, James Jeffrey. *Songs and Satires*. Boston: Tinknor and Company, 1887.

Roethke, Theodore. *Collected Poems*. Garden City, NY: Doubleday, 1966.

Rogers, James Silas. *Sundogs*. Madison, WI: Parallel Press, 2006.

Rooney-Céspedes, Aidan. *Day Release*. Loughcrew, Ireland: Gallery Press, 2000.

Ruark, Gibbons. *Passing Through Customs: New and Selected Poems*. Baton Rouge: Louisiana State University Press, 1999.

Ryan, Michael. *God Hunger*. New York: Viking, 1989.

———. *In Winter*. New York: Holt, Rinehart and Winston, 1981.

———. *New and Selected Poems*. Boston: Houghton Mifflin, 2004.

Schevill, James. *Violence and Glory: Poems, 1962–1968*. Chicago: Swallow Press, 1969.

Schuyler, James. *Collected Poems*. New York: Farrar, Straus and Giroux, 1993.

Seaton, Maureen. *Fear of Subways*. Portland, OR: Eighth Mountain Press, 1991.

———. *Furious Cooking*. Iowa City: University of Iowa Press, 1996.

———. *Little Ice Age*. Montpelier, VT: Invisible Cities Press, 2001.

———. *The Sea Among the Cupboards*. Minneapolis, MN: New Rivers Press, 1992.

———. *Venus Examines Her Breast*. Pittsburgh, PA: Carnegie Mellon University Press, 2004.

Sexton, Tom. *Autumn in the Alaska Range*. Cliffs of Moher, Co. Clare, Ireland: Salmon Publishing, 2000.

———. *The Bend Toward Asia*. Anchorage: Salmon Run Press, 1993.

Shapiro, Alan. *After the Digging*. Chicago: University of Chicago Press, 1998.

Shaughnessy, Brenda. *Interior with Sudden Joy*. New York: Farrar, Straus and Giroux, 1999.

Sholl, Betsy. *Late Psalm*. Madison: University of Wisconsin Press, 2004.

Simmons, Janice Fitzpatrick. *Starting at Purgatory*. Cliffs of Moher, Co. Clare, Ireland: Salmon, 1999.

Simpson, Louis Aston Marantz. *The Owner of the House: New Collected Poems, 1940–2001*. New York: BOA Editions, 2003.

Skinner, Knute. *The Cold Irish Earth: New and Selected Poems of Ireland, 1965–1995*. Knockeven, Ireland: Salmon Publishing, 1996.

———. *Selected Poems*. Portree, Isle of Skye, Scotland: Aquila Publishing, 1985.

Smith, R. T. *Messenger*. Baton Rouge: Louisiana State University Press, 2001

———. *Split the Lark: Selected Poems*. Cliffs of Moher, Co.Clare, Ireland: Salmon Publishing, 1999.

———. *Trespasser*. Baton Rouge: Louisiana State University Press, 1996.

Spires, Elizabeth. *Globe*. Middletown, CT: Wesleyan University Press, 1981.

Stanley, George. *At Andy's*. Vancouver: New Star Books, 2000.

———. *A Tall, Serious Girl: Selected Poems: 1957–2000*. Edited by Kevin Davies and Larry Fagin. Jamestown, RI: Qua Books, 2003.

Stanton, Maura. *Glacier Wine*. Pittsburgh, PA: Carnegie Mellon University Press, 2001.

———. *Life Among the Trolls*. Pittsburgh, PA: Carnegie Mellon University Press, 1998.

———. *Snow on Snow*. New Haven, CT: Yale University Press, 1975.

———. *Tales of the Supernatural*. Boston: D. R. Godine, 1988.

Stevens, Wallace. *Collected Poems*. New York: Alfred A. Knopf, 1978.

Swander, Mary. *Driving the Body Back*. Iowa City: University of Iowa Press, 1998.

———. *Succession*. Athens: University of Georgia Press, 1979.

Thoreau, Henry David. *Collected Poems*. Edited by Carl Bode. Baltimore, MD: Johns Hopkins University Press, 1966.

Tillinghast, Richard. *The Stonecutter's Hand*. Boston: D. R. Godine, 1995.

Tobin, Daniel. *Double Life*. Baton Rouge: Louisiana State University Press, 2004.

———. *The Narrows*. New York: Four Way Books, 2005.

———. *Passage to the Center: Imagination and the Sacred in the Poetry of Seamus Heaney*. Lexington: University Press of Kentucky, 1999.

———. *Where the World Is Made*. Hanover, NH: University Press of New England, 1999.

———. "The Westwardness of Everything: Irishness in the Poetry of Wallace Stevens." *The Wallace Stevens Journal* 27, no.1 (Spring 2003): 27–48.

Townsend, Ann. *The Coronary Garden*. Louisville, KY: Sarabande Books, 2005.

———. *Dime Store Erotics*. Eugene, OR: Silverfish Review Press, 1998.

Valentine, Jean. *Door in the Mountain: New and Collected Poems 1965–2003*. Middleton, CT: Wesleyan University Press, 2004.

Wall, Eamonn. *Dyckman–200th Street*. Galway, Ireland: Salmon Publishing, 1994.

———. *Iron Mountain Road*. Cliffs of Moher, Co. Clare, Ireland: Salmon Publishing, 1997.

Walsh, Ernest. *Poems and Sonnets: With a Memoir by Ethel Moorhead*. New York: Harcourt, Brace and Company, 1934.

Waters, Michael. *Anniversary of the Air*. Pittsburgh, PA: Carnegie Mellon University Press, 1985.

———. *The Burden Lifters*. Pittsbugh, PA: Carnegie Mellon University Press, 1989.

———. *Green Ash, Red Maple, Black Gum*. New York: BOA Editions, 1997.

Whalen, Philip. *Heavy Breathing: Poems 1967–1980*. San Francisco, CA: Four Seasons, 1983.

Whitman, Sarah Helen. *Poems*. Boston: Houghton, Osgood and Company, 1879.

———. "Don Isle" in *The Household Library of Ireland's Poets with Full and Choice Selection from the Irish American Poets*. Edited by Daniel Connolly. New York: Daniel Connolly, 1887.

Whitman, Walt. *Leaves of Grass*. Edited by Sculley Bradley and Harold W. Blodgett. New York: Norton, 1973.

Whittemore, Reed. *The Mother's Breast and the Father's House*. New York: Houghton Mifflin, 1974.

———. *The Past, the Future, the Present: Poems Selected and New*. Fayetteville: University of Arkansas Press, 1990.

Winch, Terence. *The Drift of Things*. Great Barrington, MA: The Figures, 2001.

———. *The Great Indoors*. Brownsville, OR: Story Line Press, 1995.

Wood, Susan. *Asunder*. New York: Penguin Books, 2001.

Wright, Carolyne. *A Change of Maps*. Sandpoint, ID: Lost Horse Press, 2006.

———. *Premonitions of an Uneasy Guest*. Abilene, TX: Hardin-Simmons University Press, 1983.

———. "In the Yeats Class, Summer Term" in *Blackbird: An Online Journal of Literature and the Arts* 4 (Fall 2005), www.blackbird.vcu.edu.

SELECT BIBLIOGRAPHY
FOR GENERAL READING

*Immigration, Irish and Irish American History and Culture,
History of Irish Poetry and American Poetry*

The Big Book of Irish American Culture. Edited by Bob Callahan. New York: Viking, 1987.

Bodnar, John. *The Transplanted: A History of Immigrants in Urban America.* Bloomington: Indiana University Press, 1985.

Chadwick, Nora. *The Celts.* Middlesex: Penguin, 1970.

Chermayeff, Ivan, Fred Wasserman, and Mary J. Shapiro, *Ellis Island: An Illustrated History of the Immigrant Experience.* New York: MacMillan, 1991.

The Course of Irish History. Edited by T. W. Moody and F. X. Martin. Cork: Mercier Press, 1994.

Daniels, Roger. *Coming to America: A History of Immigration and Ethnicity in American Life.* New York: HarperCollins, 1990.

Diner, Hasia R. *Erin's Daughters in America: Irish Immigrant Women in the Nineteenth Century.* Baltimore, MD: Johns Hopkins University Press, 1983.

Emigration and Irish Studies. Edited by Jim MacLaughlin. Notre Dame, IN: University of Notre Dame Press, 1997.

The Encyclopedia of the Irish in America. Edited by Michael Glazier. Notre Dame, IN: University of Notre Dame Press, 1999.

Ernst, Robert. *Immigrant Life in New York City, 1825–1863.* Syracuse, NY: Syracuse University Press, 1994.

Evans, A. G. *Fanatic Heart: A Life of John Boyle O'Reilly, 1844–1890.* Nedlands: University of Western Australia Press, 1997.

Evans, E. Estyn. *The Personality of Ireland: Habitat, Heritage, and History.* Cambridge: Cambridge University Press, 1973.

Fanning, Charles. *The Exiles of Erin: Nineteenth-Century Irish-American Fiction.* Notre Dame, IN: University of Notre Dame Press, 1997.

———. *The Irish Voice in America.* Lexington: University Press of Kentucky, 1990.

Fellows, Marjorie. *Irish Americans: Identity and Assimilation.* Englewood Cliffs, NJ: Prentice-Hall, 1977.

Foster, R. F. *Modern Ireland, 1600–1972.* London: Penguin, 1989.

Gibbons, Luke. *Transformations of Irish Culture.* Notre Dame, IN: University of Notre Dame Press, 1996.

Gilroy, Paul. *The Black Atlantic: Modernity and Double Consciousness.* Cambridge, MA: Harvard University Press, 1993.

The Great Famine and the Irish Diaspora in America. Edited by Arthur Gribben. Amherst: University of Massachusetts Press, 1999.

Greeley, Andrew M. *That Most Distressful Nation: The Taming of the American Irish.* Chicago: Quadangle Books, 1972.

Gregory, Horace and Zaturenska, Marya. *A History of American Poetry, 1900–1940.* New York: Harcourt, Brace, 1946.

Ignatiev, Noel. *How the Irish Became White.* London: Routledge, 1995.

Ireland in Exile. Edited by Dermot Bolger. Dublin: New Island Books, 1993.

Irish Identites. Edited by Jim MacLaughlin. Notre Dame, IN: University of Notre Dame Press, 1997.

Krieg, Joann P. *Whitman and the Irish.* Iowa City: University of Iowa Press, 2001.

Kreymborg, Alfred. *Our Singing Strength: An Outline of American Poetry (1620–1930).* New York: Coward-McCann, 1929.

McCaffrey, Lawrence J. *The Irish Diaspora in America.* Washington, D.C.: Catholic University Press of America, 1984.

———. *The Irish Experience.* Englewood Cliffs, NJ: Prentice Hall, 1989.

———. *Textures of Irish America.* Syracuse, NY: Syracuse University Press, 1992.

McMahon, Sean. *A Short History of Ireland.* Chester Springs, PA: Dufour Editions, 1996.

Metress, Seamus P. *The Irish American Experience: A Guide to the Literature.* Washington, D.C.: University Press of America, 1981.

Miller, Kerby. *Emigrants and Exiles: Ireland and the Irish Exodus to North America.* Oxford: Oxford University Press, 1985.

Modern Irish American Fiction: A Reader. Edited by Daniel J. Casey and Robert E. Rhodes. Syracuse, NY: Syracuse University Press, 1989.

Montague, John. *Born in Brooklyn.* Freedonia, NY: White Pine Press, 1991.

The New York Irish. Edited by Ronald H. Bayor and Timothy J. Meagher. Baltimore, MD: Johns Hopkins University Press, 1996.

Pierce, Roy Harvey. *The Continuity of American Poetry.* Middletown, CT: Wesleyan University Press, 1987.

Perkins, David. *A History of Modern Poetry: From the 1890s to the High Modernist Mode.* Cambridge, MA: Harvard University Press, 1976.

———. *A History of Modern Poetry: Modernism and After.* Cambridge, MA: Harvard University Press, 1987.

Powell, T. G. E. *The Celts.* New York: Thames and Hudson, 1983.

Scally, Robert James. *The End of Hidden Ireland: Famine, Rebellion, and Emigration.* Oxford: Oxford University Press, 1995.

Shirmer, Gregory A. *Out of What Began: A History of Irish Poetry in English.* Ithaca, NY: Cornell University Press.

Von Hallberg, Robert. *American Poetry and Culture, 1945–1980.* Cambridge, MA: Harvard University Press, 1985.

Wall, Eamonn. *From the Siné Café to the Black Hills: Notes on the New Irish.* Madison: University of Wisconsin Press, 1999.

Woodham-Smith, Cecil. *The Great Hunger: Ireland 1845–1849.* London: Penguin, 1962.

PERMISSIONS
AND ACKNOWLEDGMENTS

Abel, Colleen: "On Touring the U.N. with My Mother-in-Law" previously unpublished. Copyright © 2007 by Colleen Abel. Used by permission of the author.

Agee, Chris: "By the HARP Brewery," "First Light," "Offing," and "Thistledown" from *First Light*. Copyright © 2003 by Chris Agee. Reprinted with the permission of the author and Dedalus Press.

Ammons, A. R.: "Expressions of Sea Level," "Hymn," and "Passage" from *Collected Poems 1951–1971*. Copyright © 1972 by A. R. Ammons. Reprinted with the permission of W. W. Norton & Company, Inc.

"The Pieces of My Voice" from *The Selected Poems: 1951–1977*. Copyright © 1977 by A. R. Ammons. Reprinted with the permission of W. W. Norton & Company, Inc.

"Easter Morning," "Feel Like Travelling On," and "Night Finding" from *A Coast of Trees*. Copyright © 1981 by A. R. Ammons. Reprinted with the permission of W. W. Norton & Company, Inc.

Anderson, Nathalie: "Country Night, County Donegal," "Féis," and "Slow Airs" from *Following Fred Astaire* (Word Works). Copyright © 1998 by Nathalie Anderson. Reprinted with the permission of the author.

Archer, Nuala: "Between Swilly and Sewanee" and "Emigrant" from *From a Mobile Home* (Salmon Publishing). Copyright © 1995 by Nuala Archer. Reprinted with the permission of the author.

Berrigan, Daniel: "Dachau Is Now Open for Visitors," "Immanence," and "The Big Wind" from *Selected and New Poems*. Copyright © 1973 by Daniel Berrigan. Used by permission of Doubleday, a division of Random House, Inc.

Berrigan, Ted: "Frank O'Hara" and "Heloise" from *Collected Poems*. Copyright © 2005 by Ted Berrigan. Reprinted with the permission of University of California Press.

Berryman, John: "The Dream Songs": *279, 290, 296, 300, 307, 309, 312, 321, 355* from *The Dream Songs*. Copyright © 1969 by John Berryman. Reprinted with the permission of Farrar, Straus and Giroux, Inc.

Bogan, Louise: "Cassandra," "Hypocrite Swift," "Medusa," "Women," and "Zone" from *The Blue Estuaries: Poems: 1923–1968*. Copyright © 1977 by Louise Bogan. Reprinted with the permission of Ecco Press, an imprint of HarperCollins.

Boland, Eavan: "In Exile" from *Outside History: Selected Poems, 1980–1990*. Copyright © 1990 by Eavan Boland. Reprinted with the permission of W. W. Norton & Company, Inc.

"In a Bad Light" from *In a Time of Violence* Copyright © 1994 by Eavan Boland. Reprinted with the permission of W. W. Norton & Company, Inc.

"The Emigrant Irish" from *An Origin Like Water: Collected Poems 1967–1987*. Copyright © 1996 by Eavan Boland. Reprinted with the permission of W. W. Norton & Company, Inc.

"Home" from *The Lost Land*. Copyright © 1998 by Eavan Boland. Reprinted with the permission of W. W. Norton & Company, Inc.

Bowen, Kevin: "A Granite Stairway: St. Joseph's School for Boys," "Inchemekinna," and "Sailing to Thai Binh" from *Eight True Maps of the West* (Dedalus Press). Copyright © 2003 by Kevin Bowen. Reprinted with the permission of the author.

Boyle, Kay: "A Poem of Gratitude," "The New Emigration," and "To America" from *Collected Poems*. Copyright © 1991 by Kay Boyle. Reprinted with the permission of Copper Canyon Press, www.coppercanyonpress.org.

INDEX OF POEMS

918

INDEX OF POETS